EVIDENCE, INFERENCE AND ENQUIRY

PROCEEDINGS OF THE BRITISH ACADEMY · 171

EVIDENCE, INFERENCE AND ENQUIRY

Edited by

PHILIP DAWID, WILLIAM TWINING
AND MIMI VASILAKI

Published for THE BRITISH ACADEMY
by OXFORD UNIVERSITY PRESS

Oxford University Press, Great Clarendon Street, Oxford OX2 6DP

Oxford New York
Auckland Bangkok Bogotá Buenos Aires Cape Town Chennai
Dar es Salaam Delhi Hong Kong Istanbul Karachi Kolkata
Kuala Lumpur Madrid Melbourne Mexico City Mumbai Nairobi
São Paulo Shanghai Singapore Taipei Tokyo Toronto

British Library Cataloguing in Publication Data
Data available

978–0–19–726484–3

Typeset in Times
by New Leaf Design, Scarborough, North Yorkshire
Printed in Great Britain
on acid-free paper by
CPI Group (UK) Ltd, Croydon, CR0 4YY

Contents

Foreword

IN A DECADE as Chancellor of the University of East Anglia I witnessed the emergence of an independent school of History, schools of Management and of Business Studies and a Medical School. The debates across the range of disciplines were often ill-formed, causing the vice-chancellor (Professor Vincent Watts) to consider the introduction of a course on the nature of evidence, available to all undergraduates, to illustrate the different practices and attitudes. It was not introduced simply because it would have required an interdisciplinary, fundamental research programme.

A discussion with Sir Richard Brook in 2002 led to the Leverhulme Trust calling for research proposals 'On the Nature of Evidence'. As a result of additional funds from ESRC, two grants were awarded:

1. 'How well do facts travel'; led by Mary Morgan from LSE, and
2. 'Evidence, Inference and Enquiry: towards an integrated science of evidence'; led by Philip Dawid and William Twining at UCL.

The programme at LSE started by exploring the factors which influence the migration of 'facts' between disciplines, between different national cultures and between different periods of history. It blossomed into an integrated study which has thrown light on the factors most likely to ensure the successful transfer and uptake of knowledge and understanding.

The group at UCL recognised from the outset that there was little appreciation of the different attitudes to 'evidence' between disciplines. Accordingly they developed a partnership with Professor David Schum (George Mason University, USA) who was one of the few international figures exploring fundamental issues relating to the nature of evidence. Together they structured a multidisciplinary programme which invoked contributions from some twenty departments in UCL over a period of four years.

The British Academy held an interdisciplinary meeting in December 2007 on 'Evidence, Enquiry and Facts' at which plenary lectures given by contributors from Europe, Australia, the United States and the United Kingdom were interlaced by research contributions mainly from the programmes at LSE and UCL. It became obvious that the London groups had made significant advances.

The present book records the work carried out (across a range of disciplines) at UCL and highlights interdisciplinary differences and the beginnings of progress, albeit limited, towards addressing the basic questions about the nature of evidence. Keeping this disparate group together was no easy matter but this in itself generated new interfaces and fresh dialogue. The only omission is that no one from the schools of 'hard' science or engineering was motivated to participate. With this exception, the text gives an up-to-date perspective on the subject and shows that an evolving structure and new programmes will be required to make further progress.

Based on the 'evidence' presented in this book, each university should consider the creation of an multidisciplinary group, in which participants remain in their original departments but interact to provide interdisciplinary studies of enquiry, inference and evidence. A desirable outcome would be the promotion of courses available to all undergraduates in each university.

Geoffrey Allen
28 July 2010

Acknowledgements

DURING THE COURSE of the UCL Evidence programme and the process of preparing this book for publication we have accumulated numerous debts to individuals and organisations. Special thanks are due to the Leverhulme Foundation and the Economic and Social Research Council for the major grants that financed the programme and for support and advice throughout its life; to University College London for practical support and providing an environment that encourages and facilitates multidisciplinary cooperation; and to the British Academy for supporting and hosting the conference held at 10 Carlton House Terrace in December 2007 and for undertaking to publish this volume. It is invidious to try to list all the many individuals who have made this volume possible. We thank the contributors and readers for their cooperation and patience; and Angela Pusey and James Rivington and his colleagues in the Publications Department of the British Academy.

APD
WLT
MV

Contributors

Terence J. Anderson has been Professor, University of Miami School of Law since 1976. Prior to that he served for two years as a regional local courts commissioner in Malawi, practised for seven years with a law firm in Chicago, and taught for three years and served as academic dean for one at the Antioch School of Law in Washington DC. Since joining the UM Law faculty, Professor Anderson has continued to participate in public interest litigation. Most notably, from 1982 until 1991, he represented former US District Judge, now Congressman, Alcee Hastings in all litigation relating to his office, including his impeachment trial before the United States Senate in 1989. He is the author of *The Battles of Hastings: Four Stories in Search of a Meaning* (NIAS, 1996) and co-author (with William Twining) of *Analysis of Evidence* (2nd edn., Cambridge University Press, 2005).

Nancy Cartwright is Professor of Philosophy at the London School of Economics and at the University of California at San Diego. She specialised at the beginning of her career at Stanford University in the philosophy of physics; since coming to LSE, in the philosophy of the social and economic sciences; and most recently, on evidence for evidence-based policy. In all three areas she focuses on how science is put to use. Her most recent book is *Hunting Causes and Using Them: Approaches in Philosophy and Economics* (2007, Cambridge University Press).

Hasok Chang is Hans Rausing Professor of History and Philosophy of Science at the University of Cambridge. From 1995 to 2010 he taught in the Department of Science and Technology Studies at University College London. After his Ph.D. work in the philosophy of quantum physics (Stanford University, 1993) he has turned his attention more to earlier periods of science, focusing on physics and chemistry in the eighteenth and the nineteenth centuries. His publications include *Inventing Temperature: Measurement and Scientific Progress* (Oxford University Press, 2004), and '*Is Water H_2O? Evidence, Pluralism and Realism* (Springer, forthcoming).

David Colquhoun held the A. J. Clark chair of pharmacology at UCL from 1985 to 2004, and is now employed at UCL as a research assistant. He wrote *Lectures in Biostatistics* (Clarendon Press, 1970), and, with A. G. Hawkes developed the stochastic theory that underlies single ion channel recording, and the methods of maximum likelihood inference of mechanisms from experimental records. This has resulted in a series of experimental and theoretical papers about single ion channel mechanisms. Latterly he has taken an interest in more general problems of inference in clinical trials and in science policy and science communication, largely through his blog <http://dcscience.net/>.

Jason Davies is a Senior Teaching Fellow at UCL and researches the praxis of knowledge systems. His publications include work on ancient religion (most notably *Rome's Religious History* (Cambridge University Press, 2004)) and interdisciplinarity. He is currently preparing a book on the Evidence Programme and Interdisciplinarity with Professor Stephen Rowland and a monograph on Dreams and Divination in Ancient Rome. He has taught in Higher Education since 1995 on courses related to Ancient History, Classical Languages and Literature, and most recently about Academic Practice, Adult and HE Education, contextualising Education Policy and Interdisciplinarity at UCL.

Philip Dawid is Professor of Statistics at the University of Cambridge. Until 2007 he was in the UCL Statistical Science Department from where he directed the interdisciplinary research programme 'Evidence, Inference and Enquiry'. His research interests are largely focused on the logical and mathematical foundations of reasoning under uncertainty. He holds Guy medals in bronze and in silver from the Royal Statistical Society, and is an author of *Probabilistic Networks and Expert Systems* (Springer, 1999), which won the 2002 DeGroot prize for a published book in Statistical Science.

Grant Fisher is Associate Professor of Philosophy of Science at the Korea Advanced Institute of Science and Technology in Daejeon. He has been a Research Fellow at University College London and has taught at the University of Durham, University of Leeds and Boğaziçi University in Istanbul. He completed his Ph.D. on the philosophy of models and philosophy of chemistry at the University of Leeds in 2004. He is co-editor of the forthcoming *Oxford Handbook of Philosophy of Chemistry*.

John Fox is Professor of Engineering Science in the University of Oxford. He originally trained as a cognitive scientist but spent much of his research career running an AI research laboratory at Cancer Research UK in London. He has published widely in theoretical and applied computer science, biomedical engineering and AI and was founding editor of the *Knowledge Engineering*

Review (Cambridge University Press). Books include *Safe and Sound: Artificial Intelligence in Hazardous Applications* (MIT Press, 2000) which deals with many aspects of the use of AI in safety-critical and ethically sensitive applications. In 1996 his group was awarded the Twentieth Anniversary Gold Medal ('Laureate Prize') of the European Federation of Medical Informatics for the development of PROforma, a formal language for modelling cognitive processes and agents. He now leads COSSAC, an interdisciplinary collaboration between Oxford, UCL and Edinburgh which is concerned with the principles and practice of cognitive systems engineering <www.cossac.org>.

Tony Gardner-Medwin, Emeritus Professor of Physiology at University College London, has a research background in neuroscience and neural computation. He has a long-standing interest in the improvement of student learning experience and student assessment by getting students to judge the reliability of arguments and knowledge (Certainty-Based Marking: <www.ucl.ac.uk/lapt>). He participated frequently in the UCL Evidence Programme. Home page: <www.homepages.ucl.ac.uk/~ucgbarg>.

Trisha Greenhalgh is Professor of Primary Health Care and Director, Healthcare Innovation and Policy Unit at Queen Mary University of London and a general practitioner in north London. Her research interests include innovation in health services, policymaking and resource allocation, and developing and testing complex interventions to improve health outcomes.

Dr Amanda Hepler is a postdoctoral researcher at the Document Forensics Laboratory based at George Mason University. She served as a Research Fellow for the 'Formal Tools for Handling Evidence' project within the Evidence research programme at University College London from 2006 to 2008. She obtained her MS and Ph.D. in Statistics from North Carolina State University. Her research interests include decision analysis, evaluation and interpretation of legal evidence, probabilistic expert systems, forensic genetics, and quantitative approaches for questioned document examination.

Michael Joffe is Emeritus Reader in Epidemiology at Imperial College London. His epidemiological work has been mainly in relation to environmental chemicals and health, especially reproduction, and he has developed a widely used method of assessing biological fertility. He has also made other methodological contributions relating to causality in epidemiology. He has had considerable experience providing technical advice to government (including the EU and WHO), and was a member of the UK Committee on Toxicity of Chemicals for nine years. In addition he has postgraduate qualifications in sociology and economics.

David Lagnado is a lecturer in the Department of Cognitive, Perceptual and Brain Sciences at University College London. He has co-authored a book, *Straight Choices: the Psychology of Decision Making*, with Ben Newell and David Shanks (Psychology Press, 2007). He runs an M.Sc. course in Cognitive and Decision Sciences at UCL.

Jill Russell is Senior Lecturer in Health Policy and Evaluation, Healthcare Innovation and Policy Unit, Centre for Primary Care and Public Health, Blizard Institute at Barts and The London School of Medicine and Dentistry, Queen Mary University of London. She has a background in social policy and medical sociology and her recent research interests include discursive approaches to health policy analysis.

David A. Schum holds the rank of Professor in the School of Information Technology and Engineering and in the School of Law at George Mason University, and the position of Chief Scientist at the Learning Agents Center at George Mason. In 2003 he was named Honorary Professor of Evidence Science at University College London. Schum has had a career-long interest in the study of the properties, uses, discovery, and marshalling of evidence in complex probabilistic reasoning tasks. He has published over a hundred papers and is the author or co-author of five books on these topics. He was presented with the Outstanding Research Faculty Award in Information Technology and Engineering at George Mason University in 2006.

Jacob Stegenga is a postdoctoral fellow at the University of Toronto. Prior to completing his doctorate at University of California, San Diego, he was an epidemiologist with the Public Health Agency of Canada. His research focuses on the assessment of scientific evidence and the importance and methodological challenges of diverse bodies of evidence.

Peter Tillers is Professor of Law at Cardozo School of Law, Yeshiva University. He recently edited (with J. Jackson and M. Langer) *Crime, Procedure, and Evidence in a Comparative and International Context* (Hart Publishing, 2008). At Cardozo he teaches the law of evidence, a course in fact investigation, and other courses related to evidence.

William Twining is Quain Professor of Jurisprudence Emeritus at University College London and Visiting Professor at the University of Miami School of Law. His recent works include *Analysis of Evidence* (2nd edn., 2005, with Terry Anderson, David Schum and Philip Dawid), *Rethinking Evidence* (2nd edn., 2006) and *How to Do Things With Rules* (5th edn., 2010 with David Miers), all published by Cambridge University Press. For most years since 1983 he has taught the UCL LLM course on Evidence and Proof.

Mimi Vasilaki is completing a doctorate in Comparative Literature at UCL on the theory of criticism. She has published in the journal *Philosophy and Literature* and in *Scandal. Proceedings of the European School for Comparative Studies: The Synapsis Notebooks VIII* (ed. Rosaria Carbotti, Le Monnier, 2009).

Alison Wylie is Professor of Philosophy and Anthropology at the University of Washington. She is a philosopher of science who works on philosophical issues raised by archaeological practice and by feminist research in the social sciences: ideals of objectivity, the role of contextual values in research practice, and models of evidential reasoning. Her publications include *Thinking from Things: Essays in the Philosophy of Archaeology* (University of California Press, 2002); edited volumes such as *Value-free Science?* (with Kincaid and Dupré, Oxford University Press, 2007), *Epistemic Diversity and Dissent* (Special Issue of *Episteme*, 2006), and *Feminist Science Studies* (*Hypatia*, 2004); as well as essays that appear in *The Ethics of Cultural Appropriation* (Wiley, 2009), *Agnatology* (Stanford University Press, 2008), *Evaluating Multiple Narratives* (Springer, 2007), the *Handbook of Feminist Research* (Sage, 2007), *Science and other Cultures* (Routledge, 2003). She is currently working on a monograph, *Standpoint Matters, in Feminist Philosophy of Science*.

1

INTRODUCTION*

PHILIP DAWID

Information or evidence?

MODERN TECHNOLOGY provides for the collection and manipulation of vast quantities of data of many different kinds, and a new and all-pervading field of intellectual and practical activity, 'Information Technology', has sprung up to support these data-handling requirements. In contrast, relatively little attention has been paid to the issues of combining, comparing, linking and—most important—interpreting all these data, so turning them from *information* into *evidence*. The need to understand and interpret evidence is surely as fundamental to all human enquiry as Aristotelian logic, and just as ancient; but from classical until modern times there has been all too little interest displayed in general principles of evidential reasoning.

The gathering and interpretation of evidence are essential activities in every major intellectual discipline, from ancient history to cosmology, yet different disciplines conceive of and use evidence in very different ways. At a high level, there are broad differences in focus, approach and method between the sciences and the humanities. In many scientific areas, researchers will expend much effort on devising and implementing clever experimental designs for producing or gathering data to ensure they will have high evidential value, and may regard other methods, such as observational studies, as inferior to the point of uselessness. With the data in, their evidential impact might then be assessed by the application of more or less formal statistical methods

*We are deeply indebted to the Leverhulme Trust, not only for financial support but also for its foresight in identifying Evidence as a topic of interest, and for its continuing interest in the activities of the University College London Evidence Programme. We are also grateful to the Economic and Social Research Council for the additional support it provided to make the Programme possible. UCL provided valuable administrative support and a congenial environment, while the staff and facilities of the British Academy were crucial to the success of our closing conference. We are also indebted to the British Academy for its assistance in producing and publishing this volume.

Proceedings of the British Academy, **171**, 1–9. © The British Academy 2011.

(though many scientists will be somewhat vague as to when these are appropriate, and unaware of the deep philosophical rifts, having serious practical consequences, which divide the statistical community). But there are also many scientific subjects, such as archaeology, astronomy and epidemiology, where experimentation is difficult, impossible, or simply inappropriate to the task at hand. These raise different issues of the nature and use of evidence, drawing closer to the situation more typical in the humanities, where there may be few if any opportunities for generating new evidence, let alone for control over the quality of the evidence-generating process. It may then seem important to try and squeeze as much useful information as one can out of whatever material may be available. Workers in these areas may be sceptical of the idea that evidential value can be neatly arranged in hierarchies, and quite as interested in the evidence of reported individual experiences as that produced by double-blind randomised interventional studies.

Some disciplines have developed sophisticated methodologies for handling the type of evidence that tends to arise in their field, but it is rare that there is consideration or discussion of general approaches to evidence even within a discipline, let alone across different disciplines. In practical affairs, there are some areas, such as medicine, where the importance of basing practice on sound evidence and reasoning (what might have been termed evidence-based medicine, had that term not developed what many regard as too narrow an interpretation) is becoming increasingly appreciated. But there is also much resistance to this idea, and those attempting to spread it still more widely, for example into evidence-based policymaking (interpreted, again, in the very broadest sense) may find they are fighting a long uphill battle against politicians, administrators and other policymakers who would rather base their decisions on personal and political preconceptions and prejudices. Indeed, in public life there is all too rarely any examination of the way evidence is sought and used, nor any conception that these tasks could have an underlying rational foundation. Unintelligent use of evidence is widespread and damaging. In the face of terrorist threats, training and practice in intelligence analysis still fail to address fundamental principles. In law enforcement there is scant appreciation of the import of missing evidence, while new evidence is typically sought to try and firm up a currently favoured theory, rather than to discriminate well between the various viable alternatives. In forensic science, distinct types of evidence such as DNA, fingerprints, fibres, etc. will be handled by different teams, using different specialist methods, rather than integrated under a 'substance-blind' approach. Similar inadequacies pervade decision-making in politics, medicine, public health and commerce.

Understanding the nature and impact of evidence is a non-trivial and often counter-intuitive task. Evidence never speaks for itself, but has to be interpreted through the filters of models, assumptions and analyses. Generic attributes of evidence include accuracy, credibility, objectivity, relevance, provenance and weight. One item of evidence may corroborate another, or conflict with it, or explain away its apparent message. Items of evidence and hypotheses can form complex interrelated chains or webs, outstripping unaided human comprehension. If there were such a thing as a general theory of evidence, it would have to explicate and analyse such issues.

While there is a long history of theorising about evidence in some contexts, notably law, probability theory, epistemology and historiography, there have been relatively few attempts to make evidence itself the subject of a general theory. Jeremy Bentham, whose spirit (if such it is) still hovers over UCL where his mortal remains are housed, wrote as much about evidence as any other subject. His main work (Bentham 1827) focused on legal trials, although it had much wider implications. Another highly significant attempt, also grounded in law but of much wider relevance, was that of the American jurist John Henry Wigmore, as expounded in Wigmore (1913).[1] In more recent times, David Schum has been one of the few voices raised in support of the possibility of a general intellectual approach to understanding and handling evidence, transcending disciplines. His original and incisive book (Schum 1994) presents a thorough and thoughtful account of general principles of evidential analysis, well attuned to the needs of the intelligent common man trying to make sense of the world.

The UCL Evidence Programme

In an attempt to rectify the relative lack of attention to the nature of evidence, an interdisciplinary research programme 'Evidence, Inference and Enquiry: Towards an Integrated Science of Evidence' (generally known simply as the 'Evidence Programme') was established at UCL in 2004, with generous funding from the Leverhulme Trust and the Economic and Social Research Council. This incorporated and coordinated a collection of individual research projects across a broad range of subjects studied at UCL, including

---

[1] The third edition, entitled *The Science of Judicial Proof* was published in 1937. A modern account and development of Wigmore's ideas may be found in Anderson *et al.* (2005); see also Twining (1986).

Education, Economics, Forensic Science, Health Sciences, History, Law, Philosophy of Science, Statistics, and Psychology. It also provided a range of integrating activities, including seminars, conferences and reading groups. Further information about the UCL Evidence Programme may be accessed online at <http://www.ucl.ac.uk/jdi/research/evidence-network> which contains an archive of all its activities. The Evidence Programme culminated in a public Symposium: 'Enquiry, Evidence and Facts: An Interdisciplinary Conference' held at the British Academy in December 2007, addressed by Programme participants and distinguished external speakers: this was organised jointly with our sister Leverhulme-funded research programme 'How Well Do Facts Travel?', directed at the London School of Economics by Mary Morgan (see <http://www2. lse.ac.uk/economicHistory/Research/facts/Home. aspx>). The BA Symposium was preceded by a satellite meeting held at UCL in which researchers from the various constituent projects of the UCL Evidence Programme described their work. The present book is largely based around the findings of the UCL Evidence Programme and the presentations made at the British Academy Symposium and the satellite meeting.

The UCL Evidence Programme itself developed out of a long-standing collaboration between Philip Dawid, Professor of Statistics, and William Twining, Professor of Jurisprudence. To their own initial surprise, they had identified and developed fruitful similarities and links between the conceptions of evidence, and methods for manipulating it, as these entered into the two apparently unrelated disciplines of Statistics and of Law. This led to Dawid's contributing over many years to a course on 'Evidence and Proof' given by Twining to postgraduate law students, as well as an Appendix on 'Probability and Proof' for the associated book *Analysis of Evidence*. Twining in turn was a collaborator of David Schum, who had developed his specialist study of the use of evidence in Law and Intelligence Analysis into a more general approach to the handling of evidence. Particularly helpful tools for this enterprise were found to be certain graphical representations of complex webs of evidence: specifically, in Law, Wigmore's 'Chart Method', and, in Statistics and Artificial Intelligence, 'Bayesian networks'.

Thus when the Leverhulme Trust issued a call in 2002 for proposals for a research programme on 'The Nature of Evidence', this fell on fertile ground, with Dawid and Twining keen to take advantage of this opportunity and to involve David Schum as 'guiding guru'. In view of the special concern with 'evidence as a multidisciplinary subject', and considering that an interest in Evidence ought to be a feature of almost every university discipline, the net was spread widely to solicit interest from right across UCL. It was this quintessentially interdisciplinary approach that formed the basis for the Evidence

Programme—though, to the (perhaps unwarranted) surprise and disappointment of the convenors, there was relatively little interest or participation by workers in the 'harder' sciences.

Such a broad interdisciplinary coalition is naturally attended by both benefits and frustrations: indeed one of the projects within the Evidence Programme explored the activities and dynamics of the programme itself as a case study of interdisciplinary working (see Chapter 3, 'Disciplining the Disciplines'). On the benefit side it was pleasing to identify, explore and extend ways in which the different insights, approaches and techniques native to different disciplines could find common ground, and come together to produce genuine advances in our understanding: there was, for example, fruitful interaction between the normative principles and methodological tools developed in the project 'Formal Tools for Handling Evidence', based in Statistical Science, and their exploration in relation to actual behaviour in the project 'Human Attitudes to Evidence', based in Psychology. But serious interdisciplinary differences in points of view were also evident. For example, many researchers in the humanities took exception to the term 'science' in the subtitle of the Programme, considering that it represented an attempt by 'scientists' to expand their area of control; whereas those from the sciences understood it (as had been intended) in the non-specific sense of 'a systematically organised body of knowledge'. More significant still were differences of opinion as to whether such a 'science', even if it could be constructed, would be desirable—some participants considering that much of value would necessarily be squeezed out in the process. But such differences could themselves be turned to positive effect, as in the one-day workshop in which Evidence Programme personnel from a variety of disciplinary backgrounds examined critically the relevance and potential for their own subject of the 'substance- and subject-blind' view of evidential reasoning championed by David Schum.

In Chapter 4 of this book, Twining notes that only limited progress was made during the Evidence Programme towards addressing many of the basic general questions about the nature of evidence. To accomplish these tasks would require a different structure and strategy, and a longer time frame, and it is very much to be hoped that some new programme might one day be conjured up to take up these continuing challenges. The actual achievements of the Evidence Programme should not, however, be undervalued. Perhaps the most important—though this may not be obvious to those not directly involved—was the way in which it changed participants' perceptions of each other. Coming from many disparate backgrounds, carrying a slew of preconceptions both about 'the nature of evidence' and about disciplines other than our own, over the course of the Programme we were able to reach at least a partial understanding of just what it was that others were concerned about, and even sometimes to understand (or at least think we understood) fundamental aspects of their world view, or what they really meant by a seemingly unproblematic turn of phrase. Whether this culminated in collaboration or in reasoned debate over disagreements, it was for many of us a significant experience, even changing the way we go about our everyday business—be that as academics or as human beings.

This book

This book begins with some personal accounts of the background, genesis, execution and achievements of the UCL Evidence Programme. David Schum discusses what might be the appropriate focus and constituents of an 'integrated science of evidence', as well as the very appropriateness of such terminology, which became a source of contestation within the Evidence Programme. He offers a 'substance-blind' classification of generic properties of evidence in terms of relevance and credibility. Jason Davies follows the twists and turns of the 'interdisciplinarity project' within the Evidence Programme, whose self-referring object of study was the overall Programme, and particularly the successes and, more interestingly, failures of attempts at communication across the wide variety of disciplines and personnel it encompassed. William Twining explores the history of theorising about evidence in legal contexts and emphasises that this has long been conceived as a multidisciplinary enterprise, although in developing a general field of evidence many of the specific constraints and concerns of that specialist area have to be left behind. Twining also explores critically some of the reasons for resistance within the UCL Evidence Programme to the very idea of a single multidisciplinary field, and suggests an agenda for carrying this enterprise forward. Together these contributions offer a range of perspectives over the Evidence Programme which may give the reader some feeling for the challenges, both intellectual and organisational, of bringing together strong-minded individuals, from a divergent range of academic disciplines, to address a common goal (especially when some of the participants harbour a variety of scepticisms about that goal); as well as for the several and varied perceptions of the development of the Programme over its lifetime.

The next three chapters describe some general approaches, and associated specific issues, related to the modelling and structuring of complex patterns of evidence. Philip Dawid, Amanda Hepler and David Schum describe and compare *Bayesian networks* and *Wigmore charts*, two different ways of representing evidential relationships in graphical form, and attempt to forge a synthesis. John Fox describes a formal approach to manipulating and combining evidential propositions of less than perfect credibility, inspired by natural features of human decision-making and debate. David Lagnado, using Agatha Christie's play *Witness for the Prosecution* for illustration, considers Bayesian networks as descriptions of courtroom inferences, and reports experiments suggesting that, while human reasoning is sometimes (e.g. for alibi evidence) broadly consistent with such network models, other cognitive strategies appear to be used in other contexts, such as when assessing the impact of discredited evidence.

In the models considered above, support for specific inferences is grounded in background generalisations. Terence Anderson undertakes a detailed analysis and classification of such generalisations and their application to inferential reasoning. In a more sceptical vein, Peter Tillers discusses the limitations of approaches to modelling and handling evidential issues using hierarchical network representations, arguing that for certain important problems, especially where these concern meaning and human understandings, these need to be complemented by other methods.

A still deeper scepticism, of 'scientistic' approaches to questions involving the distribution of values, is expressed by Jill Russell and Trisha Greenhalgh. They are concerned that, for policy analysis, any systematic approach to evidence risks privileging numerical and economic considerations to the exclusion of softer and more personal inputs, such as experience, value judgements and moral preferences, which are equally valid and relevant. They develop their case with an account of deliberative processes of evidence construction within a group tasked with prioritising spending on medical care.

Policy analysis is also the focus of the chapter by Nancy Cartwright and Jacob Stegenga, who point out that the quality criteria relevant for consumers of evidence can be very different from those applied by its producers. They propose a philosophical framework for causal modelling as a helpful structure and guide. In contrast the working scientist David Colquhoun claims that the contributions of philosophers to causal understanding have been unhelpful. He puts the case for randomised studies as the safest guarantee of the reliability of scientific evidence. A somewhat different line of philosophical investigation, concerning the degree of confirmation afforded to a general hypothesis by an observation, is undertaken by Hasok Chang and Grant Fisher. They base their analysis of Hempel's celebrated 'ravens paradox' (which suggests that the observation of a white shoe lends support to the hypothesis 'all ravens are black') on the idea that the impact of evidence can not be a matter of logic alone, but must also depend on the context and nature of activities of observation and testing.

Alison Wylie adopts a philosophical perspective on evidential reasoning in archaeology. She argues that strong relativist and scientistic positions in debates within anthropological archaeology are both based on simplistic assumptions. The 'scientists' set standards of credibility that are too high, while the relativists underestimate the confirmatory power of epistemically independent lines of evidence. Drawing on philosophical theories of confirmation and model building, Wylie outlines an approach with potential significance beyond archaeology. Next, Jason Davies explores the consequences, for ancient history, of the move to conceiving of religion in terms of ritual rather than belief. This has fundamental implications for perceptions of what evidence is, and what it is evidence of, when interpreting ancient religions. He argues that the transition is incomplete, and that this threatens to distort our understanding of the subject.

Using biology as a comparator, Michael Joffe examines the extent to which mainstream economic theory can be regarded as 'scientific', and finds it wanting, most crucially in elevating elegant theorising above empirical evidence and deep causal understanding. Finally, Tony Gardner-Medwin champions the elicitation and use of probabilistic measures of uncertainty, and compares two different views (roughly corresponding, respectively, to the Bayesian and frequentist approaches to statistical inference) as to how probabilities should be used as evidence. He argues that, while the former may be a logical ideal, the latter may be more appropriate in the special circumstances of the courtroom.

The contributions to this book address many issues related to the understanding and use of evidence, starting from a broad spectrum of disciplinary and personal positions but informed and to some extent moulded by the many interdisciplinary exchanges that were a feature of the UCL Evidence Programme. Although we cannot claim to have reached anything like a settled view of 'The Nature of Evidence', we hope that the processes and the outcomes reported here might be regarded as taking at least one step towards that end.

References

Anderson, T. J., Twining, W. L. and Schum, D. A. (2005), *Analysis of Evidence* (2nd edn.) (Cambridge, Cambridge University Press).

Bentham, J. (1827), *Rationale of Judicial Evidence* (5 vols., ed. John Stuart Mill) (London, Hunt and Clarke).

Schum, D. A. (1994), *The Evidential Foundations of Probabilistic Reasoning* (New York, Wiley).

Twining, W. L. (1986), *Theories of Evidence: Bentham and Wigmore* (Stanford, Stanford University Press).

Wigmore, J. H. (1913), *The Principles of Proof as Given by Logic, Psychology and General Experience and illustrated in Judicial Trials* (Boston, Little, Brown).

2

Classifying Forms and Combinations of Evidence: Necessary in a Science of Evidence*

DAVID SCHUM

Abstract

As our work proceeded on a project entitled 'Evidence, Inference and Inquiry: Towards an Integrated Science of Evidence', I became interested in what would constitute a science of evidence and how it might compare with other areas commonly identified as being sciences. I had encountered the term science of evidence in reading other works and had used it myself on one occasion. But I had never read any form of justification for using the term science with reference to the many different studies of evidence coming from a variety of different disciplines. And I had never attempted to provide such justification myself. So, I collected my thoughts about what would justify these studies being called a science. Naturally, I had to consider how the meaning of the terms evidence and science have changed or mutated over the centuries as well as how these terms are used today. On this occasion, I will dwell upon one of the most important requisites of any activity that can be referred to as being scientific. What is necessary in any area of science, including the science of evidence, is our ability to classify or categorise phenomena and concepts. There are other requisites of scientific studies that I will mention, but the necessity for classification is perhaps the most important, being recognised as such by the eminent scientists and philosophers of science that I will mention.

If we cannot usefully classify evidence, how can we say anything general about evidence or compare the evidence in one situation with the evidence in another situation? One thing we can immediately rule out as a basis for classifying evidence is its substance or content, that varies in a

*The author is most grateful for the support of this research that was provided by the Leverhulme Foundation and the Economic and Social Research Council to University College London. The author also wishes to express his thanks to an anonymous reviewer for the many helpful suggestions that were provided.

Proceedings of the British Academy, **171**, 11–36. © The British Academy 2011.

near infinite fashion. But evidence forms the foundation for inferential reasoning in any conceivable discipline, and there are three important inferential credentials of all evidence: relevance, credibility and inferential (or probative) weight or force. Some years ago, while searching for useful ways to categorise evidence, it occurred to me that evidence could be usefully categorised on inferential grounds involving the concepts of relevance and credibility. I knew of other attempts to classify evidence but I believed that there were additional distinctions among classes of evidence that were possible. The evidence classification scheme I developed I have referred to as being *substance blind*, meaning that the classes of individual items of evidence I identify are recurrent and apply regardless of the substance or content of the evidence. There are also substance-blind combinations of evidence that are also recurrent. The term substance-blindness may cause some confusion. But I will show how substance-blindness occurs as a matter of course involving concepts encountered throughout science, logic, and mathematics.

A science of evidence

IN A BOOK I wrote a few years ago on evidence and probabilistic reasoning I posed a question concerning whether there could be a science of evidence.[1] I did not propose this science myself but borrowed it from a book written by the American scholar of evidence John H. Wigmore (1863–1943).[2] Wigmore, in turn, borrowed the idea of this science from an English mystery writer named Israel Zangwill (1864–1926). Zangwill used the term *science of evidence* in a detective story entitled: *The Big Bow Mystery*.[3] In this story the main character says that the science of evidence is hardly a matter of just common sense but is in fact the 'science of the sciences'. Wigmore used this quote as the frontispiece of his work *The Science of Judicial Proof*. I have often thought that Wigmore could just as easily have titled his work: *The Science of Evidence,* since the bulk of this book mainly concerns the properties, uses, and marshalling of different forms and combinations of evidence that come to us from different sources. Such was my respect for Wigmore that I was ready to believe there must be a science of evidence if Wigmore thought so. However, until quite recently, I had given little thought about how one would defend the idea of there being a science of evidence and how this science could compare with work in other areas that, without much controversy, are commonly said to be scientific in nature.

[1] Schum, 1994.
[2] Wigmore, 1937.
[3] Zangwill, 1891.

The objective of this paper is to show how necessary it is for any science, including a science of evidence, to be able to classify phenomena of interest. Classifying evidence seems impossible since there is a virtually unlimited variety of it as far as its substance or content is concerned. For some years now, I have advocated a scheme for classifying evidence in terms of its inferential properties or credentials. The classification scheme I will tell you about for individual evidence items and combinations of them does not depend in any way upon the substance or content of evidence. The forms and combinations of evidence I will mention are recurrent in any context. Being able to classify evidence on inferential grounds has many useful consequences. This allows us to discuss some very general properties of evidence and to meaningfully compare the meaning of evidence in different evidential reasoning tasks and within a given particular inferential task. A very kind reviewer asked if this paper bears on the philosophy of science or the psychology of science. My reply is that it bears on both, as well as upon any other discipline in which drawing defensible and persuasive conclusions from masses of evidence is of primary interest.

The UCL studies of evidence

In 2003, I was very pleased and honoured to be invited by Professors Philip Dawid and William Twining to participate in a project at University College London (UCL) entitled: *Evidence, Inference and Inquiry: Towards an Integrated Science of Evidence*. This project has enjoyed the support of the Leverhulme Foundation and the Economics and Social Research Council, and has been so capably directed by Professor Dawid. Thinking about the title of this proposal and how it involved an 'integrated science of evidence', I believed it necessary for someone to seriously consider defending the work on evidence in many disciplines as being scientific in nature. William Twining has never had any trouble convincing me that evidence is a multidisciplinary subject.[4] What was a bit troubling to me was the thought that, if there was no such thing as a science of evidence, why should we worry about whether it is 'integrated' or not? So, I spent a fair amount of time thinking about what should be considered in any defensible and persuasive argument that there is indeed a science of evidence. I was unable to find anyone who had already attempted to offer such a defence. So, I wrote a paper summarising my thoughts about a science of evidence.[5]

[4] Twining, 2003.
[5] Schum, 2005.

Our research on evidence attracted the interests of many colleagues at UCL in the fields of probability, statistics, law, medicine, geography, education, philosophy, ancient history, economics, psychology, and computer science. Clearly, as the other chapters in this volume illustrate, persons in these areas naturally have different standpoints in the study of evidence. They have different objectives and methods in their studies and have different insights into the properties and uses of evidence in their disciplines. Thus, our research on evidence at UCL certainly corresponds with Twining's claim that evidence is a multidisciplinary subject and one that can be integrated in nature if we agree to share our ideas about evidence, as we are doing in this present volume.

As our work progressed, and we enjoyed many meetings to share our thoughts about evidence, I was quite interested to hear several persons object to using the term 'science' to characterise studies based on evidence in their own areas. Others argued that the term 'science' was too strong and that we should simply say that our work involved the 'study of evidence', in spite of the fact that we had told our sponsors that we were working toward developing an 'integrated science of evidence'. There may be a variety of reasons why persons in certain disciplines may not wish to associate their work with science. One reason may be that scientists in certain areas often quite arrogantly suppose that their methods allow them access to truth more readily than do studies by persons in allegedly underprivileged areas such as the humanities and the social and behavioural sciences. Some may even reject the idea of social and behavioural research as being among the sciences.

A very elegant counterargument to these ideas has been provided recently by the logician and philosopher of science Susan Haack. In a recent work, she seeks to defend science against a variety of extreme charges.[6] On the one hand she rejects what she calls 'scientism', the exaggerated showing of deference towards science and the acceptance of any claim made by science as being authoritative, as if scientists are epistemologically privileged. On the other hand, she rejects the many current cynical critics of science who have said that scientists' stated concerns for honest inquiry, respect for evidence, and a search for truth are illusions being used as a cover for their other agenda relating to power, politics, or rhetoric. A statement she made bears repeating in our present discussions about a science of evidence:

> The core standards of good evidence and well-conducted inquiry are not internal to the sciences, but common to empirical inquiry of every kind. ... respect for evidence, care in weighing it, and persistence in seeking it out, so far from being exclusively scientific desiderata, are the standards by which we judge *all* inquirers,

[6] Haack, 2007.

detectives, historians, investigative journalists, etc., as well as scientists. In short, the sciences are not epistemologically privileged.[7]

Persons who fear that their work will be associated with a science of evidence should consider that almost certainly they use a Windows PC or a MAC every day without fear that their work will be thought to be a part of computer science. There being a science of evidence should not threaten anyone regardless of their interests, unless their work does not meet the reasonable standards Susan Haack sets for all of us.

Criteria for a science of evidence

I considered various criteria for claims that any area of research could be called scientific in nature. These criteria are more specific but are certainly consistent with the general ones Susan Haack mentioned. One of these specific criteria, perhaps the most fundamental one, involves the ability of a science to systematically classify phenomena of interest in its field. This was the view taken by an eminent scientist, Jules Henri Poincaré (1854–1912), and an eminent philosopher of science, Rudolf Carnap (1891–1970), whose works I will mention. However, as far as a science of evidence is concerned, systematic classification of evidence would be quite impossible, and useless, if we just considered its substance or content. The reason of course is that there is a virtually unlimited variety of evidence as far as its substance or content is concerned. I had earlier developed a scheme for classifying recurrent forms and combinations of evidence on inferential grounds involving its relevance and credibility characteristics.[8] I referred to this classification scheme as being 'substance-blind' since its classes are recurrent and apply to all evidence regardless of its substance or content.

But my use of the term 'substance-blindness' regarding evidence aroused some controversy. What I had said about there being a scheme for classifying *all* evidence regardless of its substance or content has occasionally been misinterpreted. One major objective in the present work is to revisit the importance of being able to systematically classify evidence, to emphasise again what I mean and do not mean by the term substance-blindness, and to show how so many concepts we encounter in every area of science, in logic, and in mathematics are substance-blind. I will also have some additional comments

---

[7] Haack, 2007, p. 23.
[8] Schum, 1994, at pp. 114–35 in both editions.

to make about a substance-blind classification of evidence and what it offers anyone concerned about evidence and its inferential uses.

Five criteria for science that I considered

There are hundreds of books written about science and its history, objectives, and methods. I searched through a number of these works hoping to find a collection of criteria for justifying an area of knowledge as being a science. Many of the works I consulted assumed a particular area of science, and some seemed to emphasise the alleged epistemological privilege about which Susan Haack complained. I finally settled on a list of five criteria for an area to be called a science that is provided by *The New Shorter Oxford English Dictionary* (*NSOED*). Here is a set of criteria the *NSOED* provides[9]:

1. Knowledge obtained by study; acquaintance with or mastery of a department of learning.
2. A particular branch of knowledge or study; a recognised department of learning.
3. A branch of study that deals either with a connected body of demonstrated truths or with observed facts systematically classified and more or less comprehended by general laws, and which includes reliable methods for the discovery of new truths in its own domain.
4. The kind of organised knowledge or intellectual activity of which various branches of learning are examples.
5. The intellectual and practical activity encompassing those branches of study that apply objective scientific method to the phenomena of the physical universe (the natural sciences), and the knowledge so gained.

I assumed that the standpoints of the writers of dictionaries and scientists themselves might be quite different. However, a fair guess is that the *OED* consulted with a number of scientists in order to evaluate the merits of this listing of criteria. In any case, in spite of its possible inadequacies, I thought this listing was a good place to start in my defence of there being a science of evidence; but I have added to it as I will explain later. In my *Thoughts about a Science of Evidence*,[10] I considered a variety of past and current research on evidence coming from the fields of law, probability, history, medicine, and other areas. Criteria 1, 2, and 4 are quite general and I had no trouble in claiming that the evidence research I mentioned met these general criteria. But criteria 3 and 5 are more specific and required additional deliberation on my part in justifying how works on evidence meet these criteria. Criterion 5 is

---

[9] *The New Shorter Oxford English Dictionary*, vol. 2, 1993, p. 2717.
[10] Schum, 2005

troublesome since it supposes that there is a settled 'objective scientific method' applicable in all scientific activity. But I was quick to note the views of respected scientists who have argued that the claim of there being a unique and uniformly accepted 'scientific method' is groundless. For example, I cited the work of a chemist Henry H. Bauer. Bauer claims that 'the scientific method' is a myth that has caused others, including scientists, educators and the general public, no end of trouble.[11] He says that 'the scientific method' is useless as a guide to what scientists actually do and that it is worse than useless as a guide to what the public might think about science and technology. In particular, this myth encourages the view that scientists are somehow not like the rest of us, but always are objective, patient, careful, and good observers. This myth sounds very much like the alleged epistemological privilege of the sciences to which Susan Haack objected.

The classification criterion and its importance

Criterion 3 concerning classification allows me to comment on what may be the most important criterion for any science, including a science of evidence. Here I draw upon the work of Jules Henri Poincaré, the celebrated French mathematician and physicist that I mentioned earlier. Poincaré emphasised the importance of classification in all of science. As he said:

> Now what is science? ... it is before all a classification, a manner of bringing together facts which appearances separate, though they were bound together by some natural and hidden kinship. Science, in other words, is a system of relations.[12]

But Poincaré went even further; he said in a later work that the most interesting facts are *recurrent* and can be used several times. He said that we are fortunate to be born in a world where there are such facts.[13] As an illustration, he asks us to suppose that, instead of there being eighty chemical elements (the number of chemical elements identified in Poincaré's time), there were eighty million elements, more or less uniformly distributed. In such instances nearly every pebble we could pick up would be unique; nothing we could say about one pebble would tell us anything about any other pebble. This would make any science of geology impossible. Similarly, if every living organism were unique this would make fields such as biology impossible. He concluded that the inability to classify would make any science impossible. If we considered

[11] Bauer, 1994.
[12] Poincaré, 1905.
[13] Poincaré, 1908.

just the substance or content of evidence there would be a number very much larger than the eighty million elements in Poincaré's example; and so any science of evidence would be impossible.

But I also considered the thoughts about science from the philosopher of science Rudolph Carnap, who also recognised the importance of classification in science.[14] Carnap argued that there are three kinds of concepts in science, as well as in everyday life: *classificatory*, *comparative*, and *quantitative*. He said that by a 'classificatory' concept he meant that an object could be placed within a certain class. As examples, he cited taxonomies in botany and zoology. Carnap's focus on comparative and quantitative concepts in science and elsewhere is also very interesting as far as concerns a science of evidence. For example, having a defensible and useful method for classifying evidence allows us to compare the force of our evidence in different problems or situations; it also allows us to compare the force of evidence at different points in the same problem or situation. Speaking of the force of evidence, Carnap's listing of quantitative concepts becomes so important in a science of evidence. On all views known to me, the force of evidence is graded in quantitative probabilistic terms. So, mathematics in the form of probability theories appears as a criterion for a science of evidence. This corresponds with the views of philosopher Carl Hemple on the importance of mathematics in the sciences including a science of evidence.[15] There are of course different ways of expressing our probabilistic views about the force of evidence. The probabilistic force of evidence can be expressed in words or in various numerical terms as Anderson, Twining and I have noted[16].

A substance-blind classification of evidence

In the classification of evidence to be described I have used the term 'substance-blindness' with reference to recurrent types or forms of individual items of evidence and to recurrent combinations of evidence. What the evidence tells us, or what information it conveys, does depend on its substance or content. In a series of challenges to some of my views about evidence, one critic said that I had generated a substance-blind 'theory of inference'. I have never said such a thing, since the actual conclusions we infer from evidence always depend on the substance or content of our evidence. Here are some further

[14] Carnap, 1966, p. 51.
[15] Hemple, 1956.
[16] Anderson, Schum and Twining, 2005.

thoughts about the concept of substance-blindness in the classification of evidence.

I first return to part of Poincaré's quote regarding classification that I mentioned earlier. He said: 'Science, in other words, is a system of relations.' This quote bears directly upon how we can think of evidence as a system of relations. A very natural question is: what exactly is evidence? Hear William Twining on evidence and relations:

> 'Evidence' is a word of relation used in the context of argumentation. (A is evidence of B). In that context information has a potential role as relevant evidence if it tends to support or tends to negate, directly or indirectly, a hypothesis or probandum. One draws inferences from evidence in order to prove or disprove a hypothesis or probandum. The framework is argument, the process is proof, and the engine is inferential reasoning from information.[17]

Combining the thoughts of Poincaré and Twining, we might say that science is a system involving the evidential relations between the observations we make and the hypotheses or probanda[18] we entertain as explanations for the occurrence of these observations. We might argue that the science of evidence is the science of these evidential relations in science. I have often wondered what was in the back of Israel Zangwill's mind when he had his character in *The Big Bow Mystery* say: 'The science of evidence is the science of sciences'. Whether the science of evidence can be said to be the science of science is not part of my present story. I note that others have studied what seems to be involved in a science of science and have argued that this science involves more than just evidential relations.[19] This acknowledged, I can now begin to discuss the dimensions of a substance-blind classification of evidence.

Classification dimensions: individual items of evidence

All evidence has three major inferential credentials or properties known to me: *relevance*, *credibility*, and *inferential force or weight*. Inferences in any imaginable area, whether you consider this area to be part of science or not, rest upon evidence having these three credentials. Two of these credentials form the basis for my classification of evidence; here is where its substance-blindness arises since these three credentials apply to all evidence regardless of the situation in which it arises. The classification of individual items of evidence I will

---

[17] Twining, 2003, p. 97.
[18] The word *probandum*, from Latin *a matter to be proved*, was a term Wigmore used in preference to the word *hypothesis*. See Wigmore, 1937, p. 9.
[19] For example see Mayr, 1982.

offer is based entirely upon inferential grounds concerning relevance and credibility. Why my classification of evidence does not rest upon the inferential force or weight credential I will discuss in a moment. It is necessary of course for me to be specific about what these three evidence credentials mean and how I will employ them in classifying individual items of evidence. Other matters arise when we consider combinations of evidence items.

The relevance dimension

First, the *relevance* credential answers the question: so what? how does this information, whatever form it takes, bear upon what we are trying to prove or disprove? Data or items of information only become evidence when their relevance to hypotheses being considered is established by defensible arguments or chains of reasoning. In many works the terms 'data' and 'information' are taken to be synonymous with the term 'evidence', but this is quite unfortunate. There are untold trillions of data or items of information in existence that will never become evidence in the inferences of concern to anyone. Here is a datum or item of information for you. As I write these words I am currently working in my basement office where my thermometer reads 64.1° F. Unless you are currently studying my working conditions, you are entitled to say: 'So what? Why should I be interested in this information about the temperature in your office?' The term 'fact' is also troublesome when it is equated with the term 'evidence'. Here comes John who tells us that it was Henry who threw a rock through his professor's window this morning. We all heard John say this and so we regard his testimony as fact. But whether Henry did throw the rock through his professor's window is not a fact but a source of doubt since we have John's credibility to consider. What this means is that we must always distinguish between evidence about an event and the event itself. I have more to say on this distinction when I consider the credibility credential.

But there are two species of relevance to consider: *direct* and *indirect*. Evidence is *directly relevant* if we can form a defensible argument or chain of reasoning linking the evidence to hypotheses we entertain. Suppose Henry will be charged with malicious threats he allegedly made toward his professor. John's evidence about Henry throwing the rock through the professor's window opens up one line of reasoning bearing on the hypothesis underlying this charge. So John's testimony is directly relevant on this hypothesis. But evidence can be *indirectly relevant* if it bears upon the strength or weakness of links in a chain of reasoning set up by directly relevant evidence. Other names given to indirectly relevant evidence are *ancillary evidence, auxiliary evidence*, or *meta-evidence*. The term meta-evidence is useful since it shows how indirectly relevant evidence is evidence about other evidence. But it also reminds us that we have an infinite regress on our hands. We have evidence, evidence about this evidence, evidence about the evidence about this evidence, and so on, ad infinitum. As examples of ancillary evidence, we first have Ralph who says that it was 5 a.m., before sunrise, when John made his observation and there were no streetlights in the vicinity. So, how can John be sure that it was Henry who threw the rock? Then, we have Ruth who tells us that John was on very bad terms with Henry and had often wished he could get Henry into trouble. Neither of these items of evidence is directly relevant on the hypothesis that Henry did make malicious threats against his professor, but they are indirectly relevant since they bear on John's credibility.

The credibility dimension

The credibility credential concerns the question: can we believe that the event(s) reported in the evidence actually occurred? Just because we have evidence for the occurrence of an event does not entail that this event did occur. This is precisely where the distinction between evidence about an event and the event itself arises. I have long thought that assessing the credibility of evidence and its sources is the most interesting but difficult task we face in evaluating the evidence we are considering in any context. Part of the reason is that we must ask different credibility-related questions for different kinds of evidence we have. Two major forms of evidence can be identified: *tangible* and *testimonial*. Tangible evidence is something that can be examined directly by one or more of the senses of the person evaluating the evidence in order to determine what events the evidence reveals. We might say that the person evaluating tangible evidence has a direct sensory interface with a tangible item in order to observe what events it reveals. For tangible evidence the questions we ask depend upon what kind of tangible evidence we have. Two different kinds of tangible evidence have been usefully discerned, at least in the field of law: *real* and *demonstrative* tangible evidence.[20] Real evidence is a thing itself such as a bullet or shell casing, a human corpse, blood samples, an original document or a contract. Demonstrative tangible evidence is not a thing itself but only a representation or illustration of this thing. Examples include such things as a floor plan of a house, a photo of a person, a diagram of a device, and a chemical analysis of a blood sample. The major credibility attribute of real tangible evidence is its *authenticity*; is this thing what it is represented as being? Authenticity is also an attribute of demonstrative tangible

---

[20] e.g. Lempert, Gross and Liebman, 2000, pp. 1146–8.

evidence, but we are also concerned about the *reliability* and *accuracy* of the process used to produce the evidence.

The credibility of testimonial evidence given by witnesses involves different questions than those asked about tangible evidence. First, there are so many instances in which the evaluator of evidence does not have a direct sensory interface with evidence; i.e., the evidence is not tangible in nature. Instead, this evaluator of evidence must rely upon the report or testimony of another person who did, allegedly, have some sensory interface with the evidence. This other person, whom we can call an *ordinary witness*, tells the evaluator what this witness saw, heard, touched, smelled, or tasted during a direct observation of something. There are two important classes of questions we must ask of this witness.

The first concerns the *competence* of this witness and there are two major questions regarding competence. The first is: did this witness actually make the observation this witness claims to have made? Another way of asking this question is to inquire: did this witness have access to the information being reported? The second question is: did this witness understand what was being observed well enough to give the evaluator an accurate and intelligible account of what was observed? Consider again John's testimony about Henry's throwing the rock through the professor's window. To what extent can we believe that John was actually in a location where and when he could have observed what he reported about Henry. Then, we must also ask whether John knows Henry well enough to identify Henry as being the person he saw throwing the rock. So, *access* and *understanding* are the two major issues concerning the competence of witnesses who report on the basis of observations they allegedly have made. But there is an entirely different class of questions we must ask of ordinary witnesses; these questions concern the *credibility* or *believability* of the witness.

In several other places I have argued that the major attributes of the credibility of witnesses are: *veracity*, *objectivity*, and *observational sensitivity* under the conditions of observation.[21] Veracity concerns whether the witness believes the events being reported actually occurred. Does John believe it was Henry who threw the rock through his professor's window? We can only say that John was truthful if he does believe what he has told us. The second question concerns objectivity and how witnesses have formed their beliefs. Did they form their beliefs on the basis of sensory evidence or on the basis of what they either desired or expected to observe? Objective witnesses base their beliefs on sensory evidence instead of desires or expectations. Did John base his belief

[21] e.g. Schum, 1989; Schum and Morris, 2007.

on sensory evidence or on the basis of his desire for it to be Henry who threw the rock? We recall Ruth saying that John expressed a desire to get Henry into trouble. This information may bear on John's objectivity or his veracity. Memory plays a role here as well since we always wonder whether witnesses have accurately recalled what they have observed. Suppose we believe that a witness is objective and has based a belief on sensory evidence. The remaining question is: how good was this sensory evidence considering both the witness and the conditions under which the observation was made? Apart from John's sensory capabilities and his physical condition at the time he made his observation, we also must consider Ralph's evidence about the very poor ambient conditions under which John made his observation.

Unfortunately, the distinction between competence and credibility is not always made when they are quite separate characteristics of witnesses. I have observed several instances, sadly in the important field of intelligence analysis, in which someone will say: 'We can believe what X said because he had good access to the information he has reported'. This is a glaring non sequitur since the witness may have had all the access in the world but be untruthful in his report about what he observed. Competence does not entail credibility any more than credibility entails competence. We might say that competence considerations allow us to decide whether to take seriously what a witness tells us and to proceed with an evaluation of this witness's credibility.

The *inferential force or weight* credential of evidence allows us to assess: how strong is this evidence in allowing us to prove or disprove some hypothesis being entertained? There are two major reasons why the inferential force or weight of evidence is not an appropriate basis for classifying evidence. The first is that there are several valuable but quite different views about what the force or weight of evidence means and how it should be assessed. In a recent work,[22] Anderson, Twining, and I have given an account of the Bayesian, Belief Function, Baconian, and Fuzzy views of what the force or weight of evidence means and how it should be assessed. Each one of these views tells us important things, but no single view says all there is to be said about the force or weight of evidence. The second reason is that the force or weight of evidence depends on assessments made regarding the other two evidence credentials: relevance and credibility. In making such assessments we ask: how strong are the links in chains of reasoning we have identified in showing the relevance of evidence on hypotheses being considered? In addition, we must ask: how strong are the credibility-related foundations for these chains of reasoning? By focusing on just the relevance and credibility credentials we

---

[22] Anderson, Schum and Twining, 2005, pp. 246–61.

have an adequate basis for the inference-based classification scheme that I have argued is substance-blind.

'Substance blindness' in other contexts

My final words on 'substance-blindness' are to observe that this is hardly a novel concept since it is one that occurs in logic, mathematics, the sciences, and in other areas as well. Consider the syllogistic arguments encountered in logic. The validity of such arguments depends on their form and not on their substance or content. Syllogisms have various forms stated by their *mood* and *figure*. The mood of a syllogism is indicated by the form and the order of the categorical propositions it contains. Mood is represented by three letters: one applied to the syllogism's major premises; one applied to its minor premises; and one applied to its conclusion. These letters can each be one of four possibilities: A, E, I, or O, characterising the subject (S) and predicate (P) of the premises and the conclusion of the syllogism. Letter **A** indicates a universal affirmative: all Ss are Ps; **E** indicates a universal negative: all Ss are not Ps; **I** indicates a particular affirmative: some Ss are Ps; and **O** represents a particular negative: some Ss are not Ps. There are sixty-four moods represented by the possible permutations of these four indications. But each of these four moods can have one of four figures indicating the position of the middle term in the premises. So there are 256 possible standard-form syllogisms, only some of which are valid.

In medieval times, words were contrived as mnemonic devices to help persons remember the mood of a syllogism.[23] Perhaps the most well known is Ba̲rba̲ra̲, a syllogism containing all As, universal affirmatives. One figure of Barbara is:

> All Ms are Ps
> *All Ss are Ms*
> ∴ All Ss are Ps.

What the Ms, Ps, and Ss are is irrelevant as long as they make the major and minor premises true. Thus, from the statement 'all dogs (M) are mammals (P)', and the statement 'all poodles (S) are dogs (M)', we can validly conclude that 'all poodles (S) are mammals (P)'. The syllogism works just as well for people as it does for dogs. Thus, from 'all people are mammals', and 'all Inuits (Canadian Eskimos) are people', we can validly conclude 'all Inuits are mammals'.

---

[23] We are told that it was William of Shyreswood (*c.*1200–71) who first contrived these mnemonics; see Kneale and Kneale, 1984, p. 231.

Mathematics and the sciences abound with substance-blind concepts. Here are two that come from probability theory. Two events A and B are said to be *independent* if P(A|B) = P(A), or equivalently, P(B|A) = P(B). What this says is that knowledge of event B does not change the probability of event A, or that knowledge of event A does not change the probability of event B. Suppose event A = you will win the lottery you just entered, and B = the event that the temperature in my office just now is 64.1° F. You would certainly be entitled to assume that event B is totally irrelevant as far as the probability of event A is concerned. Bayes' rule in probability theory is also substance blind. This rule allows you to determine the probability of some hypothesis (H) in light of evidence (E) you obtain; in symbols, P(H|E). This is called a posterior probability and Bayes' rule tells us how we can determine it. But the hypothesis H can refer to any matter we seek to prove or disprove and can be a possible medical condition, a possible terrorist incident, a possible explanation for an aircraft accident, or tomorrow's weather. Similarly, the evidence can be of any form relevant to the hypothesis whose probability is being determined. In short, Bayes' rule concerns a particular form of a probabilistic relation and not its substance.

A substance-blind classification of evidence

I have already noted the importance both Poincaré and Carnap placed on classification in the sciences. But there are other eminent persons, such as the philosophers Morris R. Cohen and Ernest Nagel, who have commented on the importance of classification in science, but they have also noted the difficulties that surround the formation of classificatory schemes.[24] They mention how difficult it has been to classify living organisms. A major reason, they say, concerns how we define the classes into which we intend to group individual organisms; this problem is still with us today. We might start with the classification schemes devised by Carolus Linnaeus (1707–78), the Swedish botanist who is regarded as the founder of modern systematic botany and zoology. Linnaeus developed a binomial or two-part scheme based on Latin names for an organism's generic name, *genus*, and a more specific name, *species*. Since that time there have been various attempts to form what are called *artificial* and *natural* classifications. Artificial classification is based on one or more characteristics that allow ease of identification. For example, birds can be classified according to their habits and habitats. Natural classification is based

[24] Cohen and Nagel, 1934.

on resemblances and is hierarchical in nature ascending from species, genera, tribes, families, orders, classes, phyla, and kingdom. A newer and somewhat controversial scheme, called *cladistics*, involves placing animals and plants into groups called *clades* that identify their evolutionary relationships. It seems safe to say that study of the process of classifying living organisms is not yet completed.

In my initial thoughts about classifying evidence I paid attention to the writings of John Locke (1632–1704) and John H. Wigmore, whom I have already introduced. In Locke's discussion of the force of evidence, which he referred to as *degrees of assent*, he mentioned several forms and combinations of evidence that are recurrent and are substance-blind.[25] For example, Locke distinguished between tangible and testimonial evidence, and discussed several matters including the credibility of witnesses, contradictory and corroborative evidence, hearsay evidence, and what we term today as accepted facts. Locke never said that his account of evidence was complete, but Wigmore did, at least as far as evidence produced in law trials is concerned. Wigmore said there are three kinds of evidence: *autoptic proference, circumstantial*, and *testimonial*.[26] Wigmore did not directly distinguish between tangible and testimonial evidence. At the time, all tangible evidence was referred to as real evidence, a term that Wigmore rejected. By *autoptic proference* (self-visible) evidence, Wigmore included any tangible item or any testimonial assertion that could be directly observed by the fact finder at trial. I have never been particularly enthusiastic about Wigmore's classification scheme, partly because he only considered evidence provided under the conditions of trials at law. I also believe that there are other distinctions that Wigmore never considered involving individual items of evidence as well as combinations of evidence, as the following classification captures.

Classifying individual items of evidence

Shown in Figure 2.1 is a two-dimensional classification scheme containing ten classes of individual items of evidence that are substance-blind and recurrent.

The credibility dimension

First, consider the rows of this scheme labelled the *credibility dimension*. This credibility dimension involves the following question: *how do you, the evaluator of the evidence, stand in relation to the evidence?* Different credibility

[25] Locke, 1691.
[26] Wigmore, 1937, pp. 11–13.

questions arise from each answer to this question. If in some way you can examine this item of evidence yourself to observe what events it reveals, then it is *tangible* evidence as shown in the first row. I have preserved the distinction between *real* tangible evidence and *demonstrative* tangible evidence mentioned above. Recall that real evidence is a thing itself, such as an object or a person; but *demonstrative* tangible evidence is just a representation or illustration of something or some person. For tangible evidence we always have authenticity questions to answer; for demonstrative tangible evidence we also have reliability and accuracy questions to answer. I have also noted the distinction between *positive* and *negative* tangible evidence, as indicated by the plus and minus signs. Positive evidence reveals the occurrence of an event of interest; negative evidence reveals the non-occurrence of an event of interest. There is often no order of precedence of the force of positive and negative evidence; evidence that an event did not occur is frequently as important as evidence that an event did occur. Perhaps the best-known examples of the importance of negative evidence come from several of the Sherlock Holmes mysteries in which Holmes solved cases based on evidence that certain events did not occur.[27]

The second row in Figure 2.1 shows *unequivocal testimonial evidence* in the form of assertions coming from another person that an event did or did not occur. This first case of testimonial evidence involves instances in which a person tells you she is certain that some event occurred; in other words she does not hedge or equivocate her testimony. Thus, unequivocal testimonial evidence can be either positive or negative. We ask this person how she knows that the event she reports did, or did not, occur. She might say that she directly observed it herself in which case we have her competence and credibility to consider. Recall that her competence rests on evidence about her access and understanding, and her credibility rests on evidence we have about her veracity, objectivity, and observational sensitivity. But she may instead say that she did not observe this event herself but she heard about this event's occurring or non-occurring from another person. In this case she has supplied us with *secondhand* or *hearsay* evidence. In another work I have discussed the complexity of credibility assessments for evidence from chains of hearsay sources.[28]

In discussing testimonial evidence I have made a distinction that Wigmore never considered. I have just mentioned instances in which sources of testimony

---

[27] For example, the mystery *Silver Blaze* in which Holmes used evidence that a dog did not bark to solve this case; see Baring-Gould, 1967, vol. 2, pp. 261–81.

[28] Schum, 1992.

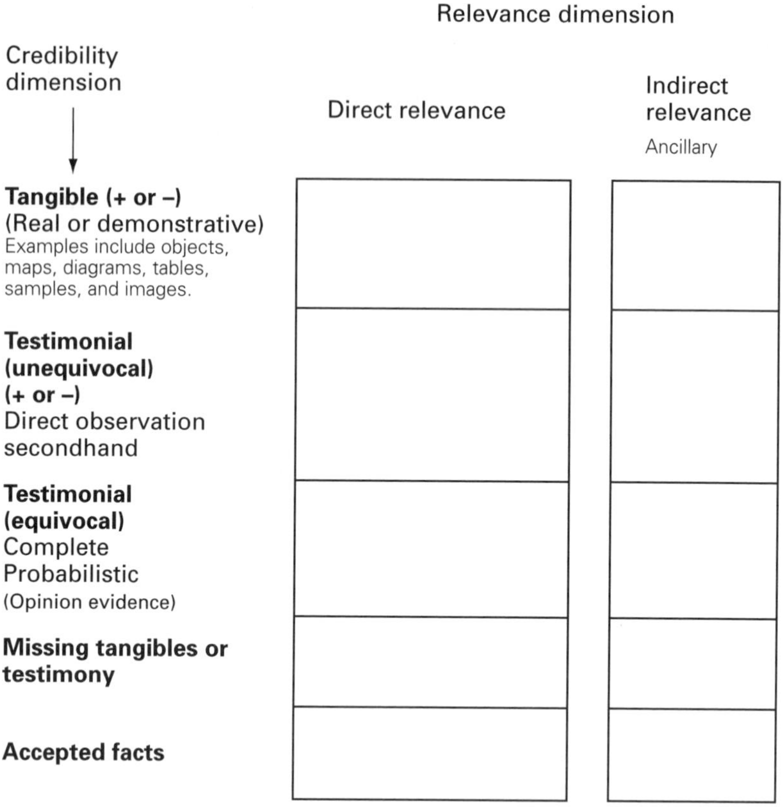

Relevance dimension

Credibility dimension	Direct relevance	Indirect relevance
		Ancillary
Tangible (+ or −) (Real or demonstrative) Examples include objects, maps, diagrams, tables, samples, and images.		
Testimonial **(unequivocal)** **(+ or −)** Direct observation secondhand		
Testimonial **(equivocal)** Complete Probabilistic (Opinion evidence)		
Missing tangibles or testimony		
Accepted facts		

Figure 2.1. A substance-blind classification of individual items of evidence.

do not hedge or equivocate in telling us that an event either occurred or did not occur. But there are instances in which persons do equivocate in various ways in providing testimony. First, a person asked whether event E occurred, may provide a *complete equivocation*; the person says: 'I don't know', 'I don't remember', or 'I'm the wrong person to ask'. The credibility issue here concerns whether this person is honestly impeaching his own credibility, he does not know or cannot remember, or whether he does know or remember but is refusing to tell us about event E because it would be against his interests to do so. Second, a person asked whether event E occurred, may equivocate probabilistically using either numbers or words. For example, the person might say: 'I'm 70 per cent sure that E occurred' or, in words, 'I'm fairly sure that event E occurred'. This forms another way a person may comment on his own credibility. But you may have evidence about this person's competence and credibility that allows you to infer that this person is actually more or less certain about event E's occurrence than what his own equivocation suggests.

Now notice that I have placed *opinion evidence* in this class of equivocal testimonial evidence in the third row of Figure 2.1. I had, until quite recently, included it under unequivocal testimony in row two.[29] The reason why I have made this revision requires a slight digression in my story about classifying evidence. Anyone who attempts a taxonomy must be prepared to answer questions about it and also be prepared to make revisions in it that seem justifiable. I will have one other revision to make concerning the relevance dimension in Figure 2.1. As far as opinion evidence is concerned, we have to consider two cases: the *ordinary witnesses* I have already described, and the *expert witnesses* who often appear in legal disputes and in other contexts.

First, consider ordinary witnesses. Suppose, in an inference about a matter that is important to you personally, you wish to know whether event E occurred, and so evidence about E's occurrence would be relevant in your inference. So, you ask Anne, a person you believe to be generally competent and credible. Anne tells you that she is 'fairly sure' that event E occurred. So you ask her the question: how do you know this? Suppose Anne replies: 'I did not observe E myself, and I did not hear about it at second hand from another person. But I did observe events C, D, and F which, when taken together, allowed me to infer that event E occurred.' But the issue now is: to what extent can you believe that event E occurred, given Anne's opinion that she is fairly sure that E occurred? The actual credibility issues here are quite complex. You must consider Anne's competence and credibility as far as her stated observations of events C, D, and F are concerned. But you must also inquire about whether you would argue that the occurrence of these three events allows the inference that event E occurred. For reasons I now discuss, the mistake I made in an earlier account was to let Anne state unequivocally that E occurred, based on her opinion resting on other events.

I now consider the *expert witnesses* who appear at trials and other tribunals. Persons having certifiable expertise in specific matters are frequently called upon by the parties in dispute or by the court to provide their opinions concerning a vast array of issues encountered at trials that go well beyond the competence of the attorneys, judges, and juries if they exist. Experts in a wide variety of scientific and technological areas are requested by one or the other of the parties in a dispute and their opinions may be requested by judges themselves. In the American legal system there are specific rules regarding the

[29] Schum, 1994, p. 115 in both editions.

admission of the testimony of expert witnesses.[30] There are many accounts of the array of topics concerning expert opinion evidence given in criminal and civil litigation and how the courts are concerned about the extent of reliability of these opinions.[31] But there are other hardly flattering accounts of the opinions sometimes provided by alleged scientific experts.[32]

But I have recently given close attention to one of the world's authorities on assessing the relevance, credibility, and force of expert opinion evidence given at trial. He is: The Honorable Judge John Coster van Voorhout, of Arnhem, the Netherlands. For the past several years I have been privileged to have fairly regular correspondence with Judge van Voorhout regarding evidential matters. In the Netherlands, judges routinely summon expert witness to help them decide cases; there are no juries in the Dutch legal system. Judge van Voorhout read my account of evidence classification and said he had one quibble, namely that I had included opinion evidence under unequivocal testimony. He said he would disregard any opinion evidence given by any person who claimed absolute certainty from an array of other information. In other words, he argued that opinion evidence is necessarily equivocal in nature. So, I had to rethink what I said about opinion evidence given by ordinary witnesses such as Anne, who based the opinion she gave you that event E occurred on the grounds of her observations that three other events had occurred. Had she said that she was certain that E occurred, you would have been justified in questioning how she arrived at this opinion on the basis of other evidence whose relevance, credibility, and force are also at issue.

Under certain conditions, either *missing tangible or testimonial evidence* can be inferentially important, as indicated in row four of Figure 2.1. But to say that evidence is missing, we must have expected to obtain it. First consider an item of tangible evidence we say is missing. Four reasons come to mind, the first three of which are not interesting: the evidence has never existed (our expectation was wrong); we are looking in the wrong place; or the evidence exists but was lost. The fourth reason is inferentially interesting and it concerns the possibility that someone is concealing from us in some way, including this person's having destroyed the evidence. For nearly three hundred years in our Anglo-American judicial system, we are entitled to draw an adverse

---

[30] *Federal Rules of Evidence 702 to 706* concern the acceptable basis for expert testimony, opinion evidence provided by experts, expert opinion on ultimate issues, the disclosure of the factual basis for expert opinion, and the permission of court-appointed experts. Rule FRE 701 concerns the admissibility of opinion evidence by lay or ordinary witnesses. See: *Federal Rules of Evidence*: 2007–8 edn.

[31] Kennedy and Merrill, 2002.

[32] Huber, 1993.

inference against a person who refuses to produce the requested evidence. The argument is that the production of the requested evidence would be against the interests of this person. Regarding missing testimonial evidence, the situation is more complex. We inquire of a person whether event E occurred and this person responds either with silence or in some evasive way. The trouble here occurs in legal situations in our Anglo-American system in which a person is allowed to refuse to testify on a matter that may be self-incriminating. Credibility questions naturally arise regarding persons who refuse to produce tangible evidence or respond with silence when their testimony is requested, the exception being instances in law in which witnesses have the privilege to remain silent.

The final form of individual items of evidence can be called *accepted facts*. In some cases we may have evidence about matters regarded as being completely credible. There are many examples including entries in tide and celestial tables, entries in mathematical tables of various sorts, and entries in tables of statistical distributions. But there are other examples that stem from common knowledge. You would hardly question the fact that the population of London is greater than that of Oxford, or that strychnine, in sufficient amounts, is a toxic substance. Centuries ago, Locke noted that some forms of evidence rise to near certainty. As examples he said: 'That Fire warmed a Man, made Lead fluid, and changed the colour or consistency of Wood or Charcoal: that Iron sunk in Water and swam in Quicksilver.'[33]

Finally, regarding the five classes of evidence just described, there is a very important attribute: *they are not mutually exclusive but can occur in various mixtures in an item of evidence*. For example, you may have a tangible document that you can examine to your heart's content, as far as its authenticity and accuracy are concerned. But what this document contains is a record of the testimony provided by a person whose competence and credibility attributes you must also consider. There is a virtually unlimited array of such mixtures. Document trails provide another example. One document presently examined makes reference to another document which, in turn, makes reference to a third document. Your passport supplies a very good example. Mixtures of these five recurrent forms of evidence involve some very difficult credibility assessments.

---

[33] Locke, 1691, p. 662.

The relevance dimension

Now consider the two columns in Figure 2.1 that concern the *relevance dimension*. The question this dimension poses for you, the evaluator of the evidence, is: *how does this item of evidence stand in relation to the major hypotheses you are trying to prove or disprove?* As noted earlier, evidence can be either *directly* or *indirectly relevant* to major hypotheses. Recall that evidence is *directly relevant* if it can be linked by a defensible chain of reasoning to major hypotheses being considered. *Indirectly relevant evidence*, also called *ancillary, auxiliary,* or *meta-evidence*, bears on the strength or weakness of links in chains of reasoning set up by directly relevant evidence. So, ancillary evidence is evidence about the strength or weakness of other evidence.

In earlier works I discussed two forms of directly relevant evidence: *direct evidence* and *circumstantial evidence.*[34] In many works, direct evidence was said to be evidence that goes in a single stage to prove some event of interest. If the source of this evidence is perfectly credible, that settles it, the event did occur. On the other hand, circumstantial evidence, even if perfectly credible, supplies only some and not conclusive grounds for showing that an event of interest did occur. In other words, circumstantial evidence is always inconclusive in nature. But in a more recent work we have, for various reasons, dropped the distinction between direct and circumstantial evidence.[35] One reason is that any particular link in a chain of reasoning can often be decomposed to reveal other links. When this happens we must reconsider which event our evidence would be direct upon. This is arbitrary of course since the decomposition might take many forms.

Classifying recurrent combinations of evidence

The individual items of evidence classified in Figure 2.1 can be combined in different ways in the masses of evidence we all encounter. There are three basic patterns of recurrent *combinations* of evidence: *harmonious, dissonant,* and *redundant*; there are two varieties of each one. Diagrammatic illustrations of these three classes of evidence combinations are provided elsewhere.[36] There are two species of harmonious evidence: *corroborative* and *convergent*. Evidential corroboration occurs when we have two or more items of either positive or negative evidence for the *same event*. Corroboration can also

---

[34] Schum, 1994, pp. 114–20 in both editions.
[35] Anderson, Schum and Twining, 2005, pp. 76–7.
[36] Schum, 1994, pp. 120–30 in both editions.

involve favourable ancillary evidence regarding the credibility of a source of evidence. Convergent evidence involves two or more items of evidence about *different events* all of which favour the same hypothesis. Convergent evidence can also possibly be *synergistic*. In other words, two or more items of convergent evidence can often mean more when taken together than they would do if considered separately or independently. In summary, harmonious evidence is always directionally consistent in favouring the same hypothesis.

The two species of dissonant evidence are: *contradictory* and *divergent*. A contradiction always involves evidence about mutually exclusive events or events that cannot occur simultaneously. One source says that event E occurred, another says that E did not occur. Divergent evidence, also called *diverging* or *conflicting evidence*, involves two or more evidence items concerning different events that can occur simultaneously but that favour different hypotheses. Patterns of dissonant evidence are always directionally inconsistent by favouring different hypotheses. Resolving evidential contradictions always rests on credibility considerations. Resolving evidential divergences or conflicts is more complex. Source credibility may be at issue, but we must also defend the claim that the events reported actually favour different hypotheses. In some cases, apparent divergence or conflict vanishes when we consider the joint occurrence of these events instead of considering them separately or independently.

Finally, there are patterns of evidence that are redundant in the sense that one item of evidence can act to reduce the force of other items of evidence. There are two patterns of redundant evidence: *corroborative* and *cumulative*. In the corroborative case, when we have multiple sources reporting the same event, the force of each new report depends upon how credible were the sources of earlier reports. In a limiting case, if we believed the first source to be completely credible, further reports of this same event would be valueless because they all tell us about an event we already completely believe to have occurred. Cumulatively redundant evidence involves different events where we seem justified in believing that the actual occurrence of one event would diminish the force of other events. Suppose we have interest in event E and event F, where F is just inconclusive regarding the occurrence of event E. But if we had completely credible evidence of E, this would make evidence about F completely redundant since F would only supply additional grounds for believing event F that we already believe completely. We might say that evidence about event F only springs to life inferentially to the extent that the evidence about event E is not perfectly credible.

My final comment about these three recurrent and substance-blind combinations of evidence is to note the obvious fact that any mass of evidence can involve different patterns of harmonious, dissonant, and redundant evidence all at the same time. This is one reason why assessing the force of masses of evidence is such a complex task.

Final comments

I have argued that a major reason for considering what I have termed substance-blind forms and combinations of evidence is that they allow us to compare the force of evidence in different parts of the same inference problem and also to compare the force of evidence in entirely different problems. I will provide two examples from my own experience. The first concerns the analysis Professor Jay Kadane and I provided regarding the evidence in the celebrated American murder case involving Nicola Sacco and Bartolomeo Vanzetti.[37] We examined 395 substantively different items of evidence provided at trial and from post-trial records. Sacco and Vanzetti were charged with first-degree felony murder in the shooting of a payroll guard in South Braintree, Massachusetts in 1920. The prosecution's case rested on three planks. The first concerned identity: where were the two defendants before, during, and after the crime and what were they doing at these times. The second involved ballistics evidence in the form of bullets, shell casings, and two weapons, an automatic and a revolver. The third involved the defendants' alleged consciousness of guilt. The first and third of these planks rested on testimonial evidence from witnesses whose credibility was seriously at issue, particularly veracity and accuracy. The second plank rested mainly on tangible evidence whose authenticity and reliability has been seriously questioned.

I was especially privileged to provide an overview of six studies that were provided in a work by Twining and Hampsher-Monk[38]. These six studies were as substantively different as anyone could imagine. The six studies involved a British law case, an analysis of ancient Sumerian cuneiform tablets, studies of the role of mountebanks in the field of theatre iconography, an analysis of Franz Schubert's possibly writing arrangements for the guitar, an examination of Dutch colonial labour relations, and an analysis of John Locke's theory of property. My task was to provide an overview of these six works. This task was made much easier by my consideration of the substance-blind forms and combinations that were recurrent in all six of these works regardless of the differences in the substance or content of the evidence each study provided.[39]

[37] Kadane and Schum, 1996.
[38] Twining and Hampsher-Monk, 2003.
[39] Schum, 2003.

I am going to let William Twining have the last words regarding my work on classifying evidence. Speaking of what I had said regarding substance-blind forms and combinations of evidence, Twining remarked:

> I would go one stage further and suggest that the core concepts of evidence as a subject are also blind to typologies of sources and matters to be proved. The main general characteristics of the subject of Evidence are substance-blind, source-blind, and hypothesis-blind. In other words the subject of Evidence at its core transcends disciplinary cultures, the objects of inquiry, and the peculiar methods and traditions of particular specialisms. ... The core of the subject is inferential reasoning.[40]

Thanks William.

References

Anderson, T., Schum, D. and Twining, W. (2005), *Analysis of Evidence* (2nd edn.) (Cambridge, Cambridge University Press), pp. 246–61.

Baring-Gould, W. S. (1967), *The Annotated Sherlock Holmes*, vols. 1 and 2 (New York: Clarkson S. Potter, Inc.), vol. 2, pp. 261–81.

Bauer, H. (1994), *Scientific Literacy and the Myth of the Scientific Method* (Urbana, IL., University of Illinois Press).

Carnap, R. (1966), *An Introduction to the Philosophy of Science*, ed. M. Gardner (New York: Basic Books), p. 51.

Cohen, M. and Nagel, E. (1934), *An Introduction to Logic and Scientific Method* (New York, Harcourt, Brace and Co.), pp. 223–44.

Federal Rules of Evidence (2007), 2007–8 edn. (St Paul, MN, Thompson/West Publishers).

Haack, S. (2007), *Defending Science—Within Reason: between scientism and cynicism* (Amherst, NY: Prometheus Books).

The New Shorter Oxford English Dictionary (1993), vol. 2 (Oxford, Clarendon Press), p. 2717.

Hemple, C. (1956), 'On the Nature of Mathematical Truth', in J. R. Newman (ed.), *The World of Mathematics*, vol. 3 (New York, Simon and Schuster).

Huber, P. (1993), *Galileo's Revenge: junk science in the courtroom* (New York, Basic Books).

Kadane, J. and Schum, D. (1996), *A Probabilistic Analysis of the Sacco and Vanzetti Evidence* (New York, John Wiley & Sons).

Kennedy, D. and Merrill, R. (2002), *The Age of Expert Testimony: science in the courtroom* (Washington DC, National Academy Press).

---

[40] Twining, 2003, p. 97.

Kneale, W. and Kneale, M. (1984), *The Development of Logic* (Oxford, Clarendon Press), p. 231.

Lempert, R., Gross, S. and Liebman, J. (2000), *A Modern Approach to Evidence: text, problems, transcripts, and cases* (3rd edn.) (St Paul, MN, West Group), pp. 1146–8.

Locke, J. (1691), *An Essay Concerning Human Understanding*, ed. P. Nidditch (Oxford, Clarendon Press, 1991), pp. 654–68.

Mayr, E. (1982), *The Growth of Biological Thought: diversity, evolution, and inheritance* (Cambridge, MA, Belknap Press of Harvard University), pp. 829–58.

Poincaré, J. H. (1905), 'The Value of Science', in S. J. Gould (ed.), *Henri Poincaré, The Value of Science: essential writings of Henri Poincaré* (New York, The Modern Library, 2001), p. 347.

Poincaré, J. H. (1908), 'Science and Method', in S. J. Gould (ed.), *Henri Poincaré, The Value of Science: essential writings of Henri Poincaré* (New York, The Modern Library, 2001), pp. 364–5.

Schum, D. (1992), 'Hearsay from a layperson', *Cardozo Law Review*, 14(1), August: 1–77.

Schum, D. (1994), *Evidential Foundations of Probabilistic Reasoning* (New York, John Wiley & Sons); paperback edn. (Evanston, IL, Northwestern University Press, 2001), pp. 6–8, 114–30 in both edns.

Schum, D. (1989), 'Knowledge, probability and credibility', *Journal of Behavioral Decision Making*, 2: 39–62.

Schum, D. (2003), 'Evidence and inference about past events: an overview of six case studies', in W. Twining and I. Hampsher-Monk (eds.), *Evidence and Inference in History and Law: interdisciplinary dialogues* (Evanston, IL, Northwestern University Press), pp. 9–62.

Schum, D. (2005), 'Thoughts about a Science of Evidence', in *UCL Studies of Evidence Science* (29 December 2005). A shortened version of this paper is forthcoming in *Law, Probability & Risk: a journal of reasoning under uncertainty* (Oxford, Oxford University Press).

Schum, D. and Morris, J. (2007), 'Assessing the competence and credibility of human sources of evidence: contributions from law and probability', *Law, Probability and Risk*, 6: 247–74

Twining, W. (2003), 'Evidence as a multi-disciplinary subject', *Law, Probability & Risk: a journal of reasoning under uncertainty*, 2(2), June: 91–107.

Twining, W. and Hampsher-Monk, I. (2003), *Evidence and Inference in History and Law: interdisciplinary dialogues* (Evanston, IL, Northwestern University Press).

Wigmore, J. H. (1937), *The Science of Judicial Proof: as given by logic, psychology, and general experience, and illustrated in judicial trials* (3rd edn.) (Boston, MA, Little, Brown and Company).

Zangwill, I. (1891), *The Big Bow Mystery* (New York, Carroll & Graf Publishers, 1986), pp. 143–4.

3

Disciplining the Disciplines*

JASON DAVIES

Abstract

Interdisciplinarity has become a field in its own right in recent decades: this chapter gives a brief overview of emergent taxonomies of disciplinarities in scholarship, and documents our engagement with these as 'the Interdisciplinary Project' within the *Evidence* programme. It then gives a situated and provisional interdisciplinary account of the process of the programme over time that is designed to evoke the experience as much as the emergent understanding of interdisciplinary work. In this way, I intend to make the unfamiliarity of the processes of interdisciplinary work more intelligible and elucidate what is at stake in an interdisciplinary approach to interdisciplinarity.

PART I
AN INTERDISCIPLINARY APPROACH
Introduction

Context and framework

IN SUMMER 2003, the Leverhulme Trust offered funding for an 'Interdisciplinary study of Evidence'. To add to a growing focus in academia (Medicine and Education in particular), 'evidence' had shot to media fame in the wake of the terrorist bombings, the search for weapons of mass destruction, the investigations and recriminations after 9/11 (Twining, in this volume, gives a more

*The Interdisciplinary Project of the UCL Evidence Programme was led by Professor Stephen Rowland. The extent of his generous and extraordinarily insightful mentorship would normally merit my crediting him with imparting 'almost everything I know about this topic' but, as will hopefully become obvious, I owe him a greater debt for his showing me almost everything I *don't* know. I must also acknowledge Roy Ecclestone ('only a schoolteacher') for so many conversations over the years that have profoundly informed my thinking. Both have repeatedly tried, frequently in vain, to save me from error. I am also very much indebted to the anonymous reviewers who endeavoured to transform delusions of grandeur into an aspiration to adequacy.

Proceedings of the British Academy, **171**, 37–72. © The British Academy 2011.

detailed picture of the context). We found ourselves deep in media- and government-driven debates about who should know what, and how, and who they should tell: evidence had become an urgent question within and beyond academia.

Led by Professor Philip Dawid (a statistician), preliminary meetings were held in University College London which would become the *Evidence* programme (some funding was also procured from the ESRC). A number of projects, which typically ended up with one or two principal investigators and one or two postdoctoral fellows, applied to participate. These projects acted as (sometimes rather nominal) points of reference for the lifetime of the project. Inevitably, not all disciplines were represented but the centre of gravity was the 'harder' Social Sciences. The programme (by which I will consistently mean the whole entity) was therefore structurally made up of individual projects. Not all of them mapped directly onto academic disciplines so the disciplinary background of the relevant staff is approximated here in parentheses with the named projects:

- *Formal Tools for Handling Evidence* (Legal/forensic)
- *Model-Contingent Interpretation of Evidence* (Economics)
- *Historical Evidence* (Ancient History)
- *Human Attitudes to Evidence* (Psychology)
- *Synthesis of Complex Evidence Practice and Policy Making* (Primary Health Care/Computer Science)
- *Evidence in Natural Sciences* (Philosophy of Science)
- *Evidence: a Case Study of Interdisciplinarity* (Education/Humanities)
- *Enquiry and Detection* (Crime Science)
- *Towards an Integrated Concept of Evidence* (Statistics/Law)

There were also informal participants from Classics, Anthropology, History (later periods), Pharmacology, Physiology, Archaeology, Comparative Literature and others, but very little input from the 'hard' sciences or the 'more relativising' disciplines.

It was clear from the start that the bulk of activity would take place within the physical confines of UCL, though the inclusion of a few outside experts and a 'sister' project at the London School of Economics did widen our horizons somewhat.

What was not clear at that early point was the form that *Evidence* would take over the next four years (or longer if you include the writing of this volume): a series of more-or-less programme-wide seminars of varying duration, overlapping and self-directing groups, an email list, a range of generally serendipitous close collaborations across individual projects and a pair of final conferences—not to mention the intradisciplinary workings between members of the same disciplines in the individual projects.

Possible accounts of *Evidence*

I wish to open by stressing emphatically that *any* account of *Evidence* is highly provisional and dependent on the context and purpose of the questioner: if asked 'did it work?', we might emphasise the breadth and depth of collaboration across UCL over several years (no mean feat in itself) by both paid and unpaid participants who were often (but far from reliably) employed at the university at the time; a course emerged for graduate students of UCL through its Graduate School which at the time of writing may also become the basis for a number of customised courses at various points across the university; the final conference at the British Academy was full to bursting and oversubscribed; a number of collaborative projects emerged and a great number of publications was produced by the various members of the different projects. These would be obvious signs of whether the Evidence programme 'worked' or not. But what would we do with the less obvious signs of a 'healthy programme' such as the fact that almost all the postdoctoral fellows found employment during or immediately after the programme? What did it mean that a whip-round to thank the chief culprits for *Evidence* led to people queuing to hand over notes of various denominations?

For sake of rhetorical argument, we might also have an account that emphasised 'failure': the programme did not produce *A Unified Theory of Evidence* to tidy up all those loose ends and usher in a new period of quasi-global certainty in all things deductive; no new discipline of 'Evidentology' was (so far) founded; the group largely dispersed at the end of the programme, though many stayed in touch professionally and personally; and the email list, supposedly a forum for collaboration, came to be dominated (in the eyes of some) by a very small number of people who were not formally within the programme. It fell into relative disuse before the funded period came to an end, though there are plans to reinvent it, not least as a focal point for the many people in UCL (both students and staff) who find the whole notion of interdisciplinary working a confusing mass (or mess) 'when you actually get down to it'.

While we could subscribe to the former ('optimistic') account much more readily than the latter (the programme members and its director deserve far more credit than the 'pessimistic' version), I do not consider that *either* would do justice to the theme of interdisciplinarity or the programme as a whole. Any account of *Evidence* must be met with the questions 'which other accounts are possible?' and 'whose position and interests are reflected here?' Some might expect the interests of the Leverhulme Trust, which provided the majority of funds, to be uppermost (but 'it's only money'); or a case can be made that the programme was in reality 'owned' by the employed participants—but then, after all, it's just a job. Was the programme primarily a research activity (exploring notions of evidence) or a teaching one (enlightening other participants as the way *we* do things, for a given value of 'we')? What follows is an account of how we found a path through *Evidence*.

Initial brief

The initial brief for the Interdisciplinary Project brief read as follows:

- to understand the different conceptions of evidence, from the different disciplinary perspectives, and how these can be brought into more productive relationships;
- to develop a conceptualisation of interdisciplinarity that is most appropriate for large-scale social science investigation;
- to study how different disciplines can engage with each other critically and to identify those features which enable or disable this;
- and as a consequence, to give coherence to the programme by enabling the different disciplines and perspectives to engage in a productive and critical manner. It will thus serve to integrate and enhance the reflexive functions of the proposal.

Finding a place to stand

Our first task as the Interdisciplinary project appeared to be to form a relationship with the broader programme, with its sets of plenary and emergent smaller ('more specialist') groupings, as well as the email list that would see many outsiders form their own relationship with what (they thought/hoped/ expected) *Evidence* was, could or 'should' be. An obvious starting point was that we[1] treat *Evidence* as an experiment to be measured against a general understanding of interdisciplinary work.

---

[1] 'I' and 'we' are problematic here: the project was a collaboration between Professor Stephen Rowland and myself, and few ideas here are easy to attribute to either one of us. Secondly, I originally joined as part of the History Project and thus had a dual identity. I shall at least endeavour to be clear by what I mean here by using 'we' only of myself and Stephen unless clearly signalled. 'I' means myself as author of this piece, looking back.

Interdisciplinarity scholarship

This was not as simple as it sounded, though. Broadly speaking, the scholarship addressed questions like 'what is it, how did it arise and why would we want it?' but, as we shall see, potentially distinct terminology is often treated as synonymous, even when the attempt is made to posit specific meanings. A survey of the literature will serve to illustrate how elusive a clear position on the subject can be.

Three principal terms provided points of reference: according to the more recent scholarship, 'transdisciplinarity', 'once one of many terms' (Klein 2004: 524) has become particularly associated with transgression of disciplinary and academic boundaries to produce synthetic and complex outcomes for 'real' issues in society; 'interdisciplinarity' is generally posited as being integrative, process-centred and providing a stimulus for reflective disciplinary working; and 'multidisciplinarity' is associated with an additive pooling of disciplinary understandings that do not endeavour necessarily to reflect on the process but rather emphasise synthetic outcomes.

However, two things must be borne in mind: first, even if these uses do indeed establish a sustained hegemony, they are relatively recent: something that *was* called 'interdisciplinary' might well *now* be classed as 'transdisciplinary' (or 'multidisciplinary' and so on). Second, these distinctions are made by (many of) those who choose interdisciplinarity as their object of study but there are no guarantees that all those who use the terms have read (or will ever read) these works or subscribe to their suggestions.[2] By definition, no single community 'owns' the terms or the practices and it seems unlikely to me that attempts to demarcate different types will escape Moran's (2002: 15) deceptively simple formulation:

> ['Interdisciplinary'] can suggest forging connections across the different disciplines, but it can also mean establishing a kind of undisciplined space in the interstices between disciplines, or even attempting to transcend disciplinary boundaries altogether ... I want to suggest that the value of the term 'interdisciplinary' lies in its flexibility and indeterminacy.[3]

What must be never far from our minds in surveying the scholarship is that the terms 'interdisciplinary' and 'multidisciplinary' in particular *can be* so loosely used for the most part that even if someone *is* trying to adhere to a

---

[2] Thus Huutoniemi *et al.* (2009: 2) lament that 'even well-argued conceptual categorizations have not found their way into empirical analyses of interdisciplinary research'.

[3] One might, however, note that someone from a field like English would inevitably be predisposed to choose a definition that embraced uncertainty and contingency.

specific sense, no one else can be sure that they are doing so unless they say so out loud (and every restatement invites at least subtle rewriting). This particularly applies to general exhortations, reports and (let's face it) descriptions of precisely what 'the funding on offer is supposed to be for'.

Beyond disciplines—transdisciplinarity

Interdisciplinarity is often linked to calls for 'solving real-life problems' rather than just those 'internally generated by individual disciplines'. A pragmatic division can be made here: first, I sidestep what are often called 'metadisciplines' with developed positions (such as Women's Studies or Marxism). For academics within these fields, most existing disciplines, as the very enactment of the wrong sort of power-relations, are often the source or at least the guardians of 'the problem' and cannot easily be seen in a favourable light. Thus, in documenting a history of Women's Studies, Bird (2001: 467) (perfectly reasonably from her perspective) says that '[d]isciplines/disciples fiercely defend their spaces, patrol boundaries, and regard those who either intrude or disrupt with suspicion'. These metadisciplines are visible and articulate their premises to those who care to listen. Because their agendas are reasonably familiar by now, we can engage with them as more or less *known* systems of thought.

There is however another strand, and this is often what is referred to nowadays by references to 'interdisciplinary work': rather than develop a distinctive position that is an inherent challenge to the status quo, they privilege 'problem-solving' as a self-evident value that requires no validation. Thus rather than seek to supplant the existing hegemonic discourse with another, they assume that they have already established the necessary hegemony. One of the cues for this strand of thought is a much-quoted phrase of Rustum Roy that 'the real problems of society do not come in discipline-shaped blocks' and the corollary that universities must move beyond the disciplines to formulate 'real' solutions to 'real' problems.[4] Who would be mad enough to argue with the idea that we need to solve 'real-life problems'? This project is increasingly associated with the term 'transdisciplinarity': it praises/legitimises/urges the inclusion of expertise from not just an eclectic range of disciplines but frequently also expertise and knowledge from 'outside the academy'.

At one 'extreme', there is a sentiment that, to us, offered (or, more often, masked) a paradoxical critique, with calls for 'an end to' or 'our liberation from the unnecessary/undesirable/dated/inadequate-for-our-needs restrictions

---

[4] Roy (1979: 165).

of what are now often treated as hopelessly over-specialised 'traditional disciplines'. Admittedly, these utopianising claims tended to appear more in talks on interdisciplinarity (used in its most generic sense) than in published literature and are not generally taken as seriously as once they were.[5] However, it is worth noting that the image some academics (and other parties) have of interdisciplinarity corresponds more to this than any other. Whether their reaction is of hostility, praise or indifference, what they know is that it needs to go on the grant application somewhere.

'Mode 2'

Excesses aside, transdisciplinarity looks, for the most part, to build on monodisciplinarity and 'overcome the problem' of over-specialisation. A key moment in the emerging field of transdisciplinarity was the coining of the terms 'Mode 1 and 'Mode 2', with the claim by Gibbons, Limoges and Nowotny (1994) that the production of scientific knowledge was being 'radically transformed'. The authors note several years later that their

> thesis was radically simplified, and collapsed into a single phrase—'Mode 2'. The old paradigm of scientific discovery ('Mode 1')—characterized by the hegemony of theoretical or, at any rate, experimental science; by an internally-driven taxonomy of disciplines; and by the autonomy of scientists and their host institutions, the universities—was being superseded by a new paradigm of knowledge production (Mode 2), which was socially distributed, application-oriented, trans-disciplinary, and subject to multiple accountabilities.

The irony was noted that the authors of an argument that refused to authorise meanings encoded in published scholarship could not complain about this simplification, and (to be fair) they duly returned to the fray as 'equal' participants.

I shirk the task of representing the epistemological and organisational complexity of transdisciplinarity here,[6] but will note that though it still characterises itself as creating a 'different kind of knowledge than disciplinarity can' by crossing boundaries and synthesising eclectic agendas and knowledge, it has largely shed the more anarchic associations of 'tearing down the [disciplinary] walls' that interdisciplinarity (as an umbrella term for transgression across disciplinary boundaries) once had.

Evidence could have been a transdisciplinary project if it had been more focused on a specific, predefined socially relevant issue. Had we (all) been charged

---

[5] Castronovo (2000: 781–3), citing Klein (1996: 10) and Lyotard (1984: 52).
[6] It is described (perhaps 'evoked' is a better term) in Klein's (2004) deceptively brief survey.

with answering the question 'how should we [academics] train Intelligence Services staff?', it might have been. That is not to say that we [the Interdisciplinary Project] would necessarily have felt there was a place for our project in such a programme: we noted an unease with what criteria should be used to judge 'exactly' what 'real-life' *is* (some anthropologists might struggle with the claim to have identified such a thing though I lack the space to explore this theme), and the implied claims to transparency (positionlessness).

We also noted a strong tendency to make claims of special urgency with regard to these 'needs' in the literature, though to note it is not necessarily to problematise it per se. While noting that it is the discourse which legitimises this urgency rather than any loquacious 'reality',[7] it does nonetheless seem to us to be a necessary 'glue' and incentive to focus and collaborate.[8] There seems little point in identifying social needs only to propose ignoring them. But *Evidence* did not, as it turned out, limit itself to a specific 'problem' and so, if it was going to fit anywhere, it was more likely to be within the frame of 'interdisciplinarity'.

Interdisciplinarity literature

In recent years, we have seen a range of publications that explicitly addresses itself to interdisciplinarity as an object of study—'interdisciplinarity' rather than 'interdisciplinary' literature. At its most naive (which is rare), it positions itself as a neutral observer but the vast majority of writers acknowledge that they cannot avoid being participants in the interdisciplinary game when writing about it. A key task this scholarship sets itself is one of clarifying terminology, and if there is any consistency, it is due to their efforts.[9] The understanding of 'interdisciplinarity' that has emerged (and may well yet establish a more reliable hegemony across the board) is of integration.[10] 'Multidisciplinary' work, in contrast, is usually defined as ('merely') additive: whereas interdisciplinary work is said to create a reflective friction and a seamless understand-

---

[7] Fish (1995: viii–x) dispenses efficiently with the 'problem' of whether disciplines are social constructions 'or not'—'post-modernist [social constructivist] accounts of how disciplines come into being are correct, but ... such accounts, rather than telling us that disciplines are unreal tell us just how disciplines came to be as real and as productive as they are.'

[8] Indeed, with logical consistency, Klein (2004) is essentially a transdisciplinary argument for the need for transdisciplinary work.

[9] See e.g. Klein (1990, 1996, 2001, 2005), Messer-Davidow *et al.* (1993), Moran (2002), Lattuca (2001), Gibbons, Limoges and Nowotny. (1994), Readings (1996).

[10] Klein's works (already cited) circle around the theme of integrating knowledge; Lattuca (2001, esp. pp. 10–21).

ing, multidisciplinary work (while valuable in the right context) is more like a 'patchwork quilt'.[11]

Much of this scholarship focuses on the (by now) vast number of interdisciplinary projects or informants and positions, taking what we might call a 'bird's-eye view'—explaining what interdisciplinarity is by 'seeing how it works'. There is usually discussion of 'how we got here', often finding a thread (sometimes not) from Plato, going via the medieval curriculum to the modern disciplinary world, which is itself depicted as being in the process of making the transition to some kind of interdisciplinary mould of knowing: this last transition is said to be driven by an alliance between a 'normal' expansion of disciplines and as a response to external pressures.[12]

These studies carve their way through an enormous amount of modern data, citing an array of other scholarship and interdisciplinary moments to reflect a smorgasbord of perceptions, hopes and suspicions about interdisciplinary work by the participants and (other) stakeholders. Making sense of outcomes is a perennial theme: 'the interdisciplinary individual' often becomes the focus of interest but this is a somewhat paradoxical focal point for something that aspires to a social or shared outcome.[13]

If the position put forward in this scholarship can be grouped, it is that an interest has arisen in response to the growing incidence of inter- (or multi-, or trans-) disciplinary work, and the conclusions drawn are that it is a necessary and desirable move away from an exclusive reliance on the ever-increasing specialism of monodisciplinary work (though these scholars would probably be the first to admit that much of it arose 'naturally' out of disciplinary work).[14] Monodisciplinary work is sometimes treated as ineluctably limited and not always able to respond to 'needs'—instead it responds to questions generated

---

[11] Lattuca (2001: 11), citing Rossini and Porter (1981). See also Klein (1990: 55–75), Moran (2002: 16–19).

[12] Claims of a continuity of knowledge from the classical world are strongly contested by classical scholars (see e.g. Flemming, 2000: 7–8 on science) and I (on firm disciplinary ground here, for once) assert simply that we gain nothing and lose credibility by making such references. Disciplinarity is a modern phenomenon.

[13] Klein (1990) concludes with a chapter on 'the interdisciplinary individual' and 'the integrative process': Lattuca (2001) grapples with in-depth interviews; Huutoniemi *et al.* (2009) end an attempt to produce a model to measure types and extent of interdisciplinarity by noting this tension between individual and group understanding as currently impossible to quantify.

[14] Indeed, despite the tendency explicitly to date the emergence of disciplinarity in the nineteenth century, and the beginning of interdisciplinary work to the early and mid-twentieth, there is a tendency to reify monodisciplinary work as monolithic when the dates given suggest rather that it is more transitory. See e.g. Becher (1989), Pryse (1998: 5), Klein (1990: 19–23). The point is perhaps more relevant when noting that interdisciplinarity has no institutional home.

'only' within the discipline, which is often treated as no longer sufficient.[15] The interdisciplinarity scholarship does repeatedly state that disciplines 'have their place' and notes that interdisciplinary enquiries do indeed arise from disciplinary questions rather than purely external pressures—nonetheless there is a vague sense at times that monodisciplinarity is the least well-dressed guest at the wedding.

Discipline all the way down

This leads me to my third group of interdisciplinarity scholarship, an even more eclectic set that the first two. My criterion for grouping them is simply that they take a position on generic interdisciplinarity that can be at least superficially described as informed by a particular discipline or field. Another way of describing them is that they worry more than the others about the incommensurability of disciplines and/or are cautious about seeing these 'new trends' as truly going *beyond* disciplines: rather, the disciplines that we (happen to) have are themselves the result of the kinds of forces that are now giving rise to interdisciplinarity and its cognates—with a contingent and undeniably *particular* history. *Plus ça change* ... interdisciplinarity is not magically immune to all the factors that 'bedevil' disciplines: it simply hasn't had enough time to realise it fully.

Fish (1994: 231) thus groups some commentators as 'all hostile to the current arrangement of things as represented by (1) the social structures by means of which the lines of political authority are maintained and (2) the institutional structures by means of which the various academic disciplines establish and extend their territorial claims'. He notes such criticisms are often informed by 'deconstruction, Marxism, feminism, the radical version of neopragmatism, and the new historicism' (his 'political left') before throwing his political 'right' into the mix as well ('it is difficult to distinguish the two ends of the political spectrum on this question' (231–2)).

He then calls 'emperor's new clothes' on this line of thought:

> partiality and parochialism are not eliminated or even diminished by the exposure of their operation, merely relocated. The blurring of existing authoritative disciplinary lines and boundaries will only create new lines and new authorities; the interdisciplinary impulse ... merely redomiciles us in enclosures that do not advertise themselves as such. ... either the vaunted 'blurring of genres' (Clifford

---

[15] e.g. Klein, 1996 closes '[t]he disciplines have not lost their power to generate new knowledge. Yet side by side other forces—propelled by new demands, interests, and technologies—have produced new subjects and new ways of looking at older subjects.'

Geertz's now famous phrase) means no more than that the property lines have been redrawn ... or the genres have been blurred only in the sense of having been reconfigured by the addition of a new one, of an emerging field populated by still another kind of mandarin, the 'specialist in contextual relations.' (Fish 1994: 237–8)

As Fish went on to argue (and develop further in Fish (1995)), the claim that one can stand outside the disciplines in a 'neutral' position is impossible because we are *always* embedded in a regime of truth, even if (especially if) part of that regime's *modus operandi* is to (pro)claim its self-apparence and universal, unchallengeable, relevance.

In a similar but independent line of thought, and during the lifetime of *Evidence*, Rowland (2006: 95) would note that transdisciplinarity, rejecting disciplinary critique, can be diverted to the lowest common denominator and thereby simply avoid the challenge of that necessary critique. As a result, it can (appear to) lack rigour. This is precisely because rigour demands discipline (that word again). His espousal of a 'critical interdisciplinarity' (*passim* but especially 90–1) depends on the interaction between scholars who recognise (rather than suppress) the incommensurability of disciplines as their own legitimating structures: to judge between disciplinary claims is to create a new discipline (find another vantage-point).

These two arguments highlight a central difficulty in interdisciplinarity studies—whose interdisciplinarity are we talking about, exactly? Fish is addressing a particular group who have a particular set of (typically universalising) claims (we might dub them 'the utopianists'). Lattuca (2001: 243) volunteers that 'the early literature on interdisciplinarity would depress even the most successful interdisciplinarian' and she may well be referring to Fish's commentators or others like them. Many interdisciplinarians might now wish to point to their own increasingly sophisticated discussions of positionality and perspectives[16] but there are still many moments in interdisciplinarity literature where a 'solution' is waved rather breezily at a 'problem': the field cannot afford to abandon Fish's or Rowland's concerns just yet.

Just to demonstrate how eclectic my grouping is, Moran (2002), like Fish, writes illuminatingly on interdisciplinarity from the perspective of English literature but is unconvinced of his colleague's arguments. For him (Moran 2002: 113), Fish does not provide 'an *intellectual* justification for the maintenance of traditional disciplinary distinctions' (original emphasis) but Fish's

---

[16] For a sustained attempt to navigate these tensions in a particular field (Women's Studies), see Pryse, 1998.

argument is that what is claimed of interdisciplinarity (a universal and 'liber-ated' perspective) is *not possible*. Fish's response to Moran's claim that 'it is better to be self-questioning than to carry on doing what we have always done for reasons of institutional practicality or intellectual inertia' might well be '*just how exactly* will you be self-questioning without taking a position? And what will inform that position except another network of implicit meanings? This is *normal disciplinary work*.'

To pick up a couple of other lone voices: Hunt (1994: 1), in her 'the Virtues of Disciplinarity' threatens to 'begin ... by striking a somewhat contrary note and insisting on the advantages of disciplinarity even to the practitioners of interdisciplinary studies'; Concerns (2001) goes further in 'Interdisciplinarity and nursing: "everything is everything," or is it?', noting grand claims being made without much explicit basis: 'many ... frequently refer to traditions and paradigms within single disciplines as doctrine or dogma or quasi-religious belief systems, ... [but] the interdisciplinarity movement appears to this author to have generated quite a lot of dogma and a strong quasi-religious belief system of its own' (276).

What my third group has in common is their sense that disciplines are regimes of truth which facilitate judgements and that there is no 'outside' that one can step into, free of constraint, limitation and (dare I say it again) *disci-pline*. Thinking outside the box (at best) means thinking in *another* box, another set of meanings, and it is worth noting that most of the difficulties noted by these authors are probably best linked to the claims made for what is 'technically' now *trans*disciplinary work rather than *inter*disciplinary.

These 'disciplinary' positions on interdisciplinarity are partly a question of emphasis or even ('just') caution rather than being defined in strict opposi-tion to my previous two groupings. Their arguments are not news to my second group of 'interdisciplinarians', though they might be to some transdiscipli-narians. Indeed, the interdisciplinarity literature struggles increasingly to be explicit about its own position (what it values, what it is for and what its own criteria for making judgements are). As such, 'Interdisciplinary Studies' as a distinctive field is, somewhat inevitably, well on the way to forming a recognis-able metadiscipline, as Fish and Rowland predicted (perhaps I should say 'warned').[17]

---

[17] Most recently, a special issue of *Critical Inquiry* (35/4—summer 2009) entitled *The Fate of the Disciplines* raised other possible ways to approach (inter)disciplinarity that may well prove fruitful, particularly in interactions between the humanities and science: see especially Biagioli (2009) and Post (2009).

Our question

I have not exhausted the range of positions in the scholarship or possible configurations of those positions, least of all dealt with the relatively uncelebrated interdisciplinary work that disciplines have 'quietly been getting on with' ever since their inception, which often leads to the foundation or recognition of new disciplines or the transformation of existing ones.[18] Nonetheless, these perspectives appeared to offer three possible approaches to *Evidence*: we could look for the synthetic benefits of boundary transgression, for the fruits of integrative collaboration or emphasise the breakdowns of the programme and the need for a (choice of) discourse to authorise judgements and conclusions. Despite having these options, we persistently found ourselves returning afresh to the question 'what does it mean to have an *interdisciplinary* study of an interdisciplinary programme?' Any reader of the publications that appeared under the auspices of (e.g.) the History Project would become *more of a historian*; a reader of statistical publications becomes *more of a statistician*. What exactly (or even vaguely) would our readers become *more of*?

The fact was that we did not know and we were unsure whether anyone could tell us. It seemed paradoxical, even dishonest, effectively to curtail these questions by lapsing unproblematically into methods and approaches that we were familiar with. Furthermore, for us surreptitiously to become the 'anthropologising and sociologising' project (for instance) would not only be intellectual cowardice, but a pretence, since neither of us are recognised in those disciplines.

As such, in an effort to preserve those tensions rather than resolve them, we developed habits (rather than methods) which were intended to honour those difficulties rather than seek closure. We had no expectation that we could avoid positionality entirely (or at all), but we wished to stand as lightly as possible in any particular place until we could honestly note that we seemed

[18] Moran (2002) charts the 'rise' of English; Grossetti (2005) examines the matrix of conditions that give rise to established disciplines. Most recently, Post (2009), writing as a lawyer, argues that science has been quick to create new disciplines, under an impetus to 'solve problems' whereas the humanities has instead 'absorbed' new approaches into 'traditional' disciplines. On the whole he is concerned about the response of the humanities and their 'institutionalised subversion' but this is at odds with his observation that new 'Studies' fields have emerged, and also implies a (somewhat legal-sounding) norm for disciplines. Moreover, I am far from convinced this observation is only true of the humanities: Douglas (1992: 248) drily notes that 'anthropologists have always been attracted to cultural relativism and I do not doubt that they have relished the iconoclastic threat.' Biagioli (2009) also discusses the 'problem-solving' approach of science, and Daston (2009) outlines divergent disciplinary developments for History of Science and Science Studies.

to have reached a place to settle. What therefore emerged (after a great deal of extremely speculative discussion) was that our first loyalty would be to the emerging programme rather than any external methodology and expectations: we would start 'from the ground up'. That was not a value-free position—it was the choice to value enquiry over conclusion, at least as long as we could sustain it. *Evidence* was a particular and unique scenario that might, or might not, reveal some more general themes about interdisciplinary work on its own terms.

We therefore engaged with *Evidence* not directly with 'what values, priorities and frameworks should we use in understanding the Evidence programme?' but a regression of that question: 'on what would we base the selection of criteria to choose values, priorities and frameworks?' Not just 'what do we think?' but 'what (and how) do we think about what we think *with*?'

Emerging discipline

Turning then to 'face' the programme through this lens of enquiry, we focused on the part of our brief to document and represent the programme's work, but there were no easy answers here either. Just what *was* the programme? At a simplistic level, the website acted as a repository of activity but that was not going to 'tell the story'. Was it the seminars, discussions and publications? Was it the private remarks made around the edges of these moments and events, in corridors and during chance meetings of participants outside the formal programme? Was the email list perhaps the location where people said what they 'really' thought? We were concerned not to reify *Evidence* unthinkingly and therefore considered any event fair game for our consideration. The only 'rule' we began with was that we would meet frequently for discussion to consider whatever had struck us and explore the reasons that we had noticed it in the first place. Typically, we would have an initial sense about why something was worthy of note. What was important to us in this was that we found out *why* something was important to us and we would set about interrogating that sense to see what had given rise to it. What we unconcealed in this way we would then subject to the same circling scrutiny.

Finite regress

Our tolerance for ambiguity was not infinite, however. Allowing strategies to emerge also meant allowing habits to establish themselves, sometimes almost while we were not looking. Even naming this process raised issues, though we settled on the phrase 'a set of contestations' more often than not. Over time we found a number of themes that repeated themselves (in our discussion, in the programme or both) such as the need to explore pejorative judgements until 'personality' had all but disappeared as a consideration; we learned quickly that putting words into people's mouths was generally to be avoided when we tried to provide written commentary on some interactions; 'mistakes' were just as meaningful as 'successes' and often more revealing; we discovered a preference for seeking underlying intellectual 'structures' that gave rise to people's remarks, responses and so on (in a manner reminiscent of Foucault's 'archaeology');[19] we also found experimenting with borrowed methodologies useful ('what would a phenomenological analysis of this look like?'; 'an anthropologist might look at the group's activities rather than the content of discussion but a psychologist might look more at individuals').

In this way, some criteria emerged that are far from free of apparent contradiction: we made a note when others referred back to earlier scenarios; or when we found ourselves doing the same, or repeating ourselves in other ways—why were we (whoever 'we' was at that moment) circling around the same theme? We found it hard not to notice when something seemed to attract widespread attention but also, on occasion, when something seemed to go unremarked which surprised us. In this way, we aspired to become responsible interpreters for the programme beyond the literal statements and events—and treated the whole culture of the programme as our object of study. We would not wish to declare that we had found any 'interdisciplinary method' in this: our understandings are pragmatic and local rather than looking towards a methodology that can be borrowed, extended or refined.

As such, the following account has certain characteristics: it invites (even demands) rewriting (as long as an account is given of what is being prioritised, and why); its hallmark is pragmatic impermanence—it has a disinclination to be quoted, refined or built on (we invite others to draw on it, to digest, then begin from scratch); it is cumulative in the sense that I attempt to represent some of the stages of our reasoning at various points, though often only to undermine them later on (in accordance with our sense that mistakes are as illuminating as successes).[20] It is therefore humble (makes no claim to hegemony) but not meek (does not consider itself inferior to any other account). As much as anything, it is an attempt not to wander too far from the 'worm's eye-view' and the question 'what is interdisciplinary work actually like'?

[19] Not an easy methodology to summarise for those unfamiliar with it but see e.g. Foucault and Gordon (1980: 61): 'the archaeology of the human sciences has to be established through studying the mechanisms of power which have invested human bodies, acts and forms of behaviour'.
[20] Davies (2009) is a briefer account.

I explicitly contrast this story of the programme with many other possibilities: disciplined judgements that are made on the basis of specialised
understanding and frameworks that either have been, or might be, articulated; with enactments of implicit values (e.g. a working assumption that the
outcomes should be privileged over the processes); with an infinite regress (we
may have found Foucault useful but I do not tip my hat to Derrida in this document); and it is certainly not based on induction, deduction or abduction—
except where we thought this useful to elicit meaning.

In this account, then, I retain a little epistemological disruption on strictly
methodological (rather than lazy or self-indulgently iconoclastic) grounds: the
programme *was* disruptive to its participants and I would be doing a disservice
to my readers to spare them *all* of the perplexity.

PART II
WELCOME TO THE PROGRAMME
The early phase

The Causality series

Evidence initially hosted open presentations (which rapidly became 'the
Causality series'): speakers gave introductions to their discipline and methods
of working to 'help us get started'. At this stage, the audience frequently felt they
had a good enough grasp of a topic to contribute suggestions and interesting
(frequently 'guiding') questions or helpful suggestions about 'how my discipline
handles this theme': there was confidence and optimism.

If these early stages can be characterised briefly, it would be a 'search for
consensus'. No particular theme was imposed in Causality beyond a general
emergent interest in the named theme (or an articulate refusal to credit it as a
useful concept): speakers framed their own agenda, and discussion alluded to
our soon 'getting on with' the task of finding common ground. This would
allow us to proceed to the 'greater' task of exploring a common understanding
of evidence.

But from the outset, another process that was to become familiar
appeared—a suggestion would be made or a question asked and the speaker
would explain why it was not appropriate or could not be answered. Or
speakers might find themselves mired in an ever-spiralling retreat from 'their
real point' ('could you talk us through that equation?' 'Thanks, but what does
that symbol *mean*, the one you read out?' 'Hmm. Why does that *matter*?')

Audiences increasingly faced the choice of abandoning any detailed understanding (thus being left only with the—often counterintuitive—concluding assertions) or bringing the speaker to a point of frustration where they did not know what they could say without 'retreating' to 'explaining the basics first'. Even this ultimate retreat did not necessarily help—there were times when this exposed the axiomatic workings of a discipline to unfavourable scrutiny by outsiders. This kind of situation created a recurring dilemma between respecting the disciplinary expertise of the speaker and bewilderment about even where to begin to make a statement meaningful. This occurred most visibly at the start with subjects like Economics and Statistics because of unmistakably unfamiliar and complex equations: it *looked as if* some disciplines were more obscure than others.

What emerged only over time was, conversely, the opaqueness of disciplines that *appeared* to use everyday language: for instance, as a historian of religion, I asserted that 'belief is not a useful concept for studying religion' which makes *superficial* sense—the words form a syntactically intelligible sentence— but its implications rapidly extend into perplexity on closer examination. Apart from anthropologists, furiously nodding, no one could find a meaningful context for this counterintuitive statement. If anything, the use of 'everyday words' simply created the extra difficulty of their specificity and richness being not just impenetrable but also *masked*. Explaining the rich (but confusing) implications of 'belief' required explaining the rich (and, in this case, equally treacherous) implications of 'religion', and this in its turn required the clarification of the very terms used to explain: the explanation process threatened to be an infinite regress. Jargon and symbols at least have the decency to advertise their strangeness to outsiders.

Thus, much broader questions arose (often in private subdiscussions) as to what exactly constituted 'understanding' and 'explanation' but these also moved with disconcerting swiftness from being 'clearly understandable' terms to a yawning abyss. Did 'understanding' mean someone could now explain the difficulties themselves or merely that they could pass on the news that 'belief is a flawed concept for studying religion with'? Some thought these were philosophical questions—but why privilege philosophy?[21] The infinite regress was ever at our shoulders: as each idea was discussed, the terms used to discuss it would (necessarily) become problematised. There usually emerged a point at which, despite travelling quite some way with the speaker, we were

---

[21] Claims of, or aspirations for, philosophy as a universal space for reflection have been made regularly since its inception: see most recently Hartog (2009). For similar claims made of English as it established itself, see Moran (2002).

ultimately reduced to 'taking someone's word for it'. It does not seem excessive to say that these breakdowns happened in literally unimaginable ways—their unpredictability was precisely the point.

When fundamental disciplinary assumptions and frameworks (the academic sense-making systems) are suddenly, almost impossibly, swept away, how (exactly) does one speak? Can we 'drop' to a more general level of shared understanding? Often we thought so—until the illusion was shattered by the realisation that this was precisely what we were doing: few claims to general applicability are as vacuous as the one enshrined in 'common-sense'. Thus, while Causality undoubtedly began the process of building bridges of mutual understanding, it also generated a growing awareness of incommensurability between the disciplines. This seemed to us the converse of a student learning their discipline (on which we like Polanyi (1962)), but a crucial qualitiative difference should be emphasised: it is very different for an 'undisciplined' student to learn than it is for someone *already* expert in a discipline. Indeed, one factor that was thrown up was the question of what is at the heart of academic expertise: is it the accumulation of (disciplinary) knowledge? Or is it the ability to make 'sound judgements'? If participants could not participate 'as' academics, then in what sense *were* they participating?

The Narrative Group

There were other issues and formats for discussion: a perception that 'generalisability' and 'universality' were the 'favoured modes' in the programme, combined with the short-term existence of 'b-list projects' whose funding had not yet been secured, gave rise to what became known as the 'Narrative Group' (though it initially referred to itself as the 'Narrative, Meaning and Persuasion Group'). This group shared a perception (which may or may not have been fair) that the programme had a great deal of momentum towards 'reductionist and universalising' modes of thinking, not least because of some of the ways we had been introduced to the work of David Schum, an external adviser. There was a sense that some in the programme were promoting Schum's work as a pre-agreed starting point and some of the group felt uncomfortable with this.[22] The participants of the Narrative Group instead had an intense interest in academic discourse as heavily contextualised persuasion, rhetoric and narrative. They took to meeting together to discuss a nominated text at regular

[22] I cannot stress enough that I am dealing with *my* sense of others' perceptions of yet others' statements. Schum himself was not a major player in this scenario though his talks inevitably summarised his ample published work into bullet points and headings.

(roughly monthly) intervals. They also took the decision rather early on that membership was invitation-only and that, by and large, each member was trusted to use their judgement on who would contribute to the culture that was arising: a single invitation sufficed to 'qualify' members as entitled to make further invitations.

Thus the group operated on a radically different basis from other areas of the programme and found an identity that was defined in contrast to the main programme. Essentially, the group sought out kindred spirits who shared a recognisable (but largely undefined) interest in a particular type of qualitative discourse—disciplines as epistemological and rhetorical strategies and the role of judgement and argument in preference to content.[23] Disciplinary specialities varied widely (from Medicine to History, with Statistics, Education, Anthropology, Literature, Computer Science, History of Science and (adamantly) *others* represented at different times) and participation (despite our best efforts with diaries) fluctuated according to people's availability. Thus the readings chosen by the group included chapters from such works as Rorty (1989), McCloskey (1990), Messer-Davidow, *et al.* (1993), Lacey (1999), Polanyi (1962) and other discursive texts that seemed to the group to offer worthwhile perspectives on issues (and typically not the normal or normativising perspective). However, readings were not limited to those that circled around disciplinary claims and epistemological constructivism: at times, policy documents concerned with Higher Education were discussed and problematised (such as QAA codes for postgraduate study or handbooks for Ph.D. supervisors).

What this generated was *discussion*: unminuted, virtually undocumented, undirected and often asynthetic discussion 'just like academics used to have' (as one participant enthusiastically put it). The skies were as blue as they can get (and fieldnotes were virtually impossible, given how multifaceted the discussion would get). To preserve this culture, there was a strong reluctance to 'account for itself' or to regulate its own activities. Thus, when the group (as a recognisable entity within *Evidence*) was asked to produce a report in line with other projects, only one was submitted, early on. Respectful (but repeated) requests for further reports were met with threats to 'meet in our own time'.

Despite the apparent freewheeling anarchy I have just described, there was an intense focus on the theme of 'evidence' through all the group's discussions, aligned with a deep suspicion about the *perceived* norm of *Evidence* whereby formulae and methodologies could (almost automatically) 'provide the answers'. Rather, the emphasis was on modes of representation, the role

---

[23] I am fully confident that this description would be ripped to shreds by the group should they reconvene to discuss this particular piece.

of judgement and the deeper implications of 'objectifying' representations in particular. There was no search for consensus as such—but there was a strongly bounded sense of identity.

Organisationally, then, the Narrative Group was almost the inverse of Causality: in the latter, there was a pooling of individual contributions in search of unity whereas Narrative *knew* they had a common identity and their interaction involved no search for consensus. Difference became 'interesting' rather than 'challenging'.

Thus the Narrative group acted as a focal point for those whose disposition (if not discipline too) predisposed them to problematise positions or methodologies that were positioned as integrative. As such, as individuals, they frequently interrupted the 'search for consensus' in wider gatherings. For instance, during a general discussion led by William Twining in November 2004, the following exchange occurred in a search for 'ways that articulate some questions'. Both speakers were members of the Narrative Group.

> Speaker 1: I'd like to be aware of what's shaping [any decision]. So my question is, how are you deciding what's a good question? Do you see what I mean? ...
> Speaker 2: So we're saying ... *is* the question, 'what is the relationship between theory and evidence' a good question? That's the question he was asking. It's a question about the question. Is the question 'what's the relationship between theory and evidence' a good question? And if we were all to say 'yes', then we've agreed that that's a good question (laughter). It *becomes* a good question.
> Speaker 1: I'm just wondering on what basis we decide.
> Speaker 2: On what evidence?
> Speaker 1: What's the evidence for it being a good question? That's it, thank you.

This disruption of plenary discussions had a gradually polarising effect at many levels: one participant (whose career has indubitably been multidisciplinary) said several times to me in private that the frequency of such questions led him to take a 'harder and more empirical position than I would ever normally take'.

As this continued, 'common ground from which to proceed' began to appear less and less accessible. This tension eventually came to a head in the 'Schum Challenge' in June 2005 (about eighteen months after the start of the programme). As already mentioned, Schum (1987) and Schum (1994) had been suggested as a starting point for collaboration and he had already given presentations to the programme (as Twining discusses, in this volume.)

A one-day seminar was held, framed largely around the participants of the Narrative Group putting their case for a different agenda and a response to their presentations. This day, and the email interchanges that followed, exposed a great deal of misunderstanding: typically, someone would say that *now* they had *begun* to realise that when they thought they understood something earlier, actually they had not—but it took lengthy discussion before familiar (and therefore overlooked) assumptions were subjected to an enquiring gaze. This process was to repeat over and over in a spiral—not of greater knowledge but greater sensitivity to *one's own* modes of understanding and its limits. Gradually we (many participants) became more sensitive to those moments where it was an unexamined assumption that was misleading us, rather than the 'point we were trying to make' being challenged. A spectacular example is that it was not for a year or so that some participants, while being aware that not all academics consider their work to be 'science', did not grasp that 'being scientific' was not a term of approval in all disciplines. I can see that 'you're being scientific, then' could have been intended as approval but it was not always received that way.

Interdisciplinary observations: private and public

During this 'first phase', therefore, the first thing we (the Interdisciplinary Project) developed was a high tolerance for ambiguity and ambivalence: in that context, we returned repeatedly to the issue of criteria and grounds for making judgements of what was important and how we should articulate what we saw as happening. Since a deliberately polemical and provisional working definition of 'discipline' characterised it for our purposes as a gaze that 'defines and presents things in ways other than they initially seem', our ignorance was complete. Could we really tell when a statistician (to pick a random example) was asking a profound methodological question or just seeking apparently trivial clarification? There were occasions when a questioner *thought* they were asking a trivial question but they accidentally cut to the heart of a discipline. Then from time to time there were also occasions when questioners seemed to have every intention of cutting to the core of a discipline ... Put simply, one could not tell in advance how a question would be received and the questioner's intentions could play what was frankly a completely random role in shaping the discussion.

What we *saw* (he said, choosing his words to advertise his attempt at neutrality) was people's language sometimes becoming dismissive or impatient. We eventually decided that our sense that such pejorative judgements ('absurd', 'nonsensical', 'trivial' and so on) should be treated as 'personal' was a red herring, and were to be treated with extreme caution (and we take credit for asserting this *before* we were the recipients of such judgements) but this was not our first thought. We *initially* found it helpful to view these frustrations as symptomatic of a breakdown of disciplinary working that 'spilled' into 'the personal' (it had to go somewhere). Put bluntly, if someone got annoyed, the indignation pointed to intellectual shock and the breakdown of normal order, as if 'the person behind the professional' was forced to appear at this point. Another way of putting this was that no disciplinary framework was available to the 'speaker' (who might by now be silent) that was appropriate to express the *scale* or *detail* of discursive breakdown. In fact, we acquired the habit of seeking out such moments as indicative of when 'something interesting' was just starting to emerge. This was put more flippantly by one participant who said in passing (and in private) that 'you knew you were doing real interdisciplinary work when you felt like punching someone'.

But however easily the distinction between 'personal' and 'disciplinary' came to mind, its fate exemplifies what happened to our thought process over time as we experimented with frameworks and metaphors. Often the decision to change our mode of questioning was based not on firm understanding but the recognition that we simply could not give a definitive answer and this turned out to be one of those cases. Was someone on the email list 'being rude' or were they merely embodying the typical culture and expectations of their disciplinary background? It may be that certain disciplinary cultures are more 'assertive' and 'dismissive' than others; equally it might be (as one participant suggested at this point without a great deal of conviction) that senior academics *can be* more impatient because their responsibilities pressurise them to a far greater degree than postdoctoral fellows experience (but postdocs on short contracts probably found it hard to see how anyone who already had a permanent job could be *that* pressurised). Or perhaps they were 'just rude people'— in which case were they 'disciplined into it'? Or 'not disciplined out of it'? Are there disciplines where such attributes are vital and deliberately cultivated?

Of course, patience, inclusivity and 'appropriate manners' sound good but they ignore the necessity of finding ways to *exclude* certain topics and methodologies for the sake of a discipline's integrity. Disciplines are as much defined by what they are *not* as what they are, by deliberate effort: Daston (2009: 804), for instance, notes that many scientists simply stopped reading the history of science when they found relativism rearing its head and Collins (1992: 188–90) explains that that 'doing science' *requires* a commitment to its being true: relativism has no place—or at least not a useful one within the paradigm. Even if one is minded to 'permit' something epistemologically alien in another field, it will be routinely excluded by one means or another from disciplinary work if it cannot be found a useful role.

That is not to say that a discipline's borders are permanently fixed: as we were told more than once, from a medical point of view there is 'no such thing as alternative medicine' since 'orthodox medicine' will adopt anything it considers efficacious—but it must do on its own terms and by its own criteria. This logic seems to hold true for all disciplines—if statistical or economic reasoning is to become a productive part of (e.g.) History, it will have to do so in a recognisably *historical* way. For our purposes, one consideration that emerged was that the style of 'rejection' was less relevant than the *fact* of rejection.[24]

We were dealing then, with three kinds of friction: firstly, 'healthy' (or even unhealthy) academic differences that are the bread-and-butter of academic practice (which *can* of course become 'personal' but that is a more familiar breakdown); secondly, situations where interdisciplinary interactions threatened to derail a particular argument; and thirdly (and distinctly) also the logical extension of those moments where such issues cascaded to a critical point when everything ground to a complete halt. The Socratic word *aporia* seems appropriate for its meaning of 'there being no path'. It was not just a case of not being able to make progress, it was that there was nowhere to go that seemed even *potentially* fruitful. Discussion sometimes reached a point where participants were apparently speechless—but what conclusions can be drawn from someone falling silent or no longer contributing to an email thread?

Aporia arose, then, when familiar disciplinary strategies were exhausted: a statement that was expected to command unproblematic assent failed to do so, further appeals to disciplinary norms merely complicated matters as they too were challenged, and so on until we reached a complete breakdown.[25] To consider that the apparent irruption of emotion (notwithstanding the difficulties of making secure judgements about 'irritation', 'frustration', 'annoyance' and so on from the relatively stark medium of (possibly) hasty emails or a momentary facial expression) was something that should abruptly catapult us into the idiom of 'being personal' risked *avoiding* rather than answering the question.[26]

[24] This paragraph of course begs a question I have been avoiding for lack of space, namely what we consider academic disciplines to *be*: for some discussion see Chandler (2009), Post (2009), Butler (2009), Moran (2002, esp. 3–14), Lenoir (1993), Hoskin and Maeve (1993), Becher (1989), Klein (1990: 104–17) and all her cited works via index. Most works cited in this article address the nature of disciplines in some way. For more culturally situated discussions, see the works of Foucault (especially Foucault, 1977), Certeau (1984).

[25] It is hard at this point not to be drawn to Rorty's (1989: 73) 'final vocabulary': 'it is "final" in the sense that if doubt is cast on the worth of these words, their user has no noncircular argumentative recourse. Those words are as far as he can go with language; beyond them there is only helpless passivity or a resort to force.'

[26] If we seem overly cautious, one junior person connected loosely with the programme told me of a harrowing experience where they were convinced the senior academic they were speaking to was scowling throughout their long conversation. He eventually 'cracked' and asked if 'everything was ok, you seem to be frowning a lot', and got the reply 'oh, sorry, apparently when I'm concentrating on something I find interesting, I do that.'

Thus our initial way of looking at such interactions, where the breakdown of the 'public/academic' mode gave way to the previously hidden 'last resort' of the personal, raises some profound questions of academic identity. Is 'private' the 'bedrock' on which 'public' is constructed and therefore 'that which is exposed when the public discourse cracks'? Or do the two have more of a symbiotic relationship?

Suddenly we needed a framework to make such judgements: there is plenty of bibliography in different areas on 'public and private', and alternative models to apply—none of which we were expert in at that point, and even fewer of which could be called an interdisciplinary approach. The instant we thought we saw a trend it would be undermined by the next interaction. We therefore became extremely reluctant to use the distinction, however obvious it seemed at first glance.

What seemed most significant to us was that, in a monodisciplinary setting, what steps into the breach at times of rupture is *discipline* itself, in all its meanings, to 'restore order': that is business as usual in monodisciplinary work (indeed it might be said to be the *point*, if one takes a Foucauldian line). In an interdisciplinary setting, that was possibly the most *un*productive thing to do and generally invited chaos because we all had a different version of what 'order' actually *was*. This conclusion seemed to merit further exploration.

A need for discipline

If I were to make a statement in an academic setting, I would be implicitly accepting the possibility of challenge by legitimate experts: 'Rome's Empire came about more by accident than design', for instance, would invite authoritative comment by ancient historians and while physicists, philosophers or statisticians might have interesting comments to make, it would be expected that these historians would have the last word on whether this judgement was to be found persuasive in an interdisciplinary setting.

The more specific the statement, the more this applies. So, while a worthwhile discussion might contingently arise about what we meant by 'accident and design, cause and effect' from non-historians, if the statement were instead 'the Roman Republican system of competitive but short-lived consulship predisposed the ruling oligarchy to repeated expansion of Rome's influence (generally military)', judgements about my statement become even more the preserve of these specialists. Conversely, statements about statistical probability, epidemiology or accelerated particles would presumably not be resolved to everyone's satisfaction by ancient historians.

But what expertise can authorise a statement during 'interdisciplinary work'? *By definition*, there is no organised and authoritative body of knowledge for academics in an interdisciplinary study, no habitual methods of judgements that have been thrashed out and debated to the point where expert discussion is even possible. How can experts in one discipline make *authoritative* judgements about the work of another discipline? There would turn out to be no shortage of 'plain and simple' *judgements* during *Evidence* but these were monodisciplinary, that is, made from the point of view of a particular discipline or set of related disciplines. Thus, for instance, contentious arguments about 'relativism' were generally informed by 'the implications for my discipline'—literary theorists were, broadly speaking, less unnerved than scientists by these implications. Reductionist approaches tailored to 'large-scale quantitative data' had roughly the opposite reception.

To refine this question a little further—if academics do make judgements, are those for their own disciplinarity (i.e. a contribution to expanding their own understanding) or (God help us) to 'help' the speaker with what is 'actually not such a difficult problem'? Attempting to proceed towards agreement/decision/resolution, so habitual and obvious, often simply enacted incommensurability between different disciplinary modes.

Another way of describing this whole process would be to centre it around the theme of ignorance, and not just run-of-the-mill ignorance, but rather *expert* ignorance which takes years of dedication to muster. It started to be useful to assume one's knowledge was less 'normal' and shared than usual. The knowledge itself was not the problem—it was our relationship with it that needed reinventing. The necessary change was almost an inversion—seeing the limits rather than the value, an unfamiliarity rather than the automaticity of our systems of knowing, yet all the while realising it was *still all we had to work with*.

The middle phase

To return to the sequence of events: at this point, which I am designating 'the middle phase', the programme 'naturally' ('instinctively?') moved towards subgroups where common interest had 'spontaneously' emerged: what had been the general Causality Seminar Series became the 'Causality Triangle', where statistical modes predominated (the website merges the two sets, though the first year (2004) of Causality was much broader than its later incarnation). The new incarnation of Causality ran until December 2005. The relative success of the original series as a well-attended plenary on the other hand (typically attracting between twenty and forty people from a range of disciplines) was seen as valuable and a successor series 'Prediction and Forecasting' was optimistically organised.

At this point an unexpected [*sic*] pair of factors arose: the institute that had hosted Causality, organised through an economist, declined to host Prediction on the grounds that 'my discipline is not interested in prediction'. Moving to a different venue saw a noticeable drop-off in interest, with numbers generally being between six and ten. Quite apart from the surprising assertion that economics does not concern itself with prediction (which came to me second-hand and is therefore perhaps best not problematised here), it brought to light a rather 'mundane' aspect of *Evidence* that was also seen in other areas: if you have no obvious audience (as recognised disciplines tend to do for seminars and talks), you will get more numbers at a busy junction. My guess is that that many economists were visiting the convenient lunchtime lectures held at the end of the rainbow in their own institutional basement (they got the apocryphal free lunch) and, while many were engaging actively in discussion, none were drawn into a long-term loyalty to the seminars. Those planning interdisciplinary studies might do well to take heed and steer towards *either* a conspicuous and broad (but perhaps rather loosely engaged) audience *or* a less visible but more focussd and specialising one.

Prediction

Prediction was, for all its subdued numbers, an extremely interesting and thought-provoking set of presentations and discussions (well, *we* thought so ...) that allowed for the development of a close group whose thinking (if the diverse series can be adequately summarised) developed around the position that prediction and forecasting were essentially a useful place to unveil disciplinary strategies and tactics. This was because methodologies and extrapolations were being extended into an empty domain of possibility (the future or, as some achronologically orientated speakers necessarily interpreted it, ignorance). This evoked a disciplinary handling of provisionally reified 'evidence' instead of actuality (the past, which can nominally at least be objectified)—a revealing exercise, as it turned out. Thus Prediction lurks in the collective memory of the programme as a space where there was *no* evidence to speak of, the 'counterfactual' flipside of causality. Once again (a response to) *not* knowing was a theme, though for the most part it was deliberately constructed. That is not to say that we did not encounter the expert ignorance we had started getting used to.

Dreams in History

Prediction ran from October 2004 to May 2005 and was organised under the auspices of the Interdisciplinary Project. I then 'switched' roles to the History Project to organise a six-month set of discursive seminars (rather than talks) on 'Dreams in History' between January and June 2006, which endeavoured to form links with the Wellcome Trust Centre for the History of Medicine at UCL. Again, the apparently straightforward aspect of hosting turned out to have a critical effect—locating the seminar at the Wellcome (a *fairly* short walk from central UCL) may have been a factor in the gradual shift of audience to being largely populated by Wellcome academics: but equally, the subject was perhaps better disposed to that community of historians of medicine. Having said that, one participant wrote to me afterwards to say '[i]n the dream seminars ... interdisciplinarity could be seen to be vulnerable to the pressure of disciplinary expression and consciousness: psychologists, historians of medicine, historians of the ancient world seem only barely able to communicate—surprisingly to me, as they might all be thought to be "social science" disciplines in the general sense of studying humans in societies.' Dreams was the last named seminar series or circle to be organised: future gatherings within the programme would take a different form.

The Bentham Defence

Thus from autumn 2004 to summer 2006 the Evidence programme completed a transition from being a widely populated group aspiring to consensus to a self-selecting, more focused (but still overlapping) series of subgroups who could cooperate beyond the banal and introductory. Sometimes these groups were reasonably formalised (such as a seminar organised around a theme, as I have outlined) but at other times they were ad-hoc sets of participants on the email list discussing a particular issue from contingent disciplines, such as the one we dubbed 'the Bentham Defence'.

This opened in August 2005, in the wake of the July bombings in London and the tragic shooting of Jean Charles de Menezes, with a problem about calculating probabilities in taking a decision to shoot a suspected bomb-laden terrorist. Contributors tended to be able to manage close arguments in statistical probabilities and/or legal propositions (no doubt because of the opening message that framed the question in those terms) and my impression (as a non-contributor) is that some useful discussion was to be had before the thread died away. Interestingly, of the last three messages, one ended with a vigorous, even straightforwardly didactic, call for 'more Bayesian thinking' on the grounds that that 'people on the whole' are poor at making judgements based on probability (and a *deeply* ironic closing remark by the male speaker— '... item 4. People, especially men, tend to be overconfident'). The thread was effectively closed by the response to this confident set of assertions with an open question:

> How has it been shown that (Bayesian) probability theory is the *only* consistent way, i.e. that no other consistent way is possible? (This is different from showing that *certain* other ways are not consistent.)
>
> And: coherent Bayesian reasoning implies that all possible future events are specified *a priori*. Do we want such a restriction, be it consistent or not?

The speaker was certainly cognisant of Bayesian reasoning, though I got the sense he does not consider himself a 'Bayesian'. His comment (if I have understood it correctly) is reminiscent of the 'pro-disciplinary commentators' on interdisciplinarity who argue that taking any position about disciplines requires a disciplined position, in that however useful Bayesian reasoning is in particular contexts, it does not help us decide on answering questions about its own suitability. It relies, like all methodologies, on excluding or fixing certain aspects. Once again, the 'self-apparent' and 'unquestionable' turns out to be a necessary prerequisite for discussion.

The homeopathy thread

Another thread on the email list that began on 1 June 2006 debating critiques of biomedicine (which we referred to as 'the homeopathy thread' though it covered 'well, *everything* really ...') served to demonstrate the extent to which *any* (disciplinary? 'informed'?) judgement requires disciplinary assumptions. The homeopathy thread began with an expectation that a rather derisive opinion about a social science critique of modern medicine would be more generally shared on the list. Reactions were mixed, and the thread slid rather helplessly across issues such as postmodernism, disciplinary borrowings, whether we should unproblematically state that the earth goes round the sun. ... For the most part we saw an enactment of a position rather than (necessarily) a sharing of understanding as each speaker exercised (or exorcised, depending on your perspective) their optimism, irritation, concern, alarm, indignation or caution at a discussion where every attempt to fix meaning, values or definitions produced more confusion. In one particularly striking case, an attempt to be genuinely helpful about terminology was apparently taken to be another head-on challenge and the last straw for one particular poster. If we were to construct a sequential narrative of *Evidence*, this thread signalled as good a moment as any where the hope of 'natural' (self-emerging and uncontestable) cross-disciplinary consensus about shared methods and approaches quietly packed its bags and left.

Emergent landscape

Nonetheless, rather than being the apocalyptic moment that people abandoned 'communicating across divides' and huddled in small, like-minded collectives where 'real' discussion could be had, this point is better thought of as the moment that the texture and landscape (so to speak) of the interdisciplinary spaces came more into striking relief. We knew now, if nothing else, that going into an interdisciplinary discussion thinking it was epistemological 'business as usual' virtually *guaranteed* that disciplinary knowledge and expertise would be transformed instantly into interdisciplinary ignorance and ineptitude.

I would venture to say that participants faced an increasingly visible (stark, even) choice at this point; either to retreat into the familiar and humour the exercise without any noticeable engagement or to begin to incorporate into their thinking, speaking and writing a much greater awareness of their understanding as *particular*.

Different forms of interaction evolved: at every point during *Evidence*, there were 'one-off' events to which the group was invited and many attended, providing a low-level kind of continuity; most people continued to participate in different aspects of the programme and a set of presentations centred on the individual projects kept attracting a core membership who were, by now, increasingly adept at dealing with each other's perspectives. Starting in September 2006 with (paid) participants of *Evidence* being urged to run presentations on their progress as projects, 'Evidence seminars' continued, a little sporadically, up to the end of the programme.

It was somewhere during this period that the marginalised, 'insufficiently funded' and altogether *secondary* Narrative Group, meeting once again to discuss a suggested chapter, realised it had accidentally become the most stable, longest-lived and possibly most influential identifiable thread of the *Evidence* programme. Typically for us, this suggestion was met with a mixed response within the group. But the sheer persistence of the group is worth remarking on and there is evidence of their (ahem) persuasiveness: when *Evidence* reached the point, in April 2007, where projects were expected to give presentations to the Leverhulme Trustees, a 'practice run' day was held, with all projects participating. My fieldnotes for the day record a relative ease between *most* speakers, by now very much accustomed to one another and deftly able to address questions that might well have floored them in the early stages of the programme—with one or two rather spectacular (and accidentally exposed) exceptions where there had clearly been a quiet surrender to the incommensurability of profoundly different outlooks. I stress that this is entirely to be expected: each discipline must form its own relationship with each other that it encounters and this will inevitably require a range of different responses. Thus, History must find its own response to Statistics, Medicine, Philosophy (to name a few random examples).[27] The borders/negotiating parties can be anything from token lines to something resembling the Berlin Wall. Without such judgements ('this is us, this is *not* us'), disciplines would simply not be distinctive.

One fieldnote of the day jumps out as simultaneously significant but unable to sustain much interpretative weight: an informal discussion with a very senior member of the programme, outside the papers and chaired discussions (i.e. holding a cup of coffee in the break) concluded a chat on the nature of disciplines with the words 'Well, yes I suppose it is *all* persuasion in a way'.

The members of the Narrative Group will be the first to seize on my rather sly claims here for a certain kind of 'progress' and would certainly puncture any claim that 'their agenda had predominated': to allow such a grand narrative to stand uncontested and unredescribed would instantly *disprove* their hegemony—yet, perhaps, it cannot be said to be entirely untrue.

'So much for seminar series': the late phase

If I am to construct a 'late phase', it might easily be based on a move to organise discussion around the disciplinary specialities (i.e. the projects, though they did not always map directly onto disciplines) that was almost accidentally embodied in that 'practice day' and some of the 'Evidence seminars' that followed. After seminars and various thematic groups, we found we were once again hearing what the individual projects had to offer. We were back to the familiar disciplines, it appeared. Had interdisciplinarity 'failed'?

This would be a very unsatisfactory conclusion. I would prefer to represent the projects, immersed for a while in thematic groupings, as 'expanding' to reclaim a more visible central role. There was a noticeable change in how they did so. Presentations and discussions that had formerly blinked uneasily in the glare of an unpredictable interdisciplinary audience could more easily

---

[27] I am not even going to begin to consider the issue of 'personalities'.

refer to/form a relationship with/politely and (relatively) effortlessly find ways to decline to engage with an exotic range of 'foreign' habits with greater confidence or at least make a show of familiarity and more clearly defined ignorance. They knew better what they were, what they were not, what they could usefully engage with and what had no place in *their* world.

The postdoc group

One small nugget might suffice to represent this: running somewhat in the background of the middle and late phases was the 'postdoc meetings'. Most of the projects were the combination of a fully or partly salaried relatively junior postdoctoral fellow who was linked to a senior (professorial) principal investigator. In June 2005 until relatively late in the project, these postdocs began meeting regularly to seek a viable kind of discourse together and the informal culture of that group precipitated a cascade of insights as they gave subject-orientated presentations to one another where 'side-tracking' questions were permitted to exhaust themselves. I, for instance, as one of the more vocal non-statistical (and certainly non-quantitative) participants of *Evidence*, was rather embarrassed to grasp (after patient and repeated explanations by other members of the group) the extent to which my historical/humanities language of 'probably/possibly/it is reasonably likely . . .' roughly corresponded 'grammatically' (in disciplinary terms) to statistical probabilities.[28] My taking 'real numbers and percentages' so literally (and then being suspicious of their apparent claims to precision) did no justice to the dexterity with which statisticians (or at least the ones to whom I was speaking) treated them as what *I* would call 'metaphors'. They have no need to *call* them metaphors because 'they all know what they mean' (which, in mitigation, is probably why none had stated the situation so baldly until that point). It was *I* who was objectifying these signifiers, not the statisticians.

Conversely, it was in these seminars that I began to grasp ever more deeply the extent to which my historical background had imbued me with a certain sense of genre in my questions and argument that had become invisible to me—thus when I was talking about 'belief' in discourse about religion, one participant turned to me and said '*I just don't understand* why it's such a big

---

[28] An early attempt to provide some kind of commentary on email exchanges and the transcript of a general seminar by Stephen Rowland and myself proved to be an act of extraordinarily annoying interpretative imperialism. I have therefore refrained from interpreting the praxis of anyone except myself in this discussion. It has the advantage, at least, of exposing fully the solipsism of this account of the programme.

deal.' Being sent back to the drawing-board proved to be an illuminating exercise as I hope my other contribution to this volume demonstrates.

Again (thinking of the subtle effects of 'background factors' such as location and lunch), I am drawn to thinking about the culture of a particular kind of group who had other bonds such as short-term contracts, fairly similar ages and the aspiration to establish ourselves academically—in contrast to the professorial culture of the principal investigators.[29]

It is impossible to gauge the extent to which these moments of revelation fed back into the programme as a whole, but they were certainly part of a fundamental reorientation in our epistemological relationships. Fewer questions brought speakers grinding to a halt (or so is my impression) around this point in the programme, and questioners began to recognise (so is my assertion) when they had all they were going to get from the speaker and what was enough to proceed, even (if only) impressionistically.

This process of gradual insight and a fluency in establishing one's relationship with other (albeit often superficially understood) disciplinary modes stands in contrast to something that we (the interdisciplinary team) had noted running through many conversations and interactions of many kinds during the programme, a propensity that we came to call 'disciplinary imperialism'. A sincere enthusiasm for, and deep grasp of the explicative power of, a particular methodology (*or* unreconstructed naivety about the nature of disciplinary knowledge and culture, as you prefer) led at times to a sense by *some* that (some) others were urging a foreign methodology upon their field rather unreflectively or at least, disrespectfully. This was not helped by a perception (particularly on the email list) that a small minority of participants were rather too quick to (for instance) 'throw Bayesianism at everyone's problems'. I, for one, found the claim that what I was doing in my historical argument was 'basically Bayesian' curiously disquieting and at first difficult to respond to adequately. My eventual answer was 'no, it's not, I'm doing *History*'.

Such accusations of being a good Bayesian seemed to the recipients to be an appropriation of something familiar of theirs without sufficient regard for context: to them, just because an approach in *your* discipline seemed to correlate with something in *mine* does not make 'calling my method by your name' a constructive move, even if it was meant as an endorsement. Such imperialism was rather easy to slip into, it seemed, and therefore my disingenuous claim that the Narrative Group's focus on rhetoric and persuasion

---

[29] I cannot imagine Professor Stephen Rowland not prompting me here with 'and what's that then?'

ultimately permeated the programme might well be set aside as an imperial reflex (though Fish would surely shrug and offer 'what else did you expect to happen? Just get on with it.')

In striking contrast, what we *did* think was useful was a scenario where someone could 'borrow' something to use in their own work and *on their own terms*—in other words, to make it their own and thereby enlarge their discipline: 'appropriate and take back home' was the order of the day. This happened many times during *Evidence* though space does not permit any expansion of the theme here.

It was these kinds of deliberate reflection and consequent reframing on the nature of one's knowledge that appeared erratically but incrementally within the presentations of *Evidence* that I would say began to characterise the late phases of the programme. To be more specific, though many had espoused such aspects right from the start, the general expectation and conduct of the overall programme began more explicitly to accommodate such considerations: they became part of the general culture of *Evidence*.

Thus I claim that the earlier activities that revealed as much breakdown as insight acted in a sense as a 'womb' that nurtured the project-centred work. We (the programme) had started from an initial 'flat' sense of the different disciplines where speakers represented their disciplines, mediated only by an awareness that they were addressing a relatively featureless audience of 'non-specialists'; we then moved to examining themes where incipient mutual familarity permitted some degree of reference to one another's methodologies and paradigms. This gave the projects an extraordinary range of stimuli which laid the basis for the 'final phase'. More colloquially, as time went by, and conversations continued in a wide range of contexts (seminars, email lists, corridors …) a mature awareness emerged amongst participants of the profundities of talking across the disciplines.

The final phase and conferences

What have I argued? Something to the effect that the fruition of this interdisciplinary programme was be a 'maturing' of the disciplines/personnel (we had difficulty separating them) in a multidisciplinary setting, such that they could 'leave home' and embody an interdisciplinary (whatever that means) mode of operation 'in the wild'—a persistent practice of reflexivity and self-awareness. This includes a willingness to experiment with perspectives or methods borrowed from other disciplines on one's own terms, the building of bridges where appropriate—but also the creation or enforcement of frontiers and the institution of border-guards. Not every discipline can easily intermingle with *all* its peers. It also includes a dexterity in all things interdisciplinary—dealing with accidental or deliberate challenges, including the art of side-stepping discipline-shattering questions where appropriate.

Let us imagine this is indeed true (a useful description): when the final conferences were held, with a mixture of long-term participants and outsiders, the 'insiders', we assert, had changed noticeably since the beginning. There was a different mode of questioning and listening; they (to use an antiquarian word) suffered more ambiguity, and had greater humility regarding their own level of understanding. There was also a more sophisticated mode of engaging with discipline-specific modes of reference (which were often assumed to be transparent by people new to interdisciplinary work). The UCL-based 'Satellite' conference was made up almost entirely of 'insiders' (though it was not without its controversies) and contrasted in that respect with the more glamorous final conference at the British Academy. This had a significant number of external speakers and it was unclear to me, at least, that it was a 'fruit' of the programme. Rather the programme was able to contribute, often powerfully and *distinctively*, to a new creation which happened to be a single conference. It was more than simply knowing the people as colleagues. Without wishing to detail particular interactions, there were moments when 'outsiders' visibly began undergoing the kinds of processes that we had suffered at the beginning of *Evidence*. It may be my imagination that active members of the *Evidence* programme managed such moments with greater fluency but that *is* one claim I choose not to deconstruct too much. If there is any truth in it, such a qualitative change is extremely difficult to substantiate—we have next-to-no 'evidence'. The reader will have to decide whether to take my word for it.

References

Becher, T. (1989), *Academic Tribes and Territories: intellectual enquiry and the cultures of disciplines* (Milton Keynes, Society for Research into Higher Education).

Biagioli, M. (2009), 'Postdisciplinary liaisons: science studies and the humanities', *Critical Inquiry*, 35(4): 816–33.

Bird, E. (2001), 'Disciplining the interdisciplinary: radicalism and the academic curriculum', *British Journal of Sociology of Education*, 22(4): 463–78.

Butler, J. (2009), 'Critique, dissent, disciplinarity', *Critical Inquiry*, 35(4): 773–95.

Castronovo, R. (2000), 'Within the veil of interdisciplinary knowledge? Jefferson, du Bois, and the negation of politics', *New Literary History*, 31(4): 781–804.

Certeau, M. de (1984), *The Practice of Everyday Life* (Berkeley, University of California Press).

Chandler, J. (2009), 'Introduction: doctrines, disciplines, discourses, departments', *Critical Inquiry*, 35(4): 729–46.

Collins, H. (1992), *Changing Order: replication and induction in scientific practice* (Chicago: University of Chicago Press).

Concerns, T. (2001), 'Interdisciplinarity and nursing: "everything is everything," or is it?', *Nursing Science Quarterly*, 14(4): 274–80.

Daston, L. (2009), 'Science studies and the history of science', *Critical Inquiry*, 35(4): 798–813.

Davies, J. P. (2009), 'The messiness of academics "speaking across the disciplines"', in L. Walsh and P. Kahn (eds.), *Collaborative Working in Higher Education: the social academy* (London, Routledge), pp. 111–18

Douglas, M. (1992), *Risk and Blame: essays in cultural theory* (Routledge, London).

Fish, S. (1994), *There's No Such Thing as Free Speech: and it's a good thing, too* (New York, Oxford University).

Fish, S. (1995), *Professional Correctness: literary studies and political change* (Cambridge, MA, Harvard University Press).

Flemming, R. (2000), *Medicine and the Making of Roman Women: gender, nature, and authority from Celsus to Galen* (New York, Oxford University Press).

Foucault, M. (1977), *Discipline and Punish: the birth of the prison* (New York, Vintage Books).

Foucault, M. and Gordon, C. (1980), *Power/Knowledge: selected interviews and other writings, 1972–1977* (First US edn., New York, Pantheon Books).

Gibbons, M., Limoges, C. and Nowotny, H. (1994), *The New Production of Knowledge: The Dynamics of Science and Research in Contemporary Societies* (London, Sage Publications).

Grossetti, M. (2005), 'Interdisciplinarity or Hybrid Disciplines: the example of "Sciences for the Engineer", in France', in *International Conference: challenges in innovation in graduate education* (Toronto), pp. 2–5.

Hartog, F. (2009), 'The double fate of the Classics', *Critical Inquiry*, 35(4): 964–79.

Hoskin, K. W. and Maeve, R. H. (1993), 'Accounting as discipline: the overlooked supplement', in E. Messer-Davidow, D. R. Shumway and D. J. Sylvan (eds.), *Knowledges: historical and critical studies in interdisciplinarity* (Charlottesville, VA, University Press of Virginia), pp. 25–53.

Hunt, L. (1994), 'The virtues of disciplinarity', *Eighteenth-Century Studies*, 28(1): 1–7.

Huutoniemi, K., Thompson Klein, J., Bruun, H. and Hukkinen, J. (2009), 'Analyzing interdisciplinarity: typology and indicators', *Research Policy*, 39(1), 79–88.

Klein, J. T. (1990), *Interdisciplinarity: history, theory, and practice* (Detroit, MI, Wayne State University Press).

Klein, J. T. (1996), *Crossing Boundaries: knowledge, disciplinarities, and interdisiplinarities* (Charlottesville, VA, University Press of Virginia).

Klein, J. T. (2001), *Transdisciplinarity: Joint Problem Solving Among Science, Technology, and Society: an effective way for managing complexity* (Basel, Birkhäuser).

Klein, J. T. (2004), 'Prospects for Transdisciplinarity', *Futures*, 36(4): 515–26.

Klein, J. T. (2005), *Humanities, Culture, and Interdisciplinarity: the changing American academy* (Albany, NY, State University of New York Press).

Lacey, H. (1999), *Is Science Value Free? values and scientific understanding* (London, Routledge).

Lattuca, L. (2001), *Creating Interdisciplinarity: interdisciplinary research and teaching among college and university faculty* (Nashville, TN, Vanderbilt University Press).

Lenoir, T. (1993), 'The discipline of Nature and the nature of disciplines', in E. Messer-Davidow, D. R. Shumway and D. J. Sylvan (eds.), *Knowledges: historical and critical studies in interdisciplinarity* (Charlottesville, VA, University Press of Virginia), pp. 70–103.

Lyotard, J.-F. (1984). *The Postmodern Condition: a report on knowledge*, vol. v. 10 (Minneapolis, MN, University of Minnesota Press).

McCloskey, D. N. (1990), *If You're So Smart: the narrative of economic expertise* (Chicago, IL, University of Chicago Press).

Messer-Davidow, E., Shumway, D. R. and Sylvan, D. J. (eds.) (1993), *Knowledges: historical and critical studies in interdisciplinarity* (Charlottesville, VA, University Press of Virginia).

Moran, J. (2002), *Interdisciplinarity* (London, Routledge).

Polanyi, M. (1962), *Personal Knowledge: towards a post-critical philosophy* (London, Routledge).

Post, R. (2009), 'Debating Disciplinarity', *Critical Inquiry*, 35(4): 749–70.

Pryse, M. (1998), 'Critical interdisciplinarity, women's studies, and cross-cultural insight', *NWSA Journal*, 10(1): 1–22.

Readings, B. (1996), *The University in Ruins* (Cambridge, MA, Harvard University Press).

Rorty, R. (1989), *Contingency, Irony, and Solidarity* (Cambridge, Cambridge University Press).

Rossini, F. and Porter, A. (1981), 'Interdisciplinary research: performance and policy issues', *Journal of the Society of Research Administrators*, 13(2): 8–24.

Rowland, S. (2006), *The Enquiring University* (Milton Keynes, Open University Press).

Roy, R. (1979), 'Interdisciplinary science on campus: the elusive dream', in J. Kockelmans (ed.), *Interdisciplinarity in Higher Education* (University Park, PA, Pennsylvania State University Press), pp. 161–96.

Schum, D. A. (1987), *Evidence and Inference for the Intelligence Analyst* (Lanham, MD, University Press of America).

Schum, D. A. (1994), *The Evidential Foundations of Probabilistic Reasoning* (New York, Wiley).

4

Moving Beyond Law:
Interdisciplinarity and the Study
of Evidence

WILLIAM TWINING*

Abstract

The purpose of this paper is to examine critically both the idea of 'a multi-disciplinary field' or 'an integrated science' of evidence and scepticism about and resistance to this idea from the standpoint of a jurist who has been involved with interdisciplinary work on evidence in law for many years. Part I presents an overview of the intellectual history of the academic study of evidence in law in the Anglo-American tradition and shows how important aspects of the field came to be recognised as inherently multidisciplinary.[1] Part II identifies some limitations of legal

*Quain Professor of Jurisprudence Emeritus, University College London. Some parts of this paper draw on longer accounts of the history and theory of evidence scholarship in William Twining, *Rethinking Evidence* (2nd edn., Cambridge University Press, 2006) (hereafter *RE*), especially chap. 15, 'Evidence as a Multidisciplinary Subject' (originally published in 2003). This version has been rewritten for a non-specialist audience and as a reflection on the UCL Evidence programme. I am grateful to two anonymous reviewers, Terry Anderson, Jason Davies, Philip Dawid, and David Schum. I am especially indebted to Susan Haack, both for detailed comments and suggestions and, more generally, for her robust approach to epistemic justification ('foundherentism') and metaphysics ('innocent realism'). See Haack (1998, 2003, 1993/2009) and her writings on Evidence in law.
[1] A note on terminology: I use capitals (The Law of Evidence, Evidence in Law, Evidence as a multidisciplinary field) to refer to names of fields or subdisciplines; other uses of evidence are in lower case. In this paper the Law of Evidence—the legal rules governing admissibility of evidence and a few other matters—is distinguished from the much broader subject of the study of Evidence in law; in ordinary usage the two ideas are often loosely conflated (see below, n. 101). I shall use 'interdisciplinary' as the generic term for all the different kinds of relations and interactions across disciplines that transcend more refined distinctions between, for example, interdisciplinarity, transdisciplinarity, cross-disciplinarity, and pluridisciplinarity. I shall use multidisciplinary when more than two recognised fields are involved. Jason Davies, who presents an outline of his

perspectives on evidence, especially when the focus is on contested trials. It recounts the story of attempts to move beyond law in the direction of constructing a general field of evidence, that formed part of the background of the UCL programme. Part III examines some of the reasons for suspicion of and resistance to the idea of 'an integrated science of evidence'. Part IV restates the case for recognition and institutionalisation of evidence as a special focus of attention at the present time and puts forward a personal agenda of general questions that still need to be tackled.[2]

Part I. The study of Evidence in Law: an historical overview of an interdisciplinary tradition

LAW IS ALMOST the only discipline in which Evidence is established as a distinct field with courses, treatises, conferences, journals, and scholars who claim it as their main specialism.[3] This institutionalisation has only occurred within the common law tradition. For example, in civil law countries rules of evidence, such as they are, are normally integrated into Civil Procedure and Criminal Procedure, which are two quite distinct areas of expertise. Forensic science and criminalistics are also generally conceived as largely separate disciplines.

In common law Evidence as a specialised field was largely the creation of eighteenth- and nineteenth-century treatise writers, most of whom were practising lawyers or judges. The raw material of the early treatises was judicial decisions, but these were scattered and unevenly reported. It was the writers

---

thinking in Chap. 3 above, argues in a forthcoming publication that that the field is in need of some more precise distinctions and a single generic term to refer to all types of inter/trans-/ multidisciplinary work, and will be suggesting that this should be 'pluridisciplinarity'. The conventional, if imprecise, generic terms are sufficient for my purposes, except at pp. 108–11 below, where some such differentiations are needed. I am grateful to Jason Davies for clarification of this point.

[2] As this is a personal interpretation of the UCL Evidence programme, I should clarify my standpoint. I was involved in some aspects of the planning and management of the programme, received the reports and other communications, and attended a dozen or so seminars and other academic occasions, including some meetings of the narrative group. I helped to plan the conference at the British Academy in December 2007 and to edit this volume. However, by the time the project started, I had retired from UCL. I live in Oxford, and spend almost half of each year abroad, so attendance at meetings and seminars was problematic. I was accordingly more observer than participant.

[3] Epistemology is a long-established subdiscipline in philosophy and some theoretical aspects of evidence have also been of sustained concern in, for example, philosophy of science and history, but they have been less extensively institutionalised.

who developed the structure, conceptual apparatus, and attempts at theorising. For most of its history the study of evidence in law has focused on the technical rules and the underlying rationales of the Law of Evidence, viewed largely as a practical subject for lawyers involved in litigation. However, there have been periods when evidence scholars have drawn heavily on a range of other disciplines.

The story starts with Chief Baron Gilbert's *The Law of Evidence*, written in the 1720s, but published posthumously in 1754. For the next 150 years a central concern of the writers was to establish the Law of Evidence on the basis of a single principle. The main pioneering efforts can be seen as a series of illuminating mistakes up to the late nineteenth century, when James Bradley Thayer of Harvard laid the foundation for the structure of the modern law.[4] Gilbert tried to establish the Law of Evidence as a coherent field on the basis of an explicitly Lockean epistemology and a single organising principle, 'The Best Evidence Rule':

> The first therefore, and most signal Rule, in Relation to Evidence is this, That a Man must have the utmost Evidence, the Nature of the Fact is capable of; for the Design of the Law is to come to rigid Demonstration in Matters of Right, and there can be no Demonstration of a Fact without the best Evidence that the Nature of the Thing is capable of.[5]

Gilbert's rigid interpretation of what constitutes 'the best evidence' took the form of a hierarchy of rules of weight 'on a Scale of Probability[6] with Public Records at the top trumping non-official documents under seal down to oral testimony by competent witnesses at the bottom. Gilbert's scheme was followed by early nineteenth-century treatise writers, but is now recognised that as an account of the English Law of Evidence it was based on two false premises: first, Gilbert failed to distinguish between weight and admissibility and, second, his scheme postulated a hierarchy of *rules* of weight.[7] There are

---

[4] Thayer was appointed to Harvard in 1874, but his *Preliminary Treatise* preceded by some classic articles, was only published in 1898, almost 150 years after Gilbert's treatise.

[5] Gilbert (1754/1979), p. 4. Gilbert recognised that 'Demonstration' is rarely attainable and in practical life decisions have to be made on the basis of judgements of probability.

[6] Ibid.

[7] Wigmore (1908) stated this forcefully: 'If there is one thing for which the common law system of judge and jury stands, it is that rules of evidence as applied by the judge, are rules of admissibility alone and for the judge alone; the weight or credibility is for the jurors untrammeled by any rules of law ... The counsel who uses this book to induce the judge to a ruling on credibility is committing moral treason to our system.' Wigmore overstated the point, for judges are sometimes involved in making judgements of weight, but the central point that there are no formal rules of weight is generally accepted. On Thayer's very similar views see below, pp. 78–9.

no formal rules of weight in the common law: there are no general rules that prescribe that official evidence should be given priority over unofficial evidence; that written evidence has more probative force than oral testimony; nor, although this is not always observed by the media, that circumstantial evidence is weaker than testimony.[8] A similar error has been repeated throughout history, most recently in more doctrinaire versions of evidence-based medicine and evidence-based policy that have tried to formalise the weighing of evidence on the basis of peremptory rules prescribing hierarchies of weight and reliability.[9]

One of Gilbert's achievements was to provide a clear, and quite soft, target to attack. Jeremy Bentham demolished Gilbert's 'False Theory of Evidence' in a classic polemic,[10] before going on to develop his *Rationale of Judicial Evidence* in five volumes.[11] Bentham did not respect boundaries between disciplines. His writings on evidence contain many important insights and over the last two centuries the Anglo-American Law of Evidence has evolved in piecemeal, halting fashion in the general direction that he charted. However, legal opinion has almost unanimously judged that he went too far in advocating the total abolition of *all* binding rules of evidence (and procedure).[12] His central precept was 'the non-exclusion principle':

> Be the dispute what it may—see everything that is to be seen: hear everybody who is likely to know anything about the matter: hear everybody, but most attentively of all, and first of all, those who are likely to know most about it— the parties.[13]

---

[8] Compare for example DNA produced as evidence of the presence of X at a crime scene, from which opportunity might be inferred, to eyewitness identification evidence that X was at the crime scene (often, but not always, a notoriously unreliable kind of evidence). Both are, in fact, 'circumstantial', in that evidence of opportunity does not establish guilt.

[9] On evidence-based medicine see below, p. 99.

[10] Jeremy Bentham, *An Introductory View of the Rationale of Judicial Evidence* (1838–53), VI, *Works*, ed. J. Bowring, pp. 1–188. It is arguable that Bentham's interpretation of Gilbert was in some respects unfair. For a detailed study of Bentham on Evidence see Twining (1985)

[11] Bentham (1827).

[12] The writer nearest to Bentham was Charles F. Chamberlayne (1855–1913), but he does not seem to have been very influential and is now seldom cited. See *RE*, pp. 65–69.

[13] Bentham (1827), vol. V, at pp. 742–3. The non-exclusion principle is not as radical as it may sound, because Bentham strongly supported the main basis for exclusion—irrelevance. Similarly Bentham accepted the common sense idea that one should always try to obtain the best available evidence, but what is 'best' depends on the particular circumstances of each case and cannot be prescribed by rigid general rules, which will almost always be over- or under-inclusive. On the survival of the idea of 'best evidence' see Nance (1988). On Bentham's illuminating distinction between rules (commands) addressed to the will and instructions addressed to the understanding, see Twining (1985), pp. 43–4, 68–9. Bentham was against any peremptory, binding rules, but a

Bentham's 'anti-nomian thesis' sounds radical to common lawyers, but in nearly all other spheres of practical life we operate under a system of 'free proof', that is an absence of formal rules in regard to weight, credibility, or quantum as well as admissibility.[14] Bentham's reason is instructive:

> To find infallible rules for evidence, rules which insure a just decision is, from the nature of things, absolutely impossible; but the human mind is too apt to establish rules which only increase the probabilities of a bad decision. All the service that an impartial investigator of the truth can perform in this respect is, to put the legislators and judges on their guard against such hasty rules.[15]

In an age of bureaucratisation and audit, this warning should still have resonance. The pressures to simplify, standardise and codify are greater than ever.

Through most of the nineteenth-century treatises on the Law of Evidence struggled to construct a coherent framework for exposition. There were some illuminating failures. Taxonomies relating to sources (e.g. witness testimony, documentary evidence, real evidence) or to types of data frequently used as evidence (e.g. classes of documents, confessions, traces, later fingerprints and polygraphs) or fields of law (evidence in torts, property, contract) just did not work as frameworks for exposition of evidence doctrine. Some legal treatises were organised around the tasks of proving particular kinds of matters to be proved (probanda)—for example, how to prove debt, arson, the causes of railway accidents, or particular crimes.[16] All of these tended to deteriorate into what can be satirised as 'the law of milk churns'—categories that were too particular and fragmented, lacking organising concepts and general principles.[17] It was only when it was realised that structured argument could

---

great deal of the substance of the law of evidence re-entered his analysis as non-binding cautionary instructions (guidelines). Bentham was against all formal rules of evidence and procedure. Whether he was an 'anti-nomian' in a more general sense depends on whether or not he was a consistent act-utilitarian, despite his zeal for codification. See the debate between Gerald Postema (1986) and Paul Kelly (1990), discussed Dinwiddy (2002), at pp. 6–7.

[14] On the various meanings of 'free proof' see *RE*, pp. 203–4, 241–2 and Twining (1997). In English law corroboration requirements, which are very limited, are the main survival from the old rules of quantum (specifying the number and types of witnesses required to prove a matter).

[15] Bentham (1825), p. 180. On two minor caveats to the anti-nomian thesis see *RE*, pp. 43–4.

[16] e.g. Roscoe (1827); S. M. Phillipps (1st edn., London 1814, 9th edn., 1843), Greenleaf (1st edn., 1842), and Taylor (1st edn., 1848), are examples of works which tried to introduce general concepts and principles, but which still were largely organised in terms of different kinds of probanda. See *RE*, chap. 3.

[17] The *locus classicus* is the story of a Vermont Justice of the Peace who, in an action by one farmer against another for breaking a churn, could find no reference to churns in any statute and so found for the defendant. This story was told by Oliver Wendell Holmes to urge lawyers to think in terms of broad rules and fundamental legal conceptions. Holmes (1896).

provide a general framework (what Wigmore called the 'logic of proof') that
the field was able to achieve some coherence.

During the nineteenth century the exclusionary rules were thinned down,
generally in the direction indicated by Bentham, but in a piecemeal fashion
that was quite contrary to the radical spirit of his proposals, and not always
because of his influence.[18] However, some of Bentham's specific targets survived, including the right to silence, the privilege against self-incrimination,
lawyer–client privilege, and safeguards for the accused in criminal cases. By
the 1870s piecemeal reforms and the decline of the Best Evidence Rule to
'an evidentiary ghost' left the Law of Evidence looking like a collection of
fragmented technical rules with no coherence or form.[19]

The next significant attempt to rationalise the field was by James Fitzjames
Stephen, who as a relatively young man drafted the Indian Evidence Act of
1872 and developed a general theory of judicial evidence based on relevance.
Stephen elegantly simplified and streamlined the rules of evidence, but his
theory was soon recognised to be 'a splendid mistake'.[20] If the Law of Evidence
is mainly concerned with exclusion of certain kinds of *relevant* evidence, then
relevance cannot itself provide the basis for exclusion. This paved the way for
James Bradley Thayer (1831–1902) to perceive that the Law of Evidence provides for a series of diverse exceptions to a general principle of admitting all
relevant evidence. Thayer pronounced two principles which today form the
foundation for the modern law of evidence in common law systems, including
the influential American Federal Rules of Evidence:

(1) That nothing is to be received which is not logically probative of some matter
    requiring to be proved;
(2) That everything which is thus probative should come in, unless a clear
    ground of policy of law excludes it.[21]

Thayer saw that the Anglo-American Law of Evidence consists of a series
of exceptions to a principle of free proof (i.e. absence of rules) and that 'free
proof', far from meaning that anything goes, refers to structured rational
argument based on ordinary principles of practical reasoning. The basis of
the Law of Evidence is a matter of fact and logic, guided by his two principles
(exclude all irrelevant evidence; include all relevant evidence, unless ...).
'Relevance' means 'tends to support or tends to negate' what is to be proved—

---

[18] On non-Benthamic influences on nineteenth-century reforms see C. Allen (1997).
[19] On 'that motley and undiscriminated character' of the common law of evidence at the end of
the nineteenth century, see Thayer (1898), at p. 527.
[20] Pollock (1899).
[21] Thayer (1898), p. 530; cf. p. 266.

the 'ultimate probandum' or 'material facts' in legal parlance. The test of relevance is a matter of logic and general experience,[22] not law. In his splendid phrase 'The law has no mandamus to the logical faculty', meaning that the law cannot tell you how to think.[23]

Thayer's own writings concentrated very largely on the Law of Evidence, which he conceived quite narrowly, but his basic insights were built on and greatly expanded by several of his students, most notably John Henry Wigmore (1863–1943).

For most of the twentieth century Wigmore was the dominant figure in the study of Evidence in the United States and beyond. For practitioners and judges his main work was his enormous treatise on the Law of Evidence, which over time expanded to fill ten substantial volumes.[24] However, we are here concerned with other aspects of his work that have recently become more prominent. Building on Thayer's work, Wigmore divided the study of evidence in law into two parts, which he called 'the Trial Rules' and 'the Principles of Proof'.[25] Although his reputation rested mainly on his work on the Law of Evidence, he argued forcefully that the Principles of Proof are prior to, and more important than, the Law of Evidence. The title of his main work on the subject is *The Principles of Proof as Given by Logic, Psychology and General Experience and illustrated in Judicial Trials.*[26] Although it focuses mainly on contested jury trials, this book is a multidisciplinary text, which contains almost no law. It deals extensively with witness psychology, forensic science as it then was, and Wigmore's own 'chart method' of constructing and representing complex arguments based on mixed masses of evidence. It is about

---

[22] On the meaning of 'general experience' see below, p. 80.

[23] Thayer (1898), p. 314. 'Logic' is used here, and in most legal contexts, in a broad sense to include various kinds of 'informal logic', i.e. not only closed system reasoning. In legal contexts nearly all reasoning about questions of fact is ampliative, that is the conclusions go beyond the premises. However, deductive reasoning occasionally plays a role, for instance in respect of alibis, for 'general experience' tells us that one person can never physically be in two different places at the same time.

[24] J. H. Wigmore, *A Treatise on the System of Evidence in Trials at Common Law* (3rd edn., Little, Brown, 1940). Since 2002 a new edition (*The New Wigmore: a Treatise on Evidence*, Richard D. Friedman (gen. ed.)), has been emerging with individual volumes edited by different scholars.

[25] The term 'Trial Rules' is misleading because the Law of Evidence has an important role in pre-trial proceedings, for example police interrogation and, to a lesser extent post-trial (see below, p. 92).

[26] (1913, 2nd edn., 1931, 3rd edn., 1937). The title of the third edition was changed to *The Science of Judicial Proof* at the instance of the publishers for commercial reasons. Wigmore's conception of 'general experience' included all of the sciences, so the explicit mention of psychology in the title was redundant.

structuring arguments about questions of fact in contested trials—key concepts, including relevance, probative force, and credibility are not governed by legal rules.

The structure is provided by an application of ideas about practical reasoning in general; the idea of 'general experience' refers to a society's stock of knowledge (or more correctly stock of beliefs)—widely held beliefs held at a particular moment in history. The link is that in ordinary reasoning every inferential step is warranted by a generalisation drawn from this stock of beliefs.[27] These may range from a citizen's 'common sense' beliefs to experience-based generalisations to more or less well-grounded propositions based on empirical research, which may range from impressionistic surveys to rigorous and repeated scientific studies. Thus almost any form of knowledge or belief can come into an argument about an issue of fact through such background generalisations. Of course, it is easy to show that many common sense beliefs are based on speculation, superstition, myth, or prejudice and that the contents of any individual's stock of beliefs vary greatly in respect of reliability. Moreover the idea of 'cognitive consensus' about common sense needs to be treated with care, especially in a multicultural society,[28] and the 'cognitive competence' of ordinary adults is sometimes challenged.[29] It is also easily shown that what passes for knowledge at any time may later be rejected or proven to be false and that even well-founded scientific generalisations are open to refinement, revision or falsification. In reaching important decisions by rational means it is sensible to rely on 'the best' information available, but often that is no more than fallible 'general experience'. What else can we rely on?

Wigmore's *Principles of Proof* was compiled in a period when forensic science, witness psychology and other cognate specialisms were relatively undeveloped. This was before genetics, data bases, DNA profiling and matching of traces transformed methods of investigation and what is generally known as 'scientific evidence'. Although between the first edition in 1913 and the last edition in 1937, he tried to keep up with scientific developments, the book now appears quaint, out-dated and poorly organised in its brave attempt

---

[27] Schum (1994/2001), pp. 82–3, 109. On generalisations, see Anderson (this volume) Chap. 8.
[28] T. Anderson, D. Schum and W. Twining *Analysis of Evidence* (2nd edn., 2005), pp. 273–6. (hereafter *Analysis*).
[29] On cognitive consensus and cognitive competence see *Analysis* at pp. 263, 273–6. Cognitive competence was the subject of a series of sharp exchanges between Jonathan Cohen (philosopher) and Daniel Kahnemann and Amos Tversky (psychologists) in the 1980s. See Cohen (1981), 317; the debate continued in *The Behavioral and Brain Sciences*, 6: 487–533 (1983).

to synthesise knowledge and assess the reliability of such matters as poly-graphs, fingerprints, and the demeanour of witnesses. But the core of his basic insights still holds good: First, following Thayer, the foundation of the subject of evidence in law is ordinary informal logic.[30] Second, the reliability and probative force of evidence can only exceptionally be made the subject of binding rules about classes of evidence. Third the basic concepts of evidence in law are not legal concepts.[31] With only minor exceptions, relevance, credibility, probative force and other key concepts are not defined by law;[32] and, fourth, that evaluating the credibility and weight of evidence depends on 'general experience' which includes the whole gamut of specialist disciplines.

Thus in an important sense, a large part of the subject of evidence in law is by its nature multidisciplinary. Unfortunately, nearly all of the scholarly legal literature since Wigmore has tended to focus largely on aspects that are peculiar to legal contexts: the exclusionary rules that are exceptions to the principle of admitting all relevant evidence, the institutional and procedural peculiarities of jury trials, issues concerning production and presentation of evidence in court, appeals and so on. It is odd that, when a subject is defined as a series of diverse exceptions to a general principle, the focus is almost exclusively on the exceptions, even when they are of diminishing importance.[33] The crucial bridge between the principles of proof and the Law of Evidence is relevance, which is not defined by law.[34]

From Wigmore's first edition of *The Principles of Judicial Proof* in 1913 until the 1980s there were spasmodic efforts by legal scholars to develop the ideas associated with the principles of proof, but most of these did not flourish.[35] The reasons for this are complex. Forensic science and its proliferating

---

[30] See above, n. 23.

[31] This is potentially a matter of controversy. For example, the Federal Rules have officially adopted the following definition: 'Rule 401. *Definition of "Relevant Evidence"*. "Relevant evidence" means evidence having any tendency to make the existence of any fact of consequence to the determination of an action more probable or less probable than it would be without that evidence.' This could be interpreted as giving an ordinary concept a special legal meaning. The definition of 'evidentiary reliability' in *Daubert v. Merrell Dow Pharmaceuticals Inc.*, 509 U.S. 579 (1993) can be similarly interpreted. However, the courts in England and the United States have generally been reluctant to treat decisions on relevance, credibility and probative force as precedents that establish a special legal meaning and when such steps towards formalisation are taken, they are almost entirely of local significance.

[32] See above, n. 23.

[33] On the narrowing of the scope and increased flexibility of the Anglo-American Law of Evidence and the variability of its application in practice see *RE*, chap. 6.

[34] See above, n. 31.

[35] See *RE*, pp. 14–30.

subdisciplines developed largely outside law schools. Contacts with psychologists interested in law were at times more frequent,[36] but most pyschological studies of witnesses, jury decision-making, and other aspects of legal process were based mainly in psychology departments. So far as legal education was concerned Wigmore's idea of 'The Principles of Proof' was perceived to be a 'non-subject', perhaps because rule-oriented academic lawyers believed that, insofar as there are no rules, there is no subject matter for lawyers to study;[37] or, if fact-determination is 'just common sense', it could be picked up without formal instruction. There is also a natural tendency for specialists to emphasise the distinctive aspects of their subject.

There was, furthermore, a feeling that interdisciplinary work was not 'practical'. This was the fate of the collaborative efforts of Jerome Michael, a brilliant legal proceduralist, and Mortimer Adler, a well-known philosopher. Their outstanding book was only privately printed.[38] In his *Elements of Legal Controversy* Michael eloquently expressed the inherent multidisciplinarity of the principles of proof:

> ... since legal controversy is conducted by means of words, you need some knowledge about the use of words as symbols, that is, some grammatical knowledge. Since issues of fact are constituted of contradictory propositions, are formed by the assertion and denial of propositions, and are tried by the proof and disproof of propositions, you need some knowledge of the nature of propositions and of the relationships which can obtain among them, and of the character of issues of fact and of proof and disproof, that is, some logical knowledge. Since the propositions which are material to legal controversy can never be proved to be true or false but only to be probable to some degree and since issues of fact are resolved by the calculation of the relative probabilities of the contradictory propositions of which they are composed, you need some knowledge of the distinction between truth or falsity and probability and of the logic of probability. Since propositions are actual or potential knowledge, since proof or disproof is an affair of knowledge, since, if they are truthful, the parties to legal controversy assert, and witnesses report, their knowledge, and since knowledge is of various sorts, you need some knowledge about knowledge, such, for instance, as knowledge of the distinction between direct or perceptual and indirect or inferential knowledge. Since there are intrinsic and essential differences between law and fact, between propo-

---

[36] In a useful review of recent contributions of Psychology to Evidence in Law, Roger Park and Michael Saks show that a high proportion of journal articles on legal evidence have been interdisciplinary in recent years, but the main focus of practitioners' treatises and students' works is still on doctrine: (Park and Saks, 2006).

[37] This involves a revealing non-sequitur: 'It is not law, therefore lawyers need not study it.'

[38] Michael and Adler (1931).

sitions about matters of fact and statements about matters of law, and between issues of fact and issues of law and the ways in which they are respectively tried and resolved, you need some knowledge about these matters. Since litigants and all those who participate in the conduct and resolution of their controversies are men and since many of the procedural rules are based upon presuppositions about human nature and behavior, you need some psychological knowledge. Finally, of course, you need such knowledge as is necessary to enable you to understand the tangential ends which are served by procedural law and to criticize the rules which are designed to serve them.[39]

Michael's vision of the subject of legal proof included the classic trivium of logic, grammar and rhetoric; forensic psychology; the detailed exploration of probability; the interconnections between law and fact; and the basic concepts, doctrines, and policies of the law of evidence. Recently that list has expanded to include more emphasis on scientific evidence, narrative, discourse analysis, and computer applications—to mention but a few. Not surprisingly, many lawyers have found such a conception of the subject daunting—a matter to which I shall return—but the immediate point is that these connections with other disciplines can be mapped within a single, quite flexible framework. For despite the complexities, the Anglo-American legal tradition has had a remarkably homogeneous mainstream.

The Rationalist Tradition

Thayer provided a coherent structure for the Law of Evidence; Wigmore expanded this to include both the Principles of Proof and the Law of Evidence in an integrated conception of the study of Evidence in adjudication.[40] These were not *a priori* constructions, but rather historically informed syntheses of the central ideas in a tradition that extends from Gilbert to the present day. This 'Rationalist Tradition' has at its core the idea of the pursuit of correct decision in adjudication by rational means through argumentation based on evidence.[41] 'Rationality' in this context is contrasted with 'irrational' means of dispute processing such as trial by battle, compurgation, ordeal, appeals to

[39] Michael (1948).
[40] On the extension of Wigmorean analysis to all stages of legal proceedings see below and *RE*, pp. 249–53.
[41] On 'the Rationalist Tradition' see below, n. 45; for details see *RE*, chaps. 3 and 4. Bentham's notion of 'rectitude of decision' captures the idea of achieving justice under the law by correct application of positive laws to true facts. This sets out an aspiration, i.e. it is normative, rather than a purported description of actual legal processes. On optimistic and complacent rationalism see *RE*, pp. 79–80.

the supernatural, or tossing a coin.[42] Most evidence scholars adopted or assumed a particular view of inductive logic in the tradition of Francis Bacon, John Stuart Mill, and modern philosophers, such as Jonathan Cohen and Stephen Toulmin. However, the Rationalist Tradition can be interpreted broadly to include alternative conceptions of rationality, including various conceptions of probability.[43]

The characteristic assumptions of discourse about evidence within the Rationalist Tradition can be succinctly restated as follows: epistemology is cognitivist rather than sceptical; a correspondence theory of truth is generally preferred to a coherence theory;[44] the mode of decision making is seen as 'rational', as contrasted with 'irrational' modes; the characteristic mode of reasoning is induction; the pursuit of truth as a means to justice under the law commands a high, but not necessarily an overriding, priority as a social value.[45]

Despite this broad consensus, legal evidence scholarship has had its share of debates and disagreements. From an early stage there was a continuing uneasiness about whether there were or should be any formal rules of evidence, what precisely might be the status of such rules (and, in particular, of judicial rulings on points of evidence) and about the scope of Evidence as a subject. There has been repeated, almost cyclical political controversy about 'balancing' efficient enforcement of criminal law with due process and protecting innocent accused from conviction. Some debates are quite specialised— for example, about presumptions, hearsay and the best evidence rule. Others represent particular applications of standard legal or juristic controversies, such as debates about the pros and cons of the jury or the adversary system or judge-made law or codification. Some, such as disagreements between util-

---

[42] On whether these were 'irrational' see *RE*, pp. 35–6, 125–30, and H. L. Ho (2004), 'The Legitimacy of Medieval Proof', *Journal of Law and Religion*, 19: 259.

[43] *Analysis*, chap. 9.

[44] I am inclined to follow Susan Haack in steering a middle course between correspondence and coherence theories in respect of epistemic justification ('foundherentism') and 'innocent realism' in respect of metaphysics (see above, n. *).

[45] These basic assumptions can be constructed into a more elaborate ideal type to which, it is claimed, nearly all Anglo-American Evidence scholars have more or less conformed for about 250 years. (See *RE*, p. 76; *Analysis*, pp. 82–3). Part A is a modified version of a Benthamite model of adjudication, presented in a way that suggests a number of possible points of departure or disagreement. Although by no means all leading Evidence scholars have been legal positivists and utilitarians, a rationalist theory of evidence necessarily presupposes a theory of adjudication that postulates something like Bentham's 'rectitude of decision' as the main objective. There is scope for divergence on a number of points of detail, but not from what might be called 'the rational core'. For a critical evaluation of the ideal type, see *RE*, pp. 80–6.

itarians and deontologists, between civil libertarians and proponents of 'law and order', between Pascalians and Baconians, and between atomists and holists, reflect wider differences. But these disagreements have by and large taken place within a shared framework of assumptions and concepts.[46]

After Wigmore

Between the First World War and about 1980, the study of Evidence was in the doldrums, partly because the field was overshadowed by Wigmore, who dominated the subject and was not inhibited about seeing off rivals.[47] Then, stimulated from several directions, there arose the variegated movement towards broadening the field that came to be known as 'the New Evidence Scholarship'.[48] The stimulus for this came from several directions. Perhaps the main ones were: (a) moves to reform the Law of Evidence, or even to codify it, gathered momentum after the Second Word War, culminating in the Federal Rules of Evidence (enacted 1975) and rather more piecemeal reform in England and elsewhere; (b) the movement to develop links between law and the social sciences, represented by the Law and Society Movement in the United States and socio-legal studies in the United Kingdom. Here the main activities relevant to Evidence involved the interface between Law and Psychology, where interest in witness psychology (especially identification evidence) revived, but went beyond this to include such matters as jury research, discourse analysis, and interaction in the courtroom.[49] (c) Forensic Science continued to develop largely independently of law, but its connections were obvious and it received an enormous stimulus from DNA analysis and IT applications; (d) Bentham studies also became established during this period and it is worth remembering that Bentham is still the leading theorist of evidence, that his writings on evidence represent a substantial proportion of his largely forgotten works, and that he was never one to respect disciplinary boundaries. And, finally (e) there was a dramatic rise in interest in the

---

[46] See above, n. 45.

[47] Thomas Barnes, Introduction to a reissue of *The Principles of Judicial Proof* in *The Legal Classics Library* (1991). After the Second World War, Professor (later Sir) Rupert Cross led a revival of scholarly interest in evidence in England, but this was largely confined to the Law of Evidence.

[48] Richard Lempert (1988) coined the label, which stuck. He interpreted this as referring mainly to debates about the use of statistics in reasoning about questions of fact in legal contexts ('the probabilities debates'); I tend to give it a much broader interpretation (see *RE*, pp. 244–8).

[49] Park and Saks (2006).

relationship between statistics and legal proof, largely stimulated by the misuse of statistics in the California case of *People v. Collins*.[50]

This last development involved a number of different concerns. The first commentators stressed the potential of statistical analysis in evaluating evidence, provided that it was properly used,[51] but in a famous 1971 paper Professor Laurence Tribe of Harvard argued that even if all reasoning about disputed questions of fact is in principle mathematical, it would be both inappropriate and dangerous as a matter of policy to encourage or allow explicit quantification of such matters as the criminal standard of proof or the likelihood of guilt in identification cases.[52] The debate moved to a quite different plane with the intervention of Jonathan Cohen, a philosopher from Oxford, who challenged the assumption that all arguments about probabilities are in principle mathematical or, as he termed it, Pascalian.[53] Law, he suggested, provides one of the standard examples of non-Pascalian inductivist (Baconian) reasoning.[54] Cohen stimulated controversies in several disciplines, notably law, medical diagnosis, and psychology.[55] Cohen's thesis provoked sharp attacks from jurists in England, Australia, and especially the United States, but gained a good deal of support from many evidence scholars who were deeply sceptical of the mathematicisation of arguments about evidence in court.[56] These largely theoretical 'probabilities debates' have rumbled on, some-

---

[50] *People v. Collins*, 68 Cal. 2d 319, 438 P.2d 33 [1968].

[51] e.g. Kaplan (1968). An important pioneer in the study of statistical applications to legal evidence was an Australian judge, Sir Richard Eggleston (e.g. R. Eggleston, 1978/1983).

[52] L. Tribe, 'Trial by Mathematics: Precision and Ritual in Legal Process' (1971). Three main reasons were advanced for this: (1) as a matter of communication, as long as judges and juries can be assumed to be innumerate, they should be addressed in a language they can understand; (2) mathematical arguments are likely to be overly seductive or prejudicial because seemingly 'hard' quantified variables will tend to push out 'soft', non-quantitative variables; and (3) it is politically improper to quantify certain matters, such as an acceptable level of risk of conviction of the innocent.

[53] See L. J. Cohen (1977) (arguing that lawyers use non-Pascalian inductive reasoning about questions of fact).

[54] See ibid. at p. 44.

[55] See ibid. at pp. 258–63. Although it was based on philosophical arguments, Cohen's thesis clearly had political implications. It served as a warning against 'the cult of the expert' and provided theoretical support for the belief in the cognitive competence of ordinary citizens to make sound judgements based on everyday practical reasoning. This is particularly significant in jurisdictions that place a high value on lay participation in the administration of justice. In this view, innumerate judges and ordinary jurors are competent to adjudicate disputed questions of fact and are usually justified in relying on 'common sense' (more precisely 'general experience'), despite its shortcomings.

[56] See above, n. 29. For a useful overview see Roberts and Zuckerman (2004), pp. 116–32. Many of the applied problems that colleagues in statistics are studying have implications for forensic

what obscuring the fact that the use of statistics in proving specific matters such as paternity, discrimination, and offender profiling has grown significantly in importance over the years.[57] The use of probability theory as a general model for evidential reasoning is one thing; the relevance of statistical data as evidence in some cases is quite another.

Undoubtedly, the literature on the Federal Rules and debates about probabilities are important examples of a widespread revival of academic interest in Evidence in law. But these represent only two parts of a much more varied picture. Since the 1980s there have been many multidisciplinary conferences and seminars exclusively devoted to Evidence in law.[58] These illustrated the liveliness in the field and the extent of the involvement of non-lawyers, but they had one major limitation: the focus was almost entirely on litigation.

Part II. Limitations of law

Many non-lawyers interested in inferential reasoning and argumentation have recognised that law provides a rich source of concrete, real-life, cases that illustrate facets of evidence, inference and proof. Toulmin (philosopher), Perelman (rhetoric), Gaskins (philosopher), the Amsterdam School of Argumentation and above all Schum (psychology and statistics) are some modern examples.[59] Schum even goes so far as to suggest that legal scholarship on evidence 'forms

---

contexts, police investigations and other legal processes. See Kadane and Schum (1996), pp. 121–31; Schum (1994/2001), pp. 243–61.

[57] Since 1983–4 the LL M course on Evidence and Proof at UCL has included a 3–4 weeks section on statistics and evidence. This was taught for over 20 years by Professor Philip Dawid and continues under Dr Rex Galbraith.

[58] These include Facts in Law (Durham, 1982), Probabilities and Inference (Boston, 1986), Semiotics and Legal Proof (Messina, 1987), Theoretical Aspects of Evidence and Proof (Oxford, 1988), and Freedom of Proof (Trento, 1988). An excellent series of workshops on Law and Psychology sponsored by the Oxford Centre for Socio-legal Studies from 1979 until the late 1980s devoted a great deal of attention to evidentiary issues (See e.g. Lloyd-Bostock (1988) (surveying work of that period). For more than a decade Professor Peter Tillers organised interdisciplinary seminars on Evidence in Litigation at the Beniamin N. Cardozo School of Law in New York. Law and Psychology work has continued to flourish, see for example, Memon, Vriej, and Bull (2003), Carson *et al.* (2007) and Cutler (2008).

[59] e.g. S. Toulmin, *The Uses of Argument* (1964); Ch. Perelman, *The Idea of Justice and the Problem of Argument* (trs. Petri, 1963); F. H. van Eemeren and R. Grootendorst, *A Systematic Theory of Argumentation: the Pragma-dialectic Approach* (2001). See also Gaskins (1992) and Schum (1994/2001).

the major source of inspiration for anyone interested in a general study of the general properties and uses of evidence'.[60]

As I am an enthusiast for my subject, I am usually delighted when I find my territory is thought to be interesting by colleagues from other disciplines. However, it is important to recognise the limitations of standard legal examples. In considering problems of evidence and inference three distinctions are crucial: the difference between past-directed and future-directed inquiries; the distinction between particular and general inquiries; and the distinction between hypothesis formation and hypothesis testing. For various reasons, including the tendency to equate Evidence in law with the Law of Evidence, the contested trial is widely perceived to be the main arena in which evidentiary issues arise. Adjudication of issues of fact in contested trials is typically past-directed, particular, and hypothesis testing—it only exceptionally deals with predicting the future, proving general empirical propositions, or hypothesis formation. These characteristics of standard legal examples may limit their significance in many other contexts.

Of course, the prototype of the contested trial, especially in common law adversarial proceedings, has certain features that do indeed make it a rich source of material for study: typically the proceedings are public, the conflict is overt, the issues are sharply defined, evidence is presented, questioned and argued about, and the legal record makes for neat packaging of complex material. Often the record contains a great deal of detail, the data and arguments are complex, and there is a mixed mass of evidence of different kinds. Above all, trials deal with 'real life' problems rather than hypothetical or fictitious examples. For those interested in inference there may be 'noise' factors that have to be filtered out such as technicalities of procedure, lawyers' tactics, artificial rules of evidence, and blurred lines between rational argument and effective persuasion. But trial records, official inquiries and like documents can provide a wealth of examples, not only for lawyers, that illustrate different attributes and credentials of evidence, the structure of complex arguments, problems of combining mixed masses of evidence, and common fallacies in reasoning from evidence.

Disputed trials are typically concerned with inquiries into particular past events in which the hypotheses are defined in advance by law—what lawyers call 'materiality'. Moreover records of cases are artificially constructed units extracted from more complex and diffuse contexts. For example, a criminal trial may be just one event in a long-drawn out feud or other conflict. These

---

[60] Schum (1994) at p. 6. This theme is developed in ibid., chap. 2.

elements—particularity, pastness, materiality, and individuation of cases—differentiate this kind of legal material from many other inquiries in which reasoning from evidence is involved.

In adjudication there is a further factor, the duty of the adjudicator to come to a firm decision. Judges determine, historians and scientists conclude (or sit on the fence). This pressure for decision has led the law to develop important ideas about presumptions, burdens of proof and standards of proof as aids to decision. These can be quite suggestive in other decision contexts.[61]

Thus historians share with lawyers a concern with particular past events, but historians lack the concept of materiality that identifies in advance the hypotheses to be proved or disproved and that helps to formulate and anchor disputed issues of fact in advance with precision and specificity. Historians are often involved not only in establishing what happened but also explaining why it happened—typically a more difficult and more interesting problem.[62] Furthermore, historians are often interested in questions that go beyond establishing and explaining a particular event. For example, a great deal of the vast literature about the Sacco-Vanzetti case assumes their innocence in order to explore wide ranging questions about the political, social and legal context of the time.[63]

Detectives, like adjudicators, are typically also concerned with particular past events—especially 'whodunit' kinds of questions—and their inquiries may be guided by legal categories such as murder, manslaughter and accident. But like historians, scientists, and many other inquirers, they have to construct hypotheses as well as test them. The typical decided case is not a good vehicle for learning about or developing skill in abduction and imaginative reasoning as part of the process of investigation.[64]

Intelligence analysts, now much in the news, are often involved with predicting future possibilities and probabilities in a changing context with the continuing prospect of further information. Sometimes they are asked to make specific predictions—for example, what is the likelihood of an attack on a particular target in a particular time period?—but they are also often concerned with more open-ended possibilities based on judgements about capabilities

[61] e.g. Gaskins (1992) and D. Walton (2008).

[62] In practice, fact-finders want to 'make sense' of a case by understanding not only what occurred, but why it occurred. For example, proving motive may not be a formal requirement or an evidentiary need in proving a criminal case, but it is often a practical necessity for police, attorneys and fact-finders. This is one of the main functions of story telling in advocacy.

[63] See the literature discussed in Felix (1965). This is not true of Kadane and Schum (1996).

[64] On the application of Charles Saunders Peirce's concept of abduction to law, see *Analysis* (2005), chap. 2.

and intentions. Moreover, they are also concerned with building up general intelligence pictures of networks, scenarios, and plots. As the post-11 September post-mortems have made clear, it is usually much easier after an event to identify bits of information that would have been useful had they been spotted and selected as significant.[65]

The prototypical inquiry in the physical sciences is concerned with the formulation and testing of *general* hypotheses, which *inter alia* form a solid basis for prediction. The classic 'problem of induction' concerns the difficulty of justifying an inferential step from particular premises to a general conclusion. In this context, the establishment and interpretation of particulars is often treated as unproblematic.[66] On the other hand, the paradigmatic adjudicative inquiry is concerned with establishing particulars—often the most straightforward part of a general scientific inquiry. Of course, where *application* of general scientific principles to particular instances is involved, for example in medical diagnosis or forensic pathology, the analogy to fact-finding in adjudication is somewhat closer.

It would, of course, be rash to say that lawyers have it easy in respect of evidence and inference, just because particular inquiries may often be easier than general ones, and because of aids to decision such as materiality, burdens of proof, and presumptions. Disputed trials are often disputed because the evidence is especially problematic—otherwise there would be a guilty plea or a settlement. *Causes célèbres* are often celebrated because there is an unsolved mystery. More important, evidence scholars have become more sensitive to the obvious fact that the contested trial is only one legal context among many. Problems of evidence and inference arise in many other legal contexts—including investigation, negotiation, mediation, anticipating future contingencies (as in drafting contracts), and law-making, where some of the elements of materiality, predictability, pastness, and individuation of cases are absent.

This overview of the development of the study of evidence in law as a multidisciplinary enterprise, has some implications for the idea of a general field of evidence. I would emphasise four in particular:

---

[65] On ex post facto wisdom about 9/11, see *Analysis*, pp. 46–60 and below at p. 96.

[66] Cf. 'In science, unlike the law, the data are virtually never problematic. What actually happened is typically the uncontroversial starting point for attempting to explain what happened.... In the law, exactly the opposite obtains ... Controversy virtually always settles on what happened.' R. Allen (1994), at p. 624.

1. For at least 250 years Evidence has been a specialised focus of attention in legal scholarship as well as legal practice. It has a rich literature of primary and secondary sources. There are concepts, rules, devices and controversies that are peculiar to law, but it is generally recognised that the study of evidence in law is a multidisciplinary field, involving borrowings by lawyers, inputs by non-lawyers, interdisciplinary collaboration and ongoing controversies not confined to law.[67]

2. Some of the problems, debates, and disagreements centring on legal process as an arena have echoes in other contexts: for example, Baconians v. Pascalians in respect of probabilities and proof; utilitarianism v. deontology; holism and atomism; narrative and argument; cognitivism v. scepticism; and empiricism v. anti-foundationalism.

3. Some of the concepts and devices developed in legal contexts have been picked up or are potentially suggestive in other contexts. For example, the dangers of trying to establish formal rules or hierarchies about weight in respect of evidence; concepts such as presumptions, burdens of proof, standards of proof (or standards for other decisions); assessing the credibility of witnesses and documents; the role of background generalisations as warrants in inferential reasoning; and methods of marshalling large bodies of evidence and structuring complex arguments based on such evidence.

4. Contested trials have attracted a great deal of attention. In that context the focus is on inquiries about particular past events in respect of sharply posed issues defined in advance by law and governed by formal rules of procedure and exclusion of evidence. This is only one type of inquiry involved in legal processes. Within a general field of Evidence distinctions need to be made and developed between past-directed and future-directed inquiries, hypothesis formation and hypothesis testing, concern with establishing the truth about particular events and about general propositions, precisely formulated and more open-ended inquiries, and rule-governed and informal inquiries. Even in law the contested legal trial typically involves only one type of inquiry among many kinds that involve inferential reasoning from evidence. A genuinely multidisciplinary field of evidence would need to differentiate between different kinds and contexts of inquiries.

---

[67] At a conference in Boston in 1986 on 'Probability and Inference in the Law of Evidence', some sharp exchanges between statisticians prompted a well-known legal scholar to remark that he felt like a Belgian peasant watching the Great Powers fighting their wars on his territory.

Part III. Moving beyond law

(a) From contested trials to total legal processes

We have seen that the classical writers on evidence in law, including Thayer and Wigmore, talked of 'judicial evidence' and treated the contested jury trial as the standard case. However, since the Second World War it has increasingly been recognised that this focus is unrealistic: contested jury trials are a small proportion of all trials and, more importantly, only a small proportion of formal legal proceedings ever reach the stage of a contested trial: most civil cases get settled out of court or are abandoned; most criminal cases end with a guilty plea or charges being dropped; and many disputes are directed to administrative tribunals or arbitration or are resolved by 'alternative' means, such as mediation and conciliation.[68] Both civil and criminal litigation are now widely conceived in terms of a 'total process model', which starts with some event, claim, or dispute, proceeds through various pre-trial stages and, if a case ever arrives in court, is succeeded by further post-trial decisions, such as sanctioning, appeals, parole decisions, and so on. Such processes are not necessarily unilinear. They involve complex sequences of decisions and events all of which are worthy of attention. Information that is conventionally talked of as 'evidence' is relevant to most of the important decisions, but in varied ways. Thus, a plaintiff deciding whether to pursue a claim, or a prosecutor deciding whether or not to prosecute, or a parole board or similar body deciding on whether a prisoner constitutes a continuing threat to society all have to weigh evidence and potential evidence from different standpoints in varied contexts. Thus the Law of Evidence does not only affect contested trials; it casts a long shadow over pre-trial and post-trial decisions and over a wide variety of adjudicative tribunals and quasi-judicial bodies.

This extension of focus naturally associates a range of other professionals—most obviously detectives and other investigators, but also probation officers and social workers (for example in looking out for sexual abuse). Thus the Law of Evidence and the Principles of Proof are an important concern of many participants in addition to lawyers in a wide variety of contexts. This raises important questions about the generality and transferability of concepts, methods, and modes of reasoning about evidence that developed within a relatively narrow legal framework.

---

[68] American commentators talk of 'The Vanishing Trial'. For example, in 1962 11.5 per cent of civil cases filed in the United States went to trial; in 2002 the proportion of trials had declined to 2 per cent of cases filed (Galanter, 2004).

(b) David Schum

A major move in the direction of constructing Evidence as an integrated field or focus of attention was the publication of David Schum's *Evidential Foundations of Probabilistic Reasoning* in 1994.[69] Schum, who was trained in psychology and statistics, had done important work in intelligence analysis for the security services, but his two volume work on *Evidence and Inference for the Intelligence Analyst* had received almost no recognition, perhaps because of its formidable size and erudition.[70] In *Evidential Foundations* Schum set out to synthesise basic insights and ideas about evidence and inference across several disciplines, including law, philosophy, logic, probability theory, semiotics, artificial intelligence, psychology, and history. The central theme is that similar problems arise in many practical and academic contexts in situations where conclusions and decisions are reached on the basis of incomplete information. Responses to these problems have varied between disciplines and the experience and attempted solutions in one discipline may be illuminating for others. He argued that the complexity of inferential tasks has often been underestimated in some disciplines, but in the crucible of litigation lawyers have routinely had to wrestle with many of these complexities. Schum was particularly impressed with Wigmore, and adapted his chart method for application in a number of other contexts, especially intelligence analysis and police investigation. He argues that Wigmore anticipated by many years modern developments in such areas as Bayes nets, but more importantly provided an unrivalled approach to marshalling and analysing complex masses of evidence.[71]

Schum's work was one starting-point for the UCL programme and for an unusual project that preceded it.[72] In 1994 Terry Anderson and I were part of a group of lawyers studying 'forensic expertise' at the Netherlands Institute for Advanced Study (NIAS), the Dutch equivalent of the Stanford Center for Advanced Study in the Behavioral Sciences (CASBS). As Fellows of the NIAS we were expected to interact with our colleagues in other specialist theme groups. The other projects were: (a) history of Dutch political concepts; (b) theatre iconography—that is the use of works of art as evidence in theatre

---

[69] Schum (1994/2001), op. cit. The work, despite its bulk, is very readable and it still contains an admirably clear, copiously illustrated, account of the application of inferential reasoning to complex problems in many contexts.

[70] Schum (1987).

[71] See further, Dawid, Hepler and Schum, Chap. 5 below.

[72] Twining and Hampsher-Monk (2003).

history; (c) magic and religion in ancient Assyria; (d) social dilemmas. In addition, there were several Fellows working on individual projects. At first sight these topics seemed rather esoteric and diverse. But on reflection it seemed to us that most of the Fellows of NIAS in that year could fairly be said to have shared methodological problems about evidence and inference. So Anderson and I decided to throw down a challenge to our colleagues to run a joint seminar on these problems. The starting-point was what came to be known as 'Twining's hypothesis':

> Notwithstanding differences in (i) the objectives of our particular inquiries; (ii) the nature and extent of the available source material; (iii) the culture of our respective disciplines (including its history, conventions, state of development etc.); (iv) national backgrounds; (v) other contextual factors, all of our projects involve, as part of the enterprise, drawing inferences from evidence to test hypotheses and justify conclusions and that the logic of this kind of inquiry is governed by the same principles.[73]

This was framed in deliberately provocative terms and I expected it to be challenged, subverted, or modified and refined in the course of discussion. However, rather than producing a general analysis of methodological issues, the seminar resulted in a series of case studies dealing with a somewhat bizarre range of topics: a lawyer and an Assyriologist analysed the evidence relating to the date of the death of the Sumerian language; a Shakespeare scholar and a jurist explored the differences in their approaches to a body of love letters that were the main evidence in a *cause célèbre*; a political theorist, an economic historian, a theatre iconographer, and a musicologist contributed individual case studies in their particular fields in light of our discussions. David Schum then contributed a general introduction to the volume that resulted, drawing out some common themes.[74]

No attempt was made to build a grand theory of evidence and inference—indeed the orientation of this group was strikingly particularistic.[75] This exer-

---

[73] Twining and Hampsher-Monk (2003), p. 4. Support for this may be found in, e.g., Haack (2003).
[74] These all feature in Twining and Hampsher-Monk (2003).
[75] The main concluding observations are worth noting:

> 'First, there was no serious disagreement that we had overlapping problems of evidence and inference and that we could usefully discuss these across disciplines. Second, the members of the group were all drawn from the humanities and the social sciences and all agreed that problems of evidence and inference could not be kept separate from questions about interpretation and narrative. Third, if representatives of the physical sciences, both pure and applied, and of cognate disciplines such as astronomy and mathematics had been represented, there would probably have been little difficulty accommodating them within the group—although there might have been more emphasis on probabilities and statistics

cise was very much an experimental first step in treating Evidence as a multidisciplinary subject in its own right. David Schum developed his 'substance blind' approach further in the context of this project. This formed one starting-point of the UCL programme several years later, but as we shall see this approach ran into a certain amount of opposition at that stage.

(c) Evidence, 'general culture', and public affairs: a subject whose time has come?

Quite independently of these academic activities during the past decade or so, evidence has recently become a much more sustained focus of attention both in the news media and what might be called 'general culture'. Of course, historical puzzles and unsolved mysteries have been a staple of popular culture; the detective story has held its place since Victorian times; and Sherlock Holmes is still the secular patron saint of evidencers. What is new is that evidentiary issues are attaining a high profile because of the convergence of a number of developments such as research on DNA profiling, other advances in police investigation, the search for weapons of mass destruction in Iraq, post 9/11 intelligence analysis, evidence-based policy, evidence-based medicine and so on. To cite just a few examples: perhaps because of advances in our understanding of DNA, forensic scientists have started to rival lawyers and spies as characters in works of fiction (e.g. thrillers by Patricia Cornwell and the forensic anthropologist, Kathy Reichs) and in television dramas, soap operas, and documentaries. Evidentiary issues have been central to news about Iraq: the efforts of the weapons' inspectors, Colin Powell's address to the Security Council, controversies about the reliability of the intelligence relied on by Bush and Blair, and the Hutton, Butler, and Chilcot inquiries in England have all captured headlines.[76] Dope testing of athletes, Truth Commissions, and problems of proving genocide are in the news. In some countries, there have been debates about 'evidence-based policy' and 'evidence-based' medicine. In 2009 the Darwin Centenary sparked a new round of public controversy about the implications of evolutionary theory for Creationism, the origins of the universe, and religious education. And in 2009 debates about the scientific evidence for global warming heated up.

---

and sharper disagreements on these issues. Difficult questions were raised about the relationship between fundamental problems of evidence and inference and the specific contexts and objectives of projects situated in different disciplinary cultures, but overall we had few serious problems of communication.' (Introduction, ibid., p. 7).

[76] Runciman (2004).

Perhaps the most obvious example of the centrality of evidentiary issues in contemporary life has been the post-mortems on the events of 11 September 2001: one standard line goes that the intelligence services had enough information to predict the event, but lacked the skills to analyse it. They did not have the capacity to 'join the dots' or methods for identifying as significant a few 'trifles' from the masses of data that flow into different agencies from a variety of sources.[77]

An article in *The New Yorker* in February 2003 reported interviews with leading figures in the CIA and the Pentagon who were concerned with improving intelligence analysis in the aftermath of 11 September 2001,[78] including Donald Rumsfeld, George Tenet, and Robert Gates. The starting-point of the article was a judgement that 'American intelligence agencies did not possess the analytic depth or the right methods of analysis accurately to assess [possible threats]'.[79] The diagnosis and the prescriptions were expressed largely in terms that are familiar to students of evidence and inference: the dangers of hypothesis-driven inquiries; the need to distinguish between constructing a hypothesis and testing it against the available data and between gathering and interpreting data; the different problems that arise from a surfeit of information and absence of evidence; the difference between ambiguity and incompleteness; the value of alternative interpretations of ambiguous evidence; the dangers of 'mirror imaging', that is 'projecting of American values and beliefs onto America's adversaries and rivals'; a tendency to confuse the unfamiliar with the improbable; the relationship between calculus of risk and thresholds of credibility; the likelihood of political bias entering into judgements where the situation is uncertain. Though the vocabulary is sometimes different, all of these ideas should be familiar to students of evidence and inference; most of them have been explored in the writings of Wigmore and Schum.

Resistance and scepticism

This is one jurist's personal interpretation of the background to the UCL Evidence Programme. When it started, I had assumed that the main focus would be on exploring the extent to which there are concepts, principles and methods relating to evidence and inference that could be developed and applied broadly across many disciplines. I expected that scholars with differ-

---

[77] See *Analysis* at pp. 46–8.
[78] Jeffrey Goldberg, 'The Unknown: The C.I.A. and the Pentagon take on Al Qaeda and Iraq', *The New Yorker*, 10 Feb. 2003, 40–7.
[79] Ibid.

ent specialisms could both contribute to and learn from such an enterprise. David Schum's 'substance blind' approach to evidence as set out in *Evidential Foundations of Probabilistic Reasoning* seemed one promising starting-point, but not the only one.[80] In short, I had assumed that this would be a multi-disciplinary enterprise bringing together the perspectives, concepts, insights, knowledge and experience of individuals from many different backgrounds to exchange experiences and to explore questions about evidence at a fairly general level.

I was not surprised that the proposed title 'Towards an Integrated Science of Evidence' provoked some resistance. I had myself opposed the use of 'science' in this context and thought the phrasing was too strong, for reasons set out below. But I was surprised at the hostility expressed to the idea of 'a substance blind approach' and to the very idea of a common enterprise. The purpose of this section is to try to identify some of the main reasons for resistance and hostility to the enterprise as I had conceived it.

Jason Davies's analysis of interdisciplinarity is helpful in identifying some of the different expectations and agendas that some participants may have brought to the programme, apart from the obvious fact that substantial funds were available.[81] Some no doubt joined in the hope of learning about concepts, methods or insights that might help to illuminate specific intractable problems in their own field; some had concerns about particular concepts or issues (e.g. causation) that might be illuminated by interdisciplinary exchanges at a less general level than the construction of a 'science' or field; some were attracted by the opportunity to explore questions about evidence within their own discipline or area of specialisation ; the term 'evidence' may have had quite different associations for some from the conception shared by the instigators of the programme (see below); some came with their own individual agendas or with no very clear ideas about what to expect. The outcome was that a loosely knit 'evidence community' was established with a rich variety of interactions. Some interesting specific projects were pursued, but it is my impression that the general tendencies were more centrifugal than centripetal.[82] In short the main benefits were what participants took back to their own

---

[80] Schum (1994/2001). Other obvious ones included writings by philosophers (e.g. Toulmin (1964), Cohen (1977), Haack (see above, n. 1), Achinstein (2001)); intellectual historians (e.g. Hacking (1975) and Shapiro (1983, 1991)); 'The New Rhetoric' (Chaim Perelman and associates); probability theory; the massive literature about miracles and proof of the existence of God; and last, but not least, Jeremy Bentham, who is claimed by several disciplines.

[81] Chap. 3 (this volume).

[82] This is in line with Davies's comment that scholars involved in interdisciplinary work tend to remain focused on their own discipline (ibid.).

specialisms rather than significant advances in a common enterprise. My personal expectations were disappointed, but as Davies makes clear, this is far from saying that the programme was a failure; but the criteria of 'success' are elusive.[83]

I still think that Evidence deserves sustained attention as a multidisciplinary field or subject, if not a science, and I want to explore some possible intellectual reasons for resistance to the idea. Anyone who has been involved in sustained interdisciplinary work is likely to encounter one or more obstacles to communication and cooperation. Some are intellectual, but others, real enough psychologically, are not intellectually interesting. For example, one's counterparts from other disciplines may be daunted by the prospect of entering into a new field or reading a lot of unfamiliar literature; they may be defensive about their own territory or challenges to their expertise or authority; or they may assume that they are there to teach and have nothing to learn from the natives; or they may just find it difficult to think outside their individual boxes. The ethnography of knowledge is replete with stories of the territorial behaviour of different academic tribes.[84] These attitudes illustrate some of the practical obstacles to sustained interdisciplinary work. Here I am more concerned with intellectual resistance to the idea of a multidisciplinary field of Evidence.

There are other forms of resistance that can be put aside. Someone may just not be interested in the subject of evidence as the term is used here; or they may be sceptical about the value, or relevance to their concerns, of a general field of Evidence; or they may think that the concept or use of evidence in their specialism is unproblematic. Sometimes, such attitudes are quite legitimate and present a challenge to proponents of a science or field of Evidence to show that it is more interesting or relevant or problematic than it may appear to be to the resister.

I shall address the more intellectual forms of resistance under the following heads:

(a) Suspicions of 'scientism' and empiricism;
(b) Varieties of scepticism;
(c) Different conceptions of 'evidence'.
(d) Strong views on the autonomy of disciplines.

---

[83] Davies, above at p. 39.
[84] Becher (2001), and Bourdieu (1988).

(a) Suspicions of 'scientism' and empiricism

As was noted above, the suggestion that the UCL programme should be called 'Towards an Integrated Science of Evidence' provoked quite widespread hostility. Although it was emphasised that 'science' was being used in this context to mean nothing more than 'systematic study', suspicion remained. This is understandable: in some quarters 'science' has acquired strong negative associations, which are broadly expressed by the pejorative term 'scientism'.[85] For example, it is sometimes assumed that inquiries in the humanities and social sciences should be modelled on the natural sciences; that only measurable quantitative data are meaningful; that policies and problems involving value choices can be resolved empirically;[86] that 'evidence-based medicine' had become a dogma which sometimes went far beyond the sensible claim that doctors should try to rely on the best information available;[87] that the label 'scientific' is often used to give spurious authority or a political advantage to bogus claims that satisfy none of the standards of well-grounded empirical sciences. Susan Haack sums up the dangers of honorific use of the term:

> 'Scientific' has become an all-purpose term of epistemic praise meaning 'strong, reliable, *good*'... In view of the impressive successes of the natural sciences, this honorific usage is understandable enough. But it is thoroughly unfortunate. It obscures the otherwise obvious fact that not all and not only practitioners of

[85] 'Scientism', characterised as 'a kind of over-enthusiastic and uncritically deferential attitude towards science, an inability to see or an unwillingness to acknowledge its fallibility, its limitations, and its potential dangers' is analysed in Haack (2009*a*).

[86] See Jill Russell and Trish Greenhalgh, this volume Chap. 10. In October 2009 Professor David Nutt was sacked as the government's Chief Scientific Adviser on Drugs by the Home Secretary, Alan Johnson. The main reason was that Nutt had roundly criticised the Government's decision to upgrade cannabis from a class C to a class B drug against the advice of the Advisory Council on the Misuse of Drugs (ACMD). The issue was hotly debated in terms of 'a conflict between science and politics' and whether classification of drugs is a political or a scientific issue. Since it has consequences for sentencing and other matters, it is hard to see how the decision could be classified as purely 'scientific'. The controversy was complicated by the fact that the Advisory Council is not composed solely of scientists, Nutt's views were expressed in an academic lecture, and even if he had broken the rules, many considered sacking to be an inappropriate response. For two views see *Prospect*, Dec. 2009, at 25 (William Cullerne Brown), and 29 (Nigel Warburton). Nevertheless, the incident sharply raises questions about the nature and limits of 'science-based policy'.

[87] On criticism of some excesses of evidence-based medicine (EBM) see, for example, M. Tonnelli, 'Integrating evidence into clinical practice: an alternative to evidence-based approaches', *Journal of Evaluation in Clinical Practice*, 12: 248–56 (2006); and comments by K. Malterud, ibid., 248–56, and S. Tanenbaum, ibid., 248–56. Insofar as some forms of EBM involve strict priority rules or precise rules for evaluation of types of evidence, to a jurist Bentham's criticism of Gilbert (above, p. 76) still appears relevant.

disciplines classified as sciences are honest, thorough, successful inquirers; when plenty of scientists are lazy, incompetent, unimaginative, unlucky or dishonest, while plenty of historians, journalists, detectives etc. are good inquirers. It tempts us into a fruitless preoccupation with the problem of demarcating *real* science from pretenders. It encourages too thoughtlessly uncritical an attitude to the disciplines classified as sciences, which in turn provokes envy of those disciplines, and encourages a kind of scientism—inappropriate mimicry, by practitioners of other disciplines, of the manner, the technical terminology, the mathematics, etc., of the natural sciences. And it provokes resentment of the disciplines so classified, which encourages anti-scientific attitudes.[88]

The wording of the title of the UCL project created further difficulty. 'Towards' suggested to some a specific goal to be achieved. 'Science' raised the hackles of those who are suspicious of 'scientism'. But it was also ambiguous: did an 'integrated science' mean a new discipline or something less ambitious like a focus of attention or a flexible framework or map for indicating connections between different lines of inquiry? Or did it mean a general theory of evidence? If the latter, what kind of questions would it address?

It is possible that the use of the term 'integrated' and Schum's 'substance blind approach' to evidence were perceived to be an attempt to impose a monolithic general theory of evidence for all disciplines. In my view, these fears were not realised: Schum's goals were more modest than this and the operation of the programme was flexible and open-ended. In fact when 'theories of evidence' are discussed one finds a wide range of views about the agendas of questions that such a theory should address.[89]

Another possible source of resistance was suspicion of 'empiricism', not least in relation to the social sciences. Questions about the epistemological foundations of any inquiry, whether empirical inquiries can be value free, the

---

[88] Haack (2003), p. 18; cf. the extended account cited in Haack (2009a). At UCL some of the resistance to the label 'evidence science' related to such abuses of the word 'scientific', especially in relation to policy-making and evidence-based medicine; some wished to emphasise contextual factors that made their particular disciplines unique and so were sceptical about cross-disciplinary generalisation; and some were attracted to diverse forms of 'postmodern' epistemology.

[89] For example, the ideal type of 'The Rationalist Tradition of Evidence Scholarship' in law (see above, nn. 44–5) identifies a coherent framework of concepts and assumptions shared by most legal evidence scholars, but is a long way from a general theory that provides an integrated set of substantive answers to basic questions in the field. To refer to the examples from law mentioned above: Thayer could be said to have formulated a theory of the Anglo-American law of evidence that has been extremely influential; Wigmore's Principles of Proof aspired to be such a theory for Judicial Evidence. It did provide a general framework for the study of evidence in law, but there is room for disagreement as to whether it deserved in its own time to be accorded the status of a general theory—that is a fully worked out coherent set of answers to a set of linked basic questions within a subdiscipline.

relationship between conceptual analysis and social facts, and the extent to which all knowledge is 'constructed' are routinely contested in many different disciplinary contexts. The late Peter Lipton neatly surveyed the battleground:

> There are almost as many empiricisms as there are empiricists, but what these views or approaches have in common is an emphasis on the importance of experience to the formation of concepts and to the acquisition of knowledge. The foil to empiricism is rationalism, which emphasizes instead the importance of thought and knowledge of material that is in some sense independent of experience. The range of empiricist positions is vast, from the shocking view that all we can think or know about are our sensations to the mundane claims that experience plays some role in the formation of some of our concepts and in the justification of some of our beliefs. Empiricism of some form may seem both obviously correct and obviously the correct philosophy for science on the grounds that it is clear that one can only find out about the world by observing it; but this innocuous looking thought has been disputed, and in any case many forms of empiricism go beyond it in their claims. It is also unclear whether empiricism ultimately supports or undermines claims to scientific knowledge.[90]

Here it should suffice to make two simple points: First, the study of evidence is concerned with empirical inquiries and is 'empiricist' in that loose sense. But to be interested in the subject involves no commitment to any particular version of empiricism or to any version at all. Most participants in the UCL programme probably subscribe to at least 'the mundane claims' referred to by Lipton, some may go further in the direction of 'the shocking view'. Second, a field or subject or 'science' with evidence as its focal point cannot but involve engagement with philosophical issues surrounding empiricism and epistemology. In short, evidence as a subject is potentially an arena of profound philosophical contestation. This is one reason for being wary of any aspirations to a single overarching Grand Theory of Evidence.

(b) Varieties of scepticism[91]

Closely related to suspicion of 'empiricism' are strong versions of epistemological scepticism that can be interpreted as challenging the very idea of evidence as a subject worth studying.[92] A simple version goes as follows: the concept of evidence as interpreted here assumes a cognitivist epistemology—acceptance of some empirical conception of truth and the idea that truth can

---

[90] Lipton (2001) at p. 4481.
[91] On 'strategies of scepticism' in regard to fact-determination in law, see *RE*, chap. 4.
[92] Goldman's 'reliabilism' is a type of non-sceptical epistemology that eschews the concept of evidence (Goldman, 1986), discussed Haack (1993), chap. 7.

be pursued by rational means. If either of these assumptions is rejected, then the very idea of a science of evidence is a delusion. That is probably correct. Most discourse about evidence proceeds on the basis of some cognitivist assumptions. Fundamental problems of epistemology arise in relation to evidence as a subject, not only in relation to confronting various forms of scepticism, but also in clarifying which version of cognitivism or empiricism is assumed by a given account of evidence. Of course, for many practical purposes, some common sense form of empiricism may suffice,[93] but a general field of evidence needs to address its epistemological foundations. However, to argue that evidence is a worthwhile *focus of attention* as a field or subject involves no commitment to a particular *theory of evidence* any more than treating epistemology as a subject involves commitment to a particular theory of knowledge.

A special challenge is presented by some varieties of postmodernism that are currently in fashion. Within the UCL programme some of the participants were attracted by one or more of these versions or more generally by the postmodern mood. Some of our scientifically minded colleagues dismissed postmodernism out of hand as a fashionable and dangerous delusion.[94] Others were ambivalent. Especially interesting were some individuals who seemed to be reacting against excesses of 'scientism' in their own academic subcultures.

'Postmodernism' means many things in a multiplicity of contexts. The issues are too complex to pursue here, but it may help to draw attention to a distinction that I have found useful in probing my own ambivalences about postmodernism in legal contexts: postmodernism as a form of epistemological scepticism or strong relativism (irrationalist postmodernism) and imaginative postmodernism as a perspective that emphasises complexity, multiple perspectives, difficulties of description, and the role of imagination in inquiry without abandoning a basic cognitivism. The first is exemplified by Richard Rorty; the second by Italo Calvino's Mr Palomar and Marco Polo in his wonderful fictional evocations of the elusiveness of reality.[95]

In Rorty's 'anti-foundationalism', 'truth' is a matter of consensus or solidarity within a particular epistemic community: 'There is nothing to be said about either truth or rationality apart from descriptions of the familiar pro-

---

[93] e.g. 'Analysis of legal fact-finding does not need to draw on any deep theory of truth', Ho (2008), at p. 56; cf. Haack (2004), at p. 45.

[94] e.g. Colquhoun, this volume, below at p. 323.

[95] Especially Italo Calvino, *Invisible Cities* (1974) and *Mr Palomar* 1986), discussed in relation to postmodernism in Twining (2001), chap. 8.

cedures of justification which a given society—*ours*—uses.'[96] If correct, this would clearly undermine the very idea of an empirical science or field of evidence, as interpreted here.[97] Calvino, on the other hand, accepts that that there is a world independent of our senses, but emphasises the complexities of that world and the immense difficulties of describing and understanding it.[98] That is quite compatible with a cognitivist position and inquiries that seek to develop true conclusions based on evidence.

I am attracted by Calvino's emphasis on the elusiveness of reality, but I strongly disagree with Rorty's sceptical epistemology as interpreted here. I also disagree with colleagues who sweepingly dismiss all 'postmodernism' as discredited,[99] but I accept a cognitivist epistemology (much influenced by my colleague Susan Haack).[100] For the not insignificant number of colleagues who are attracted by Rorty the study of evidence presents a challenge: Is it possible to reconcile Rortyian scepticism with taking the study of evidence seriously?

(c) Different conceptions of 'evidence'

So far I have assumed a particular usage of the term 'evidence' in the context of empirical inquiries. In this usage 'evidence' is a word of relation used in the context of argument (A is evidence of B). In that context information has a

---

[96] This version of Rorty's position is taken from 'Science as Solidarity', in J. Nelson, A. Magill and D. McCloskey (eds.), *The Rhetoric of the Human Sciences* (Madison: University of Wisconsin Press, 1987). More complex versions are elaborated in *Objectivity, Relativism and Truth* (Cambridge: Cambridge University Press, 1991). Interpretations of Rorty are not in issue here; suffice to say that he is widely interpreted as an epistemological sceptic, typically rejecting any distinction between epistemology and ontology. A philosophy that has no conception of truth or falsity has difficulty in accommodating as meaningful such notions as conviction of the innocent, misidentification, mistake of fact, and some central examples of miscarriage of justice.

[97] '[I]f Rorty and Co. were right, we would surely stand in need of the most urgent and radical revision not only of our legal thinking, but of our legal system itself', Haack (2004), at 43.

[98] Haack, commenting on Calvino, says: 'My examples—the various ways of describing objects on my desk or the furniture in my living room—weren't nearly as romantic: but the theme of "many different true descriptions" was one strand in my statement of Innocent Realism: though there is just one real world, and though incompatible descriptions cannot be jointly true, there are many truths, in different, sometimes irreducibly different vocabularies.

'But of course it doesn't follow from the fact that there are many true descriptions of the world that any and all descriptions are true from some perspective, that the epistemological desiderata of evidential reach and respect for evidence could be replaced by the political desideratum of inclusiveness, or that imagination is not only necessary, but sufficient for successful inquiry', Haack (2007), at 261.

[99] See above, n. 94.

[100] See above, n. 1, esp. Haack (2003), chap. 5.

potential role as relevant evidence if it tends to support or tends to negate, directly or indirectly, a hypothesis or probandum or other proposition of fact.[101] One draws inferences from evidence in order to prove or disprove a proposition of fact. The framework is argument, the process is proof, the engine is inferential reasoning from information.[102]

Of course, the term 'evidence' has a number of other associations, depending on context. Here it is useful to distinguish between what counts as 'information' in the context of inferential reasoning, particular usages that are broader and narrower than that outlined above, and ideas, such as models, that are closely associated with evidence, but which presuppose a core idea of evidence yet become loosely conflated with it.

Let me first dispose of some not very interesting examples of deviant usage. In law, it is sometimes said that 'hearsay is not evidence'; this is merely shorthand for the rule (subject to many exceptions) that hearsay may not be *used* or *admitted* as evidence under the Law of Evidence.[103] Something similar is to be found in some versions of evidence-based medicine, when some kinds of information not based on random clinical trials is barred or discouraged from being used in diagnosis: the patient's own diagnosis, the doctor's impressionistic experiences of similar cases, and 'intuition' are not to be treated as evidence.

Some people are interested in the properties and characteristics of particular materials or things that can be used as evidence, such as fingerprints, official records, or human bones or DNA. Here, the phrase 'types of evidence' is potentially misleading: documents, fingerprints, and DNA are *used* as evidence. To say 'DNA is a type of evidence' is misleading outside the context of its use in evidentiary reasoning. Of course, some scholars are especially puzzled or interested in methodological difficulties of constructing inferential arguments from especially elusive or fragmentary material—for example, an archaeologist trying to reconstruct a whole building from a few fragments[104] or a theatre historian puzzling over whether and how a painting depicting a performance of the Commedia del Arte can be used as evidence of costume

---

[101] On 'relevant evidence' cf. Federal Rules of Evidence Rule 401, cited above, n. 31.

[102] 'Information' is here confined to factual information. On other usages see *RE*, pp. 253–4.

[103] As noted above at n. 1, lawyers sometimes conflate the Law of Evidence with the subject of Evidence in Law, confining the subject to evidence doctrine either by ignoring the Principles of Proof or subsuming them under the Law of Evidence even though those principles are not governed by law.

[104] Cf. Alison Wylie (this volume, Chap. 14). For this and a wide range of other examples, see Fagan (1995).

or gesture or other aspects of an actual performance.[105] These are interesting questions, but they are not puzzles about the *concept* of evidence.

We can also put on one side loose extensions of the term 'evidence'. We talk of someone 'giving evidence' before a Committee of the House of Commons or of the US Senate. Often such presentations on a particular issue or topic involve a mixture of facts, value judgements, opinions and arguments to advance 'a position' or 'view'; whereas 'evidence' in its primary usage is confined to facts. One may use factual information, among other things, as part of an argument in support of a position or proposal or one may be doing little more than asserting an opinion.

Economic forecasts and assessments of the likelihoods of particular events often use 'models' that are based in part on data, but go beyond them. They are akin to hypotheses that are plausible according to available evidence, in the sense used here, and often serve as a substitute for evidence in arguments that cannot be settled by the available data.[106] The use of models in economics and in other contexts—debates about global warming, for example[107]—deserve to be taken very seriously in a multidisciplinary field of evidence.

One of the most interesting uses of 'evidence' relates to the much-debated topic of miracles. In Catholic doctrine 'miracles' (*miracula*, cf. Greek *terata*, *dynameis*, *semeia*) are wonderful things—'wonders performed by a supernatural power as signs of some special mission or gift and explicitly ascribed to God ... A miracle is said to be supernatural because its effect is beyond the productive power of nature and implies supernatural agency.'[108] Catholic doctrine distinguishes sharply between miracles as evidence, and what constitutes evidence of the existence or occurrence of a miracle. The main significance of miracles is 'to attest and confirm the truth of a Divine mission or of a doctrine faith, morals or true sanctity. Miracles are a sign ...'[109] However, the

---

[105] Katritzky (2003).

[106] 'Copernicus had devised a better, a more elegant system, which yet, for all its seeming radicalism, was intended in the schoolman's phrase "to save the phenomena", to set up a model which need not be empirically true, but only plausible according to the observations', John Banville, *Kepler* (1981), p. 25. On models as instruments of inquiry, see Haack (2003), at pp. 137–9.

[107] James Lovelock, author of the 'Gaia theory', who believes that global warming is largely caused by human agency, goes so far as to say: 'Observations and evidence are out of fashion; most evidence is now taken from the virtual world of computer models' ('Ground Truth', *Prospect*, Dec. 2007, 68).

[108] 'Miracle' in *The Catholic Encyclopedia* <http://www.catholic.org/encyclopedia/view.php?id= 8016> (last visited 10/09).

[109] Ibid.

existence of miracles is a question of fact based on ordinary principles of inferential reasoning from observation:

> A miracle, like any natural event, is known from personal observation or from the testimony of others. In the miracle we have the fact itself as an external occurrence and its miraculous character. The miraculous character of the fact consists in this: that its nature and the surrounding circumstances are of such kind that we are forced to admit natural forces alone could not have produced it, and the only rational explanation is to be had in the interference of Divine agency. The perception of its miraculous character is a rational act of the mind, and is simply the application of the principle of causality with the methods of induction. The general rules governing acceptance of testimony apply to miracles.[110]

On this interpretation, when a person claims to have observed a miracle we can subject the testimony to standard tests of witness credibility: veracity (does the witness sincerely believe what she reports?); observational capacity (were the witness's vantage point and sensory abilities such that the witness was capable of observing the event with her senses?), and bias (was the witness's perception or memory predisposed or influenced to believe that she observed the event?). A fourth test is whether the hearer believes that what the witness claims to have experienced is impossible or highly improbable (judged by 'general experience' or the known 'laws of nature').[111] Some sceptics about miracles rely solely on the fourth test, others on a combination of two or more such tests.[112] The Catholic position seems to be that there is overwhelming observational evidence that miracles occur and that this is in turn evidence of the supernatural.

This is not the place to explore the claims of religious experience in depth.[113] Suffice to note here that some such claims can be subjected to standard tests of witness credibility and accordingly can be evaluated as evidence of the truth, falsity or likelihood of such claims. But others, such as claims based on supposed extrasensory perception or intuition or revelation fall outside the empirical conception of 'evidence' as being based directly or indirectly on observation by one of the five senses. Similarly, it is useful to distinguish

---

[110] 'Miracle' in *The Catholic Encyclopedia*, op. cit., p. 16, n. 108.
[111] On Schum's elaborate scheme for testing credibility (mainly of witnesses) see *Analysis* at pp. 63–71.
[112] e.g. Hume doubted miracles on the basis of their 'antecedent improbability' (Hume (1748), chap. 10, but this was criticised by John Stuart Mill on the ground that this argument was only valid on the assumption that God does not exist (J. S. Mill (1859), *System of Logic*, II. xxv).
[113] Haack (2008), chap. 12.

between beliefs based on authority (e.g. a religious text, the sayings of a prophet) or on faith (acceptance or commitment not based on evidence) and beliefs based on empirical evidence. Here, I shall use 'evidence' in the narrow empirical sense, but note that many claims about what the world is like are based on other grounds for belief.

One of the most striking extensions of the term 'evidence' relates to our sister project at the London School of Economics.[114] The UCL programme is represented in this volume and nearly all of the contributions bear a direct relationship to the idea of evidence. The LSE programme is entitled 'How Well Do Facts Travel?'. Its different goals and emphasis were summarised as follows:

> It is often assumed that a fact is a fact is a fact, yet those who work across disciplinary boundaries are well aware that the life of a fact is not so simple. Even everyday experience suggests that, like gossip, facts that travel rarely remain stable. Our research programme proposes to explore the nature of evidence by adopting a consistent research design to analyse how well evidence travels between and within disciplines and to examine why evidence considered acceptable in one context retains or loses its status as evidence in another. We aim to establish a body of case work on this question of how well facts travel and to develop, for more general use, the conceptual frameworks appropriate to answering this question.[115]

The main focus of the LSE project was on how data generated in one context are received, interpreted and used in different contexts. The programme and its constituent elements excited interest and admiration, but some of us in the UCL programme wondered what it had to do with *evidence*. To be sure data generated in one context is sometimes explicitly or implicitly used as evidence to support some factual thesis or conclusion, but this is only one of many uses that can be made of such information. The focus was on what happens to supposed facts in the process of travelling rather than on the nature of evidence and its role in inferential reasoning. Initially, I shared some colleagues' doubts as to whether this was really about evidence, but I have changed my

---

[114] The Leverhulme Foundation was sufficiently impressed with the responses to their invitations for bids for funding a major project on 'Evidence' that they persuaded the Economic and Social Research Council to join them in funding two projects, one at UCL and one at LSE. There was some liaison and interchange between the two projects, but they were quite separate.

[115] <http://www.lse.ac.uk/collections/economicHistory/Research/HowWellDoFactsTravel.htm> (last visited 23/11/09). This was a statement of the original conception of the LSE programme; the findings of the programme and how it changed are summarised in Mary Morgan, 'Matters of Fact', Introduction to P. Howlett and M. Morgan (eds.) (2010). One of the general findings was that facts that travel remain stable more often than they had expected.

mind, because the publications resulting from the LSE programme can clearly be interpreted as a significant contribution to the subject of evidence as I have interpreted it.[116] Indeed, because the LSE programme was more closely integrated than the one at UCL, it promises to make a contribution to this subject at a more general level than the more disparate UCL projects:

> We expect these component projects to generate case studies that will teach us not just about how the nature of evidence and its evaluation differs between disciplinary sites, but also to generate *some general suggestions* about the receipt of facts. Are facts in a new site positively received and integrated? Or are they reinterpreted to fit? Perhaps they are inconsistent with the new site information, and, if so, how is the dispute resolved? Or do the new facts prove destructive? These are the senses in which we will seek to assess how 'well' facts travel, that is, understand the different kinds of reception and strategies for integration of facts. To help us analyse these reception issues in our cases, and so to *provide more general answers* to the overall question 'How well do facts travel?', we adopt a number of theoretical and conceptual starting points from the existing literatures on knowledge transfer.[117]

(d) Interdisciplinarity: terminology and assumptions about the relative autonomy of disciplines

Before the UCL Evidence programme, I had tended to use 'interdisciplinary' to refer to interactions between members of two different disciplines and 'multidisciplinary' to refer to interactions where more than two disciplines were involved. Jason Davies points out that these and related terms are used loosely and without consistency.[118] He has argued that there is a need for a more refined terminology to distinguish between different kinds of interaction including: (a) scholars drawing on insights and methods from one or more other disciplines in looking for solutions to intractable problems within their own discipline; (b) scholars from two or more disciplines exploring issues, concepts and methods for the sake of increased understanding for a variety purposes, with the main pay-off being illumination for each within their own discipline; (c) teams of specialists from several disciplines looking for a solution to an *extradisciplinary* problem (e.g. building a power station,

---

[116] See Howlett and Morgan (eds.) (2010).

[117] Ibid. (italics added). The conceptual frameworks that provided the starting points for the programme were: (i) expanding the notion of 'travelling'; (ii) exploring substitutes for tacit knowledge; (iii) analysing the role of cases; (iv) conceptualising how facts are used in public and official domains. See now Morgan (2010), op. cit.

[118] Davies, Chap. 3 above at p. 41.

devising responses to global warming) with members of the team typically exporting expertise without necessarily importing insights back into their own discipline.[119]

I am not familiar with the academic literature about interdisciplinarity,[120] but I have had extensive first-hand experience of the rewards and frustrations of cross-disciplinary interactions. I have found the commentary by Stephen Rowland and Jason Davies on the UCL programme and interdisciplinary relations generally illuminating, but I have one major reservation about their perspective.[121] Lurking behind much of what they say seems to be a picture of disciplines as solid, largely homogeneous, bounded entities, like fortress communities, from which individual scholars sally forth on short expeditions as importers, exporters, or explorers only to return 'home' having garnered new material or having made some specialised contribution (in the latter case typically to a practical, extradisciplinary problem). It is very risky to linger outside. This fortress image fits some academic cultures better than others. It strengthens ideas of distinct domains of knowledge and even autonomous disciplines. Such fortresses can no doubt accommodate within their walls some dissent and disagreement, some subdisciplines and other specialisms, and power struggles within and between disciplines. It contains a core of truth about the identity of specialists and the dangers of dilettanteism.[122] But it does not fit all disciplinary cultures and, more importantly, it can be epistemically misleading.

I happen to come from an academic culture which is towards one end of the spectrum of bounded and unbounded subjects. Apart from the subject of Evidence in law, which I hope to have shown is inherently multidisciplinary, my main subject is Jurisprudence. It is sometimes said that Law is a parasitic

---

[119] On the terminology used in this paper, see above, n. 1. There are, of course, other patterns of interaction between different kinds of specialists, but this characterisation is useful in differentiating between those primarily involving importing and exporting expertise, and those interacting for the purpose of mutual illumination and teamwork directed to jointly solving some practical problem that involves multiple inputs. The typology could no doubt be extended, but in the present context it is clear that my account of Evidence in law is pluridisciplinary, in that it involves all the kinds of interaction differentiated by Davies—(and some others). Similarly, the UCL Evidence programme was also pluridisciplinary and, on Davies's account, the main benefits were whatever insights and ideas each participant took back to their own discipline. (Communication to author.)

[120] See citations in Davies, Chap. 3 above at pp. 40–6.

[121] Davies this volume and Rowland (2006).

[122] In satirising the propensity of academic lawyers to be suckers for 'law and …' enterprises, a standard joke is that literature by lawyers is a harmless indulgence, economics by lawyers is third rate economics, but psychiatry by lawyers is really dangerous.

subject and Jurisprudence is the lawyer's extraversion, i.e. the main locus of law's interface with other disciplines.[123] As with other theoretical enterprises many of the central questions of Jurisprudence are shared with other disciplines. For example, the question: 'What is justice?' does not belong exclusively to ethics or analytical philosophy or political theory or economics or legal theory or any other discipline. [124] Similarly, differing conceptions of law have been a major battleground in legal theory, but these controversies are to a large extent shared with analytical philosophers, social scientists, and others interested in legal phenomena. 'Law' as a concept does not belong to jurists.

My conception of Evidence as a multidisciplinary field is rather like that: there are epistemological, logical, probabilistic, conceptual, and many other types of questions that arise within the field, but many of these questions do not *belong* to any one discipline—in the sense of depending for their more general answers on specialised methods and knowledge that are the exclusive domain of one kind of specialism.[125] Moreover, not only do questions of and about evidence and inference arise in many academic disciplines and spheres of practice, but our representative democracy and the role of juries and lay magistrates in our system of administration of justice are premised on notions of 'cognitive competence', that is the assumption that normal adult citizens have the ability to draw on their society's general stock of knowledge ('general

---

[123] Stone (1964), at pp. 15–16.

[124] Of course, there are psychological, sociological and other types of questions about justice that presuppose or adopt particular conceptions of justice and injustice.

[125] My colleague at UCL, René Weis (English Dept.) and I, quite independently of each other, analysed the case of Edith Thompson to determine whether she was rightly convicted of murdering her husband, Percy. We used significantly different methods to arrive at a similar conclusion. Weis used the methods of a social historian to gather and interpret a mass of new data and he used the lenses of a textual scholar to interpret Edith's elusive love letters. I used an adaptation of Wigmore's chart method to analyse the evidence presented at trial. The main evidence against Edith was her passionate and often cryptic letters to her lover, Frederick Bywaters. Weis and I arrived at similar conclusions about Edith's guilt but by very different routes. Rather than alter what we had already written, we collaborated in an article contrasting our two approaches. (Twining and Weis 'Reconstructing the Truth about Edith Thompson: The Shakespearean and the Jurist', repr. in *RE*, chap. 12). I have argued elsewhere that despite somewhat different data bases, we were both asking exactly the same question: does the evidence available to me support beyond reasonable doubt the conclusion that Edith was guilty of (legally responsible) murdering her husband? The meaning of that question depends on the law of murder, incitement and conspiracy and the criminal standard of proof at the time. Some of my students argue that we were asking different questions, because of differences in our data sets and methodology. My reply is that Weis and I were both adopting the standpoint of historians asking an identical question and the meaning of that question is defined by the law at the time. Neither of us was concerned with the fairness of the trial, but rather with Edith's legal responsibility as a matter of historical fact.

experience') to make sound judgements based on ordinary practical reasoning. In short, the case can be made for saying that concerns about evidence are a part of 'general culture'.[126] Of course, a multidisciplinary field of evidence requires specialised inputs. But it is misleading to see it in terms of interactions between specialists from sharply separated 'domains', who have little or no common ground.

Part IV. Conclusion

In answer to the question: why do you think evidence has special claims to be a good focus of attention, my argument is largely pragmatic. All disciplines that have significant empirical elements are connected to a shared family of problems about evidence and inference. Apart from its theoretical interest (as a contribution to understanding), evidence is of great practical importance in many spheres of decision-making and risk management. In particular multidisciplinary study of evidence should focus attention on such general questions as: (i) What features of evidence are common across disciplines and what features are special? (ii) What concepts, methods and insights developed in one discipline are transferable to others?[127] (iii) What concepts are not transferable? Why? (iv) Can we develop general concepts, methods, and insights that apply to evidence in all or nearly all contexts?

In my view, the UCL programme achieved much at particular levels, but did not make much progress in addressing more general and middle order questions. Nearly all of the activities and interactions took place at lower levels of abstraction. There were many interesting specific activities and products, but the idea of a shared enterprise that also focused on some shared general questions was lost sight of. My personal hopes were not realised. The development of a new subject is a major undertaking. From the outset it was my judgement that three to four years was much too short and a single programme much too modest to achieve the basic aspiration. The UCL programme succeeded in constituting an 'evidence community' with a considerable sharing of ideas and experience among its various members. This would have been an excellent starting-point for a further, more integrated phase, but unfortunately

---

[126] On controversy about 'general cognitive competence' and 'cognitive consensus' see *Analysis*, pp. 273–6.

[127] This question focuses on the transferability of *concepts* and *methods*, whereas the LSE project was concerned with *facts* 'travelling'. There are potentially significant connections between these inquiries.

there was insufficient interest in moving to a more general level and no one was available and willing to take over the leadership from Philip Dawid, who had done a fine job in keeping the programme together despite the diversity of the interests of members of the group.

So, in my view, there is still a need for a reasonably integrated multi-disciplinary effort to carry this enterprise forward. This would probably involve the acceptance of some broad cognitivist and empiricist working assumptions with the main focus on middle order questions. In this view, the central theoretical question should be: given such assumptions, how far can we generalise about evidence and inferential reasoning across disciplines, decision contexts, and types of inquiry?

In relation to this more specific questions need to be addressed, such as:

1. Are there principles of reasoning from evidence that transcend all or most scholarly disciplines?
2. What counts as 'evidence' has varied across time, language, cultures, practical contexts, and academic disciplines. Is it possible to construct an analytic concept or framework of concepts that transcends these various contexts?
3. Are there concepts, methods of reasoning, or types of evidence that are unique or special in one or more disciplines?
4. In what sense is any given type of inquiry or decision context-specific in relation to evidence? Can a substance-blind approach to evidence (Schum) also be context-blind?
5. Are there concepts—such as relevance, probability, probative force, and credibility, cognitive competence, ancillary evidence—that can usefully be given meanings that transcend all, most or some scholarly disciplines?
6. Are Schum's credibility indicators applicable to questions about testimony or documentary evidence in different contexts?
7. Are there general tests of authenticity applicable to documents and physical objects that are used as evidence?
8. What is the relationship between narrative and reasoning in the context of argumentation? To what extent does that relationship vary according to disciplinary and practical contexts? What exactly is meant by the claim that stories help us 'to make sense of the world'? What can legitimately be claimed can be done by narrative that cannot be done by reasoning?
9. To what extent and in what respects can concepts and methods concerning evidence developed in one discipline or practical environment be applied, with or without modification, to other disciplines and contexts?

10. What are the uses, limitations, and dangers of formal representations of inferential arguments (Bayes's nets, Wigmore charts etc.)?
11. What are the uses and limitations of evidence-based approaches to medicine, policy, or other activities?
12. What can reasonably be expected of computers and artificial intelligence as aids to marshalling and reasoning from evidence?
13. What general lessons can be learned from recent developments in handling evidence in police investigation, intelligence analysis, forensic science, forensic anthropology, and other practical operations?
14. To what extent should study of evidence be driven by questions about how people actually deal with evidence rather than how they should think and act in relation to it?

Answering such questions does not involve trying to set up a monolithic Grand Theory of Evidence. Too many perspectives are involved, the questions are too varied, and the possibilities for honest disagreement too extensive for that to be appropriate. Even if a set of answers could be welded into a single coherent 'theory', it is likely to be too abstract to be of much assistance in dealing with particular and practical questions that could benefit from the development of a multidisciplinary field—a locus for many kinds of interaction and, sometimes, an arena of contestation. Here the instincts of some resisters seem to me to be sound.

Nor, in my view, would the best approach be largely 'top down'. To be sure there already exist in the literature general concepts, principles and hypotheses that are relevant to the enterprise. But I would personally favour an approach that emphasises quite concrete comparisons and explorations of particular examples. By way of illustration (a) two or more individuals exploring in depth whether conceptions of relevance, credibility, and probative force mean exactly the same thing in each specialist context and whether judgements relating to them are reached in comparable ways; (b) Individuals with several different specialisms jointly examining the use of evidence in particular texts about climate change[128] or the Vatican's processes of sanctification or Richard Dawkins's *The God Delusion* or René Weis's use of Shakespeare plays as a source of biographical evidence.[129]

---

[128] e.g. a comparison of the conceptions and approaches to evidence in the Stern Review (Stern, 2007) and Nigel Lawson's sceptical critique in *An Appeal to Reason: a cool look at global warming* (2008).
[129] Weis (2007).

Such inquiries can be very detailed and specific, but they would be oriented to the possibilities of generalisation across specialisms, inquiries and contexts. This is just one person's agenda. No doubt it exhibits theoretical, juristic and humanistic biases. Scholars from different backgrounds would have different, but one hopes, overlapping agendas. That is one reason why interdisciplinary work is important.

References

Achinstein, P. (2001), *The Book of Evidence* (Oxford, Oxford University Press).
Allen, C. (1997), *The Law of Evidence in Victorian England* (Cambridge, Cambridge University Press).
Allen, R. (1994), 'Factual ambiguity and a theory of evidence', *Northwestern University Law Review*, 88: 604–40.
Anderson, T., Schum, D. and Twining, W. (2005), *Analysis of Evidence* (2nd edn.) (Cambridge, Cambridge University Press) (cited as *Analysis*).
Banville, J. (1981), *Kepler* (London, Secker and Warburg).
Barnes, T. (1991), 'Introduction' to a reissue of Wigmore, J. H. *The Principles of Judicial Proof*, in *The Legal Classics Library* (Delran, NJ, Gryphon).
Becher, A. (2001), *Academic Tribes and Territories* (2nd edn.) (Milton Keynes, Open University Press).
Bentham, J. (1825), *A Treatise on Judicial Evidence*, ed. E. Dumont (London, J. W. Paget).
Bentham, J. (1827), *Rationale of Judicial Evidence*, ed. J. S. Mill (5 vols.) (London, Hunt and Clarke).
Bentham, J. (1838–43), *An Introductory View of the Rationale of Judicial Evidence*, VI, *Works*, ed. J. Bowring (Edinburgh, W. Tait), pp. 1–188.
Bourdieu, P. (1988), *Homo Academicus*, trs. P. Collier (Stanford, CA, Stanford University Press).
Brown, W. C. (2009), 'Drug Classification: hazy politics, Man', *Prospect*, Dec. 2009: 25.
Calvino, I. (1974), *Invisible Cities*, trs. William Weaver (New York, Harcourt Brace).
Calvino, I. (1986), *Mr Palomar*, trs William Weaver (New York, Harcourt Brace).
Carson, D., Milne, R., Pakes, F., Shalev, K. and Shawyer, A. (eds.) (2007), *Applying Psychology to Criminal Justice* (Chichester, Wiley).
Catholic Encyclopedia, The, 'Miracles' <http://www.catholic.org/encyclopedia/view.php?id=8016>.
Cohen, L. J. (1977), *The Probable and the Provable* (Oxford, Oxford University Press).
Cohen, L. J. (1981), 'Can human irrationality be experimentally demonstrated?', *The Behavioral and Brain Sciences*, 4: 317–70 (responses, ibid., 6: 487–533 (1983)).
Cutler, B. L. (ed.) (2008), *Encyclopedia of Psychology and Law* (Thousand Oaks, CA, Sage Publications).
de Waal, C. (ed.) (2007), *A Lady of Distinctions: Susan Haack: the philosopher responds to her critics* (Amherst, MA, Prometheus Books).

Dinwiddy, J. (2002), *Bentham: Selected Writings of John Dinwiddy*, ed. W. Twining (Stanford, CA, Stanford University Press).

Eggleston, R. (1978), *Evidence, Proof and Probability* (London, Weidenfeld and Nicolson (2nd edn., London, Butterworth, 1983)).

Eemeren, van F. and Grootendorst, R. (2001), *A Systematic Theory of Argumentation: the Pragma-dialectic Approach* (Cambridge, Cambridge University Press).

Fagan, B. (1995), *Time Detectives: how archeologists use technology to recapture the past* (New York, Simon and Schuster).

Felix, D. (1965), *Protest: Sacco-Vanzetti and the Intellectuals* (Bloomington, IN, University of Indiana Press).

Friedman, R. (ed.) (2002–), *The New Wigmore: a Treatise on Evidence* (New York, Aspen Law and Business).

Galanter, M. (2004), 'The Vanishing Trial', *Journal of Empirical Legal Studies*, 1: 459–570.

Gaskins, R. (1992), *Burdens of Proof in Modern Discourse* (New Haven, CT, Yale University Press).

Gilbert, G. (1754/1979), *The Law of Evidence* (repr.) (New York, Garland).

Goldberg, J. (2003), 'The Unknown: the C.I.A. and the Pentagon take on Al Qaeda and Iraq', *The New Yorker*, 10 Feb. 2003: 40–7.

Goldman, A. (1986), *Epistemology and Cognition* (Cambridge, MA, Harvard University Press).

Greenleaf, S. (1842), *A Treatise on the Law of Evidence* (Boston, MA, Little, Brown).

Haack, S. (1993), *Evidence and Inquiry* (Oxford, Blackwell).

Haack, S. (1998), *Manifesto of A Passionate Moderate* (Chicago, IL, University of Chicago Press).

Haack, S. (2003), *Defending Science Within Reason* (Amherst, MA, Prometheus Books).

Haack, S. (2004), 'Epistemology legalized: Truth, Justice, and the American way', *American Journal of Jurisprudence*, 49: 43–61.

Haack, S. (2007), 'Law, literature and bosh: response to William Twining', in de Waal (ed.) (2007), p. 259.

Haack, S. (2008), *Putting Philosophy to Work* (Amherst, MA, Prometheus Books).

Haack, S. (2009), *Evidence and Inquiry* (2nd enlarged edn., Amherst, MA, Prometheus Books).

Haack, S. (2011 forthcoming), 'Six Signs of Scientism'.

Hacking, I. (1975), *The Emergence of Probability* (Cambridge: Cambridge University Press).

Ho, H. L. (2004), 'The legitimacy of Medieval Proof', *Journal of Law and Religion*, 14: 259–98.

Ho, H. L. (2008), *A Philosophy of Evidence Law* (Oxford, Oxford University Press).

Holmes, O. W., Jr. (1896), 'The Path of the Law', *Harvard Law Review*, 10: 457–78.

Howlett, P. and Morgan, M. (eds.) (2010), *The Facts Book* (Cambridge, Cambridge University Press).

Hume, D. (1748/2000), *An Enquiry Concerning Human Understanding*, ed. T. L. Beauchamp (New York, Oxford University Press).

Kadane, J. and Schum, D. (1996), *A Probabilistic Analysis of the Sacco-Vanzetti Evidence* (New York, Wiley).

Kaplan, J. (1968), 'Decision-theory and the fact-finding process', *Stanford Law Review*, 20: 1065–92.

Katritzky, M. A. (2003), 'The Mountebank: a case study in early modern theater iconography', in W. Twining and I. Hampsher-Monk (eds.), *Evidence and Inference in History and Law* (Evanston, IL, Northwestern University Press), pp. 231–86.

Kelly, P. (1990), *Utiliitarianism and Distributive Justice* (Oxford, Oxford University Press).

Lawson, N. (2008), *An Appeal to Reason: a cool look at global warming* (London, Duckworth).

Lempert, R. (1988), 'The New Evidence Scholarship', in P. Tillers and E. Green (eds.), *Probability and Inference in the Law of Evidence* (Dordrecht, Kluwer Academic), pp. 61–102.

Lipton, P. (2001), 'Empiricism, History of', *Encyclopedia of Social and Behavioral Sciences* (Oxford: Elsevier), 7: 4481.

Lloyd-Bostock, S. (ed.) (1988), *Law in Practice* (London, Routledge and the British Psychological Society).

Lovelock, J. (2007), 'Ground Truth', *Prospect*, Dec. 2007: 68.

Malterud, K. (2006), Comment on Tonnelli (2006), *Journal of Evaluation in Clinical Practice*, 12: 248–55.

Memon, A., Vriej, A. and Bull, R. (eds.) (2003), *Psychology and Law: Truthfulness, Accuracy and Credibility* (Chichester, Wiley).

Michael, J. (1948), *Elements of Legal Controversy* (Brooklyn, NY, Foundation Press).

Michael, J. and Adler, M. (1931), *The Nature of Judicial Proof: an inquiry into the Logical, Legal and Empirical aspects of the Law of Evidence* (New York: privately printed).

Mill, J. S. (1843/1974), *System of Logic, Ratiocinative and Inductive* (*Collected Works* 7–8) (Toronto, University of Toronto Press).

Morgan, M. (2010), 'Travelling Facts', Introduction to P. Howlett and M. Morgan (eds.), *The Facts Book* (Cambridge, Cambridge University Press), pp. 3–40.

Nance, D. (1988), 'The Best Evidence Principle', *Iowa Law Review*, 73: 227–97.

Park, R. and Saks, M. (2006), 'Evidence scholarship reconsidered: results of the inter-disciplinary turn', *Boston College Law Review*, 47: 949–1031.

Perelman, Ch. (1963), *The Idea of Justice and the Problem of Argument* (trs. Petri) (New York, Humanities Press).

Perelman, Ch. and Olbrechts-Tyteca, L. (1969), *The New Rhetoric: a treatise on argumentation* (Notre Dame, IN, University of Notre Dame Press).

Phillipps, S. M. (1814), *A Treatise on the Law of Evidence* (London, Butterworth (9th edn., 1843)).

Pollock, F. (1899), 'Review of Thayer (1898), *A Preliminary Treatise on Evidence at Common Law*', *Law Quarterly Review*, 15: 86–7.

Postema, G. (1986), *Bentham and the Common Law* (Oxford, Oxford University Press).

Roberts, P. and Zuckerman, A. (2004), *Criminal Evidence* (Oxford, Oxford University Press).

Rorty, R. (1987), 'Science as Solidarity', in J. Nelson, A. Magill and D. McCloskey (eds.), *The Rhetoric of the Human Sciences* (Madison, WI, University of Wisconsin Press).

Rorty, R. (1991), *Objectivity, Relativism and Truth* (Cambridge, Cambridge University Press).

Roscoe, H. (1827), *A Digest of the Law of Evidence in the Trial of Actions at Nisi Prius* (London, Saunders and Benning).

Rowland, S. (2006). *The Enquiring University* (Milton Keynes, Open University Press).

Runciman, W. G. (ed.) (2004), *Hutton and Butler: lifting the lid on the workings of power* (London, The British Academy).

Schum, D. (1994/2001), *Evidential Foundations of Probabilistic Reasoning* (Chichester, Wiley; Evanston, IL, Northwestern University Press).

Schum, D. A. (1987), *Evidence and Inference for the Intelligence Analyst* (Lanham, MD, University Press of America).

Shapiro, B. (1983), *Probability and Certainty in Seventeenth Century England* (Princeton, NJ, Princeton University Press).

Shapiro, B. (1991), *Beyond Reasonable Doubt and Probable Cause: historical perspectives on the Anglo-American Law of Evidence* (Berkeley, CA, University of California Press).

Stern, N. (2007), *The Economics of Climate Change* (Cambridge, Cambridge University Press).

Stone, J. (1964), *Legal System and Lawyers' Reasonings* (London, Stevens).

Tanenbaum, S. (2006), Comment on Tonnelli (2006), *Journal of Evaluation in Clinical Practice*, 12: 273–6.

Taylor, J. P. (1848), *A Treatise on the Law of Evidence* (London, Maxwell).

Thayer, J. B. (1898), *A Preliminary Treatise on Evidence at Common Law* (Boston, MA, Little, Brown).

Tonnelli, M. (2006), 'Integrating evidence into clinical practice: an alternative to evidence-based approaches', *Journal of Evaluation in Clinical Practice*, 12: 248–56.

Toulmin, S. (1964), *The Uses of Argument* (Cambridge: Cambridge University Press).

Tribe, L. (1971), 'Trial by Mathematics: precision and ritual in legal process', *Harvard Law Review*, 84: 1329–93.

Twining, W. (1985), *Theories of Evidence: Bentham and Wigmore* (London, Weidenfeld and Nicolson).

Twining, W. (1997), 'Freedom of Proof and the reform of Criminal Evidence', *Israel Law Review*, 31: 439–63.

Twining, W. (2000), *Globalisation and Legal Theory* (London, Butterworth).

Twining, W. (2006), *Rethinking Evidence* (cited as *RE*) (2nd edn., Cambridge, Cambridge University Press).

Twining, W. and Hampsher-Monk, I. (eds.) (2003), *Evidence and Inference in History and Law* (Evanston, IL, Northwestern University Press).

Twining, W. and Weis, R. (2006), 'Reconstructing the truth about Edith Thompson: the Shakespearean and the Jurist', in W. Twining, *Rethinking Evidence* (2nd edn., Cambridge, Cambridge University Press), pp. 344–96.

Walton, D. (2008), 'A dialogical theory of presumptions', *Artificial Intelligence and Law*, 16: 209–43.

Warburton, N. (2009) 'Everyday Philosophy', *Prospect*, Dec. 2009: 25.

Weis, R. (2007), *Shakespeare Unbound* (New York: Holt).

Wigmore, J. H. (1908), 'Review of C. Moore *A Treatise on Facts, or the Weight and Value of Evidence*', *Illinois Law Review*, 3: 477–8.

Wigmore, J. H. (1913), *The Principles of Judicial Proof* (Boston, MA, Little, Brown (2nd edn., 1931; 3rd edn., 1937 sub. nom. *The Science of Judicial Proof*)).

Wigmore, J. H. (1940), *A Treatise on the System of Evidence in Trials at Common Law* (3rd edn.) (Boston, MA, Little, Brown).

5

Inference Networks:
Bayes and Wigmore

PHILIP DAWID, DAVID SCHUM, AND AMANDA HEPLER

Abstract

Wigmore charts and Bayesian networks are alternative approaches to the structuring and graphical display of complex interrelationships between items of evidence and questions of interest. The technologies have many similarities but also many differences, especially in the way in which the flow of information is represented. In this chapter we provide philosophical and technical introductions to both tools, highlighting natural points of comparison as they arise. We illustrate how both approaches can be used to marshal masses of evidence, focusing for definiteness on the eyewitness evidence presented in the celebrated murder trial of Sacco and Vanzetti in the 1920s.

1. Introduction

METHODS FOR PERFORMING complex probabilistic reasoning tasks, often based on masses of different forms of evidence obtained from a variety of different sources, are being sought by, and developed for, persons in many important contexts including law, medical diagnosis and intelligence analysis. The complexity of these tasks can often be captured and represented by graphical structures now called *inference networks*. These networks are *directed acyclic graphs* (DAGs), consisting of nodes, representing relevant hypotheses, items of evidence and unobserved variables, and arcs (arrows) joining some of the nodes, representing dependency relations among them. Such inference networks may be constructed by persons with different objectives in mind and who consequently view the networks as serving different purposes. One result has been that different interpretations are placed on the ingredients of inference networks, and different network structures emerge according to the various uses to which they may be put.

Proceedings of the British Academy, **171**, 119–150. © The British Academy 2011.

Inference networks can indeed serve various purposes; a major one is to provide a foundation for subsequent probabilistic analyses. They also serve as important heuristic devices for helping us to generate new lines of inquiry and evidence during the process of discovery and investigation. Finally, they can serve as an important and useful basis for subsequent narrative accounts of the process being studied.

Here we shall describe and comment on two different approaches to inference network construction that are currently being employed in several different contexts. In the first of these approaches, a DAG network structure is explicitly constructed as a vehicle for probabilistic analyses. Since the associated computations can be regarded as generalising the use of Bayes' rule, such networks are commonly called *Bayesian networks* (BNs); they are also referred to as *Probabilistic Expert Systems* (PES). Though other formal probabilistic systems might be employed in inference network analyses, it is fair to say that Bayesian approaches to probabilistic inference network analyses are currently predominant.

The second approach we describe stems from the work of the American jurist John H. Wigmore who, to our knowledge, was the very first person to attempt a systematic study of inference networks. Wigmore's inference networks are also DAGs that can sometimes be analysed by Bayesian methods. But this is not the underlying purpose of a Wigmorean inference network, which is to help us to make sense out of a mass of evidence in a defensible way. Wigmore networks are graphical representations of argument structures, in the form of chains of reasoning that are formed in defence of the relevance, credibility and inferential force of existing evidence. All network structures are in fact arguments, but the nature of the arguments being constructed are often different in Bayesian and in Wigmorean inference networks. We believe it is important and useful to provide a comparative analysis of these two approaches to inference network construction and employment. Both approaches have distinct virtues; each also has limitations that need to be discussed.

This account has developed as a 'trialogue' between three colleagues, each of whom has been active in the study and advancement of inference network technology over many years. Dawid and Hepler represent current views about Bayesian network construction and use, while Schum represents Wigmore's approach as well as the approach taken by several of his modern advocates. Our trialogue is in no sense adversarial: rather our intention is to identify and compare both the best features and the inherent limitations of the Bayesian network and Wigmore approaches.

The final book on complex probabilistic analysis has not yet been written; on some views at least, it may never be written. Our hope in this work is to enhance understanding of the various ways in which complex probabilistic inference tasks may be structured and interpreted.

2. Inference networks and Bayes' theorem
(Dawid and Hepler)

Bayes' theorem

Bayesianism is a particular approach to evidential reasoning, based on a single simple tenet: all uncertainty, whether it be interpreted as 'objective', 'subjective', or in any other way, can be uniformly described and manipulated using the standard probability calculus. In particular, inference about any unobserved uncertain quantity, event or hypothesis is fully expressed by means of its probability distribution (typically interpreted subjectively), appropriately conditioned on whatever evidence is taken into account. In order to apply Bayesian reasoning, we need to specify the initial ('prior') joint probability distribution over all relevant quantities, and manipulate this, using the standard laws of probability theory, to derive the conditional ('posterior') distribution of quantities of interest, given the evidence.

In general the quantities involved can be of arbitrary complexity, e.g. multivariate continuous variables. However for current purposes we confine attention to discrete quantities, with a finite number of possible states. An important special case is a binary variable, with values such as 0/1, YES/NO, MALE/FEMALE, etc. Any uncertain event or proposition can be regarded as such a binary variable, with possible values TRUE/FALSE. However variables with more than two states can be handled just as easily and it is generally a bad idea to try and represent everything in terms of propositions only.

Initial uncertainty about a quantity X is described by its probability function $p(x) = \Pr(X=x)$, specified for each possible outcome x of X, with 'Pr' denoting 'probability'. (When we need to be clear about which random variable X is involved we may write $p_X(x)$; however we will often omit the suffix when it is obvious from the context.) Similarly, the revised uncertainty about X, after observing the value y for some other variable Y, is described by the conditional probability function $p(x \mid y)$ (or, when the relevant variables are not clear from the context, $p_{X \mid Y}(x \mid y)$), defined as $\Pr(X=x \mid Y=y)$, for each possible outcome x of X and y of Y. Here the vertical bar | denotes 'conditional' on, or 'given'. As we vary x for any fixed y, $p(x \mid y)$ defines a regular probability distribution for X. In particular, if, keeping y fixed, we sum it over all possible values for x, we must obtain 1. However it is important to note that there is no such relationship constraining the terms p(x | y) as y varies with x fixed. These are the probabilities assigned to the identical event 'X=x', under differing hypothetical conditions 'Y=y'. There is no logical reason why these values should be related in any way whatsoever.

In the simplest case, we have an unknown quantity X of interest, but cannot observe X directly. We can however observe another quantity Y, stochastically related to X. Our task is to make inference about X on the basis of the evidence, i.e. the observed value y_o of Y. This is expressed by means of the posterior distribution p(x | y_o).

A simple graphical representation of this problem includes a node for each of X and Y, and an arrow from Y to X to represent the fact that the desired *flow of inference* is from Y to X. See Figure 5.1 (which is in fact considered a Wigmore chart as will become apparent in the next section). We can regard the arrow in Figure 5.1 as symbolically encoding the desired 'inferential' conditional distribution of X, p(x | y), for any potentially observed value y of Y.

However, in many applications it will not be natural to assess this inferential distribution directly. For example, X might represent a patient's blood pressure, and Y the reading on the doctor's sphygmomanometer. Known properties, error characteristics, etc. of the sphygmomanometer may mean that we can make reasonably good assessments of how it would respond when applied to a patient with specified blood pressure, i.e. of p(y | x), and these conditional distributions might often be reasonably regarded as substantially stable across different patients, doctors, clinics, etc. By contrast, the distribution p(x | y) would typically not embody such stability. If we knew that the local population had particularly high levels of blood pressure, we should rationally infer a higher value of X from any given reading of Y than we would in a different population susceptible to low blood pressure. In such a case it would be misleading to regard the inferential distribution p(x | y) as if it had a clear-cut meaning and value independent of the specific context at hand.

The conditional distribution p(y | x) represents the direction of the underlying *process*, rather than of the desired *inference*. Because it will often be reasonable to regard that process as reasonably stable, it will typically be appropriate to start by modeling this, and then apply Bayesian reasoning to

Figure 5.1.   Wigmore chart, representing flow of inference.

Figure 5.2.   Bayesian network, representing flow of causality.

determine the desired inferential distribution $p(x \mid y)$ as a derived quantity. The 'process model' can be represented as in Figure 5.2, where the arrow, now from X to Y, represents the flow of causality (loosely interpreted), and symbolically encodes the assumed 'process' conditional distribution of Y, $p(y \mid x)$. With this interpretation, such a diagram is called a Bayesian network (BN).

In this example the flow of causality, from X to Y, and the flow of the desired inference, from Y to X, are in opposite directions. This is often but not invariably the case: inference can proceed either with or against the flow of causality or, in a more complex network, through paths incorporating both these aspects within them. The Bayesian network approach is to represent directly only the flow of causality, specifying the associated 'causal' conditional distributions, and from this compute any desired inferential distribution.

The 'causal' assumption that $p(y \mid x)$ is relatively stable across different circumstances can be regarded as a form of (stochastic) generalisation, supporting the specific probability values $p(y \mid x)$ utilised.[1] For the reasons rehearsed above, such causal generalisations are typically more defensible than 'inferential' generalisations, that seek to justify values for $p(x \mid y)$. However, the phrasing of generalisations in everyday language (and even in more academic discussions) often leaves it unclear whether these are to be interpreted as causal or inferential. Consider, for example: 'A policeman tells the truth 95% of the time.' The causal interpretation would be: 'If a policeman observes an event E, then with probability 95% he will testify that E happened.' The inferential interpretation is: 'If a policeman testifies that E happened, then the probability is 95% that it did.' These are quite different statements, neither of which implies the other.[2] In a Wigmore chart, which represents inferential flow, it is most

[1] This is particularly useful when (as in the use of DNA research databases) we can gather relevant statistical data to estimate $p(y \mid x)$. These data might even be gathered under a range of contexts and conditions—so long as we can regard all of these as subject to the same causal probabilities $p(y \mid x)$ relevant to the case at hand.

[2] This is related to the infamous 'prosecutor's fallacy', where, faced with forensic testimony that, if the accused were innocent, the probability of his DNA matching that at the crime scene is (say) 1%, the prosecutor misrepresents this as implying that, if his DNA matches that at the crime scene, the probability that he is innocent is 1%. For more on this see A. P. Dawid, Probability and Proof' (online appendix to 'Analysis of Evidence', by T. J. Anderson, D. A. Schum and W. L. Twining), <http://tinyurl.com/tz85o>.

natural to regard generalisations as inferential; but since these may be unstable across different contexts this can lead to distortion.

In our simple example we have specified $p(y \mid x)$, but require $p(x \mid y_o)$. In fact there is no immediate relationship between these two quantities, and to proceed we need to introduce further information, in the form of the prior (marginal) distribution $p(x)$ of X, representing the uncertainty about X before the evidence on Y is taken into account. Once we have both these ingredients, we can apply the rules of probability theory in the form of Bayes' theorem:

$$p(x \mid y_o) = c \, p(x) \, p(y_o \mid x) \qquad \qquad \text{(Eqn. 1)}$$

where c is a number that has to be chosen so that the sum of $p(x \mid y_o)$ over all values of x is 1.

Note that, in Eqn. 1, y_o is regarded as fixed, at an actual or hypothetical observed value for Y. The only variable is x, which ranges over all possible values of the still uncertain quantity X. On the right-hand side x enters in both terms. The first term, $p(x)$, is itself a distribution (the prior distribution) for X. However the second term, $p(y_o \mid x)$, is not a distribution for x (indeed, will typically not sum to 1 over all values of x); rather, x indexes a variable hypothetical condition that might have generated the observation $Y = y_o$. As a function of the condition x for fixed observation y_o, this term is called the *likelihood function* for X based on the evidence $Y = y_o$.

In words, Eqn. 1 says 'the posterior probability is proportional[3] to the product of prior probability and likelihood'. Also, given both ingredients $p(y \mid x)$ and $p(x)$, we can compute the marginal distribution $p(y)$ of Y:

$$p(y) = \sum_x p(x) \cdot p(y \mid x) \qquad \qquad \text{(Eqn. 2)}$$

where $\sum_x$ denotes a sum over all values of x. Thus if we regard Figure 5.2 as implicitly encoding the prior distribution $p(x)$ of X (unconditional because there is no arrow into X) as well as the conditional distribution $p(y \mid x)$ of Y given X (represented by the arrow pointing from X to Y), by means of Eqns. 1 and 2 we can transform this representation into one that is similarly represented by Figure 5.1, incorporating both the marginal distribution $p(y)$ of Y (which however is often of little direct interest) and the desired inferential distribution $p(x \mid y)$.

We see then that, in this very simple case, a Bayesian network, although constructed to represent the flow of causality, also has all the power necessary

---

[3] This refers to the constant c, which does not depend on x (though it may depend on the evidence observed). As indicated above, it is easy to recover the value of c, if desired, through the condition that $p(x \mid y_o)$ constitute a probability distribution for X.

to represent the flow of inference, and thus to take on (albeit indirectly) the functions of a Wigmore chart.

More complex Bayesian networks

Figure 5.3 is a Bayesian network representation of a possible set of relationships between three variables, X, Y and Z. Extending the semantics of our simple example, we regard this as encoding: a marginal distribution p(x) for X; a conditional distribution p(y | x) for Y given X; and a further conditional distribution p(z | x) for Z given X. However, to define a joint distribution for the triple (X, Y, Z), we need the joint conditional distribution p(y, z | x) of the pair (Y, Z), given X, which is not uniquely determined by the above inputs. In order to construct this, we impose an additional assumption of *conditional independence* between Y and Z, given X. This is itself regarded as encoded in the graph by the absence of any arrow between Y and Z. Then we can apply the product formula, to obtain p(y, z | x) = p(y | x) p(z | x). Combining this with p(x) we obtain the overall joint distribution for (X, Y, Z) in the form p(x, y, z) = p(x) p(y | x) p(z | x). More straightforwardly, we can regard the figure as specifying that the overall joint distribution is obtained by multiplying the constituent terms associated with it; then the conditional independence property is automatically satisfied.

An alternative set of relationships is represented by Figure 5.4, in which the arrows of Figure 5.3 have been reversed. This now encodes the marginal distributions p(y), p(z), and the conditional distribution p(x | y, z) for X given the pair (Y, Z). The joint distribution is defined as the product of these terms, p(x, y, z) = p(y) p(z) p(x | y, z), and this has the property that Y and Z are independent marginally (i.e. not conditionally on x): p(y, z) = p(y) p(z). In particular (and unlike the situation with Figures 5.1 and 5.2), Figures 5.3 and 5.4 are not simply alternative ways of representing the same overall probability structure, but impose different restrictions on that distribution.

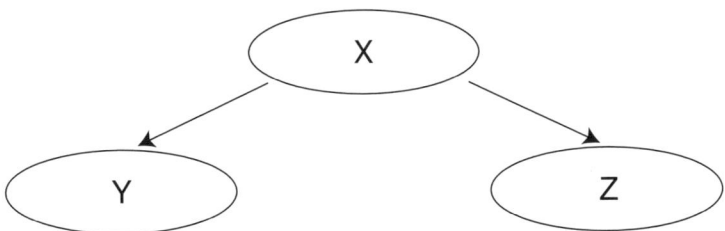

Figure 5.3.   Bayesian network incorporating conditional independence.

The above examples are special instances of a rigorous general mathematical description of the structure and meaning of a Bayesian network. In a general BN we have a collection of nodes, representing the variables in the problem, with some of these joined by arrows. There can be at most one arrow between any two nodes, and no way of following a directed path out of a node and back to the same node (in particular there can be no loopy arrow, from a node into itself). These conditions define a *DAG* (*directed acyclic graph*). Associated with any node V is a specification of its conditional distribution given its 'parents' (i.e. those nodes from which arrows lead into V)—for example, in Figure 5.4 the parents of X are Y and Z, so we have a term $p(x \mid y, z)$; since Y has no parents, there is nothing to condition on, so we have the marginal term $p(y)$, and similarly for Z. Finally, the overall joint distribution is constructed as the product of all these terms. Once we have this, we can in principle apply the standard rules of probability theory to compute any desired marginal or conditional distribution for some of the variables given some others (extending calculations such as those of Eqns. 1 and 2), so solving the problem of inference from evidence to still uncertain quantities. In practice, the required computations, if approached naively, can rapidly become prohibitively heavy; but there are efficient computational algorithms (implemented in computer software) that take advantage of the modular nature of the network to overcome this problem.

The machinery of Bayesian networks is not strictly essential to quantitative Bayesian analysis, which can proceed by algebraic and computational manipulations even in the absence of any simplifying assumptions of conditional independence. However, at this very general unstructured level it is typically extremely difficult to specify, and to justify, the high-dimensional joint distribution of all relevant quantities that is needed just to get started, as well as computationally overwhelming to process this to account for the impact of evidence. When it is possible to represent a problem by means of a

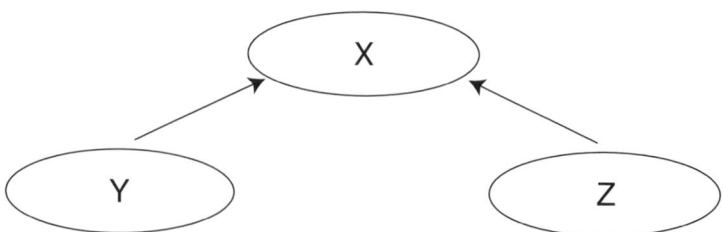

Figure 5.4. Bayesian network incorporating marginal independence.

Bayesian network, that can provide an effective means of dealing with both these problems.

Although quantitative computation is important, for evidential reasoning we can go a long way with the purely qualitative features of a Bayesian network. Indeed, in a parallel with Wigmore charts, we can regard these as fundamental, and the detailed probability specification as an optional add-on. As we have seen in Figures 5.3 and 5.4, Bayesian networks encode properties of marginal or conditional independence, which can be interpreted purely qualitatively. Thus if we assert that, given X, Y is independent of Z, we mean that, once information about X is at our disposal, further information about Z will be of no additional value for predicting Y: this is a statement that, once X is known, Z becomes *irrelevant* to Y. Properties of relevance and irrelevance are fundamental to evidential reasoning, and Bayesian networks provide a handy and logically rigorous way of representing and manipulating[4] these, even in the absence of any probabilistic interpretation.[5]

Considerations of relevance and irrelevance, and of the direction and stability of causal processes and other generalisations, can be used to guide the construction of a suitable Bayesian network representation of a problem; further conditional independencies may generally be assumed when the actual dependencies are regarded as likely to be weak. But choices need to be made, both of the network structure and (for conducting quantitative analysis) of the specific numerical probability values associated with it. There can be no definitive representation, and there will always be scope for discussion and further investigation of any specific choices made, and of the robustness of inferences to departures from them.

3. Wigmorean analysis
(Schum)

In many situations, law and intelligence analysis being prime examples, masses of information begin to accumulate as the process of discovery, investigation or inquiry unfolds. Alternative hypotheses are generated in order to explain what is being observed. Hypotheses taken seriously serve as devices for generating new lines of inquiry, new information and new or revised hypotheses. As

---

[4] The actual way in which we can read such properties off the network is somewhat subtle: see S. L. Lauritzen, A. P. Dawid, B. N. Larsen and H. G. Leimer, 'Independence properties of directed Markov fields', *Networks*, 20 (1990): 491–505.

[5] A. P. Dawid, 'Separoids: a mathematical framework for conditional independence and irrelevance', *Ann. Math. Artificial Intelligence*, 32 (2001): 335–72.

this process unfolds, and we begin to test hypotheses we have generated, natural questions arise concerning the bearing of acquired evidence on hypotheses being considered. This question concerns the *relevance* of an item of information on hypotheses being considered. Only when the relevance of an item of information on some hypothesis is established by argument can this item of information be termed *evidence*. Other natural questions concern the *credibility* or believability of evidence whose relevance has been established. Credibility considerations form the very foundation for all subsequent arguments based on evidence. At some stage in this complex process probabilistic judgements of various sorts are required concerning the *inferential (or probative) force or weight* of the accumulating evidence on hypotheses being considered.

The process just described is one that occurs when we have the task of trying to make sense out of some emerging mass of information. To use a modern phrase that has so often been applied in the wake of the 9/11/01 disasters in New York City and Washington DC, we have the task of trying to 'connect the dots'. There is nothing easy about this task. In the first place, there are different kinds of dots. Some refer to details in the information we obtain. Other dots refer to thoughts we have about these details as we construct arguments in defence of their relevance and credibility. Given masses of dots, which ones should we be trying to connect? What kinds of connections should we make among certain combinations of dots we have identified? Finally, we have the task of determining what these connections mean. It happens that the American jurist, John H. Wigmore (1863–1943) was the first person to make a systematic study of this process of making sense out of masses of evidence, or connecting the dots. He did so over ninety-five years ago.[6] In short, Wigmore was the first to study what we now call *inference networks*. Wigmore studied these networks in the context of law, a fact we need to keep in mind as we proceed. However, the methods he advocated are applicable in a wide variety of other situations in which we have the task of trying to make sense out of masses of evidence or are trying to 'connect the dots'.

Wigmore's analytic and synthetic methods

The methods Wigmore advocated concern the process of constructing arguments in defence of the relevance, credibility and inferential (probative) force

---

[6] J. Wigmore, 'The problem of proof', *Illinois Law Review*, 8/2 (1913): 77–103; J. Wigmore, *The Science of Judicial Proof: as given by logic, psychology and general experience and illustrated in judicial trials* (Boston, MA, Little, Brown & Co, 1937).

of evidence. In the process Wigmore said we need to perform two essential tasks. We first need to generate and list all the ingredients of our arguments; this is an *analytic task*. Then, we need to show how these ingredients are linked or related; this is a *synthetic task*. As I describe how Wigmore viewed these tasks we will be able to see their connection with the modern Bayesian network inference schemes Dawid and Hepler describe in Section 2. Wigmore's terms are different from those employed in contemporary work on inference networks. But there are important similarities that I will note.

The analytic task

In Wigmorean analysis we need to itemise all the ingredients of the arguments we are constructing. This itemisation Wigmore called a *key list*. Wigmore was one of the first to acknowledge that arguments consist of chains of reasoning *from evidence* to what we are trying to prove or disprove from this evidence. He referred to these chains of reasoning as involving *catenated inferences*, which he also said were inductive in nature. Each link in a reasoning chain represents a source of uncertainty or doubt. In any argument based on evidence we have hypotheses, evidence, and generalisations that license or justify the links in a chain of reasoning. But Wigmore never used the term *hypothesis*; instead he used the term *probandum* (a matter to be proved: plural *probanda*). In his terms, there are three important classes of probanda:

- The *ultimate probandum* represents the major charge a defendant is facing at trial. This ultimate probandum in most cases is a compound proposition. For example, in a charge of first degree murder, the ultimate probandum might read: 'It was defendant D who unlawfully and intentionally killed victim V with malice aforethought.'
- *Penultimate probanda* are specific binary propositions that usually result from a parsing of some ultimate probandum into main lines of argument that are necessary and sufficient to prove the ultimate probandum at some specified level of proof (such as 'beyond reasonable doubt'). In the Anglo-American legal system these penultimate probanda or main lines of argument on an ultimate probandum are given by substantive law. For example, a first degree murder charge specified in an ultimate probandum might be parsed to read: (i) Victim V was unlawfully killed; (ii) It was defendant D who intentionally killed victim V; and (iii) Defendant D fashioned the intent to kill V beforehand. Notice that each of these penultimate probanda is a binary proposition that may be judged true or false on the basis of evidence. What is interesting about inferences in the field of law is

that there are *materiality criteria* that specify what needs to be proved in any criminal or civil case. In other words, substantive law prescribes the penultimate probanda, or main lines of argument, on any ultimate probandum. These penultimate probanda are the material elements that must be proved and they provide touchstones for determining the relevance of any item of evidence that is to be admitted at trial. To be admitted at trial, any item of evidence must be shown relevant, by argument, to some penultimate probandum. Law is the only field known to me in which materiality criteria are prescribed for persons constructing arguments based on evidence.

- *Interim probanda* are also binary propositions and they refer to sources of doubt interposed between evidence and penultimate probanda. In other words, interim probanda are links in chains of reasoning from an item of evidence to one of the penultimate probanda. Determining which interim probanda reside between evidence and some penultimate probandum is an exercise in imaginative reasoning coupled with critical reasoning. There is no reference available to tell an attorney precisely how some item of evidence is linked, via interim probanda, to a penultimate probandum; this is where the necessity for imaginative reasoning arises. But it is also necessary for an attorney to carefully examine a chain of interim probanda to see that it does not have any disconnects, or non sequiturs, lurking anywhere in the chain. This is where the necessity for critical reasoning arises.

We must also, of course, list evidence items. In doing so, it is necessary to parse evidence into singular details whenever possible; this is particularly true for testimonial evidence provided by witnesses. A witness's testimony will ordinarily contain many details, some of which are relevant and others not. In principle, each evidential detail must be examined to judge whether it is true or false. This judgement is necessary in determining the credibility of the evidence. When two or more details are combined into the same evidence item it is not always possible to make such a determination. In addition, different details in the same evidence may be relevant to different penultimate probanda. Sherlock Holmes referred to these evidential details as 'trifles'; we could also call them evidential 'dots'.

Here is the first connection that can be observed between Wigmore's methods and Bayesian networks. All three types of probandum, as well as evidence items, are subject to doubt or uncertainty; they are regarded as *probabilistic variables*, and represented by the *nodes* of a Bayesian network.

Evidence nodes appear in all inference networks including Wigmore's. I have mentioned that penultimate and interim probanda are usually stated as binary propositions, which are either true or false. In constructing an argument in defence of the relevance of a certain item of evidence the person constructing the argument will have a specific sequence of propositions he/she must try to show are true. During such argument construction it is not necessary to enumerate all the specific reasons why any of these propositions might not be true. In current Bayesian inference networks the probabilistic variables need not be binary in nature; they may contain any number of mutually exclusive and exhaustive propositions. In fact, in some cases a probabilistic variable may be continuous in nature.

Finally, a key list can also contain *generalisations* that provide justification for reasoning from one probandum to another in a chain of reasoning. Generalisations are commonly if-then statements that are also hedged in some way. For example, reasoning from proposition or interim probandum E to proposition F might involve the generalisation: 'Whenever F occurs then E (usually, probably, often) occurs.' There are many different kinds of generalisations that arise in argument construction. Some are said to be matters of commonsense, but others may require specific knowledge. There is an account of the various kinds of generalisations that arise in argument construction provided by Anderson, Schum, and Twining.[7] Very often generalisations are not explicitly asserted and itemised on a key list. They would of course be listed if the person constructing an argument believed a reasoning step might be controversial.

The synthetic task

What Wigmore called his *chart method* involves linking evidence and probanda together to form coherent and defensible arguments *from evidence to penultimate probanda* or main lines of argument on an ultimate probandum. Wigmore used arrows (*arcs*) to construct chains of reasoning linking evidence to penultimate probanda through various interim probanda. In modern terms, his networks are *directed*, the arrows showing the direction of inductive reasoning *from* evidence *to* penultimate probanda. Wigmore's networks are also *acyclic*; i.e. there are no inferential reasoning loops that bring you back to where you started. Thus, a Wigmore chart is a DAG.

[7] T. Anderson, D. Schum and W. Twining, *Analysis of Evidence* (2nd edn.) (Cambridge, Cambridge University Press, 2005).

There are several points to be made about the interpretation of Wigmore's arrows or arcs. First, Wigmore charts are special DAGs, being hierarchical structures with a single node, the ultimate probandum, at the top of the hierarchy. Underneath the ultimate probandum appear the penultimate probanda, whose number and definitions depend on the ultimate probandum at issue. Then, chains of reasoning involving interim probanda link the evidence to the penultimate probanda. In most cases, two or more lines of reasoning will converge at several places in the reasoning hierarchy. So, the direction of reasoning in a Wigmore evidence chart is *upward, from* evidence *to* penultimate probanda.

The next important consideration concerns the meaning of Wigmore's directional arrows that link evidence and probanda at the various stages of the reasoning hierarchy. The direction of Wigmore's arrows reflects the flow of reasoning, and so generally differs from that of the arrows in a Bayesian network. Also, although Wigmore was no probabilist, he did understand that the linkages in a chain of reasoning are probabilistic in nature. His arrows represented what he termed the *force* of an evidence item on an interim probandum or the force of one probandum on another. Here Wigmore's lack of parsimony in his collection of symbols began to catch up with him. He attached different symbols on his arrows to indicate, in words, the strength of the inferential force of one node on another. Some of the verbal qualifiers he used were: 'strong force', 'weak force', and 'provisional force'. As noted in another work, Wigmore in fact used fuzzy qualifiers to indicate gradations of probative force.[8]

Wigmore also used a variety of different symbols for different nodes on his networks. This proliferation of symbols was one reason why, until recently, few people paid much attention to his chart method. The charting of masses of evidence can be made much simpler as Anderson, Twining, and I have illustrated.[9] Various persons who have taken Wigmore's methods seriously have attached other meanings to the arrows. For example, some might interpret the arrows to mean; 'tends to support', or 'tends to negate'. Other interpretations are possible. For example, since the major purpose of a Wigmore chart is to establish the relevance of evidence on major probanda or hypotheses, the arrows might well be interpreted as inductive relevance relations, since the direction of probabilistic reasoning is upward, from evidence to major hypotheses.

[8] P. Tillers and D. Schum, 'Charting new territory in judicial proof', *Cardozo Law Review*, 9/3 (1988): 907–66.
[9] See above, n. 7.

In modern applications of Bayesian networks a similar variety of interpretations has been used with reference to arrows or arcs.[10] In some accounts, the arrows mean simply 'probabilistic dependence' or 'probabilistic influence', or even 'is relevant to'. But in other accounts, notably Judea Pearl's,[11] the arrows can indicate supposed lines of causal influence. Wigmore's methods were basically designed to help persons establish the relevance and credibility credentials of masses of evidence. Relevance and causality are not the same, as I have argued elsewhere.[12]

Inference networks can be constructed with quite different objectives from those entertained in Wigmorean analyses. Many current Bayesian networks are designed to model a complex process of interest in which there is any number of nodes representing probabilistic variables. The arcs on such networks are said to indicate avenues of probabilistic influences or dependencies, or even causal influences, among these nodes. In another work I have described the inference networks constructed under such objectives as being *process models*.[13] The construction of a process model also involves analysis and synthesis as do Wigmore's methods. The probabilistic variables and their possible states must be described with care; this is the analytic part of the task. The synthetic part involves construction of the network showing how the person constructing the network believes these probabilistic variables are linked together. Not all nodes on a process model have observable states; those that do are usually termed *evidence nodes*. Although it does not directly represent patterns of inference or thought, a process model can be queried to determine, for any pattern of evidence, how the probability distribution at each probabilistic variable on the network would change (or fail to change) as a result of this evidence. It thus supports inferential reasoning, even though it does not represent it directly

Process models can have a quite different structural appearance from Wigmore evidence charts. In the first place, they need not be hierarchical structures as are Wigmore evidence charts. A process model may contain any

---

[10] This profusion can lead to confusion: See A. P. Dawid, 'Beware of the DAG!', in *Proceedings of the NIPS 2008 Workshop on Causality*, ed. I. Guyon, D. Janzing and B. Schölkopf, *Journal of Machine Learning Research Workshop and Conference Proceedings*, 6: 59–86.

[11] J. Pearl, *Probabilistic Reasoning in Intelligence Systems: networks of plausible inference* (San Mateo, CA, Morgan Kaufmann, 1988).

[12] D. Schum, *The Evidential Foundations of Probabilistic Reasoning* (New York, John Wiley & Sons, 1994; Northwestern University Press, paperback edn., 2001), pp. 140–56 in both edns.

[13] D. Schum, 'Alternative views of argument construction from a mass of evidence', *Cardozo Law Review*, 22/5–6 (July 2001): 1461–1502.

number of *root nodes* (nodes with no parent nodes). The probabilistic linkages in a process model may also be more intricate than those on Wigmore's
original evidence charts. As mentioned earlier, in Bayesian analyses of a process model these linkages may indicate the presence of *conditional dependencies*. These conditional dependencies are the major vehicle in Bayesian
analyses for capturing a remarkable array of evidential and inferential subtleties.[14] Again, Wigmore was no probabilist and was therefore not aware of the
conditional dependencies that his evidence charts might be made to reveal.
In one of the examples to follow I will illustrate how these conditional
dependencies can be captured using Wigmore's methods.

4. Analysis of selected evidence from
Sacco and Vanzetti trial

We shall give examples of the use of both Wigmore's methods and Bayesian
networks for making sense out of a mass of evidence. As we will illustrate,
both methods are useful in the analysis of an existing collection of evidence;
but they are also useful as aids to the process of discovery or investigation. All
of these examples come from analyses made of very large masses of evidence.
However, the examples here will involve just small portions of these analyses
to illustrate the points we wish to make about Wigmorean and Bayesian
network methods.

The following example comes from a probabilistic analysis performed on
the trial and post-trial evidence in the celebrated American law case of Nicola
Sacco and Bartolomeo Vanzetti.[15]

Opportunity evidence regarding Sacco

Briefly, Sacco and Vanzetti were accused of first-degree felony murder in the
slaying of a payroll guard named Alessandro Berardelli on 15 April 1920 in
South Braintree, Massachusetts. This forms the ultimate probandum in this
case. Sacco was specifically charged with killing Berardelli whereas Vanzetti
was charged with being an accomplice. Under Massachusetts law at the time,
the prosecution was obliged to prove beyond reasonable doubt the following

---

[14] See above, n. 12.
[15] J. Kadane and D. Schum, *A Probabilistic Analysis of the Sacco and Vanzetti Evidence* (New
York, John Wiley and Sons, 1996).

three penultimate probanda in order to sustain the charge against Sacco for first-degree felony murder.

P$_1$. Alessandro Berardelli died of gunshot wounds he received on 15 April 1920.

P$_2$. At the time he was shot, Berardelli was in possession of a payroll.

P$_3$. It was Nicola Sacco who, with the assistance of Bartolomeo Vanzetti, intentionally fired shots that took the life of Alessandro.

The only contested issue in this case was P$_3$.

Wigmorean analysis of opportunity evidence

In this example we focus attention just on Sacco. To prove P$_3$, as far as it concerns Sacco, one thing the prosecution had to prove was that Sacco had the *opportunity* to kill Berardelli; i.e. Sacco was at the scene of the crime when it occurred. The opportunity evidence in this case was given by seven witnesses, two for the prosecution and five for the defence. The two prosecution witnesses, Lewis Pelser and Lewis Wade, were labelled by the news media as being the 'star witnesses' in this case. We also consider the testimony of one of the defence witnesses named Albert Frantello. Here is the evidence given by these three witnesses:

- Lewis Pelser testified that he saw a man he identified as Sacco at the crime scene at the time the crime occurred.
- Lewis Wade testified that he saw a man who looked like Sacco at the crime scene at the time the crime occurred.
- Albert Frantello testified that Sacco was not at the scene of the crime about fifteen minutes before the crime was committed.

First consider Figure 5.5A that shows how Wigmore might have charted arguments justifying the relevance of each of these items of evidence on the penultimate probandum P$_3$. In Wigmore's original method, what are charted are propositions such as those on the following key list.

Key list

P$_3$: It was Nicola Sacco who intentionally fired the shots that took the life of Alessandro Berardelli during a robbery of the payroll he and Parmenter were carrying.

(1) Sacco was at the scene of the crime when it occurred.

(2) Lewis Pelser's testimony to (1).

(3) Someone who looked like Sacco was at the scene of the crime when it occurred.
(4) Lewis Wade's testimony to (3).
(5) Sacco was not at the scene of the crime about fifteen minutes before the crime occurred.
(6) Albert Frantello's testimony to (5).

Observe that items 1, 3 and 5 on this key list are probanda, or matters to be proved. They each state propositions that may be true or false. Items 2, 4, and 6 are also propositions, but they represent *given* items of evidence and are not probanda. Each of the probanda 1, 3, and 5 are in fact sources of doubt or uncertainty. To make a Wigmore chart amenable to probabilistic analysis, we need to have a representation that shows what these doubts actually concern. Figure 5.5B displays this same inference network in a way that does capture the major sources of doubt in the argument being constructed. Starting at the top, we have:

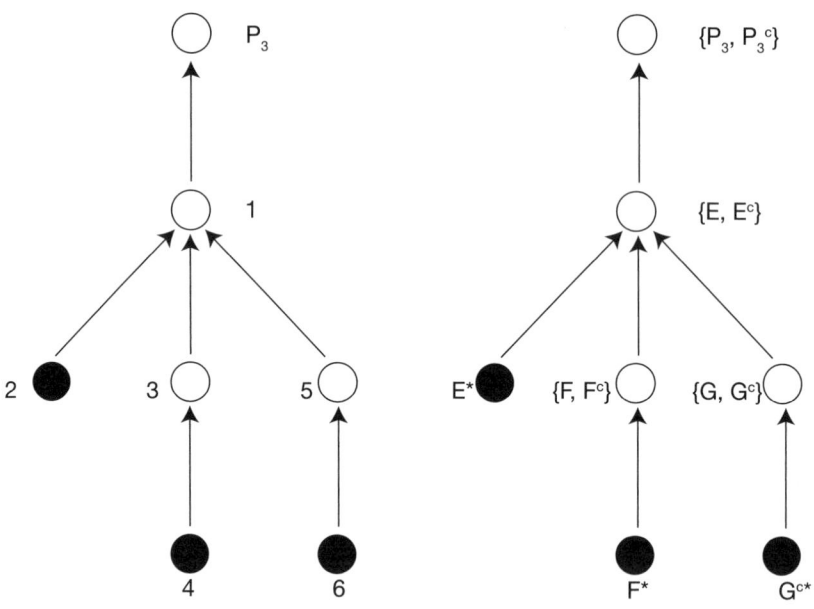

A. Wigmore Evidence Charting

B. Making Sources of Doubt More Specific

Figure 5.5.   Wigmore chart of opportunity evidence.

P_3: It was Nicola Sacco who intentionally fired the shots that took the life of Alessandro Berardelli during a robbery of the payroll he and Parmenter were carrying, and

P_3^c: It was *not* Nicola Sacco who intentionally fired the shots that took the life of Alessandro Berardelli during a robbery of the payroll he and Parmenter were carrying.

E = Sacco was at the scene of the crime when it was committed,

E^c = Sacco was not at the scene of the crime when it was committed,

E* = Pelser's testimony that event E occurred.

F = Someone who looked like Sacco was at the scene of the crime when it occurred,

F^c = No one who looked like Sacco was at the scene of the crime when it occurred,

F* = Wade's testimony that event F occurred.

G = Sacco was at the scene of the crime about fifteen minutes before the crime occurred,

G^c = Sacco was not at the scene of the crime about fifteen minutes beforethe crime occurred.

G^{c*} = Frantello's testimony that event G did not occur.

One thing Wigmore understood very well, that is also captured in modern Bayesian inference networks, is the necessary distinction between evidence about some event and the event itself. In Figure 5.5A, for example, there is a clear distinction between the event that Sacco was at the scene of the crime when it occurred (2) and Pelser's testimony that he was (1). In Figure 5.5B this distinction is preserved because E* is just evidence of event E. This distinction captures the important credibility-related foundations of all chains of reasoning. Just because Pelser tells us that Sacco was at the scene at the time of the crime does not entail that this event did occur. So, from E* we can only infer, at some level of probability, that event E did occur. How strong this inference can be depends on Pelser's credibility. As it happened, Pelser's credibility was severely challenged during the trial and was damaged further by evidence that came to light after the trial. The second Wigmorean example involves examining credibility matters in greater detail.

Bayesian network representation of opportunity evidence

When representing the opportunity evidence regarding Sacco as a Bayesian network, construction proceeds smoothly as a result of having already performed a Wigmorean analysis of the evidence. The process would prove much more difficult if one were to attempt to build the network without taking this time to think carefully about all evidential items and their interrelationships. This illustrates how a fusion of Wigmorean and Bayesian network approaches can be advantageous.

To begin, P_3 becomes a node in the network, shown in Figure 5.6. In order for P_3 to have occurred, the event E must also have occurred, and it is converted into a Boolean node in our network, labelled **At Scene?**

We next consider the supposition G: Sacco was at the scene of the crime about fifteen minutes before the crime occurred. This node is also directly converted to a Boolean node, **At Scene Early?** The direction of the arrow between **At Scene Early?** and **At Scene?** arises from the temporal relationship between these two variables. Sacco having been at the scene shortly before the crime occurred influences whether or not Sacco was at the scene during the commission of the crime. It is also important to note the absence of an arrow between P_3 and **At Scene Early?** Once we know whether or not Sacco was at the scene during the commission the crime, knowing whether or not he was there earlier does not provide any additional information helpful in determining whether or not Sacco committed the crime. Thus, these two variables are independent, conditional on the variable **At Scene?**

The advantages of formal reasoning are apparent here in that the dependence among variables, and the relevance thus implied, is expressly represented. This aids the reasoner by ensuring focus on relevant items of evidence, ignoring those having no bearing on the proposition of interest. This idea of modular reasoning is further enhanced by the use of network fragments as will be shown below in the section on 'Hierarchical Bayesian network representation of credibility evidence'.[16]

In addition to the graphical representation of Figure 5.6, a table of conditional probabilities must be specified for each node we include in our network. In forensic casework these probabilities are often difficult to specify exactly. Here we present what we feel are reasonable values, while issuing a strong caution that these are purely illustrative, subjective and evidently contestable. Appropriate values for conditional probabilities need to be determined on a case by case basis, using expert input from all informed members of the investigational team. For our purposes the numerical aspects of the BN representation are in any case secondary to the primary graphical representation, which displays the assumed qualitative relationships (of dependence,

---

[16] See below, p. 144.

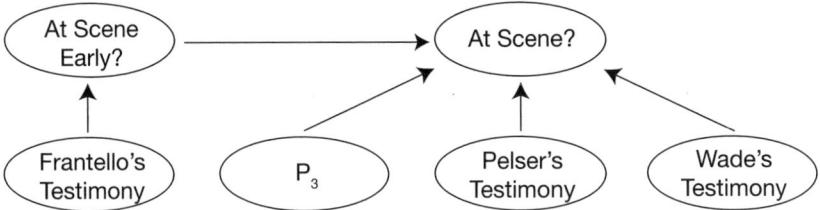

Figure 5.6.   Bayesian network of opportunity evidence.

causality, relevance, etc.) between the hypotheses, events and variables under consideration.

We first specify the (unconditional) probabilities for the states of node **At Scene Early?** At this stage, we have no evidence to suggest he was at the scene, so we make this probability suitably small, say 0.01. By subtraction, the probability of not being at the scene must be 0.99. In the next section testimonial evidence will be introduced into our network, which will in turn update these probabilities to values more appropriate for this specific case.

Reading down the columns, Tables 5.1 and 5.2 give the assumed conditional probabilities for **At Scene?** and P_3, respectively. Eyewitness accounts concurred that the two assailants had been leaning on a pipe-rail fence lying in wait for their victims. Thus, if Sacco was there, leaning on the fence, fifteen minutes prior to the commission of the crime, it is more likely than not that he would be there at the time of the crime. That is Pr(**At Scene?** = true| **At Scene Early?** = true) = 0.90. However, if Sacco was not at the scene early, there is still some positive probability (perhaps 0.01 that he arrived within this fifteen minute time span. Appealing to the law of total probability, the values

Table 5.1:   Conditional probabilities for **At Scene?**

	At Scene Early?	
At Scene?	True	False
True	0.90	0.01
False	0.10	0.99

Table 5.2:   Conditional probabilities for P_3

	At Scene?	
P_3	True	False
True	0.05	0.00
False	0.95	1.00

in the bottom row of Table 5.1 are found by subtraction. Turning now to Table 5.2, if Sacco was in fact at the scene, we can assume the probability of guilt is rather small (0.05), as no a priori evidence suggests Sacco was the perpetrator. Under the assumption that Sacco was not at the scene, there is no chance that he committed the crime, giving a probability of 0 in this cell. Again the values in the bottom row can be determined by subtraction.

At this point all that remains to describe in our network are the individual testimonies of Pelser, Wade and Frantello. Through this process we will indirectly include the proposition, F = Someone who looked like Sacco was at the scene of the crime when it occurred. This proposition solely arises as a result of the testimony Wade provided: when asked 'Did you see Sacco at the scene?' Pelser also responded to this question, and testified 'Yes I saw Sacco at the scene.'

In creating a **Testimony** node, we assume four possible states:[17]

T_1: Witness says 'Sacco was at the scene'
T_2: Witness says 'someone similar to Sacco was at the scene'
T_3: Witness says 'Sacco was not at the scene'
T_4: Witness's testimony does not relate to whether or not Sacco was at the scene

The additional flexibility afforded by multiple states is a benefit here as we can now distinguish between evidence of absence (T_3) and absence of evidence (T_4). This distinction is lost when, as in Wigmorean analysis, binary nodes are used.

Both Pelser and Wade testified as to whether or not Sacco was at the scene of the crime. Thus, there is a probabilistic dependence between **At Scene?** and each of their testimonies. The same is true for **Frantello's Testimony** and the event **At Scene Early?** Without considering any other information as to the credibility of the witness, we assume that, whether or not Sacco was at the scene, an eyewitness would testify to that fact correctly 85% of the time. When an error or equivocation is made, we distribute the remaining probability over these possible states. The resulting conditional probability table for both Pelser's and Wade's testimonies is shown in Table 5.3.

Next we turn to Frantello's testimony. He stated that Sacco was not at the scene of the crime fifteen minutes before the crime occurred. The states here

---

[17] In fact it turns out that, when we have observed the state at a **Testimony** node, only the (conditional) probabilities for that state are relevant for further analysis; so it is only ever really necessary to include two states: the actual testimony, and anything else, with their relevant probabilities. But it is nevertheless good discipline to take the prospective modelling focus of a BN seriously, and so think about what alternatives might have occurred.

Table 5.3: Conditional probabilities for Pelser's and Wade's testimonies

Testimony	At Scene?	
	True	False
T_1	0.85	0.05
T_2	0.05	0.05
T_3	0.05	0.85
T_4	0.05	0.05

are equivalent to T_1–T_4 above, replacing 'at the scene' with 'at the scene early'. Assuming again a 'hit rate' of 0.85, the probability table for **Frantello's Testimony** is similar to Table 5.3, replacing **At Scene?** with **At Scene Early?**

Decomposing links in chains of reasoning: a credibility example

An important fact that Wigmore asked us to consider years ago is that there can be no final uniquely correct chain of reasoning, or inference network for that matter. Someone can always suggest a link in a reasoning chain, or probabilistic variable, that we have left out. Other persons may of course have arguments concerning how we have defined our sources of doubt or how we have linked them together. In short, there are no unique normatively correct chains of reasoning or inference networks. Next, we consider possible decompositions of the reasoning chain between a particular event and an eyewitness' account of that event.

Wigmorean analysis of credibility evidence

As an example of how a chain of reasoning can be further decomposed to capture additional important sources of doubt, first consider Figure 5.7A. This figure shows a chain of reasoning from Pelser's testimony E* to the penultimate event class $\{P_3, P_3^c\}$ as in Figure 5.5B. Suppose someone says: 'You have said that the link between E* and $\{E, E^c\}$ concerns Pelser's credibility. But the credibility of human sources of evidence is a multi-attribute characteristic.' In particular, we are obliged to consider whether a person is reporting an event he/she truly believes to have happened; this concerns his/her *veracity*. The next question we should consider is how this person formed a belief about what he/she reported. Was this belief formed on the basis of sensory evidence obtained during an observation, or was this belief based instead on what the person either expected or wished to have happened? This concerns the person's *objectivity*. Finally, if this source's belief about the event reported was based on sensory evidence, how good was this evidence? This concerns the source's *sensory sensitivity* including the conditions under which the observation was made. As you observe, each of these three credibility attributes represents a source of doubt: (i) Was Pelser being truthful?; (ii) Was Pelser an objective observer?; and (iii) Was Pelser an accurate observer?

In Figure 5.7B we have decomposed the E*, {E, E^c} in Figure 5.7A to capture these three sources of credibility-related uncertainty. The first link concerns Pelser's veracity and involves the events:

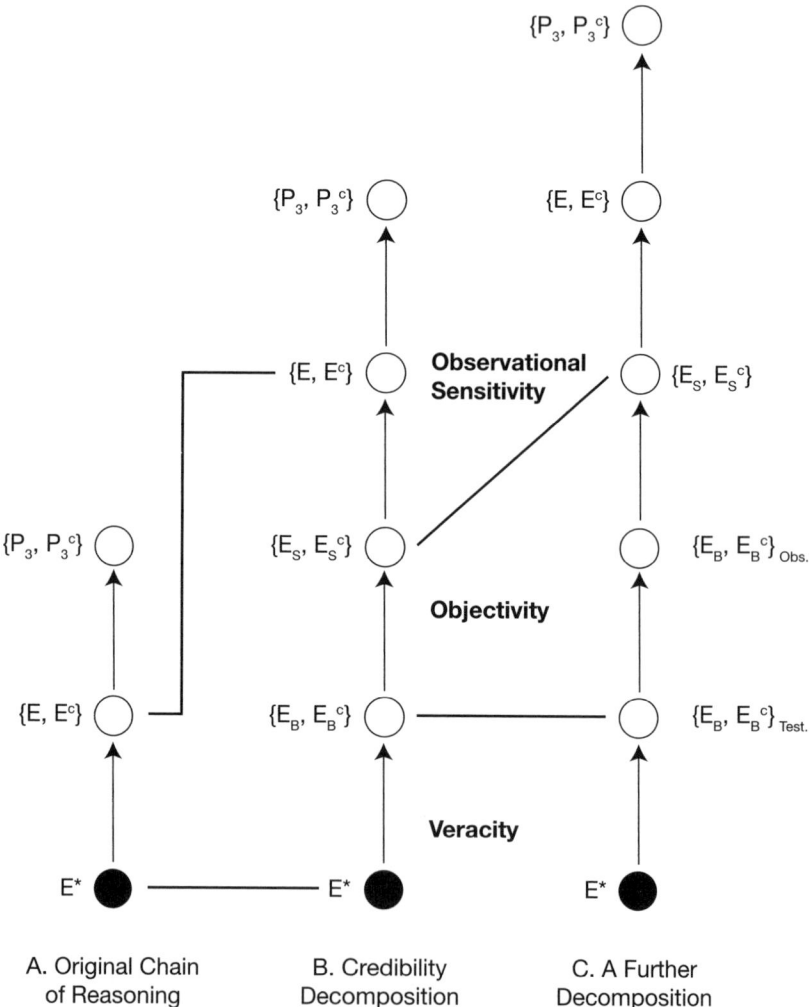

Figure 5.7.   Decomposing a chain of reasoning.

E_B = The event that Pelser believes what he testified, that Sacco was at the scene of the crime when it was committed, and

E_B^c = The event that Pelser does not believe that Sacco was at the scene of the crime when it was committed. Notice that this event incorporates two possibilities: (i) Pelser believes that Sacco was not at the scene of the crime when it was committed, or (ii) Pelser has no belief about this event one way or the other; i.e. he was instructed about what to tell the jury. (This turns out to have been a distinct possibility.)

At the next link in the chain of reasoning we consider whether Pelser based his belief about what he testified on sensory evidence he obtained, or whether he based his belief on what he expected or desired to observe; but there is another possibility we must capture. At this objectivity link we have the events:

E_S = The event that Pelser did base his belief about what he testified on the basis of sensory evidence he obtained, and

E_S^c = The event that Pelser did not base his belief on the basis of sensory evidence. Notice that the event incorporates two possibilities: (i) Pelser ignored his sensory evidence and believed what he expected or desired to observe, or (ii) Pelser obtained no sensory evidence at all; he was told what to testify.

Finally, if Pelser did obtain sensory evidence about the event to which he testified, how good was this sensory evidence; did event E occur or not? As noted above, this concerns Pelser's observational sensitivity and the conditions under which he made his observation (if indeed he made one).

If we took the decomposition in Figure 5.7B to be our final decomposition, believing we had captured all major credibility-related doubts, we would be leaving ourselves open to a critic who says the following: 'Our beliefs are known to be supple or elastic; they change over time. As far as Pelser is concerned, which of his possible beliefs are you talking about? His belief at the time he gave his testimony, or his belief at the time he made his alleged observation? There was a considerable interval of time separating these two situations; don't you have any doubts about whether Pelser changed his beliefs between the time he made an observation and the time of the trial?' So, as Figure 5.7C illustrates we must first consider events concerning his beliefs at the time he gave his testimony; these we capture by events in the class $\{E_B, E_B^c\}_{Test.}$ Then we must consider what beliefs he might have held at the time he made his alleged observation; these we capture by events in the class

$\{E_B, E_B^c\}_{Obs.}$ The idea here is that the state of Pelser's beliefs while giving testimony only provides a basis for an inference about what Pelser believed at the time he made his alleged observation.

There is literally no end to such further decomposition; this is especially true when time is involved as is the case with Pelser's beliefs. Several months elapsed between the time of the crime and the time of the trial. We might have doubts about what Pelser believed or did not believe at any point in this time interval. Many years ago[18], John Venn, talking about chains of reasoning, said 'Nature is continuous, and it depends on the degree of minuteness to which we decide to work, and upon the existence of appropriate names for the intermediate events, whether or not we impose any of these links.' There's an especially important message here for Wigmorean or any other analysis of inference networks. How finely we choose to decompose our chains of reasoning, or how many doubts we should attempt to capture, presents quite a problem. This problem is often called *paralysis by analysis*. We may be able to identify more sources of doubt than anyone could reasonably make sense of in the analysis of any inference network.

Hierarchical Bayesian network representation of credibility evidence

As mentioned, the credibility of a witness is a multifaceted construct that can be decomposed in various ways to capture additional sources of doubt. One natural way to represent this decomposition is to impose a hierarchical structure on the Bayesian network. In the hierarchical network, or *object oriented Bayesian network*, shown in Figure 5.8, we represent those sources of doubt using a decomposition similar to that shown in Figure 5.7. To describe this we will use as an example Pelser's testimony that he saw Sacco at the scene of the crime.

For this case the **Event?** node is an exact replica of the **At Scene?** node discussed earlier. **Competent?** is a Boolean node capturing the uncertainty about whether or not the witness was competent to observe the event: i.e. what were the conditions under which the observations were purportedly made? Often ancillary evidence can shed light on the appropriate probabilities that should be assigned for the competence of a particular witness. In Pelser's case we have additional testimony that he may have been under a table, which would lead to his view of the scene being obstructed. This additional evidence can be modelled in a separate network and added into the existing network and, as we will see, it has the effect of increasing the probability that Pelser

[18] J. Venn, *The Principles of Empirical or Inductive Logic* (London, Macmillan & Co. Ltd., 1907), p. 506.

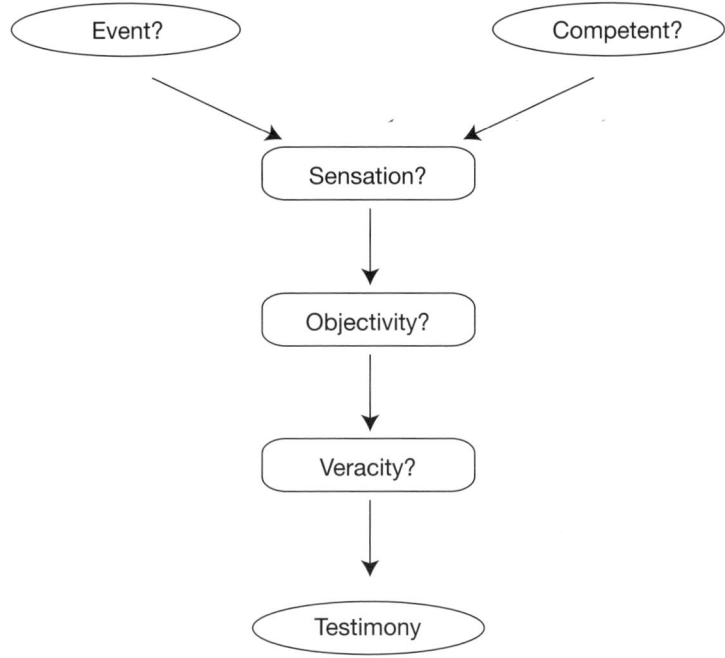

Figure 5.8.   Hierarchical Bayesian network for witness credibility.

was incompetent.[19] The **Testimony** node can take on four states, T_1–T_4, as described earlier.

The remaining rectangular nodes represent network *classes*, fragments of BNs that can be instantiated within this larger network. Each corresponds to one of the attributes of credibility mentioned earlier: Observational Sensitivity, Objectivity and Veracity.

The *Observational Sensitivity* network class is shown in Figure 5.9. The **Event?** and **Competent?** nodes are exact replicas of those shown in Figure 5.8. To model the uncertainty that exists at this level of the chain of credibility assessment, we pass the event information through a *Noisy Filter* network class labelled **Agreement?** This class is shown in Figure 5.10.

The input and output of this filter will match if the Boolean node **Correct?** is true. In this example the **In** node has two states (taken directly from the **Event?** node in Figure 5.9): Sacco was at the scene; Sacco was not at the scene.

---

[19] As a simpler approximate device, we could do this directly via the **Competent?** node.

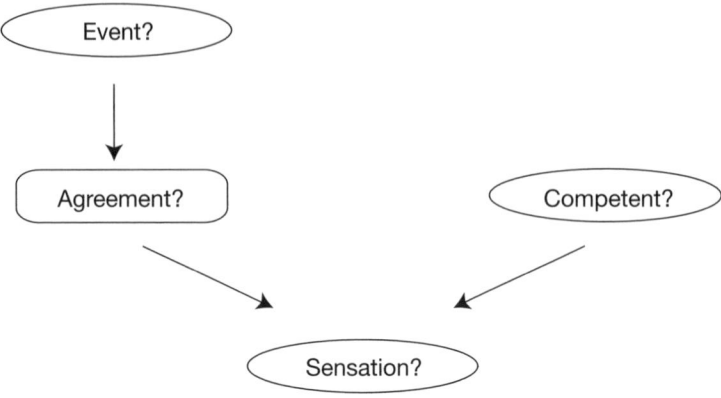

Figure 5.9.   *Observational sensitivity* network class.

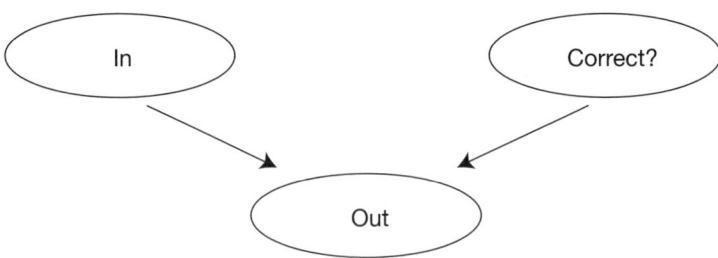

Figure 5.10.   *Noisy Filter* network class.

The **Out** node will have four states, corresponding to the four possible testimonies Pelser could have given (T_1, T_2, T_3, T_4 as defined for Table 5.5 in the previous section). When the witness is correct and the **In** node takes on the value 'Sacco at scene', the state of the **Out** node is set to T_1. If instead, the **In** node takes on the value 'Sacco not at scene' (and the **Correct?** node remains true), then the **Out** node is set to T_3.

We assume that the witness will base his belief about what he testified on the basis of sensory evidence he obtained 90% of the time, thus the probability with which the **Correct?** node will be true is 0.90. (Again, we emphasise that the specific probabilities entered here are highly subjective and must be assigned on a case-by-case basis.) In scenarios where **Correct?** is false, we assume the witness will err equally often towards the other three testimonies. So that if Sacco was at the scene and the **Correct?** node is set to false, there is a probability of 1/3 that the witness's testimony will be either (equivocally) T_2, (falsely) T_3, or (uninformatively) T_4. On the other hand, if Sacco was not at the scene the correct testimony would be T_3. Thus, when incorrect the witness will testify to T_1, T_2, or T_4 equally often. This can be seen in the probabilities shown in Tables 5.4 and 5.5.

Turning back to initial credibility network shown in Figure 5.8, the two remaining rectangular nodes are both instances of a slightly modified *Noisy Filter* class. The first corresponds to Schum's notion of objectivity: Did Pelser testify based on an objective understanding of his sensation? The output variable from the **Sensation?** node is directly copied into the **In** node for noisy filter. This differs from the previous filter as the input was a Boolean node. The graphical portion remains unchanged from Figure 5.10, however the conditional probabilities assigned to **Out** node are altered, as shown in Table 5.6.

The final rectangular node from Figure 5.8 corresponds to veracity: Did Pelser truthfully report what he believed? This is another copy of the modified *Noisy Filter* network class just described.

For simplicity, we described the credibility network specifically in relation to Pelser's testimony. However, the modular nature of hierarchical networks

Table 5.4: Probabilities for **Correct?** node from *noisy filter* network class

Correct?	
True	0.90
False	0.10

Table 5.5: Conditional probabilities for the **Out** node from the *noisy filter* network class

In	Sacco at Scene		Sacco not at Scene	
Correct?	True	False	True	False
T_1	1	0	0	1/3
T_2	0	1/3	0	1/3
T_3	0	1/3	1	0
T_4	0	1/3	0	1/3

Table 5.6: Conditional probabilities for the **Out** node from the modified *noisy filter* network class

In	T_1		T_2		T_3		T_4	
Correct?	True	False	True	False	True	False	True	False
T_1	1	0	0	1/3	0	1/3	0	1/3
T_2	0	1/3	1	0	0	1/3	0	1/3
T_3	0	1/3	0	1/3	1	0	0	1/3
T_4	0	1/3	0	1/3	0	1/3	1	0

allows us to reuse it for any other witnesses testifying either to the event **At Scene?** or to the event **At Scene Early?** We can allow the probability specifications to vary according to the individual providing the testimony, and according to any additional ancillary evidence relevant to the three credibility attributes. In general, portability of modules is an advantage of using a formal, object-oriented approach for evidence analysis. It is common to find certain patterns of evidence used repeatedly, both within a single case and across different cases. For example, eyewitness testimony commonly arises in criminal casework. Object-oriented Bayesian networks allow a user to model eyewitness testimony as a generic basic network, and then reuse this module (perhaps with some modifications) throughout the main network and/or in further networks.

Additionally, hierarchical network construction assists the reasoner by providing a formal methodology to assist in breaking down an (at times over-whelming) evidential analysis task into many smaller, more manageable analysis tasks. Thus, instead of building a network for the entire Sacco and Vanzetti case all at once, one could consider each collection of evidence in turn, creating a module for each. Once each module is created and approved, the modules are placed into a top-level network, significantly simplifying the analysis task. In addition, this architecture facilitates a 'top-down' approach, in which the details of lower level modules do not have to be specified at the very beginning.

5. Summary

We have briefly outlined the nature and interpretation of two kinds of graph for reasoning about evidence: Bayesian networks and Wigmore charts. Both Wigmore charts and Bayesian networks are helpful graphical devices for displaying, controlling, manipulating and communicating complex sets of relationships between hypotheses of interest and a mass of evidence. These relationships will generally reflect the standpoint of the individual construct-ing the graph, rather than any putative 'objective truth'. At a superficial level the two types of representation are similar, both involving directed acyclic graphs (DAGs), where evidence, hypotheses, unknown variables and other focuses of uncertainty are displayed as nodes of the graph, and some of these are joined by arrows (the graphs are *acyclic* because we can not follow the arrows to arrive back where we started). And both serve the common purpose of taking a large and complex mass of interrelated evidence and breaking it down into smaller (and thus more interpretable and manageable) modules, which fit together to make up the whole story.

However, closer attention reveals a number of significant differences. A Wigmore chart is structured like an upside down tree (or like a root-system), with a single ultimate probandum at the very top, the penultimate probanda immediately below that, and then a branching out downwards to incorporate the various other nodes. The nodes themselves are usually atomic uncertain propositions inhabiting a key-list, and the arrows between them, pointing upwards, are intended to represent inferential relevance and patterns of thought. Wigmore himself used a large palette of symbols to annotate his charts with indications of the evidential import and force by which one proposition weighs for or against another to which it points, although modern developments have abandoned most of these. The principal purpose of constructing a Wigmore chart is to help the constructor synthesise the many individual relationships between evidence items and hypotheses into a large scale system that can support synthesis of the evidence and qualitative reasoning about the way it combines together.

By contrast, in a Bayesian network there need be no single proposition of special interest, and it typically will not look like a tree. The nodes of the network can represent uncertain variables with any number of possible values, not just binary propositions, and typically are not decomposed into more specific atomic constituents. Arrows joining nodes now indicate direct probabilistic dependence, and are typically interpreted as going with the flow of the underlying causal or developmental processes, rather than with the desired inferential processes. In particular, absence of an arrow reflects a local irrelevance property, and there are formal rules for examining the whole network to answer qualitative conditional relevance questions, such as 'If I know A, would learning B teach me anything new about C?' Also, although we have emphasised qualitative aspects of reasoning, Bayesian networks can be annotated with numerical probabilities describing local relationships between variables, and used to compute efficiently the probabilities of more complex scenarios. In particular, even though a Bayesian network is constructed to represent directly the process by which events are considered to develop, it can be queried to answer inferential questions.

We believe that both these graphical technologies have positive and negative features, and that a suitable combination of the best of both worlds would supply a still more valuable technology. Thus, the ultimate objective is the development of a formal tool which jointly exploits the specific strengths of both Wigmore charts and BNs.[20]

[20] For a suggestion as to how this might look, see A. B. Hepler, A. P. Dawid and V. Leucari, 'Object-oriented graphical representations of complex patterns of evidence', *Law, Probability & Risk*, 6 (2007): 275–93.

6. Suggestions for further reading

Anderson, T., Schum, D. and Twining, W. (2005), *Analysis of Evidence* (2nd edn.) (Cambridge, Cambridge University Press).

Cowell, R. G., Dawid, A. P., Lauritzen, S. L. and Spiegelhalter, D. J. (1999), *Probabilistic Networks and Expert Systems* (New York, Springer-Verlag).

Dawid, A. P. (2010), 'Beware of the DAG!', in *Proceedings of the NIPS 2008 Workshop on Causality*, ed. I. Guyon, D. Janzing and B. Schölkopf, *Journal of Machine Learning Research Workshop and Conference Proceedings*, 6: 59–86.

Hepler, A. B., Dawid, A. P. and Leucari, V. (2007), 'Object-oriented graphical representations of complex patterns of evidence', *Law, Probability & Risk*, 6: 275–93.

Schum, D. (1994), *The Evidential Foundations of Probabilistic Reasoning* (New York, John Wiley & Sons; pbk edn., Northwestern University Press, 2001), pp. 140–56 in both edns.

6

Arguing about the Evidence:
a Logical Approach

JOHN FOX

Abstract

Evidence-based practice is the norm in law and science, and is increasingly demanded in fields like clinical medicine and social policy. As pressures for *evidence-based-everything* grow there is a concomitant need to develop clear ways of discussing evidence and, ideally, formal ways of reasoning with and about it. Unfortunately the concept of evidence differs across different domains so we must first find some unifying framework. One influential tradition has it that *evidence is any kind of information that increases or decreases confidence in a hypothesis or claim*, and that *a good tool for formalising the notion of confidence is mathematical probability*. The view developed here accepts the first part of this tradition but argues that the second part is frequently impractical. An alternative is proposed in which confidence is determined first by logical argumentation and secondly by considering the range and relative strength of these arguments. Two complementary modes of argumentation are discussed. *Evidential argumentation* builds on the common sense notion that the more supporting (opposing) arguments there are for a claim the more (less) our confidence in it. *Dialectical argumentation* builds on the equally commonplace observation that confidence is influenced by arguments that 'attack' or 'corroborate' each other as well as directly supporting or opposing claims. This framework is discussed in terms of a number of desirable features of a formal system for arguing about evidence, and is illustrated with natural examples drawn from evidence-based decision-making in medicine.

Introduction

EVIDENCE IS AN important human preoccupation. It is important, for example, when we want to decide whether some scientific or medical claim is true; when

Proceedings of the British Academy, **171**, 151–182. © The British Academy 2011.

we are considering how best to act in circumstances where there is uncertainty about the outcomes of our actions, and when one individual's opinion on some important matter might or might not be superior to that of someone else. Increasing demands for scientific evidence in legal proceedings, in formulating social policy and in the movement for *evidence-based medicine* suggest that the opinions of people who are simply deemed to be 'experts' in a subject are not trusted to the degree that they once were.

During a recent edition of the BBC discussion programme *More or Less* the presenter Tim Harford observed that

> It is hard to object to the idea of evidence-based policy making, the idea that policies should meet some sort of test, to make sure they do 'what is said on the tin'. Policies should be developed with the advice of experts, rather than spin-doctors or pressure groups, based on the best statistical evidence rather than an opinion poll. And this matters. When our children are taught to read or write, when we go to see our [family doctor], or when we negotiate some new traffic calming scheme, what we would all like to think is that someone, somewhere has found evidence, 'real evidence', that the teaching method, or the medical treatment, or the road design actually work.   (16 January 2009)

Given that a sound rationale for our beliefs and actions can be critical to success or failure—as individuals, societies and even as a species—it is surprising that people do not seem to be very good at evidence-based thinking, at least not in the statistical sense that the above quote assumes. Our everyday decisions are rough and ready rather than precise and evidential. Psychological studies of human reasoning and decision-making suggest that our reasoning about the *risk* of dangerous things happening or the *likelihood* of our actions achieving the intended effects is subject to common misconceptions and also deeper logical fallacies and biases.[1] Identification of apparent shortcomings in human judgement has led to a growing interest in developing rational, mathematical foundations for evaluating claims, and the use of computers as 'cognitive prostheses' to improve our decision-making in medicine and science and even public policy and the law.

The main exemplar of evidence-based thinking we will discuss in this chapter is evidence-based medicine, though we will make some comparative comments about evidential reasoning in science and law as well. This movement emerged in the early 1970s. Early advocates like Cochrane in the UK and Eddy in the USA[2] and many others since raised doubts about the

---

[1] <http://en.wikipedia.org/wiki/Cognitive_bias>.
[2] For a recent discussion see D. M. Eddy, 'Evidence-Based Medicine: a unified approach', *Health Affairs*, 24/1 (2005): 9–17.

reliability of subjective expert opinion, and their insistence on scientific justification for clinical decisions is spreading to other fields where society has an interest in good decision-making based on sound rationale.

As we see in the quote above it is often assumed that rational views of evidence must begin with the concept of *probability*. P. Achinstein (2001) writes: 'It is argued that evidence must supply a good reason for belief, and that the latter requires that the objective ... probability of the hypothesis on the evidence be greater than half.' The starting point for our discussion, however, is that in practice our ability to estimate probabilities can be very limited. In order to determine how effective a particular medical procedure is, for example, we need to be able to observe numbers of similar patients who have and who have not had the treatment. This kind of objective sampling can be impractical. Complex medical cases may involve uncommon combinations of conditions; legal practice frequently has to deal with newly emerging kinds of issue, such as computer fraud, and science is often concerned with trying to explain new phenomena or predict events that have never been observed at all! As J. Franklin (2001) comments 'Even now, the degree to which evidence supports hypotheses in law or science is not usually quantified, and it is debatable whether it is quantifiable even in principle.'

While the value of quantitative models of evidence and evidence-based thinking are clear I share Franklin's view that we need to appreciate its limitations as well. This is a pity because one of the great virtues of the mathematical theory of probability is that it provides clear procedures and constraints for reasoning rationally when there are significant levels of uncertainty about what is 'truly' the case. The problem, as our examples illustrate, is that there are many situations where sampling problems make it difficult to collect objective data from which to estimate probabilities. The purpose of this chapter is to explore ways in which we can be equally rigorous about how to reason about and assess uncertain evidence, using a framework that allows for uncertainty but does not depend on being able to quantify it.

In the next section we will attempt to define what is meant by 'evidence' since it has somewhat different interpretations in different fields. Over the next two sections we will attempt to develop a unified perspective. The central idea of this unification is that it is based on logic and the patterns of *argumentation* which are to be seen in deliberations and debates about evidence. Our framework does not reject the importance of probabilistic methods for reasoning about evidence but offers a broader perspective which accommodates probabilistic methods when they are practical, and offers an alternative set of methods when they are not.

Perspectives on evidence

A typical dictionary definition[3] is that evidence is:

- That which tends to prove or disprove something; ground for belief; proof.
- Something that makes plain or clear; an indication or sign: *His flushed look was visible evidence of his fever.*
- *Law*: data presented to a court or jury in proof of the facts in issue and which may include the testimony of witnesses, records, documents, or objects.

This seems to be straightforward, except of course that there are several different notions here, encompassing things that are about logic (proof, grounds etc.), things which are about observation (visible evidence) and things which are indirect forms of evidence, including testimony, documents, measuring devices and so on. It gets more complicated though because evidence is treated differently in different professional domains, as we can see by looking at how evidence is viewed in the law, in science and in medicine.

Evidence in law

Law is perhaps the most venerable domain in which the question 'what constitutes evidence?' is discussed, and in which rules that determine when evidence is acceptable are pivotal to decision-making and professional practice. In the broadest sense, 'legal evidence includes all the means by which any alleged matter of fact, the truth of which is disputed, is convincingly established in the mind of a judge or a member of a jury'. The content of an evidential statement (witness testimony, expert opinion, documents and written records, observations, including observations by cameras or other machines, laboratory procedures etc.) seems to have few limits. To remedy this situation some legal scholars have suggested that the term 'evidence' should be applied 'to the process by which the truth is established, and the term *proof* to the effect which the evidence produces upon the judicial mind. ... "Evidence" bears the same relation to "proof" that *cause* does to *effect*'.

---

[3] <http://dictionary.reference.com/>.

Evidence in science

The basic methodology of evidence collection in the sciences can be very different from that of legal processes. Scientific evidence usually goes towards supporting or rejecting a general hypothesis or theory, not what happened in a particular situation. Scientific theories are developed and tested through a combination of disputation and careful assessment of many different types of evidence, as in law, but scientific laws are predictive, legal reasoning is not. The rules for evidence used in science have evolved to eschew 'authoritative opinion' and anecdotal evidence, in favour of systematic observation of phenomena that occur in the world, or which are created as experiments in a laboratory, and formal theoretical analysis leading to empirically testable predictions.

A feature that is prominent in science is that *evidence is frequently identified and interpreted through the lens of a particular theory*. A scientific theory may be expressed formally (e.g. mathematically or in computational form) or informally (e.g. in natural language or pictures). Different representations facilitate different kinds of reasoning. Figure 6.1, for example, illustrates three different theoretical views of protein molecules—as a simple linear sequence of amino acids, as a topological model showing connected structures like helices and coils (which are made up of 'folded' amino acid sequences), and

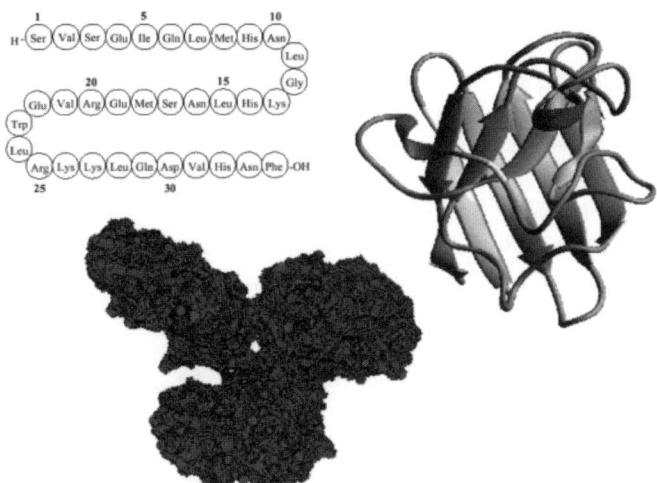

Figure 6.1.   Three representations of a complex protein molecule: linear sequence of amino acids (top); topological organisation of secondary structures (right), and 3D space-filling model (bottom left).

as a three-dimensional structure that has volume in space and a characteristic surface configuration.

Scientists often work within multiple theoretical perspectives (and with different experimental techniques), and reason about evidence with different kinds of argument depending on the perspective in use. For example, observing that two proteins have similar amino acid sequences can be used as evidence to support a claim that they have evolved to support similar cellular functions, or that they are likely to fold in similar ways; the topological representation can be used to support arguments that the molecule must fold in a particular way because of local constraints on packing, while cause–effect arguments justify claims such as 'hydrophobic' amino acid residues will tend to be inside the molecule and 'charged' residues will be on the surface because of repulsion and attraction to water molecules respectively.[4]

Evidence-based medicine

For many centuries medical practice was seen as an arcane, even occult, skill. With the growing dominance of science-based medicine, and general awareness that human decision-making and even professional judgement are fallible and can lead to errors, modern clinical practice increasingly means the combination of individual clinical expertise with the best available external evidence from scientific research. While the dominant mode of evidential reasoning in law is *disputation*, however, in medicine it is one of *deliberation*— bringing all the relevant data and arguments together to weigh up the pros and cons of alternative diagnoses or treatments for each individual patient. Doctors are expected to deliberate systematically in their decision-making, taking into account the provenance and the strength of each contributing piece of evidence, as exemplified by Table 6.1.[5]

Another contrasting feature of these three different domains is how easily they become committed, or *entrenched*. Reversing a legal judgement in an individual case often requires compelling new evidence and demanding appeal processes which try to limit the creation of precedents. Overturning scientific theories which have been widely accepted can also be difficult, but a single key observation or experiment which cannot be explained on orthodox theory can have revolutionary consequences, not only on the original theory but countless other fields that depend upon it. Interpretation of evidence in practical medical decision making can be even more open-minded. Indeed the expectation

[4] <http://en.wikipedia.org/wiki/Protein_structure>.
[5] <http://www.gp-training.net/>.

Table 6.1.   Grading of provenance and strength of kinds of evidence.

Categories of evidence

Ia	Evidence from meta-analysis of randomised controlled trials.
Ib	Evidence from at least one randomised controlled trial.
IIa	Evidence from at least one controlled study without randomisation.
IIb	Evidence from at least one other type of quasi-experimental study.
III	Evidence from non-experimental descriptive studies, such as comparative studies, correlation studies and case control studies.
IV	Evidence from expert committees' reports or opinions and/or clinical experience of respected authorities.

Strength of recommendation

A	Directly based on category I evidence.
B	Directly based on category II evidence or extrapolated recommendation from category I evidence.
C	Directly based on category III evidence or extrapolated recommendation from category I or II evidence.
D	Directly based on category IV evidence or extrapolated recommendation from category I, II or III evidence.

that we may reverse a decision is often built into practical treatment planning as in 'the evidence suggests an infection but if the medication doesn't work in seven days we'll try something else'.

Towards a unified view of evidence

Philosophers, scientists, logicians, statisticians and many others have tried to nail down a unified concept of evidence that covers all these uses, and which is objective, clear and precise. However, as we have seen evidence can take a huge range of specific forms, and even if we exclude *ad hoc* and subjective evidence we still find different kinds of evidential reasoning and argumentation in different domains. While law depends heavily on third party sources, such as witness testimony and documentation, science and medicine place more emphasis on observation and measurement. Furthermore evidence is tested through adversarial debate in legal settings, while predictions and experimental tests are the norm in science and science-based fields such as medicine.[6]

[6] This is not to say that disputes do not take place in science and medicine, far from it, but the scientific community regards disputes as at best a regrettably human way of pursuing the truth (generating 'more heat than light') while it is the principal way of arriving at a verdict in courts in many countries.

Given such a varied picture it is unsurprising that many seek a simpler, more general and flexible yet still *rational* way of representing and assessing evidence. This section proposes a model which captures a general notion of evidence and evidential reasoning, while accommodating the distinct styles of evidence characteristic of different domains. The approach is based on argumentation theory; a logical framework for reasoning about beliefs and actions which includes deliberative and disputatious forms that are not addressed by traditional techniques like those provided by probability theory.

From evidence to argument

For present purposes let us define evidence to be any information that is *relevant* to making a decision about a hypothesis (e.g. whether a patient is suffering from this disease or that; an accused is guilty or innocent; a molecule has a particular function, or children are less happy now than they were twenty years ago). Evidence also plays a key role in making decisions about actions (e.g. whether to treat a patient with this drug or that; the penalty for someone convicted of a crime; whether to carry out an experiment to test a hypothesis, or rescue a bank in trouble).

Relevant information can take many forms but we will distinguish *foreground data* about the specific situation of interest and *background knowledge* covering general facts and rules that cover situations like it (see Table 6.2). In our model foreground data are interpreted by applying background knowledge to construct arguments for and/or against the competing claims about the situation. Background knowledge can include everything from universal laws to general rules or theories that are particular to the domain of discussion.

Let us first make some informal observations about the properties we would like to capture in a theory of arguing about evidence. The aim is to gain some insight into how people naturally argue about and make decisions based

Table 6.2.   Examples of foreground and background knowledge relevant to a decision.

Decision	Relevant foreground data	Relevant background knowledge
What is the diagnosis?	A patient's family history.	General knowledge about the genetics of diseases.
Is the defendant innocent or guilty?	Information from crime scene.	Characteristic patterns in cash machine fraud.
What is the structure of a protein molecule?	The set of species that a protein is found in.	Evolutionary constraints on protein structure.
Do we need to change a school policy?	Results of a student survey.	Social factors in bullying behaviour.

on evidence, and to guide the design of rational and practical tools which can help them make decisions better.

I.   Argumentation is a process of constructing reasons for or against competing *claims*. The background knowledge which is used in constructing an argument may be specific to a particular domain such as medicine or law, or embody general principles that are applicable in all domains.

II.   Evidential arguments increase or reduce *confidence* in a claim, though we may not be able to be precise about how large the change is.

III.   All other things being equal the more independent and valid lines of argument we may construct in support of a claim the greater the confidence that is warranted in the claim (and the more independent lines of argument against the greater the doubt).

IV.   In some cases a single argument can be conclusive—it *confirms* or *refutes* a claim absolutely. Furthermore, one argument may appear to conclusively support a claim, while another conclusively supports a logically contradictory claim. Tolerance of contradictions makes intuitive sense because arguments can be based on different background assumptions; a formal theory should be similarly tolerant.

V.   Arguments and theories can themselves be objects of reasoning in discussion and debate e.g. 'I do not accept your argument that my theory necessarily predicts climate change because you are making unreasonable assumptions about the physics of the greenhouse effect.'

VI.   Some arguments may be stronger and take *precedence* over others, leading to the rebuttal of one argument by another (as in the example in V). Similarly some arguments may *corroborate* or *buttress* others, thereby strengthening the claim.

VII.   In the absence of information about relative strength contradictory arguments can still play an important part in analysing evidence and making decisions.

VIII.   Natural language provides an expressive vocabulary for discussing evidence. It would be desirable to develop techniques which use sound formal and mathematical languages for argumentation tasks but which can be translated to and from intuitive, natural language forms.

IX.   If a rational agent is forced to choose between two or more competing hypotheses or actions it should choose the one in which it has the greatest overall confidence that it is the most credible (hypothesis) or the most beneficial (action), unless there are grounds to suspect that the current order of preference is not to be relied upon.[7]

X.   A rational agent that is not forced to choose may defer a decision on the grounds that the arguments are inconclusive, unreliable or otherwise unwarranted (see also V).

In what follows I will set out a framework for arguing about evidence which accommodates these requirements. The theory is outlined in a formal style frequently used by logicians, computer scientists, philosophers and others who are interested in mathematical foundations of logical reasoning, since the aim is to be *clear* about terms, *precise* about meanings of statements, and *rigorous* in determining what may be rationally concluded from statements. However, a formal treatment as such is not on offer here. As a scientist my focus is on what people find intuitively reasonable in their considerations of evidence, because doctors, scientists, lawyers, policy makers and others will judge it irrelevant if it does not connect with their natural ways of thinking and training. As an engineer engaged in the design of cognitive prostheses for medical decision-making my concern is with practical tools as well as abstract notions of rationality, since doctors (etc.) are the end users of these tools. While an absence of formal mathematical guarantees is potentially a weakness—human intuitions are powerful but they are also sometimes mistaken—unless we can engage with the end user within his or her natural framework, then credibility is undermined and opportunities to understand mistakes are lost.

Data, knowledge and theories

People, and increasingly computers, apply knowledge in reasoning, solving problems and making decisions. Logicians and computer scientists often speak of the contents of knowledge bases as 'theories'. In his discussion of the use of evidence in scientific theorising, for example, Glymour (1980) identifies three key elements—a general *hypothesis* or claim, *evidence* such as observational data, and a *theory* which determines that the evidence is an instance or a consequence of the hypothesis. A theory is typically formalised as a collection of sentences in some well-defined language. Sentences typically include

---

[7] This chapter focuses on the first case, the confidence in a hypothesis which is warranted by available evidence, because arguing about actions raises distinct (and deep) issues about how we take cost–benefit, and utility into account in practical decision-making. Evidence may still play a key a role in choosing between actions and we discuss in more detail how the framework can be used for this purpose elsewhere (Fox and Parsons, 1998).

background 'facts', and 'if … then …' rules which can be applied to derive conclusions from foreground statements using an automated system under an agreed set of computational rules.

Although theories can be general (e.g. medical practitioners routinely draw upon widely applicable scientific theories from biochemistry, epidemiology, genetics, physiology etc., etc.) they also apply informal and empirical theories in their routine decision-making (e.g. rules which may have only temporary significance such as 'a presentation of flu-like symptoms in a child under five could be swine-flu and the child is therefore at risk'[8]). Note that theories which are widely accepted and very general are not always mutually consistent and can therefore lead to contradictory conclusions.

We allow 'common sense theories'[9] as part of background knowledge since specialist background knowledge is intimately intertwined with common sense reasoning. For example assumptions about time are involved in risk assessment or when reasoning about a patient's prognosis, and reasoning about space informs thinking about the spread of infections. Legal theory subsumes common sense principles of fairness as well as technical rules of evidence which are acceptable to courts.

I follow Glymour op. cit. in assuming that evidence, hypotheses and theories can be formalised in a first-order logic[10] but assert that 'standard' first-order logic requires significant extensions. The predicate calculus, for example, allows sentences to be true or false and includes only categorical proof rules such as *modus ponens*. In order to reason about evidence our framework needs to deviate from classical logic in a number of ways.

---

[8] At the time of writing (2009) this rule has important currency among doctors but as the epidemic wanes as expected it will cease to have such a prominent role in diagnostic reasoning. This draws attention to the important observation that argumentation varies over time, becomes refined or altered with changing knowledge etc. A general argumentation theory will presumably need to provide an account of how arguments evolve or may be maintained over time.

[9] 'Common sense' has acquired a technical meaning in computer science and artificial intelligence research, see for example, E. Davis, *Representations of Commonsense Knowledge* (San Mateo, CA, Morgan Kaufmann, 1990). These are often concerned with formalising human understanding of the world, including the kinds of objects and events that we distinguish within the world (the 'ontology'), and the patterns of reasoning about such concepts that we find intuitively sound. A common sense rule of inference, for example, is that one physical object cannot be in two places at the same time. This provides a common sense rationale for the specialised legal concept of an alibi.

[10] Wikipedia: 'First-order logic is a formal logic used in mathematics, philosophy, linguistics, and computer science. It goes by many names, including: first-order predicate calculus, the lower predicate calculus, and predicate logic. First-order logic is distinguished from propositional logic by its use of quantifiers; each interpretation of first-order logic includes a domain of discourse over which the quantifiers range.'

- In classical logic if we hold foreground fact *p* to be *true*, and we have background knowledge in the form of a rule *if p then q* then we must conclude *q* to be *true*. Since evidential reasoning may only warrant an uncertain or tentative conclusion, we need a way of representing confidence in any claim. This must capture confidence in our background knowledge and foreground data, and tell us how we should compute confidence in derived conclusions. For example we may be more confident in *q* than in *r,* or more confident in the rule *if p then q* than the rule *if r then not q.* In contrast with probabilistic reasoning, however, we do not require that it be practically possible to quantify confidence in prior beliefs, the arguments we construct or the conclusions we arrive at.

- In a classical logic if we have deduced *q* from *p* then the possibility that we may also deduce *q* from *s* adds no further information about *q*. In everyday reasoning, however, each argument increases or decreases confidence that a hypothesis will prove to be correct, or an action will have the desired outcome. In our framework we assume that the more independent lines of argument we can sustain given our knowledge for (against) a claim the more (less) our confidence should be in the claim.

- Standard logic requires that a proposition is either true or false; there can be no line of reasoning that it is true and another line of reasoning that it is false; contradictions are not tolerable in the classical framework. A corollary of this is that a classical logical agent cannot 'change its mind' believing *p* at one point in time but believing *not p* at another. This assumes that the agent either knows everything that is relevant for determining the truth of a claim when a conclusion must be drawn, and/or it will not receive any new information that would require a change of truth-value, neither of which are practically realistic. In contrast evidential reasoning requires that a rational agent be able to tolerate inconsistent lines of reasoning, allow the possibility of acting on tentative beliefs, and reverse its commitments in the light of new evidence.

- A formal treatment of argumentation must allow for the need to reason about whether an argument is valid or invalid, persuasive or not, 'good' or 'bad'. Neither classical logical inference nor probabilistic models of inference address the problem of *meta-logical reasoning;* common patterns of debate and recent developments in formal argumentation theory show that *arguments about arguments* are important and can be given formal treatment.

The next section sets out a framework for describing evidential reasoning in terms of a theory of argumentation which is expressed in a first-order language and in a manner that accommodates properties I–X. As with our discussion of the nature of evidence I will start from a standard English-language dictionary, since many scholarly definitions of 'argument' have become overloaded with philosophical and mathematical concerns that may distract from our objectives. This definition[11] includes four distinct nuances:

1.   the process of developing or presenting an argument; reasoning;
2.   the setting forth of reasons together with the conclusion drawn from them;
3.   discussion; debate; disputation;
4.   a discussion dealing with a controversial point.

These meanings can be put into two classes. The first two are concerned with the reasoning that an individual may engage in when constructing, evaluating or analysing the rationale for a claim. The second pair addresses the kind of argumentation which involves two or more parties that take different positions with respect to some claim, and may dispute the arguments for and against it.[12] We view these as distinct modes of argumentation which we call the *evidential mode* and the *dialectical mode*.

The evidential mode of argumentation

Given the theme of this chapter we will introduce the evidential mode with a medical example. The specific example is taken from a computer system which was developed for assisting general physicians in making common clinical decisions. The background medical knowledge it uses is based on a standard reference text called *Clinical Evidence* that doctors use to review the potential benefits and harms of possible clinical interventions for their patients.[13] Figure 6.3 shows an example screen from this system which was developed in collaboration with the British Medical Association (Steele and Fox 2003).

Clinical Evidence is organised around common clinical questions; in the top part of Figure 6.2 is the question 'Which treatments improve outcomes in

---

[11] <http://dictionary.reference.com/>.
[12] A single agent that is considering arguments for and against a claim might be viewed as having a debate with itself so the 'two or more parties' might also be said to include that case.
[13] <http://clinicalevidence.bmj.com/ceweb/index.jsp>.

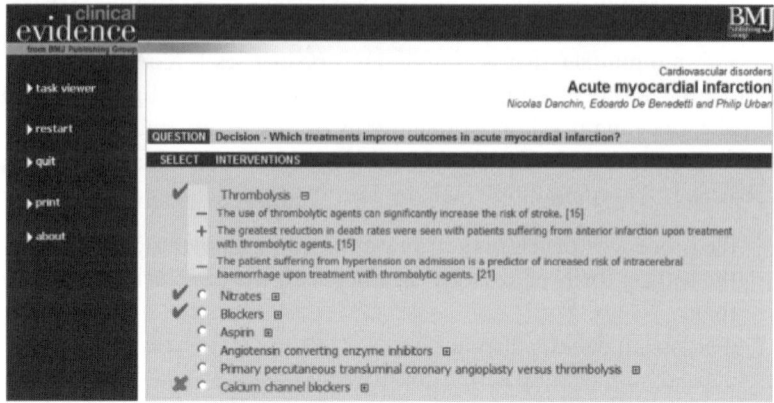

Figure 6.2.　Example of argumentation in medical decision-making (Steele and Fox, 2003).

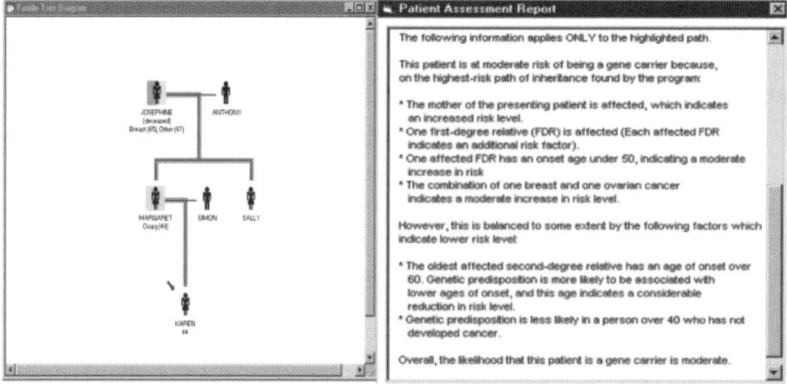

Figure 6.3.　Risk Assessment in Genetics (RAGs), takes in information about the patient (Karen) and her family history and constructs a family tree (left). It then constructs a set of arguments for and against the claim that she has a genetic predisposition to breast cancer (right).

acute myocardial infarction?' Relevant foreground data about an individual patient (e.g. symptoms, test results) have at this point already been collected by the software and the possible decision options (drugs in this case) are listed in the panel underneath the question. The treatment options are assessed against these data using knowledge of the efficacy and safety of the different drugs as reported in clinical trials.

In this system the options are presented in order of preference. If there is a tick adjacent to the option then the balance of argument is in favour; a cross indicates the option is excluded for some reason, and a question-mark says that the position is open or equivocal. The user can select any of the options shown in the middle panel, and the system will show a summary of the logical arguments for and against that option for that patient (bottom panel). In this case there is one argument for use of thrombolytic drugs and two against. If a deeper justification is required for any argument the user clicks on the index number and is linked through to the supporting evidence, typically the published research paper(s) that report the results of empirical trials in which the drug has been tested.

The presentation details in this example of evidential argumentation are not particularly important. The arguments are shown here as text but behind the scenes an evidence-based theory in the form of a set of logical rules is being applied to the patient data to construct arguments which underpin the informal presentation of the pros and cons. The software can vary the presentation in many ways, but whatever presentation style is adopted there are several key problems that need to be addressed by the underlying evidence model. These include the structure and construction of logical arguments; criteria for accepting them, how to aggregate arguments in order to assess the overall confidence we may have a claim, and when we may safely commit if there are multiple hypotheses or candidate actions.

Argument structure

In our system an argument has three parts:

  (*Claim : Grounds : Qualifier*)   abbreviated   (*C : G : Q*)

Here *Claim* is typically a foreground assertion such as 'the patient has cancer' (abbreviated 'cancer') though it could be a rule or even a collection of sentences which compose a theory. The term 'Claim' is used to indicate that it may not be categorically true as in classical logic, but has some associated *uncertainty*, or is *tentative* or subject to *counter-argument* etcetera. The claim is 'labelled' with two additional pieces of information: the *Grounds* represent one logical line of reasoning for the claim ('line of argument') and the *Qualifier* is a representation of the confidence conferred by that specific line of argument. The need to explicitly label each argument with its Grounds is that we need to be able to distinguish the different lines of argument for a claim. We also need to be able to check which lines of argument are distinct, an argument based on the grounds (elderly and weight loss) is obviously different from the argument (elderly and positive blood test) but is not distinct from (weight loss and elderly) which includes the same foreground data but in a trivially different arrangement.

Argument construction

In classical logic an argument is a set of assertions (the premises of the argument) from which we can derive another assertion (the conclusion) under some set of inference rules (the logic). For example foreground data may include 'the patient is elderly' and 'the patient has lost weight' together with background knowledge such as '*if* weight loss in an elderly patient then cancer'. If the conclusion can be derived by mechanically applying the inference rules of the logic the conclusion is taken to be proved. Classical proof procedures are extremely powerful methods of reasoning, but do not directly accommodate the uncertainty that is typical of practical domains and central to any discussion of evidential reasoning. Classical logics do not represent *degrees of belief*, accommodate *changes of mind* or *relative truth* (when a proposition is viewed as true from one point of view but false from another). In line with properties II and IV our approach is based on a less categorical system of reasoning than has traditionally been studied by logicians. Here arguments are not proofs but *reasons to believe* in some claim or *reasons to act* in some way.

We will frequently use the symbolic qualifiers '+' and '++' to represent *confidence* in an argument, where + indicates that the argument increases confidence and ++ is the *top* symbol, meaning the argument increases confidence in the claim to some maximum (though not excluding the possibility that we may subsequently argue equally forcefully against the claim). We can also use other representations or 'dictionaries'. For example it is straightforward to extend the framework to include arguments that 'oppose' (–) or 'exclude' a claim (– –) with the obvious meanings. We also discuss later the possibility that the general notion of qualifier can subsume traditional quantitative representations of uncertainty.

A general framework for constructing arguments is summarised in [1].

$$Background \cup Foreground \vdash_{LA} (Claim : Grounds : Qualifier) \qquad [1]$$

This states in general terms that the application of background theories to foreground data (the left hand side) yields an argument (right hand side) under the inference rules of some logical system LA. The $\cup$ symbol is the logical union of background and foreground information, and the turnstile $\vdash$ with the subscript $_{LA}$ indicates that the arguments that are valid are those that can be constructed under the inference rules of the Logic of Argument LA (Fox *et al.*, 1992, 1993). Schema [1] formalises informal requirement I above. However our scheme is intended to allow for different base logics such as Dung's argumentation system (1995) which is concerned with whether an argument is *acceptable* rather than whether it is deductively *valid*; we would indicate that we are using different inference rules by replacing $\vdash_{LA}$ with $\vdash_{Dung}$.

Inference rules are defined as first-order rules in a language in which variables representing claims (C_i) and grounds G_j) may be instantiated by sets of sentences in the language. We now give two examples of inference rules from LA. Suppose we are trying to diagnose a patient who is complaining of chronic indigestion and we are able to construct one supporting argument for gastric ulcer ('GastricUlcer': PainAfterMeals: +) and another argument is for gall-stones ('GallStones': PainInRightUpperQuadrant: +).[14] Logically of course it is possible that the patient is suffering from both conditions. We can construct an argument for this possibility with the following inference rule.

$$(C_1:G_1:Q') \text{ and } (C_2:G_2:Q'') \rightarrow (C_1 \text{ and } C_2:G_1 \cup G_2: \min(Q',Q''))$$

Which is to be read as: if we have some level of confidence Q' (say +) in a claim C_1 and confidence Q'' (say ++) in C_2, then confidence in the conjunction of C_1 and C_2 is the *minimum* of Q' and Q'' (i.e. +). In other words our confidence in both diagnoses can be no stronger than our confidence in the one that we have least confidence in (often called the 'weakest link').

A similar inference rule is analogous to the *modus ponens* inference rule of classical logic:

$$(C_1:G_1:Q') \text{ and } (C_1 \rightarrow C_2:G_2:Q'') \rightarrow (C_2:G_1 \cup G_2: \min(Q',Q''))$$

For example if we are maximally confident that the patient is complaining of pain in the right upper quadrant of the abdomen, but our background knowledge is that patients with gall stones often, but certainly not always, complain of pain in this position then we can only conclude that we have a supporting argument for gall stones. In such circumstances we will obviously wish to consider other clinical data about the patient and construct additional arguments for and against the competing claims.

Uncertainty in argumentation

What do the abstract symbols + and ++ (or – and – –) actually mean? We adopt the view here that they represent an agent's *confidence* in an argument

---

[14] Tony Hunter has pointed out that strictly there are insufficient premises in these examples. For example a complete presentation of one line of argument for diagnosing gastric ulcer might be (Gastric Ulcer : (Pain After Meals and causes (Gastric Ulcer, Pain After Meals) and goal (diagnosis)) : +) but we leave out these additional clauses for simplicity.

with respect to a claim. We now need to say what 'confidence' itself might mean.

A widely held opinion is that informal terms like 'belief' and 'confidence' should be formalised in terms of mathematical probability, which imposes a requirement to be able to quantify degrees of confidence. However, as noted above it is often not practical to assign explicit prior probabilities to a claim or conditional probabilities to rules as would be required for a standard probabilistic inference model. A less demanding view is that the agent can know the direction of the change in confidence if not the magnitude of the change. This takes us to a notion of *qualitative probability* similar to that proposed by Wellman (1990), Parsons (2001) and others.

Restricting the interpretation of confidence to a technical probability is not the only option, however. For example we may interpret confidence as a *propensity to act* on the claim, a measure of *trust*, a summary of the *amount of evidence*, the average *plausibility of the arguments*, or various other intuitively distinct notions. Indeed, an agent may assert that an argument increases or decreases confidence in a claim without declaring the underlying measure or representation that is being used. If we represent the confidence conferred by arguments using a simple dictionary of qualifiers such as $\{++, +, -, --\}$ we have a simple but robust representation which can be applied in many situations.

Argument aggregation

Property III says that the more arguments we have for a claim then the greater should be our confidence in it. Given that an agent has constructed a number of arguments for and against competing claims, how may it select the most plausible, probable or otherwise preferred claim based on the set of arguments? We can do this by introducing a general aggregation constraint in our evidence system.

$$| (C: G_1:+) \text{ and } (C:G_2:+) | > | (C:G_1:+) | \qquad \textit{Accumulation}$$

Here claim C has two supporting arguments with independent grounds G_1 and G_2. The vertical bars represent the aggregate confidence in C given the set of arguments between the bars. As observed above we may not be able to use a quantitative scale for representing confidence in individual arguments but we can put claims in order of our relative confidence. Suppose we have three supporting (+) arguments for, say, a medical diagnosis, two supporting arguments for a competing diagnosis, and just one argument for a third then there is an obvious natural order over these claims.

If we permit arguments *against* claims as well as arguments *for* there is a comparable 'reduction' constraint that says that we cannot have as much confidence in a claim if there is an argument against it as we would have had if we had only an argument for it:

$$| \, (C{:}G_1{:} \, +) \text{ and } (C{:}G_2{:} \, -) \, | \, < \, | \, (C{:}G_1{:} \, +) \, | \qquad\qquad Reduction$$

Given these simple constraints it is a straightforward matter to develop algorithms which collect together a set of arguments to determine the order of relative confidence over a set of competing claims. The simplest such process consists of merely adding up the pros and cons for each option in which all arguments are given equal weight. We justify assigning equal levels of confidence to all the arguments for a hypothesis on the 'principle of insufficient reason' which asserts that if there is no reason to assign different levels of confidence to competing claims the parsimonious choice is to assign equal levels of confidence to them (an argument is just a special kind of assertion).

This is consistent with property III: all other things being equal the more independent and valid lines of argument we may construct in support of a claim the greater the confidence that is warranted in the claim (and the more independent lines of argument against the greater the doubt). Despite its simplicity human decision-making can frequently be modelled by simple linear rules of this kind (Dawes, 1979). If there is sufficient reason to weight arguments differentially this can be added to yield a practical aggregation method for decision making often attributed to Benjamin Franklin.[15]

In cases where we can precisely quantify relative weights we can still understand this in terms of a general *argumentation plus aggregation* framework. If we can treat evidential argumentation as a special case of probabilistic reasoning in which the qualitative aspects of inference are made explicit as well as the quantitative we may choose to calculate the posterior probabilities of alternative hypotheses by applying a probabilistic aggregation function based on standard methods developed for Bayesian networks.[16] A general schema which subsumes a variety of aggregation methods is summarised in [2].

$$\{(Claim : Grounds : Qualifier)\} \rightarrow_{Agg} (Claim : Confidence) \qquad\qquad [2]$$

In general, an aggregation function *Agg* maps from the set of arguments about a Claim into a simpler representation of the overall confidence in it.

---

[15] Web search term such as 'pros, cons and Benjamin Franklin' produces a lot of interesting examples, but a useful starting point is <http://home.att.net/~essays/Ben_Franklin_Decision_Making.pdf>.

[16] For more about Bayesian networks see Chap. 5 of this volume, and <http://www.dcs.qmul.ac.uk/~norman/BBNs/BBNs.htm>.

Contradictory evidence

Property IV says that arguments can be contradictory; one argument may conclusively support a claim while another argument conclusively opposes it, or conclusively supports the negation of the claim. We can model this with inference rules in which contradiction is explicit.

$$(C: G_1: ++) \text{ and } (C: G_2: --) \rightarrow (C: G_1 \cup G_2: \bot) \qquad Contra\ 1$$

Contra 1 says that if G_1 conclusively supports claim C and G_2 conclusively rejects C then there is an argument with grounds $G_1 \cup G_2$ that the argumentation for C is inconsistent, indicated by the qualifier $\bot$. Tolerance of contradictory arguments is desirable if we wish to formalise everyday reasoning about evidence though it is not consistent with classical logic, in which if it is possible to both derive a proof that P is true and a proof that P is false then the reasoning system is unsound.

Some argumentation systems also deviate from classical logic and standard probability theory in their treatment of negation, (*C* and *not C*). Standard probability requires that evidence for *C* necessarily entails evidence against *not C* and in classical logic a *proof of C* necessitates a *disproof of not C*. This is not the case in argumentation systems such as LA. If we want to include the idea that *evidence for C* is necessarily *evidence against not C* then we must make this explicit, as in *Contra 2*.

$$(C: G_1: ++) \text{ and } (\neg C: G_2: ++) \rightarrow (C: G_1 \cup G_2: \bot) \qquad Contra\ 2$$

The rule of contradiction captured by *Contra 2* may seem self-evident to some readers. However, the universality of such complementation rules has been a focus of much philosophical dispute and its validity depends on the precise formal system one adopts. As Karl Popper puts it '... rules of inference need not necessarily have that "formal" character which we know from our logical studies; their character will depend rather on the character of the semantic language system under investigation' (*Conjectures and Refutations*, p. 282).

People are often willing to argue in support of some claim without being willing to agree that the same argument necessarily refutes the complementary claim. For example, while they may argue that advanced age in a patient who has lost weight is evidence for the presence of cancer, it might not be accepted that this is correspondingly evidence against 'absence of cancer' (where absence of cancer may be an indefinite set such as {gastric ulcer, gall stones, ... measles, mumps, nothing wrong, or a broken leg). In many cases they will in fact assert the argument for the claim to be irrelevant to the complement of the claim or at least overstated. In fact the use of complementation rules is not even a universal feature of formal reasoning systems. Although the complementation axiom of the 'excluded middle' is fundamental to classical logic some systems, notably intuitionistic logic[17], do not include it.

The dialectical mode of argumentation

In a recent review of argumentation methods Besnard and Hunter (2008) draw a distinction between *monological* and *dialogical* argumentation. In monological argumentation the emphasis is on how to construct the arguments for a claim, and how to draw a conclusion about the claim from the assembly of arguments for and against it. This captures the intuition behind the dictionary definitions 1 and 2 discussed earlier, and seems very close to the notion of evidential argumentation. Dialogical argumentation, in contrast, relates more closely to definitions 3 and 4. Agents involved in a debate or dispute may present an argument for a claim while other agents may challenge one or more of the arguments which have been constructed by their opponents. Lawyers disputing the guilt or innocence of an accused, and scientists debating a theory and the evidence for/against it, are examples of dialogical argumentation. The emphasis is on the nature of the dialogical interactions between the opponents and the assembly of a set of arguments on which the agents collectively arrive at a conclusion. In the system proposed here we assume that all the informal monological properties I–IV will hold in the dialogical case, though there are variants in which this may not be so.[18]

A key intuition about argumentation that we identified earlier was that we not only argue about *claims*, we may also argue about the status of *arguments* that support or oppose the claims (property V). In deliberating about evidence it is commonplace to think about whether an argument is valid, whether one argument is stronger or more persuasive than another, whether one argument contradicts another and so on. This dialectical mode of argumentation is typical of situations where two agents who are arguing about a controversial claim may produce counter-arguments to the other's arguments (seeking to 'rebut' their conclusions or 'undercut' their premises) or to strengthen their own position against counter-argument (e.g. by buttressing or seeking corroboration

[17] <http://plato.stanford.edu/entries/logic-intuitionistic/>.
[18] e.g. Dung, 1995.

for their arguments or developing counter-counter-arguments to the opponent's counter-arguments and so forth).

An early precursor of dialectical argumentation was *defeasible reasoning* (Pollock, 1987; Nute, 1994) in which one logical line of argument can falsify or *defeat* another line of argument. This concept does not exist in classical logic in which inference rules are only concerned with the truth or falsity of individual (atomic) sentences, not the validity of proofs, or the credibility of theories, which subsume collections of sentences (Dung, 1995). Defeasibility weakens the force of deductive proof by acknowledging that even if a proof is logically sound some assertion it depends upon may in fact be mistaken. In defeasible logic the traditional inference rule *For all X: $p(X)$* **implies** $q(X)$ is replaced by or extended to include a schema such as *For all X: $p(X)$* **defeasibly_implies** $q(X)$ which allows for the possibility that $q(X)$ may be implied on some set of believed facts or data, but further information may show these beliefs to be incorrect and the conclusion $q(X)$ will be withdrawn in that case.

The central idea of one argument being a counter-argument to another can again be illustrated in a practical medical situation (Figure 6.3). This shows a clinical decision support system for taking a family history and arguing the pros and cons that an imaginary patient, Karen, does or does not have a genetic predisposition to breast cancer. Arguments for the claim that there is a genetic predisposition are shown in the panel on the right. These arguments are based on personal and family factors which are known to affect risk; there are four supporting arguments shown at the top and two opposing arguments at the bottom.

This system was originally developed with a purely evidential perspective in mind but the argumentation in this example has a defeasible element as well. The last supporting argument for Karen being at risk is 'The combination of one breast and one ovarian cancer indicates a moderate increase in risk.' However, one of the arguments has been classified as simply an opposing argument for increased genetic risk but is better viewed as bringing the first argument into question: 'The oldest affected second degree relative has an age of onset greater than 60. Genetic predisposition is more likely to be associated with lower ages of onset, and this age indicates a considerable reduction in risk level.' What this is saying is that we cannot take the argument that the combination of two cancers in one of Karen's relatives is a risk factor for her at face value because both of these diagnoses were made when the relative was over 60. Since patients who contract cancer for genetic reasons usually do so at a relatively early age Karen's grandmother was more likely to have acquired the disease for non-genetic reasons so the first argument is brought into question.

A recent influential treatment of dialectical argumentation is Dung's (1995) framework in which one argument is allowed to *attack* another. In this approach a collection of arguments is modelled as a directed binary graph, in which arguments are nodes in the graph and the edge Arg2 $\Rightarrow$ Arg1 in the graph represents an attack relationship. If Arg2 is *acceptable* then Arg1 is *defeated*. However, if Arg2 is itself successfully attacked by a further argument Arg3 then Arg2 is no longer acceptable and Arg1 is reinstated.

Dung's argumentation framework has many interesting features. The traditional notion of 'truth' for example seems to give way to the idea that the only interest is whether or not arguments are *acceptable*. Verifying that an argument is acceptable is different and arguably (*sic*) simpler than verifying truth, hence avoiding some sticky philosophical issues about the fundamental nature of truth. Furthermore Dung's framework is abstract: it makes no commitments to any particular argument structure such as the *Claim:Argument: Qualifier* structure adopted for LA. The aim is to be able to explore the mathematical properties which will be common to *any* specific argumentation system.

Although Dung's framework is elegant and general it seems less helpful in exploring the practical problem of how to represent and reason about evidence in a natural way. For example it only supports the notion of 'attack' between arguments, with no notion of how an argument might 'support' something (a claim or another argument), though support for hypotheses seems natural to evidential reasoning. It also offers little guidance for developing practical tools and applications (e.g. how should we accommodate uncertainty in an argument?) Also, while Dung's treatment accepts contradictions in foreground data and background knowledge as natural states of affairs it offers little help in deciding how inconsistencies should be managed in practice.

Besnard and Hunter review argumentation theory from an eclectic and somewhat more practical position. They start with specific assumptions about the structure of arguments (as in LA arguments are constructed with respect to claims and arguments can be for or against claims). They also see the formalisation of uncertainty as a key theoretical and practical issue. In the context of any form of evidential reasoning and decision-making we have seen that this is needed for evaluating how much confidence an individual argument contributes to a hypothesis, and how collections of arguments can contribute to an overall level of confidence.

Argumentation is viewed by Besnard and Hunter in a way that accommodates both the evidential and dialectical perspectives. They see it as a process in which arguments and counter-arguments are constructed, compared (e.g. to determine whether one argument is better or stronger than another, property VI) and evaluated (e.g. to determine the status of an argument in the face of a set of counter-arguments, properties III, IV). This accommodates the intuition that arguments add or subtract varying amounts of confidence during the assessment of claims, and arguments have a 'meta-logical' aspect; they can attack or support other arguments that only indirectly affects confidence in claims as well as arguing directly about claims (properties V, VI).

Meta-logical reasoning about arguments

An important aspect of debate in general, and evidential disputes specifically, is that we do not just engage in discussions about 'the facts' (foreground data) but we may also dispute the argumentation and even the theoretical background that is used to interpret the evidence and construct the arguments (property V). There are many strategies that a skilled debater can follow, many of which can be expressed in the present framework.

For example if one agent can construct independent reasons to believe in the premises of a supporting argument for a claim then intuitively the original argument, and the Claim it supports, are strengthened (we call this 'buttressing'). For example, a witness may support another witness not by having seen the same event, but by emphasising the competence, reliability and honesty of the first. A buttressed argument is harder to defeat than one that is not, which can be expressed by the following constraint.

$$| (C:G1:+) \text{ and } (G1:G2:+) | > | (C:G1:+) | \qquad \textit{Buttressing}$$

In other words if the grounds for a claim have independent support then the claim is more credible than if there is no independent support. Another example of an argument having a strengthening role is in corroboration. Suppose we have an argument for some claim C_1, and a second independent argument for a separate claim C_2. If it were the case that C_2 could be used in an argument in support of C_1 then the corroborated claim would be stronger than the uncorroborated claim. For example when a scientist makes a prediction (C_2) based on a theory (C_1) and then shows in an experiment that the prediction C_2 is correct, then the experiment corroborates the theory. A theory that is corroborated by experimental evidence is harder to defeat than one that is not.

$$| (C_1:G:+) \text{ and } (C_2: C_1:+) \text{ and } (C_2:Exp:+) | > | (C_1:G:+) | \quad \textit{Corroboration}$$

The notion of defeasibility, and the specific notion of argument 'attack' is intuitively appealing and an important innovation in logic, but Dung's notion can be refined.

If C is a claim and Arg1, Arg2 are arguments then if one argument successfully attacks another argument it weakens it in a number of possible ways, illustrated by the following example constraints. The first *undermining* constraint says that if we have an inconclusive argument Arg1 *for* C which is successfully attacked by another inconclusive argument Arg2, then the overall effect is that confidence in C is reduced. The rule is very similar to the *reduction* schema given earlier except that it is the argument that is weakened by the attack, not the claim.

$$| \text{(C:G1:+) and (G1:G2:--)} | < | \text{(C:G1:+)} | \qquad \textit{Undermining}$$

A similar constraint is that if Arg1 argues *against* C then the effect of Arg2 will be to *increase* confidence in C. If, on the other hand, Arg1 categorically supports C, then the effect of Arg2 is to introduce some uncertainty. As before we are not saying how much uncertainty is introduced but we treat the aggregated arguments as equivalent to a single supporting argument.

$$| \text{(C:G1:++) and (G1:G2:--)} | = | \text{(C:G1:+)} | \qquad \textit{Weakening}$$

The *Undermining* and *Weakening* constraints are similar to the *undercut* rule in defeasible logics, except that in these logics there is no notion of an attacking argument having some uncertainty attached (property II).

Another important constraint highlights the feature of everyday argumentation (and evidential reasoning): arguments for or against a claim may be contradictory but contradiction does not make the underlying system unsound, it just makes the conclusion *equivocal*. Two independent arguments that both support a claim, yet are mutually contradictory, have complex effects in the sense that both arguments may be thrown into doubt.

$$| \text{(C:G1:+) and (C:G2:+) and (C:G1} \cup \text{G2: } \bot \text{)} | < | \text{(C:G1:+)} |$$
$$\textit{Equivocation}$$

Here it is difficult to know how much confidence the two arguments should contribute to the claim since both are compromised by their inconsistency. One approach to resolving an equivocation is to seek a counter-argument that defeats one of the contradictory arguments (though in practice that may not be possible). Another approach may be to disregard all such contradictory arguments, though this potentially throws away useful information since both arguments may have weak evidential value. A third strategy may be to assume that one of the arguments must be correct even if we cannot construct an explicit rebuttal for the other, we just don't know which one. Unfortunately that solution doesn't extend to the case where there are N contradictory arguments. The problem of equivocation is central to deliberation and debates about evidence. Thinking about it in terms of argumentation helps to articulate the logical circumstances that can arise and possible strategies for resolving them

Expressing confidence in everyday language

People have a very diverse and expressive language for discussing evidence that draws on argumentation conventions. At bottom we speak of arguments that 'support' or 'oppose' hypotheses but everyday language also offers a vocabulary for describing characteristic *patterns* of argumentation. We don't just say 'I'm starting a cold' but also 'it is conceivable {possible, likely, pretty certain, …} that I'm starting a cold.' Similarly a doctor doesn't just say 'you've got athlete's foot' but could also say 'I suspect, {doubt, assume, believe, am certain/uncertain} that given all the evidence you {have, may have, could have} athlete's foot' and so on. This vocabulary is further augmented by 'hedges' (e.g. {quite, very, highly …}), conventional elaborations (e.g. 'it appears to be the case that …', 'there are persuasive reasons to think that …'), the lexical and affixal negative forms of English (e.g. not possible, impossible), and many other everyday constructions.

The existence of such a large vocabulary for talking about the status of our beliefs has long puzzled linguists, psychologists, philosophers and others. For some they merely signal emphasis, or serve a practical conversational role. If I say '*it's possible that* I'm starting a cold' I may intend to communicate something like 'I have reasons to think I may be getting a cold (such as a sore throat, sneezing etc.) but there is also at least some reason to believe that I may not (e.g. (1) I already had a cold just last week; (2) I had the same symptoms yesterday but nothing happened, (3) my throat is only slightly sore).'

These examples might represent nothing more than the use of insignificant social or pragmatic conventions, of no formal interest. However, there seem to be important practical reasons for the large vocabulary of terms in that we see examples of such terms being used in relatively formal medical and other communications. A compelling example is to be found in a guideline published by the International Agency for Research on Cancer. This sets out a standard terminology for talking about categories of risk associated with chemical compounds, in that the evidence for 'chemical X causes cancer' can be classified with one of seven qualifying terms:

confirmed	there is epidemiological data and/or an established causal relationship
probable	there is better evidence than merely recognition of possible carcinogenic activity
possible	a potential hazard is recognised
improbable	possible carcinogenic activity, but strong evidence against
equivocal	hazard recognised and both evidence for and evidence against
open	no information regarding potential hazard is available
not	test case data or direct chemical analysis disconfirms carcinogenic activity

One interpretation of the richness of everyday language is that the purpose of these terms is to *summarise* common patterns of argument (as in 'Claim is possible if there is an argument that supports Claim and no argument that rebuts it') and this addresses requirement VIII above. Elvang-Gøransson *et al.* (1993) formalised this idea by proposing a set of logical 'acceptability classes' for classifying claims, basing these solely on the logical properties of the set of arguments for and against the claim. Acceptability classes define an ordered set of terms for expressing confidence in a Claim:

open Claim	if P is any well formed formula in the language of the logic
supported Claim	if an argument, possibly using inconsistent data, can be constructed for P
plausible Claim	if a consistent argument can be constructed (we may also be able to construct an Arg-consistent argument against)
probable Claim	an argument can be constructed for P, and no consistent argument can be constructed against it
confirmed Claim	if P satisfies the conditions of being probable and, in addition, no consistent arguments can be constructed against any of the premises used in its supporting argument
certain Claim	if P is a tautology of the logic (meaning that its validity is not contingent on any data in the knowledge base).

Elvang-Gøransson *et al.* do not suggest that their formal definitions necessarily capture 'standard' English or other natural language meanings. Their specific interpretations of the terms might be challenged on linguistic or more technical grounds. The approach suggests, however, that it would be possible to agree a standard set of terms for discussing evidence when we lack quantitative risk or similar data based on characteristic logical patterns. If we can agree on a standard set of terms (qualifiers) we could apply them to the task of summarising evidence in a way that is clear, consistent and computable. Even if we are unable to quantify the strength of the underlying evidence the approach yields a practical scale for comparing confidence in competing claims which can be used with clear meaning and across application domains. This would seem preferable to using *ad hoc* schemes such as that adopted by the IARC and other bodies.

Commitment

When can we *accept* a conclusion based on evidence? This question motivates the inclusion of the last two properties in the list of informal requirements given above: property IX (if we must choose between two or more competing but *uncertain* or *equivocal* claims we should choose the one in which we have the greatest overall confidence) and property X (if we are not forced to choose we may defer a decision if the arguments are *inconclusive, unreliable, equivocal* or otherwise *unwarranted*).

The commitment rule implied by property IX is appealing in its simplicity—select the candidate in which we have the greatest confidence. Unfortunately, by itself this rule is potentially unsafe because it is not always clear *when* to make a commitment. At some point the balance of argument might be strongly in favour of one choice but if we wait a while some presently unknown information could become available that would change the arguments and hence the preferred claim. In other words premature commitment can lead to error. How are we to avoid this? A stronger condition is needed that says, essentially, there are no further arguments that could alter the top preference. Two general conditions may clarify this problem:

1. If we can argue that in our current state of foreground data and background knowledge there are no unknown items of information that could lead to arguments that would change the most strongly supported conclusion then we can safely commit to the claim which is currently the most preferred.
2. If there is significant unknown information but we can argue from current data and knowledge that the expected costs of seeking that information exceed the costs of making an error then we can reasonably commit to the claim in which we currently have greatest confidence.

Despite the apparent generality of these two conditions they are problematic. First, in many practical situations we may suspect that there are missing data or that we lack some critical piece of knowledge but we may not know precisely what that information is or what the evidential consequences of its absence might be. Unless we make the unrealistic assumption that we know everything that could be relevant to a claim we cannot evaluate conditions 1 and 2 in order to arrive at a stable conclusion. Second, there may not be just one missing piece of foreground data and/or background knowledge, there may be many missing pieces whose absence is individually inconclusive but certain combinations could critically change our relative confidence in the competing claims. The demands of evaluating the implications of all possible combinations of unknowns can be computationally intractable.

For these and other reasons a firm commitment to a hypothesis or claim on the basis of a body of evidence is frequently difficult. Decisions are often taken based on practical rules, which are developed to meet the specific needs of a community. These may be based on heuristic criteria that have evolved to deal with the common challenges seen by the community rather than general assessments of confidence such as probabilistic calculations.

To take a medical example, in the UK a family physician ('general practitioner' or GP) has responsibility for deciding whether a patient should be referred for diagnosis and treatment by specialist clinical services. A GP making this decision will consider the evidence for the alternative diagnoses and apply a rule of thumb such as 'if it is possible that the patient is suffering from a serious condition then s/he should be referred to an appropriate specialist'. Suppose an elderly woman who has lost weight seeks advice from her GP because her sister had previously had breast cancer and she knows that cancer can have a genetic cause. The GP may accept this argument but also *counter-argue* that the weight loss could be a side effect of another medication and, as discussed earlier, if there were a genetic predisposition the disease would normally appear much earlier in life. Despite the pros and cons, however, the GP may accept the *possibility* of a serious condition such as cancer and refer the patient to a specialist. The use of linguistic terms such as those discussed in the previous section is often present in this kind of evidential reasoning as they can be helpful in formulating practical decision rules.

As another example, a scientist or a scientific community may be engaged in a debate about whether a particular scientific theory is correct or not. Given the experimental and other foreground evidence the status of the theory may be *plausible* but not *confirmed* because there are arguments from the evidence for and against the theory and for its rivals. Furthermore there may be *counter*-arguments to some arguments (and perhaps *counter-counter*-arguments) so the overall picture remains *equivocal*. Such a dispute cannot be resolved by some sort of probabilistic calculation of the likelihood that each theory is correct because there is no plausible basis on which to estimate the probability that a theory, or its predictions, are correct. In such circumstances the community may hold that both theories remain *plausible*, and are there-fore candidates for further experimental and theoretical investigation to resolve specific issues or test predictions. This pattern is familiar from every-day life, but is particularly striking in the history of science; as Clark Glymour puts it in his book *Theory and Evidence* '... probability is a distinctly minor note in the history of scientific argument' (p. 66).

As a last example, in English criminal law a verdict can only be arrived at if the evidence points to 'a conclusion *beyond reasonable doubt*'; in civil law the weaker criterion of '*the balance of probabilities*' is used. Both of these criteria can be understood in terms of arguments and commitments. The first criterion says that if a guilty verdict (commitment) is to be brought in the arguments that are critical to a proof of the defendant's guilt must not have been rebutted and that there are no convincing arguments that the accused is innocent, or that if there are any such arguments then they must have been defeated. The second case, 'balance of probabilities (more than a 50 per cent probability that the defendant is liable)' is harder to analyse in argumentation terms. However, there is rarely any mathematical calculation involved and despite the talk of probabilities legal practitioners frequently do something very similar to the practice in medical research where 'strength of recommen-dations' are made based on logical distinctions between commonly encoun-tered patterns of argument—e.g. 'reasonable suspicion'; 'preponderance of the evidence'; 'clear and convincing'; beyond 'the shadow of a doubt' and so on.

Conclusions

In this chapter I have sought insights on evidence and evidential reasoning from law, science and medicine. A new approach to thinking about evidential reasoning has been proposed based on logical theories of argumentation, that are developing rapidly in computer science and artificial intelligence. Among the claims that I make for the contribution of argumentation concepts is that they offer a natural way of thinking about how evidence is used in the absence of quantitative data and that they illuminate both the deliberative and disputatious aspects of evidence analysis. We have identified a small number (10) of properties of natural argumentation and discussed how formal systems of argumentation can demonstrate these properties.

The particular framework we have described is based on a logical view of argumentation, in which knowledge is seen as a collection of background theories about a specific domain, or about the world in general, which are applied to foreground data about particular situations. Unlike classical logic such theories can be inconsistent; contradictions are common and background knowledge and foreground claims are associated with varying degrees of uncertainty. Since it is often difficult to quantify degrees of uncertainty in practical settings the proposed framework is designed to accommodate uncertainty by making explicit the confidence associated with arguments and the conclusions drawn from them. Unlike evidence theories based on probability our aim is to allow use of qualitative and logical representations of confidence when uncertainty cannot be quantified.

Among the benefits of a more eclectic framework are that it provides the science of evidence with an expressive language and a natural yet precise way of thinking about evidential issues. From a practical perspective it will yield powerful technologies for automating argumentation (e.g. see <http://www.argumentation.org/>) and increasingly sophisticated applications for helping people analyse and use evidence in practical tasks such as medical decision-making. I hope it can also inform debates about social policy and similar human disputes where we require 'some sort of test, to make sure they do "what is said on the tin"' (Tim Harford in BBC discussion programme *More or Less*).

References

Achinstein, P. (2001), *The Book of Evidence* (New York, Oxford University Press).

Besnard, P. and Hunter, A. (2008), *Elements of Argumentation* (Cambridge, MA, MIT Press).

Coulson, A., Glasspool, D., Fox, J. and Emery, J. (2001), 'RAGs: a novel approach to computerized genetic risk assessment and decision support from pedigrees', *Methods of Information in Medicine*, 40: 315–22.

Davis, E. (1990), *Representations of Commonsense Knowledge* (San Mateo, CA, Morgan Kaufmann).

Dawes, R. M. (1979), 'The robust beauty of improper linear models in decision making', *American Psychologist*, 34: 571–82. See also <http://en.wikipedia.org/wiki/Unit-weighted_regression>.

Dung, P. M. (1995), 'On the acceptability of arguments and its fundamental role in nonmonotonic reasoning', *Artificial intelligence Journal*, 77: 321–57.

Eddy, D. M. (2005), 'Evidence-Based Medicine: a unified approach', *Health Affairs*, 24/1: 9–17.

Elvang-Goransson, M., Krause, P. J. and Fox, J. (1993), 'Acceptability of arguments as logical uncertainty', in M. Clarke, R. Kruse and S. Moral (eds.), *Symbolic and Quantitative approaches to reasoning and uncertainty; Proc. European Conference ECSQUARU 93* (Berlin, Springer Verlag), pp. 79–84.

Fox J., Krause, P. and Ambler, S. (1992), 'Arguments, contradictions and practical reasoning', *Proc. Eur. Conference on Artificial Intelligence*, pp. 623–7.

Fox, J., Krause, P. J. and Elvang-Goransson, M. (1993), 'Argumentation as a general framework for uncertain reasoning', *Proc. Int. Conf. On Uncertainty in Artificial Intelligence* (Washington, Morgan Kaufman), p. 428.

Fox, J. and Parsons, S. (1998), 'Arguing about beliefs and actions', in A. Hunter and S. Parsons (eds.), *Applications of Uncertainty Formalisms* (Berlin, Springer-Verlag), pp. 266–302.

Franklin, Benjamin (1772), Letter to Joseph Priestley, 19 September 1772. <http://www.jstor.org/stable/20298471?cookieSet=1>.

Franklin, J. (2001), *The Science of Conjecture: Evidence and Probability before Pascal* (Baltimore, MD, Johns Hopkins University Press).

Glymour, C. (1980), *Theory and Evidence* (Princeton, NJ, Princeton University Press).

Nute, D. (1994), 'Defeasible logic', in *Handbook of Logic in Artificial Intelligence and Logic Programming*, vol. 3, *Nonmonotonic reasoning and uncertain reasoning* (Oxford, Oxford University Press), pp. 353–95.

Parsons, S. (2001), *Qualitative Methods for Reasoning under Uncertainty* (Cambridge, MA, MIT Press).

Pollock, J. L. (1987), 'Defeasible reasoning', *Cognitive Science*, 11: 4 (Oct.–Dec.), 481–518.

Popper, K. R. (2003), *Conjectures and Refutations: the growth of scientific knowledge* (London, Routledge).

Steele, R. and Fox, J. (2003), 'Enhancing web content with intelligent knowledge processing', *Proceedings of the 9th Conference on Artificial Intelligence in Medicine in Europe (AIME-03)* (Berlin: Springer), pp. 142–52.

Wellman, M. P. (1990), 'Fundamental concepts of qualitative probabilistic networks', *Artificial Intelligence*, 44/3 (Aug): 257–303.

7

Thinking about Evidence[1]

DAVID LAGNADO

Abstract

Are there general principles for how people update their beliefs in the face of uncertain evidence? How do these relate to formal theories of evidence integration? In particular, how do everyday reasoners such as jurors draw conclusions from large bodies of interrelated legal evidence? This chapter argues that people reason about legal evidence using small-scale qualitative networks. These cognitive networks are typically qualitative and incomplete, and based on people's causal beliefs about the specifics of the case as well as the workings of the physical and social world in general. A key feature of these networks is their ability to represent qualitative relations between hypotheses and evidence, allowing reasoners to capture the concepts of dependency and relevance critical in legal contexts. In support of this claim, the chapter introduces some novel empirical and formal work on alibi evidence, showing that people's reasoning conforms to the dictates of a qualitative Bayesian model. However, people's inferences do not always conform to Bayesian prescripts. We also discuss empirical studies in which people over-extend the discredit of one item of evidence to other unrelated items. This bias is explained in terms of the propensity to group positive and negative evidence separately and the use of coherence-based inference mechanisms. It is argued that these cognitive processes are a natural response to deal with the complexity of legal evidence.

[1] This chapter has benefited greatly from the Leverhulme/ESRC Evidence project, and in particular the wise words of David Schum, Philip Dawid, William Twining, Nigel Harvey, Amanda Hepler, and Gianluca Baio. I also thank Cheryl Thomas, Tobias Gerstenberg, Norman Fenton, Tracy Ray, Adam Harris, and two anonymous reviewers for insightful feedback on earlier drafts of the chapter.

Proceedings of the British Academy, **171**, 183–224. © The British Academy 2011.

Introduction

LEONARD VOLE is charged with murdering a rich elderly lady, Miss French. He had befriended her, and visited her regularly at her home, including the night of her death. Miss French had recently changed her will, leaving Vole all her money. She died from a blow to the back of the head. There were various pieces of incriminating evidence: Vole was poor and looking for work; he had visited a travel agent to enquire about luxury cruises soon after Miss French had changed her will; the maid claimed that Vole was with Miss French shortly before she was killed; the murderer did not force entry into the house; Vole had blood stains on his cuffs that matched Miss French's blood type.

As befits a good crime story, there were also several pieces of exonerating evidence: the maid admitted that she disliked Vole; the maid was previously the sole benefactor in Miss French's will; Vole's blood type was the same as Miss French's, and thus also matched the blood found on his cuffs; Vole claimed that he had cut his wrist slicing ham; Vole had a scar on his wrist to back this claim. There was one other critical piece of defence evidence: Vole's wife, Romaine, was to testify that Vole had returned home at 9.30 p.m. This would place him far away from the crime scene at the time of Miss French's death. However, during the trial Romaine was called as a witness for the prosecution. Dramatically, she changed her story and testified that Vole had returned home at 10.10 p.m., with blood on his cuffs, and had proclaimed: 'I've killed her.' Just as the case looked hopeless for Vole, a mystery woman supplied the defence lawyer with a bundle of letters. Allegedly these were written by Romaine to her overseas lover (who was a communist!). In one letter she planned to fabricate her testimony in order to incriminate Vole, and rejoin her lover. This new evidence had a powerful impact on the judge and jury. The key witness for the prosecution was discredited, and Vole was acquitted.

After the court case, Romaine revealed to the defence lawyer that she had forged the letters herself. There was no lover overseas. She reasoned that the jury would have dismissed a simple alibi from a devoted wife; instead, they could be swung by the striking discredit of the prosecution's key witness.

This crime story is a work of fiction. It is drawn from Agatha Christie's play *Witness for the Prosecution*. The story contains twists and turns that are not representative of a typical crime case; however, it serves to illustrate the patterns of inference that recur in real-world legal contexts. The task of the 'fact-finder' (e.g. investigator, judge or juror) is to pull together all the diverse threads of evidence and reach a singular judgment of innocence or guilt. One thing that makes this task so difficult is that the different pieces of evidence are often interrelated. You cannot simply sum up the positive evidence on the one hand, and the negative on the other. The evidence interacts in complex ways. For example, in the above story, Vole's enquiry about a luxury cruise is not relevant on its own; it becomes relevant because he had recently been written into the old lady's will. Moreover, it strongly suggests that he knew that she had changed her will. Not only does this give him a motive for the murder, but it also shows that he was lying when he claimed not to know that he stood to benefit from her death.[2]

This is what makes crime stories so fascinating. They cannot be solved simply by adding or subtracting beliefs; rather, one must negotiate the intricacies of how the different parts of the puzzle fit together. Further, the pressure to reach a decisive verdict—in a criminal case beyond reasonable doubt[3]—means that a simple leaning towards one side or the other is no good. One needs to mentally bolster the case for or against the suspect, so that it clearly dominates the alternatives—crowding out other possible construals of the case. This compels one to construct a story that is both one-sided[4] and comprehensive, and thus likely to fill in many gaps left unsupported by the evidence at hand. There is seldom the leisure to tinker away slowly, as in science, accumulating support for each step; instead, one must sketch a picture all in one go, and hope that it captures the essential truths of the case.

Despite the enormity of the task, untrained jurors are expected to reach verdicts that can have life-changing consequences. For the large part they achieve this (although mistakes are made!). How do they do this? How should they do it? These are the questions that this chapter will address.

Before we start, it is important to clarify the intended domain of the chapter. It is not about the reasoning of legal experts, such as judges, barristers, or investigators. It is about the reasoning of lay people when confronted with complex bodies of evidence. This might involve an individual juror on a criminal case, but it could also be a member of the general public following the unfolding of evidence through reading snippets in the media. Moreover, it

---

[2] In the legal context it is common to distinguish between direct and circumstantial evidence. The former is supposed to prove a fact without need of additional inference (e.g. a witness testifying that he saw the defendant kill the victim) while the latter must be supported by other inferences (e.g. a witness testifying that he saw the defendant leave the crime scene; DNA evidence). This terminology is potentially misleading, because direct evidence is still open to doubt (e.g. the witness might be mistaken or lying in their testimony). Nevertheless, the fact that most of the evidence in a case is circumstantial supports our contention that items of evidence are often interrelated. In the *Witness for the Prosecution* story all of the evidence is circumstantial.

[3] In England jurors 'must be sure that the defendant is guilty'.

[4] This is most applicable to the adversarial system in criminal trials in England and the USA, but less so to the inquisitorial systems typical in Europe.

is the individual juror that is the focus of attention here, not the group of jurors that participate in the jury deliberation process. This is not to say that what we discover about the psychology of the individual juror, or non-expert, does not have implications for the jury as a whole, or for the expert judge (they are human after all). But extrapolation to these more complex cases would require a lot more argument and evidence.

Networks of relations

Evidence is typically sorted as positive or negative with respect to a particular hypothesis. For example, evidence can either exonerate or incriminate a suspect. However, there are various different ways in which the evidence can exert its influence on a hypothesis, and these different routes are masked by the simple dichotomy of positive versus negative. To illustrate, consider the distinction between *affirmative* and *rebuttal* evidence (cf. Binder and Bergman, 1984). Affirmative evidence directly supports the case made by either prosecution or defence. For example, the maid's testimony that she heard Vole talking to Miss French shortly before the murder is affirmative evidence for Vole's guilt. Rebuttal evidence is less direct; it serves to undermine a claim made by the opposing side. For instance, the maid's testimony is rebutted by the evidence that she disliked Vole, and sought to incriminate him. Affirmative and rebuttal evidence can be presented by both sides to the dispute, and thus crosscuts the distinction between incriminating and exonerating evidence. Indeed some evidence is both affirmative and rebuttal. For example, the wife's statement that Vole returned home much later than 9.30 p.m. rebuts his alibi, and also supports the claim that he was with Miss French shortly before the murder.

More generally, a crucial difference between affirmative and rebuttal evidence is that the latter is only relevant to a hypothesis (e.g. guilt or innocence) because it targets a piece of evidence presented by the opposing side.[5] Without an item of evidence to oppose, rebuttal evidence exerts no influence on the target hypothesis. Thus evidence that the maid disliked Vole is only relevant to his guilt given her testimony that he was with Miss French shortly before the time of her murder.

To capture the distinction between affirmative and rebuttal evidence, and various other structural subtleties, evidence and hypotheses need to be

---

[5] Schum (2001) makes the distinction between 'evidence about events' and 'evidence about evidence'. Here affirmative evidence is a subset of the former, and rebuttal evidence is a subset of the latter.

represented in a *network*. It seldom suffices to gather positive items on one side, negative items on the other, and compute a weighted sum (as Charles Darwin famously did when deciding whether or not to marry). Instead, account must be taken of how these items of evidence might interrelate.

Formal models of evidential reasoning

How can complex interrelations between evidence and hypotheses be represented? Before looking at how people do this in practice, it is instructive to consider how it can be done in principle. There have been substantial advances in normative models of evidential reasoning over the past decade, and a variety of network models have been developed, including Wigmore charts (Wigmore, 1913), cognitive maps (Axelrod, 1976), and Bayesian networks (Pearl, 1988). We will focus on Bayesian networks. They have well-established foundations in probability theory, and are currently applied in many practical contexts, including legal and forensic reasoning (Dawid and Evett, 1997; Dawid, Mortera and Vicard, 2007; Fenton and Neil, 2008; Hepler, Dawid and Leucari, 2007; Taroni, Aitken, Garbolino and Biedermann, 2006).

Bayesian networks

Bayesian networks (BNs) consist of two parts: a graph structure and a set of conditional probability tables. The graph structure is made up of a set of nodes corresponding to the variables of interest, and a set of directed links between these variables corresponding to causal or evidential relations. In legal contexts the variables will include hypotheses about the details of the crime, the culprit, the suspect and numerous evidence statements. This yields a directed graph that compactly represents the probabilistic relations between variables, in particular the conditional and unconditional dependencies. Thus the graph can be used to read off which items of evidence are relevant to each other, or to particular hypotheses. For example, the graph in Figure 7.1 represents a small portion of the evidence in the *Witness for the Prosecution* story outlined above.

This graph has four binary variables, each taking values of either true or false. The variable 'Vole Guilty' represents whether or not Vole murdered Miss French. The variable 'Vole Present' represents whether or not Vole was with Miss French at 9.30 p.m. on the night of the murder. The variable 'Maid Testimony' represents whether or not the maid testified that Vole was present

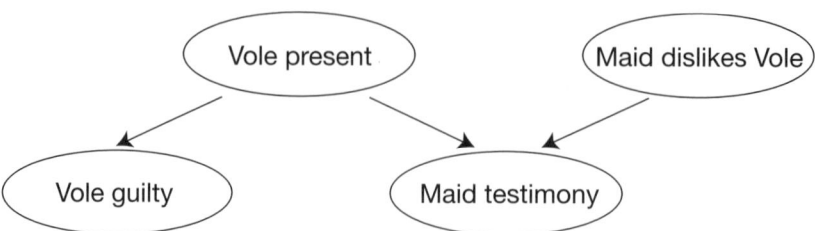

Figure 7.1. A simple Bayesian Network capturing a few variables in the *Witness for the Prosecution* story.

at that time. The variable 'Maid dislikes Vole' represents whether or not the maid disliked Vole.

The link from 'Vole Present' to 'Vole Guilty' indicates that Vole's committing the murder that night depends on his being with her at 9.30 p.m. Obviously this link is probabilistic—Vole might have been present at that time but not guilty of the subsequent murder. Moreover, Vole's presence at the crime scene is clearly not a sufficient cause of his murdering Miss French. Various additional causal factors, such as motive and intent are necessary for Vole to have murdered her. Some of these variables are represented in the fuller Bayesian Network in Figure 7.3. Nevertheless Vole's presence at the crime scene is evidence of opportunity, and thus raises to some degree the probability that he did murder Miss French. This explains the link from 'Vole Present' to 'Vole Guilty'.

The link from 'Vole Present' to 'Maid Testimony' indicates that the Maid's claim—that she heard Vole speaking to Miss French around 9.30 p.m.—depends on whether or not Vole was actually there at that time. This link is also probabilistic. Perhaps the maid misidentified Vole's voice. Indeed the defence lawyer suggested that she might have heard voices from the radio. Another alternative cause of the maid's testimony is that she fabricated it because she disliked Vole. After all, in the trial she expressed a strong dislike for him. This possibility is explicitly represented in the network by the link from 'Maid dislikes Vole' to 'Maid Testimony'.

In addition to the graph, a Bayesian network also requires a conditional probability distribution table for each variable. This dictates the probability of the variable in question conditional on the possible values of its parents (the nodes with direct links into that variable). When a node has no parents, this table simply contains the base-rate value for that variable. This base-rate corresponds to the prior probability of the variable before any of the case evidence is taken into account. In some cases the exact values of these conditional probabilities are not too important, so long as they obey the qualitative relations encapsulated by the links in the graph. For example, the presence of a link from 'Vole present' to 'Maid Testimony' requires that the probability of the testimony given that Vole is present is greater than (or less than) the probability of the testimony given that Vole is not present. However, there are various aspects that are not given by the graph structure alone, but are furnished by the probabilities themselves: for example, whether the link is positive or negative; how the values of different parent nodes combine to dictate the value of the child node. In addition, most of the algorithms that allow a BN representation to be used for inference require exact numbers.

Representation and inference

A significant bonus of Bayesian networks is that once the representation is constructed, it can be used for inference. This sets it apart from most other forms of networks (e.g. Wigmore charts and Cognitive maps), which serve mainly as descriptive tools. Indeed representation is intertwined with inference in a BN. The arrangement of nodes and links, plus the conditional probability tables for each node, dictate what inferences are licensed (via the laws of probability). One way to draw novel inferences is to set a subset of variables to particular values (instantiate the variables), and then see what effect this has on the other variables of interest (e.g. the crime hypothesis). This corresponds to standard cases of inferential reasoning in legal cases. Moreover, it enables several kinds of inference: inference based on evidence that is known for sure (e.g. the Maid's testimony), evidence that is believed with some probability (e.g. that Vole was poor), and evidence that is presumed for sake of argument (e.g. if we suppose that Vole was present at 9.30 p.m., what else follows?). The latter can be very useful at the investigative stage of enquiry, when new pieces of evidence are sought. For example, a detective might suppose that Vole was indeed present at 9.30 p.m., and then infer the likely consequences of this, such as Vole being seen and heard by the maid, or leaving some trace evidence.

Patterns of inference

The network structure captures several patterns of inference critical to evidential reasoning.

Screening-off (conditional independence)

A basic feature of BNs is the screening-off relation. This holds when two variables that are probabilistically dependent are rendered independent by the knowledge of the state of a third variable. For example, the maid's testimony depends on Vole's guilt, but if we know for certain that Vole was with Miss French at 9.30 p.m., her testimony becomes independent of his guilt. In other words, if we already know that Vole was with Miss French at 9.30 p.m., the maid's testimony does not add anything to our knowledge of whether or not Vole is guilty. Of course such certainty is often hard to come by. Even CCTV footage confirming Vole's presence at 9.30 p.m. is open to doubt. Was it really Vole? Could the footage have been tampered with? Is the timing correct? Nevertheless there are many situations where a proposition is assumed or accepted as true (or false).

The BN representation rests upon the assumption that the parent nodes of a variable screen it off from all other variables in the network (except for variables that themselves depend on that variable).[6] This is a powerful condition: it can greatly simplify the computations needed to draw inferences, allowing various items of evidence to be ignored all together. For example, if it is established that Vole was with Miss French at 9.30 p.m., then no other witness testimony about this event can influence the probability that Vole is guilty. This screening-off assumption can also aid future investigation and information gathering. Thus, if an event E is established for certain, there is no additional inferential benefit to be gained from further witness testimonies that attest to E. Of course in many cases the truth of a key event will remain in dispute; hence the adding of extra witnesses to the same event will be a reasonable policy.

In legal investigations, as in everyday life, it is crucial to distinguish between what people claim and what actually happened. The network structure

---

[6] It is important to be clear about the provisional nature of BN representations and the inferences they sanction. The 'screening-off' condition is just an assumption, and in some cases its applicability is debatable, see Cartwright (2007) and Williamson (2005). This reinforces the fact that any inference requires certain assumptions, and there is no guarantee that these assumptions hold true of the domain to be modelled. This problem strikes at the status of BNs as 'true' models of the world, but it need not undermine their status as 'useful' models. Any practical model is bound to involve simplifications and assumptions. The real test is how well they serve the inferential goals of the user. And human users, with their bounded computational abilities, might be well-served by principled simplifications such as the screening-off assumption. Indeed we will argue later that the BN framework needs to be simplified further, if it is to provide a reasonable tool for human cognition. It is also important to distinguish questions as to whether a BN is appropriate for a specific case (e.g. is there a link from H to A? Does E screen-off H from A?), and the justifiability of the 'screening-off' assumption in general.

is ideally suited to this, and readily distinguishes witness reports from the events or situations that these reports are about. Thus the maid's testimony that Vole was with Miss French at 9.30 p.m. is represented separately from the event that he was in fact with her at that time. One advantage in representing the report E* and the reported events E separately is that the probative force of the events (if true) is kept distinct from the credibility of the witness source.[7] This is important because the factors relevant to the probative force of E on the target hypothesis H are quite different from those relevant to the relation between the report E* and E. For example, there are various reasons why Vole's presence at 9.30 p.m. does not guarantee that he killed Miss French; perhaps someone else was there too, or broke in shortly afterwards. But a different set of factors potentially undermine the reliability of a witness report, and thus the inference from E* to E. This is a place where rebuttal evidence can exert its force. Perhaps the maid misidentified the voice, or heard the radio, or simply lied. The distinction between E* and E also greatly facilitates inference in situations where there are several witness testimonies to the same event, and clarifies the differences between corroborating, conflicting, or contradictory testimony.[8]

Explaining away

The screening-off relation holds when three variables are in a chain (A→B→C)[9] or a divergent structure (A←B→C). In both cases, A and C are dependent, but become independent conditional on B. The converse situation occurs with a convergent structure (A→B←C). In this case, A and C are independent, but become dependent conditional on B (or conditional on a variable that itself depends on B). This encapsulates a distinctive pattern of inference termed 'explaining away'.[10]

Explaining away typically occurs in situations where there are multiple independent hypotheses (explanations) for an observed item of evidence. The observed evidence leads to some increase in probability for all these hypotheses; however, if one of these is found to be true, the others then decrease in probability. The evidence that previously supported them is explained

---

[7] This distinction is explicitly introduced in Schum (2001), and his notation is used here.

[8] See Schum (2001) for extensive discussion of these issues.

[9] An example of an A→B→C chain, drawn from our crime story, is as follows: Vole's being a legatee in Miss French's will (A) is a potential cause of him murdering Miss French (B) (it is definitely a motive!), and his murder of Miss French is a potential cause of the blood on his cuffs (C). This chain is embedded in Figure 7.3.

[10] See Pearl (1988).

away. A notable feature of this situation is that the possible hypotheses are independent when the status of the evidence is unknown, but become conditionally dependent given knowledge of its status. This is distinct from cases where hypotheses are mutually exclusive.

To illustrate, consider again the network in Figure 7.1. There is no direct link between 'Vole present' and 'Maid dislikes Vole'. This indicates that these two variables are unconditionally independent. Whether or not Vole was present at that time is irrelevant to whether or not the maid disliked Vole, and vice versa. However, once the maid gives her testimony, these two variables become conditionally dependent—they compete as alternative explanations of her testimony. Suppose further that we are sure that the maid does have a strong dislike for Vole, and wishes to incriminate him. This hypothesis will 'explain away' the maid's testimony.

Consider another example from the *Witness for the Prosecution*. Vole's cuffs were found to have traces of blood on them (type O). This was advanced as evidence that Vole had murdered Miss French (who had blood type O).[11] However, the defence sought to explain away this evidence by claiming that the blood belonged to Vole (also type O), who had cut himself when slicing ham. This claim in turn was backed-up by a recent scar on Vole's wrist. Clearly there are two competing explanations for the presence of blood on Vole's cuffs. Moreover, these explanations were independent prior to the discovery of blood on the cuffs.

Legal scenarios, and evidential contexts in general, are replete with 'explaining away' inferences, and it is a substantial advantage of the BN framework that it models this inference so naturally. This also explicates the distinction between affirmative and rebuttal evidence mentioned earlier. Rebuttal evidence serves to explain away an opposing piece of affirmative evidence. For instance, the blood on Vole's cuffs is affirmative evidence that he murdered Miss French, whereas the claim that he cut himself slicing ham (and the scar on his wrist) is rebuttal evidence. Whether or not Vole cut himself is only relevant to the question of his guilt because it rebuts (explains away) the evidence provided by the blood on his cuffs. BNs provide a natural format for representing this kind of evidential subtlety.

---

[11] Christie's story comes from the days before DNA evidence. Nowadays DNA testing would be the standard method to determine whether the bloodstain was from Vole or Miss French. DNA tests have much greater power to discriminate, but still yield conclusions with a degree of uncertainty. In such forensic contexts, Bayesian networks provide the normative standard for quantifying the impact of DNA evidence (Taroni *et al.*, 2006).

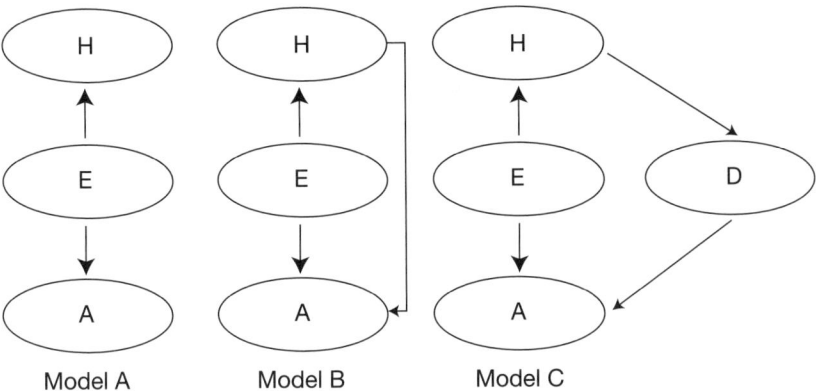

Figure 7.2. Witness vs Alibi models. Model A is an impartial witness testimony in which E screens-off H from E*. Model B is a partial alibi testimony where E does not screen-off H from A, and Model C represents the same situation as model B but with the deception variable D explicitly represented.

Alibi testimony and failure of screening-off

In the simplest case of witness testimony, the event testified to (E) will screen-off the witness report E* from the target hypothesis H (see Fig. 7.2, model A). This screening-off relation can hold even if there are serious reasons to doubt the reliability of the maid's testimony, or the probativeness of the event E. However, this will not always be the case. Sometimes the witness report E* will exert an independent influence on H. This is most clearly illustrated by considering alibi testimony.

An alibi involves the claim that the defendant was somewhere else at the time the crime was committed. Assuming that nobody can be in two places at the same time[12] an alibi is potentially very strong evidence in favour of the defendant. This is because the probability that the defendant committed the crime, on the supposition that he *was not* at the crime scene, is very low, and much lower than the probability that he committed the crime, given that he *was* at the crime scene. However, alibi evidence is often considered weak evidence, especially if it is only the defendant's word, and there is no corroborating evidence (Gooderson, 1977).

The alibi context is depicted by model B in Figure 7.2. The variable H corresponds to the hypothesis that the defendant is guilty; variable E to the

---

[12] And ignoring situations where something or someone is remotely controlled—e.g. detonating a bomb; hiring an assassin.

defendant's presence at the crime scene; variable A to the defendant's claim that he was somewhere else. The link from E to H indicates that his committing the crime depends on his presence at the crime-scene; the link from E to A indicates that his alibi statement depends on whether or not he was at the crime scene. In the case of alibi testimony the inference from H to E is usually taken to be much stronger than the inference from A to E.

There is also a direct link from H to A. This represents our claim that the event E does not screen-off H from A. Why is this the case? Recall that the screening-off relation states that once you know the value of the intermediate variable E, knowledge of A tells you nothing more about H (and vice versa). But consider the situation in which the defendant gives his alibi, but you have independent evidence (e.g. CCTV footage) that he was in fact at the crime scene. Does the fact that he said he was not at the crime scene tell you anything more about whether or not he is guilty? Well now you know that he lied.[13] And this information seems incriminating, over-and-above the fact that you know that he was at the crime scene. Of course he might be lying for other reasons: perhaps he was having an affair; or committing a different crime. But it seems reasonable to assume that the probability that he will lie in his alibi is greater when he is guilty than when he is innocent.

On this reading of the situation, the event E no longer screens-off H from A. The probability that the defendant is guilty (H) given that he was at the crime scene (E) is lower than the probability that he is guilty (H) given that he was at the crime scene (E) *and* said he was not at the crime scene (A). In numbers, $P(H|E\&A) > P(H|E)$. For screening-off to hold, these two probabilities would have to be equal.[14]

In other words, finding out that the defendant has lied in his alibi tells you more about his guilt than simply knowing that he was at the crime scene. The possibility that the alibi provider is lying can itself be represented in the graph (see Figure 7.2 model C) with an additional node D representing whether or not the defendant is motivated to lie. The link from H to D corresponds to the assumption that the motivation to lie depends on whether or not the defendant is guilty (i.e. he is more likely to lie when guilty than when innocent). The link from D to A indicates that whether the defendant says he was present at the crime scene depends on whether he is motivated to lie (i.e. he is more likely to say he was not at the crime scene if he is motivated to lie).

---

[13] It is possible that he was mistaken, for example if he suffers from severe memory loss; but in most cases this will be unlikely.
[14] For details see Hepler, Lagnado and Baio (2007).

This 'alibi network' is readily applied to Vole's alibi. Recall that Vole claimed that he returned to his home at 9.30 p.m., and therefore was not with Miss French at that time. However, if Vole is indeed guilty he would have strong motivation to lie about this. This furnishes an alternative explanation for his alibi. Therefore it is not too surprising that a defendant's alibi is often treated with scorn. The alternative explanation in terms of deception explains away the alibi testimony.

The situation changes if someone else corroborates the alibi. An impartial witness, with nothing to gain, might bolster the alibi considerably (although not always as much as expected).[15] A partial witness, such as a friend or relative, is less convincing. After all, they too have a motive to lie. Romaine knew this, and realised that the jury would not be overly impressed by a supporting alibi from Vole's beloved wife.

An intriguing consequence of the alibi network is that the failure of screening-off only seems to apply when the alibi-provider *knows* whether or not the defendant committed the crime. This is because the link from H to D is only present if the guilt of the defendant influences the alibi-provider's motivation to lie. But if the alibi-provider does not know whether or not the defendant is guilty, there is no such link. This is not to say that the alibi-provider is not motivated to lie in his favour, but just that this motivation is not dependent on the defendant actually being guilty. For example, one might expect a wife to lie for her beloved husband even if she does not know whether he is guilty or innocent. But in this case the event E will screen-off H from A. If we know that the defendant was at the crime scene (E), finding out that the alibi-provider lied to protect the defendant does not add anything extra to our assessment of guilt. Their motivation to lie was not affected by whether or not the defendant was indeed guilty.

This twist demonstrates the considerable subtleties that can arise in reasoning about witness or alibi evidence, and reiterates the need for a network representation. In a later section we will present an empirical study showing that people are sensitive to this subtlety in their inferences about alibi evidence.

Thus far it appears that BNs provide a promising framework to represent the complex interrelations between bodies of evidence and hypotheses. In particular, BNs capture important patterns of reasoning such as screening-off and explaining away, and elucidate some of the subtleties involved in alibi

---

[15] See empirical study by Culhane and Hosch (2004).

and witness testimony.[16] Moreover, it is the graph structure rather than the exact conditional probabilities that play the key role. The network representations and the qualitative 'relevance' relations between variables do much of the inferential work.

Holistic vs atomistic approaches

Bayesian approaches to legal reasoning are often criticised for their 'atomistic' evaluation of evidence (e.g. Pardo and Allen, 2008). In contrast, proponents of a holistic approach argue that evidence should be assessed as a whole—not piecemeal. This claim also draws on psychological research that jurors compose coherent stories to make sense of the evidence presented at trial (Pennington and Hastie, 1986, 1992). However, this criticism is based on a restricted notion of the Bayesian approach that does not take into account the holistic relations implicit in Bayesian networks. The network model defended in this chapter maintains that people organise evidence and hypotheses in coherent networks, and that this is often the right thing to do from a rational viewpoint. Thus, an item of evidence can only be evaluated with respect to its relation to other items of evidence and relevant hypotheses. For example, the scar on Vole's wrist is only relevant to the hypothesis of his guilt given his claim that he cut himself slicing ham, and the evidence of blood on his cuffs. This is not to say that smaller subsets of evidence cannot be analysed in isolation from other subsets. Presumably the complexities of the blood evidence are largely independent of the issues that surround the maid's testimony about Vole's presence on the night of the crime—these subsets are only linked via the superordinate proposition that Vole committed the crime. Indeed it is the possibility of isolating small subsets of evidence that makes a network approach tractable to the human mind.

A related issue is whether people's ultimate focus is on the probability of the issue in question, for example, the probability that the defendant is guilty, or on something more holistic, such as the probability (or plausibility) of the prosecution's account as a whole (as compared to the defendant's account). The Bayesian account is usually portrayed as concentrating on the former— the probability of the crime hypothesis given all the evidence. And a standard objection is that in contrast fact-finders are concerned with holistic judgements, such as how believable the prosecution story is as compared to the

---

[16] The Bayesian network framework also has the potential to formalise and explicate other patterns of legal inference, for example the distinction between cable and chain inferences (see Hamer, 1997).

defence story. However, the latter kind of judgement is readily accommodated within the broader Bayesian framework. Thus, Pearl discusses inference mechanisms that revise the probability of composite sets of beliefs rather than updating individual probabilities (Pearl, 1988). In short, the Bayesian network framework is not restricted to probability judgements about singular propositions, but can extend to judgements about sets of propositions. It supplies the tools for assessing the probability of a connected set of beliefs, as well as individual beliefs.

Bayesian networks as models of human reasoning?

Bayesian networks have considerable appeal as normative models of evidential reasoning, especially in domains with quantitative data (Aitken, Taroni and Garbolino, 2003; Dawid, Mortera and Vicard, 2007; Hepler and Weir, 2008). However, fully fledged BNs are unlikely to provide a comprehensive model for human reasoning. The specification of precise conditional probabilities, and the complex computations required to draw inferences, seem beyond the capabilities of human reasoners, especially when large numbers of variables are involved. For example, even a partial BN for the *Witness for the Prosecution*, including only a subset of the available evidence, would present an intimidating picture for the uninitiated juror (see Fig. 7.3). Indeed many psychological studies suggest that people are poor at estimating and calculating

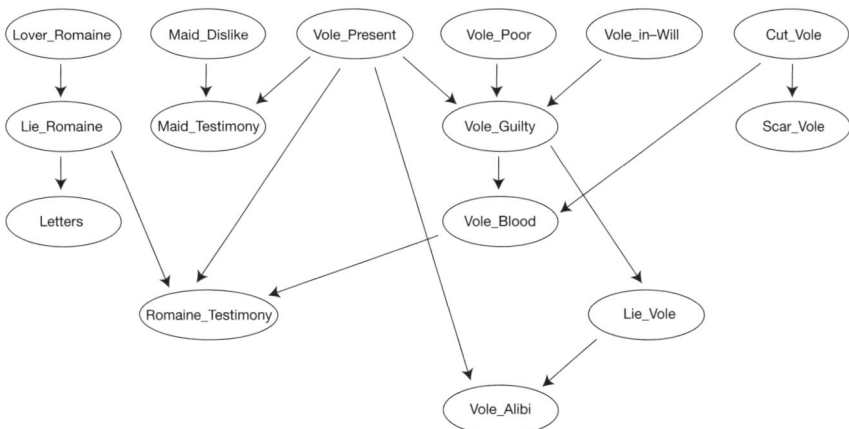

Figure 7.3. Partial Bayesian Network covering some of the major pieces of evidence in *Witness for the Prosecution*. Note that not all the items of evidence have been included in this network.

with probabilities (Gilovich, Griffin and Kahneman, 2002; Kahneman, Slovic and Tversky, 1982).

It thus appears that BNs are a non-starter as a descriptive model. However, this conclusion is premature. It overlooks the fact that key aspects of the BN formalism are qualitative rather than quantitative, and that BNs can be hierarchically structured to overcome human processing limitations.

Qualitative network models

The network structure of a BN is purely qualitative, representing the presence or absence of dependencies between variables. Thus a link from A to B tells us that certain values of A will change the probability of certain values of B, without needing to specify exactly how much. And although the standard BN framework requires a precise set of conditional probabilities, many of the important characteristics of the network are retained without a full and exact set of probabilities (Biedermann and Taroni, 2006; Wellman and Henrion, 1993).

This means that someone can construct the graphical part of a BN without having access to any precise probabilities. Moreover, in many cases they will still be able to draw inferences based solely on this qualitative structure, albeit less precise ones than with a quantitative network. Indeed most of our examples and discussions so far have relied on this qualitative sense of probabilistic relations.

Therefore the fact that people cannot estimate or calculate with exact probabilities does not undermine the possibility that they use networks to represent relations between evidence and hypotheses. Furthermore, such qualitative representations can apply equally well in domains where no precise figures are available. This is particularly significant in the legal context, where much of the evidence does not admit of quantification. For example, it might not be possible to quantify the exact probative force of a witness testimony that places the defendant at the crime scene; but most people would agree that it raises the probability of guilt, however slightly. Moreover, people will often be able to make comparative probability judgements; for instance, judging that a certain piece of forensic evidence (e.g. traces of the victim's blood found on the defendant's coat) raises the probability of guilt more than the testimony of a partial witness.

The important point is that even if people lack a fully specified probabilistic model, they can still express their uncertain knowledge in terms of a qualitative network. In a similar vein, even if people are unable to perform exact Bayesian computations over this network, they can still draw approximate inferences (perhaps using heuristic methods). And this might not be such a bad thing, especially in contexts where exact figures are unavailable, or where there are large numbers of interacting variables, so that exact inference is intractable. The restriction to qualitative networks might actually increase the applicability and feasibility of these networks to the problems faced in legal contexts.

The idea that people utilise qualitative networks is not new. And in computer science there are various qualitative reasoning systems designed to mesh with the natural propensities of human users (Druzdzel, 1996; Keppens, 2007; Parsons, 2001). These provide an impressive array of representational formats and inference algorithms. There are also several considerations from psychology that speak in favour of qualitative approaches.

First, psychophysical studies show that for a range of sensory phenomena people are poor at making absolute judgements, and instead make ordinal comparisons (e.g. Stewart, Brown and Chater, 2005). Estimates of likelihood or strength of evidence seem no exception to this. Thus, although someone might not be able to judge the precise probative force of evidence E1 on hypothesis H, they might be able to judge that E1 makes H more probable, and perhaps that E1 is stronger evidence for H than E2 is.

Second, analyses of a wide range of predictive tasks (e.g. clinical and medical diagnosis) suggest that statistical models that use unit weights often outperform more complex models (Dawes, 1979). The key requirement for these simpler models is that the sign of each variable in the model is correct; the exact weights placed on these variables is not critical. While the generalisability of these findings is open to question, the success of unit weight models in these specific environments remains impressive. One lacuna is that the models typically assume a simplistic structure, where the relevant predictor variables are independent. This assumption might work well in certain environments, but is unlikely to succeed in more complex contexts, such as the legal domain, where the interrelations between evidence and hypotheses are crucial. The proposed qualitative networks thus go beyond simple linear models, but share the intuition that precision in the weights is not a necessary condition for successful inference (and in fact might impair performance, by adding a spurious degree of precision).[17]

Third, psychological research on causal reasoning (Griffiths and Tenenbaum, 2005; Lagnado, Waldmann, Hagmayer and Sloman, 2007; Sloman, 2005) suggests that people are initially concerned with judgements about

---

[17] Note that in the judge's directions to the jury on how they should reach their verdict, the terminology used is 'the law does not attempt to provide a scale of answers to juries'.

causal structure (is there a link between A and B?) rather than causal strength (how strong is the link between A and B?). People focus on qualitative causal relations, and use these causal models to guide their inference and actions. There is also growing empirical evidence that people reason in accordance with the qualitative prescripts of causal BNs (Krynski and Tenenbaum, 2007; Sloman and Lagnado, 2005). Clearly, causal beliefs are critical in the construction of our models of the world. If these are predominantly qualitative, then so too will be the network structures that they underpin. Indeed it has been argued that people's network representations of the world are causal through-and-through. Pearl (2000) advances an argument for the primacy of qualitative causal beliefs that also serves as a strong empirical hypothesis about human cognition. He argues that the best way for people to organise their knowledge of the world is in terms of invariant (stable) qualitative causal relations. These relations, once known or assumed, will not change according to the particularities of the information we have, whereas probabilistic relations can. For example, consider a chain $A \rightarrow B \rightarrow C$. There is a probabilistic dependency between A and C, but this disappears when we know B (screening-off). Conversely, consider a common effect model $A \rightarrow B \leftarrow C$. On this model A and C are probabilistically independent, but become dependent conditional on our knowing B (explaining away). What remains constant across all these changes in the probabilistic relations are the underlying causal relations in the models. Of course we might have the structure wrong, but this is a separate issue. In essence, the argument is that people should prefer to organise their knowledge on the basis of invariant rather than unstable aspects of the world. This is not to say that causal relations do not change. They often will, especially when we interact with the world. But unlike with probabilistic relations, these changes will reflect changes in the world rather than changes in our knowledge about it. This is a powerful conjecture about human cognition, and psychologists are exploring its implications. However, it is not an essential part of the current argument, which emphasises the *qualitative* nature of our 'mental networks'.

The proposal that the fundamental building blocks of human reasoning are qualitative fits with Gilbert Harman's claim that people think and reason primarily in terms of beliefs (all-or-none) rather than degrees of belief (Harman, 1986). To speculate, one reason for the central role of categorical beliefs might derive from the close relation between thought and action. Events in the world, including actions and outcomes, are typically all-or-none; so our representations of these events are likely to follow suit. For instance, the suspect was either at the crime scene or not—he cannot have been 67 per cent present. Consequently, when reasoning about this possibility we either suppose that he was present, or suppose that he was not. It seems less plausible that we can suppose and reason with some mixed state in which he is partially there, and partially elsewhere. This is not to say that more complex situations cannot admit of gradations, or that we cannot assign probabilities or degrees of belief. The claim is that our cognitive systems have primarily developed to reason with situations involving categorical events, actions and outcomes.

Small-scale networks

Not only do people reason qualitatively, they also seem to reason with just a few variables at a time. This is not to argue that they cannot build up large-scale knowledge sets containing many variables; but the active reasoning process is likely to involve only a few variables at a time. This seems to be a natural consequence of our limited working memory capacity (Cowan, 2001; Halford, Cowan and Andrews, 2007; Miller, 1956). This restriction suggests that active evidential reasoning takes place with network fragments (e.g. the model in Fig. 7.1) rather than the full-scale networks (e.g. the larger model in Fig. 7.3). These small-scale networks are sufficient to carry out key inference patterns such as explaining-away or screening-off, but may require that some variables be 'chunked' together or ignored entirely. Reasoning with network fragments can lead to modifications in the implicitly stored knowledge base, so that in the long term people effectively represent larger structures. In other words, people construct and reason with network fragments, and these are stitched together to yield a large-scale picture of the world. On this view, working memory acts as a bottleneck between the world and our large-scale representation of this world.

Hierarchical representations

The notion of chunking is widely recognised to be a key feature of human memory, but it has not been connected with inference and reasoning in a legal context.[18] In the context of evidential reasoning, it seems that people use richly structured representations that can be unpacked at various levels of grain. In this way people can negotiate a complex problem domain with multiple interacting variables, while respecting the limitations of working memory and

---

[18] See work on chunking in expert chess players, Chase and Simon (1973), and in medical diagnosis, Schmidt and Boshuizen (1993).

active reasoning.[19] For example, in many crime cases the initial level of representation is in terms of individual people (e.g. victim, perpetrator, suspect, accomplices, witnesses), objects (e.g. weapons, blood traces, fibres), and the spatiotemporal relations and interactions between them. At a finer level of grain, each individual possesses various attributes (age, race, gender, personality traits, dispositions etc.), along with beliefs, desires and intentions that serve to explain and predict their behaviour. When reasoning about a crime case the fact-finder can switch between these levels of abstraction, at one moment reasoning about the interactions between several individuals (e.g. the locations of Vole, Miss French and the maid on the night of the crime), at another moment reasoning about the motives, beliefs and intentions of a specific individual (e.g. the maid). The key point is that by using rich hierarchically structured representations human reasoners can overcome the limitations imposed by their limited-capacity working memory.

How does this ability to chunk information fit with the idea that human reasoners use Bayesian networks? At first sight it would seem that the hierarchically structured representations used in human reasoning are far-removed from Bayesian networks, which represent all variables at the same level. However, recent work in computer science (Koller and Pfeffer, 1997; Hepler, Dawid and Leucari, 2007) has developed probabilistic systems that introduce hierarchical structures ('objects') to deal with more complex real-world domains. These systems are still based upon Bayesian networks, and exploit the notion of conditional independence, but allow for richer representations and more efficient inference procedures. This highlights an intriguing parallel between the human reasoning system and artificial systems developed in computer science. In order to cope with the computational demands of large and complex domains, both systems make use of hierarchical structured representations, and simplify inference by using network structures that exploit conditional independence relations. Thus future research into human evidential reasoning can profitably draw on advances in probabilistic graphical frameworks.

Our guiding hypothesis is that people reason about legal evidence using small-scale qualitative networks. These networks are generated on the basis of background assumptions, generic causal knowledge, and case-specific information, and utilise hierarchically structured representations to overcome computational limitations and support efficient inference. Such networks often require only comparative judgements of relevance and probability, rather than precise probability estimates. In addition, it is likely that people flexibly adopt

---

[19] For a related argument about the use of stereotypes in decision making in legal contexts, see Davies and Patel (2005).

the format that best suits the data available to them. For example, combining quantitative evidence such as that provided by a DNA match with qualitative evidence such as that furnished by a witness testimony. Reasoning and inference might also be conducted in an approximate fashion, rather than through full-scale Bayesian computation. There is a range of possible inference mechanisms, including sign propagation, belief propagation, spreading activation and constraint satisfaction. Here again the choice of mechanism might depend on the available data and the format of the network. For example, if all network links have signs (positive or negative),[20] but no strength value, then sign propagation is the most appropriate inference mechanism. If the strength of links can be ranked or quantified, then other algorithms might be more suitable.

Another important feature to note is that the qualitative network models that people construct are subjective. These models depend on an individual's background knowledge and assumptions, the evidence available to them, their interpretation of this evidence, and myriad other factors. And of course these can differ substantially from individual to individual. Presumably the prosecution's model will be very different from that of the defence. However, this does not mean that they are unconstrained, or that reasonable people cannot end up agreeing on a shared model. The requirements of consistency and coherence (and fit with real-world causal knowledge), and the need to accommodate the undisputed elements of the case, will place constraints on the viable models and inferences that can be legitimately drawn from the available evidence. The trial is a social structure that will ideally converge on a model that is an appropriate reflection of what actually happened in the case.

Sources of reasoning errors

The central claim is that qualitative networks lie at the heart of people's evidential reasoning. This is not to say that people will conform perfectly to the dictates of any specific qualitative reasoning system. Rather, the claim is that the fundamental vehicle for representation and inference is qualitative, and often derived from causal understanding. Indeed, there will be many ways in which evidential reasoning can fall short of normative theory. With regard to representation, people can err due to inadequate models, failure to include crucial variables or links, inappropriate collapsing or grouping of variables.

---

[20] The standard way of determining the sign of a link is via the following comparative probabilistic relations: A→B is +ve if P(B|A) > P(B|~A); –ve if P(B|A) < P(B|~A); 0 if P(B|A) = P(B|~A). For details see Wellman and Henrion (1993).

With regard to computation, people can err because of short-cut heuristic procedures that can lead to suboptimal inference. In both cases errors will typically arise from capacity and processing limitations, and the reasoner's attempts to overcome these by simplifying representation and inference. As with many cognitive biases, these errors are a necessary price to pay in order to maintain and use workable models of the world.

Dynamic networks

A key feature of human cognition is that it adapts to a changing environment. These changes might involve novel evidence, hypotheses and goals. Thus network construction in the face of evidence is dynamic. People adapt their network online as information is received and hypotheses are developed or thought up. This is not a strictly Bayesian process (in which a complete set of hypotheses are continually updated). Rather, people seem to introduce and eliminate hypotheses in a more all-or-nothing manner. This saves greatly on storage and computation, but can lead to biases and errors. For example, an early piece of evidence might be ignored because the right hypothesis had not yet been entertained. And the interpretation of ambiguous evidence will depend on what hypotheses are entertained at that time. This can lead to substantial order effects—the final evaluation of a body of evidence being heavily dependent on the order in which that evidence is processed (Hogarth and Einhorn, 1992).

A parallel can be drawn with action and practical reasoning. At an early stage one might not have the requisite knowledge to take advantage of an opportunity; later on one acquires the knowledge, but the opportunity has passed. This would not happen in the ideal world of flawless memory and unrestricted reasoning abilities, but will be commonplace in the bounded and imperfect world that we inhabit (especially as untrained jurors). For instance, consider a case in which the defendant is charged with assault, and pleads self-defence. According to the law it is crucial to establish whether the defendant used force that was 'reasonable' in the circumstances. But jurors are often not given a definition of self-defence until the end of trial. This can be problematic, because critical evidence about the suspect acting in self-defence might have been presented before the juror has an appropriate understanding of the legal notion.

Despite these potential shortcomings, the online generation and adaptation of a small range of hypotheses will often be a good adaptive solution to the problems that we face. People do not use full-scale (static) BN representations—they are more likely to adopt small-scale networks that undergo discrete changes as new evidence is encountered and hypotheses are refined, abandoned or augmented. The small-scale nature of these networks can facilitate rapid and flexible adjustment. Moreover, the qualitative nature of the networks spares the numerous probability estimations and computations that a full BN would require.

Current models of evidential reasoning

We have speculated about the form that a human model of evidential reasoning might take. Thus far only general principles have been articulated; desiderata that we would expect any plausible theory of human reasoning to satisfy, without specifying the cognitive processes that implement these principles. How does this network model fit with other psychological theories of evidential reasoning? There are three dominant models, each with pros and cons.

Belief-adjustment model

The belief-adjustment model is a general purpose model for how people update their beliefs in the face of new evidence (Hogarth and Einhorn, 1992). Applied to the legal context, the model assumes that people start with an initial degree of belief in the guilt of a suspect, based on background information. This prior information can include both specific details about the case (e.g. nature of the charge; gender and race of the defendant etc.) and general assumptions or knowledge (e.g. the presumption of innocence).[21]

When a new item of evidence is received, it is encoded as positive or negative in relation to the guilt hypothesis, weighted according to its judged strength, and then additively combined with the prior belief. This produces an adjusted degree of belief in the suspect's guilt, which then serves as the new prior when the next piece of evidence is received. This process is iterated until all items of evidence are integrated, and a final degree of belief is reached.

The belief-adjustment model has some attractive features. It specifies a simple processing model that avoids heavy computational or storage demands. At any one stage, the decision maker only needs to consider their prior opinion and the impact of the new item of evidence. It has been applied to a wide variety of cognitive tasks, and can account for a rich pattern of empirical results. In particular, it can explain both primacy effects—where people over-weight items of evidence that are presented early in a sequence, and recency

---

[21] See Hastie (1993) for more details.

effects—where people over-weight items of evidence that are presented later in the sequence. In the case of legal judgments, where the evidence is encoded as positive or negative relative to a target hypothesis, it predicts that later items of evidence are over-weighted relative to earlier items (Kerstholt and Jackson, 1999).

The Achilles heel of the belief-adjustment model, when applied to legal contexts, is that it treats all pieces of evidence as independent. It ignores the interrelations between items that make legal cases so compelling. This is a substantial shortcoming, even in relatively simple situations. For example, it cannot capture instances of explaining away, and thus cannot distinguish rebuttal from affirmative evidence. Consider again the *Witness for the Prosecution* story. The police had evidence that there was blood on Vole's cuffs, and this matched the victim's blood. The defence rebutted this piece of evidence by showing that Vole himself had the same blood type as the victim, and claiming that he had cut himself slicing ham. This rebuttal was in turn supported by the fact that Vole had a fresh scar on his wrist. According to the belief-adjustment model, the blood on the cuffs constitutes positive evidence of guilt, and the claim that Vole cut his hand, and the scar on his wrist, constitute negative evidence. But the fact that this negative evidence impacts on the guilt hypothesis only by undermining the positive evidence cannot be represented.

The inability to represent interrelations between items of evidence can rapidly lead to counter-intuitive consequences. For example, suppose that further forensic tests reveal that the blood on Vole's cuffs does not match the victim's. This finding rules out this piece of incriminating evidence against Vole, but it also renders the claim that he cut his hand slicing ham, and the scar on his wrist, irrelevant to whether or not he is guilty. These items of rebuttal evidence are no longer needed (the blood does not match); they no longer count as positive evidence. The belief-adjustment model cannot capture these changes. It has no mechanism, or representational structure, that allows it to re-evaluate earlier items of evidence.

It might be argued that while the neglect of interrelations undermines the model as a normative account, this feature might fit with actual human reasoning. However, there is a wealth of empirical data (see below), plus every crime writer's intuitions, suggesting that people can accommodate these patterns.

Story model

In direct contrast to the belief-adjustment model, the story model (Pennington and Hastie, 1986, 1992) places strong emphasis on the interrelations between items of evidence. This model maintains that people construct stories in order to make sense of the evidence presented in court, and these narratives are key determinants of the final verdicts reached. According to Pennington and Hastie these stories involve complex networks of causal relations between both physical events and psychological states (e.g. intentions, desires and motives). These causal networks draw on evidence presented in the case, as well as prior assumptions and common-sense knowledge. They are used to construct a plausible narrative for the unfolding of the crime.

The story model has garnered broad empirical support, but remains vaguely specified with respect to the underlying cognitive processes and mechanisms. For example, no precise account is given for how people construct or update their causal models, or how they draw inferences from them. Moreover, Pennington and Hastie argue that the story model only applies to global judgements (those made once all the evidence is processed). In the case of online judgements, people are supposed to revert to a simpler belief-adjustment model.

The qualitative network perspective argued for in this paper shares many of the insights of the story model. In particular, that evidential reasoning involves the construction of causal networks that organise and make sense of the available evidence. In contrast to the story model, however, our perspective emphasises the role of probabilistic links between evidence and hypotheses. The story model explicitly rules out any role for probabilistic evaluations.[22] Our account uses a formal Bayesian framework to represent these relations, and capture important patterns of inference. The story model is silent on these details. In addition, our account applies equally to online judgements, as the evidence comes in, and to global judgements, once all the evidence is presented.

Coherence-based models

Coherence-based models (Simon, Snow and Read, 2004; Simon and Holyoak, 2002; Thagard, 2000) also accentuate the complex interrelations between items of evidence. These models derive from earlier psychological theories of cognitive consistency (Heider, 1946), and are based on the idea that the mind strives for coherent representations of the world. Evidence and hypotheses

---

[22] Note that Pennington and Hastie's main argument against the Bayesian approach rests on participants' failure to conform to Bayes' rule for exact computations (people tend to be more conservative). However, this does not count against people's use of qualitative notions of probability.

are represented as nodes in a large-scale connectionist network. The relations between nodes are represented as bidirectional links that are either excitatory (where the activation of one node increases the activation of the linked node) or inhibitory (where the activation of one node decreases the activation of the linked node). Some of these nodes are instantiated as true statements (e.g. observational reports), while others are set at random or prespecified values.

Judgments (e.g. is the defendant guilty on the basis of the given evidence?) are supposed to emerge from an interactive process that maximises the overall coherence of the network via constraint satisfaction (Thagard, 2000). This process can lead to substantial re-evaluation of hypotheses and evidence. In particular, even the evaluation of assumed facts can shift to achieve greater coherence with the emerging verdict (Simon *et al.*, 2004).

Coherence-based models, like BNs, represent multiple interrelations between items in a probabilistic fashion, and representation is closely tied to inference. The nature of the representation is somewhat different. Whereas BNs aim to represent events and processes in the world, coherence-based models represent the flow of inference in the mind itself. Another important difference is that BNs use directed links (often corresponding to causal direction) whereas coherence-based models have bidirectional links. This is a critical difference, and means that the latter models are unable to represent basic forms of inference such as 'explaining-away'. Returning to the example of the blood on Vole's cuffs. There are two main explanations for this piece of evidence: the blood came from the victim, and thus raises the probability of guilt, or it came from Vole himself, and thus lowers the probability of guilt. However, to capture this inference, a coherence-based model must assume that the two explanations are exclusive (or at least negatively correlated). But this is an inappropriate representation of their true relation in the world. Whether or not Vole cut himself slicing ham is unrelated to (independent of) whether or not he is guilty of murder. The two explanations only become dependent given the evidence of blood on the cuffs that they both seek to explain. As noted earlier, this pattern of inference is naturally captured in a BN representation. An important question for future empirical research is the extent to which human reasoners engage in explaining away inferences, without assuming that alternative explanations are always exclusive or negatively correlated.

Recent studies on the role of network models in evidential reasoning

Most of the empirical studies conducted so far provide support for either the story or coherence models. However, the key findings, that people are sensitive to both causality and coherence, can also be explained on the network model proposed in this chapter. One major factor that discriminates between the network model and the other two models is the role of probability. Both the story model and the coherence model explicitly reject the idea that people think about evidence in a probabilistic fashion. This conclusion is largely based on the fact that people do not seem to follow the prescripts of Bayes' rule when evaluating evidence (Pennington and Hastie, 1986, 1992). In particular, people seem to be more conservative than Bayesian updating requires. We believe that although such findings militate against the notion that people carry out precise probability computations, they do not undermine the possibility that people are sensitive to the qualitative structure of probabilistic reasoning. For example, judging that one piece of evidence is relevant (or irrelevant) to a specific hypothesis does not require precise numerical estimates. We can all agree that the presence of the suspect at the crime scene increases the likelihood of guilt, especially if the suspect has no other reason to be there, even if we cannot assign exact probabilities to these events. Comparative judgements like these will often suffice to build up a qualitative network that links relevant pieces of evidence. This suggests a slightly different line of research to assess the extent to which people can engage in probabilistic reasoning: how closely does their reasoning approximate the qualitative prescripts of Bayesian networks? In the final section of this chapter we will review some recent studies that address this question.

Models of alibi evidence

Alibi evidence is often critical in criminal cases. It has great potential to exonerate a suspect—if the suspect was not at the crime scene at the time of the crime, it is very unlikely that they are guilty. However, alibi evidence is often treated with suspicion (Gooderson, 1977), especially if it is proffered by a friend or relative of the accused. This is because the alibi testimony is readily explained away by the possibility that the alibi provider is lying to protect the suspect.

Despite the ubiquity of alibis in court cases, alibi evidence has not been subjected to much formal or empirical study. The few psychological studies on alibis (Culhane and Hosch, 2004; Olson and Wells, 2004) have reached sensible conclusions; for example, that people are more convinced by an alibi when it is provided by an impartial stranger rather than by a partial friend or relative; and more convinced by physical corroboration (e.g. a time-stamped receipt) than by personal corroboration (e.g. the verbal statement of a cashier). However, this leaves open a whole raft of questions about how people evaluate and assess alibis.

Of particular interest for the current chapter is how alibi evidence is assessed in the light of other pieces of evidence. As discussed above, one subtlety of alibi evidence is that it can provide information over-and-above the issue of whether the suspect was actually at the crime scene. We developed a basic alibi model[23] that represents the network of relations in typical alibi situations. The model implies that when a suspect's alibi is refuted by another piece of evidence (e.g. CCTV footage showing that the suspect was at the crime scene) this can incriminate the suspect along two separate routes: (a) evidence that the suspect was at the crime scene raises the probability of guilt; (b) knowing that the suspect lied in their statement also raises the probability of guilt. Furthermore, we distinguished two situations: (1) when the alibi provider does not know whether or not the suspect is guilty (e.g. when the alibi provider is an impartial stranger); (2) when the alibi provider does know whether or not the suspect is guilty (e.g. when the suspect is the alibi provider). We argue that the discredit of an alibi statement incriminates the suspect along both routes in case 2 but only along route (a) in case 1.

This is captured by the two models in Figure 7.4. Model 1 represents the case in which the alibi provider does not know whether the suspect is guilty, Model 2 represents the case where the alibi provider does know. The key difference is the link from guilt to deception in Model 2 but not Model 1.

How well do these two alibi models capture people's actual reasoning when confronted with alibi evidence? We conducted an experimental study to explore this question (see Lagnado, 2010). All participants[24] in the study were given the background story to an assault case (based on the details of a real case). The gist of the case was that a young man was accused of assaulting a woman shortly after she left a nightclub. The suspect matched the description given by the victim, and he admitted to being at the nightclub on the night in question. Participants gave initial estimates for the probability that the suspect was guilty, which served as baselines for their subsequent judgements. They were then presented with alibi evidence in one of three versions. In

---

[23] See earlier section on alibis, as well as Hepler, Lagnado and Baio (2007), and Lagnado (2011).
[24] There were eighty jury-eligible participants in the study, all from the UCL student population. This experiment has since been replicated with 100 participants.

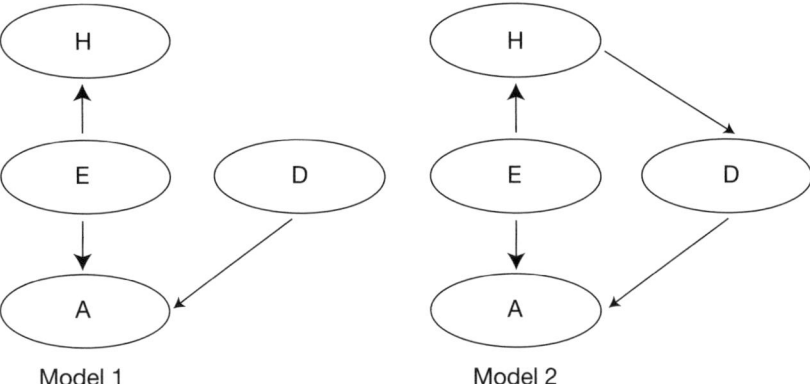

Figure 7.4. Two alibi models: (1) when alibi provider does not know whether suspect committed the crime (e.g. stranger provides alibi); (2) when alibi provider does know whether suspect committed the crime (e.g. suspect provides alibi).

condition (i) the suspect provided the alibi statement. He claimed that he caught a night bus from the club and was at home at the time of the crime. In condition (ii) the suspect's mother provided an equivalent alibi statement, and in condition (iii) the night bus driver provided it. The content of the alibi statement was kept as constant as possible across the three conditions, so that the essential difference between conditions was the nature of the alibi provider (suspect, mother or stranger). The conditions were constructed so that they varied as to whether the alibi provider was motivated to lie to protect the suspect (conditions i–ii) and whether the alibi provider knew if the suspect was guilty (condition i). See Table 7.1 for a summary.

Once participants received the alibi information they again estimated the probability that the suspect was guilty. Next, participants in all conditions were presented with a piece of evidence that undermined the alibi. This consisted in a statement to the effect that CCTV footage and face recognition analysis revealed that the suspect had followed the victim very near to the crime scene at about the time of the crime. After reading this statement, participants made their final estimates as to the guilt of the suspect. In addition to the three alibi

Table 7.1. Three conditions in the alibi study.

Alibi provider	Motivated to lie?	Knows that suspect is guilty?	Alibi model	Model prediction
Suspect	Yes	Yes	2	$P(H|E\&A) > P(H|E)$
Mother	Yes	No	1	$P(H|E\&A) = P(H|E)$
Stranger	No	No	1	$P(H|E\&A) = P(H|E)$

conditions, a control condition was run on another group of participants. This control group was presented with the background information and then the CCTV evidence, but with no alibi evidence in between. This provided a critical comparison, because it served as a measure of how much the CCTV evidence alone was judged to raise the probability of the suspect's guilt.

The results for this experiment are shown in Figure 7.5. The bars labelled 'alibi' represent the differences between the baseline probability ratings (based on the background information) and the ratings after the alibis were presented. Effectively these bars show the impacts of the three alibis. It is notable that only the stranger's alibi lowers the judged probability of guilt. In all the other conditions the alibi has little effect. This fits with our expectations that alibis from partial witnesses are treated with great suspicion—there is an obvious alternative explanation for their statement (e.g. they might be lying to protect the suspect). What happened when the alibis were subsequently undermined by the CCTV evidence? This is shown by the bars labelled 'CCTV', which correspond to the difference between baseline ratings and those given after the CCTV evidence is presented. In all three cases the judged probability

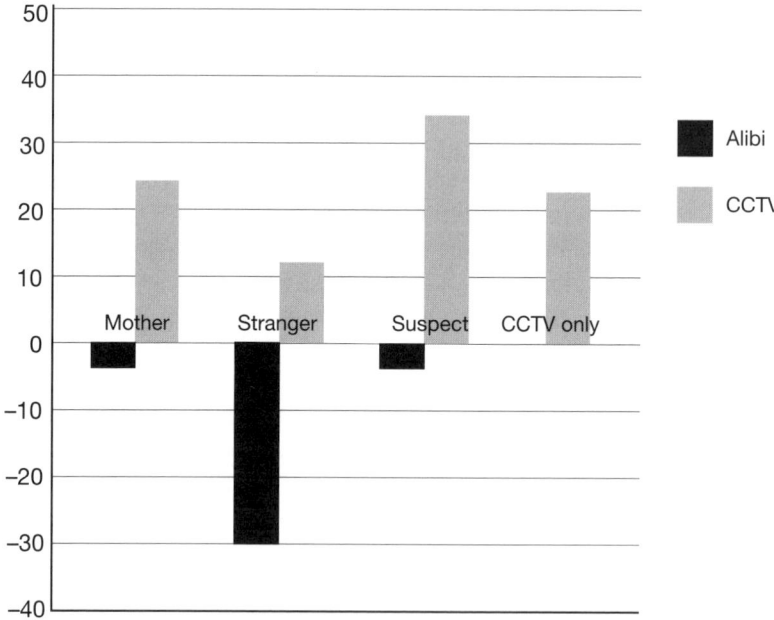

Figure 7.5. Baseline subtracted ratings for three alibi conditions and control (± standard error).

of guilt rises, reflecting the incriminating effect of the CCTV evidence. However, the level for the suspect is significantly higher than for the other alibi providers. And, most importantly, it is higher than the judged probability of guilt based on CCTV evidence in *the absence of an alibi*. (In numbers, P(H|E&A) > P(H|E).)

This pattern was predicted by our alibi model. The suspect is incriminated by the CCTV evidence along two routes: it shows (a) that he was at the crime scene, and (b) that he was lying in his alibi statement. This pattern is not predicted by an additive model of evidence integration. The CCTV evidence by itself is less incriminating than the combination of CCTV evidence and alibi statement, despite the fact that the alibi statement by itself slightly lowers the judged probability of guilt. This suggests that Model 2 best captures people's reasoning about the suspect's alibi. In contrast, Model 1 best captures people's reasoning about the mother and stranger. In the case of the bus driver, we suppose that the preferred explanation for his false alibi was error rather than deception. This would account for why the CCTV evidence does not raise the level of guilt as high as with the other alibi providers. This possibility is supported by some other studies on alibi evidence (Olson and Wells, 2004), which show that when a stranger provides an alibi for the suspect, the question of correct identification is raised (which is much less likely for a friend or relative of the suspect).

This experiment supplies initial support for the alibi models proposed earlier. More generally, it confirms the claim that people's reasoning can be sensitive to the interrelations between hypotheses and items of evidence as predicted by the qualitative aspects of Bayesian network models.

The impact of discredited evidence

Recall one of the major twists in the plot of the *Witness for the Prosecution*. Vole's wife, Romaine, fabricated the letters that undermined her own testimony against Vole. She reasoned that the jury would not believe her if she simply provided an alibi for her husband (and our studies suggest that she was right about this). Instead, Romaine thought that a better way to persuade the jury of Vole's innocence was to undercut a substantial pillar of the prosecution's case, namely, her own testimony against Vole. A more general psychological maxim can be extracted from this line of reasoning—that once a story is mounted in favour of one side (in this case the prosecution), the discrediting of one element of that story can serve to collapse the whole story, even if there still exists incriminating evidence unaccounted for.

Exactly this pattern of reasoning has been explored in a recent set of studies (Lagnado and Harvey, 2008). We were interested in how the discrediting of one piece of evidence might affect other items of evidence. According to a purely normative account, the discredit should only affect related items, i.e. those that bear some causal or evidential relation to the discredited item. For example, consider a situation in which a suspect is accused of house burglary, and a witness testifies that the suspect was loitering in the area a few days before the crime (statement A). This same witness also testifies that she saw the suspect near the crime scene on the night of the crime (statement B). What happens if it is subsequently discovered that the witness has fabricated statement B. For example, perhaps there is strong evidence that she was out of town on the night in question, but fabricated her statement because she dislikes the suspect? Clearly one should disregard statement B—it no longer provides valid evidence against the suspect. But what about statement A? Should this also be disregarded?

In the situation where the items are related (e.g. both are produced by the same individual), it seems appropriate to extend the discredit of statement B to statement A. After all, if the witness is lying on one occasion, shouldn't we doubt her other statements too? Especially now that we know that she has reason to fabricate evidence against the suspect. At the opposite extreme, it also seems clear that we should not extend this discredit to pieces of evidence that are entirely unrelated, for example, forensic evidence such as a match between the suspect's shoes and footprints found at the crime scene. There is, however, a large grey area in between, where the extent to which a discredit should be generalised is unclear, and will depend heavily on the precise details of the case. For example, should we also call into question the testimony of other neighbours? What if they are friends of the discredited witness?

We conducted a set of studies to investigate such questions. Participants[25] were presented with various crime scenarios, and judged the probability that a suspect was guilty on the basis of several pieces of evidence. In the first study people always received two items of exonerating evidence in a row, followed by information that discredited the second item. For example, at stage one they were told about a footprint match, at stage two they were told about the witness testimony, and at the final stage they were informed that the witness had fabricated their statement. Participants gave probability of guilt judgements at each stage. The key question was whether the judged probability at the final stage, after the discrediting of the second item of evidence, simply returned to the estimate given at stage one (after the first item of evidence). If it did return, this would suggest that the discrediting information

---

[25] Participants were jury-eligible students from the UCL population. In total there were ninety-eight participants across the three studies. For details see Lagnado and Harvey (2008).

had only affected the second item of evidence. If it did not, this would suggest that the discredit was being extended in some way.

There were two main experimental conditions: the two items of evidence were either related (e.g. two statements from the same witness) or unrelated (e.g. a footprint match and a witness statement). A reasonable prediction—and indeed that sanctioned by a normative theory based on BNs—would be that the discredit should only be extended to related items of evidence. For example, the discredit of a witness testimony should affect other statements from the same witness, but should not affect footprint match evidence. This can be illustrated by constructing two BN models—one for the case of unrelated evidence, the other for related evidence (see Fig. 7.6).

The results for this first study did not completely fit with the normative predictions (reinforcing the importance of empirical studies!). In those cases where the two items were related (e.g. two statements from the same witness) the final judgement was significantly lower than that given at stage one. Thus the discrediting of the second item was extended to the first (related) item. This was as expected by a normative model. If the witness has lied in one statement, there is increased reason to suppose that he had lied in another statement. However, this extension of the discrediting information also took place when the two items of evidence were *unrelated*. For example, the discrediting of a witness testimony was extended to an unrelated item of footprint evidence. This is clearly not sanctioned by the normative theory.

At first blush these findings can be most simply explained by the belief adjustment model. On this model later items of evidence are over-weighted relative to earlier items. It can therefore explain the results by assuming that the final discrediting information is over-weighted (hence the final stage judge-

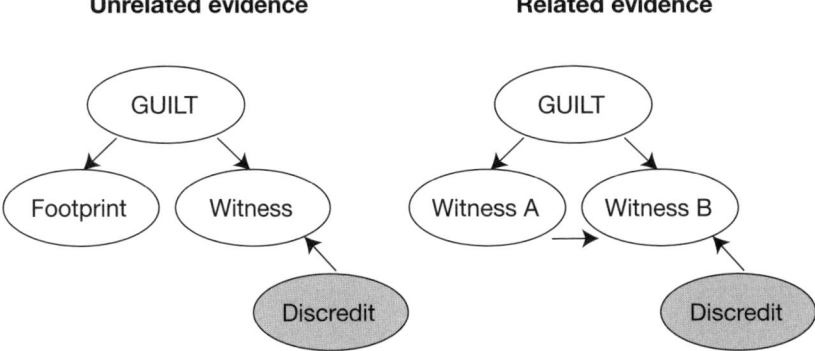

Figure 7.6. Two main conditions in the discredited evidence study.

ment is lower than the first stage judgement). This belief adjustment model also assumes insensitivity to the interrelations between items of evidence, and thus explains why this effect occurs irrespective of whether the items are causally related.

To test out this simple explanation, a second study varied the order in which the items of evidence were presented. In particular, participants received information in one of two orders: (i) *late discredit*, as in study 1, in which the discrediting information was presented at the final stage, and (ii) *early discredit*, in which the discrediting information was presented after the first stage, and then another item of evidence was presented afterwards. For example, a witness statement was presented first, and at the second stage it was discredited. At the final stage another piece of incriminating evidence was presented (either related or unrelated to the initial item).

The results are displayed in Figure 7.7. The late discredit condition replicates the finding from Study 1—the discrediting is extended irrespective of the relations between the items of evidence (and against the predictions of a normative model). In contrast, the early discredit condition falls in line with the normative predictions. The discredit of one item is only extended to the other item when they are related, not when they are unrelated.

This is a puzzling pattern of results—why should people make normatively appropriate judgements when they receive information in one order, but not when they receive it in a different order? We advanced an explanation for this pattern that draws on coherence-based models of decision making. Coherence models (e.g. Simon *et al.*, 2004) presume that the mind strives for the most coherent representation of the evidence and hypotheses in the decision problem. In particular, elements that cohere with each other will tend to be

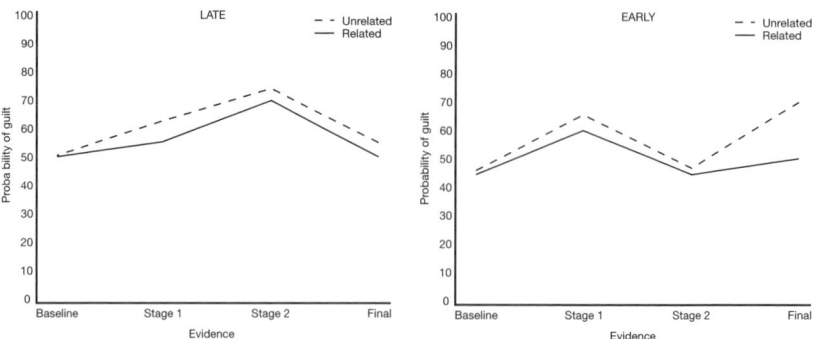

Figure 7.7.   Mean probability of guilt ratings (± standard error) for Study 2 in late condition (left panel) and early condition (right panel).

accepted or rejected together. Applied to our experiments, we assume that people tend to group items of evidence together according to whether they incriminate or exonerate the suspect. This basic division is strongly encouraged by the legal context, and the distinction between prosecution and defence evidence. During the decision-making process these two groupings (evidence for or against the accused) will compete with each other to be accepted, whereas the within-group elements will mutually cohere, irrespective of the exact causal relations between them.

On this view of the decision process, the over-extension of the discrediting information in Study 1 arises because items with a common direction (e.g. two pieces of incriminating evidence) are grouped together, and a subsequent discredit of one of these items hurts the whole group, bringing people's final estimates of guilt below their first stage estimates. It can also explain the difference between the late and early discrediting conditions in Study 2. In the late condition participants receive items A+ and B+,[26] and group these as positive evidence against the suspect (see Fig. 7.8). The two items cohere because they are both incriminating. Then participants receive information C, which discredits B. This discredit is extended to item A because of the prior grouping. The mutual coherence between A and B, and C's subsequent discredit of B, means that A and B are both undermined. In contrast, in the early condition participants receive item B+ first; this item is then discredited by C. When they receive A+ this is not grouped with B+ because B+ has already

LATE   **EARLY**

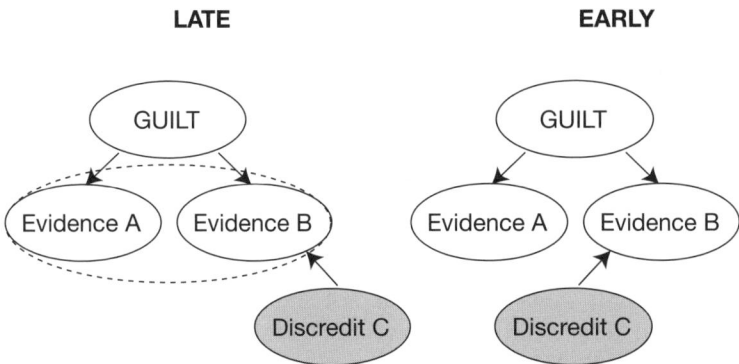

Figure 7.8. The effect of grouping on discrediting. In the late condition grouping of A and B leads to over-extension of the discredit C from B to A; in the early condition no grouping occurs, so discredit C is restricted to causally related evidence.

[26] Note: '+' = incriminating evidence; '−' = exonerating evidence.

been discredited. Thus A+ is only discredited if C applies to it directly (i.e. if there is an appropriate causal relation).

This grouping hypothesis has some testable predictions. In particular, it predicts that coherent groupings will only emerge when evidential elements share the same direction (e.g. both incriminating or both exonerating). This implies that when the two items of evidence are mixed (e.g. one item incriminating and the other exonerating) the discredit of one item will not be extended to the other. This prediction was tested in Study 3. There were four conditions:

(1) Two incriminating items (A+, B+), followed by the discredit of B+
(2) Two exonerating items (A–, B–), followed by the discredit of B–
(3) One incriminating and one exonerating item (A+, B–), followed by discredit of B–
(4) One exonerating and one incriminating item (A–, B+), followed by discredit of B+

In short, there were two *non-mixed* conditions (1 and 2) and two *mixed* conditions (3 and 4). As in the previous studies, the causal relations between the two items of evidence were also varied within each condition. For example, in condition (3) the two items were either related (e.g. item A+ and B– were both witness statements, A+ stating that the suspect was seen at the crime scene, B– stating that the suspect was seen elsewhere) or unrelated (e.g. item A+ was footprint evidence placing the suspect at the crime scene, B– a witness statement stating that the suspect was seen elsewhere at that time).

The results for Study 3 are shown in Figure 7.9. The predictions of the grouping model were supported in all conditions. In the non-mixed conditions (both items positive or both items negative) the discredit was extended irrespective of whether the two items of evidence were related or unrelated. In contrast, in the mixed conditions (e.g. one positive item and one negative item) there was no extension of the discredit, again irrespective of whether the two items of evidence were related or unrelated. This suggests that the flow of inference in people's evidential networks was dictated by the positive vs negative grouping of evidence, rather than the precise causal relations between the elements. This finding does not show that people do not use causal reasoning; they clearly used 'explaining-away' inferences when evidence was discredited. However, their reasoning does not appear to be neatly captured by a Bayesian model of inference.

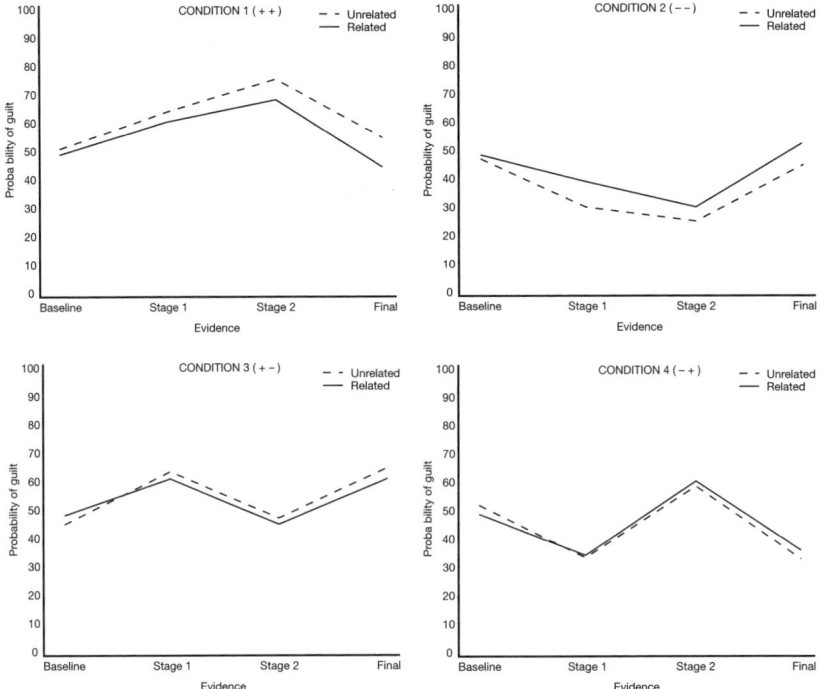

Figure 7.9. Mean probability of guilt judgements (± standard error) for the four evidence conditions in Study 3. Note: '+' = incriminating evidence; '−' = exonerating evidence.

Summary of discrediting studies

The experiments on discrediting evidence have thrown up a number of findings: that people use causal models to explain-away discredited evidence; that this explaining-away can also lead to over-extension of the discrediting information; that people's inferences are dependent on the order in which information is received. To explain these findings, we drew on coherence-based models of juror reasoning and introduced the idea that people group evidence according to its direction. Items of evidence with a shared direction are supposed to mutually cohere, irrespective of their exact causal relatedness, and mutually coherent groupings will fall together in the face of information that discredits one item of that grouping. This grouping hypothesis can explain why discrediting information is extended to causally unrelated items, so long as they share a common direction. It also explains the difference between early and late conditions: items only form a grouping in the late condition; in the early condition the discredit undermines the prior item before it can be grouped.

Returning to the *Witness for the Prosecution* story, we now see that Agatha Christie, and her character Romaine, had the right intuitions about the effect of discrediting evidence. By having Romaine testify for the prosecution, and then undermining her testimony, the case against her husband Vole collapsed. And this occurred despite the existence of independent incriminating evidence (such as the blood on Vole's cuffs, the maid's testimony, Vole being left in Miss French's will, Vole's enquiry about cruises, etc.). Our studies confirm this pattern of inference, and also suggest that had Romaine's discrediting occurred earlier in the trial, then its effect might have been less catastrophic!

These experimental findings need to be explored with a wider range of materials and conditions. If robust, they will reinforce previous studies showing that people do not integrate evidence in a fully Bayesian way (cf. Pennington and Hastie, 1992; Schum and Martin, 1982; Simon *et al.*, 2004). However, this 'over-extension' effect is a sign of a sensible cognitive mechanism at work. By grouping information people can overcome memory and processing limitations.[27] Without such organising and simplifying strategies it is unlikely that people could draw firm conclusions from complex and interrelated bodies of evidence.

One way of reconciling the current findings with previous research is to maintain that people use causal networks to represent the interrelations between evidence, but allow that they use coherence-based mechanisms for inference and decision. This separation of representation and inference-mechanisms is not uncommon in cognitive science, and might prove a fruitful path to explore in future work.

Conclusions

This chapter has argued that people integrate and evaluate uncertain evidence by constructing network models. These network models are typically qualitative and incomplete, and based on people's causal beliefs about the specifics of the case as well as the workings of the physical and social world in general. These models can differ widely from person to person according to the knowledge and presuppositions that each individual brings to the situation. Despite these differences, individuals share the common aim of producing a consistent

---

[27] Cf. 'chunking' in memory research, see above, n. 18, for references.

and coherent picture of the evidence: one that supports further inference, and the reaching of a decisive verdict.

Although we have concentrated on legal contexts, we believe that the network framework can be extended to other areas where people must integrate and reason about bodies of uncertain evidence (e.g. clinical and medical contexts, business and management, social interactions etc.). In all of these areas there are large bodies of interrelated evidence, and the decision maker must somehow combine these to reach singular judgements.

This chapter has only covered a subset of the issues arising in evidential reasoning. There are many other aspects that require careful treatment, such as the process of hypothesis generation, the search for evidence, and the social context in which evidence is proffered and judged. Indeed the role of evidence as an exchange of information between one person (e.g. defendant, witness) and another person or group (e.g. judge, investigator, jury) needs extensive study, especially in situations where this exchange involves strategic interactions between parties. Our optimistic perspective is that all of these issues will benefit from the central idea that people construct and reason with qualitative network models.

References

Aitken, C., Taroni, F. and Garbolino, P. (2003), 'A graphical model for the evaluation of cross-transfer evidence in DNA profiles', *Theoretical Population Biology*, 63: 179–90.

Axelrod R. (1976), *Structure of Decision* (Princeton, NJ, Princeton University Press).

Biedermann, A. and Taroni, F. (2006), 'Bayesian networks and probabilistic reasoning about scientific evidence when there is a lack of data', *Forensic Science International*, 157: 163–7.

Binder, D. A. and Bergman, P. (1984), *Fact Investigation: from Hypothesis to Proof* (American Case book series) (St Paul, MN: *West* Publishing Company).

Cartwright, N. (2007), *Hunting Causes and Using Them* (Cambridge, Cambridge University Press).

Chase, W. G. and Simon, H. A. (1973), 'Perception in chess', *Cognitive Psychology*, 4: 55–81.

Christie, A. (1953/2002), *Witness for the Prosecution* (London, HarperCollins).

Cowan, N. (2001), 'The magical number 4 in short-term memory: a reconsideration of mental storage capacity', *Behavioral and Brain Sciences*, 24: 87–185.

Culhane, S. E. and Hosch, H. M. (2004), 'An alibi witness's influence on jurors' verdicts', *Journal of Applied Social Psychology*, 34: 1604–16.

Davies, G. and Patel, D. (2005), 'The influence of car and driver stereotypes on attributions of vehicle speed, position on the road and culpability in a road accident scenario', *Legal and Criminological Psychology*, 10: 45–62.

Dawes, R. M. (1979). The robust beauty of improper linear models in decision making. American Psychologist, 34, 571–82.

Dawid, A. P. and Evett, I. W. (1997), 'Using a graphical method to assist the evaluation of complicated patterns of evidence', *Journal of Forensic Science*, 42: 226–31.

Dawid, A. P., Mortera, J. and Vicard, P. (2007), 'Object-oriented Bayesian networks for complex forensic DNA profiling problems', *Forensic Science International*, 169: 195–205.

Druzdzel, M. (1996), 'Qualitative Verbal Explanations in Bayesian Belief Networks', *Artificial Intelligence and Simulation of Behaviour Quarterly*, 94: 43–54.

Fenton, N. E. and Neil, M. (2008), 'Avoiding Legal Fallacies in Practice Using Bayesian Networks', Seventh International Conference on Forensic Inference and Statistics. Lausanne, Switzerland.

Gilovich, T., Griffin, D. and Kahneman, D. (2002), *Heuristics and biases: the psychology of intuitive judgment* (Cambridge, Cambridge University Press).

Griffiths, T. L. and Tenenbaum, J. B. (2005), 'Structure and strength in causal induction', *Cognitive Psychology*, 51: 354–84.

Gooderson, R. N. (1977), 'Alibi' (London, Heinemann Educational).

Hamer, D. (1997), 'The Continuing Saga of the Chamberlain Direction: untangling the cables and chains of criminal proof', *Monash University Law Review*, 23: 43–76.

Halford, G. S., Cowan, N. and Andrews, G. (2007), 'Separating cognitive capacity from knowledge: a new hypothesis', *Trends in Cognitive Science*, 11: 236–42.

Harman, G. (1986), *Change in View: principles of reasoning* (Cambridge, MA, MIT Press/Bradford Books).

Hastie, R. (1993), *Inside the Juror* (Cambridge, Cambridge University Press).

Heider, F. (1946), 'Attitudes and cognitive organization', *Journal of Psychology*, 21: 107–12.

Hepler, A. and Weir, B. (2008), 'Object-oriented Bayesian networks for paternity cases with allelic dependencies', *Forensic Science International: Genetics*, 2(3): 166–75.

Hepler, A. B., Dawid, A. P. and Leucari, V. (2007), 'Object-oriented graphical representations of complex patterns of evidence', *Law, Probability and Risk*, 6: 275–93.

Hepler, A., Lagnado, D. A. and Baio, G. (2007). *The subtleties of alibi evidence*. Paper presented at the conference 'Enquiry, Evidence and Facts: An Interdisciplinary conference' at the British Academy, London, December 2007.

Hogarth, R. M. and Einhorn, H. J. (1992), 'Order effects in belief updating: the belief-adjustment model', *Cognitive Psychology*, 24: 1–55.

Kahneman, D., Slovic, P. and Tversky, A. (1982), *Judgment Under Uncertainty: Heuristics and Biases* (Cambridge, Cambridge University Press).

Keppens, J. (2007), 'Towards Qualitative Approaches to Bayesian Evidential Reasoning'. *Proceedings of the 11th International Conference on Artificial Intelligence and Law*, 17–25.

Kerstholt, J. H and Jackson, J. L. (1999), 'Judicial decision making: order of evidence presentation and availability of background information', *Applied Cognitive Psychology*, 12: 445–54.

Koller, D. and Pfeffer, A. (1997), 'Object-Oriented Bayesian Networks', *Proceedings of the 13th Annual Conference on Uncertainty in AI (UAI)*, 302–13.

Krynski, T. R. and Tenenbaum, J. B. (2007), 'The role of causality in judgment under uncertainty', *Journal of Experimental Psychology: General*, 136: 430–50.

Lagnado, D. A. (2011), 'Adverse inferences about alibi evidence: a Bayesian network model' (Manuscript submitted for publication).

Lagnado, D. A. and Harvey, N. (2008), 'The impact of discredited evidence', *Psychonomic Bulletin and Review*, 15: 1166–73.

Lagnado, D. A., Waldmann, M. A., Hagmayer, Y. and Sloman, S. A. (2007), 'Beyond covariation: cues to causal structure', in A. Gopnik and L. E. Schultz. (eds.), *Causal Learning: psychology, philosophy, and computation* (Oxford, Oxford University Press), pp. 154–72.

Miller, G.A. (1956), 'The magical number seven, plus or minus two: some limits on our capacity for processing information', *Psychological Review*, 63: 81–97.

Olson, E. A. and Wells, G. L. (2004), 'What makes a good alibi? a proposed taxonomy', *Law and Human Behavior*, 28: 157–76.

Pardo, M. S. and Allen, R. J. (2008), 'Juridical Proof and the Best Explanation', *Law and Philosophy*, 27: 223–68.

Parsons, S. (2001), *Qualitative Methods for Reasoning under Uncertainty* (Cambridge, MA, MIT Press).

Pearl, J. (1988), *Probabilistic Reasoning in Intelligent Systems: Networks of Plausible Inference* (San Mateo, CA, Morgan Kaufmann).

Pearl, J. (2000), *Causality: Models, Reasoning and Inference* (Cambridge, Cambridge University Press).

Pennington, N. and Hastie, R. (1986), *Evidence evaluation in complex decision making*, *Journal of Personality and Social Psychology*, 51: 242–58.

Pennington, N. and Hastie, R. (1992), 'Explaining the evidence: test of the story model for juror decision making', *Journal of Personality and Social Psychology*, 62: 189–206.

Schmidt, H. G. and Boshuizen, H. (1993), 'On Acquiring Expertise in Medicine', *Educational Psychological Review*, 5(3), 205–21.

Schum, D. A. (2001), *The Evidential Foundations of Probabilistic Reasoning* (Evanston, IL, Northwestern University Press).

Schum, D. A. and Martin, A. W. (1982), 'Formal and empirical research on cascaded inference in jurisprudence', *Law and Society Review*, 17: 105–51.

Simon, D., Snow, C. and Read, S. J. (2004), 'The redux of cognitive consistency theories: evidence judgments by constraint satisfaction', *Journal of Personality and Social Psychology*, 86: 814–37.

Simon, D. and Holyoak, K. J. (2002), 'Structural dynamics of cognition: from consistency theories to constraint satisfaction', *Personality and Social Psychology Review*, 6: 283–94.

Sloman, S. A. (2005), *Causal Models: how people think about the world and its alternatives* (Oxford, Oxford University Press).

Sloman, S. A. and Lagnado, D. A. (2005), 'Do we "do"?', *Cognitive Science*, 29: 5–39.

Stewart, N., Brown, G. and Chater, N. (2005), 'Absolute identification by relative judgment'. *Psychological Review*, 112: 881–911.

Taroni, F., Aitken, C., Garbolino, P. and Biedermann, A. (2006), *Bayesian Networks and Probabilistic Inference in Forensic Science* (Chichester, John Wiley and Sons).

Thagard, P. (2000), *Coherence in Thought and Action* (Cambridge, MA, MIT Press).

Wellman, M. P. and Henrion, M. (1993), 'Explaining "explaining away"', *IEEE Transactions on Pattern Analysis and Machine Intelligence*, 15: 287–91.

Wigmore, J. (1913), 'The problem of proof', *Illinois Law Review*, 8: 77–103.

Williamson, J. (2005), *Bayesian Nets and Causality* (Oxford, Oxford University Press).

8

Generalisations and Evidential Reasoning

TERENCE J. ANDERSON

Abstract

This chapter suggests that evidence should be viewed as a field of study, one to which most disciplines could contribute and from which most could benefit, and that generalisations should be viewed as part of that field. Every argument must be based upon a generalisation that can be stated as a major premise. The relationship between a supporting proposition or propositions and an inferred proposition can be restated in a quasi-deductive form by identifying the generalisation upon which the inference depends. A datum or a proposition can be evidence if and only if it alters the probability, positively or negatively, of a proposition to be inferred. In order to demonstrate that an evidential proposition is relevant, an analyst must be able to identify and articulate a generalisation that justifies the claim that the evidential proposition alters the probability of an inferred proposition. This chapter develops these ideas and presents a method of generalisation-analysis. It also argues that generalisation-analysis is a tool in the field of evidence that could be useful in analysing and critiquing arguments in many disciplines.

THE GOAL OF THE LEVERHULME PROJECT was to develop an 'integrated theory of evidence'. From the outset, several of the project's participants expressed frustration because 'their discipline' involved much more than evidential reasoning, arguing, at the extreme, that the 'more' so permeated their discipline as to make the search for an integrated theory common to all or most disciplines fruitless or trivial.[1] Nonetheless, all appeared to agree that evidential

---

[1] On 7 June 2005, the Project held a one day workshop to challenge David Schum's theory that evidence had substance blind attributes common to evidence in any discipline. On 8 June, Philip Dawid, the project's director, circulated an email seeking comments from those who participated in the workshop. He collected the email dialogue his request generated and circulated them under the subject heading, '[Evidence] Evidence Challenge Feedback'. A copy is available from the author and may well be available in the email archives at <http://128.40.111.250/evidence/>.

Proceedings of the British Academy, **171**, 225–244. © The British Academy 2011.

reasoning constituted a necessary, even if only a small, part of the rationale for and work in their discipline. This agreement suggests that, even in the absence of an 'integrated theory', evidence could be a field of study to which most disciplines might contribute and from which most might benefit.

This chapter identifies generalisations as an important part of that field. The first section postulates that generalisations constitute a necessary element of rational justification in all or almost all academic disciplines and proposes three stipulative definitions that could be used to identify and distinguish evidential reasoning from other types of rational justification that might be involved in any discipline. The second section presents a preliminary taxonomy of generalisations that classifies the sources and kinds of generalisations and identifies characteristics that can define the strength or force of a generalisation in a particular argument. That taxonomy might be expanded, revised, or refined based upon input from any discipline.

The third section defines some of the roles that generalisations play and how the analysis of these roles might generate insights not otherwise apparent. That section presents a protocol for generalisation-analysis and provides two illustrations to demonstrate the application and utility of the protocol. The first illustrates how generalisation-analysis might be applied to a judicial decision to generate insights otherwise not apparent. Those insights might usefully have been studied and critiqued by an analytic philosopher. The second is based upon an analysis by a legal theorist (the author) of an argument developed by an Assyriologist (Mark Geller) that suggests and illustrates both the possibility of cross-disciplinary analysis and how generalisation-analysis might be applied within a discipline to assess the strength and validity of an argument. The last section presents some conclusions.

1. Rational justification and evidential reasoning

There are three forms of argument that are commonly used in the rational justification. The deductive in which the generalisation is a universal proposition. Classically:

> *All men are mortal.*[2]
> Socrates is a man.
> Therefore, Socrates is a mortal.

---

[2] In the examples the generalisations are italicised.

The inductive in which the generalisation is a plausible probability statement. For example:

> John entered Mary's house at 4.15 p.m. on 1 January.
> *Most/many people who enter a house remain in that house for more than 15 minutes.*[3]
> It is highly probable/probable that X was in Y's house at 4.30 p.m. on 1 January.

And the abductive in which the generalisation is a plausible hypothesis. For example, the investigation into the causes of the 9/11 attack revealed a hypothesis that, if pursued, might have prevented the attack:

> Foreign nationals from the Middle East, who had no prior flight training or experience, enrolled in American flight schools seeking to learn how to fly large commercial airplanes.
> *If Middleastern terrorists were planning to hijack American commercial airliners and use them as weapons, they might send terrorists to flight schools in America to learn how to fly commercial airplanes.*
> Middle Eastern terrorists might be planning to hijack American commercial airliners and use them as weapons.[4]

In each form, there is and must be a generalisation (a premise or warrant) that demonstrates why the proposed conclusion is justified based upon the proposition offered as support.

The rational justification of an evidential conclusion must be the product of the application of an evidential generalisation to evidential propositions supported by evidential data. An *evidential datum* is an observable or potentially observable phenomenon that is relevant to an evidential proposition. An *evidential proposition* is a proposition that describes an evidential datum or that can or could be inferred from, or otherwise rationally justified based upon, evidential data. An *evidential generalisation* is an evidential proposition claimed to be true[5] that can be expressed as the premise of an argument demonstrating that one evidential proposition increases or decreases the probability of another evidential proposition.[6]

---

[3] Reasonable people could question whether 'most' is an accurate qualifier. But debate can only take place if the generalisation upon which the author bases her argument is made explicit.

[4] The illustration is developed in Anderson, Twining and Schum (2005: 52–3).

[5] Most generalisations do not hold universally. In order to claim a generalisation is 'true', a generalisation usually must be qualified to express its degree of certainty, using terms such as *most, many, more often than not, some,* or *few.*

[6] Probability, as used here, includes non-mathematical probability as well as mathematical or statistical probability. I realise that some statisticians view the term non-mathematical probability as an oxymoron, but that is because they have assigned a narrow stipulative definition that excludes

An evidential generalisation is a generalisation that could be inferred from existing evidential data or evidential data that theoretically could be identified. *In many instances police will be deterred from using illegal techniques to gather evidential data relevant to the prosecution of a crime if they know that evidence so gathered will be excluded from consideration by the tribunal without regard to its probative value.* For example, 20 kilograms of cocaine found in the accused's closet would not be admissible in a United States court if the discovery of that cocaine was the product of an illegal search.[7] If the generalisation is true, then a police officer would probably be deterred from conducting an illegal search of the kind that led to the discovery of the cocaine. I am unaware of any empirical studies that have generated data sufficient to support the generalisation to any degree of certainty, but it seems intuitively sound and, in theory, the supporting evidential data could be identified.[8]

2. Beyond evidential reasoning: a preliminary taxonomy of generalisations

In order to distinguish evidential generalisations from other types of generalisations, it is necessary to identify categories and sources of generalisations. All generalisations can be assigned to one of four categories: fact-based (evidential) generalisations, value-based generalisations, faith- or belief-based generalisations, and hybrid generalisations.[9]

A value-based generalisation is a generalisation that is derived from a value adopted or held by a society or a group or an individual, without regard to whether it could be inferred from available or potentially available data. For example, the First Amendment to the United States Constitution forbids the government from regulating political speech, even speech that conflicts with other generally accepted values. An argument based upon this value

---

non-mathematical probability. The framework described here can be used in both mathematical and non-mathematical disciplines.

[7] The evidential generalisation is combined with a value-based generalisation that *all (or almost all) unreasonable searches and seizure by government officials should be prohibited* to justify the conclusion.

[8] What is the relative risk that a police officer in a jurisdiction that excludes illegally obtained evidence will use illegal techniques to gather evidence compared to the risk that a police officer in that jurisdiction that does not exclude illegally obtained evidence will use illegal techniques to gather evidence? That is a factual question that in theory could be answered, but it would be virtually impossible to design a study with the controls necessary to produce a meaningful result.

[9] For a more comprehensive description of generalisations and their roles in practical reasoning, *see* Anderson, Twining and Schum (2005: 262–79).

might be framed as follows: *In all instances, the government may not prohibit speech intended to express a political view*. A march through a largely Jewish community by a neo-Nazi group displaying swastikas is intended to express a political view. Therefore, the community's government may not prohibit the march.[10]

Religions are the source of many faith-based generalisations. The Christian belief that God created the world in seven days was the basis for generalisations that long prevented Christians from accepting Darwin's theory of evolution. Fundamentalists who promote Jihad use a fabricated generalisation to attract potential suicide bombers that might be phrased as 'any Muslim killed in Jihad goes to a heaven that is populated by virgins'.

Pejorative stereotypes provide further examples. Laws prohibiting discrimination on the basis of race, ethnicity, or gender have the effect of preventing the use of stereotypical generalisations. In 1872, prior to the enactment of those laws, the United States Supreme Court upheld an Illinois law that prohibited women from becoming lawyers based upon what would be viewed today as a pejorative stereotype. 'The paramount destiny and mission of women are to fill the noble and benign offices of wife and mother. This is the law of the Creator. And the rules of civil society must be adapted to the general constitution of things, and cannot be based upon exceptional cases.'[11] Other examples of pejorative stereotypes based upon racist, sexist and ethnic generalisations readily come to mind.

Many, perhaps most, generalisations are hybrid generalisations in that they are based upon values as well as upon evidential data. Evidence-based medicine provides current examples. An evidential generalisation that 90 per cent of persons who have symptoms x, y and z are suffering disease A would be a fact-based generalisation. A policy that was designed to prohibit further testing after a computer-generated diagnosis had reached a 90 per cent degree of certainty would be a policy based upon cost–benefit values. The fact-based and the policy-based generalisations combine to support the hybrid conclusion that a patient exhibiting symptoms x, y and z is a patient that should be treated for disease A, without further testing.[12]

There are three sources from which generalisations can be derived: instruction, study, and experience. Common-sense generalisations are derived, for the

[10] National Socialist Party v. Village of Skokie, 432 U.S. 43 (1977).
[11] *Bradwell v. Illinois*, 83 U.S. 130, 141–2 (1872). The generalisation implicit in the first sentence might also be classified as a faith-based generalisation based upon the second sentence.
[12] I recognise the difficulties inherent in maintaining a distinction between fact and value. In my experience, these difficulties are significant only at the margins.

most part, from instruction (e.g. always look both ways before you cross a street) and experience (e.g. never touch a hot stove). For scholars in a specialised discipline, the primary sources are instruction (e.g. the courses a student takes to qualify for entry into a doctoral program) and study (e.g. the additional reading and research a student does in order to complete her thesis). At this level, experience may increase a scholar's capacity to discover abductive insights. An example would be the experience in Assyriology that enabled Mark Geller to identify as a hypothesis worth testing 'the survival of cuneiform lasted at least into the third century AD' (Geller, 2003(*a*)): 122–39.[13]

Generalisations in any of these categories can be further classified as 'synthetic-intuitive' generalisations or as 'context-specific' generalisations. 'Synthetic-intuitive' generalisations are generalisations that a person synthesises or intuits from her stock of knowledge and beliefs. Sometimes an individual can explain the sources from which she synthesised the generalisation. Frequently, however, the intuitive predominates—the individual cannot identify the source of the generalisation or explain why she believes that it is sound.[14]

The generalisations necessary to support the inference that flight from the scene of a crime is evidence of guilt are examples of 'synthetic-intuitive' generalisations. I am unaware of any tests that claim to have verified these generalisations. Nonetheless, the generalisation 'persons who have committed a crime often flee from the scene of that crime' seems intuitively right. In its weakest form,[15] I would accept the transposed generalisation upon which flight inferences depend—i.e. 'a person who flees from the scene of a crime is *sometimes* a person who is guilty of that crime'. I can think of no basis for my acceptance of these generalisations, apart from a synthesis or an intuition based upon my 'common sense'.

---

[13] See also Anderson (2003: 140–73), for an illustration of the cross-disciplinary work using the methodology described in this chapter.

[14] The nature of a claim that a generalisation is 'sound' or 'well-founded' or 'grounded' is itself a complex subject. Anderson, Twining and Schum (2005: 262–79); see also, W. Wagenaar, van Koppen and H. Crombag (1993) (perspective and theory developed by Dutch psychologists examining the Netherlands criminal justice system).

[15] There are different senses in which the term 'weakest' can be applied to synthetic-intuitive generalisations (and to context-specific generalisations). A generalisation may be weak in the sense that it supplies only weak support for an inference because the quantifier is weak. A generalisation may also be weak in the sense that the individual applying it may doubt its soundness or may doubt the validity of her own intuition.

'Context-specific' generalisations[16] are generalisations made as specific to the precise inference in question as is necessary to establish a basis upon which it can be analysed and appraised. For example, a synthetic-intuitive flight generalisation might be converted into a context-specific generalisation by asking: Was the fact that this particular accused left this particular crime scene hurriedly and went to that particular place evidence of flight supporting an inference that this accused had a guilty state of mind about the particular crime charged?

Generalisations can also be classified using two axes—a generality axis and a reliability axis. The end points of the generality axis are marked by generalisations in the most abstract form and generalisations that have been made specific to the precise case or context in which they are to be applied. For example, the abstract, 'In some instances a person seen fleeing from the scene of a violent crime may be guilty of that crime', as opposed to the context specific, 'It is possible that a person who was seen emerging from a ten-unit apartment building dressed in a suit and tie walking rapidly toward a bus stop 100 yards from the building shortly after a victim had been brutally beaten with a hammer in that building may be guilty of the crime'.[17]

At one end of the reliability axis are scientific laws (such as the law of gravity); well-founded scientific opinions (such as the conclusions of a well-qualified forensic expert); and widely shared conclusions based upon common experience (for instance, everyone knows that a driver must stop for a red light). In the middle are commonly held, but unproven or unprovable beliefs (for instance, fleeing the scene of a crime is evidence of a guilty conscience). At the other end are biases or prejudices that may be strongly held irrespective of available data (for instance, women do not make good trial lawyers; men are generally poor single parents; whites cannot fairly sit as jurors when a black is on trial, etc.) and less strongly held but still operative beliefs (for instance, a person's actions usually conform to her motives).

---

[16] I chose the term 'context-specific', rather than 'case-specific' or 'situation-specific', because it better suggests the range of situation-types in which generalisation-analysis can be usefully employed. Moreover, case-specific generalisations are context-specific generalisations that are specific to a particular case. See Anderson, Twining and Schum (2005: 266–9).

[17] The flight inference has an additional step. Should the action of the individual leaving the building be classified as flight. Only if it can be classified as flight can it be used to support an inference that the individual has a guilty state of mind supporting the further inference that the individual is the person who committed the crime.

3. A protocol for generalisation analysis

There are four steps that facilitate an analysis of the role of generalisations in any type of an argument—clarification of standpoint, specification of the proposition to be justified, specification of the proposition or propositions offered as the basis for its justification, and identification and articulation of the generalisation or generalisations upon which the justification depends. The first step should be completed before the analysis begins. The rest are often reflexive.

1. *Clarification of standpoint.* The analyst must answer four questions in order to define her standpoint for any particular analysis. What is her role in this analysis? In legal contexts, for example, the role may be that of a participant in a legal process—e.g. client, counsellor, negotiator, advocate, judge, juror, etc.; or it may be that of an observer of that process—e.g. academic lawyer, historian, philosopher, probabilist, etc. In other contexts, the possible roles will vary with the purpose for which the analysis is being done. What is the material to be analysed, e.g. the evidence in a case or the arguments in an article? At what stage of what process is the analysis being done—e.g. a historian analysing the available evidence relevant to an event that occurred centuries ago or civil servant analysing data to determine whether a proposed policy should be adopted? What precisely are the purposes and objectives of the analysis—e.g. a scholar trying to improve and make more precise her arguments in an article or book before it is published?

In the *Huddleston* example developed below, the analyst was a legal theorist experienced in the application of a chart method of analysis in legal contexts. In the project described in 'Wigmore meets "The last wedge"' (Anderson, 2003: 140–73), he was a legal theorist undertaking an analysis of the arguments in an inaugural lecture, 'The last wedge' (Geller, 2003(*a*): 122–39) by an Assyriologist shortly before it was given. The purpose of the analysis was to determine whether a method of analysis developed in the discipline of law could be successfully applied to arguments made by a scholar trained in the discipline of Assyriology.

2. *Specification of the proposition to be justified.* The analysis requires that the proposition or propositions to be justified be identified and articulated with precision, but the articulation may have to be made and revised to express the proposition or propositions that can be justified in light of the available evidence and plausible generalisations.[18] This can be done for any step in an

---

[18] Wigmore (1937: 9). Wigmore defined a proposition to be justified or proved as a 'probandum' and a proposition offered as support as a 'probans'. It is important to recognise that a proposition

argument and sometimes must be done for every step. In 'The last wedge', the strongest part of Geller's argument was based upon physical evidence. One of the items he used was an astronomical diary written in Akkadian cuneiform. One of the inferred propositions necessary to his argument was:

> The scribe who wrote the astronomical diary in AD 75 believed that there were and would be enough other persons who read Akkadian cuneiform to justify the effort of maintaining an astronomical diary.[19]

3. *Specification of the justifying proposition or propositions.* Both the articulation and the function of the justifying proposition must be identified with as much precision as possible. The justifying proposition offered to support the Geller's inferred proposition was:

> An astronomical diary [has been found that] was written in Akkadian cuneiform in approximately AD 75.[20]

4. *Identification and articulation of the generalisations involved.* The processes involved in identifying and articulating synthetic-intuitive and context-specific generalisations are discussed and illustrated above and below.[21] Standpoint is critical at this stage. The analyst must understand her standpoint in order to effectively analyse the relationship between the proposition to be justified and the propositions offered as justification. In the analysis, is the proponent an advocate seeking to justify the conclusion? Is she a decision-maker who has to decide whether the conclusion has been established to the required degree of certainty? Is she a reviewer called upon to decide whether the conclusion should be confirmed, revised, or reversed? Is she a critic concerned with validity or structure of the argument or the nature and significance of the generalisations used? The articulation or articulations may vary with role and objective. In the two-proposition argument presented above, the analyst was a legal theorist trying to depict the arguments of an Assyriologist in a form that could be critiqued. The draft generalisation identified by the theorist (after interviewing the Assyriologist at some length) to justify the inferred proposition was:

---

may be both a probandum and a probans in a catenated argument. For example, evidential propositions, propositions expressing evidential data—a testimonial assertion or an item of physical evidence—may be offered to support an inferred proposition, a probandum. That probandum ordinarily then becomes a probans, a proposition offered as support, by itself or in combination with other propositions, for a further inferred proposition, another probandum.

[19] Anderson (2003: 149).

[20] Ibid.; Geller (2003(*a*): 125).

[21] See above, nn. 14–17 and accompanying text.

Astronomical diaries contained useful information that was recorded to be read and used by others.[22]

For an analysis of an argument and its justification in specific contexts, it is usually necessary to identify and articulate the abstract synthetic-intuitive generalisation and the related context-specific generalisation necessary to demonstrate the logical relationship between the probans and the probandum. The process of identification is normally reflexive—sometimes, I see the abstract at the outset and struggle to make it fit the context; other times, particularly when the role is that of an advocate, I formulate the context-specific generalisation and then 'search my mind' for an abstract, synthetic-intuitive generalisation upon which the context-specific generalisation can be defended as plausible.[23]

These steps are necessary, but hardly sufficient. They provide the foundation from which the analysis may proceed in light of the analyst's standpoint. The procedure for completing the analysis varies with standpoint and with context—points illustrated in the examples that follow.

4. Generalisation-analysis applied: two examples

1. *Huddleston.*[24] In *Huddleston v. United States,* 485 U.S. 681 (1988), a federal grand jury had indicted Gary Rufus Huddleston, charging that, in April 1985, he had knowingly sold (count one) and had knowingly possessed (count two) Memorex videocassette tapes (the 'tapes') that had been stolen in interstate commerce. It was clear that the tapes had been stolen in interstate commerce, and Huddleston had sold and had possessed quantities of the tapes. The only issue in dispute was whether Huddleston knew that the tapes had been stolen at the time he had sold or possessed them. The issue was apparently a close one. After two days of deliberations, the jury acquitted Huddleston on the charge that he had knowingly sold stolen tapes, but convicted him on the charge that he had knowingly possessed stolen tapes.

According to Huddleston, Leroy Wesby had a large quantity of the tapes, had invited Huddleston to sell them on a commission basis, and had assured

---

[22] Anderson (2003: 149).

[23] A dialogue between the theorist and the Assyriologist subsequently made it possible to refine these propositions and restate the argument. See Anderson (2003: 151–4) (for the final version of the arguments based upon the astronomical diary).

[24] The analysis developed here is drawn from a more extensive analysis developed in Anderson (1999).

Huddleston that the tapes were legitimate. Huddleston offered and sold quantities of the tapes at prices that were below the cost of manufacturing the tapes. Huddleston acknowledged that he had possessed and sold substantial quantities of the tapes, but claimed that he had no knowledge that they were stolen.

At trial, the government introduced evidence that Huddleston had engaged in two other suspect transactions. In February, Huddleston had arranged a sale of thirty-eight new 12-inch black and white television sets (the 'TV sets'), also supplied by Wesby, to a retailer, for $28 per set. In May, Huddleston had offered to sell to an FBI undercover agent a large quantity of Amana appliances that also had been supplied by Wesby. The government based its theory of relevance upon a generalisation which, according to the Supreme Court, was:

> ... the televisions were stolen, and proof that petitioner [Huddleston] had engaged in a series of sales of stolen merchandise from the same suspicious source would be strong evidence that he was aware that each of the items, including the Memorex tapes, was stolen.

Apart from relevance, the Court had to decide whether the government had offered evidence sufficient to support a finding that the TV sets had, in fact, been stolen. The Court upheld the trial court's decision to admit the sale of the TV sets, reasoning:

> In assessing whether the evidence was sufficient to support a finding that the televisions were stolen, the court here was required to consider not only the direct evidence on that point ... *but also the evidence concerning petitioner's involvement in the sales of other stolen merchandise obtained from Wesby, such as the Memorex tapes and the Amana appliances.* Given this evidence, the jury reasonably could have concluded that the televisions were stolen, and the trial court therefore properly allowed the evidence to go to the jury.[25]

Generalisation-analysis brings the problems with the two arguments to the fore.

First, the question of standpoint: For purposes of this analysis, the standpoint is that of an academic evidence theorist examining a decided case to identify the generalisations available or necessary to justify the Court's conclusions (a) that the fact that the tapes and the appliances were stolen goods supported an inference that the TV sets were also stolen goods, and (b) that the fact that Huddleston had sold or offered to sell the TV sets in February and the appliances in May supported an inference that Huddleston knew in April that the tapes were stolen. The analyst's objective was to identify and articulate

---

[25] 485 U.S. at 691 (emphasis added).

what he saw as the generalisations necessary to justify these conclusions and to identify the kinds of issues that such an articulation made it possible to address.

Second, specification of the propositions to be justified: there were two propositions to be justified in this analysis, propositions 4 and 7 below; however, an understanding of the analysis of those propositions will be facilitated by specifying the ultimate proposition, the *ultimate probandum*, that the government had to prove and its components, the *penultimate probanda*—propositions 1 through 4:[26]

1. In April 1985, Guy Rufus Huddleston ('GRH') possessed a large quantity of Memorex videocassette tapes (the 'tapes') that had been supplied by Leroy Wesby ('LW') and that had been stolen in interstate commerce, and GRH knew that the tapes had been stolen.

2. In April 1985, GRH possessed a large quantity of tapes that had been supplied by LW. [Undisputed ('U')]

3. The tapes that LW had supplied to GRH in April 1985 had been stolen in interstate commerce. [U]

4. In April 1985, GRH knew that the tapes supplied by LW had been stolen.

Third, specification of the justifying propositions: the Court thought three propositions provided sufficient justification for proposition 4—propositions 3 (set out above) and propositions 5 and 6:

5. The 12-inch black and white television sets (the 'TV sets') that LW supplied to GRH in February 1985 had been stolen.

6. The Amana appliances that LW supplied to GRH in May 1985 had been stolen. [U]

The claimed inductive relationships among these propositions upon which the Court's analysis relied are depicted in charted form in the chart set out below.

---

[26] In a legal dispute, the ultimate probandum is defined by law. In *Huddleston*, the statute prohibiting the knowing possession or sale of goods in interstate commerce constituted the major premise. The ultimate probandum was the minor premise that government had to prove was true beyond any reasonable doubt in order to justify a conviction. Given the statutory language, proposition 1 was the ultimate probandum in this case. The penultimate probanda are derived by partitioning the ultimate probandum into simple declarative propositions, here propositions 2, 3 and 4. In other contexts, the ultimate probandum is the hypothesis to be proved or tested stated as precisely as possible.

Huddleston: an inductive chart

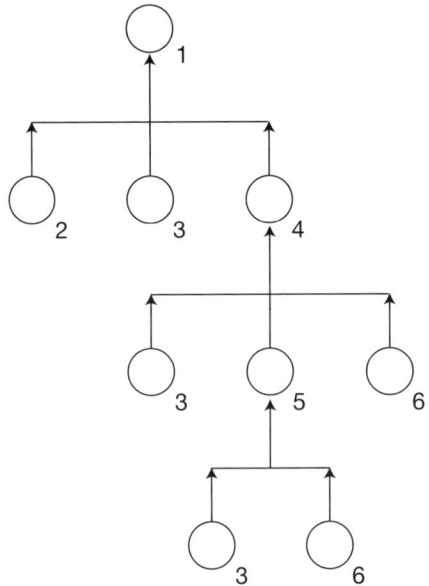

Fourth, an identification and articulation of the generalisations involved: the analysis requires the identification of two sets of generalisations—those necessary to show that proposition 3 and proposition 6 converge to support proposition 5, and those necessary to show that propositions 3, 5 and 6 converge to support proposition 4. The claim that the fact that the tapes supplied by Wesby were stolen (P_3) and the fact that the Amana appliances supplied Wesby were stolen (P_6) supported an inference that the TV sets supplied by Wesby were stolen (P_5) invokes a synthetic-intuitive generalisation that might be stated as:

7.   Goods supplied by a supplier of stolen goods are almost certainly/ probably stolen goods.[27]

In order to appraise the specific arguments made in *Huddleston*, the synthetic-intuitive generalisation must be converted into a context-specific generalisation, such as:

---

[27] I have never, to my knowledge, dealt with a supplier of stolen goods, and my knowledge of how such suppliers act is, at best, anecdotal. Nonetheless, based upon such anecdotal knowledge and my view of 'the way things are', proposition 7 seems intuitively correct, although I can think of no basis for deciding which quantifier would be appropriate.

8. In all/most/many/some instances a quantity of goods [such as the TV
    sets], which was supplied by a person who had on two *subsequent* occa-
    sions within a three-month period supplied other kinds of goods [such
    as the tapes and the appliances] that were in fact stolen goods, is a
    quantity of goods that was stolen.

The logical relationship of the generalisations in the argument that the TV
sets were stolen is depicted in the chart below.

The TV sets were stolen: a deductive chart

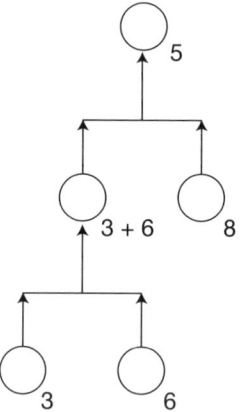

The argument that the facts that Wesby supplied Huddleston with stolen
TV sets in February (P_7) and stolen appliances in May (P_8) supported an
inference that Huddleston knew that the tapes that Wesby supplied in April
were stolen finds apparent support in a synthetic-intuitive generalisation that
might be framed:

> A person who has, on more than one occasion, offered for sale stolen goods
> obtained from the same source is a person who knew/almost certainly knew/
> probably knew that the goods were stolen goods, notwithstanding any assurances
> that the source may have given him.

The problems become apparent when the synthetic-intuitive generalisation necessary to justify the analysis that the Supreme Court adopted is converted into a context-specific generalisation because, in the Court's analysis,
the relationships between propositions 3 and 4; 7 and 4; and 8 and 4 were
convergent—that is, proposition 3 standing alone would provide some support for proposition 4 and proposition 7 standing alone would provide some
support for proposition 4 and proposition 8 standing alone would provide

some support for proposition 4. The support provided by a prior supplying of stolen goods (P_7) for an inference of subsequent knowledge (P_4) seems different in kind than the support, if any, that the subsequent supplying of stolen goods (P_8) could provide for an inference of knowledge at a prior time (P_4). For that reason the identification and articulation of three additional context-specific generalisations becomes necessary to the analysis.

The first makes it possible to consider the support that the TV sets alone (P_7) might provide for an inference that Huddleston knew the tapes were stolen (P_4):

> A person [such as GRH] who sells or offers to sell a significant quantity of goods [such as the tapes] that were in fact stolen goods on behalf of another person [such as LW] who had *previously* supplied goods of a different kind [such as the TV sets] that were in fact stolen is a person who certainly/almost certainly/probably knew that the offered goods were stolen, notwithstanding any representations to the contrary his supplier may have made.

The second isolates the claim that the *subsequent* supplying of the appliances in *May* (P_8) supported for an inference that Huddleston had the necessary knowledge when he possessed the tapes in *April*:

> A person [such as GRH] who sells or offers to sell a significant quantity of goods [such as the tapes] that were in fact stolen goods on behalf of another person [such as LW] who *subsequently* supplied goods of a different kind [such as the appliances] that were in fact stolen is a person who certainly/almost certainly/probably knew that the offered goods were stolen, notwithstanding any representations to the contrary his supplier may have made.

And finally, a formulation that enables us to consider the combined effect of propositions 7 and 8 as support for proposition 4:

> A person [such as GRH] who sells or offers to sell a significant quantity of goods [such as the tapes] that were in fact stolen goods on behalf of another person [such as LW] who had *previously* supplied and who *subsequently* supplied goods of different kinds that were in fact stolen is a person who certainly/almost certainly/probably knew [or should have known] that the offered goods were stolen, notwithstanding any representations to the contrary his supplier may have made.

Generalisation analysis of these two arguments reveals logical problems with the Supreme Court's reasoning. First, there is the double- (or triple-) counting problem. The fact that the tapes were stolen (P_3) is used to support an inference that TV sets were stolen (P_5) and used again to support an inference that Huddleston knew the tapes were stolen (P_4). Second, the Court seemingly thought that the facts that the April tapes and the May appliances had been stolen were necessary facts to enable a jury to infer it was more probable than not that the February TV sets were stolen. But Huddleston did not have this information in February and thus, insofar as the record effects, he did not have evidence sufficient to enable *him* to know that the TV sets were stolen. That diminishes significantly the degree of support that the TV sets might otherwise have had for the proposition that Huddleston knew that the tapes were stolen. Logically, the fact that the May appliances were stolen provides only weak, if any, support for the claim that Huddleston knew in April that the tapes were stolen, leaving Huddleston's claim that he did not know the tapes were stolen and had been assured that they were legitimate largely unchallenged.

My objective here has been to illustrate a method of analysis by applying it to two particular claims made by the Supreme Court in *Huddleston* to demonstrate its uses (and limitations). The analysis might be extended or broadened, if my standpoint were different, but the foregoing should provide a foundation for identifying some additional not so apparent issues and some deficiencies and flaws in the Court's reasoning that the method brought into focus. Apart from providing an illustration of the method and application, the example identified issues that would be interesting to a trained logician as well as to a legal theorist.

2. *Wigmore meets the last wedge.* In the project described in 'Wigmore meets the "last wedge"' (Anderson 2003), the legal theorist was trying to determine whether a modified version of Wigmore's chart method of analysis (Wigmore 1913 (the original method); Anderson, Twining and Schum 2005, chap. 5 (the modified version)) developed by legal theorists could be applied to an argument by an Assyriologist (Geller) to produce a useful analysis and critique. The answer was yes, but the focus here is on the nature and role of generalisations in Geller's argument.

The ultimate probandum to be tested was Geller's claim that the class of persons who could read cuneiform survived until the second or third century AD (Geller, 2003(*a*): 125).[28] Unlike a legal case, the penultimate probanda were the major points in the argument, two of which are relevant here. The first, and in the analyst's view, the one with the strongest support, was based upon the physical evidence:

---

[28] As Anderson interpreted the argument as a whole, he thought Geller's ultimate probandum could be refined to claim that the class of persons who could read cuneiform lasted until the Sassanian conquest of Babylonia in AD 256 (Anderson, 2003: 145).

The Astronomical Diary produced in AD 75, the quantity of tablets produced in the Hellenistic period as evidenced by the surviving fragments, and the Greek script inscribed on the Graeco-Babyloniaca tablets establish that the class of persons who could read cuneiform survived until the second or third century AD. (Anderson 2003: 152).

As the outsider, Anderson had no idea what an astronomical diary was; what the tablets produced in the Hellenistic period were, what the Hellenistic period, as Geller used the term, was; or what the Graeco-Babloniaca tablets were. Anderson created a draft 'key-list' of the propositions supporting Geller's argument. Geller and Anderson spent two days discussing the key-list, most of which was spent answering factual questions, such as these, and in identifying the generalisations necessary to show that each evidential proposition supported the proposition to be inferred. Those interactions produced a revised key-list with 273 propositions. Anderson and Geller discussed the propositions in the revised key-list, and Anderson did some research to answer some historical questions. The final key-list had 299 propositions, and there were still unanswered questions about some of those.[29]

The second penultimate, that the documentary record provided additional evidence that the ability to read cuneiform survived until the third century AD had, in the analyst's view, far weaker support. It was based upon what the Assyriologist metaphorically called testimony, the testimony of Iamblicus, of Elagabulus and of Lucian. Anderson did a microanalysis of the propositions necessary to support the argument based upon Iamblicus (Geller, 2003(a): 129–30 (the argument stated), Anderson: 156–67 (the argument analysed)). That argument was based upon a summary of the novel, *A Babylon Story* found in the library of Photius (AD 810–93). The story identified Iamblicus as the author. The first source of concern was the extent to which it was based upon multiple levels of hearsay—that is, what a translator said that Photius said in his summary that Iamblicus said in the novel with additional information based upon what a scholiast said in the marginal notes they made as they prepared copies of the summary. Generalisation analysis also revealed a second source of doubt. Some of the arguments were supported by implausible generalisations about the life expectancy of the tutor that Geller argued had taught Iamblicus to write Akkadian in cuneiform. According to Geller, Iamblicus was a Syrian who wrote *A Babylon Story* in approximately AD 200, the beginning of the third century, and the tutor of a Babylonian royal scribe taken prisoner by the Romans during Trajan's campaign in AD 115–16 and later sold as a slave to a Syrian. Although not impossible, the argument that

---

[29] See Anderson (2003: 141–51) for a detailed description of the process.

someone who was old enough to become a royal scribe by AD 115 lived and remembered Akkadian long enough to teach it to someone who was old enough to learn it and was still writing in AD 200 seems inconsistent with generalisations about the life expectancy of persons who lived at that time.

5. Conclusion

There are two conclusions relevant here. First, the last wedge exercise demonstrated that the chart-method and generalisation-method were analytic tools in the field of evidence that could be used to develop and critique arguments in various disciplines. The chart-method is too labour intensive for microscopic analysis of most arguments, although it is a tool useful in analysing particular phases of an argument, a point illustrated by the *Huddleston* example. Those who have taught the method in the discipline of law have concluded that it is an excellent tool for training intending lawyers. The analysis of a significant body of evidence develops sensitivity and skill analysing evidence and arguments that carry over into their work on matters that do not merit a full charted analysis. The author believes that it is a tool that could be used with similar results in training graduate students in many disciplines. The generalisation-method is an easier tool to use. As the *Huddleston* example illustrated, it can be applied to any part of an argument to identify hidden issues that should be addressed. A comparison of the analysis of Geller's argument based upon the physical evidence with those based upon the testimony of Iamblicus, demonstrates that it can be used to assess the probative force of a particular argument.

Second, the exercise made it clear that the two methods are tools that could only rarely be usefully employed to facilitate cross-disciplinary analysis. The borders of a discipline are defined by the stock of specialised knowledge and generalisations that those trained in the discipline share. Those borders are barriers that cannot be readily surmounted by those trained in a different discipline. This latter point was illustrated by 'Wigmorean analysis and the survival of cuneiform', Geller's response to 'Wigmore meets "the last wedge"' (Geller, 2003(*b*): 216–30). There, he demonstrated that an Assyriologist could do a similarly detailed analysis using only 126 propositions, and the implicit generalisation upon which the arguments were based that would be readily understood by other Assyriologists.

I suspect that some of those involved in the Leverhulme project had an unstated concern. If evidence were established as a discipline, the participants in that discipline might use their integrated theory as a licence to cross other disciplinary boundaries and seek to impose its methods and insights upon those in the invaded discipline. My own work as a legal theorist using Wigmore's chart method to analyse an Assyriologist's arguments suggests that the concern is unwarranted. That exercise yielded three insights from the outsider's standpoint that are relevant here. First, and not surprising, the principles of logic involved in marshaling evidence to support a hypothesis or to justify a conclusion were the same in both disciplines. Second, the principal barriers to cross-disciplinary analysis and communication stemmed from the fact that the outsider does not share the stock of knowledge and the knowledge-based generalisations, that are common and shared by those within the discipline. The difficulties I had in attempting to cross the boundaries between law and Assyriology were sufficient to persuade me that the effort required to obtain even limited mastery sufficient for the particular project was so great that such cross-disciplinary projects of that kind are likely to occur rarely and only in exceptional cases.[30]

Those conclusions suggest that the primary contributions to evidence, viewed as a field of study, are likely to come from those in other disciplines. The relationship would be reciprocal. Those in other disciplines could use tools developed in the evidence domain to enhance their own work. In turn, the use of those tools in other disciplines would generate insights that could be used to develop new tools and methods.

References

Anderson, T. (1999), 'On generalizations I: a preliminary exploration', *South Texas Law Review*, 40: 455–81.

Anderson, T. (2003), '"Wigmore meets the last wedge"', in *Evidence and inference in history and law: interdisciplinary dialogues*, ed. W. Twining and I. Hampsher-Monk (Evanston, IL, Northwestern University Press), pp. 140–73.

Anderson T., Twining, W., Schum, D. (2005), *Analysis of Evidence* (2nd edn.) (Cambridge and New York, Cambridge University Press).

Geller, M. (2003a). '"The last wedge"', in *Evidence and Inference in History and Law: interdisciplinary dialogues*, ed. W. Twining and I. Hampsher-Monk (Evanston, IL, Northwestern University Press), pp. 123–39.

Geller, M. (2003b), '"Wigmorean analysis and the survival of cuneiform"', in *Evidence and Inference in History and Law: interdisciplinary dialogues*, ed. W. Twining and I. Hampsher-Monk (Evanston, IL, Northwestern University Press), pp. 216–30.

---

[30] The difficulties are described and illustrated in considerable detail in Anderson (2003: 168–73).

Schum, D. (1987), *Evidence and Inference for Intelligence Analysts* (2 vols.) (Lanham, MD, University Press of America).

Schum, D. (1994), *Evidential Foundations of Probabilistic Reasoning* (New York, John Wiley & Sons, Inc).

Twining, W. (1999), 'Narrative and generalizations in argumentation about questions of fact', *South Texas Law Review*, 40: 131–65.

Twining, W. (2006), *Rethinking Evidence* (2nd edn.) (Cambridge and New York, Cambridge University Press).

Twining, W. and Hampsher-Monk, I. (eds.) (2003), *Evidence and Inference in History and Law: interdisciplinary dialogues* (Evanston, IL, Northwestern University Press).

Wagenaar, W., van Koppen, P. and Crombag, H. (1993), *Anchored Narratives* (New York, St Martin's Press).

Wigmore, J. H. (1913), 'The problem of proof', *Illinois Law Review*, 8: 77–103.

Wigmore, J. H. (1937). *The Science of Judicial Pproof* (3rd edn.) (Boston, MA, Little, Brown).

9

Are there Universal Principles or Forms of Evidential Inference? Of Inference Networks and Onto-Epistemology

PETER TILLERS*

Abstract

Although interest in evidential inference is not new—interest in the topic reaches back into antiquity—during the last two or three decades there has been a veritable explosion of scholarship and research about evidential inference. Furthermore, evidential inference (or 'factual inference') is now an important topic in virtually every field of scholarship and in virtually every kind of 'knowledge industry'. Although the models of inference generated in this latest wave of scholarship and research are varied, one thread does run through many of the new models. Many contemporary accounts emphasise the multistage nature of evidential inference; it is now very often argued or assumed that evidential inference is best viewed as a network or web of inferences Although the proponents of such models of evidential inference often have important disagreements about the properties or structure of multistage evidential inference, it is fair to say that such models generally rest on the compound proposition that real-world evidential inference usually or always consists of 'atoms' that are linked together (in some way) by 'generalisations'. If a model of this sort is a valid representation of evidential inference, the question may arise—the question has arisen—whether a model of this sort is or is not 'universal'. The answer is that this question is unanswerable. What can be

* Part of this essay was given as a lecture at the British Academy, for the conference 'Evidence, Enquiry and Facts', 13–14 Dec. 2007. The essay found here is a revised version of the chapter of the same name in J. Jackson, M. Langer and P. Tillers (2008). Permission by Hart Publishing to publish this essay here is gratefully acknowledged.

I am grateful for the comments and suggestions made by James Franklin, Mike Redmayne and William Twining. The paper's errors and flaws, however, are entirely mine.

Proceedings of the British Academy, **171**, 245–265. © The British Academy 2011.

said is that when human beings (or other agents) configure problems of evidence in a certain way, inference networks (of some sort) are inevitable and describe the structure of the problem at hand but that when problems of evidence are perceived (only or mainly) in certain other ways, representations of inference as webs of factual hypotheses connected by generalisations are of little or no use—simply because in some situations such web-like patterns of reasoning do not address the problem at hand. For example, sometimes the question is not how strongly some evidentiary phenomenon supports some hypothesis but, rather, what sort of complex of hypotheses or conceptual constructs most persuasively explains some set of phenomena. This latter sort of problem sometimes requires a constructive and imaginative conceptual activity that does not much resemble an inference network or its ingredients.

A powerful new model of factual inference: webs of inferences held together by nomological glue

DURING THE LAST SEVERAL DECADES there has been a veritable explosion of scholarship and research about evidential inference. Although the models of inference generated in this latest wave of scholarship and research are varied, one thread does run through many of those models: many contemporary accounts of evidential (or 'factual') inference emphasise the multistage, or hierarchical, nature of evidential inference; it is now commonly argued or assumed that evidential inference is best viewed as a network or web of inferences.[1]

Although the proponents of such models of evidential inference sometimes disagree (in important ways) about the properties or structure of multistage evidential inference, it is fair to say that such models generally rest on the compound proposition that real-world evidential inference usually or always consists of propositional 'atoms' (i.e. relatively granular propositional statements about states of the world) that are linked together (in some way)

---

[1] John Henry Wigmore began the parade toward inference networks many years ago. See Wigmore, 1931; Wigmore, 1937. Wigmore's approach was non-mathematical. In any event, he had few if any followers before the 1970s. In the 1970s and in the early 1980s David Schum led the way in making inference networks an important topic in probability theory. See, e.g. Schum and Kelly, 1973. Schum quickly extended his work into law. See, e.g. Schum and Martin, 1982. Other scholars, both legal scholars and scholars in fields such as probability theory and decision, then took up serious study of inference networks. See, e.g. Howard, 1980; Howard, 1990; Pearl, 1982, Tillers, 1989; Anderson and Twining, 1991; Pearl, 1995, Robertson and Vignaux, 1995. Schum continued his work on inference networks both by himself and in collaboration with others. See, e.g. Schum, 1994; Anderson, Schum and Twining, 2005.

by nomological entities of some kind, entities that are often—but not always —called 'generalisations'.[2] In this essay I refer to these sorts of models or representations of evidential inference as NAGs, which is my shorthand for 'network-and-generalisation' models of evidential inference.

The universality or non-universality of the **NAG** model of evidential inference

The case for the **NAG** model is a powerful one: **NAG**s seem to capture important properties of much evidential inference. However, even if **NAG**s are 'valid' representations of evidential inference, an important question (or family of questions) remains:

> Is a network-and-generalisation model or representation of evidential inference 'universal'? Does every problem of evidential inference take the form of a **NAG**? Does a network-and-generalisation model capture the essence of all inferential inferential problem; or—in any event—does (some version of) the **NAG** model capture an important ingredient of every problem of factual inference?

This question (or family of questions) arose within the interdisciplinary research programme and community 'Evidence, Inference and Enquiry'. Debate about the question of the universality or non-universality of the **NAG** model was provoked by a lecture given by David Schum at University College London in 2005.[3] In that lecture Schum argued that there is such a thing as a science of evidence and that evidential inference in the form of a **NAG** is applicable —at least in principle—to any investigation into the truth or falsity of any proposition about a state of the world.[4] Participants in *Evidence, Inference and Enquiry* raised a variety of questions about and objections to Schum's thesis. Schum responded to those questions and objections.[5] However, the

---

[2] William Twining has a perceptive discussion of varieties of generalisations in Twining, 1990.

Some theorists believe that the nomological glue ought to be part of the inference network itself whereas other theorists (including most legal theorists) think that entities such as generalisations should be viewed as ancillary to an inference network. This is an important disagreement.

An even more important division is between people who believe (e.g. Judea Pearl) that inference networks represent causal connections (among events in time) and those who reject this view (e.g. David Schum). The difference of opinion on this point may reflect a fundamental epistemological disagreement about the possibility of knowledge based on associations in the absence of knowledge or plausible hypotheses about causal connections.

[3] Schum, 2005.

[4] Schum's belief in the existence of a science of evidence is longstanding. See Tillers, 1989.

[5] Schum, 2006.

question of the reach of the **NAG** model of evidential inference remains unresolved—as does the question of whether any model or representation of evidential inference can achieve 'universality'.

I believe that the question of universality or non-universality of **NAG**s is literally unanswerable. In this essay I argue—once again[6]—that the only genuinely general thing that can be said about the structure of problems of evidential inference is that when human beings (or other agents) configure problems of evidence in a certain way, inference networks (of some sort) are ineluctable and do describe the structure of the problem at hand but that when problems of evidence are perceived—i.e. configured—only or mainly in some other ways, representations of an inferential process as a web of factual hypotheses connected by generalisations are of little or no use. In short, I take the arguably 'wishy-washy' position that sometimes **NAG**s have little or no epistemic value because in some situations web-like patterns of reasoning do not accurately portray the way that an observer, investigator or fact finder configures, or perceives, a problem of inference, together with the evidence that seemingly pertains to the problem that the observer, investigator, or fact finder perceives.

I support and illustrate my thesis about the relationship between (evidential) argument and configuration (or perception) by examining three situations in which network-and-generalisation representations of evidential inference—'**NAG**s'—seem to have little to say about the relationship between evidence and hypotheses. The first is a situation in which there is a question about the meanings that human beings attach to actions or events. The second is a situation in which tacit or unconscious inference—i.e. non-explicit inference—is at work. The third is a situation in which the (complex) inferential methods (strategies) employed by a 'special science' such as physics, chemistry, or genetics seem to address best the inferential problem at hand. After discussing these three examples of 'non-standard' evidential inference I conclude by pointing out some features of man and mind that are suggested by a proper understanding of inference and inferential theory.

---

[6] The general theoretical underpinnings of the argument in this essay were anticipated in Tillers, 1986.

Three examples of 'non-standard' evidential inference

Inference about human meaning—IRM

In some situations an investigator or fact finder does not focus on the question of the occurrence or non-occurrence of some event or events. Sometimes an investigator instead assumes (if only provisionally) the occurrence (or non-occurrence) of some event or events and seeks to determine the meaning or meanings of those events (or the absence of some events) to some person or persons. For example, an investigator might reasonably believe or assume (provisionally, for example) that, as expected, the sun appeared in the sky in the morning of some particular day or that a comet unexpectedly became visible to the naked eye a few weeks ago—and ask, 'What did that mean to Peter Tillers?' or 'What did that mean to the Pope?' Hence, in the hypothesised type of situation, instead of asking whether evidence such as E_L—the appearance of some new light in the sky, some apparent new light in the sky—supports the hypothesis A, the appearance (or seeming appearance) of the sun or of a comet,

$$E_L \rightarrow A \hspace{4cm} \text{Expression 1}$$

the actor or observer assumes the occurrence of some event such as A and seeks to determine M, the meaning of some event A (whether in the eyes of Peter Tillers, the Pope or some other person or persons).

The manner in which **Expression 1** portrays the relationship between some evidence E_L and some event A may suggest that it is both possible and appropriate to depict the relationship between some event or events A and some meaning or meanings M in precisely the same way: if so, perhaps the question of M given A involves nothing more and nothing other than the question of whether, and the extent to which, a mental state such as M is supported by evidence such as A. If so, questions about the meanings attached to events or circumstances—I shall sometimes refer to such questions as **MQs**—are merely problems or questions that take the form

$$E \rightarrow A \rightarrow M \hspace{4cm} \text{Expression 2}$$

In some situations it is appropriate to conceive of the relationship between a meaning M and an event such as A in this manner. However, in many instances this way of framing the relationship between some possible meaning M and some possible event such as A is inappropriate. In many situations the problem confronting an investigator or trier of fact is whether or not a meaning such as M is wrapped around, or attached to, an event such as A.

Peter Tillers

Conceived in this way, judgements about the meaning or meanings of acts are better pictured in the following way:

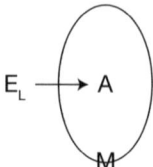

M = concept having meaning M

Figure 9.1.

Consider two possible visions of the meaning of the structure of the cosmos and one or two of its major parts.

This is one vision:

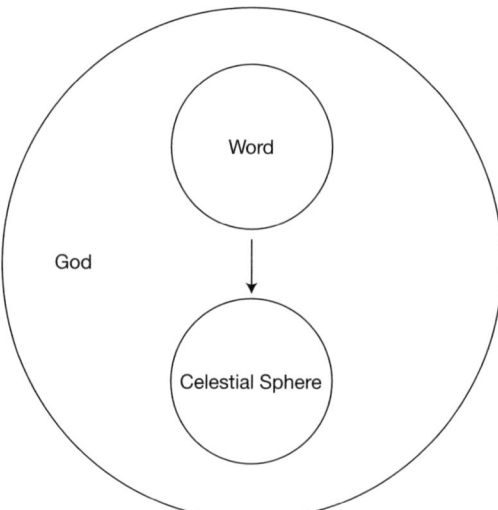

Figure 9.2.

Here is another vision:

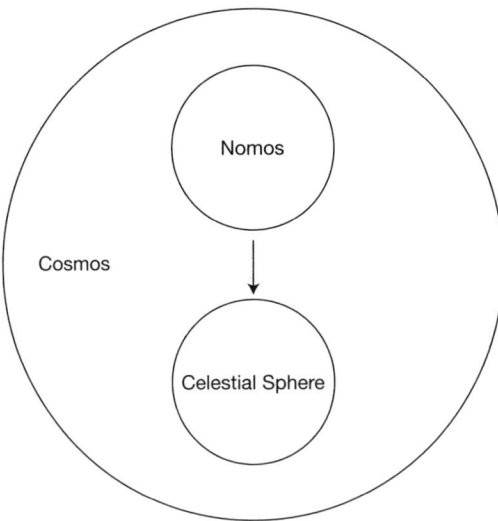

Figure 9.3.

Although these two visions (i.e. those reflected in Figures 9.2 and 9.3) are very general and lack detail, they suffice to illustrate the different ways that different people might think about the meaning or meanings of the same event. These two visions suggest, for example, that a religious person might view the appearance of a comet in the night sky as a manifestation or expression of God's Word in the cosmos, while another person might believe that celestial phenomena are manifestations of underlying natural laws that reign in the cosmos.[7]

The attempt to determine the meaning or meanings that some person or persons attach to various events and circumstances in the world is an intellectual activity that involves imagination and reconstruction. (I will occasionally refer to this sort of creative and constructive intellectual activity as the 'imaginative reconstruction of meaning', or **IRM**.) The effort to infer meanings that 'reside' in the minds of others (at certain times) involves the attempt to read other minds.[8] If done explicitly rather than intuitively, this sort of

---

[7] Note that despite their differences, both of these imaginary people might accept scientific accounts such as special relativity and quantum theory. If you doubt this, it is worth recalling that Isaac Newton believed in the existence of God.

[8] Human beings have no 'direct' access to the minds of other human beings; they cannot directly perceive the minds of other human beings. Philosophers' awareness of this point has made them

effort to discern the meanings that are at work in the minds of others perhaps must be done in a particular way.

The 'meanings' that human beings attach to events and circumstances usually involve complex concepts (or complexes of concepts) rather than only simple, or irreducible, concepts. Moreover, individual meanings (such as lust, anger, jealousy, and respect) belong to families of concepts (such as 'infidelity', 'spouse', 'love', 'children', 'class', 'chastity'). Hence, when an investigator makes a serious attempt at an **IRM**—i.e. when an investigator, or enquirer, makes an attempt to put together a reconstruction that has at least a remote chance of being representative of some actual state of affairs or some actual series of events—the investigator must try to formulate a complex of concepts (and also the complex of principles that governs the relationships among that complex of non-primitive, or decomposable, concepts) that depicts and reconstitutes, to at least some degree, the meanings that some other persons actually attach (at some point or interval in time) to events and acts that those persons think they encounter in the sort of world that they believe they inhabit.

When evidential inference takes the form of a **NAG**, evidence plays a role much like the role that symptoms play in the diagnosis of a physical disease such as cancer. In such an investigation, evidence is of interest to an investigator (or 'fact finder') because the evidence, it is thought, may speak to the truth or falsity of some proposition about the occurrence or non-occurrence of some event or condition in the world. But in investigations of **MQ**s evidence regularly serves a very different epistemic purpose. In an enquiry about **MQ**s an investigator may look to events and circumstances mainly or exclusively to see if she can find in some events or circumstances the footprint, or imprint, of some human mind or minds. In this kind of enquiry the investigator wants to see if some circumstance—such as a person's conduct—harbours a trace of— some evidence of—the structure of the thinking and beliefs of some person or persons.

An investigator who looks at evidence for this purpose and in this way— to reconstruct the meaning or meanings in the head of another person or persons—often views evidence virtually in a medieval or scholastic fashion.

---

question—philosophers are wont to raise seemingly strange questions—the existence of other minds. However, one should be wary about making too much of any argument based on our lack of direct access to others' minds. The logic of the argument for doubting the existence of other minds quite possibly implies that one must doubt the existence of anything—since, after all, there is good reason to think that human beings have no 'direct' epistemic access to anything in the world, except perhaps to their own perceptions of the world. (There is reason to doubt that human beings know even their own perceptions directly.)

An investigator or fact finder who looks to events such as human conduct for traces of the content and structure of an actor's thinking may view evidence such as human conduct as an almost literal *sign*: such an investigator may believe that circumstances in the world can embody bits of meanings, intentions, beliefs and similar matters, and that circumstances sometimes do so because fragments of human minds can be deposited in the world by the deliberate actions of intelligent beings.

Although it is rational and sensible to believe that events and circumstances in the world can echo the workings of the human mind and the human heart, the model of evidential inference as a **NAG**—as a network or web of inferences accompanied by generalisations or law-like statements of some kind—is, I believe, a powerful and compelling one. A person enchanted by inference network model of evidential inference—and I count myself as such a person—might try to shoehorn all deliberation about human meaning into the form of a **NAG**. For example, I can imagine that a dedicated proponent of inference networks might take the position that a question about what species of meaning **M** some actor attaches to some event or action (at some point or interval in time) is a question of fact like any other question of fact and that the possible relationships between evidence and a proposition about a fact of type **M** are the same as between evidence and a proposition about any other type of fact. Hewing to this line of thinking, one might then take the position that the question of whether an actor attached some specific meaning Mi to some event or act amounts to the question whether the actor did or did not have a state of mind **S** containing the specific meaning $\mathbf{M}_i$. Schematically stated, then, the issue before the trier would be

$$\{S_{M_i} \mid {\sim}S_{M_i}\} \qquad\qquad \text{Expression 3}$$

The relationship of this question to evidence such as that of the actor's possible irritation $\mathbf{E}_i$ could then be visualised thus:

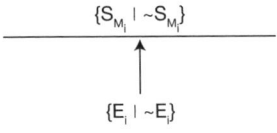

Figure 9.4.

If one grants or assumes that all questions and arguments about the meanings that human actors attach to events and circumstances can and should be formulated in this way, one can then apply the particular type of inference network that one prefers to any given question about human meaning. For example, if one has Bayesian inclinations one can follow Bayesian convention and reverse the direction of the arrow in the diagram in Figure 9.4 —and then compare (i) the probability of E_i given S_{Mi} with (ii) the probability of E_i given $\sim S_{Mi}$ and consider what impact this ratio has on one's pre-existing judgement about the probability of S_{Mi}. Alternatively,[9] one can ask whether and to what extent evidence such as E_i supports the hypothesis of S_{Mi} (the state of mind S harbouring the meaning M_i). And then if one also believes that some possible glue connecting S_{Mi} with E_i must be separately considered in any rational argument about the inferences supported by any evidence, any potentially pertinent ancillary generalisations can and should be made to envelop or to be enveloped by the sort of inference structure shown in Figure 9.4.

But the ability of a person to shoehorn deliberation about human meaning into the form of a **NAG** proves little. It might be possible to give pigs wings and to enable them to fly. But a flying pig with wings would be an unnatural and ungainly spectacle. Similarly, it might also be possible to make all deliberation about human meaning take the form of an inference network. But to do so would sometimes create an unedifying spectacle as well as an unnatural and ungainly one. As explained earlier, in many investigations (or parts of investigations) of the meanings that actors attach to events and circumstances in the world—in many investigations of 'M-assignments'—the central question is not whether some state of mind S harbouring M_i did or did not occur and the main task at hand is instead to ascertain the structure of M and the family of concepts F to which M belongs. **NAG**s do not elucidate or facilitate this latter sort of enquiry because the latter sort of activity is a creative and imaginative activity—I call it the imaginative reconstruction of meaning, or **IRM**—and a **NAG** does not elucidate or facilitate this sort of imaginative or creative activity.

When proceeding in an **IRM** mode, an investigator is engaged in hypothesis-formation. Arguments in the form of **NAG**s do not directly facilitate hypothesis-formation because **NAG**s are principally devices for assessing the strength or weight of evidence on defined—i.e. either known or assumed—hypotheses.[10]

---

[9] It is possible this alternative formulation is not essentially or necessarily different from a Bayesian formulation.

[10] Tillers and Schum, 1991 (discussing the difference between the role of evidence in argument about stated factual hypothesis and the role of evidence in the formation of factual hypotheses; the article also suggests why abduction in the form of 'inference to the best explanation' does not adequately explain or promote the formation of epistemically fertile hypotheses). For an illuminating analysis of varieties of abductive inference, see Schum, 2001.

(Hypotheses are formed within inference networks, but the hypotheses that are formed are so formed in the interstices between the two poles of inference networks, foundational evidence and ultimate hypotheses.) Furthermore, in the case of **IRM** the formation of hypotheses about human meanings is not provoked or suggested by the presence of some sensory event whose appearance seems more probable given some one possible meaning (or set of meanings) rather than some other possible meaning (or set of meanings). In much **IRM** the enquirer creates hypotheses about complexes of meanings by examining properties of events that, in the eyes of the enquirer, seem to constitute marks that are expressive or indicative of—that seem to echo—some complex of meaning-concepts and meaning-rules.

The analysis presented here of the kind of reasoning that is ordinarily (and properly) used in **IRM** is, in its broad contours, in harmony with a well-established philosophical and intellectual tradition that also holds that a distinctive method of argument, reasoning and thinking must be used to

---

By arguing that **NAG**s do not portray the workings of **IRM** I am not suggesting that **IRM** in legal proceedings should proceed without the benefit of evidence. In **IRM** as in any other type of deliberation, the formation of hypotheses that are completely unrooted in evidence is likely to lead to production of propositions about the world that may be entertaining but have little chance of being true. Legal adjudication of rights and duties cannot rest on entirely speculative propositions about events in the world.

By arguing that **NAG**s do not capture the workings of **IRM**, I am not suggesting that any judgements generated by **IRM** cannot be a constituent of an argument that takes the form of a **NAG**. Although deliberation in the form of **IRM** and deliberation in the form of **NAG**s are different, **IRM** can be an ingredient of evidential argument and inference that takes the form of a network. If this is already generally obvious, it is possible that the main service of this essay is to remind students of forensic proof that not only are meaning assignments—e.g. 'the pulling of this trigger is intended to cause death and destruction'—often the ultimate *facta probanda* in legal proceedings, but that meaning assignments—e.g., 'Switzerland is a lovely country with courteous people'—are also often part of the foundation for an argument about some ultimate *factum probandum* in a case. (The common use of **M**-assignments as a basis for further inference raises a variety of knotty inferential issues that US and UK scholarship in the law of evidence has yet to examine in a systematic fashion. For example, perhaps actors' judgements of meaning are ordinarily quite fuzzy; i.e. perhaps actors' concepts about what makes this or that event or condition or property good, lovely, vile, rotten, etc., are ordinarily very fuzzy. Moreover, perhaps the rules that actors use to reason about their fuzzy concepts of meaning tend to be fuzzy; e.g. if an actor thinks that being loud-mouthed is generally bad but that being outspoken in the defence of oppressed minorities is generally good, what sort of judgement should the actor make about a loud-mouthed defender of the rights of Italian-Americans? Furthermore, the concepts and rules that actors use to attach meanings to events and circumstances in the world may be quite unstable and changeable. If all of these baleful possibilities turn out to be true, how can investigators and fact finders draw rational or epistemically defensible inferences from the meaning-complexes that reside, or seem to reside, in the heads and hearts of actors? Is the attempt to infer action from thought always a game of blind man's buff? I am not sure of the answers to these questions.)

investigate the meaning or meanings that human beings attach to events in the world and states of the world. I am referring to the intellectual approach founded or resurrected by Wilhelm Dilthey (1833–1911). Dilthey maintained that a special method of knowing—he called it *Verstehen*—is required in the human sciences, in the *Geisteswissenschaften*.[11] However, Dilthey's thesis about a special way of knowing and studying social and cultural phenomena never quite achieved the prestige in the United States that it enjoyed on much of the European Continent.[12] Perhaps this is one reason why for the larger part of the twentieth century 'official' legal discourse in the US about factual inference rarely even hints at the possibility that courtroom investigations into matters such as cultural practices or an actor's intentions might call for the use of a type of evidentiary process that differs from the type or types of evidentiary processes that are used in courtroom investigations of so-called 'physical' or 'external' facts or events.[13]

Unconscious inference

Hermann von Helmholtz noticed more than a century ago that perception is a form of 'unconscious inference'.[14] One likely reason why we usually refer to perceptual inference with the singleton 'perception' rather than with the phrase 'perceptual inference' is that we usually still have little understanding

---

[11] Dilthey, *Der Aufbau der geschichtlichen Welt in den Geisteswissenschaften* (Stuttgart, BG Teubner, 1958, 1992) (*Gesammelte Schriften*, VII. Band), p. 205.

[12] Dilthey's notion of *Verstehen* had its roots in Kant's philosophy of law and, more broadly speaking, in the philosophical and intellectual tradition that we now call German Idealism. Although German Idealism was not wholly unknown in American intellectual circles in the twentieth century—for example, John Dewey was influenced by German Idealism—the influence of German Idealism in American intellectual circles for most of the twentieth century was not nearly as great as it was on the European Continent.

[13] However, there have been exceptions to this general indifference to, or unawareness of, Diltheyesque claims about the importance of using distinctive methods of investigation when studying matters such as mental processes, moral beliefs, cultural values, cultural practices, aesthetic sensibilities and religious practices and predilections. One important exception is Jerome Bruner. Jerome Bruner is a renowned psychologist. He is nominally not a legal scholar. However, in recent years and decades he has taken to writing about legal matters. Bruner expressly embraces the general theoretical tradition or perspective that Dilthey sired or resurrected. See, Bruner, 1990, pp. 4 and 33. It cannot be a coincidence that Bruner—a refugee from a Nazifying Europe—received his education on the European Continent.

[14] Adler, 2000; Hatfield, 2001. Helmholtz was not the first person to suggest the notion of unconscious inference; Hatfield traces the notion to antiquity. Hatfield observes that today there is some disagreement about whether sensory or perceptual processing of sensory information should be called 'inference'. For present purposes it makes eminent sense to do so.

of the underlying principles that lead biological mechanisms (e.g. perceptual organs such as eyes, ears, and so on) to generate the inferences that they do; even though in recent decades there have been great advances in our understanding of the workings of perception (visual perception, aural perception, etc), we human beings generally can do little more than marvel at the workings of our perceptual organs and we can do relatively little to make healthy sense organs work better than they naturally do. But perhaps I exaggerate: perhaps human beings sometimes can do just a bit more. For example, perhaps empirical studies can identify some generalisable situations in which error rates of various kinds are comparatively high (or low). However this may be, the simple fact is the logical workings of much subconscious inference remain elusive and cannot yet be explicitly described in a systematic fashion.[15]

Inference in the special sciences

Certain problems of evidence and inference present or are thought to present inferential issues that only a special science such as quantum mechanics or genetics can adequately address. The extent to which representations in the form of **NAG**s illuminate the logic that is deployed to address such problems depends on the presuppositions and methods of the special science that are

---

[15] The fact that the 'intelligence' of some or much human inference is largely impervious to explicit restatement by human beings does not mean that perceptual intelligence and inference do not exist. Quite the contrary: much unintelligible subconscious inference is extraordinarily intelligent. This premise is the basis of much contemporary research in fields such as artificial intelligence, cognitive science and neuroscience. This is not just a matter of believing that human thought rumbles somewhat below the plane of conscious thought and is therefore hard to grasp. The underlying premise is that some kind of logic or logics animate practically all, or all, aspects of human cognition. For example, Marvin Minsky, one of the founders of modern AI, rejects the suggestion that there are some perceptions, sensations, sensory signals, or sense *qualia* that are ... just whatever they are. He wrote:

> [S]ome people ... think that the qualities of such sensations [such as the sensation of a colour such as 'red'] are so basic and irreducible that they will always remain inexplicable.
>
> However, I prefer to take the opposite view—that what we call *sensations* are complex reflective activities. They sometimes involve extensive cascades in which some parts of the brain are affected by signals whose origins we cannot detect—and therefore, we find them hard to explain. So, I see no exceptional mystery here: we simply don't yet know enough about what is actually happening in our brains. But when you think enough about anything, then you see this is also the case with everything. (Minsky, 2005)

thought to hold the key to the inferential riddles that are presented. Not all sciences—not even all 'hard' sciences—use logic and methods that **NAGs** usefully represent.

Consider a very abstract example. Suppose that the following network of inferences along with certain ancillary generalisations correctly represents the structure of an inferential problem as understood by a scientist such as a physicist or metallurgist:

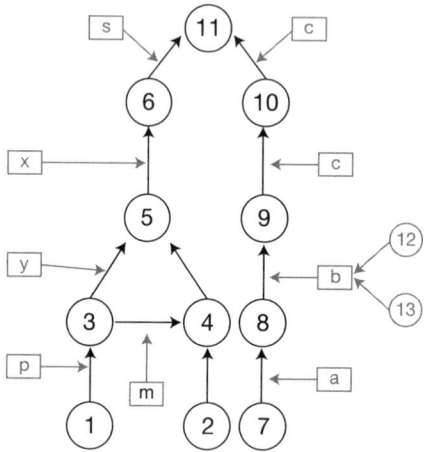

Figure 9.5. Version A.

where **node b** in the above diagram represents the following equation:

$$x = \frac{s + (m/2)}{y^b} \qquad\qquad \text{Expression 4}$$

Earlier I said that the diagram in **Version A** of Figure 9.5 accurately represents the structure of an inferential problem as understood by some scientist. So what is there to talk about? We have a **NAG**, don't we?

Yes. But the diagram in Figure 9.5, **Version A** may nevertheless fail to represent the way the scientist 'sees' the problem at hand. For example, although my hypothesised scientist concedes that the **NAG** in Figure 9.5, **Version A** accurately represents the logical structure of the problem she believes she faces, she may in fact envision the problem she faces in the way depicted in Figure 9.5, **Version B**:

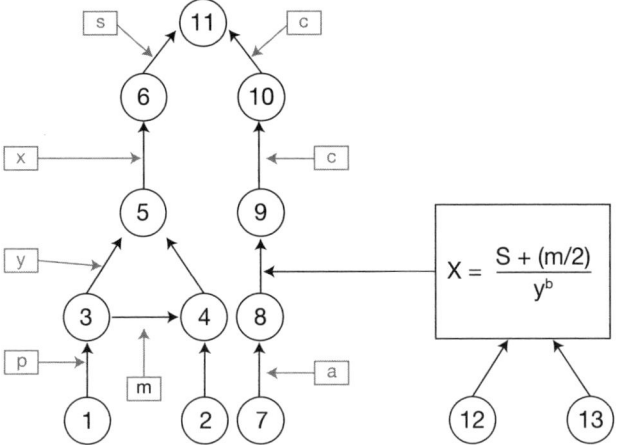

Figure 9.5.   Version B.

The two versions of Figure 9.5 are, from some logical points of view, identical. For example, from the standpoint of a graph theorist, despite the differences in the sizes and locations of some of the nodes and arrows, the problems in the two versions have the same structure and they are therefore identical. But, of course, in one version of the problem (Fig. 9.5, **Version B**) one ingredient of the problem is much 'bigger'—visually—than in the other version (Fig. 9.5, **Version A**). This difference in shape and size (but not in structure and content) is designed to suggest and represent a difference in my hypothesised scientist's attitude toward, or view of, the problem. Although this difference might be characterised as a 'psychological' one, the fact remains that my hypothesised scientist believes that the calculations, computations, and reasoning called for by **node b** are the 'really important' part of the procedure for attacking the question or problem represented by **node 11**; that is, he or she believes that the calculations and reasoning referenced and represented by **node b** are likely to be decisive for the solution of the ultimate inferential question designated by **node 11**. Given this belief and assumption (an assumption that may be well-grounded), the node-and-arrow-with-ancillary-generalisations scheme—a **NAG**—that appears in both versions of Figure 9.5 adds nothing useful (in her eyes) to the part of the problem—the equation—that **node b** designates.

Now it is true—as the structure of **Version B** of Figure 9.5 effectively acknowledges—that the upshot of the computations, calculations, and meditations required by or involved in **node b** may be affected by the other propositions and calculations represented by the entire **NAG**. But the diagram I have drawn (Fig. 9.5, **Version B**) asserts (so I proclaim!) that in the mind of the scientist the ingredients of the inference problem outside of **node b** may be ignored; she knows or believes she knows what the upshot is for **hypothesis 11** once she has properly done the calculations represented by **node b**. And what she believes is also what someone else (e.g. the trier of fact in a legal trial) may rationally and reasonably believe.

A rebirth of Aristotelian epistemology and ontology?

The root of these 'exceptions' to **NAG**s (and of other 'exceptions' that remain to be identified) is a fundamental onto-epistemological premise or hypothesis. This hypothesis begins with a firm denial that rational inference involves only explicit logic. Although human inference is a rational and logical activity, human inference—i.e. the inferential activity of the human organism—involves not just (let alone only, or even mainly) explicit ratiocinative processes. Inference is one of the activities of a sentient human organism. (The same is true of non-human organisms.) The human organism, though sentient, is 'rational' to its core: logic—a complex logic or a set of logics—is embedded in the human organism and regulates its activities.[16] It is true that many (and

---

[16] As already noted, even the human organism's sentient activities are fundamentally and deeply logical, and they are, in that sense, 'rational'.

Among students of the mind and the brain—cognitive scientists, neuroscientists, and others of this ilk—the debate today is not whether some tacit logic guides subconscious processes such as vision and memory. The debate is largely about the nature of such tacit logics and their precise source. Some scholars stress the physiological or biological roots of indwelling logics. Others stress that the nature of the indwelling logic is what matters and that human intelligence can be embedded in various kinds of material structures. But whatever position scholars take on this general question, all or almost all of them agree that (i) subconscious logics embedded in human biological material process information—such inbred logics do inference—and (ii) most human information processing—inference—occurs at a subconscious level.

Sciences such as genetics are making it increasingly plain that logical forms, or information, such as the 'genetic code', drive the development—and thus the very existence—of humanity as a species and of individual human beings. But to hypothesise that matters such as the genetic code ensure the rationality of the human animal may be taking the argument for inbred human rationality a bit too far. For example, I can imagine that a 'rational' genetic code (and any other similar 'codes' that shape or influence the development of organisms) can produce 'irrational' and inept creatures—creatures, for example, who manage to survive only because some of their biological 'friends', who do a better job of processing information, throw their inept companions a life-line. Cf. Fodor, 2007 (discussing, in part, why Mother Nature, the notion of evolutionary adaptation, and similar ideas do not explain why organisms have properties that are analogous

probably most) indwelling human logics are still poorly understood.[17] But however imperfectly we understand the subconscious logics within us, there is good reason to think that such logics are nevertheless 'there'—that a variety of indwelling logics are at work in the human organism. The bottom line is that although it is true that human beings are inferential reasoners, much human inferential reasoning—a vast amount of it—is hidden from human sight.

Since the dawn of modern artificial intelligence—and even before—man (aka his mind, aka his brain, aka his neural system, aka woman, etc.) has been analogised to a mechanical computer.[18] This analogy (which is often taken very seriously) amounts to an ontological-epistemological revolution; it amounts to a rejection of the dichotomy between mind and body, thought

---

to spandrels, which serve no purpose in architecture but accompany and must accompany certain architectural designs).

[17] That the subconscious logics at work in the human animal remain poorly understood should not occasion surprise. Although human intelligence may or may not be synonymous with the physical architecture of the human animal, almost all observers agree that the workings of tacit human intelligence do depend in a fundamental and necessary way on physical architecture of the human organism, on matters such the properties and design of human eyes and the properties and workings of the neural system (including constituents such as neurons and axons). Hence, if a full understanding of subconscious inference (including matters such as vision, hearing, taste) is ever to be possible, our knowledge of a vast multiplicity of sciences probably has to be perfected —sciences such as genetics, physics, electro-mechanics, signal detection, neural science, chemistry, biochemistry, quantum mechanics, and who knows what else. But it is possible that even comprehensive knowledge about the mechanics or physical structure of the human brain and the human organism would not fully reveal the indwelling logics that are at work in human cognition and inference. This is because one must still consider the possibility that the environment feeds information and logic and (so to speak) processing power and capacity into a human organism with a receptive architecture. So I do not mean to intimate or suggest that the logic or logics that dwell within a developed human organism in the twenty-first century are necessarily in any sense synonymous with the physical architecture of the brain, the human nervous system, or any yet broader swathe of the human organism. Fortunately, except for the hypothesis that the human mind is not separate from human matter (but is, rather, embedded in human matter), the argument in this essay does not depend on any particular solution to the vexing question of the relationship between human mind and human matter.

[18] See the exhaustive survey of the history of this idea in Boden, 2006.
There is excellent reason to think the analogy between the human mind and the computer is inexact. First, there appears to be widespread agreement that the brain uses parallel rather than serial processing. Hence, if the brain is like a computer, its operations are not isomorphic to the operations of a typical digital computer, which (I gather) performs operations sequentially. Second, some studies of the neural system suggest that signals are not transmitted only at synapses—the junctions between nerve cell extensions—but that signals are also transmitted 'along the entire length of [nerve cell] extensions and, in this way, excite the neighbouring cells' and this—one study suggests—may mean that neural information processing works 'chaotically'. 'Brain works more chaotically than previously thought', *Science Daily* (27 Feb. 2007). <http://www.sciencedaily.com/releases/2007/02/070227105247.htm>.

and matter,[19] and it restores, in modern guise, the Aristotelian notion of organism. To think in terms of organisms is to think in terms of purposes and functions.[20]

The emerging reversion to an Aristotelian ontology is, in my view, a lovely revolution; this 'new'—but ancient—way of thinking about man tends in the right direction. However, the contemporary turn in fields such as AI towards functional and teleological accounts of man frequently suffers from a serious defect. The ruling image, model, or analogy of man (or human mind) as computer does not always sufficiently stress that the 'human computer' is a *developing* computational creature.

What sort of evolution does the human inferential computer undergo? Common sense, the presuppositions of the study of evidence and inference in legal settings, and a great deal else (e.g. thermostats) suggest or suppose that it is possible, here and there, for tacit human inference—or, if you prefer, inference *simpliciter*—to emerge into the light, to become explicit. Such considerations and such examples of the victories of relatively complete explicit

---

[19] Pinker, 1997, p. 24. ('This book is about the brain, but I will not say much about neurons, hormones, and neurotransmitters. That is because the mind is not the brain but what the brain does, and not even everything it does, such as metabolizing fat and giving off heat.... The brain's special status comes from a special thing the brain does ... That special thing is information processing, or computation.

'Information and computation reside in patterns of data and in relations of logic that are independent of the physical medium that carries them....

'This insight ... is now called the computational theory of mind. It is one of the great ideas in intellectual history, for it solves one of the puzzles that make up the "mind-body problem": how to connect the ethereal world of meaning and intention, the stuff of our mental lives, with a physical hunk of matter like the brain.')

[20] It may seem a bit odd—but it seems to be a fact—that some of the best-known AI adherents to the proposition that the mind is what the brain does, to the proposition that fundamental to an understanding of the workings of the mind is an understanding of the functional logic that is embedded in the brain—are people who style themselves 'materialists' of one kind of another— people such as Daniel Dennett and Paul and Patricia Churchland, who at one time or another have favoured some kind of 'functionalism'. See, e.g. Boden, 2006, n. 19, vol. 2, 1362–9 (on Dennett) and 1376–9 (on the Churchlands). In my view such theorists have moved in the direction of an organic and neo-Aristotelian view of the relationship between man and human thought. In any event, the world of AI and cognitive science is replete with people who view human physiology and the various material parts of the human organism as being only the 'substrate' of a logical architecture, an architecture that can in principle be embedded within different material substrates—except, of course, to the extent that differences in the substrate prevent replication or installation of the necessary logical architecture. See, e.g. the amusing statement in Edelman, 2006, p. 127 that '[t]he position that the proposed artifact [having an intelligence equal to that of the human organism] must be made of biochemical components is known as biological chauvinism'.

ratiocination (i.e. examples of a fairly high degree of inferential automation) suggest, more broadly, that the human organism has some capacity (the full extent of which is as yet necessarily undetermined) to force at least some its tacit, or subconscious, logical processes into the light of consciousness and to make previously tacit inference explicit or, in any event, to make relatively tacit inferences *more* explicit and thus more subject to some explicit logical analysis and argument. This latter function is, in my view, frequently (but not always) precisely the central function of mental crutches and representations such as **NAG**s. (Sometimes—but only sometimes—inbred human logics will manage to emerge from the human animal and escape from the clutches of their creator. An example is to be seen in Isaac Asimov's *I, Robot*.[21] Less dramatically, consider once again the lowly thermostat—or the flying drones now used by the military for surveillance and even for combat operations.)

On this view of things—on my neo-Aristotelian view of the general relationship between the logic(s) in (wo)man and (wo)man's explicit ratiocination about the world (including him- or herself)—an important function of explicit reflection, analysis, argument and reason is to have the human organism wrest out of itself and its encounters with the 'world' (including its encounters with itself) some principles and logics (forms of reasoning) that the organism can hold consciously in mind or, in any event, that can be recorded and stored elsewhere, by means of marks made in the world, as in readable computer scripts and programs. The aim of such explicit expression and formulation is in part to enable the organism to facilitate and, perhaps paradoxically, improve the workings of at least some of the logics that dwell—hitherto unseen—in the human organism (and in its environment).

When such victories of explicit ratiocination (either victories that facilitate inference or those that automate inference) are achieved, they ought to be celebrated. And whenever possible, the human organism should use its emergent logic to improve its immanent logic. But on my view of things, humility about human inferential capacity—humility, that is, about the power of explicit inferential calculation—has the status of a virtual first principle. It must not be forgotten that many or most of the logical operations of the human organism remain hidden from the human organism's sight and comprehension. In many situations, therefore, the only reasonable expectation we can have of deliberation about evidence is that such deliberation will bring some shards of our indwelling logical processes to light. But we should

---

[21] Asimov, 1950.

remain alert (i) to the possibility that sometimes we will just have to trust our unanalysed hunches and (ii) to the perverse possibility that it is not always the case that explicit analysis of evidence will improve our inferential performance.

References

Adler, H. E. (2000), 'Hermann Ludwig Ferdinand von Helmholtz: physicist as psychologist', in Kimble, GA and Wertheimer, M (eds.), *Portraits of Pioneers in Psychology*, vol. 4 (Mahwah, NJ, Lawrence Erlbaum), pp. 15–31.

Anderson, T. and Twining, W. L. (1998), *Analysis of Evidence* (Boston, Little, Brown and Co.); pbk. edn. (1991) (Evanston, Illinois, Northwestern University Press).

Asimov, I. (1950), *I, Robot* (New York, Gnome).

Boden, M. (2006), *Mind as Machine: a history of cognitive science*, vols. 1 and 2 (Oxford, Clarendon Press).

Brain works more chaotically than previously thought, Science Blog (27 Feb. 2007), at <http://www.scienceblog.com/cms/brain-works-more-chaotically-than-previously-thought-12682.html>.

Bruner, J. (1990), *Acts of Meaning* (Cambridge, MA, and London, Harvard University Press).

Dilthey, W. (1958, 1992), *Der Aufbau der geschichtlichen Welt in den Geisteswissenschaften* (Stuttgart, BG Teubner) (*Gesammelte Schriften*, VII. Band).

Edelman, G. M. (2006), *Second Nature, brain science and human knowledge* (New Haven and London, Yale University Press).

Fodor, J. (2007), 'Why pigs don't have wings', *London Review of Books*, 20 (18 Oct.): 29.

Hatfield, G. (2001/2), 'Perception as Unconscious Inference' (University of Pennsylvania Institute for Research in Cognitive Science Technical Report No. IRCS-01-04, 1 April 2001) (available at <http://repository.upenn.edu/ircs_reports/9/>, posted 7 Aug. 2006, and in D. Heyer and R, Mausfeld (eds.), *Perception and the Physical World: psychological and philosophical issues in perception* (Oxford, Oxford University Press), pp. 115–45).

Howard, R. A. (1980), 'Influence Diagrams' (unpub. report).

Howard, R. A. (1980), 'From influence to relevance to knowledge', in R. M. Oliver and J. Q. Smith (eds.), *Influence Diagrams: belief nets and decision analysis* (New York, John Wiley), pp. 3–23.

Jackson, J., Langer, M. and Tillers, P. (eds.) (2008), *Crime, Procedure, and Evidence in a Comparative and International Context* (Oxford, Hart Publishing).

Minsky, M. (2005), *Interior Grounding, Reflection, and Self-Consciousness*, <http://web.media.mit.edu/~minsky/papers/Internal%20Grounding.html> (accessed 23 Nov. 2007; paper originally published in, *Brain, Mind and Society, Proceedings of an International Conference on Brain, Mind and Society* (Graduate School of Information Sciences, Brain, Mind and Society, Tohoku University, Japan, September 2005)).

Pearl, J. (1982), 'Reverend Bayes on inference engines: a distributed hierarchical approach', in *Proceedings, AAAI National Conference on AI, Pittsburgh Pennsylvania* (Aug. 1982), pp. 133–6.

Pearl, J. (1995), *Bayesian Networks*, UCLA Cognitive Systems Laboratory, Technical Report (R-216); revision I, in M. Arbib (ed.), *Handbook of Brain Theory and Neural Networks* (Cambridge, MA, MIT Press), pp. 149–53.

Pinker, S. (1997), *How the Mind Works* (New York and London, W. W. Norton).

Robertson, B. and Vignaux, G. (1995), *Interpreting Evidence* (New York, John Wiley).

Schum, D. (1994), *Evidential Foundations of Probabilistic Reasoning* (New York, John Wiley; repr. Evanston, IL, Northwestern University Press, 2001).

Schum, D. (2001), 'Species of abductive reasoning in fact investigation in law', *Cardozo Law Review*, 22: 1461–1502.

Schum, D. (2005), 'Thoughts about a Science of Evidence' (29 Dec.) (research report), at <http://www.evidencescience.org/pubs/pubs_detail.asp?pubID=70>.

Schum, D. (2006), *A Reply to the 'Schum challenge' at UCL* (6 Sept.), available at <http://www.evidencescience.org/pubs/pubs_detail.asp?pubID=52>.

Schum, D. and Kelly, C. (1973), 'A problem in cascaded inference: determining the inferential impact of confirming and conflicting reports from several unreliable sources', *Organizational Behavior and Human Performance*, 10: 404–23.

Schum, D. and Martin, A. (1982), 'Formal and empirical research on cascaded inference in jurisprudence', *Law and Society Review*, 17: 105–51.

Tillers, P. (1986), 'Mapping inferential domains', *Boston University Law Review*, 66: 883–936; repr. (1988), in, Tillers, P. and Green, E. (eds.), *Probability and Inference in the Law of Evidence: The Uses and Limits of Bayesianism* (Dordrecht, Boston and London, Kluwer Academic Publishers), pp. 277–336.

Tillers, P. (1989), 'Webs of things in the mind: a new science of evidence' (review essay) *Michigan Law Review*, 87: 1225–58.

Tillers, P. and Schum, D. (1991), 'A theory of preliminary fact investigation', *University of California at Davis Law Review*, 24: 931–1012.

Twining, W. L. (1990), 'Narrative and generalizations in argumentation about questions of fact', *South Texas Law Review*, 40: 351–65.

Wigmore, J. H. (1931), *The Principles of Judicial Proof, or, The process of proof as given by logic, psychology, and general experience and illustrated in judicial trials* (Boston, Little, Brown and Co.).

Wigmore, J. H. (1937), *The Science of Judicial Proof, or, The process of proof as given by logic, psychology, and general experience and illustrated in judicial trials* (Boston, Little, Brown and Co.).

10

Rhetoric, Evidence and Policymaking: a Case Study of Priority Setting in Primary Care*

JILL RUSSELL AND TRISHA GREENHALGH

Abstract

The idea that policy should be based on best research evidence might appear to be self-evident. But a closer analysis reveals a number of problems and paradoxes inherent in the concept of 'evidence-based policymaking'. The current conflict over evidence-based policymaking parallels a longstanding 'paradigm war' in social research between positivist and interpretivist approaches. We begin this chapter by drawing from this debate in order to inform the discussions over the appropriateness of evidence based policymaking and the related question of what is the nature of policymaking. We suggest that the positivist world view that underpins the theory and practice of evidence-based medicine fails to address key elements of the policymaking process. In particular, a narrowly 'evidence-based' framing of policymaking is inherently unable to explore the agency of policymakers, the 'meaning-making' practices of those actors and the situated, contingent nature of evidence. We suggest that rhetorical theory and discourse methods offer opportunities for developing a richer understanding of how policymaking is enacted in practice, and of how evidence is constituted at the micro-level of social interaction. We present data from an empirical study that aimed to explore how a group of policymakers charged with prioritising health care at a local level in the NHS

*This research was funded by a grant from the Leverhulme Trust and Economics and Social Research Council (ESRC), as part of the UCL Programme on Evidence, Inference and Enquiry. We gained ethical approval for the study (reference no. 04/Q0509/39, Nov 2004). We thank the members of the Primary Care Trust Priorities Forum who agreed to us observing and recording their meetings. We would also like to acknowledge the contribution of our colleagues, Emma Byrne and Janet McDonnell, who made significant contributions to the development of key ideas underpinning the research reported in this chapter.

Proceedings of the British Academy, **171**, 267–289. © The British Academy 2011.

talk about, deliberate and reason with evidence. Our findings highlight the dialogical tension that exists between a scientistic and rhetorical rationality within the policymaking process, and the ways in which a scientistic rationality may serve to constrain rather than enhance critical, reasoned thinking about 'wicked problems' in health care policymaking.

Introduction

THIS CHAPTER DESCRIBES a study we undertook as part of the UCL Evidence programme to explore how policymakers talk about and reason with evidence (Russell and Greenhalgh, 2009). Specifically, we were interested in researching the micro-processes of deliberation and meaning-making practices of a group of people charged with prioritising health care in an NHS Primary Care Trust in the UK.

Our research connects with a substantial 'evidence into practice' literature concerned with how healthcare policymaking might be improved by greater use of more and better research evidence (Dopson and Fitzgerald, 2005; Innvaer *et al.*, 2002; Walshe and Rundall, 2001). However, in contrast to the hortatory stance of much of this literature, the starting point for our study was a concern to study the use of evidence 'as is', rather than addressing the question of how we might get decision makers to behave more evidentially (policymaking as 'ought to be'). In other words, the focus of the study was on the 'real life' enactment of policymaking, rather than any idealised or prescriptive model of how evidence should be used in practice (Braithwaite, 2004).

A study of 'evidence in use' is essentially a study of language in use. As Green has suggested, *'evidence does not speak for itself, but must be spoken for'* (Green, 2000). Thus to explore how a group of people talk about and use evidence we required a framework of ideas and methods that foreground the role of language in human meaning making. In this chapter we describe how our research study brought together ideas from rhetorical theory and methods of discourse analysis to develop an innovative approach to exploring how evidence is constituted at the micro-level of social interaction and communication. We present empirical data to illuminate the representation and meaning of evidence within one particular policymaking forum, and to highlight contrasting constructions of the policymaking process.

The value of rhetoric

> ... decision science ... ignores the best capacities of human beings—to reason with and learn from each other; it encourages our submission to technical, knowledge-based solutions for what are social, value-based problems. The 'rhetorical turn' in recent scholarship challenges the assumption that intellectual and social progress demand the certainty sought by the instrumental reason of scientism. As an art, not a science, rhetoric reaffirms the value of that which cannot be wholly systematized, that which is subject to human influence. A humane and honest theory of choice, therefore, should be based on rhetorical art, not on scientism—or technicism. Decision science, which resists the fundamental uncertainty of human life, should not replace rhetorical deliberation, which helps us to live with it. (Miller, 1990)

In its idealised form, evidence-based policy represents a form of decision science (Sanderson, 2003; Wells, 2007). Decision science can be defined as

> the social-scientific approach to decision making, [which] aims to formalize the elements of complex decision problems so that a set of logical axioms can be used to analyze and compare alternatives, one of which will, it is presumed, emerge as an 'obvious' choice. (Miller, 1990)

Similarly, the notion of evidence-based policy implies that the making of a policy decision is essentially a technical, logical process comprising the selection, synthesis and critical evaluation of best research evidence, from which the obvious (or at least, a preferred) answer to a particular policy problem will emerge and can then be implemented.

As the above quote indicates, rhetorical theory provides a compelling contrast to the theory of decision science. Miller identifies three salient differences between a scientistic and rhetorical approach—their conceptualisations of uncertainty, their attention to an audience and their understanding of human rationality; we look at each of these differences in turn.

Conceptualisations of uncertainty

Much conventional scientific thinking about the relationship between evidence and policymaking construes uncertainty in terms of an 'evidence gap'. The assumption is that more and better evidence, implemented with more commitment and skill from practitioners, will eventually abolish uncertainty (Black, 2001). By contrast, Aristotelian deliberative rhetoric suggests that uncertainty generally concerns questions not of 'what do we know?' (problems of evidence) but of 'what should we do?' (problems of action). The error of decision science, and evidence-based policy, according to rhetorical scholars, is that it reduces the latter to the former (Miller, 1990).

A rhetorical perspective recognises that problems of action involve conflict between people; they are 'essentially contestable' (Garver, 1978). And so the task in solving a problem of action is not necessarily to acquire more information, but to exercise what Aristotle called practical reason. Practical reason involves deliberation, persuasion, reflection upon values, prudential judgement, and free disclosure of one's ideas (Miller, 1990). In this sense it is suggested that rhetoric offers a theory of choice about human action (Brown, 1997).

Attention to an audience

Decision science disregards its audience:

> The decision problem is cast in an absolute form: a problem of knowledge measured against omniscience. The method is algorithmic, a procedure that can ideally be performed by a computer. Since the method is, by definition, rational, the adherence of an audience is irrelevant. A decision is not judged by an audience but is justified in the abstract by the rational procedure with which it complies. By contrast, deliberation about problems of action presupposes an audience ... (Miller, 1990)

In Aristotelian rhetoric the art of persuading an audience comprises three elements: *logos*—the argument itself, *pathos*—appeals to emotions (which might include beliefs, values, knowledge and imagination), and *ethos*—the credibility, legitimacy and authority that a speaker brings and develops over the course of the argument (Van de Ven and Schomaker, 2002). A rhetorical perspective therefore requires us to move away from any sense of disembodied evidence, towards not only how evidence is constructed but also by whom and for whom it is constructed, how the evidence and the speaker are received, and the meaning the evidence holds for its audience. Evidence can no longer be considered as abstract knowledge separate from its social context. Wood *et al.* argue that:

> There is no such entity as "the body of evidence". There are simply (more or less) competing (re)constructions of evidence able to support almost any position. Much of what is called evidence is, in fact, a contested domain, constituted in the debates and controversies of opposing viewpoints in search of ever more compelling arguments. (Wood *et al.*, 1998)

Critics of rhetoric denigrate it as a form of manipulation. However, Garsten draws an important distinction between persuasion and manipulation—'The speaker who manipulates his audience so as to bring them to a belief or action without their consent ... has not persuaded but coerced' (Garsten, 2006). To persuade someone is to induce them to change their own beliefs in light of what has been said. 'Though we speak of "being persuaded" in the passive voice, we recognise the difference between being persuaded and being indoctrinated or brainwashed; the difference lies in the active independence that is preserved when we are persuaded' (Garsten, 2006). Garsten suggests that a politics of persuasion—in which people try to change one another's minds by appealing not only to reason but also to passions and beliefs—is a mode of politics well worth defending:

> Persuasion is worthwhile because it requires us to pay attention to our fellow citizens and to display a certain respect for their points of view and their judgments. The effort to persuade requires us to engage with others wherever they stand and to begin our argument there, as opposed to simply asserting that they would adopt our opinion if they were more reasonable.   (Garsten, 2006)

Perspectives on rationality

Decision science defines rationality in terms of what is *provably* true (the evidence of logico-deductive reasoning) and what is *probably* true (the evidence of Bayesian reasoning). Rhetoric allows for a rationality based also on what is *plausibly* true. In other words, rhetorical theory allows us to shift from equating rationality with procedure to considering rationality as a situated, contingent human construction: 'The constructive activity of rationality occurs through the discovery and articulation of good reasons for belief and action, activities that are fundamental to deliberation. Rationality concerns a process or activity (not a procedure) that guarantees criticism and change (not correctness)' (Miller, 1990). Miller expands on how a rhetorical perspective redefines what we understand as rationality:

> Scientistic rationality emphasizes substance when it assumes that objectively correct decisions are achievable. It emphasizes procedure when ... it assumes that they are not; what procedure can guarantee, rather than correct results, is optimal results from any given starting point. Rhetorical rationality, on the other hand, must emphasise the interdependence of substance and process. As a process, deliberation both requires and creates substance, that is, systems of meaning. The deliberative processes of reason-giving, inducement, and change can yield at least temporary agreements, the substance of which depends upon the substance of previous of previous beliefs and the effects of rhetorical art upon them. History, convention, insight, emotion, and value all become rational, this is, possible 'good reasons'. And the process of deliberation, or argumentation, as Perelman and Olbrechts-Tyteca note, 'alone allows us to understand our decisions' ...   (Miller, 1990)

A rhetorical perspective on rationality therefore recognises the validity of a range of forms of knowledge, including practical and experiential as well as empirical and theoretical expert knowledge.

Methods

The setting for our research was a Priorities Forum of an NHS Primary Care Trust (PCT). Priorities Forums are a relatively recent development in the history of resource allocation within the NHS, and aim, according to the PCT in which we undertook our study, to 'provide a mechanism within the PCT to ensure a robust ethical and evidence-based process for identifying treatment priorities'. An exploration of Priorities Forum deliberations therefore provided an opportunity to study the use of evidence in practice. We were interested in exploring how policy problems were 'named and framed'; how Forum members talked about, and reasoned with, evidence; how they legitimated their knowledge claims, values and opinions, and how they sought to persuade one another through deliberation.

The Priorities Forum is made up of specialists in public health, commissioning and finance managers of the PCT, local general practitioners, and patient/public representatives, and chaired by the Medical Director of the Trust. It meets on a bi-monthly basis and over a two and a half year period we attended nine meetings of the Priorities Forum (which in total comprised approximately twenty-five hours of discussion), and recorded and transcribed discussions of twenty substantive agenda items. Items discussed included whether the PCT should invest more money in existing services (for example, assisted conception services); invest money in new services (for example, a fracture liaison clinic); withdraw funding from existing services (for example, referral to the Royal London Homeopathic Hospital); and shift funding from one form of service provision to another for a particular patient group (for example shifting patients from secondary to primary care for dermatology services).

During the research period we also engaged in regular ongoing discussions with the Chair of the Priorities Forum and responded to requests to facilitate training sessions for members of the Forum, which provided further contextual data for our analysis of Forum deliberations. We undertook context-setting interviews with members of the PCT to better understand the Forum and its role within the work of the PCT. We gained ethical approval for our research study from the local research ethics committee.

Our theoretically driven interest in the processes of rhetorical deliberation led us to employ discourse methods that enabled an in-depth focus on 'language in use'. A defining characteristic of discourse analysis is its recognition that language is not a neutral transparent medium through which a person simply conveys thoughts, but is *constitutive* of social life. In other words, discourse methods examine how language actively constructs social worlds rather than simply reflecting and revealing it (Phillips and Hardy, 2002). Language does 'work' in producing human meaning. The advantage of discourse analysis is the way in which it helps illuminate and develop understanding of the practice of professional work as it unfolds by enabling a 'slowing down' of the activity being researched. This detailed unpacking of what is going on can, we suggest, provide a new lens for looking at practice and inspire new understandings of work activity (Sarangi and Roberts, 1999).

Discourse analysis has developed within many different academic disciplines, each with its own perspective on what discourse actually is, and hence what kind of activity the analysis of this discourse involves. There is no unitary discourse 'method'. In our study, following writers such as MacLure, who adopts an 'intentionally impure' approach to discourse analysis in her investigation of discourse in educational and social research, we drew pragmatically on various discourse theories to help explore and illuminate our specific questions of interest (MacLure, 2003). For example, we drew on analytic ideas from the discourse traditions of interactional sociolinguistics and the ethnography of communication to explore how language is used to construct particular framings of policy issues and what norms of interaction and 'rules of speaking' are discernible within speech communities (Goffman, 1974; Hymes, 1972). We were also interested more broadly in discourses as systems of representation, drawing on Foucauldian ideas about the ways in which particular discourses in society facilitate transmission of basic values at a cultural level and have the capacity to shape the way we think, feel and do particular things (Wetherell *et al.*, 2001). And, we were interested in the ideological role of language and gained insight from the work of Bakhtin on language as a site of social struggle (Maybin, 2001).

Gee draws a useful distinction between 'big D' and 'little d' discourses (Gee, 1999), the former referring to broad discourses in society 'which are the ways of acting, thinking and valuing to enact identities and practices which privilege certain groups and ways of knowing over others' (Roberts and Bailey, 2008). 'Little d' discourses, on the other hand, are examples of language in use at the micro-level of social interaction. Our approach to discourse analysis was concerned with exploring both 'big D' and 'little d' discourses in health care policymaking and the ways in which they co-construct one another. Specifically, we were interested in exploring how 'big D' discourses in UK health policy such as 'evidence-based policy' and health care rationing are represented, reinterpreted, shaped and constituted at the micro-level of the policymaking table. This sort of analysis, as Sarangi and Roberts (1999) suggest, 'attends to the smallness of things and aims to understand them in all their interpretive complexity. It also acknowledges the overarching social order in which they interact and which binds and regulates as it re-invents itself.'

Gee (1999) identifies seven broad 'building tasks' of language and uses these to identify generic questions a discourse analyst might address in any discourse-oriented research study. We used these questions as exploratory devices to facilitate the interrogation of our research data and its analysis:

- Building significance—how is language used to make certain things significant or not and in what ways? How is language used to give things particular meaning or value?
- Building activities—what activity or set of activities is language being used to enact?
- Building identities—what identities and roles/positions is language being used to enact?
- Building relationships—what sort of relationships is language seeking to enact with others?
- Building politics—what perspective on social goods is language communicating (i.e. what is being communicated about what is taken to be 'normal', 'right', 'good' etc.)
- Building connections—How does language connect or disconnect things; how does it make one thing relevant or irrelevant to another?
- Building sign systems and knowledge—How does language privilege or disprivilege specific sign systems or different ways of knowing and believing or claims to knowledge and belief?

Analysis of our data involved an iterative process of sense-making. Our initial impressions from observing Forum meetings provided the basis for early discussion of ideas between us. One researcher (JR) listened to the recordings of each of the Priorities Forum meetings we had attended, and followed this with careful reading and rereading of transcripts, alongside the field notes we had taken from observation at the meetings. These readings and analysis led to the construction of case studies of selected agenda items. Further analysis of case studies developed through discussions between the two main researchers (JR and TG) and also through discussion with colleagues with a specific interest in discourse analysis and our project.

Findings

The central research question addressed by our study was how a group of people around a policymaking table talk about and reason with evidence. We applied the concept of 'framing' to explore the representation and meaning of evidence within Priorities Forum discussions. The metaphor of the frame, like metaphors generally, conveys the idea of some parts of reality being represented at the expense of others (Fischer, 2003). In a policy context, Rein and Schon define framing as

> a way of selecting, organizing, interpreting and making sense of a complex reality to provide guideposts for knowing, analyzing, persuading and acting. A frame is a perspective from which an amorphous, ill-defined, problematic situation can be made sense of and acted on.   (Rein and Schon, 1993)

Lewis describes framing of policy issues in the following way:

> Naming and framing a problem puts a boundary around the rest of the discussion about what might be done in terms of policy change. It influences what is seen in relation to a particular policy problem. Once an area has been labelled and a boundary has been drawn around what will and will not be discussed, this influences what is visible and what is invisible, and creates beliefs about what policy can change and what it cannot touch. It also structures the discourse of a particular area, limiting what can be talked about, and defines who has a right to be involved in this discussion, who can claim an interest, and what kind of power they will have.   (Lewis, 2003)

Framing by numbers

In the Priorities Forum, framing begins with a background paper that accompanies each agenda item. This is typically a 10–15-page document produced by a public health specialist within the PCT that gives an overview of the problem to be discussed and summarises a range of research evidence, local and national policy documents and financial information, ending with recommendations to the Priorities Forum. At the beginning of each agenda item the author of the background paper takes the Forum members through the paper, summarising the key points, which are then resummarised by the Chair, before the agenda item is opened for discussion.

A striking characteristic of the background papers and oral summary is the way in which policy problems are constructed in terms of quantitative information, with an emphasis on numerical patterns, quantities, and levels. The starting point for exploring a particular policy problem is typically 'looking at the data'. So in the case of an agenda item about hospital discharge of elderly people, the starting point of the background paper is an analysis of Health Resource Group 'trim points' (the point at which additional costs per day are incurred if a patient exceeds the average anticipated stay for a particular condition or procedure). The following extract, reported in full to convey this emphasis on numerical information, is taken from the author's summary of the background paper, introducing the item to the Priorities Forum:

> So what we did was, was to go back and have a look at the data. And basically, what we did, was to run off—erm, the information, is now stored on our Information Systems, related to the number of patients who exceed their length of stay in hospital. Now this information is now monitorable. And what we call this, we call this the HRG—and the HRG is linked to the length of stay, and each length of stay is, in some respects, set to the diagnosis and the procedure that each patient undergoes.... Hospital length of stay is linked to the Health Resource Group and, in practice, this means the length of stay is linked to a number of factors and this could be the patient's diagnosis and the procedures, whether admitted through A & E or through elective admission, where the patient has had a booked admission. And linked to that HRG is set a number of days that you would expect the patient to be in hospital. And linked to that also is the cost, so the cost to the PCT of say, a patient going into hospital for an appendectomy for ten days, is paid. If the patient exceeds their 10 day length of stay, then the PCT pays for every day that the patient exceeds that standard length of stay. Okay? So, obviously not all patients can be discharged at that exact point. Some people need to stay in. All we did was to look at the excess costs incurred by the PCT for a number of specialties and treatments. And particularly those where you would expect a high proportion or a higher proportion of people to be in the older age group. So, in other words, it definitely missed out things like paediatrics and some of the other services that would be particularly accessed by the younger patient group. Now, the first figure that came out was that we could potentially reduce the cost to the PCT of excess length of stay by £2.7 million. Now, to achieve that 100% is probably asking the impossible. But what I have done is to look at it by different areas, particularly, say, by reducing it 10% or just reducing the length of stay in geriatrics. This is the excess length of stay. By reducing it in general surgery and general medicine. So there are a number of options that we could examine. And certainly, even a 10% reduction across the board, which, in theory should not be unachievable, would release a potential reinvestment sum of nearly £300,000. Now that's significant. So the next step really was to think about, 'Well how can we release this money, how can we improve services so that we can enable people to be discharged and to have the appropriate discharge?' And what the paper suggests is that we appoint a consultant physician who can offer us, not only clinical time, but particularly clinical time going in to developing the community support services particularly for older people, such as the ... rehabilitation care, intermediate care services, continuing care, primary care and perhaps even palliative care, so that we can

get a good continuum of care. But also to be able to build a balanced network of services, so people have a smooth transition from one care to the other. But this person could also offer clinical time and training time to, particularly to discharge coordinators and other commissioners, and the important aspect of the role of this person, who would be PCT appointed and representing the interests of the PCT as well as the patients', he or she could link with the clinicians, because the success of the project would be winning the hearts and minds of the clinicians. The benefits coming out of this, if we can reduce, particularly, even 10%, although I think we can probably achieve higher than that over the years, is obviously a significant year on year cost savings. (Public health specialist, Priorities Forum transcript 2)

The argument being constructed here is that there are potential savings of £2.7 million to be made from earlier discharge of elderly people from hospital, although it is acknowledged that to achieve this full level of savings is 'probably asking the impossible'. Nevertheless, the general point that there are considerable savings to be made is established by presenting 'trim point' data showing how much money the PCT spends on patients whose length of stay exceeded the trim point and defining this as 'excess costs' and thus potentially reducible.

In the above extract, and in the ensuing discussion, we can see how PCT members of the Forum use various linguistic strategies to help construct a particular framing of the problem. Firstly, as indicated above, the description of the policy problem is primarily through numbers. Numbers, in the form of excess trim point costs, are invoked to authenticate a specific story about hospital discharge. As Stone has pointed out, numbers have come to have such a pre-eminent status in our scientific culture that their pervasiveness as a mode of describing society in policy discussions tends to be taken for granted rather than interpreted as just one of many ways of describing and understanding the world (Stone, 1997). Second, the numbers being put forward have been 'run off' from the computer: 'the first figure that came out was £2.7 million'. The suggestion is that numbers are the result of an impersonal, mechanical routine and thus the figures are presented as computational fact rather than a social construction, subject to human influence and interpretation. Thirdly, the numbers are supported by other pieces of evidence explicitly labelled as 'facts'—in the background paper there is a short section headed 'facts that demonstrate differences in hospital lengths of stay' that quotes figures from one study of differences between US and English hospitals (but without further contextual information). These 'facts', the background paper suggests, 'demonstrate that there is considerable scope for reducing hospital length of stay'. Fourthly, the various numbers are presented in such a way that they roughly tally, with the suggestion that the equation neatly adds up, thus invoking the idea that the proposal offers a conveniently tidy way of dealing with a complex problem. This is a commonly used technique in Forum discussions—in this particular agenda item, the number of delayed discharges from acute hospitals is presented as approximately the same number of unfilled beds in the community hospitals:

> There are a number of beds. This number varies slightly on a day to day basis. But there are a number of beds which are unoccupied at [the local community hospitals]. Just concentrating on [the local acute hospital], which is where we've looked at … but I'm sure a similar principle applies at [another nearby acute hospital]. There are a number of people who are defined as being, with having delayed discharges. Very, very roughly, the number of delayed discharges at [the local acute hospital] is the same as the number of unfilled beds in [the local community hospitals]. Now that is not saying it's exactly the same number every day. It is not to say that on clinical grounds, it would be appropriate for all those people to be discharged from [the local acute hospital] into [the local community hospitals].   (Chair, Priorities Forum transcript 2)

We see similar examples of 'framing by numbers' with other agenda items. In the case of an item about prioritising funds to establish a fracture liaison service, for example, the policy issue of elderly people suffering from osteoporosis is constructed primarily in terms of quantitative measures. On a number of occasions there is reference to the difficulties of interpreting the data and of understanding what actually is happening in practice; however, at no point in the verbal summary or the background paper are other types of evidence, such as qualitative interpretive data, introduced.

We suggest that discernible within the PCT's framing of policy problems is what Tsoukas refers to as 'information reductionism'. Tsoukas' argument is that there is a danger that information becomes a surrogate for the world—'what is going on tends to be equated with what the relevant indicators say is going on':

> In the information society, the abundance of information tends to overshadow the phenomena to which information refers: the discussion about crime easily slips to debating crime rates and spending on police; the debate about quality in education more often than not leads to arguing about league tables; the concern with the performance of hospitals leads to debating readmission rates and other indicators. In short, the more information we have about the world, the more we distance ourselves from what is going on and the less able we become in comprehending its full complexity.   (Tsoukas, 1997)

In Priorities Forum discussions we see the way in which evidence is drawn upon so that the discussion about improving hospital discharge for elderly people slips into a discussion about HRG trim points, a discussion about the value of establishing a fracture liaison service leads to debating local prescribing rates of bisphosphonates and other indicators, and a discussion about the management of mental illness leads to a debate about episodes of care statistics. In the latter case, focused on a discussion about talking therapies, a GP member of the Forum indicates that he finds the information in the background paper 'very difficult' because all the evidence in it is based on the assumption that mental illness can be defined as episodes of care,

> when in fact in the real world it is clear that mental illness is a dynamic condition and can't be easily categorised and expressed as episodes of care ... the science and research base will give very precise definitions and use these to measure interventions but in real life this preciseness does not exist. (GP Jan. 2008 Priorities Forum)

The suggestion is not that these sorts of statistical indicators are unimportant, but that the privileging of them results in other types of knowledge being marginalised or left unidentified as relevant to discussion. For example, although the background papers for discussions about hospital discharge make brief reference to a literature review and to a consultation with local staff with responsibility for discharge planning, this evidence is given only a cursory mention in discussion and the knowledge from these potentially rich data sources is not drawn upon. In a paper on making evidence fit for purpose in decision-making in the case of hospital discharge of older people, Glasby et al. argue that 'theoretical evidence' and 'experiential evidence' (see Table 10.1) be considered equally important sorts of evidence for decision makers to seek and act on (Glasby et al., 2007). Surprisingly, although the main thrust of the proposal in the hospital discharge discussion is for the PCT to employ a consultant physician 'to give strong leadership to the management of hospital discharge procedure' no evidence is given or asked for to help the Forum members understand how this intervention might work in practice, nor how it might compare with other models of service provision for improving hospital discharge of elderly people. And in a discussion about cardiac rehabilitation, despite a lengthy background paper and discussion, one of the main conclusions of the group is that they don't have an understanding of how the service is being provided locally, and have numerous unanswered questions about the inherent practices of the service.

Espeland and Stevens suggest that information reductionism can be understood as a form of 'commensuration'. Commensuration, they argue, is the process by which qualities are transformed into quantities, and has become so much taken for granted as a natural feature of social life that it is largely

Table 10.1.   A typology of evidence for decision-making (Glasby *et al.*, 2007).

Type of evidence	Description	How it contributes to knowledge
Theoretical evidence	Ideas, concepts and models used to describe the intervention, to explain how and why it works, and to connect it to a wider knowledge base and framework	Helps to understand the programme theories that lie behind the intervention, and to use theories of human or organisational behaviour to outline and explore its intended working in ways that can then be used to construct and test meaningful hypotheses and transfer learning about the intervention to other settings
Empirical evidence	Information about the actual use of the intervention, and about its effectiveness and outcomes in use	Helps to understand how the intervention plays out in practice, and to establish and measure its real effects and the causality of relationships between the intervention and the desired outcomes
Experiential evidence	Information about people's experiences of the service or intervention, and the interaction between them	Helps to understand how people (users, practitioners and other stakeholders) experience, view and respond to the intervention, and how this contributes to our understanding of the intervention and shapes its use

invisible to us as an instrument of social thought. Commensuration, as with Tsoukas' information reductionism, creates a particular understanding of the world:

> In abstracting and reducing information, the link between what is represented and the empirical world is obscured and uncertainty is absorbed. Everyday experience, practical reasoning, and empathetic identification become increasingly irrelevant bases for judgment as context is stripped away and relationships become more abstractly represented by numbers.   (Espeland and Stevens, 1998)

At an ideological level, 'framing by numbers' reflects and helps to create a view of priority setting as a science, as a technocratic endeavour. As others have pointed out, the discursive device of quantification is vital to the representation of information as 'fact' and serves to achieve specific persuasive and argumentative ends (Petersen and Lupton, 1996; Porter, 1996; Potter *et al.*, 1991). Furthermore, through skilful use of data from both evidence-based medicine literature and from local financial and activity data, we see a 'double discursive alliance of scientism and managerialism' (Webb, 2001) that creates a context within which the main concerns come to be data about economic performance, efficiency and effectiveness. In the process, as Espeland and Stevens suggest in the quote above, everyday experience, practical reasoning and empathetic identification become increasingly irrelevant bases for judgement. Our findings concur with other studies of how health authorities talk about their priority setting role, suggesting an increasing 'economisation' of discourse. Greener and Powell suggest that their respondents consciously used

> the language of management, finance and economics to present a rational picture of their decision-making processes, making sure that they correspond with national agendas in health care. They are trying to demonstrate they are 'talking the talk', or using the prevailing acceptable discourse. (Greener and Powell, 2003)

The role of rhetorical deliberation

Alongside this 'framing by numbers', however, our data highlight the potential of rhetorical deliberation to reframe policy problems. As indicated earlier, rhetorical deliberation is an exchange of speech that invokes practical knowledge, drawing an audience into exercising its capacity for judgement (Garsten, 2006). Whereas the 'deliberative ideal' model of communication (an ideal which has gained increasing acceptance in recent health policy debate and has directly informed the setting up of bodies such as the Priorities Forum) defines rational speech as that which is purified from rhetoric (a background paper circulated to Priorities Forum members, for example, states that 'focusing on the logical structure of argument can help ensure that rhetorical devices are not used to make an invalid argument persuasive' (Parker and Hope, 2000)), a model of communication as rhetorical deliberation both acknowledges rhetoric as a necessary part of any communication, and emphasises its positive contribution in the practice of deliberative democracy.

In the Priorities Forum discussions we see instances of Forum members, in particular GPs, invoking particular and personal forms of knowledge, talking with powerful rhetorical effect from 'the frontline of general practice' for example, and in this way putting forward different framings of a problem to the dominant one on the table. One illustration of this comes towards the end of a lengthy discussion about hospital discharge and consideration of the proposal to employ a consultant physician to expedite the discharge of elderly people from acute hospitals, when a GP member challenges the view put forward by PCT staff that, in addition to the not aggressive enough discharge procedures of some clinicians, the payment system between acute trusts and PCTs creates perverse incentives for the acute trusts to keep patients in hospital:

> I just think, I'm just trying to clarify one thing. I think we're in danger of making a great big supposition, and that is, this has been mentioned twice about the

perverse incentive to keep patients in beds. I don't know where the evidence comes from. You probably are better informed than I am. But I would have thought it's quite unlikely, certainly from where I'm looking from as a GP.... I get the impression that they certainly want them off the beds.... So I think we're in danger of making a supposition that there is a perverse incentive. I'm not that convinced that it's being exercised. I don't think it's really that.   (GP, Priorities Forum transcript 2)

This comment prompts the following response from the Chair:

I actually get the impression that may be we do need to do some more work around that. And I just wondered if the outcome of that work ought to come back here before moving on.   (Chair, Priorities Forum transcript 2)

This action point is followed up by staff in the health improvement directorate, and a second paper on the subject of hospital discharge is brought back to the Priorities Forum the following year. Interestingly, in contrast to the previous discussion, the follow-up paper suggests that in fact very few patients exceed the 'trim point' and that in fact 'there was no evidence of a culture or expectation that patients should not be mobilised and that the appropriate discharge arrangements should be made'. The author of the paper concludes in her presentation to the Forum: 'this study has been quite useful, because it's blown away some of the myths and some of the sort of conjectures that people were making as to what was going on.'

Whilst this is a particularly clear example of how a persuasive contribution seems to prompt a significant reframing of a policy problem, our data contains other isolated examples where members appear to draw on the combined effects of ethos and pathos to persuade the audience of a different framing of an issue. These contributions to discussion can be characterised as being less about engaging with 'the evidence' as constituted in the dominant discourse outlined above, and more about offering particular and personal knowledge situated in practice and experience and often involving the expression of a personal judgement.

In the following example a GP member of the Forum makes a fairly forceful response to a comment by a non-executive PCT member who is arguing that IVF treatment should not be afforded any higher priority than that given at present by the PCT:

Non-executive member: 'I'm saying that I find it personally difficult to place it above other priorities which I know we have. I would find it impossible to go to the Board and say, "We actually need to put more resources into it." I could be persuaded that we need to put less in. But I certainly feel that we should assume this is the maximum, that's purely personal.'

GP: 'I agree with the first part of what you said, but I'm sorry I just completely disagree about the priority of it. I think it's difficult sitting here, for me, like this, to be divorced from the real front line of general practice, and community medicine. It is a very important area of women's health and health of couples, that actually plays on the practice every day. The results of providing a successful outcome are extremely important and helpful to the couple and the individuals involved.' (Priorities Forum transcript 1)

And the same GP, during a discussion about an individual patient whose care costs are considered so excessive as to warrant them coming to the Forum for consideration of a proposal to make changes in her care arrangements, makes the following quite dramatic contribution to discussion:

GP: 'You know, we've got some information, but I'm afraid we haven't got a lot here to be able to—I've got a feeling that we could get drawn in to making a judgement because it's been written on behalf of the PCT and I feel quite uneasy actually. I suspect the status quo should not exist, but I think you're in a Catch 22, you've brought yourselves here, and I'm not sure that this is the right forum to bail you out frankly. Sorry.'

Chair: 'No, no, no.'

GP: 'It's not very helpful.'

Chair: 'No, I think it's a very helpful point.' (Priorities Forum transcript 7)

A little later in the same discussion another GP reinforces this point:

GP: 'We don't have any sort of clinical input here. We've got none of her medical records, her history. I mean whether she would consent to that, but I think that as a GP, I would feel more comfortable, getting some, you know, have more medical background and what, you know, hospital reports have said. There may well be, you know, elements of truth in all this, but a PCT spin put on this, which is making us all very doubting and dubious. Now, that may or may not be fair to the patient, I don't know. But speaking as a doctor, we need to see the patient's perspective.' (Priorities Forum transcript 7)

And in another extract, taken from the follow-up discussion about hospital discharge, we see a GP member making a point from her experience 'on the ground' about the significance of 'failed discharges', which is subsequently acknowledged by the Chair and other members as highlighting an important aspect of the policy issue not presented in the data. We also see this member appealing to the specific concerns of her audience of PCT managers, by addressing the cost issues of failed discharges:

GP: 'I thought there was another [point] as well about failed discharges. And they often have a very short period of time, they call it within 24 hours if you have to get readmitted, but there are lots of cases of patients, within say a week would seem, you know—I haven't got a set figure for what's appropriate, but failed discharges, although you're paying, are you paying twice? Or would they consider that the lengthening of the original stay, because we're seeing more and more of those ... if you cannot cope at home, for example, I had a patient a few weeks ago, a hip replacement lady discharged after two days, couldn't walk, lives in a flat, can't cope—has to go back. Is that a second stay or?'

Public health specialist: 'Well, we did look at the data actually to see if there were readmissions, we only found one.'

Chair: 'But the question is, is it a separate admission?'

GP: 'Yes.'

Public health specialist: 'Yes'

Chair: 'It's a separate admission and we'd pay all over again.'

GP: 'And if you look at those figures, I'm sure other GPs would feel the same, I would assume it's going up and up as the length of stay is reducing. So we're in a lose-lose situation. We're paying more because we're having to support them at home, we're paying more because they're having to go into hospital more, and we're all paying twice.'　(Priorities Forum transcript 6)

In the final example, the focus on practical knowledge has been prompted by the Chair describing the case of a particular patient, whose circumstances have, unusually, formed a case-study in the background paper for an agenda item to identify the ethical considerations that should be taken into account when the PCT is determining who should receive continuing care and where it should be provided. One of the interesting features of this exchange is the apparent ambivalence the Chair expresses towards the status of more personalised, practical knowledge, simultaneously drawing on it to powerful effect whilst playing down the value of a singular example ('one example doesn't prove anything'), and responding to the patient representative who is drawn into the specifics of the case with a comment about not getting 'too bogged down with specific examples'. The Forum member nevertheless continues to make her point, drawing on her personal knowledge and experience as a district nurse, although unlike some of the GP contributions above, does not seem to manage to reframe the discussion, which the Chair brings back to a consideration of the Forum's framework of principles.

Chair: 'And there's a real example, although it's anonymised in this paper, about a patient we've got, who is paralysed from the neck down, he's on a ventilator for nearly 24 hours every day, he's being cared for at home at an absolutely massive cost. About £350,000 a year. Always assuming that it was clinically appropriate for him to be at the Royal Hospital for Neuro-Disability, and having discussed the generality of this with them, it would probably cost about £200,000 for him to be in the Royal Hospital for Neuro-Disability. And in terms of clinical effectiveness, because of the skills that they've got there, because of the equipment that they've got there, because of the expertise and experience, it's very likely he'd have a very much better quality of care, a more clinically effective care. The disadvantage of course is that he wouldn't be at home, and his mates and his family would have to travel further to see him.'

GP: 'And it's a long way to go.'

Chair: 'It is quite a long way to go, yes.'

Patient representative 1: 'What are the chances of his rehabilitation?'

Chair: 'I don't want to get too tied down with that particular individual, but ... but as a concept, and at that particular hospital, some people stay there for many, many years. Years, and years and years. But one example doesn't prove anything. If I just give you one which stuck in my mind—there was a guy who had been involved in a motor accident, and had severe brain damage. He eventually got to the Royal Hospital for Neuro-Disability and they helped him to use a computer, because there are special ways of using a mouse and whatever. And the first thing he wrote was a message to his wife, who he hadn't spoken to for 16 years, and he said, 'I love you.' They were able to enable him to do that, which nobody else had been able to do, because they didn't have the expertise, the occupational therapy or whatever. Now, I don't want to get bogged down in that one case, but in terms of clinical effectiveness the argument could be that in certain circumstances, care in a special unit is more clinically effective than care at home or in the local hospital or whatever that might be.'

Patient representative 2: 'But you'll never change the person's ...'

Chair: 'I don't want to get bogged down with particular examples.'

Patient representative 2: 'But I'm saying, from what, from the experience I've had as a district nurse for many, many years, home is home and you know, you know, deep down inside that they probably would be much, much better off with better care than any district nurses could give, we visited—but we didn't have the amount of backup that they have now. But still, people would prefer to go, to have less chances if you like and still be in their own bed and in their own home than the most wonderful places that you can think of. And I think that is something you just never can get over. Unless you turn round and say, 'We will not be paying for certain types of patients to be nursed in their own home,' and then wait for the bomb to drop.'

Chair: 'That was actually my very next point because our second principle is cost effectiveness. And we say that we should not be paying for things which are not cost effective, other than in certain exceptional circumstances. And it may be that certain types of care are better provided in an institution, a hospital, special type of home, whatever it might be, than in the community. Or in a place that people just want to go to because it appears to them to be a nice place to be. And then there's an issue of equity and there are two components to that. Cost, at the moment, because there's an opportunity cost for everything, and if you spend money on one thing, you can't use that same piece of money for something else. Therefore if you spend a disproportionate sum of money for one person, you are depriving somebody else of those resources. But equally, we should not be forcing people into organisations which are on, for example, cultural grounds or on religious grounds, are inappropriate for them. So I'm trying to suggest in this paper that you may be able to take a transparent, but also robust approach to helping to, contributing towards controlling what is an escalating cost of continuing care, by following the main principles that we have.' (Priorities Forum transcript 2)

Our overall argument is that in the above examples Priorities Forum members are drawing on a different sort of knowledge to that invoked by the 'framing by numbers' discourse. The distinction Aristotle drew between formal, theoretical knowledge, 'episteme', i.e. knowledge focused on objects and ideas abstracted from a social context, and 'phronesis', a 'practical wisdom' concerned with prudent action in a social world, is relevant here. We see instances of Forum members talking from their own professional and personal experiences, expressing values from the 'life-world' rather than 'system-world' (Habermas, 1987), and using words that convey their emotional connection to what they are saying: 'it's difficult for me sitting here', 'I feel quite uneasy ...', 'I would feel more comfortable ...', 'from the experience I've had ... for many, many years', and so on. Although it is difficult to convey the overall sense and scope of individuals' contributions from these short extracts, we suggest that what we see are examples of 'phronesis', as members direct attention to what they see as the morally relevant features of a situation or argument through particular rhetorical moves.

The paradox is that whilst these sorts of contributions are an apparent part of the use of evidence in practice, and can be seen sometimes to have a powerful effect on discussion, they remain largely unacknowledged in formal and public accounts of the Forum's work. The ideas of the discourse theorist, Mikhail Bakhtin, can help in understanding this apparent paradox. According to Bakhtin (Maybin, 2001), language is conceptualised as a constant struggle between *centripetal forces* (the wider authoritative discourses of science and religion, for example) and *centrifugal forces* (the diversification of language associated with different genres, professions and historical periods. This tension can be observed at all levels of language use, from individual conversations to wider cultural discourses. Davies *et al.*, describe the way in which:

… centripetal forces attempt to create a communicative totality with defined and seemingly fixed features, to systematise and prescribe, and to identify and enforce 'proper ways of talking' and proper modes of conduct and interaction which signify, produce and reproduce social institutions. Centrifugal forces at the same time disorganise systems, create exceptions and resist attempts at order.   (Davies *et al.*, 2006)

The rhetorical deliberation of members can be seen as part of a 'centrifugal force', but struggles against the dominant discourses of evidence-based policy and decision science.

Conclusion

In this chapter we have illuminated how evidence is talked into practice. Evidence is not a stable entity that can be separated from its social context. Rather, evidence is constructed through social interaction and through argument. As Green (2000) has suggested, there is no simplistic way in which evidence can be 'put into practice'. Rather, it is practice which, in part, constitutes that evidence.

Our findings suggest that priority setting, and policymaking generally, can be interpreted as a 'decision science', with its privileging of an instrumental, technical rationality, reflecting and shaping the discourse of evidence-based policy. At the same time, priority setting can be conceptualised as the enactment of rhetorical deliberation, with its emphasis on human judgement, personal knowledge and experiential wisdom.

Hammersley (2001) has argued that the effect of the dominant culture of evidence-based policy has been to erode practitioners' confidence in their ability to make judgements by marginalising professional experience and tacit knowledge and devaluing democratic debate about the ethical and moral issues faced in policy choices. More generally, the application of scientific method to contemporary life has led to the deformation of practical wisdom:

> To resist the 'colonization' of social and political life by expert knowledge based on method and to restore a sense of 'praxis' (in both public and civil society), many believe that we must recover the understanding that praxis involves judgement (phronesis), it requires moral wisdom, engagement and practical application to oneself.   (Schwandt, 2001)

References

Black, N. (2001), 'Evidence based policy: proceed with care', *British Medical Journal*, 323: 275–9.

Brown, R. H. (1997), 'New roles for rhetoric: from academic critique to civic affirmation', *Argumentation*, 11: 9–22.

Davies, C., Wetherell, M. and Barnett, E. (2006), *Citizens at the Centre: deliberative participation in healthcare decisions* (Bristol, Policy Press).

Dopson, S. and Fitzgerald, L. (2005), *Knowledge to Action? Evidence-based health care in context* (Oxford, Oxford University Press).

Espeland, W. and Stevens, M. (1998), 'Commensuration as a social process', *Annual Review of Sociology*, 24: 313–43.

Fischer, F. (2003), *Reframing Public Policy: discursive politics and deliberative practices* (Oxford, Oxford University Press).

Garsten, B. (2006), *Saving Persuasion: a defense of rhetoric and judgment* (Cambridge, MA, Harvard University Press).

Garver, E. (1978), 'Rhetoric and essentially contested arguments', *Philosophy and rhetoric*, 11: 156–72.

Gee, J. P. (1999), *An Introduction to Discourse Analysis Theory and Method* (New York, Routledge).

Glasby, J., Walshe, K. and Harvey, G. (2007), 'Making evidence fit for purpose in decision making: a case study of the hospital discharge of older people', *Evidence and Policy*, 3(3): 425–37.

Goffman, E. (1974), *Frame Analysis: an essay on the organization of experience.* (Cambridge, MA, Harvard University Press).

Green, J. (2000), 'Epistemology, evidence and experience: evidence based health care in the work of Accident Alliances', *Sociology of Health and Illness*, 22(4): 453–76.

Greener, I. and Powell, J. (2003), 'Health authorities, priority-setting and resource allocation: a study in decision-making in New Labour's NHS', *Social Policy and Administration*, 37(1): 35–48.

Habermas, J. (1987), *The Theory of Communicative Action* (Boston, MA, Beacon).

Hammersley, M. (2001), 'Some questions about evidence-based practice in education', in R. Pring and G. Thomas (eds.), *Evidence-based practice in education* (Milton Keynes, Open University Press), pp. 133–49.

Hymes, D. (1972), 'Models of interaction of language and social life', in J. Gumperz and D. Hymes (eds.), *Directions in Sociolinguistics: the ethnography of communication* (New York, Holt, Rinehart and Winston).

Innvaer, S., Vist, G., Trommald, M. and Oxman, A. (2002), 'Health policymakers' perceptions of their use of evidence: a systematic review', *Journal of Health Services Research and Policy*, 7: 239–44.

Lewis, J. (2003), 'Evidence-based policy: a technocratic wish in a political world', in V. Lin and B. Gibson (eds.), *Evidence-Based Health Policy: problems and possibilities* (Victoria, Oxford University Press).

MacLure, M. (2003), *Discourse in Educational and Social Research* (London, Sage).

Maybin, J. (2001), 'Language, Struggle and Voice: the Bakhtin/Volosinov writings', in M. Wetherall and S. Taylor (eds.), *Discourse Theory and Practice* (London, Sage).

Miller, C. R. (1990), 'The rhetoric of decision science, or Herbert A. Simon says', in H. Simons (ed.), *The Rhetorical Turn: invention and persuasion in the conduct of inquiry* (Chicago, Chicago University Press).

Parker, M. and Hope, T. (2000), 'Ways of thinking about ethics', *Medicine*, 28(10): 2–5.

Petersen, A. and Lupton, D. (1996), *The New Public Health: health and self in the age of risk* (London, Sage).

Phillips, N. and Hardy, C. (2002), *Discourse Analysis: investigating processes of social construction* (London, Sage).

Porter, T. (1996), *Trust in Numbers* (Princeton, NJ, Princeton University Press).

Potter, J., Wetherell, M. and Chitty, A. (1991), 'Quantification Rhetoric—cancer on television', *Discourse and Society*, 2(3): 333–65.

Rein, M. and Schon, D. (1993), 'Reframing policy discourse', in F. Fischer and J. Forester (eds.), *The Argumentative Turn in Policy Analysis and Planning* (*Durham, NC, Duke University Press*).

Roberts, C. and Bailey, J. (2008), 'What counts as discourse and what use is it?' *British Medical Journal*, 337(a879, rapid response).

Russell, J. and Greenhalgh, T. (2009), *Rhetoric, Evidence and Policymaking: a case study of priority setting in primary care* (UCL: London, Research Department of Primary Care and Population Health). <http://eprints.ucl.ac.uk/15560/>.

Sanderson, I. (2003), 'Is it "what works" that matters? Evaluation and evidence-based policy-making', *Research Papers in Education*, 18(4): 331–45.

Sarangi, S. and Roberts, C. (1999), *Talk, Work and Institutional Order: discourse in medical, mediation and management settings* (Berlin, Mouton de Gruyter).

Schwandt, T. (2001), 'Understanding dialogue as practice', *Evaluation*, 7(2): 228–37.

Stone, D. (1997), *Policy Paradox: the art of political decision making* (New York, W. W. Norton).

Tsoukas, H. (1997), 'The tyranny of light: the temptations and the paradoxes of the information society', *Futures*, 29(9): 827–43.

Van de Ven, A. and Schomaker, M. (2002), 'The rhetoric of evidence-based medicine', *Health Care Management Review*, 27(3): 89–91.

Walshe, K. and Rundall, T. (2001), 'Evidence-based management: from theory to practice in health care', *Milbank Quarterly*, 79(3): 429–57.

Webb, S. (2001), 'Some considerations on the validity of evidence-based practice in social work', *British Journal of Social Work*, 31: 57–79.

Wells, P. (2007), 'New Labour and evidence based policy making: 1997–2007', *People, Place and Policy Online*, 1(1): 22–9.

Wetherell, M., Taylor, S. and Yates, S. (2001), *Discourse Theory and Practice: a reader* (London, Open University/Sage).

Wood, M., Ferlie, E. and Fitzgerald, L. (1998), 'Achieving clinical behaviour change: a case of becoming indeterminate', *Social Science and Medicine*, 47: 1729–38.

11

A Theory of Evidence for
Evidence-Based Policy

NANCY CARTWRIGHT AND JACOB STEGENGA

Abstract

Evidence-based policy is all the rage now. But no one knows quite how to do it. Policy questions do not generally fall neatly within any one of our scientific or social science disciplines, where the standards and rules of evidence for the questions studied are fairly clearly delineated. There is by now a variety of guides available on standards of evidence for evidence-based policy. But these focus narrowly on only part of the problem. For policy we want credible evidence that speaks for (or against) the policy and we want to know how to evaluate policy effectiveness in light of the evidence. This suggests three questions: (1) When are evidence claims credible? (2) When is a credible claim relevant to the truth of a claim to effectiveness? (3) What is the probability that a policy will be effective given a body of evidence of varying credibility relevant in different ways?

Current guides tend to focus on question 1, ranking evidence claims according to the methods by which the claims are produced, that is, according to how much certainty the method confers on the claim. In an attempt to address all three questions in one fell swoop, this paper starts not from question 1, but from question 3. A sure-fire way to evaluate what the effects of a policy implementation will be is to mimic the procedures by which nature herself decides what effects to produce: survey all the causes for the targeted effect that are in place in the target situation, including those you introduce in implementing the policy; then predict the effect from nature's own rules for calculating what happens when those causes act in consort. Answers to questions 1 and 2 can then be geared to this strategy. Of course mimicking nature properly is out of the question. But we suggest first that doing so well enough may not be such a tall order and second that whether we want to mimic nature's method or not, when we bet that a policy will be effective we are willy-nilly betting on such a simulation.

Proceedings of the British Academy, **171**, 291–322. © The British Academy 2011.

I. Preliminaries

The project

WE AIM HERE to outline a theory of evidence for use. More specifically we lay foundations for a guide for the use of evidence in predicting policy effectiveness *in situ*, a more comprehensive guide than current standard offerings, such as the Maryland rules in criminology, the weight of evidence scheme of the International Agency for Research on Cancer (IARC), or the US 'What Works Clearinghouse'. The guide itself is meant to be well-grounded but at the same time to give practicable advice, that is, advice that can be used by policy-makers not expert in the natural and social sciences, assuming they are well-intentioned and have a reasonable but limited amount of time and resources available for searching out evidence and deliberating.

We go into the project with some assumptions. The first is a delimitation of the topic. The guide for which we aim to lay a theoretical base is to be concerned with the use of evidence to estimate, if only roughly, whether, were a proposed policy to be actually implemented, a specific, identified outcome would be produced. We thus do not discuss the broader issue of how to settle on goals. Nor do we discuss how to recognise when a result of a scientific study, formulated using concepts that can be tackled with the procedures of the study, is relevant to the more abstractly and vaguely set out goals that are often the real aims of policy.[1] Nor do we present ideas here on how to come up with a set of candidate policies for achieving a given goal. It is also important to keep in mind that whether a policy will achieve its stated goals is only one of many considerations that should go into policy decisions.[2] We treat here only the far simpler but already difficult problem of judging whether a particular proposed policy is likely to achieve a particular already well articulated goal.

Our second starting assumption is that the project needs to be approached from the point of view of the evidence user, not the evidence producer.

Third, we assume that rigour is a good thing, so that the advice should be firmly rooted in sound principles; but we must not be pseudo-rationalistic. A rigorous argument with nine well-grounded premises and one weak one does not make for a rigorously established conclusion. For the most part, esti-

---

[1] For instance we may want an educational program that makes children better adapted to live full, independent lives and to become contributing citizens but proper scientific method requires the study of precisely defined, measurable outcomes, like reading scores on an Iowa Test of Basic Skills.

[2] For examples of the many other types of issues that need consideration see section on 'Effectiveness' at pp. 294 below.

mates of whether a policy will be successful made in real time will be both rough and uncertain. That is important to keep in mind as policy decisions are made. But it is also important to keep it in mind as advice guides are devised. If advice is to be practicable, it may not be hugely reliable, even if it is ultimately well-grounded. We should aim for advice that improves decisions even if we cannot do the job perfectly. The best should not be the enemy of the good.

Fourth, and closely connected with the third, is that we should not expect policy effectiveness judgements to be very reliable. There are a variety of different reasons conspiring to make these judgements especially difficult, including the obvious difficulties of doing what we propose here as necessary for reasonably reliable judgements. We shall not rehearse these reasons but just offer one remark to make vivid how difficult the task is. Asking if a policy of a specific design will achieve a targeted result is structurally just like asking whether a laser of a specific design will produce a coherent beam when we plug it in. It is difficult to answer that question reliably before actually plugging the laser in—it is similarly complicated to produce advice about what counts as evidence for or against an answer and about how to marshal that evidence to settle on a prediction. Social effectiveness will be even harder since the systems under study are more open, our theories and knowledge of the materials are less secure, and the choice of targeted outcomes is generally dictated by social need, not by an assessment of how achievable they are.

How to think about the problem

Viewpoint

When it comes to evidence-based policy, viewpoint matters. Whether wittingly or not, typical advice guides focus on the *production side* of scientific evidence and not on the *use* side. They tell us what counts as good science, not how to use that science to arrive at good policy.

Most available guides, like the Maryland rules, the IARC scheme and What Works, provide ranking schemes for the 'quality' of evidence. These schemes police the credibility of results that can be counted as evidence. Evidence claims are ranked according to the methods by which they are tested. High quality means that the tests are stringent: Results that pass the tests are very likely to be true. *Randomized controlled trials* (*RCTs*) are necessary for strong evidence according to the dominant guides. Many object on the grounds that this can mean throwing out a lot of good evidence that we ought to be attending to. This issue is not our concern here. The central concern we raise is that these rankings focus on too narrow a range of *claims that need evidencing*, not that the kinds of evidence admitted are too narrow. Why?

Truth is a good thing. But it doesn't take one very far. Suppose we have at our disposal the entire encyclopaedia of unified science containing all the true claims there are. Which facts from the encyclopaedia do we bring to the table for policy deliberation? Among all the true facts, we want on the table as evidence only those that are *relevant* to the policy. And given a collection of relevant true facts we want to know how to assess whether the policy will be effective in light of them. How are we supposed to make these decisions? That is the problem from the *user's* point of view and that is the problem of focus here.

Here is how Dr Sean Tunis, director of the Center for Medical Technology Policy, a US organisation concerned with ways to get better medical evidence, puts the problem: 'There's this gulf between what questions researchers have found interesting to study and what questions industry and the N.I.H. have chosen to fund and what users of information most want to know.' In our terms, the focus has been on the side of evidence *production*, rather than evidence *use*: 'One starts from the head and the other starts from the tail and they don't meet in the middle' (cited in Kolata, 2008).

Effectiveness

There are a great many things we need to evaluate in considering whether to adopt a policy or not. Will the policy work? Does it have unpleasant side effects? Does it have beneficial side effects? How much does it cost? Have we made the correct choice of target outcomes? Is the policy morally, politically and culturally acceptable? Can we get the necessary agreement to get it enacted? Do we have the resources to implement it? Will enemies of the project sabotage it in various ways? Every one of these questions needs answering and in each case evidence will help get the right answer.

We shall confine our discussion, however, to the *question of effectiveness:*

> *Question of Effectiveness.* Will the proposed policy produce the targeted outcomes were it to be implemented in the targeted setting and implemented in the way it would in fact be implemented there?[3]

---

[3] Of course there will seldom be a highly certain yes or no answer. So at some point an assessment of the probabilities will have to be made in light of the evidence, even if only roughly. But reasonable probability assessments depend first on understanding the structure of the problem, which is the topic to be tackled first.

A structure for the problem

Start then from the point of view of the policy deliberator trying to estimate whether a proposed policy will be effective. *For a reliable decision one wants credible evidence that, all told, speaks for (or against) the policy.* This simple observation suggests that from the point of view of the user three different issues need addressing:

1 *Quality:* When are evidence claims credible?
2 *Relevance:* When does an established result bear on a policy prediction and how does it do so?[4]
3 *Evaluation:* How should predictions about policy effectiveness be evaluated in the light of all the evidence?

The first is an issue about the production of knowledge by the social and natural sciences; it is the meat of evidence-ranking systems. The latter two are the more neglected questions we focus on.

The fact that the three questions are distinct should not suggest that their answers are unrelated. Despite the common emphasis on question 1, it seems *prima facie* as if the natural starting point is with question 2. First establish what kinds of evidence are relevant to effectiveness. Then, for question 1, provide guidelines that police the quality of evidence of those kinds; and for question 3, propose some scheme for amalgamating or combining evidence.

In aid of this approach one could adopt one or another of the characterisations of relevance on offer from philosophy and methodology of science, where the topic has been explored and debated for years; then follow on with one or another of the schemes available for combining evidence or adapt weighing schemes with known characteristics from other areas, like those for amalgamating preferences or expert testimony.

We adopt a different strategy. We propose to start with an account of how to evaluate claims of effectiveness and work backwards to figure out what kinds of evidence would be relevant for the evaluation, finally returning to the first issue of how to assure that the kinds of evidence claims needed are sufficiently credible to enter into deliberation.

Before beginning with this account, we want to stress the importance for the success of evidence-based policy of covering all three questions. Question 1 is a question for knowledge producers: What is necessary in order to ensure that a claim entered as evidence is likely to be true? Users have in addition to

---

[4] But, as mentioned above in fn. 1, there are many important aspects of this issue that we will not discuss here, including how to relate the concepts of scientific studies to those in which goals are often framed.

face questions 2 and 3.[5] Yet most of the rigour and most of the attention is to question 1. We are urged to extreme rigour at one stage, then left to wing it for the rest.

But: a chain of defense for the effectiveness of a policy, like a towing chain, is only as strong as its weakest link. So the investment in rigour for one link while the others are left to chance is apt to be a waste. To build the entire chain one may have to ignore some issues or make heroic assumptions about them. But that should dramatically weaken the degree of confidence in the final assessment. Rigour isn't contagious from link to link. If you want a reasonably secure conclusion coming out, you'd better be careful that each premise is secure enough going in.

II. Evaluating effectiveness

How philosophy can help

We propose to borrow our three central principles of the theory of evidence for use from philosophy. The first two provide the basis of the theory and the third, some practical help in implementing it.

- Truth values for causal counterfactuals are fixed by causal models.
- Causes, as J. L. Mackie explains, are INUS conditions.
- In understanding how causes operate and how they operate together, mechanisms matter.

Causes and counterfactuals

For sound policy we need to evaluate whether, if the proposed policy were implemented as it would in fact be implemented, the targeted outcome would

---

[5] Is relevance really, as we say, a question for the user rather than the knowledge producer? Many think not. Indeed it is a common criticism of studies in the social sciences that they do not say what they show, what the results bear on, at a practical level. We don't think they can. Perhaps they can do better, but there will always be a great number of relevance judgements that must be left to the user. Whether a given fact is relevant as evidence for a given claim depends on a host of other assumptions, both theoretical and local to the situation. (This is the lesson of the famous 'Duhem–Quine' problem in the philosophy of science.) For causal counterfactuals of the kind we assess in effectiveness evaluations, relevance will depend in addition on *how* the cause is supposed to produce the effect. (See Part V below.)

occur in consequence. We are looking for the probability of what in causal decision theory is called *a causal counterfactual.*[6]

There is good reason to expect an intimate connection between causes and these special kinds of counterfactuals. Nature forges it. Consider: How does nature decide what effects to produce in a particular situation? First she surveys the causes that will be operating. Next she consults her rules of combination to calculate what should happen when they all act at once. Then she produces the prescribed effects. We can't lose by imitating nature.

That is our proposal. To predict what will result if we introduce some new policy or programme, follow Nature's lead: Reconstruct Nature's list of causes and mimic Nature's calculation.[7] This provides us with a good way to predict the effects of our policy implementations and we can't go wrong if we succeed. Moreover, any method that does not directly mimic Nature's processes will only get predictions about causal counterfactuals right (or 'right enough') if it has some way of achieving just the same results. Later (in Part IV) we consider 'cheap heuristics' that might get the same conclusions enough of the time in specific kinds of circumstances. These are great when they are available. But their conclusions are only warranted to the extent that we have good reason to believe that they will produce near enough the same results as would a causal model that mimics Nature's procedures.

Since it is often not possible to make life easier and getting the causal model 'right enough' is usually very difficult, any reasonably comprehensive guide will also need to remind policy analysts to expect a great deal of uncertainty and to adopt strategies for dealing with it—strategies like not introducing big policy changes that are difficult to reverse and adopting a muddling through rather than grand planning approach.[8]

---

[6] These are commonly called 'counterfactuals' despite the fact that it is generally possible for the antecedent to obtain, and were it to obtain, the consequent would obtain as well, if the 'counterfactual' is true. Some find 'subjunctive conditional' a more apt label, but the term 'counterfactual' is what is generally used throughout philosophy and we will follow that usage here.

[7] A referee expresses concern over the concepts 'Nature's causes' and 'Nature's calculations'. Perhaps this is an expression of a David Hume-inspired scepticism about causes. There is, however, a large, articulate and compelling body of literature arguing that contrary to this sceptical position causal notions make good sense and are essential for a useful and accurate description of the natural and social world and especially for understanding and evaluating claims about the effects of intervening.

[8] Thanks to a referee for encouraging us to mention this. The referee also suggests consulting William Dunn, 2003 and Charles Lindblom, 1979.

Causal models

We propose then to adopt standard philosophic advice as the first principle of the theory of use: To evaluate causal counterfactuals, build a causal model (see Reiss, 2007). But the term 'causal model' should not carry a lot of baggage with it, either from philosophy or from the sciences, where various different kinds of specialised causal models are on offer.

What is a causal model?

For our purposes a *causal model* has two essential ingredients, where we separate the first into two parts to highlight issues about implementation that we know policy makers need to take into consideration.

1   A list of the causes relevant to the targeted effect that will operate in the target situation. This includes

    1.a   the causes present in the situation independent of the policy action

    1.b   any changes in this set of causes introduced in implementing the policy.[9]

2   A rule of combination that calculates what should happen vis-à-vis the targeted effect when those causes operate together.

Consider a simple case. Later we shall look at both some real and some pastiche social policy cases. But for now we illustrate using everyday physics. We do so because the reasoning is simple, well-understood, and we are not likely to get involved in subject-specific debates in education or criminology or health policy. More importantly, we choose this kind of case to start with because it is one where our knowledge of the principles and of the aptness of the concepts is secure so that we can focus on the structure of the reasoning needed.

> *The case of the desk magnet versus the industrial magnet.* We have access to a desk magnet and to a large industrial magnet. We know the exact strengths of these with a very high degree of certainty—claims about their efficacy for lifting objects have passed far more than two good RCTs; they have centuries of study behind them. Shall we use one of them to lift an object in my driveway? That depends on the other features of the target situation.
>
>   First, magnets need helping factors to be effective at all. A desk magnet is useless for lifting a matchstick; it is only the *combination* of a magnet and a

[9] Remembering, as a referee stresses, to include recipient reactions that can affect the outcome. For instance as the referee points out, 'Whether something is effective in a public policy system depends on whether people like the policy outcome, or even the policy mechanism in its own right (e.g. in the case of some 'effective' or 'coercive' labour market and welfare policies)'.

ferrous object that produces a magnetic force. Then the acceleration caused by the magnet is still only one part of the story, often one very small part. To know what happens when we apply the magnet we need to know the other forces as well. Here, especially gravity. The desk magnet may lift a pin but it is hopeless for a car, where we need the industrial magnet. We also need to attend to what other forces we introduce in the course of getting the magnet in place. Perhaps the industrial magnet would have lifted the car if only we hadn't thrown the heavy packing case for the magnet into the boot.

Finally we need to know how all these factors combine to produce a result. Often in social contexts additivity is assumed: Add a good thing and the results can only get better. But that doesn't work in even this simple physical case. We get so used to vector addition that we forget that it isn't simple (scalar) addition of effect sizes. Add a magnetic acceleration of 42 ft/sec/sec to that of gravity's 32 ft/sec/sec and you won't usually get an acceleration of 74 ft/sec/sec.

The point is that whether the magnet will be effective at all in the target situation and to what extent depends on nature's causal model of the situation. So the most direct way of predicting its effects is to construct our own causal model in imitation of nature.

We know no one wants to hear this since it seems difficult. But consider: Industrial magnets would pass any number of RCTs, of any degree of stringency. But that's not anywhere near enough to know. None of us would rent an industrial magnet to remove a load of rubbish without looking at the rubbish. Knowledge that magnets just like this *can* lift is only a small part of what one would consider in evaluating whether renting the industrial magnet will be effective in removing our rubbish. If this is so in everyday calculations and in applied science and engineering, why should we expect it to be substantially different—and substantially easier—in social engineering?

Of course constructing causal models is hard, even if the models are rough and we have figured out ways to tolerate uncertainties. Sometimes there are shortcuts, 'cheap heuristics' that get us, more-or-less, well-enough, the same conclusions that the causal model generates. As decision makers we can opt for a heuristic if we want. But there is no avoiding the fact that the choice of the right heuristic depends on the right causal model. We may not wish to build a causal model; we may not know how to; we may think it takes too much time or money, intelligence or attention. That does not alter the fact that when we buy a policy we are betting on a causal model, willy-nilly, whether we wish to think about it or not.

Had we world enough and time

A great deal more can be said about causal models. But it is subject- and discipline-specific and almost always requires expertise and training to do at all properly. Moreover, many scientific models do less than what we demand of a causal model, though they provide more detail and zero in, usually very precisely, on specific features of interest.

Consider a joint effort to explore the causes of delays in emergency rooms (Lane, Monefeldt and Rosenhead, 2000). The modelling expertise was provided by the Department of Operational Research at LSE, while orientation to the problem area, judgements on design choices, and introductions to stakeholders were supplied by Casualty Watch, a project organised as a response to public concern that cuts in the NHS were producing an inadequate emergency service and harming patients. System dynamics was selected as the appropriate modelling medium and the model was calibrated with information from an inner London teaching hospital.

Here's what the model looks like:

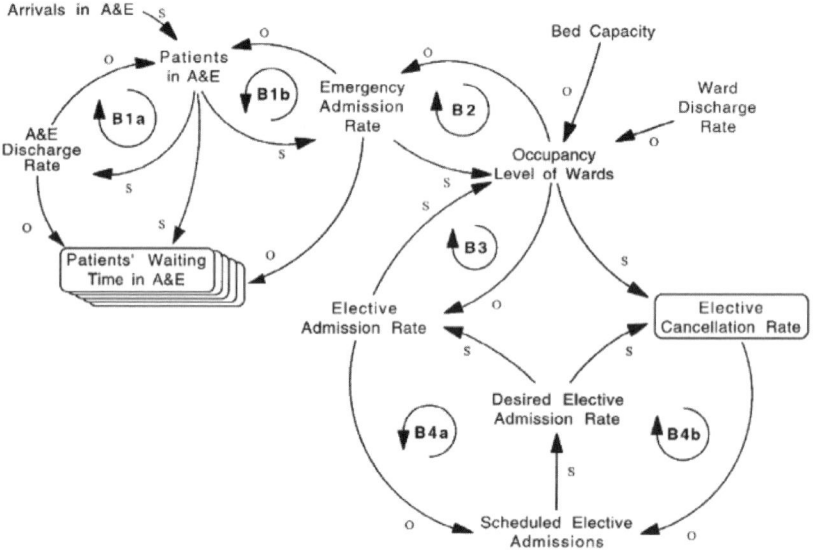

Figure 11.1.   Model of delays in emergency rooms.

What's important about this model is its ability to detect and represent feedback loops and its dynamic structure. For instance it makes clear that the number of beds available in the wards both affects and is affected by the number of admissions from A&E and that the number of patients being tended in A&E affects and is affected by the number of patients being admitted to the wards from A&E. It also shows a number of pathways by which an initial cause, say arrivals at the Accident and Emergency Department, influences the final effect, patient waiting time at A&E.

As we shall explain in Part V, tracing through the dynamics like this, step-by-step, can be a big help in constructing a significant part of the second component we demand in a causal model—an account of how causes act together to produce the targeted effect—because it focuses on what auxiliary causes are needed at each step if the salient cause is to produce the next step in the process. Notice, however, that this information is not explicitly represented in the model since the model treats causes singly. At the head of the arrow—at the causes end—is a single variable; e.g. bed capacity, ward discharge rate, and emergency admission rate are all pictured as separate causes of the ward occupancy rate. There is no information encoded about how these different causes combine, in particular which causes must act together before they can contribute to the effect at all. Thus this model, like most professional models, does less than we require, though what it does, it does more precisely and in more detail.

Another example (Figure 11.2 below), this from Judea Pearl (1995: 669–70).

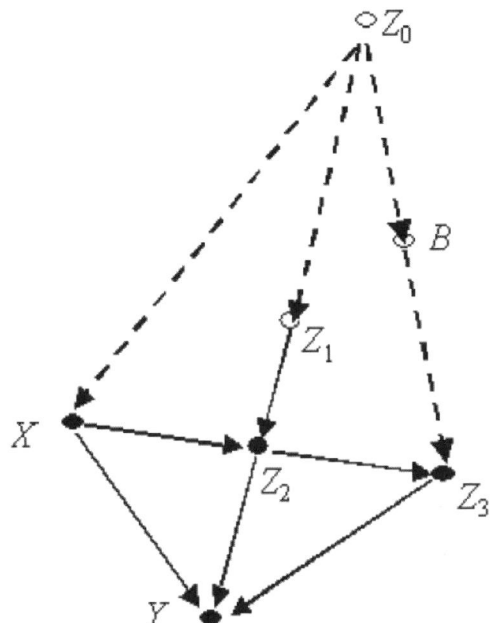

Figure 11.2.   A causal Bayes net.

Variables: X: fumigants; Y: yields; B: the population of birds and other predators; Z_0: last year's eelworm population; Z_1: eelworm population before treatment; Z_2: eelworm population after treatment; Z_3: eelworm population at the end of the season.

In this model, as in the last, causes are at the top of the arrow, effects at the tip. By calling it a causal 'Bayes net' special assumptions are made about the relations among the variables that may not hold in every causal model; for instance causes and effects pictured in the graph are all supposed to be probabilistically dependent. Generally this kind of model comes with numbers as well, ideally the conditional probability for each effect conditional on all the immediately prior causes leading into it. So these models contain more information than is required by our two conditions for a causal model, information of special use[10] in the particular kinds of causal systems that satisfy the special axioms that relate causes and probabilities in a Bayes net.[11] But like the dynamic-systems model for emergency room admissions and hospital beds, it also contains less since the model does not show how the causes interact among themselves to affect yields. We know from the graph that Z_2 can influence Y but even if we add to that knowledge of the conditional probability of Y on Z_2 we don't know from the graph whether the presence or absence of X is essential to the ability of Z_2 to influence Y.[12]

This kind of missing information is readily supplied by models presented in the form of equations, if they can be constructed. Here for instance is the final equation from a causal model we shall discuss in *Part V*:

[10] This information plus the graph, assuming the graph is causally correct and the Bayes-nets axioms are satisfied, is tantamount to having the full probability measure over all the variables in the graph. It is thus possible to predict the probability of any outcome conditional on values of antecedent variables, which naturally can be very useful. But this raises an important point about modelling to predict singular counterfactuals. A full probability over the relevant variables will allow us to predict how probable a desired effect is given that the policy variables take the proposed values. But only if the probability is over the individual events that will be implemented in the specific way they will be at the specific place and time under consideration. It is just this probability that is so difficult to find—if it exists at all, which many of us doubt.

[11] For instance, one axiom requires that immediately prior causes on the graph and their effects are always probabilistically dependent, which means that no causes act both positively and negatively by different paths that cancel each other. A second requires that a full set of prior causes screens off a factor from anything except its causal descendants. This implies, among other things, that no causes produce their effects probabilistically in tandem. For instance, no purely probabilistic causes produce a particular effect just in case they produce a particular side effect. Rather all effects are produced independently of all others (cf. Pearl, 2000).

[12] Many of those developing the theory of causal Bayes nets describe them as a method for 'causal discovery'. We think that's right. They are tools on the knowledge production side; a way to sidestep the need for RCTs by establishing efficacy with the same degree of rigour as an RCT but using population, not experimental, data. They may even be of more immediate relevance to policy than an RCT if the data comes from a population reasonably deemed similar in the right respects to the target population. Still, without further additions, they are not enough to evaluate causal counterfactuals. (Though see Judea Pearl's (2000) beautiful work on how to use them to evaluate the probability of causal counterfactuals, given input probabilities for exogenous factors and given that the special Bayes-nets axioms hold in the system under study.)

(*) $y_t = \theta\beta[p_t-p_{t-1}] - \theta\beta\pi + y_{pt} + \varepsilon_t$

Here y_t is output at t and p_t is price at t so $[p_t-p_{t-1}]$ is a measure of inflation; ε_t is a random 'error' variable.[13] This equation yields as a next step the classic Philips curve representing a trade-off in which rising inflation causes decreasing unemployment. Once the parameters, θ, β, and π, are filled in the equation shows how the two causes represented—inflation, $[p_t-p_{t-1}]$, and earlier output, y_{pt}—combine to produce later output, y_t: in this case, simple linear addition.[14]

   We will present a simple physics example (see *Illustrations of INUS conditions*, below, p. 305) where a complete set of causes is also laid out in an equation, but the rules of combination for the causes are more complicated involving not simple (scalar) addition but also multiplication and vector addition.

   Equations for calculating the exact result of a given set of causes are wonderful when one can get them. But they may not be possible even in principle for many cases. Even a complete set of causes may act only probabilistically, not fixing a value for the effect at all but only a probability. In fact we hazard that that is more often the case than not. And even that may be wishful thinking. Nature herself may proceed with less quantitative precision, not fixing even a final probability, perhaps only a direction of change. Whether she does so or not, this level of precision is generally well beyond the ability of normal policy deliberators. Also, as our colleagues at a recent conference on causality urged: Our list of causes will almost always be incomplete; the very best we can hope for is a probabilistic assessment of the outcomes and even that should generally not be too precise. So don't get hung up trying to produce equations.

   But that is not advice to ignore the need to get a grip on the dominant causes that will affect the outcome or the need to bet on what they do in combination. It is just advice not to expect a degree of precision or a degree of confidence that neither the subject nor our capabilities can support.

---

[13] Hence ε_t has a probability measure over it. This variable does not refer to any 'known quantity' but serves at one and the same time to stand for omitted causes and measurement errors and as a representational device to allow a deterministic-looking equation to represent a purely probabilistic connection between the designated causes and the designated effect.

[14] When ε_t is included, the causes will not fix a value for the effect but merely its probability.

INUS conditions

Introduction

To evaluate a causal counterfactual one needs to consider the major causes at work and how they combine. One characteristic of causes widely accepted in philosophy can help with both enterprises. As J. L. Mackie (1965) argued, causes are INUS conditions.[15]

> An *INUS condition* is an **I**nsufficient but **N**ecessary part of an **U**nnecessary but **S**ufficient condition.

The factors we normally call causes are, according to Mackie, INUS conditions. Causes—in our usual sense of the word—are not enough on their own to produce an effect. Causes work in cooperation; they need helping factors. It takes both a lighted match and a good stack of logs and brush to produce a bonfire. Together a set of factors that are SUFFICIENT to produce an effect make up what we shall call 'a complete causal complex'. Each factor in the complete causal complex—for example, the brush or the logs or the lighted match—is INSUFFICIENT by itself to produce the effect. Still, each has got to be there or that complex won't produce the effect. That's why the separate factors in the complex are NECESSARY.

The whole complex itself however, while sufficient for the effect to occur, is generally UNNECESSARY. That's because there are almost always other ways—other 'complete causal complexes'—to produce the same result: One can also make a bonfire with a stack of dry straw and packing cases and a cigarette lighter, or with dry straw, packing cases and a well-aimed bolt of lightening. Each of these different complete causal complexes is sufficient to make the effect occur but none is necessary since each of the other complete complexes will do as well. And each complex contains a number of cooperating factors, like the lighter or the brush, each one of which is insufficient by itself for the effect but is necessary if the complex of which it is part is to do the job.

INUS conditions are not just a topic for philosophers. Epidemiologists have developed a compelling way to understand INUS conditions with the use of pie graphs to represent sufficient and component causes. Each slice in a given pie represents a component cause and a whole pie represents a sufficient cause, a 'complete causal complex'. A single pie slice on its own is insufficient to cause a disease; the whole pie is needed. So in the philosopher's vocabulary a single pie slice is an INUS condition.

---

[15] That is, all causes are INUS conditions. But not all INUS conditions are causes.

Below are two complete causal complexes for a disease with the component causes shown as pie slices. There are some shared component causes (C1 and C2) and some unique component causes (C4 and C8, for example). Also, we indicate the unknown component causes as CN in the left pie and CM in the right pie.

Here is an example. Smoking causes lung cancer but not all smokers develop lung cancer. There are other factors, perhaps genetic factors and other life-style and environmental factors, that contribute to developing lung cancer. So in Figure 11.3, Sufficient Cause A would be the constellation of factors, including smoking, that together cause lung cancer; smoking could be C3. But people also develop lung cancer without ever smoking. So in Figure 11.3, Sufficient Cause B would be a constellation of factors not including smoking (C3 is not present) that together cause lung cancer. Working in a coal mine for example could be C8.

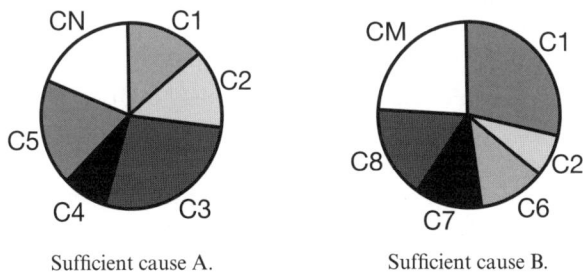

Sufficient cause A.   Sufficient cause B.

Figure 11.3.   Two sufficient causes and their component causes.

Illustrations of INUS conditions

In this section we provide examples from different subjects to illustrate what INUS conditions are and how they work together to produce an effect. The first is an example about the effectiveness of laws requiring bicycle helmets in reducing head injuries among cyclists.

BICYCLE HELMET EXAMPLE

Vigorous debate regarding the efficacy of bicycle helmets to reduce head injury has been published in the pages of the *British Medical Journal* (see especially Robinson, 2006: 722–5 and numerous letters in response). Case–control studies suggest that cyclists wearing helmets have fewer head injuries than cyclists not wearing helmets, whereas time-series studies in jurisdictions that have passed helmet laws do not show a clear decrease in the rate of head injuries after helmet laws have been implemented and in some cases these studies suggest an *increase* in head injuries after the law is implemented.

At first glance this is paradoxical. Our intuitions, supported with evidence from case–control studies, say that helmets should reduce head injuries whereas helmet compulsion laws fail to show much benefit and in some cases possibly show an *increase* in head injuries.

There are methodological reasons that could partly explain the differences between these studies. A worry about confounders in the case–control studies could exaggerate the estimated efficacy of helmets: There is some evidence suggesting that helmet wearers are overall safer bicycle riders, are involved in less severe accidents, are richer, and more likely to be white. A worry about confounders in the time-series studies could dampen the result of introducing helmet laws: Over the periods of these studies there have been more cars on roads and these cars have increased in size and speed.

Leaving aside a discussion of the methodological quality of case–control studies versus time-series analyses, this paradox can be understood by thinking about INUS conditions. The case–control studies give one piece of a causal pie: Helmets can cause a reduction in head injuries. But those studies don't tell about the other pieces of the pie, that is, other factors that are causally relevant to a cyclist's head injury, things like driver behaviour, cyclist behaviour, and road conditions. Now, there is evidence to suggest that at least some of these things change with helmet wearing.[16] Drivers give less space to cyclists who are wearing a helmet and cyclists take more risks (a 'false sense of security' phenomenon). So helmet compulsion laws don't just change one piece of a causal pie, they change several pieces. And that could partly explain the discordance between the two kinds of studies.

The nice thing about this bicycle example is that it illustrates two lessons at once. First, the importance of identifying the other INUS conditions that go into a complete causal complex, i.e. the other slices in the same pie—which one can think of as 'helping factors' necessary in order for the policy lever to work: Helmet wearing in combination with usual driver behaviour will decrease head injuries from bicycle accidents; helmet wearing with more dangerous driving may increase head injuries.

Second, it reminds us that in thinking about INUS conditions we need to pay attention to the unintended consequences of our actions. In implement-

---

[16] This naturally suggests that a feedback model as with the A&E study above would be a good one to try if one wants to lay out the steps in the causal process in aid of producing what is called a causal model here.

ing a policy we may not only produce unwanted side effects; we can, as in this case and in the Lucas example to be discussed, introduce factors that undermine the effectiveness of the very policy lever we employ. Of course we will always be plagued by uncertainty. We are in no position to predict many of the unintended outcomes of our policies. But some we can predict if only we think about them in the right way.

The failure of the California class-size reduction programme may well be a case in point. The reduction in class-size was rolled out state-wide over a very short time. That necessitated the hurried hire of a large number of new teachers and in consequence teaching quality went down (Bohrnstedt and Stecher, 2002). But teaching quality is a slice of the same pie as small class size: Reducing class size cannot be expected to increase reading scores without the cooperation of good teaching. The point is that this unintended consequence of the policy implementation is the kind that might well be foretold if careful thought is put towards it. So in producing a practicable guide based on the principles here, one will have to figure out ways to remind users to think about the unintended consequences of their policies and implementations and to help them do so.

PHYSICS EXAMPLE

An object of charge q_1 with centre of mass at a distance $\mathbf{r}'$ from the earth's centre is accelerating at a distance $\mathbf{r}$ from a second object of charge q_2. It is also, of course, subject to the earth's pull. Letting M represent the mass of the earth, the object's acceleration is given by:[17]

$$\text{Acc} = \varepsilon q_1 q_2 / \mathbf{r}^2 + GM/\mathbf{r}'^2$$

The first term (the 'Coulomb acceleration', $\varepsilon q_1 q_2/\mathbf{r}^2$) is **sufficient**—it is enough—to obtain a contribution to the acceleration. But it is **unnecessary**. There are a lot of other causes that can contribute to the acceleration even if the Coulomb force isn't there. So too with the second term (the 'acceleration due to gravity', $GM/\mathbf{r}'^2$): The presence of the earth's mass a distance $\mathbf{r}'$ away is sufficient for producing a contribution to the acceleration but it is not necessary.

Consider next q_1. Without it there is no Coulomb force. So it is a **necessary** part of the first term. But it is **insufficient** since it cannot produce a contribution to the acceleration on its own but only in consort with another charge (q_2)

[17] Assuming there are no other forces at work and ignoring the generally negligible gravitational attraction between the two objects themselves.

and some separation ($\mathbf{r}$). The same is true of each of the other factors appearing in the first term, as well as of the factors M and $\mathbf{r}'$ in the second term.

The factors q_1, q_2, $\mathbf{r}$, M, and $\mathbf{r}'$ are all *causes* of the acceleration in anybody's books. And they are each, as Mackie claims, INUS conditions; each is insufficient but necessary to a causal complex that is sufficient for obtaining a contribution to the acceleration, but no one of these sufficient causal complexes is necessary for a contribution. Moreover, we know the functional form of the relation between the factors.

Functional form

Merely knowing what the INUS conditions are is less helpful than knowing the formal relationship among the factors—but we need to know what the factors are before we can investigate their relations. In the physics example we know the *full functional form* for the production of acceleration: We know all the possible causes; we know which ones combine together to make a single complex sufficient for producing a contribution; we know the functional form for their mutual relations within the complexes—e.g. the distance in the Coulomb term appears in the denominator and is squared; and we know how the contributions combine to produce an overall effect—by vector addition.

There are standard methods used in the social sciences, and especially in econometrics, for teasing out aspects of the full functional form of the relations between causes and effects, and clearly physics has been very successful at this. That's ideal for predicting causal counterfactuals. Most often for real policy cases in real time, however, there is little hope for much headway on the full functional form. That is why we have opted to focus on INUS contributions—at least with a reasonable understanding of these one will know what auxiliaries are necessary if the policy variable is to have a hope of being effective. But it is worth having the ideal in mind since it is structurally like the less ideal cases that must be dealt with in social policy.

Some philosophical niceties

DICHOTOMOUS VARIABLES VERSUS CONTRIBUTIONS

Mackie introduced INUS conditions in the context of dichotomous variables, that is, a variable that takes yes/no values. Does the patient survive; does the magnet lift the pin; does the bicyclist sustain a head injury? For Mackie a complete cause is a sufficient condition for an effect in the logician's sense of 'sufficient': The presence of the complete cause implies the presence of the effect. In this case there is no question of how different complete causes combine. If C implies E then C and C' implies E, no matter what C' is. So if any one sufficient condition for an effect is present, the effect is present; adding more makes no difference.

Many of the effects of interest in social policy are not dichotomous however but can take a variety of values, like acceleration in our second example. That is, the variables of interest are multi-valued rather than dichotomous. In these cases each complete causal complex operating on its own will produce some value for the effect. But when they act together the effect will be different from that produced by any one alone. Each affects the value of the outcome but does not determine it. When this happens, one can talk about the *contribution* the complete causal complex makes to the effect, as we did in the physics example. Then the possibilities for the rules about how causes combine multiply. The most obvious are simple addition and subtraction. But there are many other possibilities, as in the vector addition of mechanics or log linear combination prevalent in economics. These are the rules needed for the second component of an ideal causal model of the kind we urge above (*What is a causal model?*, p. 298).

Now that we have made explicit the difference between how causes work together in the case of dichotomous versus multi-valued effects, it is time to tidy up an earlier formulation. We urge 'Causes are INUS conditions'. But we did not say *for what* they are INUS conditions though our language in discussing the examples reveals that there are two different answers. For dichotomous effects a cause is an INUS condition for the existence of the effect. For multi-valued effects causes are INUS conditions for the existence of *a contribution to the effect*. In the physics example for instance where both the Coulomb force and the force of gravity contribute to the acceleration, q_1 and q_2 are both insufficient but necessary parts of a causal complex, $\varepsilon q_1 q_2 / r^2$, that is itself sufficient for a contribution to acceleration but not necessary since a contribution to acceleration can come from other sources, like gravity (for more on 'contributions' see *inter alia* Cartwright, 2007 and 2009). Throughout we will continue to use the expression 'INUS condition for effect X' ambiguously to refer to INUS conditions for the presence of X when X is dichotomous and to refer to INUS conditions for a contribution to X when X is multi-valued.

NOT ALL INUS CONDITIONS ARE CAUSES

Causes, we say, are INUS conditions. Beware. We do not say, 'INUS conditions are causes'. The reason is the well-known problem of spurious correlation. Two factors can be correlated without either causing the other; similarly two factors can be sufficient for each other without either causing the other.

Consider a simple case of dichotomous variables, where one factor C causes both E and E', neither of which has any other causes. Then both E and E' occur if and only if C occurs, which implies that E occurs if and only if E' occurs. So E and E' are each sufficient for each other. So we don't claim that all INUS conditions are causes. But we agree with Mackie and other philosophers that causes are INUS conditions, either for their effects or for contributions to the effects.

Why fuss about INUS conditions?

Usually when discussing policy one focuses on a single cause, that is, a single INUS condition. But it is not possible to predict the effect of that cause without considering *all the other INUS conditions* and *the relations among them.*[18] Thinking in terms of INUS conditions then serves several purposes:

- It focuses attention on the fact that there are usually a number of distinct causal complexes that contribute to the effect. (So one doesn't expect the match to light the logs without the dry brush.)
- It focuses attention on the other factors that are necessary along with the policy variable if the policy is to have any effect at all. (So we don't bother to rent the magnet if the rubbish isn't ferrous.)
- It focuses attention on the functional form of the relations of the variables within a single causal complex. (So we expect that increasing the separation between charges does not increase but decreases the Coulomb acceleration because the separation is in the denominator.)
- It focuses attention on the overall functional form: How do the separate causal complexes combine? (Recall our earlier remark. Often in social contexts one assumes additivity. But that doesn't work in even simple physical cases. The vector addition of classical mechanics is after all a long way from the simple linear (scalar) addition of effect sizes.)

And the notion of INUS *contribution* is useful because it more adequately accounts for the facts that most effect variables, or outcomes of interest, are not dichotomous and that most causal factors themselves contribute to the effect to varying degrees rather than dichotomously.

---

[18] Sometimes we are only interested in estimating what difference the policy will make and even then sometimes only the direction of change so that we can get by without an estimate of size. For that we clearly need somewhat less information. To be discussed in Part IV.

Two central principles for a theory of use

We now have two assumptions that form the core of a theory of evidence for policy effectiveness:

> *Principle 1*: A good way to evaluate whether a policy will be effective for a targeted outcome is to employ a 'causal model' comprising
> - A list of causes of the targeted outcome that will be at work when the policy is implemented
> - A rule for calculating the resultant effect when these causes operate together.
>
> *Principle 2*: Causes are INUS conditions.

III. The neglected questions

With these two theoretical principles in place we return to the three issues of quality, relevance and evaluation. If one is to evaluate policy counterfactuals via causal models, as we propose, this imposes criteria of relevance and also affects the standards of quality. A causal model, even if rough and approximate, requires a great deal more information than we are in the habit of looking for.

> *Requisite information for evaluating policy effectiveness*: Information is needed about:
> - The causal factors that will operate:
>   - o   What factors causally relevant to the targeted outcome are in the situation? This breaks naturally into two questions:
>   - What's there?
>   - Is it causally relevant?
>   - o   What factors that are introduced during implementation will be causally relevant? Again this breaks into two questions:
>   - What will we do?
>   - What factors among those we introduce will be causally relevant?
> - How these combine in producing the effect. Here one should pay particular attention to
>   - o   What auxiliary factors are necessary along with the policy variable to produce the targeted effect?
>   - o   How do different factors within a single complex (different segments of the same pie) combine?
>   - o   How do different causal complexes (different pies) combine?

These are empirical questions and any answers that are proposed should have evidence to support them. This sets our criterion of relevance:

An empirical claim is *evidentially relevant* to a policy effectiveness estimate just in case it helps to establish:

i.   What's there in the target situation
ii. What will be introduced in implementing the policy
iii. The causal relevance of any of the above factors for the targeted effect
iv. The method of calculating joint effects.

This formulation does not eliminate questions of relevance; it only pushes them back a level. One still needs to know what kinds of evidence are relevant for establishing what's there, what factors are causally relevant, and for claims of how they combine. The point at the moment is that relevance is a far broader church than the one we are used to practising in. In principle one should have evidence for all the components that need to be used in supporting an effectiveness claim. In practice some facts will be fairly obvious and not need much evidencing; and one will necessarily take a good many shortcuts. But the task for this paper is not to jump into shortcuts but rather to lay a principled foundation for judging policy effectiveness, including evaluating shortcuts and deciding how much to bet on them.

The broad-church relevance criteria in turn affect issues of quality. Most current guides focus on the quality of *efficacy* claims. Depending on context and philosophical leanings, these can be read as claims that the policy can work, or that it does work under specific conditions, or about its average effect in a particular population under special implementations across some range of conditions. Efficacy claims help support the causal relevance of the policy variable, which is part of category iii. The usual ranking schemes police the quality of efficacy claims. But how should the quality of the other kinds of claims needed as evidence for the remainder be policed?

This issue needs to be faced and dealt with, however fallibly, in designing a well-grounded comprehensive advice guide, convenient as it would be to ignore it. Recall our cautions about chains of argument. It is no use having one or two highly certain premises in arguing for or against policy effectiveness. The conclusion can be no more certain than the weakest premise. In adopting a policy, one is betting, willy-nilly, that all the requisite questions have the right kinds of answers. One can do that on a wing and a prayer. But that is not an evidence-based decision. So it is important to figure out reasonable and usable sets of advice about how to manage the need for evidence and not to institutionalise ignoring the need.

Here is probably where Nancy Cartwright first got into trouble with those who maintain that RCT-backed policies are the only ones with a reasonable evidence base. We are happy to take RCTs as a gold standard—for something. In our view they are provably good at establishing efficacy conclusions, as are a number of other methods, such as deduction from sound theory and certain econometric methods (See 'Causal Claims: Warranting Them and Using Them', in Cartwright, 2007). But that is from the point of view of the evidence producer.

Evidence users want to know if a policy will work for them. That, as everyone has really known all along and as we have been stressing here, requires a lot more information than the information supplied by an RCT or a good econometric model that establishes the efficacy of the policy variable; and that information needs evidence, including evidence about what can often be a really tough question—how the causes combine.

Things look very different when one surveys the problem from the user's point of view from how they do when looked at from the point of view of the scientist charged with producing sound results to offer up as evidence.[19] Imagine we are offered two policies. One has very good RCT evidence in favour of its efficacy but we have very weak ideas and information about what the requisite helping factors and major inhibitors for it are. The second is a policy that comes with a theory that suggests what helping factors are needed—and these are ones that are either in place for us or cheap to put in place. Suppose the theory has some reasonable evidence in its favour and the associated policy has some evidence for efficacy, but not gold standard? Which has stronger evidential support in favour of its claim to be effective if we implement it?

This is a question that depends on the actual details and in many cases there won't be any very good answer. But sometimes normal educated judgement will—and should—reasonably go for the second policy though the evidence for its efficacy is clearly less compelling. That's why we made such an issue at the start of this paper about chains of support, which are only as strong as their weakest link. Adding more rigour at one point can raise the overall probability that the policy will be effective but that increase in probability can be offset by too much guessing later on. We do not have guides that provide enough of the right kind of advice considering all that is required.

---

[19] It is because we are concerned with evidence users rather than evidence producers that we do not talk of 'external validity'. External validity starts with a result and asks where outside the experimental context it will obtain. The answer is generally 'not many places', especially for RCT results where there is good reason to expect the same result only in situations where the effect has the same set of causal factors and the probabilities over these are the same. The problem for users is not how to use some special nugget of well-established result but rather how to assemble and treat all the evidence that can help with all the issues involved in estimating what will happen in their specific case.

It would be wrong of course to suggest that these other issues have not been tackled at all. A lot of hard work and serious thought has been put into what is already available. But much of it is piecemeal, directed at specific problems, starting from specific places in midflow. We need a foundation that considers the problem of evaluating effectiveness of counterfactuals as a whole. It is only on the basis of such a foundation that one will be in a position to judge how reasonable it is to leave out specific considerations, to take specific shortcuts and to make specific heroic assumptions. The theoretical foundation proposed here is meant to do that job. It is not the only one possible but it is a foundation laid specifically with a view that practicable advice needs to be built up from it.

IV. Making life somewhat easier

Perhaps suggesting that we want to provide an advice guide based on the idea of constructing a causal model sounds like a tall order. Sometimes it is, particularly when there is a demand for very precise predictions or predictions that one can be very sure of. But we should not be too frightened of the project. For it is one we are well used to. We regularly build causal models in making decisions in our daily lives as we think through the possible effects of our actions and policies. Consequently the schema should not be seen as too exotic or impractical. It, or something like it, is used all the time.

For example, recently Nancy's favourite red-and-white-striped tee shirt was soiled looking. Should she wash it in hot water? Well: Hot water only works if the shirt has a reasonable amount of cotton in it and it won't work against coffee or ink stains. Even with cotton it can be counterproductive if the hot water makes the stripes run. And she knows that she has to be especially careful in loading a hot wash since the shirt will go grey if some dark socks are inadvertently included. All told, given her cotton shirt with garden dirt and the determination to be careful in loading the machine, she reckoned (correctly) that the shirt would come out clean in a hot water wash.

This is a homely example but it illustrates our claim that people build what we call 'causal models' all the time when making policy decisions. The problem for evidence-based policy is how to use evidence to build them better and to estimate the degree of confidence policy analysts should have in the results of their efforts.

Perhaps you do not find this familiar kind of example comforting. The idea of insisting on causal models stills sounds too daunting. Nevertheless, Nature will use a causal model to decide what outcomes to produce when we implement our policies whether we wish to follow her lead or not. The right answers to the questions of quality and relevance will depend on the models she chooses. So, daunting or not, advice on these questions should reflect that.

We can, however, sometimes make the job less daunting. Consider: We would in general like to be able to predict the actual value of the effect that would follow the implementation of a proposed policy. By *just how much* will household burglaries drop if a community-wide property marking program is adopted? But often that will be difficult because we do not know how to predict what else will be going on. What other causes of burglaries will be in place at the time? Often we cannot assume that the causes will be the same then as they are now. (This is the reason J. S. Mill said economics cannot be an inductive science.) So we can't estimate what other 'sufficient' causal complexes will be at work contributing to the outcome, let alone what their combined effect will be. In these cases we may be satisfied with reasonable assurance that the policy will produce an improvement in the effect over what would be the case without it, whatever that is. If so, life is somewhat easier.

In this case establishing just a couple of facts will allow us to ignore the other sufficient causal complexes (all the other 'pies') and concentrate on those that include the policy variable.[20] What we need to know is that no alternative complex of causes will be so dominant that it swamps the policy complex, either positively or negatively, making its effects negligible. For instance, there is no point offering a low cholesterol diet to improve longevity to a man who will be executed in the morning. Nor in installing a fancy electronic lock on Nancy's old Rover sedan since, her daughter assures her, there is no chance that it will be stolen.

So ... if we are content to settle for the claim that the policy will make an improvement on what would otherwise have been the case were the policy not implemented and we have good enough reason to think that nothing will swamp the effects of the policy, then we are justified in focusing just on the policy variable and the factors necessary for it to succeed in producing the targeted effect.

A warning reminder is worth making however. We all know that a successful policy—one that did indeed produce an improvement over what would have been—can easily be judged a failure if it does not produce an improvement over what used to be. Policy consumers are apt to be unimpressed by the

---

[20] Complex relations between the sufficient causes are possible however, so sometimes even for these kinds of cases it is not a good idea to ignore other causal complexes. Suppose, for example, that adjusting one component cause of a cluster (one slice of a pie) modifies another component cause of the same cluster—the example about bicycle helmets illustrated this—then, if the secondary modified component is also a component of another cluster, the effect of the second sufficient cluster will be modified.

claim: 'Yes things have got worse. But they would have been far worse still if we hadn't acted as we did' even if it is true. In these cases one needs to have a good account of what other causes operated to counter the policy effects and good evidence that that is really the correct story.

V. Mechanisms: a principle in aid of practical advice

The primary purpose of the 'theory of evidence for use' is to provide principled grounds for practical advice. To this end we propose to borrow one more tenet from our colleagues in philosophy to add to the basic principles of the theory, albeit one more informally put.

   Principle 3: Mechanisms matter.

Methodologists like RCTs in part because RCTs provide evidence for causal relations without our having to know the mechanisms by which the cause produces its effect. Policy makers generally share this lack of interest in mechanisms. They are concerned only with whether the policy will produce the targeted results and do not care about the mechanisms that will drive the result. Still, when we want to try to put a cause to work, getting a better understanding of the mechanism can make a big difference. The importance of mechanisms for causal discovery, causal understanding, and causal prediction has been heavily stressed in recent philosophical literature. What though is a mechanism?

   Causation is all the rage in philosophy now; mechanisms are centre stage in the discussion. Not surprisingly then there are a wide variety of different characterisations on offer.[21] Here we are not going to rely on any of these

---

[21] We shall describe some of these approaches in order to stress by contrast that none of these are what we mean by 'mechanism' here. Here we mean an answer to a 'how' question that can help in finding INUS auxiliaries. As to other senses of mechanism: Judea Pearl explores causal models that take the form of linear equations, one equation for each effect variable on the left-hand-side, laying out a complete set of causes for it on the right-hand-side. Many people call these equations 'mechanisms', as in a simple supply and demand model in economics where the equation for the quantity supplied is said to describe 'the supply mechanism'; that for the quantity demanded, 'the demand mechanism'. Nancy Cartwright (cf. Cartwright, 1999 and 2007) talks about a mechanism (or a 'nomological machine') as a fixed (enough) arrangement of parts that when set running can give rise to stable in-put/out-put relations. For our UCSD colleague William Bechtel, 'A mechanism is a structure performing a function in virtue of its component parts, component operations, and their organization. The orchestrated functioning of the mechanism is responsible for one or more phenomena' (Bechtel and Abrahamsen, 2005). Alternatively Peter Machamer, Lindley Darden and Carl Craver (2000) define mechanisms as 'entities and activities organized such that they are productive of regular changes from start or set-up to finish or termination conditions'.

(including Cartwright's) since they are generally both too narrow and too abstract to be of help to those non-expert in the sciences. Rather, we make use of an informal notion of mechanism common to many of the formal accounts. This is a notion that can provide a help for policy makers—a prod for the imagination—in identifying the auxiliary factors (the other INUS conditions) that are necessary along with the policy variable to produce the targeted effect. For these purposes we take a mechanism to be an answer to the question:

How would the policy variable bring about the desired effect?

Two different ways of answering can help in finding auxiliary factors:

1   Trace out the causal pathway from policy variable to effect. Seeing what should come next at each step helps focus on what would be required in addition to the policy variable to make the next step happen.

2   Many social results are achieved by calling into play general, often familiar, routine phenomena, such as loyalty, mother-love, fear of punishment, desire to conform, desire to be recognised. Different helping factors will be required besides the policy variable to set different general mechanisms into operation. So recognising which general mechanisms will be called on can be a big help in identifying the necessary auxiliaries.

Tracing the causal pathway: an example from economics

Robert Lucas famously argues that it is generally counterproductive for governments to intervene to regulate the economy on the basis of observed regularities (1976). That's because people will figure out what is happening and act differently, thereby undermining the very regularity the government depends on for predicting the effects of its policies. One of his striking examples is that of the Phillips curve, the empirically observed trade-off between inflation and unemployment that was used by policy makers in the 1950s and 1960s to control unemployment via inflation. Lucas uses a 'rational expectations' model to show that the Philips curve will break down if people know what the government is doing. His model reflects a story that answers the question, '*How* does rising inflation produce a lowered rate of unemployment?' In so doing it unearths some crucial auxiliary factors that have to be in place besides inflation if inflation is to reduce unemployment.

We have seen a version of the Phillips curve already, above, p. 299, in 'Had we world enough and time'.

$$(*) \ y_t = \theta\beta[p_t - p_{t-1}] - \theta\beta\pi + y_{pt} + \varepsilon_t.$$

According to this equation an increase in p should make for an increase in output. We can suppose that an increase in output will in turn lead to an increase in employment. Hence the equation describes a trade-off between inflation and unemployment. But it is of no use for policy, says Lucas. His story goes like this: How much output suppliers produce depends on the price they expect their good to sell for and on what they expect their expenses to be. In the Lucas model the average price for goods in the economy serves as a proxy for expense. So in the model the amount of a good supplied in a given period depends on the ratio of the price of the good to the expected economy-wide price for goods in that period. Lucas assumes that suppliers will be good guessers about the economy-wide price: The economy-wide price that they expect is the average economy-wide price that actually obtains. In this case overall output of a good will be proportional to the ratio of the price of the good to the mean of economy-wide prices. So the output of a good will be greater when the price of the good exceeds the mean of prices across the economy. That means that there will be a positive relationship between output and price increase. Another causal process that we won't describe provides Okun's law, under which increases in output lead to increases in employment. The two processes together thus imply that rising prices will reduce unemployment.

What happens if the government decides to intervene to increase inflation over what it would have been? Assuming that the Phillips curve (along with Okun's law) still holds, unemployment should go down. Not so, Lucas argues, because suppliers are good estimators of the effects of the government action on average price. If they know about the government's actions, they will predict the average price rise that will in fact occur. The expression for output of a good has price for the good in the numerator and, assuming suppliers are good estimators, average price rise in the denominator, recall. So the rise in price suppliers see for their product, which appears in the numerator, will prompt an increase in output only if it is not offset by the increase in the average prices in the denominator that inflation will entail. Indeed, if the denominator goes up proportionately faster than the numerator, the government policy to increase prices in the economy can even create a drop in output and thereby cause an increase in unemployment.

Where in equation * do we see this important factor—the average of economy-wide prices? It is hidden in θ. But rehearsing the causal process step-by-step, as in the Lucas story, brings it out of hiding. The only way that inflation can increase output is if the average price rise this involves does not result in an increase in the overall price rise expected by suppliers big enough to offset the rise in price the suppliers see for their own products. The trade-off between inflation and unemployment holds when it does because suppliers do not expect the overall rise in prices. Thus the requisite helping factor on the Lucas story—the INUS factor necessary to allow inflation to work its lowering effects on unemployment—is the failure of the suppliers to foretell the inflation. That suggests that if the government is going to succeed in the strategy of encouraging inflation in order to reduce unemployment it had better not let people know that that is what it is doing.

This case illustrates two points of interest here. Equations are nice because they express precise quantitative relationships. Still, true equations may leave a lot out and especially a lot we need to know for policy success. Even equations that are 100% descriptively accurate can fail to lay out all the INUS factors necessary to enable the cause they picture to produce the expected effect. Second, thinking through the causal process step-by-step—answering a *how* question—can make these helping factors apparent.

Identifying the means of production: a criminology example

We quote an example from Nick Tilley (2009) at length to illustrate how thinking about the general mechanisms called into play by the policy variable in order to produce the effect can also help in identifying auxiliary factors:

> Take property marking. What is it about it that is expected to 'work' as a crime prevention measure? Property marking might increase the risk to offenders by making it more likely that they will be caught with stolen property, successfully prosecuted and punished. This in turn may mean:
>
> 1   More offenders are incapacitated,
> 2   Some offenders are deterred from future crime,
> 3   And/or other prospective offenders are deterred as they come to appreciate what will happen to them if they try to commit the crime.
>
> Alternatively (or in addition), the perceived increased risk of apprehension, regardless of the reality:
>
> 4   May lead (some) prospective offenders not to commit crime in the first place.
>
> For property marking to 'work' in relation to any individual offender in the first way,
>
> (a)   Property that is liable to be stolen has to be marked,
> (b)   Offenders have to fail to remove or disguise the marks,
> (c)   Authorities have to check that property that might be stolen has property marks on it,
> (d)   Police have to link the marked property back to those from whom it has been taken,
> (e)   Those found with the stolen property have to be unable to cook up a plausible enough story about why they legitimately have it in their possession,
> (f)   The prosecutor has to be persuaded that the case is worth taking to court,
> (g)   The judge/jury have to be persuaded by the evidence,

(h)   A custodial sentence has to be passed, and

(i)   There have to be offences that the incarcerated person would otherwise be committing but for the fact that he or she is in prison.

For property marking to work in the second way, (a–i) have to be in place, and

(j)   the penalty has to be sufficiently salient that the offender makes decisions that do not lead to further offences or which lead to fewer offences.

For property marking to work in the third way (a-j) have to be in place, and

(k)   Prospective offenders need to know, appreciate and sufficiently fear the penalties applied that they will make decisions not to commit offences that they would otherwise commit.

For property marking to work in the fourth way (a–k) need not be in place, but,

(l)   Prospective offenders must know that property is (or may very likely) be marked

(m)   Prospective offenders must be persuaded that the marking significantly increases their risks of being caught and penalised if they steal the marked goods, and

(n)   The expected penalties must be sufficient to lead them to decide not to commit the offences they would otherwise commit....

Thus, what might work to bring about a crime drop through property marking depends on contextual contingencies.

Tilley's 'contextual contingencies' are just the auxiliary factors we have been talking about in discussing INUS conditions, factors that must be in place along with property marking in order for property marking to bring about a drop in crime. Focusing, as he recommends, on *how* property marking is supposed to achieve these results directs attention to these essential factors.

VI. In sum

Our aim has been to lay the foundations for constructing a comprehensive advice guide for evaluating policy effectiveness claims, a guide that is practicable and at the same time rests on sound general principles. To this end we propose three principles. First, policy effectiveness claims are really causal counterfactuals and the proper evaluation of a causal counterfactual requires a causal model that (i) lays out the causes that will operate and (ii) tells what they produce in combination. Second, causes are INUS conditions, so it is important to review both the different causal complexes that will affect the result (the different pies) and the different components (slices) that are necessary to act together within each complex (or pie) if the targeted result is to be achieved. Third, a good answer to the question 'How will the policy variable produce the effect' can help elicit the set of auxiliary factors that must be in place along with the policy variable if the policy variable is to operate successfully.

A guide based on these principles will have to help users construct their own causal models and use evidence to judge how good they are. It should also provide shortcuts, what Gerd Gigerenzer has called 'cheap heuristics', that can achieve near enough the same conclusions with less input (Gigerenzer, Todd, and the ABC Research Group, 2000). Most of these will apply only in special conditions. Part of the job before offering them to users will be to show that these shortcuts are indeed good ones in the right circumstances, then to describe the circumstances for the users in a way that can be understood and applied.

All this is something of a tall order for users. That just makes our job hard. We need to do the best we can to help those who need to evaluate effectiveness do so as well as possible, even if the process will inevitably be flawed. Recognising that it will be flawed means making clear that policy effectiveness judgements will almost never be very secure; and so far as possible, one should hedge one's bets on them. It does not mean giving up on the attempt to construct a causal model, or alternatively defending that a particular short cut will do almost as well. For, as we have stressed, when one bets on an effectiveness counterfactual, one is betting, willy-nilly, on the causal model that underwrites it. The whole point of evidence-based policy is that bets like this should be taken consciously and be as well informed by evidence as is practicable. It's no good ducking the problem. We'd better just get on with figuring out how to make this as simple and user friendly as possible.

References

Bechtel, W. and Abrahamsen, A. (2005), 'Explanation: a mechanistic alternative', *Studies in History and Philosophy of the Biological and Biomedical Sciences*, 36: 421–41.

Bohrnstedt, G. W. and Stecher, B. M. (eds.) (2002), 'What we have learned about class size reduction in California' (Sacramento, CA, California Department of Education).

Cartwright, N. (1999), *The Dappled World* (Cambridge, Cambridge University Press).

Cartwright, N. (2007), *Hunting Causes and Using Them* (Cambridge, Cambridge University Press).

Cartwright, N. (2009), 'Causal laws, policy predictions and the need for genuine powers', in Toby Handfield (ed.), *Dispositions and Causes* (Oxford, Oxford University Press), pp. 127–58.

Cooper, H., Robinson, J. C. and Patall, E. A. (2006), 'Does homework improve academic achievement? A synthesis of research 1987–2003', *Review of Educational Research*, 76: 1–62.

Dunn, W. (2003), *Public Policy Analysis* (New York, Prentice Hall).

Gigerenzer, G., Todd, P. M. and ABC Research Group (2000), *Simple Heuristics that Make Us Smart* (New York, Oxford University Press).

Kolata, G. (2008), 'New Arena for Testing of Drugs: Real World', *New York Times*, 4 Nov. 2008. Accessible at: <http://www.nytimes.com/2008/11/25/health/research/25trials.html?_r=1>.

Lane, D. C., Monefeldt, C. and Rosenhead, J. V. (2000), 'Looking in the wrong place for healthcare improvements: a system dynamics study of an accident and emergency department', *Journal of the Operational Research Society*, 5: 518–31.

Lindblom, C. (1979), *Usable Knowledge* (New Haven, CT, Yale University Press).

Lucas, R. (1976), 'Econometric Policy Evaluation: A Critique', *Carnegie-Rochester Conference Series on Public Policy*, 1: 19–46.

Machamer, P., Darden, L. and Craver, C. (2000), 'Thinking about mechanisms', *Philosophy of Science*, 67: 1–25.

Mackie, J. L. (1965), 'Causes and conditions', *American Philosophical Quarterly*, 2: 245–64.

Pearl, J. (1995), 'Causal Diagrams for Empirical Research', *Biometrika*, 82: 669–88.

Pearl, J. (2000), *Causality: models, reasoning and inference* (Cambridge, Cambridge University Press).

Reiss, J. (2007), *Error in Economics: towards a more evidence-based methodology* (London, Routledge).

Robinson, D. L. (2006), 'No clear evidence from countries that have enforced the wearing of helmets', *British Medical Journal*, 332: 722–5; numerous letters in response, available online at: <http://www.bmj.com/cgi/eletters/332/7543/722-a>.

Tilley, N. (2009) 'What's the "what" in "what works?"? Health, policing and crime prevention', in J. Knutsson and N. Tilley (eds.), *Evaluating Crime Reduction. Crime Prevention Studies*, vol. 24 (Monsey, NY, Criminal Justice Press).

12

In Praise of Randomisation:
The Importance of Causality in Medicine
and its Subversion by Philosophers
of Science

DAVID COLQUHOUN

Abstract

It sounds like an easy job to find out whether a proposed medical treatment works or not. In fact it is surprisingly difficult and expensive to do properly. The necessary principles of randomisation and blindness were all laid down by R. A. Fisher in the 1930s, and have since been elaborated into fairly foolproof ways of getting the answer.

The problems arise when randomisation can't be done, or isn't done because of ignorance or laziness. It is because of the difficulty of randomisation of diets that so little is known about important subjects like the effects of what you eat on your health. That field is rife with dubious assumptions of causality, exemplified by the question of whether eating red meat really causes colon cancer. The hazards of epidemiology are illustrated by the case of hormone replacement therapy in which impeccable cohort studies on large numbers of people gave the wrong answer, and the policy based on the non-randomised studies was responsible for unnecessary deaths.

It would be nice to think that the philosophy of science had made some contribution to this effort. Sadly, though, many of the contributions made in recent years have taken us a step backwards. One of the reasons for this lies in the fact that some sections of the philosophy of science seem to show an influence of the long-discredited postmodernist school of thought. The intellectual standing of their relativist viewpoint appears to be not very different from that of the parallel universe school of thought favoured by homeopaths and other pedlars of ineffective medicines.

Proceedings of the British Academy, **171**, 323–343. © The British Academy 2011.

I TAKE IT TO BE the job of scientists to try to distinguish between what is true from what is false by means of observation and experiment. That job has been made harder by some philosophers of science who appear to give academic respectability to relativist, and even postmodernist, postures. Luckily it has not been made very *much* harder, because these philosophers argue mainly with each other and practising scientists are hardly aware of their existence.

There is, I maintain, no real problem of any importance in the nature of evidence in most laboratory experiments. My real job is investigation of single ion channels. The results come in the form of distributions so they are perfectly suited to analysis by likelihood methods (Colquhoun *et al.*, 2003; Lape *et al.*, 2008). Of course there are problems in ambiguities about how likelihood is calculated, in indeterminacy of free parameters, in the distinguishability of reaction mechanisms and so on, but these are all quite well understood. Clinical studies are much harder, but when they are designed properly they too can give consistent and strong evidence for the efficacy of a treatment. The problems arise only when it is impossible to do properly designed experiments, or when commercial considerations prevent properly designed experiments being done even when they could be done.

I shall concentrate mainly on clinical studies, because they are where most of the problems arise.

The problems that I see in obtaining evidence to justify the correctness of a proposition fall into several categories. Some of these impediments to discovering the truth are nothing to do with profound principles, but merely reflections of human frailty. Here are some of them. I shall deal here with only the first and last.

1 *Causality.* It isn't always possible to do a proper experiment. In large areas of medicine, the lack of clear evidence for causality is a major problem. Nowhere is that problem greater than in studies of the effect of diet on health. How what we eat affects our health is a question of enormous interest, yet it is a question that is almost impossible to answer.

2 *Commercial bias.* This has been documented widely (e.g. Lexchin and Light, 2006).

3 *Hubris and self-promotion.* The management culture that has engulfed universities has promoted dishonest self-promotion. Bibliometrists, with their futile attempts to sum up scientific achievement with a few numbers, have done as much harm to science as homeopaths and postmodernists

4 *Relativism and postmodernism.* I have left this category to the last, because, harmful though the effects of some philosophers of science may be, they have little influence.

Classification of diseases

In addition to these problems of principle, one suspects that a very major problem arises from the inadequate labels that are given to the conditions that are being tested. If you are testing a treatment for tuberculosis or malaria, the definition of the condition is pretty clear, but if you are trying to treat epilepsy or depression it is very far from clear. Even for conditions that are caused by single amino acid mutations in proteins of known function, it has turned out that there isn't just a single mutation that causes the disease, In conditions like slow channel congenital myasthenic syndrome (mutation in the nicotinic acetylcholine receptor), or hyperekplexia (mutation in the glycine receptor), there are almost as many single amino acid mutations as there are families with the condition. Each mutation causes a rather similar malfunction of the protein, and so a rather similar phenotype, but there is not just one hyperekplexia but dozens. The same, presumably, will turn out to be true of much more complex conditions like epilepsy and depression. This may be a big problem but it can't stop one trying and isn't a problem of principle so it won't be discussed further here.

I shall use the case of hormone replacement therapy to illustrate the importance of randomisation, and the case of processed meat and cancer to illustrate the problems that arise in the absence of randomised tests. Finally I shall discuss the opposition to randomisation that has come from some philosophers of science.

Causality and randomisation

It was clearly established in the 1930s, largely by R. A. Fisher, that random assignment of treatments to patients (or in his case, usually field plots) was the essential underlying condition for causal inference. He also established the idea of estimation by maximising likelihood and so provided a solution to the problem of inverse probability.

Randomisation is a rather beautiful idea. It allows one to remove, in a statistical sense, bias that might result from all the sources that you hadn't realised were there. If you are aware of a source of bias, then measure it. The danger arises from the things you don't know about, or can't measure (Senn, 2003, 2004). Although it guarantees freedom from bias only in a long run statistical sense, that is the best that can be done. Everything else is worse. The one essential bit of reading is Fisher's parable of the Lady Tasting Tea (Senn, 2003).

Everyone knows about the problem of causality in principle. *Post hoc ergo propter hoc*; confusion of sequence and consequence; confusion of correlation and cause. This is not a trivial problem. It is probably the main reason why ineffective treatments often appear to work. It is traded on by the vast and unscrupulous alternative medicine industry. It is, very probably, the reason why we are bombarded every day by conflicting advice on what to eat. This is a bad thing, for two reasons. First, we end up confused about what we should eat. But worse still, the conflicting nature of the advice gives science as a whole a bad reputation. Every time a white-coated scientist appears in the media to tell us that a glass of wine per day is good/bad for us (delete according to the phase of the moon) the general public just laugh.

Ben Goldacre has referred memorably to the newspapers' ongoing 'Sisyphean task of dividing all the inanimate objects in the world into the ones that either cause or cure cancer' (Goldacre, 2008). This has even given rise to a blog, 'The Daily Mail Oncological Ontology Project' <http://thedailymail oncologicalontologyproject.wordpress.com/>.

It wouldn't be so bad if the problem were restricted to the media. It is much more worrying that the problem of establishing causality often seems to be underestimated by the authors of papers themselves. It is a matter of speculation why this happens. Part of the reason is, no doubt, a genuine wish to discover something that will benefit mankind. But it is hard to avoid the thought that hubris and self-promotion may also play a role. Anything whatsoever that purports to relate diet to health is guaranteed to get uncritical newspaper headlines.

At the heart of the problem lies the great difficulty in doing randomised studies of the effect of diet and health. There can be no better illustration of the vital importance of randomisation than in this field. And, notwithstanding the generally uncritical reporting of stories about diet and health, one of the best accounts of the need for randomisation was written by a journalist, Gary Taubes, and it appeared in the *New York Times* (Taubes, 2007).

The case of hormone replacement therapy

In the 1990s hormone replacement therapy (HRT) was recommended not only to relieve the unpleasant symptoms of the menopause, but also because cohort studies suggested that HRT would reduce heart disease and osteoporosis in older women. For these reasons, by 2001, 15 million US women (perhaps 5 million older women) were taking HRT (Taubes, 2007). These recommendations were based largely on the Harvard Nurses' Study. This was a prospective cohort study in which 122,000 nurses were followed over time, starting in 1976 (these are the ones who responded out of the 170,000 requests sent out). In 1994, it was said (Manson, 1994) that nearly all of the more than thirty observational studies suggested a reduced risk of coronary heart disease (CHD) among women receiving oestrogen therapy. A meta-analysis gave an estimated 44% reduction of CHD. Although warnings were given about the lack of randomised studies, the results were nevertheless acted upon as though they were true. But they were wrong. When proper randomised studies were done, not only did it turn out that CHD was not reduced: it was actually increased.

The Women's Health Initiative Study (Rossouw *et al.*, 2002) was a randomised double blind trial on 16,608 postmenopausal women aged 50–79 years and its results contradicted the conclusions from all the earlier cohort studies HRT increased risks of heart disease, stroke, blood clots, breast cancer (though possibly helped with osteoporosis and perhaps colorectal cancer). After an average 5.2 years of follow-up, the trial was stopped because of the apparent increase in breast cancer in the HRT group. The relative risk (HRT relative to placebo) of CHD was 1.29 (95% confidence interval (1.02–1.63) (286 cases altogether) and for breast cancer 1.26 (1.00–1.59) (290 cases). Rather than there being a 44% reduction of risk, it seems that there was actually a 30% increase in risk. Notice that these are actually quite small risks, and on the margin of statistical significance. For the purposes of communicating the nature of the risk to an individual person it is usually better to specify the absolute risk rather than relative risk. The absolute number of CHD cases per 10,000 person-years is about twenty-nine on placebo and thirty-six on HRT, so the increased risk to any individual is quite small. Multiplied over the whole population though, the number is no longer small.

Several plausible reasons for these contradictory results are discussed by Taubes (2007): it seems that women who choose to take HRT are healthier than those who don't. In fact the story has been a bit more complicated since then: the effect of HRT depends on when it is started and how long it is taken (Vandenbroucke, 2009).

This is perhaps one of the most dramatic illustrations of the value of randomised controlled trials (RCTs). Reliance on observations of correlations suggested a 44% reduction in CHD, the randomised trial gave a 30% increase in CHD. Insistence on randomisation is not just pedantry. It is essential if you want to get the right answer.

Now back to the 'Sisyphean task of dividing all the inanimate objects in the world into the ones that either cause or cure cancer'.

The case of processed meat

In 2008, just about every newspaper carried a story with a headline like 'Why eating just one sausage a day raises your cancer risk by 20 per cent'. What was the basis for this statement? It was not made by a diet crank or supplement huckster but came from the World Cancer Research Fund report, *Food, nutrition, physical activity, and the prevention of cancer: a global perspective* (Marmot, 2007). This is a very weighty piece of work, chaired by Professor Sir Michael Marmot, famous for his pioneering work on the relationship between poverty and health. As one would expect of an eminent epidemiologist, it considers carefully the problem of causality: chapter 3 is devoted to it. Nonetheless, because most diet studies are not randomised, no amount of careful scrutiny can solve the problem. The recommendations of this study include the following.

1   Don't get overweight.

2   Be moderately physically active, equivalent to brisk walking for at least thirty minutes every day

3   Consume energy-dense foods sparingly. Avoid sugary drinks. Consume 'fast foods' sparingly, if at all.

4   Eat at least five portions/servings (at least 400 g or 14 oz) of a variety of non-starchy vegetables and of fruits every day. Eat relatively unprocessed cereals (grains) and/or pulses (legumes) with every meal. Limit refined starchy foods.

5   People who eat red meat to consume less than 500 g (18 oz) a week, very little if any to be processed.

6   If alcoholic drinks are consumed, limit consumption to no more than two drinks a day for men and one drink a day for women.

7   Avoid salt-preserved, salted, or salty foods; preserve foods without using salt. Limit consumption of processed foods with added salt to ensure an intake of less than 6 g (2.4 g sodium) a day.

8   Dietary supplements are not recommended for cancer prevention.

These all sound pretty sensible but they are very prescriptive. And of course the recommendations make sense only insofar as the various dietary factors *cause* cancer. If the association is not causal, changing your diet won't help. In section 3.4 the report says

> ... causal relationships between food and nutrition, and physical activity can be confidently inferred when epidemiological evidence, and experimental and other biological findings, are consistent, unbiased, strong, graded, coherent, repeated, and plausible.

The case of processed meat is dealt with in chapter 4.3 (p. 148) of the report.

> Sausages, frankfurters, and 'hot dogs', to which nitrates/nitrites or other pre-
> servatives are added, are also processed meats. Minced meats sometimes, but
> not always, fall inside this definition if they are preserved chemically. The same
> point applies to 'hamburgers'.

The evidence for harmfulness of processed meat was described as 'convincing', the highest level of confidence in the report, though this conclusion
has been challenged (Truswell, 2009).

Meat is only harmful if the association is causal. How well does the evidence obey the criteria for the relationship being causal? Twelve prospective
cohort studies showed increased risk for the highest intake group when compared to the lowest (Fig. 12.1), which was statistically significant in three. One
study reported non-significant decreased risk and one study reported that
there was no effect on risk.

> Meta-analysis was possible on five studies, giving a summary effect estimate of
> 1.21 (95% CI 1.04–1.42) per 50 g/day with low heterogeneity (Figs. 12.2 and
> 12.3).

This is presumably where the headline value of a 20% increase in risk came
from.

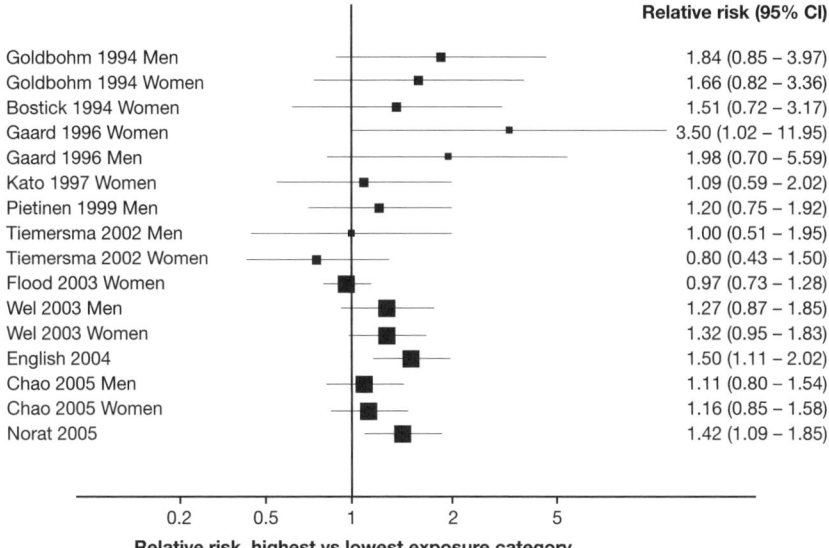

Figure 12.1. Processed meat and colorectal cancer: cohort studies (fig. 4.3.5 in Marmot, 2007).

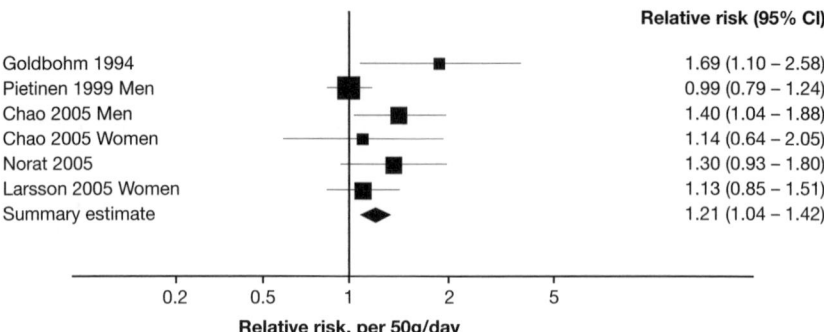

Figure 12.2.   Processed meat and colorectal cancer: cohort studies (fig. 4.3.6 in Marmot, 2007).

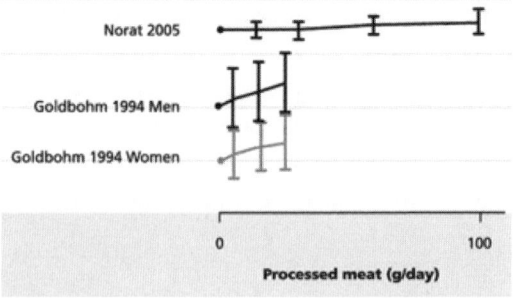

Figure 12.3.   Processed meat and colorectal cancer: dose response (fig. 4.3.7 in Marmot, 2007).

Support came from a meta-analysis of fourteen cohort studies, which reported a relative risk for processed meat of 1.09 (95% CI 1.05–1.13) per 30 g/ day (Larsson and Wolk, 2006). Since then another study has come up with similar numbers (Sinha *et al.*, 2009). This consistency cannot be taken as evidence for causality. Observational studies on HRT were just as consistent, but they were wrong.

The accompanying editorial (Popkin, 2009) points out that there are rather more important reasons to limit meat consumption, like the environmental footprint of most meat production, water supply, deforestation and so on.

So there is certainly some tendency for the relative risk to be just above 1. But being observational data there can be no guarantee that they are unbiased. The size of the effects is quite small. It is smaller than the reported beneficial effect of HRT in observational studies and that effect too was quite consistent, but it was plain wrong.

The other criteria for causality are 'graded, coherent, repeated, and plausible'. Graded means that there is a relationship between intake (dose) and response. The report says

A dose–response relationship was also apparent from cohort studies that measured in times/day (Fig. 12.4).

It is at this point my credulity gets a bit strained. Any pharmacologist looking at the six dose–response curves in Figures 12.3 and 12.4 would say that the technical description would be 'bloody horizontal'. They are certainly the least convincing dose–response relationships I have ever seen. Nevertheless a meta-analysis came up with a slope for response curve that just reached the 5% level of statistical significance.

The conclusion of the report for processed meat and colorectal cancer was as follows.

> There is a substantial amount of evidence, with a dose–response relationship apparent from cohort studies. There is strong evidence for plausible mechanisms operating in humans. Processed meat is a convincing cause of colorectal cancer.

But the dose–response curves (Figs. 12.3 and 12.4) look appalling, and it is reasonable to ask whether public policy should be based on a 1 in 20 chance of being quite wrong (1 in 20 *at best*—see Senn, 2008). I certainly wouldn't want to risk my reputation on odds like that, never mind use it as a basis for public policy. So we are left with plausibility as the remaining bit of evidence for causality.

Anyone who had done much experimental work knows that it is possible to dream up a plausible explanation of any result whatsoever. Most are wrong and so plausibility is a pretty weak argument. Scientists should take heed of the journalist, H. L. Mencken, who said, in 1917,

> there is always a well-known solution to every human problem—neat, plausible, and wrong.

Much play is made on the fact that cured meats contain nitrates and nitrites, but there is no real evidence that the amount they contain is harmful.

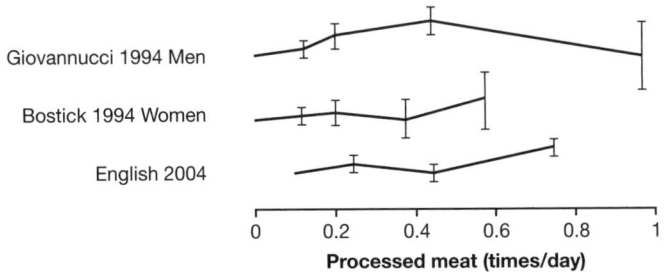

Figure 12.4.   Processed meat and colorectal cancer: cohort studies (fig. 4.3.8 in Marmot, 2007).

The main source of nitrates in the diet is not from meat but from vegetables (especially green leafy vegetables like lettuce and spinach) which contribute 70–90% of total intake. The maximum legal content in processed meat is 10–25 mg/100g, but lettuce contains around 100–400 mg/100g with a legal limit of 200–400 mg/100g. Dietary nitrate intake was not associated with risk for colorectal cancer in two cohort studies (Food Standards Agency, 2004; International Agency for Research on Cancer, 2010).

To add further to the confusion, another cohort study on over 60,000 people compared vegetarians and meat-eaters. Mortality from circulatory diseases and mortality from all causes was not detectably different between vegetarians and meat eaters (Key *et al.*, 2009*b*). Still more confusingly, although the incidence of all cancers combined was lower among vegetarians than among meat eaters, the exception was colorectal cancer which had a *higher* incidence in vegetarians than in meat eaters (Key *et al.*, 2009*a*).

Mente *et al.* (2009) compared cohort studies and RCTs for effects of diet on risk of coronary heart disease. 'Strong evidence' for protective effects was found for intake of vegetables, nuts, and 'Mediterranean diet' and harmful effects of intake of trans-fatty acids and foods with a high glycaemic index. There was also slightly less strong evidence for effects of mono-unsaturated fatty acids and for intake of fish, marine ω-3 fatty acids, folate, whole grains, dietary vitamins E and C, beta carotene, alcohol, fruit, and fibre. But RCTs showed evidence only for 'Mediterranean diet', and none of the others.

As a final nail in the coffin of case–control studies, consider pizza. According to La and Bosetti (2006) data from a series of case–control studies in northern Italy lead to

> An inverse association was found between regular pizza consumption (at least one portion of pizza per week) and the risk of cancers of the digestive tract, with RRs of 0.66 for oral and pharyngeal cancers, 0.41 for oesophageal, 0.82 for laryngeal, 0.74 for colon and 0.93 for rectal cancers.

What is one meant to make of this? Pizza should be prescribable on the National Health Service to produce a 60% reduction in oesophageal cancer? As the authors say 'pizza may simply represent a general and aspecific indicator of a favourable Mediterranean diet'. On the basis of this sort of study, the finding is uninterpretable.

Is the observed association even real?

The most noticeable thing about the effects of red meat and processed meat is not only that they are small but also that they only just reach the 5 per cent level of statistical significance. It has been explained clearly why, in these circumstances real associations are likely to be exaggerated in size (Ioannidis, 2008*b*; Ioannidis, 2008*a*; Senn, 2008) and why many, even most, claimed effects are not real anyway (Ioannidis, 2005). The inflation of the strength of associations is expected to be bigger in small studies, so it is noteworthy that the large meta-analysis by Larsson and Wolk (2006) comments 'In the present meta-analysis, the magnitude of the relationship of processed meat consumption with colorectal cancer risk was weaker than in the earlier meta-analyses.'

This is all consistent with the well known tendency of randomised clinical trials to show initially a good effect of treatment but subsequent trials tend to show smaller effects. The reasons, and the cures, for this worrying problem are discussed by Chalmers (Chalmers, 2006; Chalmers and Matthews, 2006; Garattini and Chalmers, 2009).

What about randomised studies?

The only form of reliable evidence for causality comes from randomised controlled trials. The difficulties in allocating people to diets over long periods of time are obvious and that is no doubt why there are far fewer RCTs than there are observational studies. But when they have been done the results often contradict those from cohort studies. The RCTs of hormone replacement therapy mentioned above contradicted the cohort studies and reversed the advice given to women about HRT.

Three more illustrations of how plausible suggestions about diet can be refuted by RCTs concern nutritional supplements and weight-loss diets.

Many RCTs have shown that various forms of nutritional supplement do no good and may even do harm (see Cochrane reviews <http://bit.ly/krkcr7>). At least we now know that anti-oxidants *per se* do you no good. The idea that anti-oxidants might be good for you was never more than a plausible hypothesis, and like so many plausible hypotheses it has turned out to be a myth. The word anti-oxidant is now no more than a marketing term, though it remains very profitable for unscrupulous salesmen.

The randomised Women's Health Initiative Dietary Modification Trial (Prentice *et al.*, 2007; Prentice, 2007) showed minimal effects of dietary fat on cancer incidence, though the conclusion has been challenged on the basis of the possible inaccuracy of reported diet (Yngve *et al.*, 2006).

Contrary to much dogma about weight loss, Sacks *et al.* (2009) found no differences in weight loss over two years between four very different diets. They assigned randomly 811 overweight adults to one of four diets. The percentages of energy derived from fat, protein, and carbohydrates in the four diets were 20, 15, and 65%; 20, 25, and 55%; 40, 15, and 45%; and 40, 25, and 35%. No difference could be detected between the different diets: all that mattered for weight loss was the total number of calories.

The impression one gets from RCTs is that the details of diet are not as important as has been inferred from non-randomised observational studies.

So does processed meat give you cancer?

After all this, we can return to the original question. Do sausages or bacon give you colorectal cancer? The answer, sadly, is that nobody really knows. I do know that, on the basis of the evidence, it seems to me to be an exaggeration to assert that 'The evidence is convincing that processed meat is a *cause* of bowel cancer.'

In the UK there were around five cases of colorectal cancer per 10,000 population in 2005 <http://info.cancerresearchuk.org/cancerstats/types/bowel/incidence/>, so a 20% increase, even if it were real, and genuinely causative, would result in six rather than five cases per 10,000 people, annually. That makes the risk sound trivial for any individual. On the other hand there were 36,766 cases of colorectal cancer in the UK in 2005. A 20% increase would mean, if the association were causal, about 7,000 extra cases as a result of eating processed meat, but no extra cases if the association were *not* causal.

For the purposes of those making public health policy about diet, the question of causality is crucial. One has sympathy for the difficult decisions that they have to make, because they are forced to decide on the basis of inadequate evidence.

The decision about whether to eat bacon and sausages has to be a personal one. It depends on your attitude to the precautionary principle. My own inclination would be to ignore any relative risk based on observational data if it were less than about 2. The National Cancer Institute (Nelson, 2002) advises that relative risks less than 2 should be 'viewed with caution', though they do not say what 'viewing with caution' means in real life. Hardly any of the relative risks reported in the WCRF report (Marmot, 2007) reach a relative risk of 2. Almost all are less than 1.3 (or greater than 0.7 for alleged protective effects). Perhaps it is best to stop worrying and get on with your life. At some point it becomes counterproductive to try to micromanage people's diet on the basis of dubious data. There is a price to pay for being too precautionary. It runs the risk of making people ignore information that *has* got a sound basis. It runs the risk of excessive medicalisation of everyday life. And it brings science itself into disrepute when people laugh at the contradictory findings of observational epidemiology.

The 2007 report has been updated in <WCRF/AICR Systematic Literature Review Continuous Update Project Report> [pdf file]. This includes studies up to May/June 2010. The result of addition of the new data was to reduce slightly the apparent risk from eating processed meat from 1.21 (95% CI = 1.04–1.42) in the original study to 1.18 (95% CI = 1.10–1.28) in the update. The change is too small to mean much, though it is in the direction expected for false correlations. More importantly, the new data confirm that the dose–response curves are virtually flat. The evidence for causality is weakened somewhat by addition of the new data.

If it were not already obvious, the examples discussed above make it very clear that the only sound guide to causality is a properly randomised trial. The only exceptions to that are when effects are really big. The relative risk of lung cancer for a heavy cigarette smoker is twenty times that of a non-smoker and there is a very clear relationship between dose (cigarettes per day) and response (lung cancer incidence), as shown in Figure 12.5 (Doll and Peto, 1978). That is a 2000% increase in risk, very different from the 20% found for processed meat (and many other dietary effects). Nobody could doubt seriously the causality in that case.

The question of how diet and other 'lifestyle interventions' affect health is fascinating to everyone. There is compelling reason to think that it matters. For example one study demonstrated that breast cancer incidence increased

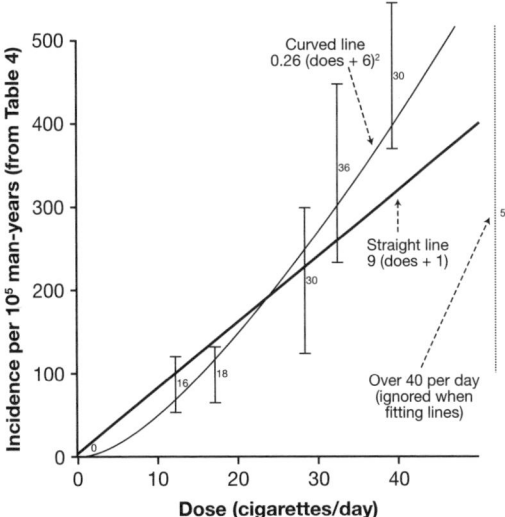

Figure 12.5. Dose–response relationship standardised for age. The numbers of onsets in each group is given, and 90% confidence intervals are plotted (Doll & Peto 1978).

almost threefold in first-generation Japanese women who migrated to Hawaii, and up to fivefold in the second generation (Kolonel, 1980). Since then enormous effort has been put into finding out why. The first great success was cigarette smoking but that is almost the *only* major success. Very few similar magic bullets have come to light after decades of searching (asbestos and mesothelioma, or UV radiation and skin cancer, count as successes). The WCRF report (Marmot, 2007) has over 4,000 references and we still don't know.

The negative contribution of some philosophers of science

It seems surprising that the value of randomisation should still be disputed at this stage, and of course it is not disputed by anybody in the business. There is, though, a body of philosophers who do dispute it. And of course almost all practitioners of alternative medicine dispute it (because their treatments usually fail the tests). I had not come across the philosophers until I joined the London Evidence group, perhaps because I had long since decided that it was Fisher, rather than philosophers, who had the answers to my questions.

'Why there's no cause to randomize' is the rather surprising title of a report by Worrall (2004; see also Worral, 2010) from the London School of Economics. The conclusion of this paper is

> don't believe the bad press that 'observational studies' or 'historically controlled trials' get—so long as they are properly done (that is, serious thought has gone in to the possibility of alternative explanations of the outcome), then there is no reason to think of them as any less compelling than an RCT.

In my view this conclusion is quite wrong—it ignores the enormous difficulty of getting evidence for causality in real life, and it ignores the fact that historically controlled trials have very often given misleading results in the past, as illustrated above. Worrall's fellow philosopher, Nancy Cartwright (2010), has made arguments similar to those of Worrall.

Many words are spent on defining causality but, at least in the clinical setting, the meaning is perfectly simple. If the association between eating bacon and colorectal cancer is causal then if you stop eating bacon you'll reduce the risk of cancer. If the relationship is not causal then if you stop eating bacon it won't help at all. No amount of 'serious thought' will substitute for the real evidence for causality that can come only from an RCT: Worrall seems to claim that sufficient brain power can fill in missing bits of information. It can't. I'm reminded inexorably of the definition of 'Clinical experience. Making the same mistakes with increasing confidence over an impressive number of years' in Michael O'Donnell's *A Sceptic's Medical Dictionary.*

At the other philosophical extreme, there are still a few remnants of post-modernist rhetoric to be found in obscure corners of the literature. Two extreme examples are the papers by Holmes *et al.* and by Christine Barry. Apart from the fact that they weren't spoofs, both of these papers bear a close resemblance to Alan Sokal's famous spoof paper, *Transgressing the boundaries: towards a transformative hermeneutics of quantum gravity* (Sokal, 1996). The acceptance of this spoof by a journal, *Social Text*, and the subsequent book, *Intellectual Impostures* (Sokal and Bricmont, 1998), exposed the astonishing intellectual fraud of postmodernism (for those for whom it was not already obvious). A couple of quotations will serve to give a taste of the amazing material that can appear in peer-reviewed journals. Barry (2006) wrote

> I wish to problematise the call from within biomedicine for more evidence of alternative medicine's effectiveness via the medium of the randomised clinical trial (RCT).

> Ethnographic research in alternative medicine is coming to be used politically as a challenge to the hegemony of a scientific biomedical construction of evidence.

> The science of biomedicine was perceived as old fashioned and rejected in favour of the quantum and chaos theories of modern physics.

> In this paper, I have deconstructed the powerful notion of evidence within biomedicine, ...

The aim of this paper, in my view, is not to obtain some subtle insight into the process of inference but to try to give some credibility to snake-oil salesmen who peddle quack cures. The latter at least make their unjustified claims in plain English.

The similar paper by Holmes, Murray, Perron and Rail (Holmes *et al.*, 2006) is even more bizarre.

> **Objective** The philosophical work of Deleuze and Guattari proves to be useful in showing how health sciences are colonised (territorialised) by an all-encompassing scientific research paradigm 'that of post-positivism' but also and foremost in showing the process by which a dominant ideology comes to exclude alternative forms of knowledge, therefore acting as a fascist structure.

It uses the word fascism, or some derivative thereof, twenty-six times. And Holmes, Perron and Rail (Murray *et al.*, 2007) end a similar tirade with

> We shall continue to transgress the diktats of State Science.

It may be asked why it is even worth spending time on these remnants of the utterly discredited postmodernist movement. One reason is that rather less extreme examples of similar thinking still exist in some philosophical circles.

Take, for example, the views expressed in papers such as Miles, Polychronis and Grey (Miles and Loughlin, 2006), Miles, Loughlin and Polychronis (Miles *et al.*, 2007) and Loughlin (2007). These papers form part of the authors' campaign against evidence-based medicine, which they seem to regard as some sort of ideological crusade, or government conspiracy. Bizarrely they seem to think that evidence-based medicine has something in common with the managerial culture that has been the bane not only of medicine but of almost every occupation (and which is noted particularly for its disregard for evidence). Although couched in the sort of pretentious language favoured by postmodernists, in fact it ends up defending the most simple-minded forms of quackery. Unlike Barry (2006), they don't mention alternative medicine explicitly, but the agenda is clear from their attacks on Ben Goldacre. For example, Miles, Loughlin and Polychronis (Miles *et al.*, 2007) say this.

> Loughlin identifies Goldacre [36] as a particularly luminous example of a commentator who is able not only to combine audacity with outrage, but who in a very real way succeeds in manufacturing a sense of having been personally offended by the article in question. Such moralistic posturing acts as a defence mechanism to protect cherished assumptions from rational scrutiny and indeed to enable adherents to appropriate the 'moral high ground', as well as the language of 'reason' and 'science' as the exclusive property of their own favoured approaches. Loughlin brings out the Orwellian nature of this manoeuvre and identifies a significant implication.
>
> If Goldacre and others really are engaged in posturing then their primary offence, at least according to the Sartrean perspective adopted by Murray *et al.*, is not primarily intellectual, but rather it is moral. Far from there being a moral requirement to 'bend a knee' at the EBM altar, to do so is to 'violate one's primary duty as an autonomous being'.

This ferocious attack seems to have been triggered because Goldacre has explained in simple words what constitutes evidence and what doesn't. He has explained in a simple way how to do a proper randomised controlled trial of homeopathy. And he dismantled a fraudulent Qlink pendant, purported to shield you from electromagnetic radiation, which turned out to have no functional components (Goldacre, 2007). This is described as being 'Orwellian', a description that seems to me to be downright bizarre.

In fact, when faced with real-life examples of what happens when you ignore evidence, those who write theoretical papers that are critical about evidence-based medicine may behave perfectly sensibly. Although Andrew Miles edits a journal that has been critical of EBM for years, when faced with a course in alternative medicine run by people who can only be described as quacks, he rapidly shut down the course (see account by Colquhoun, 2010)

It is hard to decide whether the language used in these papers is Marxist or neoconservative libertarian. Whatever it is, it clearly isn't science. It may seem odd that postmodernists (who believe nothing) end up as allies of quacks (who'll believe anything). The relationship has been explained with customary clarity by Alan Sokal, in his essay 'Pseudoscience and Postmodernism: Antagonists or Fellow-Travelers?' (Sokal, 2004).

Conclusions

Of course RCTs are not the only way to get knowledge. Often they have not been done, and sometimes it is hard to imagine how they could be done (though not nearly as often as some people would like to say).

It is true that RCTs tell you only about an average effect in a large population. But the same is true of observational epidemiology. That limitation is nothing to do with randomisation, it is a result of the crude and inadequate way in which diseases are classified (as discussed above). It is also true that randomisation doesn't guarantee lack of bias in an individual case, but only in the long run. But it is the best that can be done. The fact remains that randomisation is the *only* way to be sure of causality, and making mistakes about causality can harm patients, as it did in the case of HRT.

Raymond Tallis (1999), in his review of Sokal and Bricmont, summed it up nicely

> Academics intending to continue as postmodern theorists in the interdisciplinary humanities after S & B should first read *Intellectual Impostures* and ask themselves whether adding to the quantity of confusion and untruth in the world is a good use of the gift of life or an ethical way to earn a living. After S & B, they may feel less comfortable with the glamorous life that can be forged in the wake of the founding charlatans of postmodern Theory. Alternatively, they might follow my friend Roger into estate agency—though they should check out in advance that they are up to the moral rigours of such a profession.

The conclusions that I have drawn were obvious to people in the business a quarter of a century ago. Doll and Peto (1980) said

> If we are to recognize those important yet moderate real advances in therapy which can save thousands of lives, then we need more large randomised trials than at present, not fewer. Until we have them treatment of future patients will continue to be determined by unreliable evidence.

The towering figures are R. A. Fisher and his followers who developed the ideas of randomisation and maximum likelihood estimation. In the medical area, Bradford Hill, Archie Cochrane and Iain Chalmers had the important ideas worked out a long time ago.

In contrast, philosophers seem to me to make almost no contribution to the accumulation of useful knowledge, and in some cases to hinder it. It is true that the harm they do is limited, but that is because they talk largely to each other. Very few working scientists are even aware of their existence. Perhaps that is just as well.

References

Barry, C. A. (2006), 'The role of evidence in alternative medicine: contrasting bio-medical and anthropological approaches', *Social Science and Medicine*, 62: 2644–57.

Cartwright, N. and Munro, E. (2010), 'The limitations of randomized controlled trials in predicting effectiveness', *J Eval Clin Pract*, 16: 260–6.

Chalmers, I. (2006), 'Biased underreporting of research is unethical and should be outlawed', *Z Arztl Fortbild Qualitatssich*, 100: 531–5.

Chalmers, I. and Matthews, R. (2006), 'What are the implications of optimism bias in clinical research?', *Lancet*, 367: 449–50.

Colquhoun, D., Hatton, C. J. and Hawkes, A. G. (2003), 'The quality of maximum likelihood estimates of ion channel rate constants', *J Physiol (Lond)*, 547: 699–728.

Colquhoun, D. (2010), 'University of Buckingham does the right thing. The Faculty of Integrated Medicine has been fired', <http://www.dcscience.net/?p=2881>.

Doll, R. and Peto, R. (1978), 'Cigarette smoking and bronchial carcinoma: dose and time relationships among regular smokers and lifelong non-smokers', *J Epidemiol Community Health*, 32: 303–13.

Doll, R. and Peto, R. (1980), Randomised controlled trials and retrospective controls, *Br Med J*, 280: 44.

Food Standards Agency (2004), 'UK Monitoring programme for nitrate in lettuce and spinach 2000–2002. 2004' (London, Food Standards Agency).

Garattini, S. and Chalmers, I. (2009), 'Patients and the public deserve big changes in evaluation of drugs', *BMJ*, 338: b1025.

Goldacre, B. (2007), 'The Amazing Qlink Science Pedant', <http://www.badscience.net/2007/05/the-amazing-qlink-science-pedant/>.

Goldacre, B. (2008), 'Still no cure for cancer hysteria', *Guardian* (19 July), 10.

Holmes, D., Murray, S. J., Perron, A. and Rail, G. (2006), 'Deconstructing the evidence-based discourse in health sciences: truth, power and fascism', *International Journal of Evidence-Based Healthcare*, 4: 180–6.

International Agency for Research on Cancer (2010), 'Ingested Nitrate and Nitrite, and Cyanobacterial Peptide Toxins', *IARC Monographs on the Evaluation of Carcinogenic Risks to Humans*, Vol. 94 (Lyons) <http://monographs.iarc.fr/ENG/Monographs/vol94/mono94.pdf>

Ioannidis, J. P. (2005), 'Why most published research findings are false', *PLoS Med*, 2: e124.

Ioannidis, J. P. (2008*a*), 'Effect of formal statistical significance on the credibility of observational associations', *Am J Epidemiol*, 168: 374–83.

Ioannidis, J. P. (2008*b*), 'Why most discovered true associations are inflated', *Epidemiology*, 19: 640–8.

Key, T. J., Appleby, P. N., Spencer, E. A., Travis, R. C., Roddam, A. W. and Allen, N. E. (2009*a*). 'Cancer incidence in vegetarians: results from the European Prospective Investigation into Cancer and Nutrition (EPIC-Oxford)', *Am J Clin Nutr*, 89/5: 1620S–1626S.

Key, T. J., Appleby, P. N., Spencer, E. A., Travis, R. C., Roddam, A. W. and Allen, N. E. (2009*b*). Mortality in British vegetarians: results from the European Prospective Investigation into Cancer and Nutrition (EPIC-Oxford). *Am J Clin Nutr*, 89/5: 1613S–1619S.

Kolonel, L. N. (1980), 'Cancer patterns of four ethnic groups in Hawaii', *J Natl Cancer Inst*, 65: 1127–39.

La, V. C. and Bosetti, C. (2006), 'Diet and cancer risk in Mediterranean countries: open issues', *Public Health Nutr*, 9: 1077–82.

Lape, R., Colquhoun, D. and Sivilotti, L. G. (2008), 'On the nature of partial agonism in the nicotinic receptor superfamily', *Nature*, 454: 722–7.

Larsson, S. C. and Wolk, A. (2006), 'Meat consumption and risk of colorectal cancer: a meta-analysis of prospective studies', *Int J Cancer*, 119: 2657–64.

Lexchin, J. and Light, D. W. (2006), 'Commercial influence and the content of medical journals', *BMJ*, 332: 1444–7.

Loughlin, M. (2007), 'Style, substance, Newspeak "and all that": a commentary on Murray *et al.* (2007) and an open challenge to Goldacre and other "offended" apologists for EBM', *J Eval Clin Pract*, 13: 517–21.

Manson, J. E. (1994), 'Postmenopausal hormone therapy and atherosclerotic disease', *The American heart journal*, 128: 1337.

Marmot, M. (2007), *Food, Nutrition, Physical Activity, and the Prevention of Cancer: a global perspective* (Washington DC, AICR, 2007, World Cancer Research Fund / American Institute for Cancer Research).

Mente, A., de K. L., Shannon, H. S. and Anand, S. S. (2009), 'A systematic review of the evidence supporting a causal link between dietary factors and coronary heart disease', *Arch Intern Med*, 169: 659–69.

Miles, A. and Loughlin, M. (2006), 'Continuing the evidence-based health care debate in 2006. The progress and price of EBM', *J Eval Clin Pract*, 12: 385–98.

Miles, A., Loughlin, M. and Polychronis, A. (2007), 'Medicine and evidence: knowledge and action in clinical practice', *J Eval Clin Pract*, 13: 481–503.

Miles, A., Polychronis, A. and Grey, J. E. (2006), 'The evidence-based health care debate—2006. Where are we now?', *J Eval Clin Pract*, 12: 239–47.

Murray, S. J., Holmes, D., Perron, A. and Rail, G. (2007), 'No exit? Intellectual integrity under the regime of "evidence" and "best-practices"', *J Eval Clin Pract*, 13: 512–16.

Nelson, N. (2002), 'Epidemiology in a nutshell', <http://www.cancer.gov/newscenter/benchmarks-vol2-issue7/page2>.

Popkin, B. M. (2009), 'Reducing meat consumption has multiple benefits for the world's health', *Arch Intern Med*, 169: 543–5.

Prentice, R. L. (2007), 'Observational studies, clinical trials, and the women's health initiative', *Lifetime Data Anal*, 13: 449–62.

Prentice, R. L., Thomson, C. A., Caan, B., Hubbell, F. A., Anderson, G. L., Beresford, S. A., Pettinger, M., Lane, D. S., Lessin, L., Yasmeen, S., Singh, B., Khandekar, J., Shikany, J. M., Satterfield, S. and Chlebowski, R. T. (2007), 'Low-fat dietary pattern and cancer incidence in the Women's Health Initiative Dietary Modification Randomized Controlled Trial', *J Natl Cancer Inst*, 99: 1534–43.

Rossouw, J. E., Anderson, G. L., Prentice, R. L., Lacroix, A. Z., Kooperberg, C., Stefanick, M. L., Jackson R. D., Beresford, S. A., Howard, B. V., Johnson, K. C., Kotchen, J. M. and Ockene, J. (2002), 'Risks and benefits of estrogen plus progestin in healthy postmenopausal women: principal results from the Women's Health Initiative randomized controlled trial', *JAMA*, 288: 321–33.

Sacks, F. M., Bray, G. A., Carey, V. J., Smith, S. R., Ryan, D. H., Anton, S. D., McManus, K., Champagne C. M., Bishop, L. M., Laranjo, N., Leboff, M. S., Rood, J. C., de J. L., Greenway, F. L., Loria, C. M., Obarzanek, E. and Williamson, D. A. (2009), 'Comparison of weight-loss diets with different compositions of fat, protein, and carbohydrates', *N Engl J Med*, 360: 859–73.

Senn, S. (2003), *Dicing with Death: chance, risk and health* (Cambridge, Cambridge University Press).

Senn, S. (2004), 'Controversies concerning randomization and additivity in clinical trials', *Stat Med*, 23: 3729–53.

Senn, S. (2008), 'Transposed conditionals, shrinkage, and direct and indirect unbiasedness', *Epidemiology*, 19: 652–4.

Sinha, R., Cross, A. J., Graubard, B. I., Leitzmann, M. F. and Schatzkin, A. (2009), 'Meat intake and mortality: a prospective study of over half a million people', *Arch Intern Med*, 169: 562–71.

Sokal, A. D. (1996), 'Transgressing the boundaries: towards a transformative hermeneutics of quantum gravity' ('Science Wars'). *Social Text*, 46/47: 217–52.

Sokal, A. D. (2004), 'Pseudoscience and postmodernism: antagonists or fellow-travelers?', in *Archaeological Fantasies*, ed. G. G. Fagan (London, Routledge), pp. 286–359. <http:www.physics.nyu.edu/faculty/sokal/pseudoscience_rev.pdf>.

Sokal, A. D. and Bricmont, J. (1998, new edn., 2003), *Intellectual Impostures* (London, Economist Books edn., Profile Books).

Tallis, R., Sokal, R. and Bricmont, J (1999), 'Is this the beginning of the end of the dark ages in the humanities?', <http://www.physics.nyu.edu/faculty/sokal/tallis.html>.

Taubes, G. (2007), 'Do we really know what makes us healthy?', *New York Times* (16 Sept.), <www.nytimes.com/2007/09/16/magazine/16epidemiology-t.html>.

Truswell, A. S. (2009), 'Problems with red meat in the WCRF2', *Am J Clin Nutr*, 89: 1274–5. See also <http://www.wcrf.org/PDFs/Colorectal-cancer-CUP-report-2010.pdf>.

Vandenbroucke, J. P. (2009), 'The HRT controversy: observational studies and RCTs fall in line', *Lancet*, 373: 1233–5.

Worrall, J. (2004), 'Why there's no cause to randomize. Causality: metaphysics and methods' (Centre for Philosophy of Natural and Social Science Causality: Metaphysics and Methods Technical Report 24/04).

Worrall, J. (2010), 'Evidence: philosophy of science meets medicine', *J Eval Clin Pract*, 16: 356–62.

Yngve, A., Hambraeus, L., Lissner, L., Serra, M. L., Vaz de Almeida, M. D., Berg, C., Hughes, R., Cannon, G., Thorsdottir, I., Kearney, J., Gustafsson, J. A., Rafter, J., Elmadfa, I. and Kennedy, N. (2006), 'The women's health initiative. What is on trial: nutrition and chronic disease? Or misinterpreted science, media havoc and the sound of silence from peers?', *Public Health Nutr*, 9: 269–72.

13

What the Ravens Really Teach Us: the Intrinsic Contextuality of Evidence

HASOK CHANG AND GRANT FISHER

Abstract

We advance a contextual view of evidence, through a reconsideration of Hempel's paradox of confirmation (the 'ravens paradox'). Our initial view regarding Hempel's paradox is that a non-black non-raven does confirm 'All ravens are black', but only in certain contexts. Thus we start by reformulating the paradox as a puzzle about how the same entity can have variable evidential values for a given proposition. Then we offer a three-stage solution to the reformulated paradox. (1) The situation makes better sense when we reach a deeper propositional understanding of evidence, recognising that each entity can be represented in multiple observational propositions. (2) Some anti-contextualist intuitions can be defused by distinguishing two different senses of the word 'evidence', one applying to objects or events and the other applying to propositions; only the latter is relevant to inference. (3) A fuller understanding comes from analysing the constitution and use of evidence in terms of epistemic action. Our reflections on the ravens paradox suggest a general philosophical framework more suitable for understanding the function of evidence in scientific and everyday practices.

1. Introduction

THE MAIN POINT we wish to argue in this paper is that formal analysis is not sufficient for a full understanding of evidence. By 'formal analysis' we mean a consideration of propositions and logical relations between them. Contemporary Anglophone philosophers' penchant for formal analysis of evidence is largely responsible for the regrettably clear sense of disconnection between philosophical debates on confirmation-theory and concerns of evidence in scientific practice (as well as practices of ordinary life). From the new

Proceedings of the British Academy, **171**, 345–370. © The British Academy 2011.

philosophical viewpoint we propose in this paper, evidence acquires its meaning and significance only in the context of evidential activities. In order to reach a full understanding of evidence we must consider the purposes of these actions, the circumstances under which they are carried out, and our capabilities that make them possible.

Instead of expounding on the nature of evidence in general terms, we would like to build up our general view through a reconsideration of a classic point of debate in philosophical confirmation-theory, namely Carl Hempel's 'paradox of confirmation'. Hempel's paradox, affectionately known as the 'ravens paradox', has puzzled epistemologists and philosophers of science for many decades now. We propose a solution to this old problem, which will also shed some fresh light on the concept of evidence in general. What we offer is a multilayered solution, aimed at a thorough elucidation of evidence as an intrinsically contextual concept. Our solution to the ravens paradox is not entirely new, and we will be referring to congenial predecessors, starting with Hempel himself. However, what we offer is a more fully fledged and integrated solution than can be found in the sources we refer to. For example, we agree entirely with Susan Haack (2007: 83) that evidential support is 'not a purely formal matter, but depends on the substantial content of predicates, their place in a mesh of beliefs, and their relation to the world'. To her list of contextual factors we wish to add those that arise from the nature of human actions.

Our action-centred view on science in general is inspired by a few classic sources. First, we take note of Michael Polanyi's argument that science consists of skilled practices with tacit elements, many of them unarticulated, and some inarticulable (Polanyi 1958). A more direct inspiration comes from Percy Bridgman's operationalism (see Chang 2009), which he characterised as 'an attitude or point of view generated by continued practice of operational analysis'. He added: 'So far as any dogma is involved here at all, it is merely the conviction that it is better, because it takes us further, to analyze into doings or happenings rather than into objects or entities.' (Bridgman 1956: 76) Bridgman started by privileging physical operations in the laboratory in comparison to purely theoretical thinking, but later acknowledged that there were various types of operations: 'instrumental', 'mental' (or 'verbal'), and 'paper-and-pencil' (Bridgman 1959: 3).[1] This points to an analysis of all things epistemic in terms of physical and mental actions. One main insight absent in Bridgman's thinking is provided by Ludwig Wittgenstein (1953): we need to consider how different operations fit together to constitute an activity.

---

[1] Bridgman (e.g. 1938: 114) was clear about the importance of including 'paper-and-pencil' operations into considerations quite early on.

Bridgman used the terms 'operation' and 'activity' in a more or less synonymous way. But if we take and extend the later Wittgenstein's point of view, we can begin to see how various operations need to fit together in order to constitute an activity (or, as Wittgenstein himself called it, a language-game, or a form of life).

2. A basic contextual understanding of the ravens paradox (reformulation of the paradox)

Let us start with a very brief, informal review of the ravens paradox: 'All ravens are black' is logically equivalent to 'All non-black things are non-ravens'; a non-black thing that is not a raven serves as confirming evidence for the latter proposition; therefore, a non-black non-raven also confirms 'All ravens are black'. As Hempel put it (1945: 14), 'any red pencil, any green leaf, and yellow cow, etc., becomes confirming evidence for the hypothesis that all ravens are black'. But surely things that aren't ravens cannot confirm a proposition about ravens? What we have here is a 'surprising consequence of two very adequate assumptions', namely the 'equivalence condition', and the assumption that a general rule receives confirmation from a straightforward instance of it ('Nicod's criterion').[2] Hempel's own solution was to bite the bullet, and to admit that the observation of, say, a white shoe does confirm 'All ravens are black'. Hempel rendered this paradoxical solution sensible by reminding us that 'All ravens are black' does make a statement about the state of any given thing in the universe, namely that it is either black or not a raven. So any and every object provides relevant evidence regarding any universal proposition. It is only because of certain background assumptions that we find this result strange. Hempel declared (1945: 18): 'the impression of a paradoxical situation is not objectively founded; it is a psychological illusion'.[3]

We believe that Hempel was correct in an important sense, but we also believe that his viewpoint was overly narrow and uninstructive. An attempt to explain our position will lead us to a broader consideration of the nature of evidence, resulting in the conclusion that evidence is intrinsically contextual. We start by arguing that the same entity may or may not constitute evidence for a given proposition, depending on how the evidence is collected. And then we offer a three-layered solution to this paradox. (1) The situation already

[2] See also p. 11, for Hempel's initial formulation of the paradox.
[3] See also p. 14. This illusion is quite akin to the common logical error exhibited in the Wason selection task; see Godfrey-Smith (2003: 49–50) for an illuminating parallel.

makes better sense if we just reach a deeper propositional understanding of evidence, recognising that each entity can be represented in multiple observational propositions. (2) We can avoid some confusion by recognising two different senses of the word 'evidence', one applying to objects or events and the other applying to propositions; only the latter is useful for inference. (3) For a fuller understanding, we must analyse the constitution and use of evidence in the context of various epistemic activities; we will show the potential of this direction of thinking by offering such an analysis of theory-testing in the framework of the hypothetico-deductive model.

The preliminary argument we want to make is that there are *some* circumstances under which a white shoe does serve as evidence for 'All ravens are black'. We agree with Hempel that the white shoe can give us confirmation, but we think it does so only under particular circumstances. This context-dependence is essential to the epistemology of evidential reasoning, not merely an accident of psychology. We can imagine situations in which we would be intuitively convinced of the evidential relevance of the white shoe, which will also help us to see why in most cases we are not convinced at all.

This point is more vividly illustrated through a fictional story based on a real scientific example, rather than the tale of the ravens.[4] A key component of Antoine-Laurent Lavoisier's new chemistry that heralded the Chemical Revolution in the late eighteenth century was his theory that all acids contained oxygen; the idea that oxygen was the essence of acidity was the very basis of Lavoisier's neologism 'oxygen', meaning 'acid-begetter'.[5] This little bit of history allows us to consider the confirmation of universal generalisations through an actual scientific theory that was of undisputed significance in its time.

So we have the proposition 'All acids contain oxygen', which is equivalent to 'All oxygen-free substances are non-acids'. Could the former proposition ever be confirmed by a non-acidic substance that does not contain oxygen, which ought to confirm the latter? Well, possibly. To show how, allow us to engage in a bit of history-of-science fiction. Imagine an evil English chemist,

---

[4] Our illustration arises from the experience of one of us (HC) in teaching the paradox. When I started teaching philosophy of science to undergraduate students (many of whom were primarily interested in history or social studies of science rather than philosophy, and many others from science departments), I quickly realised that most of them couldn't see the point of worrying about this paradox at all, as it seemed to them just an annoying logical trick that had nothing to do with scientific practice. In order to keep them engaged, I have over the years come up with a couple of devices like the fictional story given here.

[5] This idea also gave rise to a stronger version of the oxygen theory of acidity, according to which any oxygen compound would be an acid. Lavoisier seems to have held this stronger conception initially, but he could not maintain it after he learned that the oxide of hydrogen was pure water, not an acid.

a determined opponent of Lavoisier. After Lavoisier's imprisonment in Paris (which actually happened in 1794 during the Revolutionary Terror, for his involvement in tax-collecting), the malicious Englishman sends taunting letters to Lavoisier through his anxious wife. In one letter he says: 'Dear Lavoisier, I have recently isolated a new chemical substance. I am certain from my analysis that the compound contains no oxygen at all. It might be an acid, but I have not carried out the test of acidity. I am about to get on to that work, and I shall write again afterwards.' Having read this, poor Lavoisier sits in his prison cell worrying that his beloved theory would be refuted (if the English compound turns out to be an acid), in addition to worrying about himself being guillotined any day (which did happen shortly). Then the next letter arrives from England, which says: 'Dear Lavoisier, you needn't have worried. The substance is not an acid at all.' Lavoisier breathes a sigh of relief, and declares: 'Of course I was right! This oxygen-free compound that is non-acidic vindicates my theory of acids.' After this process is repeated several times, Lavoisier will have gained a new set of favourable test-results for his theory, though no one has observed any new acids.

The logical structure of the above case is exactly the same as a non-black non-raven vindicating 'All ravens are black'. We can concoct an imaginary situation in which the white shoe, too, will seem like relevant evidence for 'All ravens are black' in an intuitive way, though it is hard to come up with a *realistic* scenario for that case. Suppose you have bet your life savings on the proposition that all ravens are black. Then the contents of the universe are stuffed into a very large bag, and a cosmic game-show host takes things out one at a time from that bag, and announces what he sees. You are not allowed to look for yourself; you have to sit on the sidelines and listen to the observations as they come. You hear: 'Object No. 435,234 is certainly not black. But is it a raven? Well, it could be. Hang on a moment ...' You would be at the edge of your seat, until you hear that it is not a raven. Peter Godfrey-Smith (2003: 48) has a simpler version of this tale: 'You believe that all ravens are black, and someone comes up and says, "I have a white object behind my back; want to see what it is?" You should say yes, because if he has a raven behind his back your hypothesis is refuted. He pulls out a shoe, however, so your hypothesis is OK.'[6]

---

[6] We regret that we did not read Godfrey-Smith's excellent textbook until after we had formulated our own ideas. Hempel's case of sodium salts burning yellow is also similar, though the moral we derive from it is quite different from Hempel's own: 'In the seemingly paradoxical cases of confirmation, we are often not actually judging the relation of the given evidence, *E* alone to the hypothesis *H* ... instead we tacitly introduce a comparison of *H* with a body of evidence which consists of *E* in conjunction with an additional amount of information which we happen to have at our disposal ...' (Hempel 1945: 19–20).

What matters here is the way in which the evidence is collected (and presented)—more particularly, as Godfrey-Smith emphasises, what matters is the order in which different aspects of the evidence are learned. If Lavoisier learned first that the new compound was non-acidic, he would not be interested in it at all as potential evidence for his theory of acidity.[7] But the situation is very different if Lavoisier learns the compound's oxygen content first. Then the new compound is of interest; it matters to the theory whether this compound is acidic or not. Likewise for black ravens and white shoes: defenders of raven-blackness will let out a sigh of relief if a non-black object turns out to be a shoe, rather than a raven. As we will see in the next section, it is also quite possible to accommodate our intuition in Hempel's own hypothetico-deductive framework, though not in the framework of naïve instance-confirmation represented by Nicod's criterion (that a general rule is confirmed by a positive instance of it).

Popperians should not find any of this strange, since an object that is known to be a non-raven is not a potential falsifier of 'All ravens are black', while a non-black object whose identity is unknown is clearly a potential falsifier. John Watkins's (1964: 111) quasi-Popperian solution to the paradox rests upon the introduction of background knowledge: ' "Every *A* is *B*" is (strongly) corroborated by evidence (whether *AB*'s or non-*A*'s) if and only if such evidence is rendered (considerably) more probable by the hypothesis than it was by background knowledge alone.' A severe test of a hypothesis consists of seeking evidence that is highly unlikely given background knowledge alone, but far more likely given both the hypothesis and background knowledge. Background knowledge cannot be excluded, on pain of rendering the idea of 'testing' unrealistic and unintelligible. In Hempel's scenario confirmation is indiscriminate: anything that is black or non-raven is welcomed as equally good evidence for the raven hypothesis.[8] The falsificationist, in contrast, seeks potential falsifiers capable of severely testing a hypothesis. What constitutes a potential falsifier only makes sense in situations where our observations are

---

[7] Cf. the idea of 'field of application', which Hempel considers and rejects; see Hempel (1945), section 5.12, pp. 17–18.

[8] Tony Lawson (1985) argues that background knowledge both determines the scope of a generalisation and the evidential value of observations (cf. pp. 396–400). He rejects what even Hempel regarded as a 'methodological fiction'—the assumption of no background knowledge— saying 'there is no good reason to accept Hempel's strictures that we should observe such a "methodological fiction". Background information is generally considered as relevant to reasoning and thus its role must be accounted for in any theory of confirmation' (ibid., p. 400). Lawson's solution seems to exclude any confirmatory function for contrapositive cases, unlike ours.

directed to likely counter-evidence. In the absence of background knowledge there can be no directed observations and no means for the assessment of the severity of the test.[9]

What we have given so far is not so much a solution of the ravens paradox, as a reconceptualisation of its real point. Contrapositive instances are not always confirmatory; they give us positive confirmation (or corroboration) under some circumstances but not under others. The truly paradoxical thing in need of better understanding is not the strangeness of a seemingly irrelevant observation providing evidence, but the variable evidential value of the same object depending on the circumstance of its observation.

3. A deeper propositional understanding of evidence (first-layer solution)

Having reformulated the ravens paradox, our task now is to solve the puzzle. We will proceed in three steps, with increasing innovativeness. We have already given intimations of the first step, and it does not require any other conceptual resources than what Hempel himself employed: an analysis of epistemic situations in terms of propositions and the logical relations between them. The crux of this solution is the uncontroversial recognition that an observation has to be rendered into a proposition in order to function as evidence in the hypothetico-deductive scheme of confirmation, and that there are different ways of observing the same object that result in different propositions.

Take the hero of our paradox: a black raven. What we have, objectively, is something like the image in Figure 13.1. There are multiple propositional representations of this object, even if we restrict our attention to its ravenhood

---

[9] Note that Watkins (1957: 117) refers to a Popperian solution to the ravens paradox prior to his (1964). In the scenario introduced by Hempel, hypotheses are instantiated by a vast amount of evidence but falsifiable by comparatively little counter-evidence. For the Popperian, a hypothesis could never be 'confirmed' by 'irrelevant' evidence because a corroborated hypothesis is one that has resisted genuine attempts to falsify it by seeking potential falsifiers. In response, Stove (1959) argues that Watkins's appeal to attempts to test a hypothesis is irrelevant. Failure to falsify amounts to the same thing as successful confirmation by observing supporting instances irrespective of whether one set out with the intention of deliberately falsifying or confirming through seeking positive instances (or even merely stumbling across either) of a hypothesis (p. 150). According to Stove, what matters are the observations themselves, not how one makes them (ibid., p. 151). For Watkins (1959: 241), the attribution of a 'Labour Theory of confirmation' by Stove is mere folly. And it was in response to Stove that Popper's formulas for degree of corroboration came to underpin Watkins's objective account of test severity (ibid.; see also Watkins 1960).

Figure 13.1.   Black raven.

and its blackness out of all the myriad of possible predicates, and keep strictly
to the simple subject–predicate form. Our observation may be 'This raven is
black.' Or it may be 'This black thing is a raven.' Or it may be 'This object is
a black raven.' Hempel's notation of 'Raven(a).Black(a)' does not effectively
distinguish between these different observations, or the different circumstances under which they may be made and used. Later we will want to enrich
the descriptive apparatus, but for now we can get quite far simply by noting
the order in which the different predicates are registered.[10]

What is predicted by the following hypothesis, H, regarding any object
whatsoever in the universe?

H: 'All ravens are black.'

It implies that whatever object a is, it is either black, or it is not a raven, which
we can write as follows (see Hempel 1945: 18):

P: 'Black(a) v ~Raven(a).'

Now consider the white shoe. Suppose that the first thing we note about it is
that it is a shoe (and therefore not a raven); our common intuition is that to
learn anything further about this object is irrelevant to hypothesis H. This
intuition is born out in the formal propositional formulation of the situation,
as follows. The observation we have is:

O_1: '~Raven(a).'

Now, O_1 already satisfies prediction P; anything additional is superfluous, and
irrelevant for the purpose of confirming H. On the other hand, if what we first

---

[10]This is the sort of move considered and rejected by Mackie (1963: 270–1) as 'extreme', which
Horwich (1982: 58) views more favourably.

observe is that object *a* is white (and therefore not black), then our initial observation is:

O_2: '~Black(a).'

In that case it is certainly relevant to make a further observation of the object, to check whether it is a raven or not. We have two possible outcomes:

O_{2a}: '~Black(a), and then, ~Raven(a).'
O_{2b}: '~Black(a), and then, Raven(a).'

Clearly O_{2a} satisfies *P*, but O_{2b} does not. In other words, if we first observe that something is not a raven, then any further information about that object is useless; if we first observe that it is not black, then it is of interest to find out whether it is a raven or not. Put more colloquially, 'This shoe is *white*' is not relevant evidence for *H*, but 'This white thing is *a shoe*' is.

So far so good: our earlier argument is reinforced, and we have not even gone against Hempel.[11] However, Hempel himself would have disagreed with the general lesson we want to draw from this reasoning. And we expect that many others will share a basic discomfort about our position: surely the order in which we register different properties of a given object cannot have a real effect on the objective evidential import of that object? Even those who dispute Hempel's argument that a white shoe confirms 'All ravens are black' would tend to agree with Hempel that *either it does, or it does not*. What we are trying to argue will seem like 'a psychological illusion'.

We argue that the illusion is in fact on the part of our critics. This is what we call the 'shoebox illusion' regarding the nature observation (continuing with the theme of the white shoe). It consists in imagining that the object of observation is like a shoe in a box, which is permanently there, static in all its detail; we suppose we can open the box any time we please, in order to observe any aspects of the shoe that we might like to note. The shoebox illusion creates a seemingly irresistible intuition that the observation of a raven that is later seen to be black, and the observation of a black object that is later seen to be a raven, are really the same thing because they are just different ways of registering the same aspects of the same object.

---

[11] The preceding reasoning is entirely in accord with Hempel's own theory of confirmation, which he calls the 'satisfaction criterion of confirmation' (Hempel 1945: 107 ff.), with an explicit definition on p. 109. An observation report *B* confirms a hypothesis *H* if *B* entails the 'development' of *H*. The development of *H* for a finite class of individuals *C* 'states what *H* would assert if there existed exclusively those objects which are elements of *C*' (p. 109). In other words, the development of *H* is a description of the world which would be true if the world consisted solely of the objects in *C*. If *B* entails that development, then *B* satisfies and hence confirms *H*.

Most scientific observations are not like that. We can only observe some aspects of a phenomenon as it occurs, and then the phenomenon is gone. The naïve objectivist will reply, can't we observe, at least in principle, all aspects of a phenomenon as it occurs? Or at least all aspects that are likely to be relevant for all imaginable purposes? But we cannot simply record all the properties we are interested in, because representation is subject to an inherent restriction: representing some properties precludes representing others. The point has been made forcefully by Dominic Lopes (1996: 120) in the context of pictorial representation in the arts. Pictures are 'aspectually structured' in that they present selective aspects of a subject according to certain commitments and non-commitments: 'A representation (of any kind) is "committal" with respect to a property F provided that it represents its subject as either F or not-F. If it does not go into the matter of F-ness, it is "inexplicitly non-committal" with respect to F. Finally, a representation is "explicitly non-committal" with regard to F when it represents its subject as having some property (or properties) that preclude it from being committal with regard to F.'

Take an ordinary picture of a black raven. In Lopes's terminology, the picture is explicitly committal about the property of blackness, but it is explicitly non-committal about the colour of its internal organs. Representing the opaque external colour of ravens *precludes* the possibility of representing any property of the internal structure of the bird. Conversely, an X-ray photograph of a raven is explicitly committal about its bone structure but explicitly non-committal about the colour of its feathers. In each case, representing one set of properties precludes the representation of another. This sort of restriction is widespread, and not only in the realm of pictorial representations. For example, a chemist might be interested in a molecule that has a particular configuration of atomic nuclei and bonds, which is essential to explaining some properties of the substance such as its reactivity and its melting and boiling points. The chemist might also be interested in the molecular envelope (the 'surface' of a molecule) whose properties explain the extent to which the molecule interacts with a solvent, for example. But our chemist cannot simultaneously represent both of those things. A model of a molecular surface is explicitly non-committal about the molecular skeleton (the nuclei and bonds) because in representing the molecular surface the model obscures the 'inner' structure of the molecule.

There will also be situations in which competing predicates are more strictly incommensurable with each other. It may be a cheap trick to bring in quantum mechanics here, but it makes the point conveniently: the observation of a particle as having a definite position x at time t is not commensurable with the observation of the same particle as having a definite momentum p at the same time t. If we ascertain 'This electron had position x at time t', then we will never know for certain what the observation of its momentum at time t would have revealed, so we cannot say whether it would have confirmed some statement involving its momentum. It is impossible, in principle, to observe the wavefunction of the electron in all its aspects.

Generally speaking, in observing a given object, some properties cannot be recorded if we choose to record certain other properties. The restrictions may be inherent to the properties themselves, not just their representations. Therefore the product of an observation is a particular proposition, and it may not be possible to translate that proposition into the statement of what we might have got had we made a different observation of the same object, even if we assume that there is an object with lasting identity underlying the different observations.

4. Different meanings of the term 'evidence' (second-layer solution)

The second step in our solution of the paradox is really a point of intuitive clarification. In our experience, even those who accept our argument against the shoebox illusion often display a substantial residue of objectivist intuition that insists, deep down: 'evidence is evidence is evidence' (Snyder [1994] 1998: 477). This makes it very difficult for them to accept any significantly contextualist view of evidence. We find that there is a common linguistic equivocation that fuels unwarranted naïve objectivist intuitions about evidence, and it is necessary to expose this equivocation before we proceed further. First of all, we must stop talking about an *object* serving as evidence for a *proposition*, because that is a category mistake. Hempel himself was in the end quite clear that evidence was in the form of a proposition, since the H-D model of confirmation concerns inferential relations between propositions.[12] Now, there *is* a sense in which we can talk about an object being a piece of evidence, but this sense is irrelevant for our present purposes, so we wish to articulate it and then set it aside. This sense of 'evidence' continues to support the objectivist intuition, but it is not the concept of evidence that is involved in evidential inference or in evidence-based *reasoning* more generally. This argument is not

---

[12] Hempel (1945, section 6, esp. p. 22) stated that the proper characterisation of confirmation was as a 'relation between sentences'; therefore evidence took the form of a statement, not an object or even a fact. This is despite his locution in the earlier parts of the paper (1945: 11, 14, etc.), in which he tended to speak of objects confirming hypotheses.

strictly necessary to support what comes before and after it, but we think it is intuitively very helpful.

It is helpful to recall that the term 'evidence' is used in a variety of ways in the English language. (Those who are tackling related problems in a different language would need to see if a similar analysis is required in that language.) What we are about to engage in now may seem like ordinary-language philosophy in the manner of J. L. Austin, especially as exhibited in *How to Do Things with Words*. If so, we see no shame in it. With the help of the *Oxford English Dictionary* as a convenient heuristic guide, we have distilled two salient senses of the word. On the one hand, evidence is a 'manifestation; display' (meaning 2), or 'an indication, mark, sign, token, trace' (from meaning 3). On the other hand, evidence is 'ground for belief; testimony or facts tending to prove or disprove any conclusion' (from meaning 5). We want to sharpen this distinction further, by explicitly defining two different senses of 'evidence' as follows:

> (1) X is evidence$_1$ of Y, if Y causes X to be present; X is a trace left by Y. Here X and Y are entities, by which we mean material objects or events.
>
> (2) P is evidence$_2$ for Q, if P gives us a positive reason to believe Q. Here P and Q are propositions.

A suggestive way of remembering these two senses of 'evidence' is to say that sense 1 is about an entity being evidence *of* another entity, and sense 2 is about a proposition being evidence *for* another proposition. What is fundamental to evidence$_1$ is an intuitive sense of causality; what is fundamental to evidence$_2$ is warrant for inference.

In some straightforward cases, the distinction between the two senses of evidence may seem quite pointless. If a sneer is evidence$_1$ of disrespect, then surely we can also take 'X is sneering at Y' as evidence$_2$ for 'X disrespects Y'? What is a sign of something, unless one can make an inference from the sign to that something? This seems to be the view of the *OED* lexicographer as well. In motivating the first sense of evidence, we quoted from *OED*'s definition 3: 'an indication, mark, sign', etc.; we did not quote an earlier part of the definition, 'an appearance from which inferences may be drawn', which is much closer to our second sense. The *OED* also lists 'indication' and 'trace' in one breath, betraying an equating of effect with inference-ticket. A correspondence between evidence$_1$ and evidence$_2$ is undoubtedly present in many cases, when A causes B and we can also infer something about A from observing B. In natural language the two senses of 'evidence' probably developed in close relation to each other, and our intuitive grasp of evidence is perhaps most secure when both senses are present and cleanly coordinated. However, such 'nice' cases are also apt to lead us astray by making us conflate the two concepts of evidence all the time.

Causality and inference do not always line up so nicely. Some inferences have nothing causal corresponding to them; for example, if I know that x is a natural number, I can infer that it is a real number, but one state of affairs here does not cause the other. Even when there is a clear causal process involved, the observation of the effects may not warrant an inference back to the cause. Red cheeks may be evidence$_1$ of embarrassment, of physical exertion, of drunkenness, of a skin condition, of having been in a sauna, etc.; in the absence of further information, 'Your cheeks are red' may not constitute sufficient evidence$_2$ for any particular proposition. And even if we can see a clearly delineated causal path firmly warranting inference, the directions of causality and warrant may line up in different ways. Suppose a certain force exerted on an object causes a definite acceleration in its motion, according to Newton's second law ($F=ma$). I can infer the force from observing the acceleration: the acceleration is evidence$_1$ of the force, and observing the acceleration gives me evidence$_2$ for my belief about the force. But I can also calculate the acceleration from the force. In that case, the proposition that there is a certain force on a body serves as evidence$_2$ for the proposition that the body undergoes that amount of acceleration, but it still remains the case that acceleration is evidence$_1$ for force, not vice versa. Likewise, we take blushing as evidence$_1$ of embarrassment, not embarrassment as evidence$_1$ of blushing, though the direction of inference can go either way. In a process of inquiry, the direction of inference is in large part fixed by what we come to know first; in the arrow of causation (as ordinarily conceived) there is no such epistemic contextuality.

There is an interesting illustration of the confusion that can arise from not distinguishing the two senses of evidence, from a recent debate that one of us had on the nature of evidence with Peter Achinstein.[13] One of the examples occurring in Achinstein's *Book of Evidence* is an imagined case in which Bill Clinton has bought 999 tickets in a fair lottery in which there are a total of 1,000 tickets. He states that the fact that Bill Clinton owns 999 of the 1,000 tickets is evidence that he will win the lottery (Achinstein 2001: 70, 171, 27). I raised the objection that it was a strange locution to talk about 'evidence' for something that had not happened yet, because evidence had to be the sign or a consequence of something, and we cannot yet have a consequence of a future event. Achinstein did not accept this argument, and we did not quite

[13] Presentation by Achinstein at the Centre for Philosophy of Natural and Social Science, London School of Economics, 16 March 2005, with comments by John Worrall and Hasok Chang.

reach agreement on this matter. Now I can see clearly that we were simply talking about different senses of 'evidence': the fact that Clinton has a near-monopoly on the lottery tickets of course gives him a nearly certain prospect of winning, so it is evidence$_2$ (grounds for our inference) that he will probably win. If we are talking about the second sense of evidence, then it is perfectly sensible to talk about evidence *for* predictions of future occurrences (for example, doctors give evidence-based prognosis for patients). On the other hand, if we are concerned with the first sense of evidence, Clinton's ticket-hogging is not at all evidence *of* his winning; if anything, it is the other way around—his winning will be the evidence$_1$ of his ticket-hogging.

Armed with our distinction, let us return to the ravens. What is a black raven the evidence$_1$ of? That is actually not easy to say. When we are dealing with the first sense of evidence, we are asking what causes a black raven to be there, or what manifests itself in it. A black raven might be evidence$_1$ of the Black Raven gang, who leave a black raven at the scene of their crime as a signature. Biologically, a black raven would be evidence$_1$ of other black ravens that existed before (starting with its parents). But when we are discussing the ravens paradox, we are not looking for such answers. Is there something that a black raven is evidence$_1$ of, in any way that is relevant to the ravens paradox? The blackness of all ravens? Perhaps, but only if we take a rather odd onto-logical stance that the blackness of all ravens is a metaphysical object that causes individual ravens to be black. We can entertain such notions if we wish, but it is by no means necessary, and it is not at all clear what would be gained from such a move. A much more straightforward view is that when we look for evidence for 'All ravens are black', we are not seeking to establish causality, and we are not looking for evidence$_1$. What matters is what gives us grounds for affirming the target proposition (the grounds may or may not be sufficient for proof). As reasonable grounds for believing 'All ravens are black', something like 'We have seen lots of ravens and they are all black' will work well enough for everyday purposes. So will 'All birds of the crow family are black'. Or even 'The Bible says so', if you are so inclined.

The two concepts of evidence we have distinguished are still vague, insofar as we have left unspecified the notions of causation and inferential warrant. But these vague concepts are good enough to support the main point we want to make at present, which is the following. The persistence of the first sense of evidence supports two interlinked intuitions: that an entity can serve as evidence, and that evidence is an entirely objective thing that is not affected by the way it is collected, conceptualised, or presented. It is a mistake to apply these intuitions to the second sense of evidence; this can lead to a misguided refusal to admit contextuality in evidence$_2$, on the ground that evidence$_1$, being a matter of causality, has to be an objective relation. Evidence$_2$, which gives some-one the reason to believe a proposition, is dependent on the particular nature and circumstances of that person, and this contextuality does not arise from any lack of objectivity in causal laws. It may clarify matters if we could get people to stop talking about both of these notions as 'evidence' (and perhaps only speak of 'cause' in one situation and 'inference' in the other), but they are both present in the meaning of 'evidence' in natural language, and it would be futile for us to try legislating the usage completely. That is why we content ourselves with introducing a rather inelegant distinction.

To sum up: distinguishing the two senses of evidence as we have done makes it much easier to see that an object in itself does not possess a determinate evidential value for a proposition. The intuition that a white shoe should either always confirm or never confirm 'All ravens are black' is actually incoherent, and only arises from a confusion between the two different senses of evidence. An attempt to formulate a coherent version of that intuition will return us to the fully propositional analysis of the kind we gave earlier, and make us realise that the matter is not simple. The intuition that evidence is entirely objective (unaffected by the way it is collected, conceptualised, or presented) is valid when it comes to the first sense of evidence, but this intuition should not be applied to the second sense of evidence. In the discussion of the ravens paradox we need to stick to the second sense of evidence, because the paradox is about confirmation, which concerns inferential relations between propositions, not causal relations between entities.

5. Evidential reasoning in the context of action (third-layer solution)

Testing as an activity

Having (hopefully) neutralised some misguided intuitions, let us proceed with broader considerations aimed at a complete resolution of the ravens paradox. The considerations made in Sections 2 and 3 strongly suggest that we need to contextualise the concept of evidence, and we now want to argue that it needs to be embedded into the context of action. This is the third and most important step in our solution of the paradox. Once again, Godfrey-Smith (2003: 214) has an approach that is very congenial to our own: 'we should analyze evidence, confirmation, and testing by focusing on *procedures*. If an observation provides support for a theory, that will be by virtue of the procedure that the observation was embedded within.' We will endeavour to build on and extend Godfrey-Smith's discussion of the ravens paradox in this vein, and present *epistemic activities* as a broader framework to describe what he calls procedures. A comprehensive rethinking of evidence is beyond the scope of this paper, but in this section we would like to take some initial steps to indicate the directions in which such an analysis would go, and carry out just enough of the actual analysis to tie up the loose ends in our account of the ravens paradox.

Let us consider the epistemic activities in which evidence plays a role, the most obvious of which is the activity of theory-testing. There are various ways of testing theories, but for the sake of simplicity and clarity let us stay with the basic hypothetico-deductive (H-D) scheme. The H-D model is, of course, overly simplistic, but that is actually very pertinent and useful for our purposes, for two reasons. First, the H-D model is the broad framework in which the ravens paradox was formulated, so there is some justice in seeing the story through in that framework. Secondly, if we can show that even such a simplistic model of evidence as H-D testing requires a full activity-based analysis, then it will become evident that more sophisticated models require such an analysis.

In the H-D model, the testing of a hypothesis involves three epistemic operations: (1) make a prediction; (2) make an observation; (3) match up the prediction and the observation. These steps are usually assumed to be simple logical operations involving propositions, but we will argue that they are much more than that. Checking the agreement between the prediction-*statement* and the observation-*statement* is not the whole story. The ravens paradox is just one illustration that such agreement cannot unconditionally be taken as positive evidence. What we need for evidential support is *coherence* between the prediction-activity and the observation-activity. In the following discussion we will try to spell out what we mean by coherence here, and this is at the heart of the additional insight provided by our activity-based analysis which cannot be had from a proposition-based analysis, however contextualised it might be.

As we are trying to think of evidence in the context of action, it would be appropriate to seek some insight from philosophical theories of action. Unfortunately for our purposes, standard philosophical discussions of human agency have mostly been conducted in the context of ethics or the philosophy of mind,[14] and they are not well adapted to the analysis of epistemic actions. However, there is one basic thing that any theory of action would consider,

---

[14] Jennifer Hornsby (2004: 1) makes this point clearly.

which is usually left out in the philosophy of science: that is the intentional aspect of agency, which is the most crucial thing that distinguishes actions (doings) from other types of events (happenings). This has two important methodological consequences. First, if we keep in mind that we are dealing with intentional agents, then we are reminded that they make choices; our analysis cannot presume that epistemic actions are fully determined by external factors, or demand that they should be explained by external factors only. Second, if we take care to identify the purpose of each activity, then we will be able to think about the coherence of the activity in terms of how the different parts of it fit together in order to serve that purpose. This functional coherence is not reducible to the logical consistency of the propositions involved.

In such a framework of intentional action, a piece of information or an observation-statement can function as evidence only in the context of an *evidential epistemic activity*. By 'activity', we mean a system of operations; by 'system' we mean a coherent and organised set of elements governed by certain rules and expectations that are motivated and constrained by some overall purpose. An 'operation' in the narrow sense of the term does not have a purpose beyond its completion. For example, placing a weight on one side of a balance would be an operation; adding up all the weights needed to balance the object on the other side is an operation; writing down that number is an operation, too; these and various other operations, fitted together coherently, constitute the activity of weight-measurement using a balance. This distinction between operation and activity is not meant to be absolute; it is relative to the focus of our analysis. The main purpose we identify in our actions will define what the level of 'activity' is for our analysis; then, relative to that, it will be clear what the operations constituting the activity are; in turn, each of those operations could be taken as an activity consisting of other, more detailed operations.

Prediction

Let us now take a closer look at the activity of H-D testing, starting with the operation of prediction. The first thing we need to highlight here is the dimension of choice, which we have implicitly noted already: various different predictions can be derived from a given hypothesis, and we need to choose which prediction to use in our testing activity. The choice is made in order to serve whatever purpose we might have in making a prediction. For the purpose of H-D testing, what we require is a *realisable prediction*, the kind that gives an outcome in the form of 'If I do X, then Y will happen', in which X is an operation I can perform, and Y is an event that I or someone else can observe.

(For this purpose, it is no good to predict, say, that the end of the world will come in 6,000 years.) Among the realisable predictions, there are also better and worse ones to choose from. Return to the ravens for the moment, for the sake of illustration. From 'All ravens are black', we may predict:

(P_1) 'If I find a raven, it will be black.'
(P_2) 'If I find a non-black thing, it won't be a raven.'
(P_3) 'If I find any object at all, it will be either black or non-raven'.

Which one to go with? For this case, the question about choice may seem silly, since all of these deductions fall out at a glance. But in real-life cases in science, prediction often takes a lot of work (consider, for example, working out the prediction for the precise position of the moon 48 hours from now). The three types of predictions exemplified by P_1–P_3 are related respectively to prospective, retrospective and cross-sectional sampling schemes in statistics. We should want to make the kind of prediction that can lead to an effective testing of the hypothesis in question. Judging which prediction will lead to effective testing requires that we know something about the state of the world, and about our own abilities to produce the kind of observations suitable for comparing with the predictions.[15] This is an important part of the coherence of testing-activity, to ensure that the types of prediction and observation we make are well-suited to each other.

Suppose, for the moment, that we are pursuing the ideal of proof by complete enumeration (within the H-D framework). In that context, if we believe that there are fewer ravens than non-black things in the world, and that ravens are reasonably easy for us to spot, it would be prudent to go with P_1 above. If we were only constrained by logic, we could easily go with P_2, since we can actually prove 'All ravens are black' by checking all non-black things in the universe and seeing that none of them are ravens. But in the world as we know it that will be much more work than testing through P_1, which only requires the rounding-up of all ravens. Going through P_3 is the worst option of all, as it would require the examination of all objects in the universe. An exhaustive check on P_1 would be daunting enough in practice, but an exhaustive check on P_2 or P_3 is in the realm of God, or at least Laplace's demon. Checking non-black things to see if they are ravens can be a relevant and meaningful testing operation, but only in the context of an utterly impractical test-activity. Common sense is vindicated: what we ought to do to test 'All ravens are black' is go looking for ravens, not to go looking for non-black things (to check P_2)

[15] We would also need some kind of a confirmation measure, which the H-D model itself does not specify.

or to go grabbing things randomly (to check P_3). Similar intuitions ground the Bayesian treatments of the ravens paradox that focus on the very small confirmatory value of the white shoe given certain assumptions about the populations (Horwich 1982: 56–7; Howson and Urbach 1993: 128). Things could be different, however. If most things in the world were black, then the more effective way of testing 'All ravens are black' may well be to scan for the few non-black things to see if they are or are not ravens. To take the most extreme imaginable case, suppose that there is just one non-black thing in the universe. In that world, the most efficient way of testing 'All ravens are black' would be to check that one non-black thing; if that's not a raven, then all ravens are black; if it is, then not all ravens are black.

This kind of consideration is usually taken as contextuality at the level of propositions: we need to consider certain propositions that express relevant background information or beliefs, which would affect the probability of the proposition(s) involved in the test, or the logical relationships between them. We cannot emphasise more strongly that what we are talking about is not just a matter of adding background propositions into the mix in logical deductions or probability calculations. Many of the contextual factors do change the relevant probabilities that affect the likelihood ratio or some measure for the severity of the test being employed, but that is not always the case. If we add propositions like 'I am good at rounding up ravens', that does not at all affect the truth or probability of any statements that would be considered relevant by formal theories of confirmation. Nonetheless, such background factors do make a real difference in determining the shape and significance of our activities, and whether they are properly considered and accommodated will strongly affect the coherence of the testing-activity in question.

Observation

Let us now consider more carefully the second leg of the H-D procedure, observation. We have already indicated that observation is not just a passive and automatic recording of information. But we have not yet given a full analysis of observation as an intentional activity, either in its own right, or as an operation fitting into a testing activity. For example, our propositional analysis of the ravens paradox given in Section 3 did not give a full and positive account of why the order of observing different aspects of the same object should matter. What underpins the difference between '~Black(a), and then, ~Raven(a)', and '~Raven(a), and then, ~Black(a)'? The answer emerges clearly if we give a full description of these observations as actions, or doings: on one side we might have the action-sequence of first searching for non-black objects, finding one, and then checking its other properties, and concluding that it is not a raven; on the other side, searching for non-ravens, finding one, and then checking its colour, and concluding it is not black. This kind of difference is not only clear but highly significant when we consider cases such as the collection of statistical data by different strategies of sampling. A formulation like '~Black(a).~Raven(a)' is an entirely impoverished representation of the act of observation that produces it. The time-ordered representation '~Black(a), and then, ~Raven(a)' is better, but its clumsiness is an ample hint of the inadequacy of the formalism in which it is expressed.

The time order exhibited in observation is only a very partial manifestation of the active nature of observation, which is responsible for the fact that the product of observation is irreducibly dependent on what it is that we do in making and reporting our observations. The whole view of observation must include not only the *result* of our observation-act, but what *methods* we adopt for the observation, and to what *purpose* we adopt the methods of our choice. The purpose of observation is not something that philosophers have discussed very much. Perhaps that is because it is considered too obvious, but on reflection it is easy to see that there is actually no consensus on the matter. Very generally, we could say that the purpose of observation is to learn anything that is external to ourselves. But in the context of H-D theory-testing, we must also worry about making observations that can be compared with the predictions we have made from the theory in question, or at least the kinds of predictions we could make. Although observations are not always made for the purpose of theory-testing, when they *are* made for testing, that context does impose certain specific constraints on the observation-activity.

These constraints may or may not be satisfied, depending on our physical and mental capabilities. In the case of the ravens, prediction P_1 ('If I find a raven, it will be black') cannot be checked meaningfully by observation if the only way we know of identifying a raven is as a 'large, black, crow-shaped bird' (which is probably about the level of ornithology that most people can boast).[16] Thus, P_1 would practically be a tautology for most of us, not empirically testable by any observations that *we* are able to collect. In contrast, we ignorant folk could at least do some unskilled labour in the enterprise of checking P_2 or P_3 by collecting non-black things or random objects. Our observational capabilities significantly affect the determination of effective testing-strategies. That general point is illustrated even more clearly through

[16] Haack (2007: 83) quotes Webster's Dictionary for a definition of raven as 'a glossy black corvine bird'.

the real-science example of Lavoisier's theory of acids. To test 'All acids contain oxygen', we need to have a method for testing a chemical for acidity, and an analytical method for determining its oxygen content. Until quite some time after Lavoisier's own work, it was by no means an easy task to analyse a chemical sample for its oxygen content. In contrast, there were some simple standard operational tests of acidity (although the theoretical definition of acidity remained a challenge for a long time). And it was known that the number of acids in the known chemical world was not so great. So the effective thing was to predict 'If X is an acid, it contains oxygen', and subject the small number of acids to analysis to check for oxygen content. However, we can imagine the opposite situation in which relatively few things are oxygen-free, chemical analysis is easy and cheap, and the test of acidity is tricky (imagine a world without litmus, etc.). Then we ought to start by predicting 'If x is oxygen-free, it is not an acid', and check the oxygen-free substances for acidity. Again, some of the background factors (the difficulty of chemical analysis for oxygen, and the availability of acidity indicators) do not affect the probabilities or likelihood-ratios attached to the propositions representing the hypothesis and evidence in question.

Matching and interpretation

Thinking about the mutual constraints between prediction and observation within the testing activity brings us to a more nuanced consideration of the third essential operation in H-D testing, namely the comparison between the prediction and the observation. Generally this is taken to be too trivial to deserve much comment: we simply see if the prediction-statement agrees with the observation-statement.[17] Sometimes things *are* that easy, usually when the prediction-activity and the observation-activity have already been tailored to ensure that they produce propositions that are straightforwardly comparable. So, if we have predicted 'If I find a raven, it will be black', then what I can make sure to do is to go looking for ravens, rather than do anything irrelevant.

In real life, things are usually not so straightforward. Quite often we have predictions and observations that have been made without considering their fit with each other. To construe *evidence* in this situation requires an act of *interpretation*. The possibility of such interpretation, and its requirements, will depend on some specific features of the particular situation. (This is why there aren't universally applicable answers to epistemological puzzles concerning evidence, such as the ravens paradox and the argument about the

---

[17] Hempel's account was a bit more sophisticated; see above, n. 11.

relative evidential value of prediction and accommodation.) Suppose, for example, that we have collected 1,000 black objects by grabbing anything black in a certain geographical area, among which there were twenty black ravens (alongside pieces of charcoal, strands of someone's hair, and the New Zealand rugby team). From this result, how do we discern evidence for 'All ravens are black'? We need to match it up with one of predictions P_1–P_3 discussed earlier. If we were to go for a match with P_1 ('If I find a raven, it will be black') we need to infer what our observation implies about what we would have got if we went collecting ravens. Without making additional assumptions, all we can infer is quite uninformative: e.g. that if we went and collected all the ravens in the world, we would have got at least twenty black ones. We can get something more interesting only if we have some further knowledge that will allow us to gauge the significance of the twenty black ravens.

Note that the inference needed is hypothetical, about *what would have happened* if we had got involved in some other observational activity. Such inferences rely on imagination, and some background knowledge and assumptions, both about the world and the exact observational procedures. *Interpretation* is required in the matching of prediction and observation that are not precisely controlled to suit each other. (It is a feature of the 'shoebox illusion', discussed in Section 3, to assume that an observation-result can always be reinterpreted to suit precisely whatever need that might arise later.) Of course, the case of the ravens is a toy example not reflecting the complexities of real cases. Again, that only helps our argument: in complex real cases, there will be even stronger needs for interpretation. There will be an untold number of cases in which H-D type theory-testing involves significant interpretations, such as the use of sociological or epidemiological data in areas where it is difficult or impossible to perform controlled experiments. Generally speaking, H-D testing is a process of finding *interpretive coherence* between a prediction-activity and an observation-activity, not a simple yes–no comparison of two propositions.

Contextuality

To sum up our discussion of theory-testing as an epistemic activity: even if we stick to the simple H-D method, testing is a complex activity whose details are necessarily shaped by various contextual factors reflecting not only background beliefs, but also the aims and capabilities of the inquirers conducting the test. The evidential value of a given piece of information depends on whether and how it fits into a coherent and viable testing activity. There are contextual factors that are constitutive of the testing activity, which cannot be dismissed as merely psychological. These contextual factors explain why things like the time-order of observed predicates may represent a substantial difference in evidential value.

Hempel's stance was to be aloof from all these contextual and contingent factors. He declared that the hidden background assumptions that sway our intuitions this way and that should be disregarded in our philosophical theory of confirmation. In testing 'All ravens are black', Hempel would deduce the prediction 'If we come across anything, it will be either black, or not a raven'. Finding a white shoe, or any shoe, or anything at all indeed, does have relevance in checking that prediction. But it is difficult to imagine any real testing activity carried out in this way. Hempel is giving us a logical exercise in consistency-checking, not a realistic scheme for scientific hypothesis-testing. That is why it is so difficult to get pragmatic people interested in the ravens paradox, after all. It is important to note that even Hempel's thinking is not context-free. Rather, his is the kind of reasoning operative in a logic class, which is a particular kind of epistemic activity as much as any other. Hempel made no errors in that context. His only error was to imply that what holds in the consistency-checking game should apply to the kinds of epistemic activities carried out in scientific inquiry, not to mention practical applications of scientific knowledge. We are certainly not saying that epistemic activities in empirical science do not involve logical thinking; we are only saying that they involve much more, and that the particular and contingent constraints involved in those activities are essential features of the situation, not irrelevant aberrations or incidental add-ons.

In Hempel's defence, we could note that he was only giving a non-contextual account of what *potentially* counts as evidence (only 'the *logic* of confirmation', as he put it in the title of his classic paper), not what would actually count as evidence in each particular context. So we might say: what Hempel did was to consider all possible predictions from a hypothesis, and tell us which observations would satisfy those predictions; all of that is a matter of logic, and independent of context. There is a certain robustness to that viewpoint, but its poverty is clear. What we have seen in this section is that the essential epistemic operations involved in the simple testing of a hypothesis are shaped by a variety of factors that are only determined by the contingent and particular situations and purposes that frame them in each case. Since evidence$_2$ only exists in such an epistemic setting, it is an inherently contextual notion.

6. Broader prospects

We hope to have given a reasonably complete defence of our reformulation and solution of the ravens paradox: a proposition can be confirmed by a contrapositive instance, if and only if the observation of that instance is a part of a coherent and viable epistemic activity aimed at testing the proposition in question (or at least can be reinterpreted as such). Our analysis has opened up a new point of view, that of seeing evidence as operating within well-defined epistemic activities, not existing in the world of objects and properties without actors. This point of view can and should be extended, and we would like to close by suggesting three lines along which we hope to make such extensions.

First of all, so far we have only considered testing in a simple version of the H-D (hypothetico-deductive) framework. A fuller analysis would need to consider other possible modes of testing as well. For one thing, there are ways of testing something without making explicit predictions. We would also need to consider the difference between contrastive and non-contrastive testing, depending on whether or not we are considering the relative merits of competing hypotheses. To each coherent mode of testing there will be a corresponding concept of evidence, and an appropriate theory of confirmation to go with it. We cannot enter fully into that discussion here, but we predict that any sophisticated account of testing would reveal the same kind of contextuality as we have already seen, perhaps to an even greater degree. Testing activity and confirmation theory are mutually constitutive. The role of interpretation uncovered in Section 5 actually suggests that it may make sense to connect theory-testing to inference to the best explanation (where explanation goes beyond the deductive–nomological model).[18]

Secondly, in this paper we have only considered evidence as a means of hypothesis-testing. But evidence has a role to play in all aspects of empirical inquiry. In particular, evidence is used in *generating* hypotheses as well, and sometimes justification may be found in the discovery process itself. What is involved in discovery will sometimes be a relatively straightforward activity of inductive generalisation, but more often the process of hypothesis-generation on the basis of evidence will be abductive (see Hanson 1958). Inference from evidence to hypothesis may even be deductive, given sufficiently strong background assumptions.

Thirdly, even the general context of hypothesis-focused inquiry is not broad enough to encompass the concept of evidence entirely. Evidence also has a key role to play in the *application* of hypotheses: we routinely put together general theories and concrete evidence to deduce various types of predictions to direct our action in various practical situations. Evidence is also used in the activity of giving causal *explanations*. This may be where evidence$_1$ has its use:

---

[18] This is similar to what Haack (2007: 83) calls 'explanatory integration', which underpins the 'supportiveness of evidence'.

if we already know that entity A is manifested in entity B, then we can explain the presence of B by reference to A, even if we cannot obtain convincingly high probabilities for inferring anything about A on the basis of observations about B. This is a kind of activity we can engage in after we have already acquired knowledge, not in the process of acquiring it (for the latter, we need evidence$_2$). When there is a close interaction between inquiry and explanation, a good link is established between the two concepts of evidence.

We are unable to give a full account of the uses of evidence in all of these various contexts of epistemic action in this paper. However, we have reasonable hopes for the general applicability of the analytic framework we have generated here for the purpose of solving the ravens paradox. On the one hand, we should be able to use the framework in order to make advances on some other thorny classic problems in epistemology as well, such as the 'grue' paradox (through an activity-based notion of projectibility), and the debate on the relative evidential weights of prediction and accommodation. On the other hand, it would allow us to give richer, more informative and more sophisticated analyses of complex cases of evidential reasoning in empirical science, and also in more practical areas such as engineering, law, business and medicine.

Note. This work was supported by a grant from the Leverhulme Trust and the ESRC, through the research programme 'Evidence, Inquiry and Inference' at University College London (principal investigator: Philip Dawid). We would like to thank Peter Lipton, Eleonora Montuschi, Michela Massimi, Juha Saatsi, David Lagnado, Donald Gillies, Phil Dawid, Gianluca Baio, Nigel Harvey, and anonymous referees for helpful discussions and suggestions. We also thank those who gave helpful comments when this paper was presented at the LSE and at Durham University, including Nancy Cartwright, Robin Hendry, Jonathan Lowe and Barry Gower. Hasok Chang would like to thank Jim Woodward, who first taught him the ravens paradox and facilitated some of the early ideas that developed into this paper. He also thanks his students in the introductory philosophy of science course (HPSCB111) at UCL over the years, as they forced him to sharpen his own intuitions about the paradox.

References

Achinstein, P. (2001), *The Book of Evidence* (New York, Oxford University Press).
Austin, J. L. (1962), *How to Do Things with Words* (Oxford, Clarendon Press).
Bridgman, P. W. (1938), 'Operational analysis', *Philosophy of Science*, 5: 114–31.
Bridgman, P. W. (1956), 'The Present state of operationalism', in P. G. Frank (ed.), *The Validation of Scientific Theories* (Boston, Beacon Press), pp. 75–80.

Bridgman, P. W. (1959), *The Way Things Are* (Cambridge, MA, Harvard University Press).

Chang, H. (2009), 'Operationalism', *Stanford Encyclopedia of Philosophy*, <http://plato.stanford.edu>.

Godfrey-Smith, P. (2003), *Theory and Reality (An Introduction to the Philosophy of Science)* (Chicago, The University of Chicago Press).

Haack, S. (2007), *Defending Science—Within Reason: between scientism and cynicism* (Amherst, NY, Prometheus Books).

Hanson, N. R. (1958), *Patterns of Discovery: an inquiry into the conceptual foundations of science* (Cambridge, Cambridge University Press).

Hempel, C. G. (1945), 'Studies in the logic of confirmation', *Mind*, 54: 1–26, 97–121; also repr. (1966), in *Scientific Explanation: essays in the philosophy of science* (New York, The Free Press), pp. 3–51.

Hornsby, J. (2004), 'Agency and actions', in J. Hyman and H. Steward (eds.), *Agency and Actions*, Royal Institute of Philosophy Supplement, 55 (Cambridge, Cambridge University Press), pp. 1–23.

Horwich, P. (1982), *Probability and Evidence* (Cambridge, Cambridge University Press).

Howson, C. and Urbach, P. (1993), *Scientific Reasoning: the Bayesian approach* (Chicago, Open Court).

Lawson, T. (1985), 'The context of prediction (and the paradox of confirmation)', *British Journal for the Philosophy of Science*, 36: 393–407.

Lipton, P. (2004), *Inference to the Best Explanation*, 2nd edn. (London and New York, Routledge).

Lopes, D. (1996), *Understanding Pictures* (Oxford, Oxford University Press).

Mackie, J. L. (1963), 'The paradox of confirmation', *British Journal for the Philosophy of Science*, 13: 265–77.

Musgrave, A. (1974), 'Logical versus historical theories of confirmation', *British Journal for the Philosophy of Science*, 25: 1–23.

Polanyi, M. (1958), *Personal Knowledge: towards a post-critical philosophy* (Chicago, University of Chicago Press).

Snyder, L. ([1994] 1998), 'Is evidence historical?', in M. Curd and J. A. Cover (eds.), *Philosophy of Science: the central issues* (New York, Norton), 460–80.

Stove, D. (1959), 'Popperian confirmation and the paradox of the ravens', *Australasian Journal of Philosophy*, 37: 149–51.

Watkins, J. (1957), 'Between the analytic and empirical', *Philosophy*, 33: 112–31.

Watkins, J. (1959), 'Mr. Stove's blunders', *Australian Journal of Philosophy*, 37: 240–1.

Watkins, J. (1960), 'Reply to Mr. Stove's reply', *Australian Journal of Philosophy*, 38: 54–8.

Watkins, J. (1964), 'Confirmation, the paradoxes, and positivism', in M. Bunge (ed.), *The Critical Approach to Science and Philosophy* (London, The Free Press of Glencoe), pp. 92–115.

Wittgenstein, L. (1953), *Philosophical Investigations* (New York, Macmillan).

14

Critical Distance: Stabilising Evidential Claims in Archaeology

ALISON WYLIE

Abstract

The vagaries of evidential reasoning in archaeology are notorious: the material traces that comprise the archaeological record are fragmentary and profoundly enigmatic, and the inferential gap that archaeologists must cross to constitute them as evidence of the cultural past is a perennial source of epistemic anxiety. And yet we know a great deal about the cultural past, including vast reaches of the past for which this material record is our only source of evidence. The contents of this record stand as evidence only under interpretation, but however much a construct it is, archaeological evidence has a striking capacity to disrupt settled assumptions, redirecting inquiry and expanding interpretive horizons in directions no one could have anticipated. It is this capacity for constraining inference and interpretation that I am concerned to understand. I outline a model of evidential reasoning based on archaeological practice that integrates insights drawn from philosophical theories of confirmation, model building and hypothesis testing. Given growing interest in the uses of material evidence in fields that had been resolutely text-based, the archaeological principles of evidential reasoning may have much wider reach than this particular social/historical discipline.

WHY FOCUS ON archaeological evidence? The vagaries of evidential reasoning in archaeology are notorious: the material traces that comprise the archaeological record are fragmentary and profoundly enigmatic, and the inferential gap that archaeologists must cross to constitute them as evidence of the cultural past is a perennial source of epistemic anxiety. If hard cases make bad

Proceedings of the British Academy, **171**, 371–394. © The British Academy 2011.

law, surely a discipline known for the challenges posed by its evidence is an unpromising basis for formulating a model of evidential reasoning.

What I find philosophically intriguing about archaeological evidence is its paradoxical nature: it is famously ephemeral and enigmatic, yet resolutely tangible and often epistemically consequential. In the last 150 years, for example, the time depth of human history has been dramatically expanded, a hard won accomplishment that was realised against stiff resistance on a number of fronts, and that required not only the discovery of crucial material evidence (e.g. stratigraphically sealed deposits in which evidence of human presence was juxtaposed with that of Pleistocene fauna), but new ways of seeing and interpreting this evidence that drew on a number of quite different (then-emerging) fields of inquiry: geology, human osteology, palaeobotany, ethnohistory, as well as archaeology.[1] Crucially, archaeological evidence that proved to be pivotal in these protracted debates was often discovered by accomplished antiquarians like the Reverend William Buckland who steadfastedly refused to interpret it as challenging a biblical timeframe.[2] As Sommer shows, Buckland's arguments were not just dogmatic and rhetorical, but turned on close critical examination of the geological context and an articulation of alternative hypotheses that could account for key features of the find within a diluvial framework. This is a history which richly illustrates both how complicated it is to read surviving traces as evidence and how stubbornly recalcitrant, indeed, transformative, these data can be.

This central paradox is illustrated by any number of other cases in which, for example, previously unknown cultures and key transitions in prehistory have been discovered which defy deeply held convictions about the form that specific antecedents must have taken. No less an archaeological forebear than Thomas Jefferson made judicious use of excavated burial goods and comparative osteology to demonstrate that then-contemporary Native Americans were almost certainly descended from the prehistoric peoples who had built the monumental earthworks and mounds encountered along the central

---

[1] See, for example, Goodfield and Toulmin (1965) for a classic account of the complex, extended, multidisciplinary process by which this was accomplished. Grayson (1983) provides an especially thoughtful discussion of the various contingencies at play that ultimately made it possible for French and later British excavators (not yet identified as archaeologists) to recognise geological time depth and stratigraphic sequencing in the context of which the association of Pleistocene fauna and evidence of human occupation could be identified.

[2] Sommer (2007) details the history of debate and reinterpretation of the ochre-stained skeleton known as the 'Red Lady of Paviland', discovered by Buckland in a limestone cave in Wales in 1823. This skeleton ultimately proved to be male and to date to the Upper Palaeolithic (approximately 26,000 BP) but, as indicated, Buckland maintained, to the end of his long career, that it could be no older than the biblical flood.

waterways of North America by Euro-American travellers and settlers. This was a striking reproach to the presumption, fundamental to a doctrine of Manifest Destiny and related justifications for the expropriation of land, that the mounds must have been built by some long-vanished race or by incomers as diverse as Druids and Atlantans.[3] A later example along these lines is the archaeological investigation of deeply stratified sites in Central Plains of North America which decisively challenged the assumption that Native Americans lacked the cultural and technological resources to have developed agriculture in this region: diagnostic plant remains and evidence of settlement made it clear that 'the late nomadic and hunting life of the Central Plains appears merely as a thin overlay associated with the acquisition of the horse' (Strong 1936: 362; 1935). In an historic timeframe, the multidimensional analysis of skeletal remains recovered from Roman cemeteries in England demonstrates the potential for multiple lines of evidence—in this case trace element and stable isotope analysis, in conjunction with reconstructions of the mineral composition of groundwater and isotopic signatures of various types of diet, as well as analysis of skeletal morphology and artefactual evidence—to substantially extend and in some cases correct canonical text-based accounts of population diversity and mobility in the Roman Empire (Eckardt *et al.* 2009; Leach *et al.* 2009).

Even where the broad outlines of major cultural transitions are well understood, much remains to be learned about the conditions and consequences of change. Often this is not just a matter of discovering something unexpected or counterintuitive, but of reassessing empirical and theoretical foundations of contemporary archaeological inquiry. Conventional assumptions about the linear, often teleological course of cultural evolution are substantially undermined by the growing weight of evidence that allows for the reconstruction of fine-grained chronologies of site occupation and regional interaction. In the case of the 'moundbuilder' research mentioned above, repeated patterns of occupation and abandonment are increasingly understood to require systematic rethinking of the assumption that Hopewell and Mississippian societies must somehow fit the categories of tribe or chiefdom, on a trajectory to state formation. Indeed, as Chapman (2003) argues in a comparative review of evidence for state formation processes around the world, the very concept of 'complexity' must be rethought, a challenge he

---

[3] This is a case I have discussed in connection with archaeological uses of old evidence (Wylie 2010).

takes up in empirical as well as theoretical terms.[4] Consider, finally, the kind
of evidence required to refine reconstructive, explanatory models of the
processes responsible for major cultural transitions, once their broad contours are established; I have in mind research designed to address questions
about the kinds of farming practices that were adopted in various locales as
horticultural and agricultural subsistence patterns were taking shape, and
were instrumental in reconfiguring settlement patterns, social relations and
mobility. These prove to be exceedingly complex, not least because all contemporary analogues involve suites of plants (cultigens and weeds) now adapted
to ecological settings that have been continuously and dramatically reconfigured in the course of some 10,000 years of intensive human activity. The challenge of addressing these questions has catalysed innovative work in plant
science and archaeobotany (the development of archaeological applications
of functional plant ecology) as well as experimental archaeology (recreating
posited farming practices to see how they work), that make it possible both to
define a range of hypotheses about plant husbandry practices and to determine what sorts of archaeological and palaeobotanical evidence might discriminate between them (Bogaard 2004). The successes realised here in
determining, for example, when and where intensive rather than extensive
agriculture was adopted depends on advances in a range of fields (e.g. in
understanding the growing conditions and interactions of species), reinforcing the point that the paradoxes of evidential reasoning in archaeology—its
ambiguity and its capacity decisively to canalise inquiry—are often as much a
function of developments in collateral fields as in archaeology itself.

As we move beyond the antinomies of the science wars a fascination with
material evidence has taken root in social and historical studies of science
and, indeed, in a wide range of fields where inquiry has traditionally been
text-based or ethnographic. In a classic of the genre, the collection *Things that
Talk: object lessons from art and science*, Daston (2003: Preface) describes the
objects that ground each contributor's narrative as 'neither the pure texts of
semiotics, nor the brute objects of positivism'. As dependent as 'things' are on
our capacities of recognition and interpretation, they have a striking capacity
to challenge the conceptual categories in terms of which we apprehend and

---

[4] As a framework for assessing half a dozen contending models of the formation of 'complex'
state societies in south-eastern Spain (5000–1500 BCE), Chapman (2003: 130) identifies five principles
which call attention not only to the robustness of specific lines of archaeological evidence, but
also to the interaction between different kinds of evidence, and the crucial role played by the
background knowledge or assumptions that inform interpretations of archaeological data as
evidence. In what follows I outline a complementary set of principles that pick up exactly these
dimensions of evidential reasoning.

describe them.[5] In short, things are good to think with in a number of key senses. The question archaeologists have long grappled with is how, exactly, we can (or should) think with them. Precisely because archaeological material is both so rich and so persistently perplexing there is a great deal to be learned from archaeological practice about evidential reasoning.

I. Proxy evidence

Archaeologists have been intensely reflective about the fact that they have no alternative but to depend on evidence that is, as one commentator put it, 'remote from and uncertainly coupled to the systems [they] seek to study' (Chippindale 2002: 606). This 'proxy status' (as Chippindale describes it) of archaeological evidence has provoked a series of crisis debates within anthropological archaeology that follow a predictable pattern.[6] The catalyst is usually

---

[5] Daston (2003: Preface) observes, in this connection, that 'what things are made of and how they are made shapes what they can mean'. The question of exactly how things 'shape' meaning (in their original contexts of use and significance, and as evidence of these contexts) is at the centre of the long-running archaeological debates I refer to here.

[6] These epistemic (meta-methodological) crisis debates have erupted every twenty to thirty years since the early twentieth century (coinciding with major wars, hot and cold); the historical dynamic of these debates is discussed in detail in 'How New is the New Archaeology' (Wylie, 2002, Section II).

The most recent of these debates—the focus of my discussion here—was generated by the New Archaeology of the 1960s and 1970s. This was a self-consciously positivist research programme committed to scientific goals (law-governed explanation, framed in terms of processes operating at the level of cultural systems) and forms of practice (systematic hypothesis testing, designed to set interpretive, explanatory conclusions on a secure empirical foundation). By the late 1980s, this New Archaeology faced strong objections from 'post-processual' (or 'anti-processual') critics who insisted that these goals leave out of account a great many important questions (e.g. about cultural lifeworlds, social relations, local historical dynamics) that can only be addressed by means of particularistic, interpretive modes of inquiry. Most relevant for present purposes, they also drew attention to the myriad ways in which archaeological evidence is itself interpreted and archaeological inquiry inflected by the presuppositions and interests of its practitioners.

Sharp contention between archaeologists of a broadly scientific, as opposed to humanistic, interpretivist bent dominated internal debate through the 1990s. In the last decade a number of attempts have been made to articulate mediating positions (e.g. VanPool and VanPool 1999; Hegmon 2003) and, in reviewing the current state of these debates within archaeology, Johnson (2010: 215) recently declared that 'peace has broken out in the realm of epistemology'. As Johnson makes clear, however, although contestation over starkly opposed positivist ideals and the threat of relativism is less visible, deep differences persist between divergent research programmes, and fundamental questions remain about how highly theorised archaeological data-cum-evidence actually functions as a 'network of resistance'. At this juncture the issues that are

a challenge to conventional practice, or a critical argument of more pro-grammatic cast, that brings sharply into view the inescapable fact that the evidential significance of archaeological data is an interpretive construct; it is 'theory-laden' and therefore defeasible. From this the worry arises that the theory archaeologists bring to bear predetermines what they will find. At best, what we count as archaeological evidence reflects a sampling bias (a function of what resources we have to recognise data as evidence); at worst evidential reasoning in archaeology is nothing but the projection of contem-porary preoccupations onto the past, vulnerable to the free play of contextual values.

At each juncture when these anxieties have taken hold some internal critics have embraced subjectivist and relativist conclusions, usually on the grounds that they are inescapable, but sometimes with an ironic enthusiasm. As capti-vating and richly empirical as archaeological narratives may be, they are more about the present than the past: they should be judged as much on aesthetic and political as on empirical grounds. Inevitably these arguments generate the reaction that, whether exuberant or reluctant, 'hyperrelativism'[7] is a *reductio* of the very enterprise of archaeology. It must be possible, argue those who resist relativist conclusions, to eliminate speculation and subjectivity from archaeo-logical practice, if only archaeologists were to implement sufficiently rigorous scientific modes of practice. Typically, to sustain scientific goals, they recon-ceptualise the cultural subject in terms that render it empirically tractable, limiting the scope of inquiry to data and forms of inference that hold the pros-pect of setting archaeological claims on a firm foundation. The final turn in these debates is frustration: either that what counts as scientific is so narrowly defined that it drains the enterprise of anthropological interest; or, if ambi-tions are not tailored to the tools at hand, that resolutely scientific research programmes end up relying on forms of evidential reasoning that are vulnerable to just the kinds of insecurity that the advocates of renewed scientism had hoped to escape.

---

most contentious have to do with accountability to descendant communities and a range of other stakeholders, especially where the ownership, control, use and disposition of archaeological sites and materials (understood as cultural heritage) is concerned. I note, however, that although these debates are centrally ethical and political, they have an explicitly epistemic dimension; they have become a context in which the long-running dynamic of crisis debate I describe here is reasserting itself (e.g. in objections to repatriation that configure these as a challenge to scientific rationality: see Clark (1996) and discussion in Wylie (2005)).

[7] I use here the terms of Trigger's (1989) discussion of these debates.

In the context of crisis debates, these polarised positions figure as a dilemma.[8] The premise is that archaeological data radically underdetermine claims about their origins and cultural significance. If accepted, so the argument goes, archaeologists have just two options. If they are committed to epistemically responsible (scientific) practice, they must confine themselves to the pursuit of narrowly descriptive goals. A variant on this theme is the recurrent claim that archaeologists *qua* archaeologists should be primarily concerned with documenting the contents of the archaeological record as completely and systematically as they can, deferring any more expansive goals to later stages of inquiry.[9] Those who insist, by contrast, that anthropological, historical goals should not (or cannot) be set aside must be prepared to embrace the speculative horn of the dilemma.

Note, however, that these options are mutually exclusive and exhaustive—they are genuinely dilemmic—only if you accept two further presuppositions: you must assume that the connections between surviving material evidence and antecedent events or conditions are all equally and extremely tenuous; and the bar defining what counts as epistemic responsibility must be set unattainably high. That is to say, the thesis of radical underdetermination that structures crisis debate only follows given a very strong substantive assumption about the nature (the disorderliness) of the subject domain, and only given epistemic commitments that assimilate epistemic credibility to ideals of truth and certainty

One of the few places where these suppressed premises are made explicit is in a discussion note published in the mid-1950s by M. A. Smith (1955: 4) in the (British) *Archaeological Newsletter*. She argues that there is 'no logical relation' between the social, cultural past and its surviving record by which she seems to mean no truth-preserving relation of deductive entailment. As she develops this point it has both an epistemic and an ontological aspect.

---

[8] I characterise this as an 'interpretive dilemma' and develop this analysis with reference to crisis debates generated by the New Archaeology (processual archaeology) of the 1970s and 1980s in Wylie (1989).

[9] I have identified this stance as a 'sequent stage' approach to inquiry, articulated in the first decades of the twentieth century and then again in the 1930s and 1940s. The principle animating this approach is that interpretive and explanatory, historical and anthropological goals should be deferred until the data are in ('How New is the New Archaeology?' (Wylie 2002)). By contrast, the advocates of a variety of 'integrationist' approaches insist that, if broader goals are ever to be addressed, they must inform primary investigation of the record (data collection, analysis); this objection is raised, and alternatives to a 'sequent stage' approach are explored, at each juncture at which arguments have been made for deferring more ambitious goals. They figure prominently in the most recent crisis debates between processual and post- or anti-processual archaeology.

The nature of the subject domain—the contingencies of social meanings and actions, the complexity of how these relate to material culture and material traces, and the vagaries of preservation—precludes the possibility of establishing inferential premises that could secure interpretive conclusions with the degree of certainty she requires. Given this, Smith argues, it must be accepted that all archaeological claims about the past, including evidential claims, incorporate an 'element of conjecture which cannot be tested' (Smith 1955: 4–5). The result is the Diogenes problem: archaeologists 'may find the tub but altogether miss Diogenes' (1955: 1–2) and, crucially, they may have no way of ever knowing what they have missed.[10]

So what begins as a problem of contingent and local under-determination is generalised: the potential for pervasive and undetectable error is inferred from specific instances of error fortuitously detected or counterfactually projected. The dilemma-generating conclusion is that, because no archaeological evidence can be treated as foundational, all archaeological evidence (and the claims based upon it) are equally and radically insecure.

II. Intuitions from practice

And yet, as I argued at the outset, we know a great deal about the cultural past. More to the point, we know a great deal about the details of culture history and cultural process for which there is no evidence but the surviving material record. However much these insights reflect contingent histories of situated interest, systematic engagement with the *materiel* of the archaeological record pushes to the limit categories and concepts rooted in the familiar. Even the sharpest critics of scientistic ambitions in archaeology acknowledge that archaeological evidence does significantly constrain what we can claim about the cultural past: it may always be multivocal and enigmatic but it does also function as a 'network of resistances to theoretical appropriation' (Shanks and Tilley 1989: 44) that routinely destabilises settled assumptions, redirects inquiry and expands interpretive horizons in directions no one had anticipated.[11]

---

[10] Diogenes was a fourth-century BCE philosopher associated with the Cynics, famous for carrying to an extreme their renunciation of worldly wealth and ambition. He is said to have lived for a period in a large tub in a public square in Athens.

[11] In an especially sharp rebuttal to the central claims made by the New Archaeology, Shanks and Tilley (1987, 1989), and Hodder (1983), took a strongly constructivist position in opposition to the positivist New Archaeology, insisting that archaeological evidence cannot provide a basis for testing interpretive claims about the past because it is always already theorised. However, when they qualified these claims, repudiating the 'essential irrationality of subjectivism or relativism'

On closer examination, then, the polarised positions that dominate crisis debates do not exhaust the available epistemic and methodological options. Indeed, the dilemmic structure of these debates obscures a range of strategies for building and adjudicating evidential claims that archaeologists routinely deploy in practice and that directly counter the suppressed premises (ontological and epistemic) necessary to turn local and contingent uncertainty into a domain-wide, dilemma-generating scepticism. Although archaeological evidence is widely recognised to be thoroughly a construct, the actual practice of building and adjudicating evidential claims reflects two sets of epistemic intuitions that call into question the first premise (about the radical insecurity of proxy evidence). The first is that the theory-dependence of archaeological evidence does not in any strict or comprehensive sense entail a vicious circularity by which expectations dictate what archaeologists will find or recognise as evidence.[12] And the second, by extension, is that the inferences linking surviving traces to inferred antecedent events are differentially insecure; they are not all irreducibly or equally speculative. In short, archaeologists trade in a much more nuanced range of judgements about degrees of credibility or comparative strength of evidential claims than can be recognised when, on the second suppressed premise, the measure of epistemic adequacy is deductive certainty.

The key to understanding these discerning uses of evidence is to disambiguate what counts as the 'theory' (or 'theorising') that is said to load, overreach, or render insecure the use of archaeological data as evidence. Virtually any belief or knowledge claim can figure in the inference chains by which archaeologists establish evidential claims, from the most narrowly specified empirical fact through to the most theoretical explanatory schema; from the convictions of common sense to the esoteric insights of nuclear physics; from claims established within archaeology to those supplied not only by its closest

---

(Shanks and Tilley 1987: 110), they did not revisit the constructivist premises of their argument. Despite a renewed interest in archaeological methodology and in 'how [archaeologists] reach their conclusions' (Hodder 1999: 20), it is not clear, on their account, how archaeological evidence constrains despite being radically a construct. This analysis is developed in Wylie (2002: 172; 1992).

[12] By vicious circularity (here and below), what I have in mind is the kind of worst-case scenario in which the presuppositions you bring to inquiry guarantee that what you recognise as archaeological data, and the significance you ascribe to it as evidence, will conform to your expectations or, more specifically, confirm the interpretative or explanatory hypotheses you have in view when you start. An extreme example, recently examined in detail by Gere (2009), is Arthur Evans's projection onto Minoan culture of modernist, early twentieth-century hopes and fears. Knossos became the icon of a pacifist, idyllic matriarchy, defined by contrast to subsequent (and then-contemporary) patriarchal and violent societies, but at the expense of systematically misinterpreting and ignoring evidence of conflict and militarism in Bronze Age Mycenaean Greece.

neighbour disciplines but also by an expanding range of social, life, and natural sciences. Whether a given claim should be considered an instance of 'theory', in the sense of 'theorising about the cultural past', or theory in the mediating sense—theory that plays a role constituting data as evidence (linking principles, auxiliary hypotheses, gap-crossers, 'middle range theory')—depends not on its content or its target, but on the role it plays in the specific inference at hand. This means that no unitary judgement can be made about the epistemic status (the security or credibility) of these claims as a class.

It is also important to recognise that the threat of vicious circularity arises only given an implausibly seamless holism.[13] Only if you assume that all the empirical and theoretical claims involved in evidential reasoning form a hyper-integrated web of belief is inferential nepotism inescapable as a matter of principle. In practice, the many different kinds of 'theory' that play functionally different roles in archaeological inference are disjoint in epistemically consequential ways.

There is one further point that I will not develop here, but that informs my thinking about evidential reasoning. It is a recommendation that, in the philosophical analysis of archaeological practice, we shift the focus of our attention from theorising to modelling, along lines proposed more generally by Morgan and Morrison (1999) a decade ago and extended, for example, in recent work on scientific representation (e.g. van Fraassen 2008). In practice, what archaeologists build and test are typically models, not isolated theoretical or factual claims, much less systems of laws or law-like propositions. In some cases these are models of particular past activities or events that could have produced, or likely did produce, specific elements of the archaeological record. In other cases they are models of the contexts in which these events and activities took place: communities or culture histories, conceived at a human scale (temporally and socially). In still others they are meant to capture the structure and dynamics of large scale sociocultural systems operating over centuries or millennia. Models at one scale, or models of one dimension of a cultural system or lifeworld, are the basis for testing and refining models pitched at other scales or addressed to other dimensions. Claims about evidential significance are typically claims about the credibility of a model component, itself a narrowly

---

[13] I use the term 'holism' here in the sense of confirmational holism associated with Quine. This is the thesis that theoretical claims are never tested in isolation; they are dependent on other mediating hypotheses and assumptions, and stand or fall as components of a theoretical system. More broadly, Quine argued that scientific theory constitutes a 'web of belief' on which empirical (sensory) input impinges as whole, at the margins (e.g. Quine 1970). In principle, discordant empirical input can always be accommodated by adjusting beliefs internal to the web; it is this possibility that gives rise to worries about vicious circularity.

specified model of some aspect of the past cultural context or process or system under study. On a modelling approach, as will become clear, evidential constraints are diffuse, impinging on our understanding of a particular cultural past, or of cultural processes and dynamics, at a number of points; their force arises from mutually constraining or reinforcing relations with one another rather than from a presumption that any of them constitute a self-warranting epistemic foundation.

III. A model of evidential reasoning

To make these initial observations more systematic, I begin with a philosophical commonplace articulated with particular clarity by Clark Glymour (1980) in connection with his bootstrapping model of confirmation.[14] Evidential reasoning involves (at least) three functional components: empirical input of various kinds (itself often already richly theorised); theory—background knowledge, auxiliary hypotheses—that mediate the interpretation of empirical input as evidence; and the claims (hypotheses, theories) on which this interpretively constituted empirical input bears as evidence. In assessing the robustness and import of archaeological evidence (and in this, countering the threat of vicious circularity and of radical, undifferentiable insecurity), it is standard practice to make use of bootstrapping and triangulating strategies that exploit various forms of critical distance between these constituents of evidential reasoning.

Here, then, are three principles of evidential reasoning that I find at work in archaeological practice.

Vertical independence

The classic situation in which vicious circularity threatens arises when the theory on which you rely to establish evidential claims also underpins the models or broader interpretive and explanatory claims you base on (or test against) these claims. In old school language, the hypotheses that are the target of inquiry, and the auxiliary hypotheses that mediate their empirical testing, all derive from a single theoretical framework; evidence is interpreted in terms supplied by the theory it is meant to test. Glymour considers a range of cases, from astronomy and physics to psychiatry and experimental psychology,

---

[14] For a more detailed analysis of Glymour's model and its implications for archaeological inference, see Wylie (2002: 179–84; Wylie 1986).

where worries about nepotism arise for just this reason.[15] But as Glymour has argued, close attention to the way data are interpreted as evidence makes it clear that, even in these seemingly worst cases, the vicious circularity of self-confirmation is not inevitable. Evidence can 'bootstrap-confirm' a theory, in Glymour's terms, if the internal structure of the theory is such that the auxiliaries you rely on do not guarantee a confirming outcome, even though they are supplied by the theory under test.[16] As Glymour (1980: 127) puts this point: 'using the theory, we can deduce from the evidence an instance of the hypothesis ... and the deduction is such that it does not guarantee that we would have gotten an instance of the hypothesis regardless of what the evidence might have been'. Note that what distinguishes virtuous from vicious circularity is not the content or foundational status of evidential as opposed to theoretical claims, but the structure of relations that hold between the components of the encompassing theory.

In many cases, and certainly in archaeology, this worst case scenario rarely threatens in its pure form because no one theory is so comprehensive that it can provide all the resources needed both to generate and to test hypotheses about its subject domain. Of necessity, archaeologists draw resources for interpreting data as evidence from widely disparate fields, many of which have little to do with the sources that inform their thinking about the social structures and cultural dynamics that are their primary focus of investigation. In short, the 'theory' that ladens archaeological data (as evidence) is very often unconnected to the theory that underpins the models, and the broader reconstructive or explanatory claims, that archaeologists base on this evidence.

Consider a hypothetical example based on a case that figured prominently in the crisis debates provoked by the New Archaeology of the 1960s and 1970s.[17]

---

[15] These include, for example: concern that the orbital patterns identified by Newton as evidence of the force of gravity were discernible in the astronomical observations available to him only given the assumption that they reflect the constant force of gravity; and objections that Freudian slips and dream symbolism only stand as evidence of the workings of an unconscious given prior commitment to psychodynamic theory (Glymour 1980).

[16] To extrapolate from another example of Glymour's, a theory that posits a particular relationship between, say, hunger and aggression in rats may also supply operationalising hypotheses that identify hunger and aggression with specific types of behaviour. But this does not guarantee that the behaviour actually observed will conform to a specific hypothesis about its frequency or co-occurrence, even if these observations are interpreted in the terms of operationalising auxiliaries supplied by the encompassing theory.

[17] I base this on Binford's discussion of the Allchin hypothesis (1968: 18–19): a case in which the lack of archaeological material linking formally similar African artistic traditions had been grounds for scepticism that there could be any resolution in favour of one or the other competing hypothesis (about parallel independent development versus interaction between these traditions). I

An archaeologist posits a model of trade interaction between two distant and otherwise distinct cultural groups, separated by a wide geographical margin in which no evidence of a common record has been found. Perhaps this is inspired by structuralist analysis of the grammar of design traditions evident in the burial goods and elite ceramics characteristic of these two prehistoric communities. He or she might rely on radiocarbon dating and various types of materials analysis to determine whether it is possible that the artefacts thought to have been traded into one context could have originated in the other: whether they are contemporaneous and whether they are made of materials or by means of technologies possessed by the source culture. Although each of these lines of evidence is insecure in its own way, the types of error to which they are vulnerable are not likely to be a function of commitment to, or expectations generated by, the model of interaction they are used to support (or refute). There is no obvious (or likely) interdependence between the chemistry and physics required to establish the source and the dates of the archaeological material, on the one hand, and, on the other, the linguistics and sociocultural anthropology presupposed by the model of cultural interaction.

In short, *contra* standard interpretations of the premises that set up the dilemmic structure of crisis debate, the fact that all archaeological evidence is theory-laden does not entail that it will necessarily conform to theoretically informed expectations about the past.

Security

Clearly, vertical independence is no measure of evidential robustness or relevance taken on its own. The evidential claims brought to bear on models or hypotheses must be credible in their own right. Assessments of security in this sense—that is, assessments of the security of individual lines of evidence—depend on an appraisal of the background knowledge (auxiliaries, linking principles) on which archaeologists rely to interpret their data as evidence, both within contexts in which it originates, and with respect to its relevance and reliability when applied to archaeological subjects. This requires both source and subject side work: a recursive process of working back and forth between evidential constraints that arise, on one hand, from the sources that

discuss this case in more detail in Wylie (2002: 77). Vertical independence is a key feature of several of the examples cited at the outset. For example, the thesis that agriculture was practised prehistorically in the Central Plains was established, in part, by palaeobotanical evidence the interpretation of which depended on background knowledge about cultigens that was completely independent of the hypothesis about their use in this particular context.

inform analogical model building and, on the other, from surviving traces of the archaeological subject.[18]

On the source side of this equation I include linking principles, theoretical and technical resources, that originate outside archaeology—in a vast range of physical, biological, and social sciences—as well as those generated internally by research programmes designed to establish 'middle range theory' specifically relevant to archaeological problems: for example, experimental archaeology and ethnoarchaeology.[19] At its best, source-side work takes up directly the challenge posed by the first of the two suppressed premises made explicit by M. A. Smith: it is a matter of establishing a jointly empirical and/ or theoretical basis for assessing just how robust or tenuous the linkages are that connect surviving archaeological traces to antecedent events. In practice this is typically a matter of appraising not only the determinacy of the causal link posited by a claim about the connection between surviving archaeological material and antecedent, but also the overall length and complexity of the causal chain in which specific links are embedded.[20]

At the high end of security are biconditional (if-and-only-if) linking principles that establish a unique causal pathway by which a particular material signature could have been produced, in a medium that would not have degraded over time: examples include lithic reduction sequences established by means of replication experiments and some types of trace element analysis. Declining from this are principles of standard conditional form which establish that a given trace would have resulted if a specified condition obtained, but leaves open the possibility that other antecedent or intervening conditions could also have produced the trace. Analysis of patterns of edgewear on stone tools realises security of this sort: attributions of use are plausible insofar as there is no evident risk that the breakage patterns were produced by geological processes (e.g. by rock slides). Likewise, chemical analyses designed to identify trace elements or the isotopic signature of bone composition are diagnostic so long as it is possible to exclude complex dietary interactions, as well as complicating formation processes (like leeching effects), or the effects of recovery

---

[18] This way of characterising the process of building and adjudicating evidential claims comes from a discussion of analogical inference by Patty Jo Watson (1979: 281; Wylie 1985, 2002: 150–2).

[19] In archaeological discussions the term 'middle range theory' designates the range of background knowledge (theoretical or empirical, of widely varying degrees of generality or abstraction) that functions as interpretive principles or auxiliaries in establishing the evidential significance of archaeological data. See Raab and Goodyear (1984) for a useful account of how this term was introduced and used. Bogaard's study of plant husbandry practices in the early Neolithic (cited at the outset) illustrates with particular clarity how important the targeted development of relevant background knowledge can be in addressing pivotal archaeological problems.

[20] This is a point developed in compelling detail by Kosso (2001).

and analysis (contaminants, sampling error). Finally, there is the enormous range of background knowledge that enables archaeologists to identify physical conditions, behaviours, practices, forms of life that have the capacity to produce a particular type of material trace or record with some degree of likelihood, but do not necessarily or uniquely produce it. These include most ascriptions of function or social affiliation, or of symbolic significance based on ethnohistoric sources.

There is something of a common pattern in the life history of new scientific tools of data recovery and analysis when they are imported into archaeology.[21] One after another external technical resource is expected to raise evidential claims to a new level of security: methods of absolute dating (e.g. radiocarbon dating), geological sourcing, stable isotope and trace element analysis to determine lifetime dietary profile and mobility. But even in the best cases, of which radiocarbon dating is in some sense the paradigm, the vagaries of confounding factors are legendary. The linking principles drawn from the physics—the half-life of radioactive carbon—may be unimpeachable and may meet the requirement of determinism, establishing a unique causal event (cutting or burning at a specified date) that must have obtained for the trace to have been produced. But the causal chains linking that event to its surviving physical trace, as recovered and analysed archaeologically, are long and can be complicated by a great many potentially confounding factors. The ratio of radioactive to stable carbon (C^{14} vs C^{12} and C^{13}) in the organism that originally produced the trace may diverge from the atmospheric norm given differential rates of carbon uptake (e.g. as these vary among plant species) or the degree of carbon exchange in the context in which it lived (e.g. deep sea carbon sinks); the baseline ratios of C^{14} to C^{12} and C^{13} in the atmosphere have, themselves, changed dramatically given the impact of growing reliance on fossil fuels and bomb effects; the vagaries of reuse, disposal and preservation can mean that the date at which organic matter stopped exchanging carbon with the atmosphere significantly predates the periods of use that are of cultural interest; and then there are all the risks of contamination that can arise

---

[21] There is an extensive literature on the history of reception and calibration necessary to make radiocarbon dating viable in archaeology (e.g. Marlowe 1999, Reimer 2001, Shott 1992, Currie 2004). Consider, also, Sillen, Seally and van der Merwe (1989) on the history of stable isotope analysis and Burton and Price (2000) on trace element analysis in palaeodietary studies; Chippindale (2002) on the vagaries of trace element analysis in metalurgical sourcing; Cooper and Poinar (2000) on the ambitions and pitfalls of ancient DNA analysis. I thank Gundula Müldner for references to debate about DNA and trace element analysis, and for a particularly helpful discussion of these life histories in her presentation in the Leverhulme Evidence Seminar at Reading University (10 Feb. 2010).

in the process of handling and processing of samples (see, e.g. Reimer 2001, Browman 1994, Shott 1992).

Even with significant refinements in our background knowledge of these physical processes, the difficulty remains that the auxiliaries drawn from physics and biochemistry typically establish archaeologically relevant facts only given assumptions about a number of other aspects of the archaeological context. They may determine the cutting date of building timber, but reconstructing a construction sequence from a dated sample depends on collateral evidence that rules out (or indicates) practices of curation or reuse. It may be possible to determine the chemical composition of bone recovered from a burial, but reconstructing diet from isotope values requires palaeobotanical information about the resources actually available, and evidence of subsistence practices that specifies what a given individual or population was likely to have consumed.[22]

It is here that subject-side, archaeological research plays a critical role, not as a final court of appeal, the context of verification to which you turn when you move from the speculative, hypothesis-generating context of discovery, but as a complementary source of evidence to be recruited in a dialectical process of building and refining analogically based models of archaeological context.[23] The difficulties are real and numerous, but a concatenation of empirical considerations—drawn both from background sources and from archaeological investigation—can allow for a grounded appraisal of the likelihood that one candidate cause rather than another was (or could have been) at work in a given past context.

The key point is that assessments of the security of evidential claims typically do not and, indeed, cannot proceed on a trace-by-trace, auxiliary-by-auxiliary basis.[24] Of necessity, evidential reasoning depends on multiple strands of argument: it emanates from disparate elements of the archaeological record, draws on background knowledge that originates in diverse source fields, and bears on an array of conditions and events that constitute the

---

[22] This is the point Chippindale (2002: 605) makes when he urges a terminological shift from 'data' to 'capta'.

[23] In describing this dialectical process elsewhere, as a matter of 'tacking back and forth' between source and subject, I draw on and extend Geertz's analysis of the process of ethnographic interpretation (Geertz 1979; Wylie 1989, reprinted in 2002).

[24] One case where this interdependence of lines of evidence is especially clear is in the examples of research designed to get at the form of, and changes in, gender relations in prehistory (Wylie 2002: 199–200; originally 1996). Another is the tortuous history by which human antiquity came to be recognised. As detailed by Grayson (1983), this was a process in which key advances in establishing the security of particular lines of evidence (e.g. geological evidence), as well as the critical weight of a concatenation of a number of lines of evidence, played a key role.

complicated lives of the material things that make up the archaeological record. The strength of an evidential argument depends on whether, or how, all these elements can be integrated into a coherent model (or set of models) of the archaeological subject.

Horizontal independence

In archaeology, then, appraisals of evidential credibility typically concern bodies of evidence, and depend crucially on strategies of triangulation that exploit degrees of independence between them. The principle is that cables are stronger than chains,[25] given a capacity for mutual constraint between constituent strands of evidence. To draw on Hacking's account of microscopy (1981, 1983: 186–203), we believe what we see through optical and acoustic and scanning electron microscopes, not just because each of these instruments depends on well understood physical principles—they are, in that sense, secure—but because, when used in conjunction with one another, it is implausible that images produced by such different means should converge as a consequence of confounding influences that generate compensating error in each distinct line of evidence. By extension, when multiple lines of evidence fail to converge, they have a capacity to expose error that might not be detected in assessment of the security of each taken on its own.

Perhaps the most obvious archaeological example of this is the use of multiple dating techniques. Consider, for example, evidential arguments that turn on the juxtaposition of measures of radiocarbon decay, magnetic orientation, tree ring counts, and stylistic variability over time (e.g., as manifest in the regular battleship curve pattern that reflects ebbs and flows in the popularity of stylistic traditions). Taken together these establish a basis for the attribution, respectively, of absolute burning, deposition, and cutting dates, and of production dates relative to an evolving cultural tradition. The causal processes are distinct and the relevant technologies of detection—including instruments, skilled know-how and background theoretical and empirical knowledge—are also substantially independent. Whatever the insecurities inherent in each line of evidence, their congruence raises the credibility of the claims they support insofar as the conditions or assumptions that might produce error in a C^{14} date are not the same as those that might bias a date based

---

[25] This point is inspired by Geertz and by Peirce (Wylie 2002: 164; 1989). The discussion that follows, of the implications of Hacking's arguments from miscroscopy for archaeology and of epistemic independence, is excerpted from an essay on theses of 'disunity' in science (Wylie 2002: 206–8; originally 2000*a*, *b*).

on tree ring sequences or rates of stylistic change. Similar intuitions figure when, for example, historical archaeologists point out the advantages that accrue to their subfield, given the possibility of working back and forth between archival and archaeological sources.[26] This, they insist, is not just a matter of augmenting texts with material detail (or vice versa), but of bringing independent lines of evidence to bear on one another in ways that sometimes substantially challenge settled assumptions about the security and the import of each.

Two distinct kinds of (horizontal) independence are at work in these cases: causal and conceptual independence. The first (the causal), is realised when different trace-generating causal pathways emanate from the same entity or event but do not interact; triangulation is possible when it can be assumed that distortion in the transmission of one type of trace is not likely to be reproduced in the transmission of another, producing an artificial congruence in the signals they transmit. Independence in a second sense—conceptual independence—holds between the bodies of background knowledge and technical practice that are necessary to reconstruct these distinct transmission pathways. Here it must be assumed that there is sufficient independence between these resources that a coincidence in the evidence secured by them is not an artefact of a confounding dependence between them. Often disciplinary independence is invoked as a proxy for causal and, more directly, conceptual/inferential independence.

In many cases it is reasonable to assume that causal, conceptual, and disciplinary independence coincide. The multiple dating techniques I have mentioned are often taken to be a case in point, although in practice assumptions about their independence are complicated by pervasive use of one technique to calibrate another (for example, tree-ring sequences and radiocarbon dating). But horizontal independence of these three kinds is by no means self-evident, and none can be assumed to entail the others. In the case of historical archaeology, the contents of trash pits and the records that make up an official state archive may have been produced by such different means and for such different purposes that they can be regarded as causally independent; and historians and archaeologists may have had to develop such different techniques and bodies of background knowledge to deal with their distinct kinds of record that their interpretive frameworks are, indeed, epistemically independent. But

---

[26] I have in mind, for example, the arguments made by Leone and Potter (1988), and by a number of their antecedents, for recognising that historical archaeology has distinctive strengths, rather than being a poor substitute for text-based history or secondary to prehistoric archaeology (Wylie 2002: 205–6).

these are empirical assumptions that may not hold. In some contexts the disposal of trash may reflect the same principles of decorum as writing for the public record and, as demonstrated by the advocates of 'history from below', there is often plenty of scope for critical triangulation between documentary sources: personal diaries may put pressure on the official picture presented in public archives. In short, causal independence cannot be assumed just because, on conventional ontologies or disciplinary divisions of labour, these seem to be different kinds of evidence.

In addition, a history of cross-disciplinary traffic between disciplines, or the influence on both of common cultural and social factors, may well undermine the assumption of conceptual independence. Feminists and critical race theorists draw attention to the myriad ways in which practitioners across the social and historical sciences reproduce a common stock of gender-normative assumptions and racial or cultural/ethnic stereotypes, despite using very different kinds of data bases and research tools. They show how categories of analysis and narrative conventions reflect, on the one hand, the assumption that the normatively male or white or European can be assumed to stand for the whole, reading out of the account (as literally inscrutable) any evidence of divergent experience, traits, accomplishments; and, on the other hand, a conviction that sex/gender or race differences are so fundamental they can be treated as a given, projected and naturalised as a fixed binary in which the marked term (the non-male, non-white, non-normative) is alternately romanticised and demeaned.

In short, appearances of disciplinary and conceptual independence may be deceiving. But this should not be taken as a counsel of (epistemic) despair. The vagaries of establishing epistemic independence do not so much return us to the speculative horn of the interpretive dilemma as specify what needs to be done.

IV. Changing the epistemic question

To conclude, on the model of evidential reasoning I have outlined here, much of the action is off-stage. It is at least as crucial to establish the security and relevance of a robust body of background knowledge—on the source side of the equation—as it is to work in the foreground, recovering and recording the material record that survives of an archaeological subject. This is certainly not news: it is something that archaeologists who were on opposite sides of the most recent crisis debates—the advocates of a scientific processual archaeology, and their most humanistic critics—have made central to their research programmes. But it is equally important, and less clearly entrenched in disciplinary practice, that assumptions about epistemic independence between lines of evidence must also be the object of systematic empirical evaluation. This requires (at least) two lines of inquiry. One is an extension of established traditions of source-side research: it is a matter of determining, empirically and theoretically, the extent to which the processes that generate different kinds of trace are, in fact, causally independent of one another. But, in addition to this, a second quite different line of inquiry is required to determine whether the background of technical expertise, empirical and theoretical knowledge that makes it possible to detect and interpret these traces as evidence are, in fact, conceptually independent. This is a programme of second order, social/historical and philosophical investigation designed to trace confounding interactions between disciplinary traditions, systematically appraising the proxies for epistemic independence on which practitioners typically rely.[27]

I have argued that, given the potential for adjudicating security and for making use of multiple lines of evidence, no one should accept the premises that frame the interpretive dilemma. Evidential claims in archaeology (as elsewhere) are a product of inquiry: they are always contingent and defeasible. As such, they are undeniably an interpretive construct, not distinct in kind from the interpretive or explanatory claims they are pressed into service to support or refute, test or substantiate.

But when you consider the multiple sources of structural and epistemic constraint that can be brought to bear on archaeological claims about the cultural past, it is clear that they are by no means all equally and radically insecure; they lie along a broad spectrum of degrees of epistemic credibility defined only at its extremes by speculative projection and deductive certainty. Evidential claims may never figure as incontrovertible epistemic foundations, but they do function as a scaffolding, a contingent stopping point in warranting arguments. The question to ask of them is not whether they meet an ideal standard of epistemic infallibility, but how to make best use of the resources at hand to adjudicate their credibility. When the analysis of evidential reasoning is reframed in these terms, it is clear that there is lot of knowledge worth having that falls short of M. A. Smith's ideal.

---

[27] An example of this second order analysis is the kind of historical, genealogical work archaeologists routinely undertake in order to make old data useable in new contexts of inquiry (Wylie 2010).

Note. I am most grateful to the organisers of the British Academy conference on *Enquiry, Evidence and Facts* for providing me the opportunity to integrate into a single account elements of an analysis of evidential reasoning in archaeology that I have developed over a number of years in connection with a range of different issues and debates in archaeology and in philosophy of science. I also thank the Leverhulme Trust for generous funding that made it possible for me to visit Reading University as a Visiting Professor for six months in 2010; this appointment, hosted by the Department of Archaeology, provided the perfect opportunity to revisit and refine this analysis of evidential reasoning in archaeology.

References

Binford, L. R. (1968), 'Archaeological perspectives', in *New Perspectives in Archaeology*, ed. L. R. Binford and S. R. Binford (Chicago, IL, Aldine), pp. 5–32.

Binford, L. R. and Binford, S. R. (eds.) (1968), *New Perspectives in Archeology* (Chicago, IL, Aldine).

Bogaard, A. (2004), *Neolithic Farming in Central Europe: an archaeobotanical study of crop husbandry pratices* (New York, Routledge).

Browman, D. L. (1994), 'Review: *Radiocarbon After Four Decades*, edited by R. E. Taylor, A. Long and R. S. Kra; and *Proceedings of the 14th International Radiocarbon Conference*, edited by A. Long', American Antiquity, 59(2): 377–8.

Burton, J. H. and Price, T. D. (2000), 'The use and abuse of trace elements for paleo-dietary research', in *Biogeochemical Approaches to Paleodietary Analysis*, ed. S. Ambrose and M. A. Katzenberg. (New York, Kluwer Academic), pp. 159–71.

Chapman, R. (2003), *Archaeologies of Complexity* (London, Routledge).

Chippindale, C. (2002), 'Capta and data', *American Antiquity*, 65(4): 605–12.

Clark, G. A. (1996), 'NAGPRA and the demon-haunted world', *Society for American Archaeology Bulletin*, 14(5): 3.

Cooper, A. and Poinar, H. N. (2000), 'Ancient DNA: do it right or not at all', *Science*, 289(5482): 1139.

Currie, L. A. (2004), 'The remarkable metrological history of radiocarbon dating, *Journal of Research of the National Institute of Standards and Technology*, 109(2): 185–217.

Daston, L. (ed.) (2003), *Things That Talk: object lessons from art and science* (Cambridge, MA, MIT Press).

Eckardt, H., Chenery, C., Booth, P., Evans, J. A., Lamb, A. and Müldner, G. (2009), 'Oxygen and strontium isotope evidence for mobility in Roman Winchester', *Journal of Archaeological Science*, 36: 2816–25.

Geertz, C. (1979), 'From the native's point of view: on the nature of anthropological understanding', in *Interpretive Social Science: a reader*, ed. P. Rabinow and W. M. Sullivan (Berkely, University of California Press), pp. 225–42.

Gere, K. (2009), *Knossos and the Prophets of Modernism* (Chicago, IL, University of Chicago Press).

Glymour, C. (1980), *Theory and Evidence* (Princeton, NJ, Princeton University Press).

Goodfield, J. and Toulmin, S. (1965), *The Discovery of Time* (Chicago, IL, University of Chicago Press).

Grayson, D. (1983), *The Establishment of Human Antiquity* (New York, Academic Press).

Hacking, I. (1981), 'Do we see through a microscope?', *Pacific Philosophical Quarterly*, 18: 305–22.

Hacking, I. (1983), *Representing and Intervening: introductory topics in the philosophy of natural science* (Cambridge, Cambridge University Press).

Hegmon, M. (2003), 'Setting theoretical egos aside: issues and theory in North American archaeology', *American Antiquity*, 68(2): 213–43.

Hodder, I. (1983), 'Archaeology, ideology and contemporary society', *Royal Anthropological Institute News*, 56: 6–7.

Hodder, I. (1999), *The Archaeological Process: an introduction* (Oxford, Blackwell).

Johnson, M. (2010), *Archaeological Theory: an introduction* (2nd edn.) (Oxford, Wiley-Blackwell).

Kosso, P. (2001), *Knowing the Past: philosophical issues of history and archaeology* (Amherst NY, Humanity Books).

Leach, S., Lewis, M., Chenery, C., Müldner, G. and Eckardt, H. (2009), 'Migration and diversity in Roman Britain: a multidsciplinary approach to the identification of immigrants in Roman York, England', *American Journal of Physical Anthropology*, 140: 546–56.

Leone, M. P. and Potter, P. B. J. (1988), 'Issues in historical archaeology', in *The Recovery of Meaning*, ed. M. P. Leone and P. B. J. Potter (Washington, DC, Smithsonian Institution), pp. 1–22.

Marlowe, G. (1999), 'Year one: radiocarbon dating and American archaeology', 1947–1948', *American Antiquity*, 64(1): 9–32.

Morgan, M. S. and Morrison, M. (eds.) (1999), *Models as Mediators: perspectives on natural and social science* (Cambridge, Cambridge University Press).

Quine, W. V. O. (1951), 'Two dogmas of empiricism', *Philosophical Review*, 60: 20–43.

Quine, W. V. O. and Ullian, J. S. (1970), *The Web of Belief* (New York, Random House).

Raab, M. L. and Goodyear, A. C. (1984), 'Middle-range theory in archaeology: a critial review of origins and applications', *American Antiquity*, 49(2): 255–68.

Reimer, P. J. (2001), 'A new twist in the radiocarbon tale', *Science*, 294 (21 Dec.): 2494–5.

Shanks, M. and Tilley, C. (1987), *Re-Constructing Archaeology* (Cambridge, Cambridge University Press).

Shanks, M. and Tilley, C. (1989), 'Questions rather than answers. Reply to comments on archaeology into the 1990s', *Norwegian Archaeological Review*, 22: 1–14, 42–54.

Shott, M. J. (1992), 'Radiocarbon dating as a probabilistic technique: the Childers site and late woodland occupation in the Ohio Valley', *American Antiquity*, 57(2): 202–30.

Sillen, A., Sealy, J. C. and van der Merwe, N. J. (1989), 'Chemistry and paleodietary research: no easy answers', *American Antiquity*, 54(3): 504–12.

Smith, M. A. (1955), 'The limitations of inference in archaeology', *The Archaeological Newsletter*, 6: 1–7.

Sommer, M. (2007), *Bones and Ochre: the curious afterlife of the Red Lady of Paviland* (Cambridge, MA, Harvard University Press).

Strong, D. (1935), *Introduction to Negraska Archeology*, Smithsonian Miscelaneous Collections 93 (Washington DC, Smithsonian Institution).

Strong, D. (1936), 'Anthropological theory and archaeological fact', in *Essays in Anthropology*, ed. R. H. Lowie (Berkeley, CA, University of California Press), pp. 359–69.

Trigger, B. G. (1989), 'Hyperrelativism, responsibility, and the social sciences', *Canadian Review of Sociology and Anthropology*, 26(5): 776–97.

van Fraassen, B. C. (2008), *Scientific Representation: paradoxes of perspective* (Oxford, Oxford University Press).

VanPool, C. S. and VanPool, T. L. (1999), 'The scientific nature of postprocessualism', *American Antiquity*, 64: 35–53.

Watson, P. J. (1979), 'The Idea of ethnoarchaeology: notes and comments', in *Ethnoarchaeology*, ed. C. Kramer (New York, Columbia University Press), pp. 277–87.

Wylie, A. (1985), 'The reaction against analogy', *Advances in Archaeological Method and Theory*, 8: 63–111.

Wylie, A. (1986), 'Bootstrapping in un-natural sciences: an archaeological case', in *PSA 1986: Proceedings of the Biennial Meeting of the Philosophy of Science Association*, ed. A. Fine and P. Machamer (East Lansing, MI, Philosophy of Science Association), pp. 314–22.

Wylie, A. (1988), ' "Simple" analogy and the role of relevance assumptions: implications of archaeological practice', *International Studies in the Philosophy of Science*, 2(2): 134–50.

Wylie, A. (1989), 'The interpretive dilemma', in *Critical Traditions in Contemporary Archaeology: essays in the philosophy, history, and socio-politics of archaeology*, ed. V. Pinksy and A. Wylie (1st edn.) (Cambridge, Cambridge University Press), pp. 18–27.

Wylie, A. (1992), 'On "Heavily Decomposing Red Herrings": scientific method in archaeology and the ladening of evidence with theory', in *Metaarchaeology*, ed. L. Embree (Boston Studies in the Philosophy of Science) (Boston, MA, Kluwer), pp. 269–88.

Wylie, A. (1996), 'The constitution of archaeological evidence: gender politics and science', in *The Disunity of Science: boundaries, contexts, and power*, ed. P. Galison and D. Stump (Stanford, CA, Stanford University Press), pp. 311–43.

Wylie, A. (2000*a*), 'Questions of evidence, legitimacy, and the (dis)unity of science', *American Antiquity*, 65(2): 227–37.

Wylie, A. (2000*b*), 'Rethinking unity as a working hypothesis for philosophy of science: how archaeologists exploit the disunity of science', *Perspectives on Science*, 7(3): 293–317.

Wylie, A. (2002), *Thinking from Things: essays in the philosophy of archaeology* (Berkeley, CA, University of California Press).

Wylie, A. (2005), 'The promise and perils of an ethic of stewardship', in *Embedding Ethics*, ed. L. Meskell and P. Pells (London, Berg Press), pp. 47–68.

Wylie, A. (2008), 'Agnotology in/of archaeology', in *Agnotology: the making and unmaking of ignorance*, ed. R. N. Proctor and L. Schiebinger (Stanford CA, Stanford University Press), pp. 183–205.

Wylie, A. (2010), 'Archaeological facts in transit: the "Eminent Mounds" of Central North America', in *How Well do 'Facts' Travel?: the dissemination of reliable knowledge*, ed. P. Howlett and M. S. Morgan (Cambridge, Cambridge University Press), pp. 301–22.

15

Believing the Evidence

JASON DAVIES

Abstract

The study of ancient religion, partly in response to anthropology, moved in recent decades away from thinking in terms of 'belief' to studying 'ritual': this has a fundamental effect on how we treat the evidence (or decide what evidence is, and what it is evidence *of*). I argue here that the transition is incomplete and explore some of the deeper implications of thinking in terms of 'belief' (whether implicitly or explicitly) and argue that these continue to hamper our perspective on ancient religion. The 'otherness' of ancient religion does not reside in the 'rationality' of their thinking: rather, it is axiomatic (their crediting ritual with power to effect changes in the wider world).

1. The naturalness of belief

SOMEWHERE AROUND 2000, there was an international movement which encouraged people to put 'Jedi' as their religion in censuses. The homepage of the Jedi Church says:

> The Jedi Church believes that there is one all powerful force that binds all things in the universe together ... So quiet your mind and listen to the force within you!

The interesting aspect of this for our purposes is the prominence of the word 'believes', which frames everything that follows. Apparently, if you want to start a religion, even as a joke, you talk about beliefs.[1] To a modern reader, it seems absurd even to note this: how can a religion *not* be about belief? A more interesting question for our purposes is whether it is a useful historical

[1] Even more confusingly for us, it seems that it *started* as a joke but appears to have gained momentum of its own.

Proceedings of the British Academy, **171**, 395–434. © The British Academy 2011.

category when talking about ancient religions or indeed any religion that does not reside with a broadly secular framework.[2]

Modern scholarship of religion is built on the attempts since the end of the Victorian era to form a discourse of religion that struggled with the cultural effects of European empire, namely the confrontation with 'primitive' religions: typically the question was built around the assumption of European superiority. Thus what needed to be explained was how we got from 'there' to 'here', so we had schemas posited where magic had 'evolved' into religion, which had (in our case) been superseded by science. To be associated now with such schemes (the chief culprits are Frazer and Tylor)[3] is now academic death: if we centre our discussions on some kind of evolution from religion to science as they did, anthropology and history become the exhaustive cataloguing of others' fallibility. It was Emile Durkheim who brought light where there had been darkness, delved into the mysteries and triumphantly returned with the laws for anthropology, and like all hero-founders, has found his words used for contrasting positions ever since. The principle that persists the most powerfully was that of religion as a projection of a group or society—'from Durkheim onwards insistence on the social as the primary area of analysis has been a commonplace in anthropology and now also in modern history'.[4] Freed from answering the question 'how could they be so wrong?', 'religion' becomes a broad point of access to how a society functions, since for the most part, 'religion' and politics are impossible to disentangle.[5]

That is not to say that the anthropology and history of religion now has a secure and agreed basis: it might be said that we are still grappling (albeit with greater sophistication) with the original difficulty, namely the shock that underlies the experience of confronting for the first time a culture who take it for granted that the cosmos is a very different place from the one that we are convinced it is (and when I say 'we' I mean a typical Western intellectual with

---

[2] Given an expected interdisciplinary readership, I have (in contravention of normal historical practice) cited as few representative secondary sources as is feasible, often with the criterion that they are the best place to start, especially for further reading: I have also shamelessly referred to my own work for further details, not least because this article is best considered as a gloss on matters not fully treated there rather than a new venture in itself. For the most recent general accounts of Roman religion see Rives (2007) and Rüpke (2007*b*).

[3] Original publication dates: Tylor (1871), Frazer (1915), but they have both been reprinted (and in the case of Frazer) profoundly abridged.

[4] Price (1986: 11). For a full history of the emergence of ritual as a focal point in studying religion, see Bell (1997: 1–90).

[5] See e.g. Stewart (2001) for this anthropological and historical commonplace; Rüpke (2007*b*: 6–8, 17–36) is one of the most efficient recent versions for newcomers to Roman religion but this has needed little argument since Beard *et al.* (1998), if not before.

a secular outlook).[6] Of course I might usefully explore non-secular perspectives but space does not permit that and, secondly, those perspectives would have their own distinctively orchestrated blind-spots. My project here is to extend secular discourse, not to circumvent it.

One of the results of this ongoing discourse is that we have become far more sensitive to what we are bringing to the evidence: when we talk about 'religion' and 'belief' we are generally drawing on a predominantly Christianised perspective that emphasised inner experience, spirituality, the well-being of the soul (as more important than the body) and some kind of 'core belief' (which is suspiciously similar structurally to the Catholic creed).[7] If we look for these, we frequently look in vain (often even when we are looking at Christianity).[8] That is not in dispute: the difficulty is that the expectations are often unconscious or unacknowledged.

The study of Roman religion has a similar history: most twentieth-century scholarship found Roman religion wanting because it did not 'fit the bill'. Their apparent obsession with ritual, the impossibility of agreeing with the propositions that we inferred underlay their religious practice and a distinct lack of recognisable 'spirituality' led to the impression that the 'original', more vibrant and altogether more spiritual Roman religion had become ossified to the point of meaninglessness by the time we reach the historical (i.e. decipherable) period. Thus we were looking for spirituality, rich inner conviction and a preoccupation with the well-being of the soul, but all we found was fastidious legalism and an attachment to 'sticking to how things have always been done'.

The persistence of this well-preserved corpse of Roman religion was accounted for by the suggestion that the elite, more intelligent and discerning than the credulous masses (that is, coincidentally unwilling to believe what modern scholars happen not to believe either), had kept up a pretence for political reasons but clearly signalled to those that could read between the lines their disapproval of all the nonsense. This position was reasonably consistent with itself: it accounted for rather a lot of the evidence we had. So when a

---

[6] Thus different approaches to religion confront this differently (and I am certainly not in a position to document them all. See Lambek (2002) as one introduction. On secularism (briefly) Stewart (2001) and (in greater depth) Asad (2003).

[7] Thus Asad (1993: 48) 'it is preeminently the Christian church that has occupied itself with identifying, cultivating and testing belief as a verbalizable inner condition of true religion' in the midst of arguing that this is (wrongly) generalised as an assumption applicable to all religion(s).

[8] Lindquist and Coleman (2008: 9), with references.

change began it was not so much in the evidence as a wholesale questioning whether the position was plausible as a whole.[9]

Moving our focus back to anthropology, a major landmark was the publication in 1972 of Rodney Needham's *Belief, Language and Experience*. A systematic synthesis of philosophical and anthropological scrutinies led him to conclude that we should abandon all use of the word 'belief' in discussing religion:

> Anything that we might please to say, and which in common speech is usually hung on to the handy peg of 'belief', will be better said by recourse to some other word; and if we are clear about what we want to say, we shall find that it can be said clearly only by another word.[10]

Thus, as Lindquist and Coleman (2008) put it, we are drawn to think 'against' belief rather than 'with' it.

Building partly on Needham's legacy and the resulting anthropology, ancient history also turned its attention away from aspects of belief, experience and spirituality towards ritual.[11] The advantages of studying Roman religion from the point of view of ritual instead of some (usually inferred) belief is precisely that most of the evidence that we have is *already* intensely focused around ritual actions.

The march of ritual meant that Feeney (1998) could rhetorically derail the expectation that we should organise our analysis by 'belief': it seemed dead in the water.

> A dynamically changing polytheistic system is an exceedingly problematic place in which to find the grounding for a question like 'what were the religious beliefs of Augustus?' This man ... was participant in an object of various new and traditional cults at Rome and throughout the empire, and initiate into the mysteries of Eleusis since the age of 32. He was acclaimed in marble, bronze, papyrus and song as the descendant of Venus and the son of divus Julius. He was the vice regent of Jupiter, founder of a new temple of Jupiter's founder, and always

---

[9] Rives (1998) is a useful summary of the various permutations of scholarship in the twentieth century. Feeney (1998: 3) dates the beginning of the change to the publication of Jocelyn (1966).

[10] p. 229, after a painstaking epistemological and lexical set of arguments that sought in vain for a reliable index of what 'belief' means or can usefully mean. A case can be made to distinguish the implications of the uses of 'believe' and 'belief(s)' but space does not permit a full explanation here. For my purposes, any cognate form refers to both the verb and the noun. Nor am I referring here to the 'polite' uses such as 'I believe we've already met' but rather those with religious overtones which have a special significance, as we shall see.

[11] The scholars most closely associated with this process are Price, North, Beard (culminating in their joint publication *Religions of Rome* in 1998, and John Scheid (most recently Scheid (2005)). In particular, North's 1968 dissertation has become probably the most cited D.Phil. in the field. Other notable landmarks include Pouillon (1982), Price (1986) and Phillips (1986).

carried a sealskin with him as protection against thunderstorms. In which of these contexts is the core of belief to be found?   (13–14)

The abandonment of belief as an organising principle also led to the acknowledgement that we still have difficulties if we search for a 'core' else-where. When we speak of Roman religion, it is not a simple (single) entity: should we describe 'official' religion (as organised or at least sanctioned by the state)? Or the constellation of practices at other levels (such as family)? There is perhaps one persistent feature—ritual to get the gods (back, if neces-sary) on your side (a state of affairs known in Rome as the *pax deum*, 'peace of the gods').[12] But beyond that general feature (which Rome shared with almost every ancient European culture that we know of), we cannot briefly present any definitive examples, image or 'essence'. We know that Rome embedded ritual practice deeply into civic life via a rich calendar of sacrifices and several colleges of priests who reported to the Senate rather like expert committees—essentially, an institutionalised habit of getting the gods on their side as often as possible.[13] In Republican Rome, at state level, a key part of what we call religious practice was concerned with prodigies, adverse signs that warned of future problems because they were evidence of a rupture of the peace of the gods (*ira deorum*, the anger of the gods).[14] A prodigy essentially meant that something had begun to go amiss with the cosmos but there was usually time to put it right through ritual appeasement.[15] Sacrifice allowed for the prac-tice of certain kinds of divination (the entrails of the animal were examined for signs by specialist diviners, the *haruspices*)[16] though that is only a subset of the enormous range of divinatory practices we find in antiquity. The point about ritual is that it not only gave access to the gods' mood, it was also the remedy for their anger: if the signs continued to be adverse, one could continue making offerings until they were appeased (a process known as *perlitatio*).

[12] A full account of 'how one might influence a god' is much longer than just ritual, but it will function here as a shorthand for asking for a god's help with the expectation of thanks to the deity.

[13] For the formal priesthoods and their role in Rome, see Beard *et al.* (1998: 18–30); more generally Horster (2007), Beard and North (1990), Rives (2007) and Rüpke (2007*b*) (via index).

[14] For a less brief, but nonetheless introductory, account of Roman religion see Dowden (1992), North (2000), Scheid (2003): for a summary of recent scholarship on specific themes Rüpke (2007*a*).

[15] Technically, with *your* cosmos—Rome was happy to ignore signs that did not apply to her business or field of influence (MacBain 1982: 29–31). I have argued elsewhere that Fate was a 'higher' order of unavoidable outcomes, and part of religious practice was to decide whether you were faced with a rupture that could be put right by sacrifice to the relevant gods or things were unavoidable (Davies 2004: 106–15, 171–6, 211–21 and 271–82.)

[16] On whom see Haack (2003).

In a state that placed great emphasis on divine support, getting rituals right was a serious matter: a 'pious' nation in antiquity was one that diligently looked for adverse signs and appeased the gods promptly. So if we take a look at one of our best (and, we assume, fairly representative) sources for Roman religion, the annals of the Arval Brethren (a 'minor' priesthood) we see not debate about one's inner relationship with any divinity but rather what appears to be a 'technology of supplication'.[17] Whatever Roman religion was, it seems to have put a great emphasis for the most part on expecting *practical* results: the gods had an overweening influence on the outcome of events and if you failed and could not find a plausible cause in the human realm there was a good chance it was down to ritual error.[18]

The Roman state did not attempt 'personal' conversion in the modern sense nor even enforce participation in civic ritual (to our knowledge) for centuries until a perceived crisis in AD 249.[19] None of this is to say that individuals had no personal input or practices, just that ritual practice appears to be the best place to start our enquiries. The 'ritual turn' creates a different map of ancient religion from 'belief'. What becomes important is *whose* gods, *which* gods: they were not universal or personal in the same way that they are in monotheism and they could be induced to join (or change) sides. Rome had a history of bringing foreign gods into their fold, thus obtaining greater support (and also depriving their enemies of their protecting deities).[20] And though we had put a personal focus on religion, it became obvious that it was often more useful to think of it at a state level—thus we now speak of 'civic paganism'.[21]

Thus in recent decades, Roman religion has seen a massive expansion of interest, and the vast majority of studies focus on identity (what does it mean to be Roman/not Roman?)[22] Needham's argument won the day, it seems. All of which makes a recent resurgence of interest in some quarters in 'belief' all the more challenging.[23]

---

[17] John Scheid has published extensively on the Arval Brethren; the evidence is most recently collected in Scheid (2005)—*Quand faire, c'est croire* ['Believing is doing'].

[18] Davies (2004: 9–19, 90–4), drawing heavily on Horton and Finnegan (1973).

[19] For enforced participation in rites (or not), Rüpke (2007b: 7–8) has an overview and further references. I am not referring to instances where individual cults or groups were suppressed, but the general enforcement of the whole population's involvement in communal ritual.

[20] A process known as *euocatio* (on which see Beard *et al.* (1998) via index and Ando (2008: 113–19, 128–48)).

[21] A model that is not immune to criticism: see Bendlin (2000).

[22] See, for instance, the collection of Schultz and Harvey (2006).

[23] A phenomenon not limited to ancient history: Lindquist and Coleman's (2008) introduction exists in the tension of their wishing to side with Needham but finding that 'belief' just 'keeps coming back' in anthropology.

2. The return of belief

King's (2003) 'The organisation of Roman religious beliefs' is one of the most sustained attempts to restore 'belief' explicitly as a frame of reference for studying ancient religion: it is therefore worth examining the arguments both for specific points, but also as opportunities to explore other issues that are relevant, but perhaps less explicit, elsewhere.

> It will be argued here that the arguments that have been employed against the use of the word 'belief' are not self-consistent, and the calls to banish the term from Roman studies seem premature, for the term 'belief' is appropriate and useful for describing some aspects of the Roman religious experience.

He asserts firstly that Needham rejected the term 'belief' 'on the grounds that it could not be translated into the language of the Nuer people of Sudan'. Second, he argues that 'the word "belief" has a wide range of definitions ... the lack of a consistent meaning makes the term useless for analysis'. He continues by saying that these two arguments contradict each other, on the grounds that one needs a specific definition to know whether or not it can be rendered into Nuer. Needham's argument, so the logic goes, is thus 'disabled' and we must discard his claim that 'belief' should be abandoned.[24]

This objection seems unconvincing to me on two counts: in order to establish that 'belief' is particular (indeed, peculiar) to the modern West, Needham examines far more languages than just Nuer[25] but even if he had limited himself to one language and culture, I also see no logical problem with asserting that something's vacuity or lack of specificity makes it impossible for it to be translated. There is no contradiction in asserting that the English word 'thing' has so many meanings and allusions that it does not have a single Latin equivalent and that we are therefore well advised to avoid using the word in translation from Latin since a different word can always be used with more accuracy. This is precisely analogous to what Needham said of belief.

King goes on to note rhetorically that the term 'ritual' can also be said to have too many meanings to be of use but has not been discarded.[26] Thereby

---

[24] King (2003: 276–7).

[25] I note: Penan (which he opens the enquiry with and returns to at intervals); Nuer: 14–44; Meru: 24; his chapter 'Comparison' (32–9) deals with Anuak, Navaho, Hindi, Kikchi, four dialects in the Philippines, Uduk, Piro, Huichol, the Wewewa dialect in Indonesia, Roti, Chinese and Sanskrit. By the time the reader reaches page 42 and finds themselves facing a table covering Indo-European, Hebrew, Greek, Gothic, Old English, Late Old English and Middle English (with more languages mentioned in the running text), the phrase 'bewildering array' seems appropriate. Needham deserves more credit than this even (especially) from his critics and detractors.

[26] p. 278, citing Goody (1977).

discounting the argument that a lack of an agreed unified meaning invalidates the use of 'belief', King (278) proposes we test a redefined version of the term against the Roman evidence:

> belief is a conviction that the individual (or group of individuals) holds independently of the need for empirical support.

He cites an example, an inscription by a mother grieving for her daughter which he translates as 'I believe (*credo*) that some deity or another was jealous of her'.[27] Here we surely have a circular argument—the act of translating this way is supposed to prove that the troublesome concept has relevance. The case might be more persuasive if we had more examples of this type that allowed for comparison. Thirdly, and even more damagingly, King seems to have promoted *credo* to a higher status in the sentence than it deserves: I would prefer 'some god, I suppose (*credo*), begrudged her existence'.[28]

Is 'belief' the most appropriate translation here, and if it is, is this sufficient evidence to restore its general use? Even within this tiny text, vastly divergent readings are possible: do we see almost impossibly heartbreaking acquiescence to what everyone was saying to a distraught mother who has finally come to agree that there is no other explanation that makes sense of a senseless nightmare?[29] Or, at the other extreme, does *credo* indicate a flippant disdain for whatever the cause of death was, an irritation with the bother of deciphering a diagnosis? We simply cannot tell since this example could be used for either position (though my preference is for pathos). But to make this statement positive evidence for one particular frame of mind that is precisely the one under suspicion is unconvincing: since elsewhere *credo* is used of accepting an inference from visible evidence,[30] we should probably settle nearer to 'I suppose/I conclude/I accept/I realise/I deduce/I cannot avoid what seems evident'. It seems we could not wish for a better example of the plasticity of apparently straightforward statements: this evidence is almost entirely at our methodological mercy.

---

[27] *quam nei esset credo nesci[o qui] inveidit deus*, citing Warmington (1940: 22).

[28] An improvement by C. S. Kraus on my initial attempt.

[29] Compare the way Polanyi (1962: 290), drawing on Levy-Bruhl (1928: 44–8), relates an episode where a tribesman comes to accept that he must have turned into a lion and attacked a neighbour because he *must* think within the cultural frameworks and categories that he inhabits ('It is clear to us that K. had not actually experienced turning into a lion and tearing S. to pieces, and so at first he denied having done so. But he is confronted with an overwhelming case against himself. The interpretative framework which he shares with his accusers does not include the conception of accidental death ...')

[30] Davies (2004: 40).

The statement that a conviction was held without the need for empirical support is surely a reasonable representation of what most people understand 'believe' to refer to but it is one that can only be meaningful if we make certain limiting assumptions about its interpretation and application. At face value, it permits not just 'anything goes' but *'everything* goes' (as long as we ignore evidence). It only becomes meaningful when we use it of conclusions that others have already come to which we cannot accept at face value and therefore call 'beliefs' rather than 'deductions' or 'conclusions' (and so on). It cannot refer to the process by which 'they' arrived at their 'beliefs' because 'they' have applied *some* process of discrimination to arrive at a particular proposition. We must distinguish firstly, their gathering of 'evidence' and only secondly its use in a 'reasoned' argument and their formulation of conclusions (beliefs).

To begin with, the Romans would have vigorously contested the claim that they had no evidence for religious deductions: the historians of ancient Rome (i.e. historians who lived and wrote in antiquity) went to great lengths to display processes of checking the 'religious' facts at every step of the process— verification (if possible) of signs, scrutiny of witnesses and the weighing of testimony. They were certainly sensitive to how evidence was more or less plausible in different political and social contexts (e.g. adverse signs were more likely to be noticed during times of crisis). Beyond that, they were at pains to enshrine the deductive process in their reporting, clearly distinguishing observation of phenomena from the deductions derived from those phenomena (foregrounding language such as *uideri* ('to appear to be/to be evident'), from which we get 'evidence').[31]

I do not wish to imply that King does not know all this (indeed I have rather unfairly used him as a spokesman for a more general position). He must mean not that they thought they had no evidence but that the conclusions they came to (the gods were angry) are so far from our own that from our perspective they *might as well* have had no empirical evidence. Our interpretation of lightning striking a temple—a regular prodigy—is utterly different from theirs (routine expiation of the god's wrath through sacrifice). In other words, his definition amounts to saying *they were mistaken*, because there *are* no gods and we routinely use 'believe' to signal this paradox—they accepted that Jupiter was king of the gods but we do not (and find it hard to imagine how they did). At this point a non-historian might well acerbically remark 'we knew that', as indeed they did to me during the *Evidence* programme. Is that the beginning or end of our enquiry? Using 'belief' in this

---

[31] For detailed exposition of this kind of handling of evidence in one area of Roman genre (historiography) see Davies (2004).

way seems to me more about explaining religion *away* than exploring their epistemological world.

Something does surely have to be explained—it is just that this cannot be done at the level of evidence or evidential reasoning: it is at the level of the axioms upon which the identification of meaningful evidence and the subsequent evidential reasoning were based. Our secular rejection of the existence of gods in the form that we think *they* conceived them in does not need to be proven or repeatedly highlighted. We can disregard any serious discussion of truth-content because we already know that we do not agree with the ancient Romans. Their difference—which is what makes them historically interesting—is precisely what is avoided by definitions that amount to (simply) reasserting that that 'they were not like us' ('they accepted things with a lack of empirical evidence'). The drawback of this sweeping (and profoundly disorientating, when you think it through) approach is that we never get *near* to seeing the contours of their thinking.

Can we then adapt King's strategy and redefine belief (but differently)? After all, historians are accustomed to problematising almost every term that they use—'state', 'society', 'the self' ... but the crucial difference, it seems to me, is that with a little practice these problematise *themselves*. It does not take much study of history to realise how difficult notions such as 'state' are in practice. Such terms refuse to be reductive and insist, by their very usage, on evoking a range of possibilities that must be constantly renegotiated by the writer. 'Belief', on the other hand, is utterly reductive (requiring the answers 'yes', 'no' and having only one grey area—'don't know'); rather than demanding enquiry, it conflates closure (the reasonable ceasing of enquiry) with conclusion (an exhaustion of enquiry). Thus, using 'belief' cannot be historically useful. The most carefully factual account, when framed in terms of 'belief', becomes an extended confirmation of their collective insanity—but our purpose is to make ancient Rome more intelligible. The project of rehabilitating 'belief' as a subtle lens of enquiry must defeat itself very rapidly simply because 'belief' is a simplifying designation.[32]

This is in fact what happens in King's analysis. He proposes that we use beliefs as a reference point in considering Roman paganism and Christian pagan beliefs but that the former be treated as a polythetic set, highly tolerant of variation and in contrast to the highly organised and regulated Christian beliefs. He refers to an anthropological commonplace—that a different inter-

---

[32] Even if we allowed some scope to a redefined 'belief', it is hardly as conspicuous in ancient discussions as it is in the modern world, where references to the gods/God are peppered with 'belief' clauses.

pretation of the same ritual can unproblematically and simultaneously be held by different people about the same ritual.[33] Paradoxically, his persistent application to the evidence for a lack of cohesion at the level of interpretation means he is ineluctably drawn into arguing that *ritual* is the single most reliable organising principle:

> Instead of attempting to reconcile the contradictions of those beliefs and assert an orthodox theology, the state priests instead focused on encouraging conformity in ritual practice [orthopraxy] ... The same rituals could be employed by those who held different beliefs within the context of state-encouraged ritual conformity. (298)

It seems to me that this is equivalent to saying that the defining difference between paganism and Christianity is that one organised itself around ritual and the other around belief, even though he set out to say that they are both organised around beliefs but differently. Arguing that we should see religious organisation as organised on the basis of largely unregulated assumptions/interpretations (which are highly variable, therefore unpredictable, *therefore* not the most useful focus for 'organisation') rather than the ritual (whose form was strenuously maintained and altered with the greatest of reluctance in ancient Rome) seems to me to invert an order of priority. It was the very lack of importance placed on belief that allowed it to be so utterly variable, whereas ritual shows an extremely *high* level of regulation and conformity in its performance.[34]

Implicit belief

Thus far we have dealt with explicit use of 'belief' by rounding on King's expression of more widely held positions but it also causes difficulties when implicit: even in the scholarship that orientates itself around ritual rather than belief, there is a tendency for the occasional but trenchant use of deprecatory or sneering remarks, as if the writer wishes to signal their distaste, albeit discreetly. Though far from universal, such remarks are not uncommon even in

[33] On p. 292, he notes that the Ahka of Burma and Thailand all agreed that a particular ceremony removed rats but no one agreed on the precise mechanics. Feeney (1998: 128) cites a Shintoist ritual of which a senior priest said 'I'm not really sure [what the meaning of the ritual is] ... there are many theories ... but we are not sure which of them are true.' These discrepancies may be deliberate, since stages of initiation can include the revelation that 'everything you've been told up to now is not actually true', for which see e.g. Keane (2008: 111).
[34] Rüpke (2007b: 9–13) outlines ways that religious understanding (not the same as ritual) was transmitted in the apparent absence of institutionalised education and we know that priesthood—a predominantly technical activity—involved what can reasonably described as apprenticeship.

studies that begin by claiming to offer a more sympathetic and nuanced picture of religion. I will argue that the resurgence of belief and the apparently innocuous occurrence of deprecatory remarks are different responses to the same underlying phenomenon. To appreciate the 'stickiness' of belief we must move next beyond a focus on the 'inner' and 'personal' aspects to the broader social implications.

3. The utility of belief: the fiduciary contract

The usefulness (and therefore what lies behind the impulse to rehabilitate it) of 'belief' lies, I suggest, in its invocation of a 'fiduciary contract' (almost an appeasement gesture, in a secular society). In a nutshell, 'I believe' encapsulates (and permits) both *my* certainty but also *your* doubt. If you did not doubt (or I did not care in the slightest whether you did), I would say 'I know' or otherwise treat my position as 'real' and self-evident. In other words, when two or three are gathered together who believe the same thing, the word 'believe' is at liberty to disappear from their language. Christians '*know*' that Jesus is risen, and so on. Conversely, from the point of view of the secular hegemony, to declare something to be a belief effectively says that the truth claims are bracketed out of secular ('normal') discourse: as Wittgenstein, cited by Needham (1972: 73), put it 'it isn't a question of my being anywhere near him [a religious "believer"], but on an entirely different plane'.[35] As a modern secularist, I might (to put the position at its bluntest) think you're mad but I will grudgingly allow you to believe what you want—as long as you say and/or act as if 'it's a belief' and thereby keep it 'private' (which carries the implication of 'innocuous to society'). Though Needham discusses this regularly, he focuses on the inner state rather than the social compromise involved and (more to my point) the fact that this compromise is essential for the continued hegemony of secularism.

Lindquist and Coleman (2008) offer an anecdote about an acupuncturist, called to treat a participant in their workshop who described his own practices as 'beliefs'.[36] They draw our attention to some of the dynamics of the fiduciary

[35] This is a strong version of the observation by Lindquist and Coleman (2008) that 'in using these terms in the way that we do, we have already constructed a hierarchy of value between distinct epistemological systems'.

[36] I confess to a fascination with their failure to comment explicitly on whether the patient actually reported any relief. If not, then perhaps they were avoiding offence by what might have appeared to be gloating; on the other hand, if the patient did report improvement, they would have put themselves in a partisan position by drawing attention to it. By their silence, they thereby (very understandably) *enact* rather than challenge the fiduciary contract, even in a piece called 'Against Belief'. I will return to the awkward fit of the 'religious' term to unorthodox medical practice.

contract of belief but implicitly deal with it as if it were the spontaneous position of 'the religious' without much external pressure. It seems to me that the
self-positioning in a secular (possibly critical) environment of the 'religious' as
'believers' who are acutely aware that they are marginal, is better viewed as an
unequal compromise whose violation by 'believers' would be met with great
resistance by 'non-believers'.[37]

I should emphasise that I am avoiding any attempt to describe what 'religious people' do with 'belief'.[38] I am specifically interested in the way that it is
deployed in secular discussion *of* 'religious people', often under the impression
that the term can be unproblematically borrowed from those people to whom
'it belongs'. When a Christian says 'I believe in God' to another Christian, it
means something very different in practice from when they say it to a secular
audience, and it means something different again when a non-believer says of
another person 'they believe in God'. In the second case, they are (like the acupuncturist) positioning themselves on Wittgenstein's 'other plane altogether',
and frequently do so as a defensive move (to protect their discourse from interrogation on what they would consider inappropriate criteria, such as 'material
evidence'). In the third case, while (obviously) a whole range of meanings are
possible, the situation will generally involve an element of abandoning 'normal'
discussion. I will briefly discuss the second before focusing more fully on my
third distinction.

If we think that the secular 'conceptions' of 'belief' and 'religion', whatever
their origins (my first distinction), are in their current usage somehow 'spontaneous' and 'natural', we might as well also conclude that most members of
ethnic minorities in the modern West are 'instinctively hard-working' and
'naturally polite' (especially to high-status white native Anglophone men) and
that women, instinctively happy to be routinely interrupted and 'put straight'
by men in discussion, just *prefer* to do the lion's share of the housework (they
even enjoy grumbling about it—that's just what women do).[39]

We should not then be so surprised by the acupuncturist's proclamation of
his practice as a set of beliefs. He appears to be under no illusions about where
the boundaries lie, and he kept them dutifully even while practising his art.

---

[37] One word will probably suffice to evoke the forces unleashed by the breaking of the fiduciary
contract—creationism. On the other side, there is the violation of religious privacy when Richard
Dawkins put forward the idea of 'memes' to medicalise (pathologise) religion, with the most
obvious threat to the truce being his direct calls for children not to be taught religion.

[38] On which see, amongst thousands of possible references, Keane (2008: 123–4).

[39] Thus, even words like 'concept' become problematic when used to describe 'beliefs' and 'religion':
they are better seen as strategies or transactions by virtue of their implicit claims to neutrality
and naturalness.

Had he begun to 'attempt to convert' his patient or audience (merely reporting his practices as 'factually based' rather than as 'beliefs' would probably have sufficed), the breaching of the boundary would no doubt have been made very clear to him.

Focusing now on my third distinction, the ascription of 'belief' by a 'non-believer', anything circumscribed as a belief becomes a deliberately constructed epistemological black box, impenetrable by usual methods and publicly acknowledged to be idiosyncratic and non-hegemonic.[40] Thus, whereas a discussion framed entirely within a shared paradigm can potentially end with mutual agreement and understanding between peers, when 'religion' and 'belief' enter the frame, 'toleration' (admittedly, often impatient) is the only realistic form of closure or truce (unless one wants an insoluble argument).

We can now begin to appreciate more fully the propensity to invoke 'belief': since the boundary must be ongoing redrawn and reaffirmed in secular discourse, and since the scholar of religion is constantly confronted by alien material, an enactment of secular identity is as much a necessary part of the historiographical art as is footnoting sources responsibly. Put differently, 'beliefing'—discerning explicit or inferred propositions and thereby constituting strange practices or statements as beliefs—is the primary way that we manage 'the other' and its normality is such that it would be conspicuous if absent, raising suspicions that the historian or anthropologist had 'gone native'. Put rather forcibly into a nutshell, if it doesn't make sense to us, it's best called a belief. Since the function of calling things 'beliefs' is protectively to define secularity's modes and axioms, it is not surprising that it becomes a handicap to a sympathetic treatment of the past—it is not *supposed* to be sympathetic but rather to establish unequal positions. Thus 'explaining' ancient religion in terms of 'belief'—a *refusal* to be drawn into a discussion— is a self-defeating venture. The following discussion is therefore more an exploration of our historicising, 'beliefing' gaze than about the historical objects of our analysis—it is about what we risk doing *to* evidence rather than *with* it.

4. Beyond Needham

There is a particular consequence of 'beliefing' which makes historical description very difficult: framing any 'knowledge system' or 'thought system' within

---

[40] We shall return below to the theme of 'believing in' non-hegemonic medical practices.

'belief' has a flattening, homogenising and unifying effect on its propositions, dilemmas and epistemological functioning—which is easy to demonstrate with an example.

If I were to mention 'Roman knowledge', my sense is that it would evoke an expansive sense of possibility in the reader: they would expect something nuanced, no doubt rather hit-and-miss 'compared to modern understanding' (but in the right sort of area)—complex if somewhat muddled and operating by recognisable or at least discernible rules. If, however, I speak of 'Roman religion', I instead evoke a bounded jumble of beliefs, all of equal value to us (none) and of equal interest (as oddities). Thus, if someone asked me 'what did the Romans know?' it would be an odd question that they would surely not expect a complete answer to (my response would be something like 'pull up a chair and bring refreshments ...'). Yet I am routinely asked 'what did the Romans believe?' with the 'natural' expectation that I can somehow identify and briefly render something intelligible. My greatest difficulty is that, apart from the fact that we have extensive information that can be called 'religious' (which by no means lends itself to great brevity), their *relationship* with their practices was not 'religious'. By this I mean it was not a private relationship with one or two 'simplistic and bizarre propositions' that were viewed with great suspicion by mainstream society: they *were* mainstream society.

Thus, bringing 'belief' in implies a preference to constitute its objects of interest as a single entity or set of conjoined and virtually inseparable entities so that the boundary of 'rationality' can be drawn. What gains more from this process in our society is secular rationality rather than 'religion' (which gains nothing from the transaction apart from knowing where the ghetto begins and ends). By identifying what we cannot or will not accept or engage with as equals ('that's a belief', 'so is that ... and that too ... I don't have to work them out') we are also defining what we *can*. Intellectually, there is now 'us' and 'them'. Since what 'they' have in common is that they are 'not us', we lean towards grouping them into one category and can then act as if they are 'all the same'.

This is an inevitable aspect of identity-building and (I stress) one I wish to explore (rather than decry). The particular drawback for the historian that I wish to draw attention to is that this flattening and grouping perspective does not equip us to find out what is 'abroad' in any detail.[41] Imagine a world traveller returning home triumphant with discovery—'they're all foreign!'

---

[41] Lindquist and Coleman (2008: 8) similarly offer that, when we speak of beliefs, we are 'assuming that a homogeneous, hegemonic worldview prevails in the culture of others in contrast to the heterogeneous, contested, nuanced character of culture in our own society'.

Needham might have challenged such a traveller to attempt a description of the places visited without mentioning 'foreignness' as an exercise not in truth ('but they are foreign') but towards a more informative description. We would tire of a description that ran 'they had foreign buildings for the foreign people, with foreign animals ...' yet we are accustomed to accounts of other cultures (or subcultures) that repeatedly invoke 'belief' (preferably in a familiarly monotheistic divinity).[42] The sheer embeddedness of the fiduciary contract means that the impact of this taxonomic gesture on how we see the evidence is virtually invisible to us.

As a result of this unifying process that makes all religions equal (or perhaps 'equally unequal'), distinctions made within the 'religious' realm are meaningless to us—all the food was equally foreign. In addition, belief's binary overtone strongly predisposes us to look actively for its shadow, complete scepticism. With all practices and propositions singularised any single (even isolated) criticism of a religious judgement or action by its practitioners can easily (almost automatically) therefore taken to be dismissing *all* religious judgements. Any ancient writer who criticises a particular instance (e.g. a misdiagnosed prodigy that was just a coincidence) is in danger of being held up as a (suspiciously modern-sounding) 'sceptic' as if a single example of less-than-total affiliation with a single proposition acts like a needle to a balloon.[43] The anthropologist Mary Douglas used to tell an anecdote about a tribal elder she had spent time with who laughed as he said 'if it's really important, we consult the oracle again the next day, just to check it got things right'. This is unscholarly since it cannot be referenced but the most noteworthy point is that she added that she usually refrained from introducing it into discussion because 'people wouldn't understand': she was concerned that once it was conceded that they were not unwaveringly and completely sure about their greatest oracle, the entire edifice of their religion would look ready to topple over. Even scholarship that talks of plural 'beliefs' and demonstrates a complex set of reasonings struggles to escape this unifying and flattening tendency—multiplying black boxes does not change the fact that all the ideas are still of an equal order in their impenetrability. With this gaze, it is virtually impossible for us to see any distinction between the different orders of reasoning or appreciate what can and cannot be criticised. At best, the description we end up with lacks any nuance or depth: in a narrative (whether fictive or

---

[42] For a compelling glimpse into the power of language to render the familiar (sensible) into the bizarre, see the satire of anthropological writing that is the account of the Nacirema (Miner 1956).

[43] For examples of this kind of reading, see Davies (2004: 44 and 94).

'factual') written in ancient Rome, there might be mention of a prodigy in passing but we cannot tell whether this is a trivial detail or a deeply significant clue to the ancient reader about how events look like unfolding.[44] With regard to 'religious' cues, our sensitivity to ancient narratives is probably akin to a modern child watching a disaster film who barely registers, let alone understands, the scene where the hydraulic brakelines on a car entering the uninhabited desert are accidentally ruptured or the bolt works loose from the aeroplane's wing on take-off. Even if they do, they cannot see its significance for later events or the different magnitude of another, trivial, scene in the ordering of events.

If this is what belief 'actually means' in the way we use it, is it possible to work historically with this meaning, of this singularising gaze? This seems pointless to me, as well as self-defeating. Firstly (pointless), it abandons the main advantage of using the term (drawing a line between us and them by instead asserting that 'they' were drawing a line between themselves and another 'them'). Secondly (self-defeating), if we *are* moved to redefine belief, we must take responsibility for the fact that we are projecting its effect back in time: that is to say, if we were to say that 'group X believed in Y/believed Y' then we would be concluding that a group in antiquity took up a position comparable to a modern religious group—declaring their allegiance to a framework or set of propositions that they *knew* took them out of step with mainstream society, to whom their discourse was rather impenetrable and also rather trivial. In such a scenario, some slippage of details as we apply the term would be tolerable (as it is in notions like 'state', 'power' and 'society'). But such a project is doomed: it would present even more convoluted problems than our current concerns, as a simple example will show.

One group that set itself apart in such a way in the early Roman Empire was the sect that would eventually establish its own hegemony—Christianity. If we say that 'early Christians believed in their God', our problematised and nuanced meaning would be that by doing so, they vehemently asserted their adherence to a singularised proposition and thereby established their contrary identity and mutual solidarity. But because we are so accustomed to using the word unproblematically, our subtlety becomes completely invisible, and it reads like an unproblematised and unreconstructed version whose redundancy is obvious—*of course* early Christians believed in God (otherwise

---

[44] Such difficulty is of course not exclusive to religion: as the Evidence programme found, a similar set of problems occur across disciplines and paradigms. But only religion and the 'wrong' kinds of medicine (which the reader will have noted is a shadowy and undeclared theme here) are automatically and pre-emptively marginalised, whereas disciplinary thinking at least has an initial established and accepted claim to legitimacy in most quarters.

they would not be Christians). There is no way to use 'belief' to indicate that this was their forging a (or even inventing *the*) fiduciary contract in a particular context rather than *our* enacting a fiduciary contract in response to them. It is much easier (as Needham pointed out) to use a different expression. Thus even this attempt to rescue the term 'belief' collapses in on itself.[45]

The insistence on believing is partly what has made defining religion itself such a notoriously insoluble problem—as a family, 'religion' and 'religious things' (things to believe, even when they are actions rather than propositions) are united only by that which they are *not*—intelligible and meaningful to secular discourse. Thus it is only when working towards an anthropology of secularism—articulating *our* means of judgement—that Asad can give us a more meaningful and negative description of 'religious beliefs' as 'everything the modern state can afford to let go'.[46] For our purposes, 'beliefs' accordingly become 'anything that secular thinking cannot (and does not wish to, and can afford not to) meaningfully engage with' and is an *actively attributed* status rather than a neutral and innocuous description. The implication is that the full range of epistemological handicaps that Needham so painstakingly documented as something accidental and largely unconscious actually reveal a valuable purpose—to declare that we can do without certain things.[47] It is therefore the elasticity of the criteria rather than the nature of the propositions that allows almost anything we choose into the 'category' of belief. Thus, though Needham can say, after discussing the issue of conviction as a defining aspect of belief, that in the final analysis 'evidentially it could not possibly be

[45] In fact, this also forms part of a broader historical issue, namely that verbs are generally unproblematisable (for lack of a suitable discourse or method), whereas nouns lend themselves rather well to it (either that or we have developed stronger habits). So if we say (outside the bounds of religion) that the Romans 'questioned what a state should be', we can easily indicate a difficulty with translating modern concepts into any historical period ('state' is an example I have used already). It is much more difficult to problematise 'question' with any succinctity and in a way that advertises our problematisation. If we cannot easily problematise an 'ordinary' verb, the project of doing so with one as complex as 'believe' seems a poor place to start.

[46] Asad (2003: 147). Asad's study of secularism informs this discussion to a great extent but space does not permit engagement with the fullness of his account. See Keane (2008: 110) for similar sentiments and difficulties ('if we define [religion] in terms of strange beliefs, then explain why, when properly understood, those beliefs are not strange, what remains of the category?').

[47] I wish to stress that this analysis is not a complaint: this account is not tempting the reader into the abandonment of all judgement in a world where 'anything goes' and all thoughts are equal. *All* knowledge systems have an identity (i.e. actively defines what they are and what they are not) and flattening things down to a literal relativity where everything is equally meaningful leads to a situation where nothing is meaningful. But it *is* an exploration to make us more aware of the contours of our own thinking—i.e. an extension of the secular project of analysis rather than a denial of that project.

said that the members of a society believed anything in common' (1972: 92), he does not see that it might be supremely convenient for us to *speak as if they did*. Given, then, that secular discourse routinely (ideologically) discards the religious as meaningful in itself (while nonetheless noting the existence of religion), could we not simply discard the religious as an object of serious historical study? It *is* profoundly alien to us, why not just admit it and spend our time on more promising areas?

The most obvious difficulty is that 'religion' and 'politics' are usually inseparable outside the modern West, which means that avoiding 'religion' is not really an option. We must make the attempt—in all historiography, there is a constant tension as we endeavour to make the unfamiliar as accessible as we can without disguising their particular difference and this should be no exception. But equally, we cannot acceptably equate all knowledge-systems— that would lead to a catastrophic loss of meaning. Secularism has probably reached the point where 'calling everyone else a foreigner' is no longer enough —it must explore more nuanced ways of dealing with alterity on its own (but necessarily expanded) terms (and the best opportunity for this is the current interest in reflexivity).[48]

But this project (which goes well beyond History) is not served by continuing to enact the fiduciary contract: 'belief' has continued to appear in our accounts because the line must be drawn and pointing out the inadequacies (as Needham did) of the only tool we have for the job does nothing to complete the task that must be done. In a sense, Needham's admirable study just made everything harder by making the term 'belief' illegitimate (or at least, contested).[49] As a result, when moderns describe ancient religion they either insert (or argue for the right to insert) 'belief' deliberately or they follow the letter of the Zeitgeist (but miss the spirit) by avoiding the term but nonetheless find themselves ineluctably tempted to signal to their colleagues that they have not been infected by their material by the use of trenchantly placed and mildly (mild will usually suffice) derogatory remarks. Paradoxically, Needham's legacy has undermined one of his conclusions that we are only dealing with

[48] Stewart (2001).

[49] For this reason, I suspect Stewart's (2001) thoughts on integrating anthropologists' personal convictions into secular discourse is unlikely to succeed until secularism has found a more nuanced approach to its 'other': 'religious' conviction has already 'lost' a central and unproblematic place in public discourse—that's why it is 'private'. Put differently, such a project could not be restricted to anthropology if it were to be successful. We will return to this in due course.

'belief' if someone actually brings the word into the conversation: we now have a 'belief that dare not speak its name'.[50]

To sum up so far, before we move to the second part of my argument, 'belief' creates far more problems than it solves for historical enquiry. To begin with, it forces the reader to confront and hold in their mind the complexities, difficulties, and distortions of the attached framework rather than requiring the author to do that part of the work. More programmatically, it shifts the emphasis of our study, as has been said, to propositions we infer underlie their practices rather than those things which we can identify (namely rituals) as what *they* seem to have considered central to their practice. Crucially, even an alert reader will struggle not to reduce ancient religion to a series of binary relationships—they believed, or they didn't. But the most telling objection is that enacting the fiduciary contract (even with acknowledgement of its difficulties) cements the otherness that we are trying to demystify by writing about them in the first place. We are effectively abandoning the attempt to familiarise as soon as we start thinking in terms of 'beliefs'. Aligning ourselves with the secular project does not require us to invoke 'belief'—indeed the temptation to do so should sound a warning bell that we have slipped into anachronism. And it is not just our understanding of 'religion' that will suffer—we cannot grasp the history of Rome without addressing their *cultus deorum* (roughly, 'the cultivation of the gods'). This is still only a partial explanation, both for the explicit calls for the refurbishment of 'belief' and the perceived need for distancing (as a substitute for evoking 'belief') through dismissive remarks. Deprecating 'belief' by cataloguing its drawbacks is like cutting off the heads of the Hydra—it has not yet achieved its purpose even in the case of many who endeavour to heed it. We have to dig a bit deeper.

5. Sincerity

Many discussions of belief have noted that one 'cannot will oneself to believe'.[51] But the discussion has tended to end at that point, thus only alluding to a shadowy negative aspect. It comes more into focus if we invert it: a 'believer' cannot will themselves not to believe and belief could be described as the

---

[50] 'Where, then, do we get the notion of belief from? ... statements of belief are the only evidence for the phenomenon; but the phenomenon itself appears to be no more than the custom of making such statements' (Needham 1972: 108).

[51] Needham (1972: 84–6).

absence of will (automony) between the believer and the believed.[52] I would suggest we refer to this identification as 'sincerity' and it is my contention here that is actually the block that we stumble over most of all in connection with 'belief'.

If we provisionally define 'sincerity' as the identification of the self with a belief,[53] many of Needham's confusingly disparate qualities are easier to group. We might redescribe his project as an analysis of the *expectations* we have of belief: it is the sincerity implicit in invoking 'belief' that brings the expectation of total conviction, lack of contradiction and long-term and unwavering commitment (transience implies shallowness of sincerity) amongst religious believers. This demands the singularisation of the 'believed' already touched upon—how else could one be sincere about it? It is also sincerity that implies that action (based on belief) is required by the believer.[54] Put differently, though 'belief' is fairly reasonably assumed to have begun life among 'the religious' as an expectation they have of themselves, in secular discourse it is appropriated as a standard to which we intend to hold religious people to: an aspiration of one group for themselves thereby becomes a more rigid demand and expectation that one group has of another. That is too complex to explore here but it does not help matters when one religion functions very differently from another, which is the situation we have here. With these expectations of sincerity, the older models of Roman religion asserted vehemently (in language that denied 'belief') that the elite were insincere (sceptical but still performing their rituals). As it became obvious that this was insufficient for the evidence, we drifted towards the polar opposite—a conclusion of 'insincere' was replaced by one of 'yes, sincere'.[55] This has caused us almost as many problems as the old charge of insincerity and disbelief.

It is easy to see how the subtle unifying perspective of 'beliefing' a society or group leads to a perceived need for sincerity rather than (e.g.) critical reflection. Since secular discourse permits the existence of belief-systems yet cannot make fine-tuned judgements *within* those worlds, it must take the word of adherents as it stands as the only hope of engaging meaningfully with them. 'Insincere belief' is therefore a contradiction in terms: we might say, for

---

[52] Perhaps the most famous example from antiquity is the process described in his *Confessions* whereby Augustine of Hippo struggled to align himself with God's will rather than his own.

[53] I might therefore have used the radical sense of 'identity' (still visible in 'identical') but as a methodological tool, 'identity' has become more associated with difference than sameness.

[54] Needham deals with these aspects throughout his work and though he debunks them as reliable definitions, the fact that he needs to indicates the extent to which they are widely felt expectations.

[55] Given the strangeness of their practices to us, this is still a little unpalatable so phrases such as 'taking their religion seriously' became common.

rhetorical effect, that if one *must* have a belief, it really ought to be one worth dying for or certainly going to *some trouble* for. Beliefs that are convenient or apparently superficial are rather unconvincing. What would Lindquist and Coleman have made of the acupuncturist if he had said as he left 'You know, I'm never completely sure whether it will work as it's supposed to!'? Would we think less of the Archbishop of Canterbury if he admitted that he only joined the Church because he had nothing better to do and had just muddled along ever since? Those seem unlikely to gain an understanding indulgence, yet a modern computer specialist (engineer, lawyer, teacher …) might say these things with relative impunity because we would 'just understand' them without it necessarily undermining our opinion of their practice. We take it for granted that sincerity is 'a good thing' that makes some small compensation for the 'wrongheadedness' of being religious in the first place, as it were.[56] But the high value placed on sincerity in religion is not 'spontaneous' and 'natural': deliberately cultivated within many religious movements for their own purposes, sincerity is then implicitly demanded by the secular world as the guarantee of meaningful and predictable dealings with people who do not operate by the same rules. 'If you are going to have different axioms (and therefore deductions) from the mainstream, then please at least be predictable so we know how to relate to you'. This, I suggest, is why sincerity is so important in religion, and we are uncomfortable in its absence.

The high value of sincerity is so important that it is protected from harmful scenarios: in situations where even grudging acceptance seems inappropriate, 'sincerity' is avoided (the preferred alternative is something like 'fanatic') because the category of 'sincere' would be damaged by such an association. Thus 'sincere' (the praiseworthy guarantee that 'the business of the other' will be kept away) *must* pertain only to what is constructed as private—religious fanatics are therefore characterised by the fact that they have crossed the line into the public sphere (that is one way we can tell they are 'fanatics').[57] Sincerity and belief are so intertwined as to make it impossible to have meaningful 'belief' without sincerity (although the opposite is not true).

---

[56] Based on experience, I must again stress that I am endeavouring to make visible the secular position (to which I am personally committed, albeit with Rortian irony) with rhetorical exaggeration and mild parody, rather than stating a sincerely hostile opinion, as I hope will become clearer.

[57] For deconstruction of the claim that religion is 'a source of violence', see Asad (2003: 8–12). Notwithstanding his argument, it is often more convenient for the secular state to construct terrorism as religious (impossible to fathom or deal with through dialogue) in origin where possible. For other brief consideration of 'beliefs' as (constructed as) 'private' see Lindquist and Coleman (2008: 9).

I can therefore extend my earlier contention and say that the project to restore 'belief' is actually a sympathetic but flawed project to rehabilitate ancient religion by restoring this implicit sincerity to our subjects, because in the binary choice imposed by 'belief', the only alternative seems to be to deny it, and we (historians and anthropologists) nowadays find that distasteful and unconvincing. On the other hand, deprecatory remarks may then reflect our disappointment that they do seem to have sincerely believed some rather strange things (and we had been thinking they were so rational).

Can we perhaps use sincerity as the basis of enquiry (as has been attempted with 'belief')? To do so seems to me hopeless and inappropriate: arguing for 'hopeless' is fairly straightforward—Needham concluded his study with the assertion that 'the solitary comprehensible fact about human experience is that it is incomprehensible' which is not a promising place to start. Even taking textual statements 'at face value' (sincerity) is methodologically suspect: classicists (who are not the same as ancient historians) are more interested in the opposite (irony) and, given that an important movement of recent decades in the exploration of the authorial *persona* (as opposed to 'person') sincerity is a point of reference that is being further and further left behind.[58] Statements are 'strategic' (rhetorical and persuasive) rather than enactments of sincerity, because we have become attuned to the fact that even a phrase like 'mean what you say' is far from transparent. As a corrective to the days when textual analysis consisted of assembling statements that could be represented as 'what the author really thought', this is entirely appropriate—no one would argue for such position in a modern author (especially of fictive material). The intractable difficulty is that meaning requires context to be usefully intelligible—and this context will change, often rapidly. A statement like 'I am an academic' has a vastly changed meaning in the modern day from thirty years ago. Making it intelligible to an outsider demands an extended and nuanced commentary. So it seems that textual approaches—the disciplines that specifically address explicit statements—warns us against this project.

Are there then other methodologies we can apply to consider the sincerity of our subjects? There is a discourse about sincerity centred around the writings of the philosopher Habermas, but (from my limited forays into it) that is organised around the notion of 'an ideal speech community' of equals—

---

[58] On 'authorial intention' and especially the case that the author is no more privileged than any reader to prescribe the interpretation of a statement, the most accessible general starting point for literature is Fish (1994: 183). For the rhetorical aspects of Roman historiography, Lendon (2009), while arguing against such readings, collects a great number of relevant references (though he has missed their point).

emphatically not applicable here. The historical and textual account of sincerity and authenticity given by Trilling (1972) (and drawing on textual approaches) is at once more and less than we need here. But his situating sincerity (and move to 'authenticity') in a range of historical and literary contexts does permit us to broadly comment that sincerity only exists as a 'natural' and unproblematised state until we actually begin to examine it: its unitary and 'naturalness' (i.e. implicit claim of being unchanging and common to all humanity) dissolves as it becomes clear that, like virtually every other object of historical enquiry, its particular relevance and meaning becomes differentiated depending on which specific time and place we are interested in. More than ever, then, we should be wary of assigning 'sincerity' to historical individuals.

The lack of suitable methodology should not surprise us: 'sincerity' is simply not an appropriate mode of enquiry for history. Even if we did have a way of assessing the total affiliation of a person(a), historians must marginalise it. We could say 'Cicero genuinely wanted the Roman Republic to survive' without too much controversy, but what is of more historical interest is that he formed an opinion about this in the first place. It was only an issue because of the threats to the political order and even if we were to begin with this proposition about Cicero's sincerity, our historical gaze would slide off it rather rapidly as the assertion prompts more usefully historical questions such as 'who exactly was Cicero to want this?' (an ideologically committed oligarch? merely someone who had succeeded in that system? the philosopher? the man who knew nothing different?). Assessing sincerity (and interior state) cannot be a valid part of the historical gaze—it must yield to other, more appropriate, questions.

For all these reasons, I doubt very much that many historians would explicitly address the issue of 'sincerity' and religious experience in their subjects—Green (2007) struggles to address some of its implications in connection with a particular cult, with mixed results. But all the reasons that they instinctively avoid it *should* apply also to 'belief' (including the implied search for belief that I have tentatively diagnosed). Put bluntly, as long as it is in a historian's mind, however far back it is pushed, it will colour the enquiry.

If we shift to 'ritual' without fully problematising sincerity we therefore run the risk of merely displacing the search for sincerity from propositions to practices by looking for some kind of unifying or unified meaning or participation, and this search goes on even when the evidence refuses to be organised this way. That is, much of our current exploration, rather than being along the lines of 'Romans (sincerely) believed that Jupiter was king of the gods' is now implicitly in the domain of 'Romans (sincerely) believed that ritual would get the gods on their side and that future events would then play out as they wished'. We therefore reach the point where sincerity must, like belief, be unveiled and then excised from our gaze and I propose to do that by the judicious use of irresponsible open questions that draw on our modern (familiar) understanding of how knowledge-systems function (or rather, of how people function within knowledge-systems). Given my irresponsibility in what follows, I must first offer a disclaimer.

By and large, history is a discipline centred on honouring the distinctiveness and contingency of its subject material, and building (often creative) representations of other societies.[59] To introduce an analogy risks going against this ethos: analogies have a levelling effect and making things look more similar is to risk being not just *un-* but *a*-historical. This historical emphasis on distinctiveness means that the introduction of analogy simply provides more material that needs historical explanation. Thus analogies from other historicised societies (e.g. from mediaeval France to the ancient world) run the risk of multiplying rather than solving our problems. Conversely, analogies with the modern day run the risk of appearing to invite relativism by putting modern propositions on the same footing as those of the ancient world. If this was not problematic, we would not be discussing 'belief' in the first place. Direct comparisons of content (knowledge, beliefs) damns us either to Frazer's shadow (documenting the steady rise of humanity from the murky befuddlement of the past to the shining enlightenment of the present) or, depending on one's audience, the crippling charge of relativism—once invoked, such a description (when used as an accusation) utterly obscures enquiry. So I must ask my reader actively to ward off the shade of Frazer and Tyler on the one hand, and the suspicion of a relativising argument on the other and, armed only with the modern magical amulet of careful wording, make a strictly limited foray into analogy with the modern age.

I stress that my invocation of modern knowledge is limited to one purpose only (and it is nothing to do with *content* or the truth of propositions): it is to evoke the relationship that we have with modern knowledge and suggest that it is closer to a Roman relationship with their 'religious' practices than the way modern secular thinkers claim that modern religious people relate to *their* religion. And my intention is strictly limited to a negative purpose—to strip away the unconscious habit of seeing ancient religious events programmatically through the filter of sincerity (we can still *choose* to consider it, it just loses its default priority). I make no claims to contribute to the field of

---

[59] Jenkins (1995) (and his other, similar, publications, all of which draw on the writings of the pragmatic philosopher Rorty (especially Rorty (1989)). For an account tailored to Roman historiography see Batstone (2009) (*contra* Lendon (2009)).

anthropology more widely (though their habitual disinterest in Roman religion is a puzzling phenomenon in itself, as Rüpke (2007*b*: 9) also notes in passing): my arena is strictly ancient Rome.

These analogies are not introduced in a move towards greater knowledge, but greater *ignorance*; towards discarding a methodology that handicaps our enquiry by confronting it with rhetorical comparisons in the form of some simple questions. It is a slightly uncomfortable venture, but in this situation it seems inescapable: we already have an *implicit* analogy since belief and sincerity, in their complexity, amount to an analogy in themselves. The choice is therefore not between 'no analogy' and inappropriate modern ones, but of *which* flawed analogy to use.

Lengthy disclaimer aside, let me therefore pose some very brief questions. Are we interested in whether the lawyers who drafted the human rights act were sincere? Does a judge *have to be* sincere to fulfil his or her role? Do we consider that rocket scientists should be sincere in their work? Philosophers? Engineers? Is 'sincere' the right word to use when querying a medic about a diagnosis? Does it make sense to ask whether physicists are sincere about string theory? If that one seems vaguely plausible, given the confusion and difficulties of string theory, how many scientists would not consider the following question provocative: 'do you believe in gravity?'

It is a strain to answer questions like these. Sincerity is not easily accommodated within the relationships that we have with these kinds of knowledge and to introduce it hinders our understanding of the scientist's relationship with physics, or a lawyer's relationship with what she or he is drafting (and so on). In fact, we can envisage a situation where a professional does their duty while gritting their teeth in a personal maelstrom of objection, or conversely, a shoddy job done by someone who is wholeheartedly behind a project. Of course *some* kind of answer can be given to my questions but the sense of dislocation (even offence) and inappropriateness that accompanies the attempt is precisely my point: if our interest is in understanding something rather than protecting ourselves from it, 'sincerity' and 'belief' should be avoided.

I intend to gain two interlinked freedoms here: firstly, to illustrate that sincerity is simply irrelevant to *any* knowledge-system's appropriate operation if we are thinking as or like historians. This does not mean that our subjects do not have feelings, opinions and so on: it acts as a backdrop to give those personal matters some meaning. In interaction with our knowledge systems, we think of aspects such as professionalism, integrity, considered judgement and performance of roles rather than sincerity. I do not wish to suggest that the ancient world was an exact mirror of the present, merely to raise the possibility that we should expect a potential spectrum not unlike ours.

Experience shows that a number of my readers will react to the very idea of judging sincerity in modern agents precisely because it is unfair, unknowable, irrelevant, divisive and unprofessional. They may also object to the implicit comparison of a 'level playing field' of modern discourses against ancient, but again, it seems to me we are jumping at shadows. Let me be clear that firstly, this is an experiment in perspective, intended to have a bearing on our understanding of antiquity (not the present) and secondly that by exploring this, I am in fact extending (not diminishing) the secular project. If secular history cannot meaningfully explain the religious (the other) on its own terms, then it has effectively failed.

Sincerity is a vast topic, larger than belief, and could easily merit a far greater study than is offered here—but then, our purpose was to unveil it just enough to shoo it away. I have argued that we should actively refuse to seek it in an account of ancient religion since it is both irretrievable and—when you get down to it—irrelevant. We should be looking instead, with fewer preconceptions, at how people managed in societies (or, conversely, how societies managed people). For the most part we see people interacting with complex thought-systems and finding their way through life in relation to those, negotiating understandings, tolerating uncertainties, making judgements within the explanatory frameworks they inhabited.

6. Beyond Belief

Our enquiry has been less about what we can say about the ancient world than what we should not. What then can we talk about? I have suggested 'ritual' but, having cleared some space, we should consider whether there are other potentially fruitful options. A first encounter (through text, at least) with the ancient world confronts the modern reader perhaps most of all with what appears to be a pervasive interest in prediction (divination). Space does not permit any disentanglement of divination from religion but the two are closely linked in ritual at least. But we cannot characterise the ancient world as somehow 'obsessed with prediction' if we are seeking what is genuinely different from our own. Prediction (forecasting, guessing, planning) is just as pervasive in our lives as it appears to have been in theirs. Indeed, as the anthropologist Robin Horton found, an interest in 'prediction, control and explanation' seems to be a universal concern.[60] Once again, though we are confronted by

---

[60] Horton and Finnegan (1973).

strange practices, they have a certain logic that derives from deeper assumptions: if there are gods who define future tendencies and who care about the world of men, it makes sense to try to find out what they intend. So divination confronts us with a similar situation as 'religion'—axiomatic difference underlying complex local practices.

If I were to give the briefest possible account of the most challenging question and the *locus* of genuine alterity in the study of ancient (not just Roman) religion it would be not concerned with the thought-system they built up around a different set of axioms (which we refer to in its totality as 'their religion(s)' or 'their beliefs') but rather with the fact that it was almost universally axiomatic that one could influence gods through ritual, which was usually animal sacrifice.[61] I am unconvinced we are currently in a position to explore this but more optimistic that if we treat the practices and interpretations that derive from it as reasonably intelligible corollaries, we can gain more insight than locating our perplexity at the level of those deductions and practices. This is not a particularly distressing state of affairs—it is unclear to me whether we would benefit from directly tackling the question 'why was ritual sacrifice an almost universal feature in antiquity (not to mention an extraordinary number of other cultures)?'[62] Directions for that enquiry might emerge as other studies continue to mature.

The interesting question, it seems to me, is how textured our response can become when we consider questions that, sidestepping the hugely divergent axioms, assume that their relationship with those axioms was not entirely unlike ours with our secular ones. Can we have an account of ancient religion that embraces the full spectrum of possible responses? Antiquity was replete with people who were deeply committed at a personal level, extraordinarily adept and knowledgeable as state officials, sceptical, iconoclastic, averse to authority, relatively indifferent, particularly interested, pragmatic, cheeky, unconsciously out of step with everybody else, confused, addicted, competent, incompetent, opportunistic, ignorant, hyperbolic, anachronistic ... but for the vast majority of the time wholly *within* the paradigm of their society. Furthermore, we have tended to privilege the extant voices of dissenters and critics who are distinctive and contrary by definition but we should not underestimate the power of 'business as usual': 'the speculative religious ideas of [a few, mostly aristocratic and idiosyncratic] individuals cannot be our yardstick' (Rüpke (2007*b*: 12).

---

[61] For a summary of ritual practices in Rome, see most recently Scheid (2007), also Rüpke (2007*b*: 137–53) and Beard *et al.* (1998: 35–8).

[62] Which is not to say that it has not been broached: see e.g. Burkert *et al.* (1987) for a set of propositions and Dowden (1992) is one of those who foreground sacrifice to the newcomer.

At this point, it is only fair to mention the Epicureans, philosophers whose resistance to organised religion is well documented: but the existence of a small (if apparently vocal) subset of iconoclastic intellectuals proves nothing other than the existence of a small subset of intellectual intellectuals. That in itself does not seem unduly surprising in a society as sophisticated as Rome. They may have been the fiercest organised critics of religion in antiquity but their influence does not seem to have led to any discernible changes in ancient practice, even though it is clear that some effort had to be made to respond to it in a way that disabled its extreme claims by the time of the late Republic. They were emphatically a rather inevitable end of a spectrum rather than the last word on whether 'one should believe': an ancient Roman's relationship with religion was not a 'yes/no' scenario, where the existence of a 'better' argument would bring down the entire edifice, any more than the presence of one or two vocal left-wing politicians in a position of moderate but genuine influence makes it impossible for a right-wing government to function.

Believing in medicine

There is an interesting comparison that can be made (fairly fortuitously) with the world of ancient medicine that permits one last warning against expecting sincerity as an authenticating feature of 'believing strange things' in the ancient world. There is a striking parallel between the treatment of ancient religion and the treatment of ancient medicine insofar as much scholarship in both spheres can be peppered with deprecatory remarks.[63] These two are the areas in which the ancient Romans and Greeks seem most different—and often incomprehensible—to us. The word 'believe' is close to hand when talking about their medicine.[64] We do not say that the medic Galen made deductions *without* evidence even though we do not agree with any item of his reasoning or his prescriptions: indeed it has been argued that, within the understanding of his day, he did the best job possible (Hankinson (1989)). What is useful for us is that ancient medicine is broadly divided (by us) into

---

[63] Scholars are actively moving away from the distinction as ananchronistic (Lloyd 1979) and impoverished (e.g. Nutton (2004: 12, 16), van der Eijk (2004)) but the habit is as engrained as it is convenient.

[64] Which allows us to return to our acupuncturist: my impression is that the more orthodox presses on 'alternative' medicine, the more the fiduciary contract is invoked by supporters of the latter, with varying success. The contract will probably not be enough, since medics are unlikely to tolerate a rival model of the body, whereas they do not try to construct a rival model of divinity.

what we call the 'rational' (Hippocratic/humour-based) and the 'irrational' (religious).[65]

However, ancient medicine is intelligible to us in two ways that religion is not: firstly, we can follow (without agreeing with) their humoral reasoning, which is extensively documented, but also because we grant it an easier hearing since it is orientated around the body (which we grant to exist) rather than 'supernatural forces' (which we do not). The analysis of the deployment of terms such as 'irrational' to describe 'religious' medicine—the inconceivable within the realm of the misguided—is a particular form of the fiduciary contract that sits uncomfortably because no sooner has the distinction been made than scholars point out the epistemological seamlessness of the two domains in ancient thinking. van der Eijk (2004: 189–90) highlights this difficulty in connection with the *Hippocratic text Regimen IV (De Victu IV)* which deals with medical interpretations of dreams:

> on the one hand, this work has sometimes been dismissed as one of the most 'primitive' and 'unscientific' treatises of the *Corpus Hippocraticum* ... on the other hand ... it expounds a comprehensive medical philosophy about the connections between nature, man, the world and the divine ... as such, perhaps paradoxically, the work represents Greek 'rational'. i.e. philosophically inspired, medicine to a very high extent.

The difference is that the medical material has proven fertile ground for understanding ancient culture and the negotiation of identity in recognisable terms as an epistemological enactment of their broader values.[66] In that field then, we are accustomed to detecting nuances in their thinking, even though we would not consider it usefully applicable. What would happen if we assumed that 'religious' thinking had the same (or greater) level of internal coherence and integrity whose landscape is *far* more differentiated and nuanced that we have hitherto considered, reflecting a truly sophisticated and variegated engagement with 'matters religious'? I wish to close with some speculation and experiment in that vein.

Trouble with divination

Firstly, in the study of individual texts, especially 'troublesome' ones, the charge of scepticism has been a persistent one and I shall briefly discuss possibly the most influential of these, Cicero's *On Divination.* Cicero wrote a great

---

[65] The situation is not helped by the existence of a school of medical thought in antiquity known as 'the rationalists'.
[66] For instance Flemming (2000).

deal across several different genres that seem to represent different positions (they can be broadly as a political orator, philosopher and as letter-writer). *On Divination* belongs firmly in his philosophical works, and is often treated as the text where he 'speaks his mind most obviously' (sceptically) even though it differs from the position adopted in many of his other writings.

This text, written in 45–44 BCE (Wardle 2006: 42–3), has attracted a great deal of attention over the years. It is written in the form of a discussion between his brother Quintus (book one) and 'Cicero himself' ('Marcus', book two): Quintus puts forward a case for divination, and Marcus then sets out a rebuttal. Many scholars have considered the second book to have the last word on the issues and then ascribed this conviction to Cicero himself. But it is not that simple: discussion of this text's significance has been sporadic but intense since 1986 and opinions are starkly divided. Though attempts have been made to complicate the reading of this text as a straightforward refutation of divination, many remain convinced that the text represents a clear statement of scepticism.[67] Given the interwoven relationship of divination and religion, it is a short step to say that he also rejected the entire religious apparatus.

I am not in a position to enter here into the debate about how to read the text beyond outlining some lines of enquiry, though it will become obvious I favour a version that precludes the idea that a single (albeit eminent) statesman held a position so profoundly out of step with his contemporaries. For now, I shall address the 'so what anyway?' factor.

What if he *was* sceptical? What is that evidence of? Treating him as sceptical would force us to posit all kinds of profound changes in his thinking where (to simplify grossly) his political and legal writings are broadly conservative, a supporter of religious institutions, but his philosophical works are utterly unconventional. He would be somewhere between an arch-hypocrite and a man who single-handedly thought his way out of his entire cultural framework—hardly a typical venture in any society. Comparisons from our world of a young religious man becoming an old atheist are emphatically not directly applicable: it would be more like an internationally recognised scientist being converted in our day. That will appear plausible as an analogy—but only with the assumption that the proportion of people who undergo such a change is

---

[67] Complex: Beard (1986), Schofield (1986), Krostenko (2000), Rasmussen (2003). Wardle (2006: 8–28) seems rather unconvinced; Harris (2003: 27) is more emphatic ('attempts to show that Book 2 of *De divinatione* does not represent Cicero's views, or does not mainly mean what it seems to mean, are to be firmly rejected') and his position in Harris (2009: 172, 183 for example) is unchanged.

roughly the same in both societies. What if sceptical (in our sense) philosophers then were even rarer (if prominently loquacious) than religious converts in the modern age? What sort of witness to 'normality' would he be, in that case? We can be adamant that Cicero was not typical of his age, even just by pointing at his voluminous literary output. The more positive we are that Cicero was out-and-out sceptical, the more we emphasise his difference. By thus marginalising him we devalue him as a historical witness of the mainstream. So, if we work on this basis that he formulated such a clear and extreme position, we should also minimise his historical impact.

This is unfortunately the opposite of what has happened. Rather, he has become an icon towards which our attention has gravitated, and 'sceptic' has become the biggest and most clearly labelled sticker on the map of religious Rome: the fact that we are not so sure what to write on the other labels does not help (and 'believed'/'pious'/'took it seriously' do not seize our attention in the same way as something familiar).[68]

I would prefer to argue that even if he was an absolute sceptic, it is more interesting to see his arguments virtually *buried* in the context, to offset the ease with which we diagnose belief/disbelief: it is just too easy to focus, not without some relief, on the one position we think we can relate to in the strange world of Roman religion. Of course, it might be objected that I am assuming that the rest of the aristocracy did not share a sceptical position and cannot prove this, even though that general model has been discarded for the most part, but I base my assertion on two brief observations. Firstly, we know that he did not do away with Roman practices, even if that was what he was trying to do: the Roman state and people continued to perform rituals for centuries until sacrifice was forcibly stopped by the Christian emperors (Beard *et al.* (1998: 375, 387–8)). Further, to pick one example of many, arguments from another of his philosophical works (*On the Nature of the Gods*) in favour of traditional divination are cited over four centuries later by the historian Ammianus Marcellinus (21.1.13–14). In other words, he did not convince his contemporaries to throw the towel in on the 'elite pretence' and abandon divination. Either he failed to convince them of the sceptical case or they understood that he was not making that straightforward case (as Beard and others have argued.) Secondly, if any of the foregoing argument is accepted, things just did not boil down to the simple yes/no answers that we, conditioned by 'belief' keep expecting: Cicero expected a far more nuanced response to his challenges.

---

[68] e.g. Haynes (2003) draws on 'the sceptical Cicero' as a symbol at intervals. It does not invalidate her many insights but it does overly privilege scepticism in the overall picture.

If we refuse to apply a binary 'beliefing' approach and insist on a more contextual and complex one, other positions can come into better focus. The broad historical answer (why this text? why then? why that way?) can then be located in the social and political domain and give us a more historically satisfactory commentary. Thus, in this vein, Krostenko (2000) argues that though the text is taken to argue for intellectual reasons against the entire edifice of divination at all levels to modern 'fiduciary-minded' scholars, it is driven by an urgent political agenda. Cicero is critical of the position taken in *both* books, in response to the extreme problem of Julius Caesar's meteoric rise to power and attempts to appropriate the influence available through divinatory means. His chosen method was to problematise profoundly the status of divination and contextualise all its offerings within other considerations (something I intend to explore in more detail on another occasion.) He did this knowing full well that the role of divination was deeply enmeshed in Roman life and was not going to disappear because he wrote some philosophical works that encouraged his peers to be reflective and critical (as opposed to sceptical, in the modern sense.)

Just for comparison, several academics have said to me in recent years that they are worried about the future of science, which they describe as being 'stalled' and 'deeply problematic': comic websites such as <http://www.phdcomics.com/> and <http://xkcd.com/> lampoon science from the most deeply committed scientific position and expertise: their interest is not in debunking science but in redeeming it. That does not mean they know where the next step lies except to carry on going. Thus when Cicero explicitly says that his account is aimed at 'educating the young' by emancipating philosophy from its Greek origins, we should not dismiss the claim even if we find it extremely hard to chart the assumptions he is negotiating within. We should not assume that our lack of understanding is proof of his incoherence or map the methodology of belief onto his dialogue, however well it seems to fit: it is impossible to square this claim with his complex, multivalent and undeniably critical account as long as we think sincerity should have anything to do with it.

I should not overstate this case—many such rich accounts do already exist, though perhaps the most sophisticated (such as Cicero's text) have not yet been given the fullest treatment that they might attract. Given the poverty of extant texts that expose the inner workings of divinatory and religious reasoning, to be handed a severe critique as a starting point is quite a handicapped beginning. But as time goes by, more and more authors are accommodated to a methodology that explores their negotiation of identity—complex thinking *within* their system that takes us away from the simplifying mould of 'belief'. We are also retreating from giving the greater priority to written texts when it comes to 'understanding' 'what they thought', since so often 'individual exaggerations, alternatives and misunderstandings constitute the rule rather than the exception' (Rüpke 2007*a*: 5): while belief persists as a methodology, we risk taking one step forward and two back.

A more difficult area is the broader one, of ancient society as a whole. We run the risk of unnecessarily alienating the reader with a litany of strange practices as we describe Roman religion (however factually). With the historiographical shift to more 'ironic' and polyvalent description, it becomes possible to experiment more: we are moving away from privileging a single model and becoming more accustomed to looking tentatively at societies through more than one particular lens ('just to see how it looks') without thinking that the model exhausts the truth, and this tentativeness is, in my opinion, a way out of some of our difficulties.

So, for instance, if Mary Douglas, when writing *Natural Symbols*, had chosen to dwell on Roman evidence, she might have posited, as example of a hierarchy, the Roman Republic (*c.*509–31 BCE) (high grid/high group, to use her terms).[69] It exhibited a strictly regulated social hierarchy and a high degree of internalised expectations of members of that society. The Dionysiac cult of 186 BCE, with its wild unkempt behaviour, erosion of differences (gender, class, free/servile status and so on) would represent a sudden irruption of sect ('low grid/high group') at a time of stress.[70] The Empire (from 31 BCE), on the other hand, with its greater 'cultic' aspects across the political and social spectrum (high awareness of the otherness of the outsider, emphasis on the contrasting 'good' leader who purifies the group by his charisma and special qualities) would have had been a society that laid less stress on the rigidity of a hierarchy, become more articulate, been prone to factions and not-infrequently violent changes of leadership. Gordon (1990)—similarly then—compares the Roman Emperor to 'a bottle of Vim'.[71]

I am informed that the grid/group model (generally known as Cultural Theory) is a marginal one in anthropology, and exhaustive application of Roman material in this framework would arguably do more for Cultural Theory than for History (so it must be applied only lightly, and to see what it provokes). But it does allow us to generate more questions with a broader scope than hitherto: all the 'religious' behaviour in the upheaval going from

---

[69] Douglas (1970).

[70] On the elision of normal boundaries, North (1979); on the cult in greatest detail Pailler (1986), Pailler (1988); most recently Rüpke (2007*b*: 31–3), Beard *et al.* (1998: 91–6) and via index.

[71] Gordon (1990: 255).

Republic to Empire can be purposefully explored as a failed attempt to reassert hierarchy in face of charisma to see what that approach yields. We already knew about that as a political change, but if we follow the logical extent of Douglas's model, it prompts us to consider grouping the formerly disparate religious changes to see if historically legitimate patterns emerge (and prompts questions like 'was Cicero supporting hierarchy or unconsciously going with the times and aiding the rise of charismatic leadership'?)

In addition, many oddities when comparing the Republic to Empire can be recast: the strange transition in the status of hermaphrodites as prodigies makes more sense within this perspective, with a change to 'high group/low grid'. For a period during the Republic, hermaphrodites were treated as highly toxic occurrences (untypically for prodigies) in their own right that had to be disposed of and expiated with great urgency.[72] Yet under the Empire, Pliny informs us that though they were once considered as prodigies (indicating a significant violation of cosmic boundaries), they are classified 'now amongst exotic treats'[73] (an insignificant violation of boundaries). Given that a major concern of 'high group/high grid' societies is the preservation of norms, hermaphrodites would attract greater attention than in a society with 'low grid'. In the latter society, they would indeed just be curiosities.

This tentative exploration does not exhaust the enquiry and indeed never could (we would be going native in anthropology). But it does allow us to detach ourselves from our first impulsive sense of non-sense by refusing to privilege one model (especially an anachronistic one). Perhaps in the meantime medicine had accommodated this strange phenomenon just as eclipses went from having a predictive value to being accepted as a routine part of the workings of the cosmos (and therefore being non-significant).[74]

I do not wish to retrospectively turn Roman history into a lost footnote, albeit of a great scholar and my examples have proven we don't need it (Gordon (1990), for instance, does not cite Douglas). Cultural Theory is too reductive for our purposes: the main value of introducing it is to bring to our awareness that we could configure our approach to ancient religion in a great number of ways before settling on one explicitly *chosen* rather than supplied as 'natural'. The greatest benefit of such a polyvalent approach would be the

---

[72] Beard *et al.* (1998: 80 n. 25).

[73] Pliny *Natural Histories* (7.34) *olim androgynos uocatos et in prodigiis habitos nunc uero in deliciis.*

[74] Davies (2004: 98–9). A common feature of prodigies is that they were not 'natural' but space does not permit discussion of what the Romans meant, and did not mean, by 'nature'. Lindquist and Coleman (2008: 6), building on Pouillon (1982) note that the categories of 'natural' and 'supernatural' are a modern construct that does not always bear useful relation to other cultures' perspectives

constant reminder of the ideological power of our chosen approach: further-more, multiplicity is the approach that anthropology has taken towards ritual, so at least we are in good company.[75] It is more interesting to see what the experimental application of that model provokes as a response than to estab-lish it as a hegemonic model for ancient religion. A generalising synthetic model is not likely to be helpful in teasing out the particularity of ancient Rome—unless it allows us to identify better which questions are useful, then appropriate them, by taking a cue from comparative studies.

Resolutely abandoning talk of 'belief' and the sympathetic task of estab-lishing an anachronistic sincerity forces our attention onto deciphering the particular constellation of power that Roman religion reflected and author-ised. *That* is currently a historical universal, and we can work with it irrespec-tive of the degree of our familiarity of cultural axioms. The diffusion and concentration of power is something 'we understand' and are accustomed to working with, and is a preferable option to re-enacting our own culture-shock. For instance, adopting non-secular perspectives, which some suggest as a 'solu-tion' to 'the problem of religion', only displaces the incommensurability (we must choose those we understand, i.e. those that we can build a relationship with and/or fit into the secular gaze in the process).

Instead of masking the privilege of *our* distinctiveness in these ways, we need to unpack deliberately what we instinctively brand as 'religious' so that we can explore how each society's '[religious] possibilities and authoritative status' gained their particular character as 'products of historically distinctive disciplines and forces' (Asad 1993: 53–4). I have argued that the best site for that in our case is ritual, for two reasons: firstly, it is vastly more appropriate than propositional beliefs, and secondly because anthropology is also busy endeavouring to exhaust what ritual-centred discussion has to offer.

Many will feel that the argument presented here is too late: as I have docu-mented, there are plenty of studies that do successfully evade the traps of 'belief': but my sense is that we have not fully abandoned it, and continue to have an unconscious fascination that quietly hampers our understanding. The true—and currently insoluble—alterity of the ancient world is the presump-tion that gods, and therefore the world, can be influenced: 'the rest' follows fairly intelligibly from that. If we look the real 'otherness' in the eye without blinking and without being drawn into questions of how they could be so different from us, we are in a position to write better history, describing and redescribing to ourselves another bunch of people doing what people do.

---

[75] Bell (1997: 91), after surveying the major approaches offers that 'the lack of any definitive winner in the history of theory does not mean that scholarship on ritual has not forged useful tools for analysis and reflection.

Note. These thoughts have had an extremely long gestation and therefore I must acknowledge firstly the Wellcome Trust (the History of Medicine Programme) for funding a postdoctoral position at UCL during 2000–3, where some of this began to take clearer shape. The Leverhulme Evidence Programme allowed me to continue the process of simplifying them to the point of being this article, not least by allowing for a second participation with the Wellcome Trust, at their Centre for the History Medicine at UCL, who were kind enough to host a series of seminars on an interdisciplinary study of ancient dreams. Finally, I must acknowledge the guidance offered by the anonymous referees.

References

Ando, C. (2008), *The Matter of the Gods: religion and the Roman Empire*, vol. 44 (Berkeley, CA, University of California Press).

Asad, T. (1993), *Genealogies of Religion: discipline and reasons of power in Christianity and Islam* (Baltimore, MD, Johns Hopkins University Press).

Asad, T. (2003), *Formations of the Secular: Christianity, Islam, modernity* (Stanford, CA, Stanford University Press).

Batstone, W. W. (2009), 'Postmodern historiographical theory and the Roman historians', in Feldherr (2009), pp. 41–62.

Beard, M. (1986), 'Cicero and Divination: the formation of a Latin discourse', *The Journal of Roman Studies*, 76: 33–46.

Beard, M. and North, J. A. (eds.) (1990), *Pagan Priests: religion and power in the ancient world* (Ithaca, NY, Cornell University Press).

Beard, M., North, J. and Price, S. (1998), *Religions of Rome* (Cambridge, Cambridge University Press).

Bell, C. M. (1997), *Ritual: perspectives and dimensions* (New York, Oxford University Press).

Bendlin, A. (2000), 'Looking beyond the civic compromise: religious pluralism in late republican Rome', in E. Bispham and C. Smith (eds.), *Religion in Archaic and Republican Rome and Italy: evidence and experience* (Edinburgh, Edinburgh University Press), pp. 115–35.

Burkert, W., Girard, R. and Smith, J. Z. (1987), *Violent Origins: ritual killing and cultural formation.* (Stanford, CA, Stanford University Press).

Davies, J. P. (2004), *Rome's Religious History: Livy, Tacitus, and Ammianus on their gods.* (Cambridge, UK, Cambridge University Press).

Douglas, M. (1970), *Natural Symbols: explorations in cosmology* (2nd edn.) (London, Barrie and Jenkins).

Dowden, K. (1992), *Religion and the Romans* (London, Bristol Classical Press).

Feeney, D. C. (1998), *Literature and Religion at Rome: cultures, contexts, and beliefs.* (Cambridge, Cambridge University Press).

Feldherr, A. (ed.) (2009), *The Cambridge Companion to the Roman Historians* (Cambridge, Cambridge University Press).

Fish, S. (1994), *There's No Such Thing as Free Speech, and it's a good thing, too* (New York, Oxford University Press).

Flemming, R. (2000), *Medicine and the Making of Roman Women: gender, nature, and authority from Celsus to Galen* (New York, Oxford University Press).

Frazer, J. (1915), *The Golden Bough: a study in magic and religion* (London, Macmillan).

Goody, J. (1977), 'Against "Ritual": loosely structured thoughts on a loosely defined topic', in S. Moore and B. Myerhoff (eds.), *Secular Ritual* (Assen/Amsterdam, Van Gorcum), pp. 25–35.

Gordon, R. (1990), 'Religion in the Roman Empire: the civic compromise and its limits', in Beard and North (1990), pp. 233–256.

Green, C. M. C. (2007), *Roman Religion and the Cult of Diana at Aricia* (Cambridge, Cambridge University Press).

Haack, M.-L. (2003), *Les haruspices dans le monde romain* (Bordeaux, Ausonius).

Hankinson, R. (1989), 'Galen and the best of all possible worlds', *Classical Quarterly*, 39: 206–27.

Harris, W. V. (2003), 'Roman opinions about the truthfulness of dreams', *The Journal of Roman Studies*, 93: 18–34.

Harris, W. V. (2009), *Dreams and Experience in Classical Antiquity* (Cambridge, MA, Harvard University Press).

Haynes, H. (2003), *The History of Make-Believe: Tacitus on Imperial Rome* (Berkeley, CA, University of California Press).

Horster, M. (2007), 'Living on religion: professionals and personnel', in Rüpke (2007a), pp. 331–42.

Horton, R. and Finnegan, R. H. (1973), *Modes of Thought: essays on thinking in Western and non-Western societies* (London, Faber).

Jenkins, K. (1995), *On 'What Is History?': from Carr and Elton to Rorty and White* (London, Routledge).

Jocelyn, H. D. (1966), 'The Roman nobility and the religion of the republican state', *Journal of Religious History*, 4: 89–104.

Keane, W. (2008), 'The evidence of the senses and the materiality of religion', *Journal of the Royal Anthropological Institute*, NS 110: S127.

King, C. (2003), 'The organization of Roman religious beliefs', *Classical Antiquity*, 22(2): 275–312.

Krostenko, B. A. (2000), 'Beyond (dis)belief: rhetorical form and religious symbol in Cicero's *de Divinatione*', *Transactions of the American Philological Association (1974–)*, 130: 353–91.

Lambek, M. (2002), *A Reader in the Anthropology of Religion* (Oxford, Blackwell Publishing).

Lendon, J. E. (2009), 'Historians without history: against Roman historiography', in Feldherr (2009), pp. 24–40.

Levy-Bruhl, L. (1928), *The 'Soul' of the Primitive* (London, George Allen and Unwin).

Lindquist, G. and Coleman, S. (2008), 'Against belief?', *Social Analysis*, 52(1): 1–18.

Lloyd, G. E. R. (1979), *Magic, Reason and Experience: studies in the origin and development of Greek science* (Cambridge, Cambridge University Press).

MacBain, B. (1982), *Prodigies and Expiation: a study in religion and politics in the Roman Republic* (Collections Latomus, vol. 167) (Brussels, Latomus).

Miner, H. (1956), 'Body ritual among the Nacirema', *American Anthropologist*, 58: 503–7.

Needham, R. (1972), *Belief, Language and Experience* (Oxford, Oxford University Press).

North, J. A. (1968), 'The inter-relation of state religion and politics in Roman public life from the end of the Second Punic War to the time of Sulla', unpublished D.Phil. thesis, University of Oxford.

North, J. A. (1979), 'Religious toleration in Republican Rome', *Proceedings of the Cambridge Philological Society*, 25: 85–103.

North, J. A. (2000), *Roman religion* (*Greece and Rome* New Surveys in the Classics, vol. 30) (Published for the Classical Association, Oxford, Oxford University Press).

Nutton, V. (2004), *Ancient Medicine* (Routledge, London).

Pailler, J.-M. (1986), 'Lieu sacré et lien associatif dans le dionysisme romain de la Republique', in *Collection de l'École français de Rome*, vol. 89. (Rome, École Française de Rome), pp. 261–73.

Pailler, J.-M. (1988), *Bacchanalia: la répression de 186 av. J.-C. à Rome et en Italie*, vol. 270 of BÉFAR (Rome).

Phillips, III, C. R. (1986), 'The sociology of religious knowledge in the Roman Empire to AD 284', ANRW II, 16(3): 2677–773.

Polanyi, M. (1962), *Personal Knowledge: towards a post-critical philosophy* (London, Routledge and Kegan Paul).

Pouillon, J. (1982), 'Remarks on the verb "to believe"', in M. Izard and P. Smith (eds.), *Between Belief and Transgression: structuralist essays in religion, history, and myth* (Chicago, IL, University of Chicago Press), pp. 1–8.

Price, S. (1986), *Rituals and Power: the Roman imperial cult in Asia Minor* (Cambridge, Cambridge University Press).

Rasmussen, S. W. (2003), *Public Portents in Republican Rome* (vol. 34) (Rome, L'Erma di Bretschneider).

Rives, J. (1998), 'Roman religion revived', *Phoenix*, 52: 345–65.

Rives, J. (2007), *Religion in the Roman Empire* (Oxford: Blackwell Publishing).

Rorty, R. (1989), *Contingency, Irony, and Solidarity* (Cambridge, Cambridge University Press).

Rüpke, J. (ed.) (2007*a*), *A Companion to Roman Religion* (Blackwell Companions to the Ancient World) (Malden, MA, Blackwell Publishing).

Rüpke, J. (2007*b*), *Religion of the Romans* (Cambrdige, Polity Press).

Scheid, J. (2003), *An Introduction to Roman Religion* (Bloomington, IN, Indiana University Press).

Scheid, J. (2005), *Quand faire, c'est croire: les rites sacrificiels des Romains* (Paris, Aubier).

Scheid, J. (2007), 'Sacrifices for gods and ancestors', in Rüpke (2007*a*), pp. 263–72.

Schofield, M. (1986), 'Cicero for and against divination', *The Journal of Roman Studies*, 76: 47–65.

Schultz, C. E. and Harvey, P. B. (eds.) (2006), *Religion in Republican Italy* (Yale Classical Studies, vol. 33) (Cambridge, Cambridge University Press).

Stewart, C. (2001), 'Secularism as an impediment to anthropological research', *Social Anthropology*, 9(03): 325–8.

Trilling, L. (1972), *Sincerity and Authenticity* (Oxford, Oxford University Press).

Tylor, E. (1871), *Primitive Culture* (New York, Harper).

van der Eijk, P. (2004), 'Divination, prognosis and prophylaxis: the Hippocratic work "On Dreams" (De Victu 4) and its near eastern background', in H. Horstmanshoff and M. Stol (eds.), *Magic and Rationality in Ancient Near Eastern and Graeco-Roman Medicine* (Leiden and Boston, Brill), pp. 187–217.

Wardle, D. (2006), *Cicero on Divination: De divinatione, Book 1* (Oxford, Clarendon Press).

Warmington, E. (1940), *Remains of old Latin IV* (Cambridge, MA, Harvard University Press).

16

What Would a Scientific Economics Look Like?

MICHAEL JOFFE

Abstract

David Schum has made the case for a unified science or discipline of evidence based on a detailed methodological analysis. His focus is almost entirely on the single-event context, raising the question to what an extent a similar case can be made in the context of repeatable or generalisable events and their causes. This chapter takes a substantive rather than a methodological approach to this issue by comparing the use of evidence in biology and in economics. There are some similarities between the two disciplines, for example complex causal relations and open-endedness, that have led several economists from Marshall onwards to favour biology rather than physics as a model for economics, even if the actual causal processes involved are completely different.

For biology, the use of evidence is described in the context of the three major types of system—how the body works, population dynamics and the evolutionary process—and from epidemiological associations in the absence of systematic relationships (exogenous causation). In economics, the main focus is on the need for evidence to inform core theory, especially on the properties of markets. This is done in relation to two topic areas: growth and the theory of the firm. This survey of practice in the two disciplines shows that biological theory is derived from description and experimentation. In contrast, despite a great deal of good and important empirical work, the ideal in mainstream economics is to derive theory from axioms. When economic theory is compared with the available evidence, a disjunction is found between the empirical findings and conventional theory as depicted in textbooks and still dominant in the economics profession.

Further investigation shows that the disjunction is explained not primarily by the often-criticised unrealistic assumptions and/or allegedly oversimple models of mainstream economics, but by a fundamental mismatch between the evidence and the basic theoretical categories and structure.

Proceedings of the British Academy, **171**, 435–464. © The British Academy 2011.

For example, the still-dominant neoclassical (Solow) model of growth is framed in universal not system-specific terms, even though the evidence clearly shows a repeated pattern of exponential growth in certain types of economy but not others. And firms exist, whereas mainstream theory predicts that they should not do so because trading individuals would be more efficient. In addition, economics textbooks present a model of firms' cost curves that is portrayed as universal, even though this is empirically false, but the model is included because it is necessary for theory; the implications of this approach for the use of evidence is explored.

The central issue is the relationship of evidence to theory: to put it simply, which should come first? The conclusion is that regularities that emerge from a comparative historical perspective, including use of econometric, statistical and qualitative studies, could provide the type of evidence that could form a secure foundation for theorising in economics. This would be analogous to the way that convergent evolution has been used in biology to address the question, 'is evolution predictable?'

Is a scientific economics possible?—or desirable?

THERE HAS BEEN a long history of discussion as to whether social 'science' is possible. Many issues have been involved, including the extent to which events in the social realm are predictable, the difference between causation in the natural sciences and agency in human affairs, and the role (if any) of a sympathetic understanding of the motivations of social actors (*verstehen*). The aim of this paper is more modest, and does not cover all these topics, nor does it review the rich literature on the philosophy of economics. It merely asks what lessons one particular social science, economics, can learn from methods that the natural sciences, and especially biology, have used so fruitfully in understanding how the world works.

Within economics the focus is on theory—causal explanation and modelling—especially core mainstream theory, as depicted in textbooks, on the characteristics of markets and firms that affect growth and bubbles; macroeconomics and econometrics, for example, are not covered. Since this type of theory is widely regarded as the core of orthodox economics—macroeconomists tend to refer to the desirability of 'micro foundations'—this focus goes to the heart of the discipline.

One motivation is that some economists claim economics to be scientific in some sense, so the issue needs to be considered to what extent and in what ways this may or may not be justifiable. It is true that important elements appear to resemble natural science, and indeed are borrowed from it, but I will argue that the resemblance is only superficial—at a more fundamental level the methodologies are quite different.

A second is that orthodox economics is widely perceived as not being fit-for-purpose, that purpose being to understand how the economy works—a perception shared not only by non-economists but also by many economists, as exemplified by the Institute for New Economic Thinking, which includes Nobel laureates (INET 2010). A substantial minority of economists now identify themselves as 'heterodox', in opposition to mainstream economics; they tend to belong to organisations such as the Association for Heterodox Economics (AHE) and the International Confederation of Associations for Pluralism in Economics (ICAPE).

It could also be argued that the events in the economy in recent times, together with the almost-universal inability of the economics profession to understand what was happening until too late, reinforces that view. Variants of such a position have been put forward by such eminent mainstream economists as Krugman, Shiller and Eichengreen. Alan Greenspan (2008) stated that 'he had put too much faith in the self-correcting power of free markets', and that he had 'found a flaw' in his ideology adding 'I've been very distressed by that fact'. And a feature in *The Economist* magazine (2009)—a bastion of free-trade orthodoxy—recognised that modern economic theory 'went wrong'; they located the problem in two branches, financial economics and macro-economics, saying that they are rightly being re-examined. But the centrality of the bubble phenomenon to the financial crisis suggests the need to revise fundamental ideas about the nature of markets, a topic central to economics, something that mainstream economists have long resisted.

A third motivation, related to the second, is that it is important to go beyond reactive mode, in which standard theory perpetually and fruitlessly confronts direct criticisms of how it is done. An example is the issue of whether or not assumptions need to be realistic; being locked in this dispute is liable to distract participants from the deeper question, whether it would be better to base theory on evidence and place less reliance on assumptions of all kinds.

This paper therefore compares one particular natural science, biology, with the practices of economics, hoping to act as a guide to a better methodology. The focus on methodology rather than substance is important: biological processes are not a good model for social processes, as the causal mechanisms are quite different (Hodgson 1993). The analogy is at a more abstract level.

In taking biology as the model, a judgement is clearly involved that it is successful, whereas economics is not, or rather, less so than it could be. The first part of this is easy to justify: biology has developed a large body of causal knowledge, covering for example how the body works (physiology, biochemistry, cell biology, etc), and evolutionary theory which explains how the diversity of living forms originated. The basis of this knowledge was accumulated in a remarkably short time. In 1855 biology could scarcely be said to exist. By 1955 the work of Mendel, Darwin, Snow, Pasteur, Koch, Bernard, Ross, Krebs, Crick, Watson and others had established the laws of genetics and evolution, and their interrelation (the neo-Darwinian synthesis), plus the main features of physiology/biochemistry, including the mechanistic basis for the neo-Darwinian synthesis, as well as a substantial body of knowledge about the causes of disease. The success of biology has resulted from the ability of biologists to generate theory from evidence, even when confronting a reality of bewildering diversity and change.

A second judgement is that the two are sufficiently similar for the analogy to be useful. This has been the view of several important economists, most notably Marshall (1885), as well as non-economists (Gillies 2004). One reason is that causal relations in biology are complicated and multiple as well as often stochastic, as in economics and more generally in the social sciences, albeit that biology has the advantage of a physical basis and a greater degree of regularity than the social world. Another is that both economic and biological systems are dynamic; and that they share the feature of open-endedness, i.e. that the future is not wholly determined by the present.

The arguments presented here do not require that social sciences in general, or economics in particular, need to be seen as being just like the natural sciences. Those who believe that it is undesirable for the social sciences to attempt to be like the natural sciences, or that the very idea of a social 'science' is misplaced, might still agree that some useful lessons can be drawn from the comparison—if only to understand why the mainstream economists' claim of similarity is false. My own view is that similar methods can be used in the social and natural sciences when they are appropriate to the subject matter. However, social science is more difficult, because it involves human agency as well as the type of causation invoked by natural sciences, and this introduces complications.

Before starting the main discussion, the issue of values needs to be raised. It is assumed here that the aim of an economic account is to illuminate the processes involved, not to pass judgement on them nor to use economic events to try and justify a particular moral and/or ideological position. The aim then is to produce an account which finds as much agreement as possible about how the system works, because it corresponds well with the real world. This can be personally difficult, as the task of disentangling what appears to be true from what one would like to be true is unpleasant, even painful, requiring moral courage. It is almost inevitable that the account that emerges will be distasteful for people of various moral positions; for example, a free-marketeer will dislike some aspects, a traditional socialist will dislike others—but they may still agree that, like it or not, this is how things are. Get over it.

Is economics not already scientific?

First, what do we mean by 'economics'? Contrary to the impression gained by many non-economists, it is far from monolithic (Mäki 2002; Davis 2006). As an academic discipline, it may well be the most diverse of all, including as it does:

- neoclassical (traditional textbook) microeconomic theory and macro-economics
- econometrics and other statistical methods
- game theory
- information economics
- specialised areas e.g. transport, healthcare, business
- behavioural economics and neuro-economics
- experimental economics
- institutional economics, evolutionary economics and historical accounts
- many other 'heterodox' traditions, including post-Keynesian, feminist, Marxist and Austrian perspectives.

And yet it is no accident that many people believe economics to be mono-lithic. Economics textbooks, and the courses that use them, provide a particular view of the discipline which is widely regarded as its core. Many people have studied economics but are not professional economists, and this is the view that they receive of what the subject is about. When I refer to the possibility of making economics more scientific, it is 'mainstream' economics of this type, as represented in textbooks and standard training courses, that I mean.

As is clear from the above list, research in economics is very different from the image that is portrayed by this mainstream view; and much of it is of excellent quality. In addition, many practising economists dissociate themselves from some or all of the textbook dogma, and/or its consequences in non-academic public debate. The central issue here is the view that 'the market' is self-adjusting and produces optimal outcomes, at least under specified conditions such as 'perfect competition'. This dissociation is itself intriguing—no biologist disavows the standard account of biology given in textbooks, except to say that it is outdated and/or over-simplified, and the same is true in all the sciences.

It is instructive to compare economics textbooks with those of the established natural sciences. On the surface, economics and physics textbooks are quite similar-looking, with a predominance of theory and mathematics, whereas those in chemistry and biology have a great deal more empirical content. Does this mean that the claim of the scientific nature of mainstream economics could be valid, if the processes described are sufficiently regular? A closer look shows that even this defence is invalid: the two types of textbook differ radically in the *basis* for the theoretical and mathematical statements. With physics they are empirically based, the result of centuries of observation and experimentation. Economics textbooks are typically almost free of empirical content. Where it occurs, it is included as case-study material for *illustration*, and no attempt is made to ground the theory in reality. Unlike any of the sciences, but like mathematics, it is grounded in axioms that have been derived from idealised formalism rather than from evidence.

The role of description and experimentation

Natural scientists have one methodological tool that is of only limited use in the social sciences: experimentation, the ability to manipulate nature by altering some conditions while holding others constant. But this advantage is easy to overstate, because a great deal of the empirical content of the natural sciences results not from experiments but from careful and systematic description. Astronomical observations played a major role in the development of physics. Biology in particular is largely a descriptive science, from van Leeuwenhoek's discovery of a previously unsuspected world of invisible organisms using the newly developed microscope, through Darwin's painstaking work on the subtle variations within and between species that gave rise to his evolutionary theory, up to today's research, for example using microarrays to study gene expression.

The problem in economics is not so much what is impossible, but what is possible yet not practised. Economic history has a strong tradition of accurate description, and much of this goes beyond telling an individual story to the comparative study of different experiences, usually in terms of countries (Maddison 1964; Maddison 1969; Maddison 1970; Landes 1998; Pomeranz 2000). Unfortunately, historical accounts have in general not explicitly informed core mainstream theory, nor been used to subject it to systematic revision.

Within economics too, there is a great deal of excellent empirical work, of an observational kind and also the increasingly influential experimental economics, in which a group of subjects is given a structured task (Smith 2008). In addition 'natural experiments' are widely used, in which causal inferences can be made from events in the real world that were not created by the scientists. A nice example is a study of the effect of family size on the mother's work status: to distinguish a direct causal effect from confounding (e.g. her preference for career as against childbearing) and from reverse causation (e.g. promotion leading to a decision not to have a further child, or not yet), the authors used the sex of the first two children as a natural experiment (Angrist and Evans 1998). If they were of the same sex, the parents are more likely to want another child, for reasons unconnected with the labour market, so this plays the same role as deliberate assignment would if it were possible.

The issue is that *evidence is not systematically used as an input to core theory and modelling*, which is regarded as central and high status. It does not have a fundamental place, but tends to be restricted to relatively specialised areas, as in the example just given, or in studying the effects of education/training on later earning capacity. In particular, evidence is not allowed to question the central theoretical foundations that have been passed on for generations.

One topic that could usefully be presented descriptively, and which would inform theory building, is what types of market are, or are not, prone to bubbles. This phenomenon is increasingly well understood (Kindleberger 1989; Shiller 2005; Levine and Zajac 2007), but if it is an inherent property of markets this would radically alter the self-regulating notion of markets depicted in textbook theory, and held as a default belief by many economists. On the other hand if it is restricted to certain types of market, the implications would be different but could still be far-reaching. One suggestion is that liquid trading markets are especially bubbles-prone (Turner 2009); another possibility is that markets for which the price has no well-established relationship with costs are likely to develop bubbles. The issue is not whether economists are studying bubbles—which they now are—but whether their findings are being used to challenge traditional beliefs about the fundamental properties of markets.

Another is the competitive behaviour of firms and the resulting distribution of their size. There is an empirical literature on this (Cabral and Mata 2003; Bartelsman *et al.* 2004), which is already rich descriptively and promises to uncover important causal processes. Yet in textbook economics the usual practice is for models to *assume* a particular market structure as an ideal type, such as perfect competition, typically starting with a word such as 'suppose' or 'consider'. This use of modelling language, where a scientist would use empirically established information, treats the assumption as primary; even if evidence is given a role it is treated as secondary (see discussion below on the place of

modelling). Ideal-type modelling may have a role in elucidating the consequences of different market structures for example, but only if it illuminates
what is observed empirically. This position differs from the oft-encountered
reactive argument that perfect competition rarely occurs in practice.

A third topic is the rate of return on capital. It has long been known that
the distribution is continuous and rather broad, including a small proportion
of firms having a negative value (in the short term) (Farjoun and Machover
1983). This contrasts sharply with the neoclassical assumption (also found in
some heterodox accounts) of a uniform rate of profit equal to the standard
rate of return—an assumption that implies that firms cannot fail, which is obviously false. Such an assumption needs to be used in very limited circumstances,
and with great care.

One major failure to question core theoretical foundations is exemplified
by Schumpeter's important insight that capitalism is a process of 'creative
destruction', whereby firms and industries rise and fall in a turbulent manner—very different from the neoclassical model of convergence towards a
static equilibrium position (Schumpeter 1980 [1911]; Schumpeter 1992 [1942]).
His work, although widely seen as a radical break from neoclassical economics,
explicitly retained the conventional vision of a static economy ('circular flow'
in his terminology), merely adding entrepreneurial 'new combinations', and
the resulting turbulence, on top. This resulted in a dualistic model of the
economy, seen as composed of neoclassical-like and entrepreneurial sectors.
However, this would predict a semi-continuous distribution of the rate of
return on capital (a cluster of observations at 'zero', the standard rate, plus a
separate positive distribution). As already noted, the distribution is continuous,
and it has no peak at the standard rate of return.

Schumpeter's conception of capitalist dynamism therefore conflicts with a
basic observation. However, rather than abandoning the conventional static
theory altogether and replacing it with a new one that is compatible with the
evidence and with Schumpeter's own description, the traditional view was
merely *supplemented* with an additional element. The possibility that the basic
theory needed to be completely rethought was apparently not entertained.
This could be called *incremental mode*, and is related to reactive mode in that
they are both oriented to existing theory, respectively attacking or supplement-
ing it. Incremental mode is justified when the existing theory is sound but
incomplete, but not when it is fundamentally inaccurate, as here in predicting
a cluster at zero profit. In such a situation the selective replacement of its
poorly functioning elements is needed.

Schumpeter's important ideas have become influential in recent decades,
more than half a century after their first expression, for example in endog-

enous growth theory. Here again it has been done in an incremental fashion, starting from the neoclassical growth model of Solow, then adding some Schumpeterian features to the model (Aghion and Howitt 1998). For example, some form of externality is introduced into the conventional aggregate production function model, over-riding the alleged diminishing returns that were a feature of the original. In fact Solow himself has pointed out that such models require the restrictive assumption that the externality is just sufficient to balance the diminishing returns (Solow 2000). Thus Schumpeter's reluctance to let go of old theory that contradicted his observational analysis is reproduced in this more formal context. The structure is the same: a core that predicts convergence to a static equilibrium, plus an additional component with the role of overcoming that in order to predict growth.

Another example relates to a classic paper by Ronald Coase. In 1937, he observed that 'the distinguishing mark of the firm is the supersession of the price mechanism', in other words that within firms people do not trade with one another, rather the coordination is done by means other than price.[1] He then asked, given the efficiency of the price mechanism, 'why a firm emerges at all in a specialized exchange economy' (Coase 1937). Mainstream economic theory, then and now, would predict that the economy would be composed of individual traders, this being the most efficient arrangement. It is remarkable that he had to point this out, and even more remarkable that the question has been largely ignored in the textbook version of the theory of the firm, which ignores the main characteristics that distinguish it from a sole trader, and treats it as if it were an individual.

Firms not only exist, they have become the dominant type of economic organisation. The glaring contrast between theory and reality makes this one of the most important questions in economics. What answer did Coase himself give to his own question? He considered four possible explanations:

- people prefer to work for a master
- those who wish to direct a firm would accept lower pay
- consumers prefer to buy from firms
- market transactions have a cost, e.g. relating to contracts.

He dismissed the first three, and decided that the fourth must therefore be correct. This insight has in fact been fruitful, in that it has given rise to a whole school of research based on the idea of transaction costs, which are far from trivial. But they do not solve the problem: a substantial body of research has

[1] In this context, a 'firm' indicates an organisation that employs wage labour, as contrasted with a self-employed worker.

tested how well transaction costs explain the boundaries of particular firms—
for example, the decision whether to make a component in-house or to buy it
from a supplier, and more importantly, the effect of this decision on firm performance. Its success in this has proved to be patchy (Poppo and Zenger 1998;
David and Han 2004; Carter and Hodgson 2006). In addition, the transaction
costs approach faces special challenges in explaining innovation and the
entrepreneurial firm (Hodgson 2007), which are central to studying growth.

If this concept has only limited success in accounting for the boundaries
of firms, it is *a fortiori* difficult to accept it as an important part of the answer
to the original question, why firms exist *at all*. By accepting the necessary
truth of conventional market theory, and merely adding another element in
the spirit of incremental mode, Coase failed to consider that other explanations might be possible. The real answer appears rather to be that firms exist—
and are ubiquitous in the modern world—because systems dominated by
them ('capitalist' real economies) vastly outperform all other types of system.
According to this viewpoint, the source of capitalist growth is the combination of market trading between firms with non-market coordination within
them; crucially, firms have not only the incentive but also the capacity to
reduce production costs, and more generally to radically reorganise production (Joffe 2011). A further issue is that Coase framed his question in an ahistoric manner, as a functional statement, rather than as a causal account in
historical time. This is discussed further below.

A strategy for systematic description in economics

Could economic theory learn from the practice of biology? It is true that the
workings of the body are easier to study, because a physical basis exists that
can be examined using microscopes, chemical methods, etc. Even more important, it has a high degree of regularity, so that it is meaningful to speak of 'the'
kangaroo pouch or 'the' human pancreas. Evolutionary biology, however, does
not have these advantages; even though it has a known mechanistic basis, this
only enables explanations of past evolutionary change to be made, not predictions of the future. In this respect economics is in a somewhat similar position.
However, there is no need to be pessimistic about the possibility of systematic
description in such circumstances.

The key is that while evolution is open-ended in respect of individual
'events', certain patterns recur. It is common to find convergent evolution, in
which apparently similar features have evolved independently. This can be
whole animals, which have similar features and inhabit similar ecological

niches, as in the case of the ostrich and the rhea, which look almost identical but evolved respectively in the old world and the new world. Similarly, three types of anteaters have evolved, in Australia, Africa and America, with similar features adapted to a diet of ants. Or it can be a major feature, such as the wings of bats and birds, which evolved separately from the vertebrate forelimb. Some such features can be subtle, if vital: fish in the Arctic and in the Antarctic are protected from freezing of their body water by molecules that have an antifreeze action, but which are different in the two cases. Such examples are all based on careful description, not experimentation. Observations of this kind have led Dawkins (2005) to ask the question, 'Is evolution predictable?' (see also Dawkins 2004).

Moreover, the theory of evolution itself is an example of convergent evolution: Darwin was provoked into publishing *On the Origin of Species* by the realisation that Wallace had similar ideas; if Darwin had not existed, the theory and all its ramifications would doubtless have been discovered, it would just have taken longer to elaborate fully.

The reason that this is important for economics is that by analogy it suggests the possibility of using economic history as a source of the type of systematic description that mainstream economic theory has tended to lack.[2] If a particular train of events has occurred once or even twice, this could be dismissed as case-study material that is attributable to particular individuals or decisions, or to chance. But if something similar recurs many times then there must be some consistent force bringing about this repetition, as long as it is due neither to imitation nor to direct influence such as could occur for example with foreign direct investment. It might even be possible to calculate the probability of a collection of parallel stories being true by chance, for use as the equivalent of a P-value in statistical work. The historical methods used to collect such stories could themselves include narrative and/or statistical techniques, including but not limited to econometric analysis.

A set of observations that emerges from this process provides an empirical generalisation that can then become the starting point for understanding what structures or mechanisms could be capable of generating it. Another way of expressing this is that it uncovers a regularity at a deep level, as contrasted with the search for event regularities which Lawson (2003) has criticised. The

---

[2] Other sources of empirical information are also potentially useful as a basis for theory, for example econometric studies of structural changes—see e.g. Summers (1991) and Juselius (2010) An advantage of comparative economic history is the magnitude of the contrast between, say, Ghana and South Korea; or, South Korea in 1960 and 1990: the contrasts are sufficiently great that they outweigh any uncertainties of data and statistical method.

corollary is that once a set of parallel stories has been assembled, it then becomes possible to examine differences between them as well, which can also be highly informative.

An example of good practice here is the work of the economist Peter Lindert. In a magisterial and forensic study of the growth of social spending in the past 200 years, the convergent and divergent forces are elegantly dissected (Lindert 2004). He shows how social spending increased in all economically dynamic societies, tracing its origin to the political circumstances of each rather than to imitation, and that its characteristics differed from society to society. For example, poor relief was a major feature in England and Wales, whereas education was given priority in Germany and in the United States. (He also demonstrates that social spending had no restrictive effect on economic growth, contrary to the expectations of the standard model.)

A similarly repetitive pattern can be seen in the type of sustained *per capita* growth that has occurred in some economies but not others during the last two hundred years, but was unknown before that. Starting in Britain, this pattern was next seen in continental western Europe plus the United States and other 'European offshoots'. These were followed by Japan and subsequently other countries in East and South Asia, initially on the basis of importation of technology and (sometimes) capital, but then becoming self-sustaining after a few decades. These are often grouped together as capitalist economies (Baumol 2002), and as with Lindert's study, the convergence is accompanied by sharp divergences, sometimes called 'varieties of capitalism'. In contrast, technology imports into other countries led to an initial industrial/modernisation process, but sustained dynamism did not follow; these include less successful capitalist economies, for example in much of Latin America, as well as economies run on communist principles such as the USSR.

Often the onset of sustained growth in the various Asian economies followed economic reforms, generally informed by a type of economics very different from what textbook theory would recommend. The empirical literature on these experiences has raised many important issues, notably on the role of the state (Amsden 1989; Wade 1990; Westphal 1990). The dazzling success of the developmental state that deliberately distorted the free market, for example by inducing the 'wrong' relative prices (Amsden 1989), is a direct challenge to core textbook theory on the nature of markets. Twenty years on, the textbooks have responded by ignoring the issue. Furthermore, during much of this period international economic policy has been dominated by the Washington Consensus, which is based on the same traditional flawed view of markets. The belief in the superiority of private ownership is also undermined by the stellar growth performance of China and Vietnam while they retained substantial publicly owned industrial sectors, but after capitalist-style reforms of the real economy (Qian 2003; Pritchett 2003). Clearly the 'capitalist' element that makes for sustained growth is different in important ways from the 'free market' as portrayed by orthodox economics (Joffe 2011). Yet they continue to be confused (Baumol 2002).

The place of modelling

Modelling is used both in biology and in economics, but its role is different. In biology, it is mainly used to model causal processes that have been established by other means. It is unusual to find a mathematical account that has no basis in causal understanding, as sometimes happens in physics (Cartwright 1994), and is rife in economics. Mainstream economics goes further, by relying on models that are tautologically true: they are consistent internally and with the assumptions that are used as inputs, but have no point of contact with evidence. Corroboration or falsification by empirical information is impossible.

Biological models include the Hardy–Weinberg equilibrium formula in population genetics; single- and multiple-hit models of carcinogenesis; the physics underlying the control of muscular movement; the kinetics of biochemical reactions; the sequence of chemical reactions leading to energy generation known as the Krebs cycle; air dispersion models of biologically relevant pollutants, which can include chemical reactions (formation of ozone); and statistical models of air pollution and mortality.

An instructive example is the law of independent segregation, also known as Mendel's second law. This states that when two different genes are transmitted from parent to child, they assort independently of each other, so that a random combination ends up being passed on. The basis for this is the mechanical process of meiosis, the process of cell division that leads to the formation of sperm and egg cells. It would be possible to model this law in the style of economics, as a general relationship. However, this would miss the fact that sometimes segregation is *not* independent, because when the genes are on the same chromosome they tend to be passed on together. This is known as linkage. Furthermore, the closer they are to each other on the chromosome, the more likely they are to stay together in meiosis; if they are far apart there is a chance that they will be separated by crossing over of the chromosomes. So these exceptions to the law of independent segregation in turn lead not only to the concept of linkage, but also to a classical piece of evidence for locating genes on particular chromosomes, which in due course has led to modern genetics.

In economics, the role of modelling is traditionally different from in the natural sciences. There is rarely a separate explicit concept of a causal explanation preceding modelling as there is in biology. Economists generally present a model with a plausible 'story'. The model is not totally arbitrary, but neither is it solidly rooted in causal understanding. It is admittedly more difficult to establish causal relations in economics than in biology, but that does not explain why the *ideal* is to base models on axioms, even when empirically unsupported, rather than on reality.

Accordingly, tractability, parsimony and elegance are the primary criteria by which models are judged, rather than empirical adequacy. This tends to be true even in models that are explicitly intended as the basis for statistical testing, but is at its most extreme in textbook theory. Simplicity is treated as if it were an end in itself, whereas a biologist would see it as secondary to the main task of constructing a model that corresponds to descriptive and causal reality. As economists are fond of saying, simplicity is positive when a simple model captures the essence of a situation. The problem arises with models that fail to capture the essence, or even distort and obscure it.

Distortion is quite distinct from simplification, but many economists appear not to realise this. The classic example of simplification is the application of Newton's laws of motion to a projectile in the Earth's atmosphere. The basic model ignores air resistance, and is therefore only an approximation. This can readily be remedied by introducing air viscosity into the model—an example of incremental mode. In contrast, *to say a model is distorted means that it cannot be remedied in this way*. Under these conditions, incremental mode will not solve the problem.

An important example, central to the neoclassical theory of the firm and ubiquitous in textbooks, concerns the relationship of costs to the scale of production. The standard model is that as the scale of production rises, beyond a certain point the average total costs begin to increase, producing a U-shaped curve. (Strictly speaking the theory concerns firms' *perceptions* of the cost curve, rather than objective reality, but the implication must also be that the true cost structure is the same, given the standard neoclassical assumption of perfect information.) Textbooks differ in how they present the U shape, in particular whether they attempt to justify it. Many just present it without any rationale, perhaps with the word 'typical' attached, presumably to deflect students' attempts at critical thinking. The better ones at least give examples and a plausible rationale.

The problem is that the classic U shape appears to be wrong, at least for a large proportion of firms. In industry, costs are usually stable or fall with scale, rather than rising. Empirical research, based on taking a sample of firms and asking the appropriate person within each of them about their perceived cost structure, indicates that it applies to rather a small proportion, variously estimated at between 5 and 11 per cent, with the first paper having been published in 1952 (Eiteman and Guthrie 1952; Scherer and Ross 1990; Blinder *et al.* 1998). So although the textbook account may sometimes apply, its presentation as a general description is false.

Unfortunately, the 1950s debate became deflected away from the observation that the standard account is empirically wrong. This was because the conclusion of Eiteman and Guthrie's paper was in reactive mode, 'that ... theory should be revised in the light of reality'. The issue became whether or not the findings invalidated marginalist theory, which is a bad choice of ground given that the theory is tautologously true. To dissipate the force of the criticism, the defenders of orthodoxy merely had to assert the internal coherence of their theory even without the U-shaped curve, which was portrayed as not central to it ('merely pretty pictures') (Ritter *et al.* 1953). The battle was fought on their territory, the detailed specification of the theory, rather than on the scientific grounds that deliberately spreading an untruth is wrong. And the 'pretty pictures' are still there several decades later.

If the practice in economics were to give prominence to description, such falsehood would be impossible. It survives as a standard model because it fits with the requirements of neoclassical theory, not because it has any relationship to reality. At least for this example, the closer one gets to the theoretical core of textbook-style economics, the more distorted is the analysis of how the economy works. This is unique among academic disciplines.

The basis of the U shape is a thought experiment, combining one fixed and one variable factor of production, which is a defensible procedure. However, it raises an important further question: whether the firm's decision making process that is being modelled actually occurs in real firms. The answer is no, firms do not recognise it as a description of what they do (Lee 1998). Thus the model also fails to correspond in respect of mechanism.

Certain textbooks go further than merely presenting as universal a model that is empirically false in most instances. An extreme example is 'Intermediate Microeconomics' by Varian (1987 to 2010), which is widely used. The following situation is postulated:

> Suppose that a firm has chosen a long-run profit-maximizing output ... [with] constant returns to scale and that it is making positive profits in equilibrium.

> Then consider what would happen if it doubled the level of its input usage. According to the constant returns to scale hypothesis, it would double its output level. ... its profits would also double. But this contradicts the original assumption that its original choice was profit maximizing! We derived this contradiction by assuming that the original profit level was positive; if the original level were zero there would be no problem: two times zero is still zero. This argument shows that the only reasonable long-run level of profits for a competitive firm that has constant returns to scale at all levels of output is a zero level of profits[3] (emphasis in the original).

Everything here hinges on assumptions. This is not the familiar criticism of economic theory that its assumptions are unrealistic—that would merely be a reactive response. *It is giving assumptions the role that evidence should have.* The entire sequence of reasoning is concerned only with the set-up of the thought experiment and reality has no role, but this does not prevent a conclusion being drawn that appears to be about real-world profits for a firm under conditions of perfect competition. Some might see this as a paradigm case of the relationship of textbook economic theory to the real world: the substance is merely an artificial construction, but an inference is drawn that makes apparent reference to reality.

This example may seem extreme, but it is not unique. The following section has:

> When a profit-maximizing firm makes its choice of inputs and outputs it reveals two things: first, that the inputs and outputs used represent a *feasible* production plan, and second, that these choices are more profitable than other feasible choices that the firm could have made ... This equation is our final result. It ... comes solely from the definition of profit maximization. Yet it contains all of the comparative statics results about profit-maximizing choices!' (emphasis in the original).   (Varian 1987 to 2010)

The definition of feasibility here is intriguing: a production plan is feasible if it is chosen by a firm that we have brought into existence for our thought experiment. And we know that it is the most profitable such plan because we have assumed the firm to be profit maximising. From this a series of statements is made as if they had the backing of some reality.

These two passages are (admittedly extreme) examples of theories that are tautologically true. They cannot be confirmed or refuted; evidence has no role. That this textbook is now in its eighth edition, and is widely recom-

---

[3] Note that 'a competitive firm' here does not mean a firm that is good at competing, but rather a firm in a sector characterised by perfect competition; and that the term 'profits' does not include return on capital, which is non-zero.

mended, says a great deal not only about the approach of its author, but of the mainstream of the economics profession more generally. As far as I know, economists have not criticised the strangeness of reasoning in these two passages.

Boundary compatibility—relationship with knowledge in neighbouring disciplines

The relationship between the different natural sciences is one of complementarity. They fit together neatly. For example, in considering the toxicity of an environmental chemical, a biologist has to consider the chemical aspects of the problem as well as the biology. There is not, and cannot be, any conflict between them. Indeed, the relationship is stronger than just compatibility: most biological research is devoted to finding chemical mediating pathways that can explain how a particular biological system functions. Physics also makes an important contribution to the understanding of biological systems, for example analysis of the mechanical forces in the heart and circulatory system. Physico-chemistry is the *mechanistic* language of biology. There is also an *emergent* language which is specifically biological; the study of life cannot be reduced solely to its physico-chemical elements.

The situation is different in the social sciences, and especially in economics. Neoclassical economics seeks an individual-level (mechanistic) account, yet is famously dismissive of psychological reality in formulating its models: one of the traditional criticisms is of the assumption of rationality. This can lead to a particular variant of incremental mode, in which behaviour is first depicted as rational, then the discrepancy of actual behaviour from this construct is added in. A double error is thereby created: the original distorted model, and the discrepancy that owes its existence to it. A preferable approach is directly to study the behaviour in its own right, for example as an evolved heuristic that the brain actually uses.

The most important contributors to the critique of rationality in traditional economic theory are H. A. Simon (1976), who coined the term 'bounded rationality' to contrast with the conventional assumption of perfect rationality, and Tversky and Kahneman (1981). The limitations of human calculating ability were also stressed by Hayek (1937).

Change is underway in this respect, largely resulting from the influence of Tversky and Kahneman. The subdiscipline of behavioural economics is thriving, and is now regarded as mainstream (Smith 2008). This move towards boundary compatibility is undoubtedly constructive. Currently there is tension, which is potentially creative, between this more realistic account of behaviour and the tradition of parsimonious modelling with unrealistic psychological assumptions.

Rationality is not the only issue, only the most prominent of them. Neoclassical theory also traditionally assumes perfect information/knowledge, which has been thoroughly explored by information economics. A third assumption is perfect foresight, which is especially important in respect of causality, because it relegates time and causation to an automatic extension of the agent's motivation. A theory that does this cannot encompass unintended consequences, with dire results. Indeed the term 'agent' here is inaccurate, as the absence of uncertainty and the other elements that enter into human decision-making remove agency from the scene, transforming it into an automatically realised optimum.

Criticisms of the assumption of perfect foresight have been around for many decades (Knight 1985 [1921]; Keynes 1937; Hayek 1937), largely in reactive mode in relation, for example, to equilibrium analysis and the analysis of risk; nevertheless they remain relevant today, because the assumption still underlies much current theory (Keen 2001). One of the dire results is that risk becomes reduced to a probability distribution, but one with known parameters, radical uncertainty being excluded (Keen 2001). The incorporation of such a perspective into apparently sophisticated financial models in the last few decades is a large part of the reason why the financial sector collapsed in 2008. This should have been foreseen because a smaller version of the same type of crash occurred ten years earlier with the demise of Long Term Capital Management, a company that boasted the most brilliant brains in economic finance, including Nobel laureates (Lowenstein 2002). Theoretical weaknesses have real consequences.

Another far-reaching outcome is that the theory is impoverished by its inability to build unintended consequences into the conceptual model of how the economy works. This is deeply ironic, as the cornerstone of modern economics is Smith's 'invisible hand' underlying the price mechanism, which is basically an account of unintended consequences at the aggregate level of the market. It is a simple system of balancing (negative) feedback, and it is this that creates the endogenous causal processes that lead to the balancing of supply and demand. It thereby generates an emergent property—the language is now economics not psychology.[4]

---

[4] The relationship of systems containing feedback with endogenous causal processes and with emergent properties is discussed below.

The tendency towards a stable equilibrium dominates mainstream economics, but it fails to account for key economic phenomena such as bubbles and capitalist growth. However, the same conceptual structure of unintended consequences, endogenous causation and emergence is not limited to such convergent systems. For example, when applied to an economy dominated by firms, unintended consequences at the aggregate level have been shown to explain why successful capitalist economies tend to grow inexorably (Joffe 2011).

A deeper problem is therefore the perception that if only economic theory would adopt a more realistic view of human nature, it would develop a good model of the economy. Partly this results from the lack of realisation that any social structure, including an economy, is not simply the summation of the actions of all its included individuals. The price mechanism, and capitalist growth, are not only unintended consequences, they also importantly operate at the aggregate level of the market or sector. The development of institutions is an example of this type of emergence, which Vernon Smith (2008, following Hayek) terms 'ecological rationality'. Not all social phenomena are the result of conscious design (Hodgson and Knudsen 2006).

The traditional reactive criticism of neoclassical economics, that behaviour is not rational in the real world, completely misses this. Reactive mode has meant a decades-long and still-continuing confrontation between proponents and opponents of rationality, which has obscured the fact that important aspects of economic life are not reducible to behaviour *at all*. These would not be adequately addressed by an incremental solution that substitutes new decision rules for old. Another way of expressing this is: economic phenomena are partly the result of behaviour, but there is also an emergent level of specifically economic relations. They cannot be reduced solely to psychology, however accurate.

Causal explanation: mechanism and emergence

In addition to compatibility with neighbouring disciplines, a natural scientist would generally expect all three major components of a theory, model or hypothesis—evidence and assumptions (input), mechanism, and predictions (output)—to be compatible with existing knowledge. There are of course exceptions to this, and they are famous not least because they are exceptions. For example in physics, quantum electrodynamics theory has no plausible causal mechanism and yet is able to make predictions that are accurate to eleven significant figures (Feynman 1990). Such exceptions tend to occur in fundamental physics, where the scale is unimaginably small or large. Sciences (including physics) that deal with more familiar-scale reality tend to have this three-fold compatibility.

For example, an important question in neurophysiology during the 1920s and 1930s was how impulses are relayed from nerves to muscles through the neuromuscular junction, so enabling control of posture and movement. The focus was on the mechanism by which this occurs. The inputs—observations rather than assumptions—were taken as common ground, the big controversy being electricity versus chemistry: is transmission an electric current (electrons) crossing the space between the nerve and muscle fibres? Or is there a chemical mediator? This was solved by measuring the time that elapses between the firing of the two types of fibre, which was far too long to be an electric current.

If a chemical mechanism was involved, this would predict that its apparatus was present in the nerve and muscle fibres. This prediction was then confirmed by other methods, for example visualising vesicles of the transmitter in the nerve-fibre ending using the new technique of electron microscopy, chemically analysing the substance and finding it to be acetylcholine, finding the enzymes that synthesise it, and reproducing the effect on the muscle fibre by introducing acetylcholine instead of stimulating the nerve. Interestingly, all except the last of these is an observation not an experiment.[5]

This is typical of how biology progresses. What starts off as two rival hypotheses becomes a description of the underlying process, in terms of the key components of the system and their properties or capacities (Cartwright 1994). Mechanistic explanation is description at a deeper level, and economics typically seeks an equivalent when relying on individual behaviour, rational or not, to account for economic phenomena. The alternative to a reductive account based on the deeper level is in terms of emergent properties.

Convergent economic history could provide a starting point for seeking causal understanding of either type. An example is the historical record outlined above, that appears to show that under certain conditions, a transition occurs after which a particular economy experiences sustained *per capita* growth. The most likely explanation is that some *shared* feature of the capitalist system has the potential to cause this, despite capitalism's variety, for example an institutional change (Joffe 2011). A more conventional view, based on extrapolation of human action directly to consequences, is Schumpeter's view that entrepreneurs' innovations are responsible for capitalist dynamism.

---

[5] Also, only the first one is measurement, so that the statement 'Science is measurement' (Cartwright 1994) is false.

But if this were true, one would have to ask: why are such innovations more frequent and/or more successful in these economies (Joffe 2010)? (Schumpeter (1992 [1942]) himself explicitly denied the capitalist specificity.) Any explanation in terms of individual behaviour needs to be able to answer such questions.

The methodological issue is that it is likely to be an *endogenous* feature of the economic system. If it were an exogenous force, such as Schumpeter's entrepreneurial innovation and/or technological change as in the Solow model, this would have to have been constant in magnitude to explain, for example, why growth of the US economy has been so close to exponential over a period of two hundred years.

One way of analysing endogenous causal processes is to use system dynamics. As Forrester pointed out, specifying the causal processes operating in complicated systems, and especially their feedback loops, illuminates the endogenous causality involved (Forrester 1970; Lane 2007). It then becomes possible to model how the feature of interest, growth in this case, is generated by the structure of the system, rather than having to portray it as a response to a shock, disturbance, or other outside influence. Even where an exogenous cause or shock is involved, it is necessary to examine its effects on the endogenous causal processes of the system—just as one can only understand the effect of burning on human skin if one has a good account of how skin tissue operates and how it repairs itself. Rather than having to rely on exogenous causes such as behaviour, or scientific/technological innovation, or resources (Pomeranz 2000), this systems approach thus allows the analysis of endogenous causation and of emergence, bringing economics back into economics.

Returning to the behavioural assumptions underlying economic theory, if the theory gave good predictions, would it matter that the proposed mechanism were incompatible with the known properties of human behaviour? It could be, for example, that lack of rationality merely results in noise, so that the assumption of rationality produces a good estimate of the central tendency. The vagaries of observed individual behaviour would then be like a statistical distribution around the mean. For a scientist, this would be a step forward in achieving the prediction, but also a source of frustration that the real mechanism is obscure, as in the quantum electrodynamics example.

A contrary view was put forward by Friedman (1953) in an influential paper. He stated that assumptions can be justified, however unrealistic they appear, as long as they give good predictions. The subtext to this was that he was defending mainstream economics from the standard reactive criticism of unrealistic assumptions. That the paper is still clearly relevant today is indicated by the publication of a recent book with the same title (Mäki 2009*a*), that reproduces it as 'the classical essay in twentieth century economic methodology'. The book shows that its interpretation is highly contested. While it is true that not everybody shares Friedman's views on methodology, in Mäki's view the 'popular legacy' of this article has influenced research presentations as well as textbooks, for example in stating that assumptions can be unrealistic, and that 'as-if' explanations are valid (Mäki 2009*b*). I will just comment on two examples that directly involve biology.

One example given was of an expert billiard player, the aim being to predict the shots. The point was that Newtonian mechanics would enable the calculations to be made, even though the player did not actually use Newton's equations while playing. Friedman considered that this was a good analogy for what economists do when their equations describe economic behaviour in terms that the economic agent would not recognise. The model describes the behaviour 'as if' it were a calculation, while acknowledging that the actual neurophysiological processes do not correspond to the description. In philosophical terms, this is an instrumentalist view whereas natural scientists set out to provide a realist account of mechanism (although some dispute this interpretation (Mäki 2009b)).

More importantly, Friedman's account is scientifically impoverished. It seeks a model that will predict the shots[6] (events), whereas a biologist would aim for a *causal theory of mechanism*. Elements could then be modelled mathematically. For example, a neurophysiologist would seek to explain how expertise in billiard playing is developed and executed in terms of neuronal pathways and neurotransmitters. The historical success of biology has been the result of posing and solving such causal questions.

The practice of theoretical economics has been largely based on modelling without causal understanding, and this affects even those economists who do not share Friedman's methodological views. (This may be why economics has such a poor record in prediction.) The serious consequence is that important features of reality are missed; whereas a model needs to be rather simple to be useful, a causal theory can explore connections of a widely differing type—especially important in the complex reality that economics deals with. The reduction of theory to modelling could be termed 'model dependence'. As *The Economist* magazine (2009) stated in relation to the financial crisis:

> By assuming that capital markets worked perfectly, macroeconomists were largely able to ignore the economy's financial plumbing. But models that ignored finance had little chance of spotting a calamity that stemmed from it.

---

[6] In Lawson's terms, 'event regularities'—see Lawson (2003).

Models need to be embedded in broader causal theories. This enables the overarching theory to guide the use of a component model for a specific purpose. If this is not done, the alternative to dependence on a single type of model, with no possibility of systematic thought outside it, is to have a range of models—with the choice of which to use being left merely to intuitive judgement.

A second example given by Friedman is pure biology, so is directly relevant to the analogy being explored in this paper. He considers the leaves on a tree, which are distributed 'as if' designed to catch the maximum sunlight. It is true that the observation about the distribution of the leaves is not trivial. But a biologist would go further and try to *explain* this distribution. For a situation like this there is a ready-made explanatory framework in the theory of natural selection: the trees with a genetic tendency towards the most beneficial leaf arrangement are more likely than others to survive and pass on their genes. The biologist's task would be to identify the particular pathways in the general framework, for example, what competitive pressures are acting on the tree, perhaps in terms of climate or of a changing environment; identifying the development process and relevant genes, establishing the biochemical pathways by which they act; and so on. The idea that an 'as if' explanation is satisfactory would be difficult to comprehend.

Methodologically, Friedman's statement is functional: the distribution of leaves fulfils the need of the tree to capture maximal sunlight. The problems of such potentially teleological arguments are well recognised by scientists, and in the philosophy of science (Stanford Encyclopedia of Philosophy, n.d.). Philosophers of biology have long realised that they can readily be overcome *in the biological context*, because it is straightforward to make a 'translation of talk of functions into terms of talk of adaptations', i.e. a causal one based on differential survival and reproduction (Ruse 1973); it then also becomes a historical account in real time. Outside biology such a translation cannot in general be made; a functional statement may not correspond to any real causal processes.

When Coase tried to explain why firms exist, his conclusion was phrased in functional terms, which comes naturally to mainstream economists, nowadays as it did in 1937: firms are said to exist because they fulfil the need to reduce transaction costs. It posits a reality which is nicely interconnected *at any given moment*: if firms exist, it must be because they have current cost advantages. Such an approach excludes the possibility that the causal mechanism operates in *an open-ended fashion across real historical time*: for example that firms exist—and prosper—because their control over production enables them to compete more successfully than sole traders (Joffe 2011). This is an argument in terms of differential consequences.[7]

In contrast, a biologist (or other scientist) would start by observing how firms come into being. Generally, a firm exists because it is set up by someone with initiative who either has resources or can obtain them; this creates an authority structure which normally then persists. Coase's question is still relevant, but it becomes, 'if trading between individuals is more efficient, why do firms not disintegrate?'. This leads to examining the type of firm that does break up, for example because in a high-tech context the 'workers' are themselves at the cutting edge of innovation, and they therefore have both the opportunity and the motivation to establish their own firms. In the general case, however, firms do not break up in this way, and show great capacity for persistence. A biological equivalent of Coase's explanation would be if a biologist tried to explain multicellular organisms, and their constituent organs and systems, in terms of the coming together of different types of cells. This would seriously harm embryology!

Thus, scientific methodology aligns the theoretical account with a process occurring in historical time. It is phrased in terms of consequences, not of neatly fitting together. It has been highly successful in biology.

Some of these issues have direct relevance to economic research, for example the impact of a changing business environment on the survival probability of firms in different sectors, and the tracing out of mediating causal pathways (Foster *et al.* 2008). Oddly, Friedman's view is that such pathways do not really matter. Thus he defends the assumption that firms maximise profit as being justified, irrespective of whether it is brought about by the *motivation* of the manager to maximise profits (behaviour—the standard neoclassical assumption) or alternatively by the *differential survival* of firms such that those that maximise are more likely to survive (consequences). It is not just that it may be difficult to make this distinction empirically, which is true, but that they are regarded as *equivalent*—causal mechanism does not matter. It is actually an important practical point, because the widespread perception that the private sector performs better than the public sector could be justified if managers' motivations were the operative factor. But if it is merely that the private sector is better at getting rid of poor performers, then this would be a bad argument for private sector involvement in running, say, a city's hospital or a small town's school, where ceasing to exist is not an option.

---

[7] It is true that Coase's view could also be expressed in this way, rather than in an ahistoric form, but it would not be the only such explanation. Evidence would then be the deciding factor.

Friedman's conclusion is that assumptions can be justified, however unrealistic they appear, as long as they give good predictions. Strangely, he does not provide evidence for predictive success of any mainstream economic theories, apparently regarding it as self-evident that they must be correct. This is the most disturbing part of the essay, from a scientific viewpoint: a lack of exposure to empirical evidence. The theory is deemed to be true by definition—tautologically true. Lest this be seen as an over-reaction, recall that mainstream textbooks all portray the cost curves of firms as universally having a shape that is in fact uncommon. This type of methodology leads to a hermetically sealed, circular conception of the world, structurally similar to theology, in which any accurate relationship to reality is accidental. Whereas scientists set out to make ontological statements, all too often economists are imprisoned in epistemology.

Conclusions

Mainstream core economic theory may superficially resemble some types of natural science, but it behaves as a set of mathematical modelling techniques rather than as a science. This is reflected in the ideal of basing core theory on axioms, even if empirically unsupported, and in the still-widespread practice of producing simple, elegant models based on assumptions rather than evidence. Simple models are useful *if* they capture the essence of a situation but not if they distort it. In a science like biology, a prior stage is to generate a broader theory, a causal understanding of the possibly multiple influences involved in the situation under study, based on systematic description. This helps to prevent both distortion and the risk of tunnel vision as occurred with recent models in macroeconomics that ignored finance.

One practical way of achieving a sound empirical basis would be to seek examples of convergent historical processes, analogous to convergent evolution in biology, and to examine both the similarities and the divergences between the different instances. More generally, a scientific economics would pay greater attention to causal accounts where the assumptions, mechanism and outcome are all compatible with the empirical evidence.

Much current economic research does aim at an empirical basis and a broad causal understanding. The issue is what to do about the residue of unscientific practices—not only in specific research projects, but particularly in integrative activities such as textbooks and teaching, and in methodological writings. This would mean letting go of some traditional items such as:

- believing that markets are all alike, and all have the property of self-regulation;
- focusing on convergence and stability while ignoring divergent forces and bubbles;
- reducing economics to behaviour;
- seeking 'to predict the shots' (events) rather than to uncover the underlying causal explanation;
- obscuring the open-endedness of historical time by the assumption of perfect foresight;
- mistaking functional or 'as-if' statements for causal explanations;
- and especially, reproducing apparently 'factual' statements that are in fact wrong.

A scientific economics would abandon reactive mode and limit the use of incremental mode, removing the aspects of theory that are not based on evidence, and replacing them with a well-founded empirical basis. This could be called selective replacement mode. It would then look like the best practice in current/recent research, organised around a core that is worthy of it. There is some distance to go.

References

Aghion, P. and Howitt, P. (1998), *Endogenous Growth Theory* (Cambridge, MA, The MIT Press).

Amsden, A. H. (1989), *Asia's Next Giant. South Korea and Industrialization* (New York, Oxford University Press).

Angrist, J. and Evans, W. (1998), 'Children and their parents' labor supply: evidence from exogenous variation in family size', *American Economic Review*, 88: 450–77.

Bartelsman, E. J., Haltiwanger, J. and Scarpetta, S. (2004), 'Microeconomic evidence of creative destruction in industrial and developing countries', IZA Discussion Paper No. 1374, World Bank Policy Research Working Paper No. 3464. Available from SSRN at <http://ssrn.com/abstract=612230> [accessed 27 July 2010].

Baumol, W. J. (2002), *The Free-Market Innovation Machine* (Princeton, NJ, Princeton University Press).

Blinder, A. S., Canetti, E., Lebow, D. and Rudd, J. (1998), *Asking About Prices: a new approach to understanding price stickiness* (New York, Russell Sage Foundation).

Cabral, L. M. B. and Mata, J. (2003), 'On the evolution of firm size distribution: facts and theory', *American Economic Review*, 92: 1075–90.

Carter, R. and Hodgson, G. M. (2006), 'The impact of empirical tests of transaction cost economics on the debate on the nature of the firm', *Strategic Management Journal*, 27: 461–76

Cartwright, N. (1994), *Nature's Capacities and Their Measurement* (Oxford, Oxford University Press).

Coase, R. H. (1937), 'The nature of the firm', *Economica*, repr. (1988), in R. H. Coase, *The Firm, the Market and the Law* (Chicago, IL, University of Chicago Press), pp. 33–55.

David, R. J. and Han, S.-K. (2004), 'A systematic assessment of the empirical support for transaction cost economics', *Strategic Management Journal*, 25: 39–58.

Davis, J. B. (2006), 'The turn in economics: neoclassical dominance to mainstream pluralism?', *Journal of Institutional Economics*, 2: 1–20.

Dawkins, R. (2004), *The Ancestor's Tale* (London, Weidenfeld & Nicholson).

Dawkins, R. (2005), 'Is evolution predictable?' <http://www2.lse.ac.uk/newsAndMedia/news/archives/2005/Richard_Dawkins.aspx> [accessed 27 July 2010].

The Economist (2009) 'What went wrong with economics?', Leader, 18 July, p. 11,

Eiteman, W. J. and Guthrie, G. E. (1952), 'The shape of the average cost curve', *American Economic Revue*, 42: 832–38.

Farjoun, E. and Machover, M. (1983), *Laws of Chaos* (London, Verso)

Feynman, R. P. (1990), *QED: the Strange Theory of Light and Matter* (London, Penguin).

Forrester, J. W. (1970), 'Counterintuitive behaviour of social systems', in *Collected papers of Jay W. Forrester [1975 collection]* (Cambridge, MA, Wright-Allen Press), pp. 211–44.

Foster, L., Haltiwanger, J. and Syverson, C. (2008), 'Reallocation, firm turnover, and efficiency: selection on productivity or profitability?', *American Economic Review*, 98: 394–425.

Friedman, M. (1953), 'The methodology of positive economics', repr. in *The Philosophy of Economics: an Anthology*, ed. D. M. Hausman (1994), 2nd edn. (Cambridge, Cambridge University Press).

Fullbrook, E. (ed.) (2003), *The Crisis in Economics* (London, Routledge).

George, D. A. R. (ed.) (2008), *Issues in Heterodox Economics* (Malden, MA, Blackwell Publishing).

Gillies, D. (2004), 'Can mathematics be used successfully in economics?', in *A Guide to What's Wrong with Economics, ed.* E. Fullbrook (London, Anthem Press), pp 187–97.

Greenspan, A. Congressional testimony on 23 October 2008 <http://www.nytimes.com/2008/10/24/business/economy/24panel.html> [accessed 27 July 2010].

Hayek, F. A. (1937), 'Economics and knowledge', *Economica*, 4: 33–54.

Hodgson, G. M. (1993), *Economics and Evolution: bringing life back into economics* (Cambridge, UK, and Ann Arbor, MI, Polity Press and University of Michigan Press), p. 24.

Hodgson, G. M. (2007), 'An interview with Oliver Williamson', *Journal of Institutional Economics*, 3: 373–86.

Hodgson, G. M. and Knudsen, T. (2006), 'Why we need a generalized Darwinism, and why generalized Darwinism is not enough', *Journal of Economic Behavior and Organization*, 61: 1–19

INET (2010), *Inaugural Conference of the Institute for New Economic Thinking* <http://ineteconomics.org/initiatives/conferences/kings-college> [accessed 27 July 2010].

Joffe, M. (2010), 'What causal processes underlie creative destruction?', Paper presented to the Schumpeter Conference 2010, Aalborg, Denmark, <http://www.schumpeter2010.dk/index.php/schumpeter/schumpeter2010/paper/viewFile/338/84> [accessed 28 July 2010]. Fuller version to be published in Andersen, E. and Pyka, A. (eds.) (forthcoming 2012), *Proceedings of the Biannual Conference of the International J. A. Schumpeter Society in Aalborg 2010* (Springer, Berlin Heidelberg).

Joffe, M. (2011), 'The root cause of economic growth under capitalism', *Cambridge Journal of Economics*, 35/5: 873–96. <http://cje.oxfordjournals.org/content/early/2011/03/22/cje/beq054>.

Juselius, K. (2010), 'On the role of theory and evidence in macroeconomics', paper for the Inaugural Workshop of the Institute for New Economic Thinking, Cambridge, 2010, <http://ineteconomics.org/sites/inet.civicactions.net/files/INET%20C%40K%20Paper%20Session%205%20-%20Juselius.pdf> [accessed 27 July 2010].

Keen, S. (2001), *Debunking Economics* (Annandale, NSW, Australia, Pluto Press).

Keynes, J. M. (1937), 'The general theory of employment', *Quarterly Journal of Economics*, 51: 209–23.

Kindleberger. C. P. (1989), *Manias, Panics and Crashes: a history of financial crises*, 2nd edn. (London, Macmillan).

Knight, F. H. (1985 [1921]), *Risk, Uncertainty and Profit* (Chicago, IL, University of Chicago Press).

Landes, D. (1998), *The Wealth and Poverty of Nations* (London, WW Norton & Company Inc.).

Lane, D. C. (2007), 'The power of the bond between cause and effect', *System Dynamics Review*, 23: 95–118.

Lawson, T. (2003), *Reorienting Economics* (London, Routledge).

Lee, F. S. (1998), *Post Keynesian Price Theory* (Cambridge & New York, Cambridge University Press).

Lee, F. S. (2009), *A History of Heterodox Economics* (Abingdon and New York, Routledge).

Levine, S. S. and Zajac, E. J. (2007), 'The institutional nature of price bubbles' <http://papers.ssrn.com/sol3/papers.cfm?abstract_id=960178> [accessed 27 July 2010].

Lindert, P. (2004), *Growing Public* (Cambridge, Cambridge University Press).

Lowenstein, R. (2002), *When Genius Failed* (London, Fourth Estate).

Maddison, A. (1964), *Economic Growth in the West* (London, Allen & Unwin, and New York, WW Norton).

Maddison, A. (1969), *Economic Growth in Japan and the USSR* (London, Allen & Unwin, and New York, WW Norton).

Maddison, A. (1970), *Progress and Policy in Developing Countries* (London, Allen & Unwin, and New York, WW Norton).

Mäki, U. (2002), 'The dismal queen of the social sciences', in U. Mäki, *Fact and Fiction in Economics* (Cambridge, Cambridge University Press), pp. 3–34.

Mäki, U. (ed.) (2009a), *The Methodology of Positive Economics* (Cambridge, Cambridge University Press).

Mäki, U. (2009*b*) 'Reading *the* methodological essay in twentieth-century economics: map of multiple perspectives', in Mäki (2009*a*), pp. 47–67.

Marshall, A. (1885), *Principles of Economics* (London, Macmillan & Co. Ltd.).

Ormerod, P. (1994), *The Death of Economics* (London, Faber and Faber).

Pomeranz, K. (2000), *The Great Divergence* (Princeton, NJ, Princeton University Press).

Poppo, L. and Zenger, T. (1998), 'Testing alternative theories of the firm: transaction cost, knowledge-based, and measurement explanations for make-or-buy decisions in information services', *Strategic Management Journal*, 19: 853–77.

Pritchett, L. (2003), 'A toy collection, a socialist star, and a democratic dud? Growth theory, Vietnam, and the Phillippines', in *In Search of Prosperity. Analytic narratives on Economic Growth*, ed. D. Rodrik (Princeton: Princeton University Press), pp. 123–51.

Qian, Y. (2003), 'How reform worked in China', in *In Search of Prosperity. Analytic narratives on Economic Growth*, ed. D. Rodrik (Princeton: Princeton University Press), pp. 297–333.

Ritter, L. S., Kaplan, M. and Bronfenbrenner, M. and rejoinder by Eiteman (1953) *American Economic Review*, 43: 624–30.

Ruse, M. (1973), *The Philosophy of Biology* (London, Hutchinson & Co. Ltd.), p. 195.

Scherer, F. M. and Ross D. (1990), *Industrial Market Structure and Economic Performance,* 3rd edn. (Boston, MA, *Houghton*-Mifflin).

Schumpeter, J. A. (1980 [1911 in German, 1934 in English]), *The Theory of Economic Development* (New Brunswick, Transaction Publishers).

Schumpeter, J. A. (1992 [1942]), *Capitalism, Socialism and Democracy* (London, Routledge).

Shiller, R. J. (2005), *Irrational Exuberance*, 2nd edn. (Princeton, NJ, Princeton University Press).

Simon, H. A. (1976), *Administrative Behavior*, 3rd edn. (New York, The Free Press).

Smith, V. L. (2008), *Rationality in Economics* (New York & Cambridge, Cambridge University Press).

Solow, R. M. (2000), *Growth Theory: an Exposition*, 2nd edn. (New York, Oxford University Press).

Stanford Encyclopedia of Philosophy, 'Teleological notions in biology' <http://plato. stanford.edu/entries/teleology-biology/> [accessed 27 July 2010].

Summers, L. H. (1991), 'The scientific illusion in empirical macroeconomics', *Scandinavian Journal of Economics*, 93: 129–148.

Turner, A. (2009), 'The financial crisis and the future of financial regulation' <http://www.fsa.gov.uk/pages/Library/Communication/Speeches/2009/0121_at.shtml> [accessed 27 July 2010].

Tversky, A. and Kahneman D. (1981), 'The framing of decisions and the psychology of choice', *Science*, 211 (4481): 453–8.

Varian, H. (1st edn. 1987 to 8th edn. 2010), *Intermediate Microeconomics. a modern approach* (New York, WW Norton), sections 18.9 and 18.10 (19.10 and 19.11 in the 8th edn.).

Wade, R. (1990), *Governing the Market: economic theory and the role of governance in East Asian industrialization* (Princeton, NJ, Princeton University Press).

Westphal, L. E. (1990), 'Industrial policy in an export-propelled economy: lessons from South Korea's experience', *Journal of Economic Perspectives*, 4: 41–59.

17

Reasonable Doubt:
Uncertainty in Education,
Science and Law

TONY GARDNER-MEDWIN

Abstract

The use of evidence to resolve uncertainties is key to many endeavours, most conspicuously science and law. Despite this, the logic of uncertainty is seldom taught explicitly, and often seems misunderstood. Traditional educational practice even fails to encourage students to identify uncertainty when they express knowledge, though mark schemes that reward the identification of reliable and uncertain responses have long been shown to encourage more insightful understanding. In our information-rich society the ability to identify uncertainty is often more important than the possession of knowledge itself.

In both science and law there are fundamentally different kinds of uncertainty at issue. There is uncertainty whether a particular hypothesis is correct, and there is uncertainty about observable data that may be generated if a particular hypothesis is correct. Both are expressed in terms of probabilities. Each has its own domain of application and its own logic, but the interrelationship is complex and sometimes misunderstood. Hypothesis probabilities are always open to error through possible failure to take account of realistic alternatives, while the proper inferences that can be drawn from data probabilities (often in the context of significance testing) are quite limited and easily over-interpreted.

When considering these two kinds of probability in a court of law it is possible to interpret the phrase 'reasonable doubt' in different ways. It can be seen as addressing data uncertainty: whether such incriminating evidence might with reasonable probability arise to confront an innocent person. Or (the more conventional view) it can be seen as some sort of threshold level on the probability that the defendant is guilty (a hypothesis probability). Each typically involves elements of subjective judgement,

Proceedings of the British Academy, **171**, 465–483. © The British Academy 2011.

but fewer issues and uncertainties arise when considering the data probability and it is argued that this is often the more critical and proper issue for a jury to address. This has particular repercussions for cases involving identification of a suspect through trawl of a DNA or other database.

Uncertainty and misconception in educational assessment

As a university teacher (in medical science) I have tried to raise students' awareness of uncertainties in their own knowledge. In conventional educational assessment students are often motivated to hide uncertainties. This is perverse, because it is obvious that it is a good thing to be able to distinguish between reliable and unreliable aspects of one's knowledge. Students should in fact be rewarded for acknowledging uncertainties that they have. By rewarding them, for example with simple but carefully designed mark schemes, they can be encouraged to reflect on the nature of any doubts, and on the evidence that they may be able to bring to bear to resolve these doubts. Instead of doing this, conventional marking usually encourages students to bluff their way through: it treats lucky guesses in the same way as well justified knowledge, and firm misconceptions as no worse than acknowledged ignorance. The result is a 'go-for-it' culture in which decisions may be taken in the light of a marginal or superficial preference for some option, with little further thought.

The dangers of such behaviour are very obvious in a field such as medicine, where lives can be lost through reluctance to acknowledge uncertainty. Even in ordinary discourse however, it is a sign of weakness to shy from proper awareness and acknowledgement of one's uncertainties. It is disturbing, when talking to students familiar with essay writing—where you might think the discussion of uncertainties would be paramount—that they often say they would not normally mention doubts about a fact or argument they are tempted to include. Anyone who has marked exam essays knows that in practice a qualification, perhaps a question mark in the margin, will make little difference to one's judgement if the point made is correct, while it makes a big difference if uncertainty is acknowledged about something incorrect.

It may at first seem paradoxical to reward someone for acknowledging uncertainty. Perhaps it runs counter to society's modern guidelines for '*How to get on in …*' *politics, business,* and maybe sometimes even *science* or *law*. But the rewards for caution in the face of uncertainty are fundamental to biological survival. Children and young animals learn these lessons often through games, and it is no coincidence that the relevant mathematics comes under the heading 'Game Theory' (von Neumann and Morgenstern 1944). Of course certainty also brings its own rewards—just as long as it is certainty about something that is correct. To pursue a cricketing analogy, the decision to try to hit a ball for six is fine, so long as one is pretty sure one can succeed: the price of failure tends to be high. If one is uncertain of success, then a more modest stroke will on average be better rewarded. Exactly the same principle is employed in the certainty-based mark scheme we employ for self-tests at UCL and Imperial College in London (Gardner-Medwin 1995, 2006). Acknowledging uncertainty (<67% estimated probability of being correct) gives 1 mark for a correct answer and 0 if incorrect. Claiming a high level of certainty (>80%) gives 3 marks or –6, while an intermediate level gives 2 marks or –2. This is a 'proper' or motivating mark scheme, in the sense that a student always expects to gain by giving an accurate indication of how reliable he/she thinks the chosen answer is (Dawid 1986). With this scheme there is no benefit to be gained by the student trying to 'play the system': pretending to be either more or less confident than he/she really is. It is remarkable how readily students take to this scheme, appreciating the good sense and utilitarian value of settling for modest rewards and penalties when unsure.

Uncertainty about the expression of knowledge or understanding is an example of uncertainty about ideas. Much of educational testing revolves around ideas that are generally accepted (at least within an agreed framework) as definitely either true or false, though students with partial knowledge may assign probabilities less than 1 and those with serious misconceptions may assign very low probabilities to what is correct. There are of course many elements to educational experience where there is no certainty and the task is to generate or discuss ideas that are neither known nor agreed to be objectively correct or incorrect. Here we come closer to the issues that arise in scientific research and in courts of law.

Uncertainty about ideas: the driving force in science

Scientists work with two fundamentally different kinds of uncertainty, though they don't always distinguish them very clearly. The first is an intrinsically subjective probability: *How certain is it that a particular idea or hypothesis is correct?* This is obviously fundamental within science, but the answers to such questions are always subjective in the sense that they may differ even between well informed and intelligent individuals. By gaining additional evidence one may shift such subjective probabilities in ways that all agree are rational and occasionally even quantifiable. Indeed, as Popper (1959) pointed out, one can sometimes demonstrate that an idea is certainly wrong, though never that it is certainly right as a general truth. Different levels of scepticism and uncertainty amongst individuals, about what is correct, may never be eliminated. Nevertheless, there are of course great swathes of scientific conclusions that are regarded, by more or less all who have studied them, as essentially certain. It is the power of science that the accumulation of evidence, given enough time and effort, tends to become overwhelming on one side or the other of any argument. However, evidence does not always diminish uncertainty, and even firmly embedded ideas can occasionally be challenged or overturned, even by simple pieces of evidence. Uncertainty about ideas is the motivation for progress in science, despite its nebulous and largely unquantifiable nature. It drives the testing of predictions and the devising of alternative theories and experimental challenges.

Darwin's theory of natural selection is a prime example of an idea that was conceived with a huge element of uncertainty, not least in Darwin's mind. Darwin's great success was that he amassed a vast amount of evidence in its favour before going public: enough evidence to diminish his own uncertainty and to shake the conviction of many sceptics. There never was (and never will be) a time when Darwin's theory is totally certain, beyond any meaningful threshold. Of course, nearly every scientist believes, as I certainly do, in this theory. Darwin's idea is as firmly embedded as any in science, thanks to the progressive elucidation of biological mechanisms and the accumulation of data that are all (so far as I know) consistent with the core elements and predictions of this theory. But there can be no certainty that new ideas and observations could not change it. A scientist's natural response to the question 'Is Darwin's theory beyond reasonable doubt?' is to say 'What doubt? Let's see if we can devise a test for any ideas about how it may be wrong.' Scientists love coherent scepticism, just so long as the ideas are testable. The history of science teaches them to regard dogmatic beliefs as pointless and arrogant. The strength of the chief tenets of science is not that they are certain, but that to overturn them would require not only observations inconsistent with them, but also a new explanation for all the evidence that has hitherto appeared to support them. Darwin achieved this in relation to the notion of divine creation, as did Einstein with classical mechanics. Scientists seldom of course achieve such dramatic revolutionary impact; but even when the pursuit of uncertainty doesn't overturn or strengthen existing ideas, it often throws light on facets that were previously unclear.

Uncertainty about expected data

The second kind of uncertainty is conceptually more straightforward and quantitative, though often underpinned by complex mathematics. This is uncertainty about the data that will arise in an experiment, given that the relevant mechanisms and principles are either fully understood or fully defined by a hypothetical model. Statistical analysis of such uncertainty is part of any scientific training (and the bane of many students!). It gives a framework for evaluation of new results, since a novel claim is of little value if the novelty or interest of the evidence could quite likely have arisen with conventional or uninteresting assumptions. The commonest format is that of 'significance testing', initiated by Fisher (1925). The assumptions on which a significance test is based are described as a 'null hypothesis' H_0. A point of potential interest is encapsulated in a statistic from the observations, quantifying a difference from the mean or median value expected on H_0. The outcome of the test is the probability ('P-value') based on H_0 that, with the procedures adopted in the research, at least as large a value would be observed.

Since the use and misuse of significance tests and P-values has a huge and controversial literature (see for example very approachable reviews by Royall (1997) and Senn (2003)), I shall present here just a personal perspective on some of these issues. A fundamental point, clear I hope in the description above, is that a P-value is a probability of observing data, conditional on a specific hypothesis. It does not express uncertainty about hypotheses. P-values are hugely valuable in science because they quantify the degree to which data are consistent with some conventional or postulated idea. Perhaps the most useful role they perform is when the P-value is large and the result is 'not-significant': this means that the point of interest in the data would be quite likely to arise even if H_0 is true, so there is little reason to pay attention to this aspect of the data as any kind of challenge to H_0. One can conclude this quite straightforwardly, without any consideration of alternative hypotheses or the rather nebulous business, discussed in the last section, of addressing the probabilities that hypotheses may be correct.

A hazard in the interpretation of P-values arises from terminology often used to express conclusions based on them. Low P-values are often said to justify 'rejection of H_0' at a particular significance level. This is only true in a very restricted formal sense, when a P-value is used as a decision criterion between two actions that would be appropriate if there were solid reasons to accept or reject H_0. For example one might decide to ignore the data because it is consistent with H_0, or start researching alternative hypotheses if the data would be surprising on the basis of H_0. If there are alternative hypotheses already formulated, with some basis for assigning them relative probabilities, then a result with a low P-value doesn't necessarily even argue against H_0, let alone justify rejecting it. An interesting result may be so extreme that it is very unlikely on H_0, but it may be even less likely on whatever alternative hypotheses are considered plausible. As an example, suppose that ten tosses of a coin yield nine heads and one tail. Does this result, surprisingly far from 50 : 50 (P-value=2 per cent) argue for rejection of a hypothesis (H_0) that this is a fair coin? If the only alternatives seem to be that a coin might have two heads or two tails, then the data clearly shows both of these false, supporting H_0. However, if one envisages the possibility that a coin might be biassed so as to be more likely to land one way, and considers this plausible, then the data lend more support to this idea than to H_0. Whether one ends up considering H_0 more or less likely than at the outset depends on the initial probabilities one assigns to any of these (and possibly other) ideas—one's prior probabilities. In science, especially at the frontiers, the alternatives to a well-formulated hypothesis are often simply a matter of speculation. In that situation all one can sensibly say about data with a low P-value is that the parameter of interest is surprisingly far from expectation on the basis of H_0 (or similar hypotheses) and that other hypotheses, not necessarily very plausible or even thought of, could have rendered it less surprising.

The borderline between uncertainty about hypotheses and data

A useful extension of significance tests is the calculation of so-called 'confidence limits': a range of null hypotheses that would yield P-values above a specified level for a result of interest in the data—in other words, they would make the result unsurprising. This practice helps to clarify how useful the observations are: how well they serve to discriminate between different values of a parameter within a hypothetical model; but it still says nothing about the probability that one should assign to the correctness of any of these models. The commonly used terminology is again, in my view, misleading because the term '95 per cent confidence limits' for a parameter in a model can easily be understood to mean that there is a 95 per cent probability that the true parameter lies within these limits. This is simply not so, as is evident if you think about an experiment that tries to measure an effect that you consider to be almost certainly non-existent (perhaps extrasensory perception or homeopathy). Whatever the protocol for the experiment, you should expect on 5 per cent of occasions that a result will be obtained for which a nil effect is outside the calculated confidence limits. If you happen to experience one of these results it would obviously be inappropriate to adopt a belief that there is a 95 per cent probability that the postulated effect is real. Perhaps 'consonance limits' (Kempthorne and Folks 1971) would better convey the true meaning, which is a range of models for which the data would be relatively commonplace—falling within the 95 per cent most likely outcomes.

In general it is important to make a category distinction between the probability that data will arise and the probability that a hypothesis about the generation of data is correct. Sometimes, however, there is a simple relationship between the two. For example, an experiment may estimate (by sample measurements) the mean value of a parameter that is considered at the outset equally likely to take any of a wide range of values: perhaps some characteristic of a newly encountered substance, object or species. Then (with a few, often justifiable, assumptions)[1] the posterior probabilities of different hypotheses about the true mean are the same as the data probabilities that would be calculated for sample means, on the hypothesis that the true mean is what was actually measured. Returning to terminology, this means that when no hypothesis initially has preferred status, the limits cautiously described above as '95% consonance limits' are truly '95 per cent confidence limits'—they identify a range that one can be fairly confident includes the true mean (with 95 per cent probability based on only these data). Examples like this where one can convert directly from a data probability to a hypothesis probability are not rare, but they lead to confusion if their limitations are not properly taken into account.

When alternative hypotheses are well defined and do have special status in an experiment, for example rival causal explanations of the data, then updating of probabilities for the alternatives requires Bayesian analysis (Lindley 1972). As we saw above (in the coin example) attempts to make such inferences using P-values can be quite misleading since an unlikely result on a hypothesis H_0 may actually be evidence in favour of H_0. Bayesian analysis involves identifying prior probabilities for the various hypotheses and updating these in the light of the data, using likelihood ratios (the relative probabilities that the data would be observed on the different hypotheses). The technicalities need not concern us here, but the procedure is demonstrably successful in situations where alternative hypotheses have clear prior probabilities. Even when this is not the case, and prior probabilities are little more than guesses, sufficient data can sometimes lead to highly reliable inferences (see for example,

---

[1] For example, measurements that are normally distributed random variables with mean μ, where the prior probability distribution for μ is essentially uniform over a range much larger than the measurement standard deviation.

MacKay 2003). The main reservation is that conclusions can be wholly mis-leading if the correct hypothesis has been omitted from consideration or assigned an inappropriate probability. If this is a major risk, as it can of course be at the frontiers of research, then the more limited logic by which significance tests challenge individual hypotheses can be a more comfortable basis for scientific progress.

An important application of Bayesian analysis is in medical diagnosis. Here one starts with fairly objective probabilities that different hypotheses might be true, for example that a person with a persistent cough may have each of a number of different diseases. Then these probabilities are updated on the basis of data from the patient's history and tests carried out, using information about how frequently the data would arise in the population for each of the conditions. This process may simply occur in the doctor's mind, leading eventually either to confidence about specific diagnoses or to residual uncertainty. Alternatively, a Bayesian computer algorithm may process the data to generate explicit posterior probabilities. Which is better is debatable, given the possible unreliability of the doctor's compilation of inferences set against his or her ability to take into account subtle aspects of the data ignored by a computer algorithm. But there is no disputing the appropriateness of this strategy to resolve medical uncertainties and to help make decisions.

Uncertainty in criminal trials

The uncertainties in a criminal trial have superficial similarities to the prob-lems of medical diagnosis. The endpoint is a decision that turns graded uncertainties into specific actions: whether to convict a defendant, or apply treatment for a specific diagnosis. The relative utilities of right and wrong decisions may in part determine what level of doubt is acceptable for a final decision. In medicine this uncertainty is normally explicit, since the patient usually makes the final decision about whether to accept treatment, and must therefore be informed of doubts and likely outcomes. In law, the criterion for conviction ('beyond reasonable doubt') is substantially open to a jury's inter-pretation, with only partial knowledge of the utilities involved since a sentence for conviction may only be determined at a later stage by a judge. But these are not profound differences.

Legal cases often have many layers of complexity, for example concerning facts, motives, identification, intention and witness credibility. Final decisions may hinge on a complex synthesis of many types of doubt (Cohen 1977; Anderson *et al.* 2005), and it is far from clear that mathematical approaches are helpful in coming to appropriate conclusions. Alternative conceptions of probability (for example Cohen's inductive probability based on qualitative eliminative reasoning) may sometimes be more rational (or at least more manageable for a jury) when deciding whether facts are 'beyond reasonable doubt' in a trial. Such issues are much debated in the legal literature (see for example Tillers and Gottfried 2006) with cogent arguments from many perspectives. However, the debate that follows naturally from the discussion here on the nature of uncertainties in science is not about whether probabilities should be quantified but whether we should be dealing with uncertainties about hypotheses or about data. Ideally, of course, one would like court decisions to be based on certainty rather than uncertainty, but this is rarely the case. If the evidence does support certainty, then concluding that defendant D definitely committed crime C (an assertion about a hypothesis probability) is equivalent to concluding that the evidence could not have arisen if D were innocent (an assertion about a data probability): each conclusion follows from the other. But if uncertainties are present, these become different questions.

I have argued elsewhere (Gardner-Medwin 2005) that it can be rational for a jury to come to the conclusion that the hypothesis of guilt is very probably correct, while acquitting on the grounds that the evidence could with reasonable likelihood have arisen for an innocent person. It may at first seem that these issues are opposite sides of the same coin, which would make my assertion either paradoxical or merely a matter of setting different thresholds for judging the two probabilities. I will first set out a caricature example, based on cases that first drew my interest (as discussed by Dawid 2002) to show that this is not the case.

Suppose multiple infants in a family have died in circumstances consistent with either sudden infant death syndrome (SIDS: a rare medical condition that leaves no specific signs post mortem) or infanticide by the mother. This may reasonably lead to suspicion of crime, and indeed cases have come to court with little more in the way of pertinent evidence. It is obviously relevant to ask questions analogous to those underlying tests of significance: 'How likely is it that such evidence would arise in an innocent family with comparable genetic, medical and socio-economic background, and how often would such cases be expected to arise in an innocent population?' Such questions cannot be answered with precision, but competent experts should be able to give reasonable ranges for the answers. Unfortunately the supposedly expert testimony in recent UK cases was not competent, raising serious concerns about how expert testimony should be validated (Royal Statistical Society 2002); but this does not detract from the relevance of proper answers. The conclusion might be that the risk of the deaths that have brought this mother to court arising in her family without crime was at least a probability *P*, and that similar multiple deaths in families with no greater risk factors for multiple SIDS might be expected to arise somewhere in the UK once every X months. A jury might reasonably decide to acquit simply on the basis of such testimony, justifying their decision by saying that if juries convict on such evidence they might be responsible for convicting innocent mothers at the rate of one every X months in the UK, which they deem unacceptable. The acceptability criterion is of course a subjective matter: how many false convictions of this sort might be acceptable in a given population per year, decade or century in the interests of justice. But it is no more subjective than what constitutes 'reasonable doubt' on any other basis.

An alternative approach is to decide such a case based on the probability that the hypothesis of guilt is correct, that is that this defendant is guilty within the meaning of the law. This view is often implicit in the legal literature and the media. It was clearly expressed in the letter from the Royal Statistical Society (2002) to the Lord Chancellor in the UK concerning the multiple SIDS case of R vs. Sally Clark, and was analysed in relation to this case in more detail by Dawid (2002). To quote the letter: 'Two deaths by murder may well be even more unlikely [than two deaths by SIDS]. What matters is the relative likelihood of the deaths under each explanation, not just how unlikely they are under one explanation.' The implication (made explicit by Dawid (2002) in Section 2.3 of his paper) is that a jury should use evidence about the incidence of this type of murder in the population, and convict if this is sufficiently greater than that of SIDS, taking account of all the known circumstances. This is certainly a rational way to infer probability of guilt in light of the evidence, but it has uncomfortable consequences when used as the basis for conviction or acquittal. In particular, it means that a defendant who would be acquitted on the grounds that the evidence is reasonably consistent with innocence (the argument of the last paragraph) might find herself convicted because sufficiently many other people have committed the crime of which she is accused (Gardner-Medwin 2005). This seems ethically improper and probably unacceptable in law, because the voluntary criminal acts and intentions of people in other legal cases cannot reasonably be used as an argument to establish that a particular defendant has broken the law. Such evidence might be admissible to demonstrate, in unusual cases, that people are indeed sometimes capable of surprising behaviour (for example, a mother killing her own children). But a liberal society would not be content, I think, with legal practice based on a utilitarian principle that if crime is rife then the law should convict with lower standards of evidence, so as to suppress crime at the cost of imprisoning the innocent (Gardner-Medwin 2005). This would be the action of a totalitarian state. An enlightened jury must be prepared to acquit if the evidence could plausibly have arisen without guilt, however likely it may seem that the defendant is guilty on statistical grounds. If common crimes go unpunished as a result, this needs to be rectified by improving the quality of evidence rather than by lowering the threshold for conviction.

Uncertainty in trials with evidence of a definite crime

Trials are of course usually more complex and less amenable to quantitative analysis than the caricature discussed above. Commonly there is clear evidence of a crime, and amongst the many hypotheses that might account for this evidence there are two of primary concern: those put forward by the prosecution and defence. The prosecution case entails guilt on the part of the defendant, while that of the defence may not identify at all who is guilty, merely offering alternative explanation for evidence brought against the defendant and adding further evidence that may tend to prove innocence. Both the prosecution and defence hypotheses are typically composite in the sense that there are unknown elements for which there may at best be a reasonable set of assignable probabilities (for example that the victim either walked or got a lift from A to B). The situation is somewhat similar to comparison of two scientific hypotheses, where the relative likelihood of the data arising through the alternative explanations can provide a rational basis for increasing belief in one or the other. However, as we saw above, there can be fundamental problems in this process.

The first problem is the need for prior probabilities, from which to generate posterior probabilities in the light of the evidence. With scientific theories we saw how there may simply be no way of resolving differences of opinion about such priors. Similarly, in court the priors may depend on such dubiously subjective factors as a juror's expectation on being summoned to take part, suppositions about the rigour of the prosecution services, or how the defendant is dressed in court. Aspects of the background history of the defendant, which may or may not be allowed to emerge in court, may reasonably be considered relevant to prior probabilities and thereby to the posterior probability of guilt, but constraints and debate often centre round the fairness of admitting such evidence and the legal balance between potential prejudicial and probative value (see for example Roberts and Zuckerman 2004: chaps. 4, 11).

A second problem about the use of posterior probabilities arises from the composite and incomplete nature of the hypotheses under consideration.

The defence hypothesis seldom specifies who actually committed the crime. Anyone familiar with detective fiction (and probably, though I do not have experience, detective fact) knows that a prosecution case can look overwhelmingly stronger than a defence case up to the point when a new idea or emerging fact suddenly makes plausible a hitherto unconsidered suspect, motive or opportunity. In an ideal world such a development would have arisen and been investigated before trial, but miscarriages of justice can occur if this does not happen. This is analogous to the simple coin tossing example above, where the same evidence was seen either to support or negate the hypothesis that a coin is fair, depending on details of the alternative hypotheses that may have been thought of, and whether these were assigned significant prior probabilities. Miscarriages of justice can very easily occur if the true criminal is absent from consideration or seems above suspicion.

These problems concerning probability of guilt are analogous to the problems that make scientists shy from debate about the probability that a particular hypothesis is true. The probability of guilt cannot however be avoided altogether, because it would obviously be unreasonable to convict someone without somehow concluding that there is a high probability of guilt. But we have seen both ethical concerns and logical problems about treating this as a well-founded sufficient criterion for conviction. Hence, as in science, it is also constructive to focus on the more limited but in some respects more direct inferences that may be drawn from data probabilities. In court, a relevant probability is whether an innocent person could have been brought to court to face at least the weight of incriminating evidence that has been seen for the defendant. This can be a substantial concern where there is a high profile crime, intense police effort and the opportunity to trawl a wide population: it becomes quite possible that an innocent suspect may be found against whom a convincing case can be made. The murder in London of Jill Dando and the subsequent conviction and acquittal of Barry George come to mind. A jury must be prepared to recognise that a seemingly strong case can often be made against a person innocent of the crime at issue.

In court there is not such a clear distinction to be made between hypothesis and data probabilities as there is in science. This is because hypotheses and explanations of data in court are not the well defined stochastic models that are the usual basis for calculation of data probabilities in science. There are subjective elements to the probability that evidence might arise without guilt, for example how likely it is that a particular scenario would develop or that witnesses may lie. Uncertainty about whether evidence might arise for an innocent defendant is therefore in some respects just as subjective and arguable as is uncertainty about the hypothesis of guilt. However, it involves fewer priors and can be judged within a more limited framework. This framework focuses largely on the things that could happen to innocent people, rather than on the behaviour of criminals. An incidental advantage (though hardly a reason in itself for preferring this approach) is that such scenarios may be easier for a jury to envisage.

Selection of suspects: the DNA database controversy

A hazard familiar to statisticians is the potential use of data twice over, once to select a hypothesis of interest (in this case, to pick a suspect from a population) and then again as evidence that the hypothesis (guilt of this suspect) is true. There can be an element of this in police protocols (as in the SIDS/murder cases, probably the Barry George case and many cases involving DNA matching). The procedures to avoid logical errors due to double use of data are not always appreciated by scientists, so it is unsurprising that juries may have difficulty handling the issue correctly. They may even not be aware that a suspect came to attention through a trawl of police records rather than through a connection with the case, since the fact that a suspect had a police record may be considered prejudicial in court (see e.g. Kaye 2009 for examples and court rulings in relation to DNA testing). There are diverse views and heated debate in legal and statistical circles about how to handle evidence that serves these dual roles. For example, the American National Research Council Committee on DNA Forensic Science (1996), Stockmarr (1999) and Devlin (2000) advocate downgrading the weight of evidence when the suspect is identified by a single match in a database trawl, while Balding (2002, 2005), Dawid (2002), Kaye (2009) and others claim that the use of a database does not diminish the evidence—indeed strengthens it, albeit usually only slightly, by ruling out those in the database who test negative. The differences can correspond to large factors in the estimated probability of a false conviction: factors comparable (as shown below) with the number of potential suspects. As Dawid (2002) points out, differences between statistical approaches to uncertainty must rarely have such serious potential consequences for those affected.

The issues can be somewhat clarified by considering the safety of convictions—how likely the procedures are to incriminate innocent persons. Suppose that the person who left DNA at a crime scene is considered certain to be the true perpetrator of a crime (TP), and that the technical probability of the sample matching a random person other than the TP is a very small number (p), with no possibility that a match would fail to be evident if the TP is tested. Suppose there is a prime suspect who is estimated on the basis of non-genetic evidence to have a 50 per cent probability of being guilty ($s = 50\%$: strong suspicion, but certainly not enough on its own to convict). If the DNA profile of this suspect is tested and matches the crime sample, then the probability that this match is false is $p/(1+p)$, or almost exactly p. Conviction on this basis has a small estimated probability p of being a miscarriage of justice. The risk is greater if the evidence against the prime suspect is weaker ($s<0.5$), though with only a small number (M) of possible suspects this would make little difference for a test that confirms a prime suspect.[2]

Cases involving trawl of a DNA database are more complex. Suppose there are initially no prime suspects based on non-genetic evidence, but a large number N of potential suspects (perhaps all the males of a plausible age within a city on a given day). Suppose a DNA database contains profiles for a random subset including D of these possible suspects, and that a search of the database has revealed exactly one of these as matching the DNA at the crime scene. There is at the outset a probability D/N that the database includes the true perpetrator (TP), and therefore a probability $(D/N)(1-p)^{D-1}$ that he would give rise to a unique match, taking account of the probability $(1-p)^{D-1}$ that no additional match arises by chance for any of the $(D-1)$ innocent persons in the database. But there is also a probability $(1-D/N)pD(1-p)^{D-1}$ that the TP is not in the database and that exactly one of the innocent persons in the database does match. Given the fact that a unique match has been found, the probability that this is the TP is $1/(1+p(N-D))$. There is a complementary probability (approximately $p(N-D)$ if this is $<<1$) that this is a false match, typically much greater than the probability of a false match when a single test is carried out on a prime suspect.[3] The factor by which this risk is increased compared with the illustrative example in the last paragraph is $(N-D)$, the number of potential suspects outside the database—potentially 100,000 or more in some cases (Kaye 2009).[4] Of course a match found in a DNA trawl

---

[2] If the prior probability of guilt of the matching suspect is s, based on non-genetic evidence and elimination of any previously tested suspects, then the probability that this match is false is approximately $p(1-s)/s$ (assuming this itself is small). Even if s for the prime suspect is considered unquantifiable, but there are at most M suspects who are at all plausible, s must rationally be taken as at least $1/M$ on the basis that his probability of guilt must be considered at least as high as each of the others. This sets an upper bound on the probability of a false match as $p(M-1)$.

[3] A different derivation of the same conclusion is given by Song *et al.* (2009).

[4] Note that a larger and more relevant database (larger D) reduces the risk that a unique match will be a false match. This can be seen as an argument in favour of maintaining large DNA databases. Large databases would also increase the frequency with which database use would generate suspects for investigation. However, there might be legitimate concerns that inappropriate handling in court of the statistical and technical issues surrounding database use might lead to more false convictions.

leads to investigation of the suspect and further non-genetic evidence. In some cases this may lead to confident conviction (e.g. if the suspect turns out to match a CCTV image from the crime scene) or elimination or acquittal if the match is clearly false (e.g. if there is a definite alibi). But DNA evidence often appears to the jury to be the strongest evidence in a case and conviction following a DNA trawl may even result when all other evidence seems to weigh in the defendant's favour (Donnelly 2005; Kaye 2009). It is crucial in such cases that a jury should recognise that the DNA data comes from a trawl and carries a much greater risk of false incrimination than if it were confirming suspicion of a prime suspect. Without this, such trials must be considered unsafe.

How are we to reconcile this conclusion with the seemingly contrary Bayesian argument presented by Dawid (2002) and Kaye (2009) that the order in which DNA and non-genetic data are obtained is immaterial. They argue that since a trawl eliminates suspects as well as identifying one who matches, when combined with other evidence it will rationally lead to greater probability of guilt than would be inferred if the same person had been tested as the prime suspect. This argument is illustrated in Figure 17.1 for the simple case considered above, where there is strong non-genetic evidence (E) against a defendant, either emerging at the outset to justify confirmatory DNA testing of the defendant as a prime suspect or else emerging after the suspect has been identified in a trawl. This shows how the odds on the suspect's guilt are accumulated to similar outcomes, simply in a different order. This near

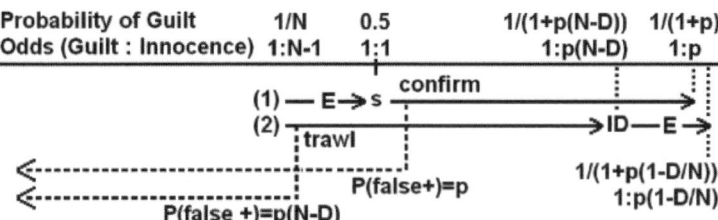

Figure 17.1. Comparison of Bayesian treatments of probability of guilt. Arrows show successive changes in probability of guilt and associated odds, for a suspect identified (1) by non-genetic evidence (E) followed by a confirmatory DNA test, or (2) through trawl in a DNA database followed by investigation and discovery of E. The non-genetic evidence on its own leads to a probability of guilt (s) that is taken here to be 50 per cent. *N*, *D* and *p* are explained in the text. Dashed arrows show the (approximate) probability of a DNA match being false with each procedure. If such a match were known to be false this would lead, given assumptions in the text, to certain acquittal.

equivalence of outcomes has been used to challenge the notion that juries need to be informed of the special facts and statistical considerations when suspect identification occurs through trawls or multiple testing (Balding 2002, 2005; Kaye 2009).

I would wholly accept this argument if the collection and evaluation of non-genetic evidence were rigorous, quantitative, free of selection bias and uncertainties, and derived from investigation of all possible avenues. But this is unrealistic, sometimes even for evidence backed by science. The reality is that much evidence depends on hunches and qualitative argument, and thorough investigation has often been restricted to just one or a few of the possible suspects. The degree of suspicion appropriate for a prime suspect is often highly uncertain, and the discovery of a positive DNA match provides strong vindication of the potentially uncertain arguments that led to the status as prime suspect. When a suspect is instead identified by DNA trawl, the arguments constructed around non-genetic evidence obtained after identification will lack that test of authenticity and must retain all their caveats and uncertainties. Contrast for example, two situations.[5] In (A), S becomes a suspect because an unreliable informant asserts 'S did it', S is DNA tested and proves to match the crime scene. In (B), S is suspected because trawl of a database reveals that he is a DNA match and then the informant adds his assertion 'S did it'. In neither case will the informant's bland assertion carry significant weight, but it is essential that a jury should know which scenario applies to the case, because the probability that the procedure would produce a DNA match incriminating an innocent person is much greater in (B) than (A), by a factor equal to the number of plausible suspects within the database. A worthwhile approach is for a jury to consider in trawl cases whether, if subsequent non-genetic evidence had been established at the outset, it would have justified the defendant being tested as the prime suspect. Only then is the probability of false incrimination by DNA as low as the random match probability p. In case (B) above this consideration would highlight the crucial importance of knowing whether the informant's post-trawl assertion was made with or without knowledge that S was by then a suspect.

My thesis here is that courts need to address the probability that police procedures (including trawls for suspects) could have produced evidence against an innocent person that is at least as incriminating as that presented. This is a form of data probability and is how the court should ultimately judge the safety of a conviction. It is a judgment that takes account of more than just facts linking the defendant to the case, but so it should. The defend-

---

[5] I am grateful to D. Kaye for suggesting consideration of this scenario.

ant is in court due to operation of these procedures, which must therefore be under scrutiny just as much as the defendant himself. A judgment that focuses only on the probability that this defendant is guilty will necessarily be deficient. It would essentially apportion probability between all possible suspects, only one of whom is fully investigated and presented, while the true culprit and nature of the crime may not even have entered consideration. There is a strong analogy here to the difficulty of judging how likely it is that a particular scientific hypothesis is correct: this is always uncertain because we simply never know if we have had the luck, insight or imagination to consider the correct explanation of the data we observe.

Conclusion

Acknowledgement and characterisation of uncertainties are key elements in the application of knowledge and evidence. A lack of awareness of the nature or extent of uncertainty can lead to confusion and inappropriate decisions in areas of education, science and law. My focus here has been on a distinction that cuts across the major debates that often emerge in statistics (about the definition of probability in frequentist or Bayesian terms) and in law (about the merits of quantitative or qualitative approaches to decision making in court). The distinction I am concerned with is between probabilities assigned to hypotheses and probabilities for the observation of data, conditional on a specific hypothesis. There is not a choice between addressing just one or the other: each has its own logic and its domains of rigorous application in both science and law. Both are central to the process of establishing knowledge, which itself consists of gradations of belief in hypotheses—justified, at least partially, by evidence from data. The link between hypothesis and data probabilities is seldom rigorous in either science or law. There are grey areas where conclusions may be matters of opinion. Science in general gets round this problem by relying on the indefinite accumulation of evidence that will ultimately swamp all but the most extreme differences of opinion. Criminal law relies more on the moderating effect of a jury decision to generate an outcome that is generally accepted as reasonable. In the legal context however, I argue that the usual focus on probability that the defendant is guilty (a hypothesis probability) is inadequate. Clear benefits arise if a verdict is considered to be ultimately constrained by a data probability: how likely is it that such incriminating evidence could have arisen for an innocent person?

Note. I am grateful to D. Kaye and D. Balding and to the editors of this volume for constructive comments.

References

Anderson, T., Schum, D. and Twining, W. (2005), *Analysis of Evidence*, 2nd edn. (Cambridge, Cambridge University Press).

Balding, D. J. (2002), 'The DNA database search controversy', *Biometrics*, 58: 241–4.

Balding, D. J. (2005), *Weight-of-Evidence for Forensic DNA Profiles* (Chichester, John Wiley).

Cohen, L. J. (1977), *The Probable and the Provable* (Oxford, Clarendon Press).

Dawid, A. P. (1986), 'Probability Forecasting', in *Encyclopedia of Statistical Sciences*, vol. 7, ed. S. Kotz, N. L. Johnson and C. B. Read (New York, Wiley-Interscience), pp. 210–18.

Dawid, A. P. (2002,) 'Bayes's Theorem and weighing evidence by juries', in *Bayes's Theorem*, ed. R. Swinburne, *Proc. Brit. Acad. 113*: 71–90

Devlin, B. (2000), 'The evidentiary value of a DNA database search', *Biometrics*, 56: 1276

Donnelly, P. (2005), 'Appealing statistics', *Significance*, 2: 46–8.

Fisher, R. A. (1925), *Statistical Methods for Research Workers* (Edinburgh, Oliver and Boyd).

Gardner-Medwin, A. R. (1995), 'Confidence assessment in the teaching of basic science', *Association for Learning Technology Journal*, 3: 80–5.

Gardner-Medwin, A. R. (2005), 'What probability should a jury address?', *Significance*, 2: 9–12. Available online at <http://www.ucl.ac.uk/~ucgbarg/doubt.htm>.

Gardner-Medwin, A. R. (2006), 'Confidence-based marking—towards deeper learning and better exams', in *Innovative Assessment in Higher Education*, ed. C. Bryan and K. Clegg (London, Routledge, Taylor and Francis Group).

Kaye, D. (2009), 'Rounding up the usual suspects: a legal and logical analysis of DNA database trawls', *North Carolina Law Review*, 87: 425–503.

Kempthorne, O. and Folks, L. (1971), *Probability, Statistics and Data Analysis* (Ames, IA, Iowa State University Press).

Lindley, D. V. (1972), *Bayesian Statistics: a review* (Philadelphia, PA, Society for Industrial and Applied Mathematics).

MacKay, D. J. C. (2003), *Information Theory, Inference and Learning Algorithms* (Cambridge, Cambridge University Press).

National Research Council Committee on DNA Forensic Science (1996), *An Update: the evaluation of DNA forensic DNA evidence* (Washington, DC, National Academy Press).

Popper, K. (1959), *The Logic of Scientific Discovery* (London, Hutchinson).

Roberts, P. and Zuckerman, A. (2004), *Criminal Evidence* (Oxford, Oxford University Press).

Royall, R. M. (1997), *Statistical Evidence: a likelihood paradigm* (London, Chapman and Hall).

Royal Statistical Society (2002), Letter from the President to the Lord Chancellor regarding the use of statistical evidence in court cases. <http://www.rss.org.uk/statsandlaw>.

Senn, S. (2003), *Dicing with Death: chance, risk and health* (Cambridge, Cambridge University Press).

Song, Y. S., Patil, A., Murphy, E. E. and Montgomery, S. (2009), 'Average probability that a "Cold Hit" in a DNA database search results in an erroneous attribution', *J. Forensic. Sci.*, 54: 22–7.

Stockmarr, A. (1999), 'Likelihood ratios for evaluating DNA evidence when the suspect is found through a database search', *Biometrics*, 55: 671–7.

Tillers, P. and Gottfried, J. (2006), 'A collateral attack on the legal maxim that proof beyond a reasonable doubt is unquantifiable', *Law, Probability and Risk*, 5: 135–57.

von Neumann, J. and Morgenstern, O. (1944), *Theory of Games and Economic Behavior* (Princeton, NJ, Princeton University Press).

Index